Joel Vos's *The Economics of Meaning in Life* is the vanguard of a revolutionary new approach to economics that finally removes that field from the domination of capitalist ideology and materialist reductionist views of human nature. Progressives in universities should insist that their own departments of economics hire at least one person who promotes this book and further develops the creative ideas that Vos presents.

Rabbi Michael Lerner, editor of Tikkun and
Author of *The Politics of Meaning* and, most recently,
Revolutionary Love: A Political Manifesto to Heal and Transform the World
(University of California Press, 2019)

There seems to be an almost universal dread about in this modern world. Everywhere I travel, there is worry that life as we know it is tearing apart at the seams. People talk with me about inequality, scarcity, and corruption at the highest levels, environments plundered, homelands turned inhospitable, oceans filling with plastic and dwindling life, and changes to society, work, family, and culture coming so fast and frequent it feels impossible to keep up. Despite true passion, concern, fear, anger, or love, discussing these vital matters sometimes feels like trying to use our hands to waft away the towering columns of crimson smoke on our horizons. It is as if humanity has built itself inside of a colossal, whirling centrifuge and forgot the 'off' switch outside it. In this ambitious book, Joel Vos works to assemble a blueprint for reconstructing this imposing machine of 21st century capitalism. He offers a vision of a Meaning-Oriented Economy, in which the fundamental currency and marker of progress is dignity, security, and a meaningful life. Using tools from history, social criticism, political science, psychology, economics, and philosophy, among others, Vos describes Capitalist Life Syndrome as a multifaceted perspective adopted by those of us who live within a system that may be destructive to the values we hold dear, and yet about which we feel hopeful and obliged. The alternative—creating social systems that support and celebrate the highest human aspirations for meaningful life—is inspiring, and, as thousands of research studies show, not only practical, not only necessary, but also glorious.

Professor Michael Steger, Director of the Center for Meaning and Purpose,
Colorado State University

This book is an impassioned and well-reasoned plea to restore meaning at the heart of politics. In a society where people feel increasingly alienated and disenfranchised this is an important and necessary argument and enterprise.

Professor Emmy van Deurzen,
Principal of the New School of Psychotherapy and Counselling, London

Joel Vos's *The Economics of Meaning in Life* is a brilliant analysis of both the ways in which capitalism colonizes and destroys not just any viable notion of economics but also the very spirit of humanity. How we live our lives far exceeds the dictates of a market and its pernicious values. Vos makes clear that the lived experiences, values, sense of social responsibility, and compassion are at the heart of what it means to live life meaningfully in a society that takes seriously the meaning of democracy.

Professor Henry Giroux, one of the founding theorists of critical pedagogy in the United States, with more than 68 books, 200 chapters, and 400 articles, including *America on the Edge*, *Education under Siege* and *The Mouse that Roared.*

Joel Vos is a brilliant scholar with an astonishing sweep of knowledge across economics, history, philosophy, psychology, and culture. He offers a compelling analysis of contemporary ills, crisply distilled as the Capitalist Life Syndrome enacted with its materialistic, hedonistic, and self-oriented values. These pursuits have not culminated in pervasive happiness and benevolent, well-functioning societies. Rather we see gaping inequalities and rampant mental health crises. In stark juxtaposition, Vos portrays an alternative: a meaning-oriented economy that is human, intuitive and existential; it is a place where individuals are both free and responsible to lead meaningful lives motivated by more than economic gain. Despite the hard-hitting critique of functionalistic, neoliberal economics, his book is ultimately hopeful and utopian, not as fantasy, but as concrete steps toward building better societies anchored in meaning-oriented educational systems, community life, research, and mental health care. The book is a must read for reflective citizens who care. There is inspiration to be found in embracing its core idea—that leading a meaningful and fulfilling life is a basic human right.

Carol D. Ryff, Hilldale Professor of Psychology, University of Wisconsin-Madison

Joel Vos is a radical psychologist for our time. His subject is the global pandemic of mental anguish under neoliberal capitalism. His work on what he calls *The Capitalist Life Syndrome* fills a huge gap in our understanding of the compound crisis of a world system that is driving us to climate catastrophe, social breakdown, and mass despair. His is a powerful voice for radical transformation. Every activist should read this book.

Dr Neil Faulkner, historian and archaeologist, author of *Creeping Fascism: Brexit, Trump, and the Rise of the Far Right, A Radical History of the World,* and *A People's History of the Russian Revolution*

Joel Vos has provided a challenge for us, individually and collectively, to examine what the mainstream of a capitalist economy has had upon, what we consider to be, the meaning of our lives. Basically, he has found that the system has established standards of what has worth that contains an important paradox. To whatever degrees we measure up to the markers of success, we find something missing when we consider what meaning we find in our lives. The economic system has left an imprint on our minds in which a disconnection from others and our ecology leaves us feeling anxious and unresolved. As Vos points out, the impact has been so pervasive through culture that its place as a source of our psychological distress is typically out of view. The contribution of this well researched and highly readable book is to remove the veil. In it we find a way to remake our economic system in ways that allow us to appreciate the deeper reaches of our connection to life, to our communities, and to our habitat.

Marc Pilisuk, Professor Emeritus, The University of California; Faculty, Saybrook University, author of *The Hidden Structure of Violence: Who Benefits from Global Violence and War* and *Peace Movements Worldwide.*

What a wonderful contribution to the study of meaning in all its varieties! For far too long meaning oriented scholars and practitioners have limited themselves to the personal or interpersonal domain. While this is of course a crucial focus, it's not a complete analysis. The personal can't be everything and Vos elegantly and clearly helps us think about the economic domain beyond capitalism 'as a landscape', but as an active constructor of experience and of meaning.

In this book, Vos delineates the mechanisms whereby neoliberalism sculpts, allows, and disallows meaning and is both astute and persuasive, partly due to the diverse types of evidence drawn upon. He considers economic theory, phenomenology, social science, and case study. Because of this, the book will no doubt speak to a range of readers, whether they be economists trying to explore the meaning of their discipline, existentialists wanting to explore being-in-the-(capitalist)-world, or many an everyday reader noting and exploring the dissatisfaction that besets so many of us as we navigate contemporary life.

In the age of the corporation as individual and the billionaire classes wielding power, this is a timely, informative, and provocative read, nicely culminating in an exploration of what else is possible, what a meaning-oriented economics might actually look like.

Professor Martin Milton, Regent's University London

A ground-breaking examination of the symbiotic relationship between our states of mind and the globally organised economy. It is also a look at where we need to be heading if we are to build a viable future. I thoroughly recommend it.

Ron Roberts Author of *Psychology and Capitalism, and The Off-Modern*

The Economics of Meaning in Life:

From Capitalist Life Syndrome to Meaning-Oriented Economy

Joel Vos
PhD, CPsychol, MSc, MA, FHEA

University
PROFESSORS PRESS
www.universityprofessorspress.com
Colorado Springs, CO

First Published in 2020, University Professors Press.

Print ISBN: 978-1-939686-57-2
ebook ISBN: 978-1-939686-58-9

University Professors Press
Colorado Springs, CO
www.universityprofessorspress.com

Front Cover Art by Paola Minekov
Cover Design by Laura Ross

For everyone who feels stuck in the Capitalist Life Syndrome: remain hopeful.
For everyone who fights for a meaning-oriented society: be meaningful.
For everyone who studies the economics of meaning in life: become wise.

Because everyone deserves to live a meaningful life.

Table of Contents

Chapter 1

Introduction

Economics is not about things and tangible material objects; it is about men, their meanings and actions. Goods, commodities, and wealth and all the other notions of conduct are not elements of nature; they are elements of human meaning and conduct. (Von Mises, 1949, p. 92)

The Spirit of Capitalism

When I look back, I see that my life has been taken hostage by the economic system in which I lived. I grew up during the economic revival of the '50s. When we came out of the war, the country was in shambles and we had little wealth. But we had our dreams. We wanted to become like these smiling people in the bright-coloured adverts. We thought that life would be perfect if we would have that house, that hoover, that TV set, that fridge... The problem was that the adverts did not tell the costs of this new lifestyle. I wanted to buy a house to start a family, so I got a mortgage, but to afford this I had to take a well-paying job in a bank, which was not what I really wanted.

I worked long days with meaningless numbers, first on paper, later with calculators, and at the end of my career behind a computer screen—changing zeros into ones and the other way around. I could not see the bigger picture; as my colleagues handed over numbers to me, I merely did some re-calculations and gave these to other colleagues. That was my life. I had never dreamt of becoming a number manipulator. My manager expected me to sit at my desk for eight hours a day, if not longer.

When I came home, my children were often already in bed, and I was too exhausted to do anything; many nights I fell asleep in front of the TV. I was stuck in this unwanted career path because we decided to have children. But to give them the space they needed, we had to get a bigger house, and thus a bigger mortgage and I could not risk changing my job. To find some fun, I went out with my mates on the weekends, as this was what we were told would

make us quickly happy: party to the max! Yes, we laughed a lot, and I was
drunk often, but I did not feel really satisfied with my life.

Do not get me wrong. We had good times, and I have been enjoying my
big house, my BMW, my holiday home. But there was always this gnawing
discomfort deep inside, telling me that there is more to life. Now that I am
retired, I realise that my life has not been as meaningful as it could have been.
But now it is too late to change.

This is part of one of the first interviews that I conducted as a young psychology student. At the time I put his story aside as merely an elderly man's whining. Now several decades and much life experience later, I understand his concerns about the economic system better. Similarly, somber life stories have come up in my conversations with participants in scientific studies and with clients in my psychology practice. They have described how they have had their major life decisions led by economic motivations and not by what felt the most meaningful for them.

The example of the elderly man shows that our economic system is more than a market of production, consumption and finances. It gives us a lifestyle and this lifestyle is double-edged. On the one hand, the growth in material wealth has offered opportunities which previous generations did not have, and which enable individuals to choose their own lifestyle. Like the elderly man could afford a house, a TV set, a BMW and much more luxury. The invention of the washing machine and dryer also enabled individuals—traditionally women—to spend their time on more meaningful activities than the household. On the other hand, the abundance of options in our wealthy society makes it hard for individuals to know which decisions to make and which direction to go in life. People desperately try to buy any existential guidance, from lifestyle magazines to spiritual retreats. Thus, capitalism can be associated with paradoxical feelings. On the one hand, capitalism offers material opportunities to realise what is meaningful but, on the other hand, these meanings may not offer deep long-term satisfaction. Such was experienced by the elderly man who described how he did find some temporary happiness by buying his house, going out and travelling, while he also acknowledged that this lifestyle did not give deep life satisfaction.

This book offers neither a one-dimensional eulogy about the meaningful opportunities of capitalism nor a complete denunciation of anything capitalist. Rather, it will search for something below the materialist surface, which has become known in sociology as the 'spirit of capitalism'. This spirit is not about tangible objects or observable behaviour but about the lived experiences, attitudes, norms, and values that are uniquely associated with capitalism. The populariser of the term 'spirit', Max Weber, believed that protestantism had stimulated the emergence of the capitalist spirit. Although his protestantism hypothesis has shown to be correct in the specific German region that he had studied, Weber's hypothesis does not explain the worldwide hegemony of capitalism, including non-protestant countries (Swatos &

Kaelber, 2016; Tubadji, 2014; Ryman & Turner, 2007; Lehman & Roth, 1995; Furnham et al., 1993).

Weber was right that capitalism brings a specific approach to life and a specific way of making sense of the world, regardless of the culture in which someone lives. However, his term 'spirit' often remains impersonally abstract in sociological and behavioural economic studies. Instead, I will examine the most concrete and personal aspect of this spirit of capitalism: the individual meaning in life that people experience in capitalist countries. For example, some individuals could perceive being a bank employee as their ultimate meaning in life, whereas others could see their environmentalist fight as most important. These meanings are more than what economists have called 'values' or 'preferences', as meaning is much more complex than 'I want A more than B'. The idea that we can reduce meaning to such materialist and functionalist terms is the result of the capitalist spirit, as meaning is, for example, viewed totally different in less capitalist countries. Obviously, our individual thoughts and feelings about our meaning in life are influenced by the system in which we live because we have internalised what our parents and teachers have told us how we should live our life. Vice versa, the meanings of individuals shape the socio-economic system. For example, when all individuals in a country start to believe that driving cars is bad for the climate and preventing climate change becomes meaningful for them, they can switch to using public transport and consequently disrupt the car manufacturing and oil industries. Thus, the experience of individual meaning describes the spirit of capitalism in personal terms, in a dynamic interaction between the concrete daily life of individuals and the macro-economic processes.

What is 'meaning in life'? Many myths exist about this—myths that are often the result of capitalist perspectives on meaning. Let us break some of these myths (Vos, 2017). It seems that the best way is to speak about meaning as an adjective, describing our general experience of how we live our life: *Are you living a meaningful life?* Thus, meaning is not necessarily about a religious or absolute meaning of life, although some individuals may describe it in such terms. Most of the time we are not aware of our meanings, as we are simply immersed in the flow of daily meaningful activities. We make many decisions unconsciously and do not need to reflect on the meaning of each activity. We usually only start to ask questions about meaning when our meaningful flow of daily life is blocked—for instance, when we lose our job or when we feel financially insecure due to the collapse of the housing market. Meaning is also not necessarily about success or happiness, although they could go hand in hand. A good example of this is the CEO with the pseudonym Robert, who said that although he was described by journalists as one of the most successful business leaders in the city of London, his professional success did not give him a deep sense of life satisfaction. He thought that his job was his main meaning in life, and any frustration in his business was felt as a personal loss. After several sessions, Robert started to realise that he did not feel satisfied with life as he had been focusing merely on professional success while ignoring other meanings in his life such as his relationship with his wife and children.

Thus, to understand the meaning of economics, we need to get rid of such myths about meaning and base it on systematic scientific research. Meaning is a well-defined psychological concept in the same way as psychological terms such as depression or extraversion are widely accepted. Thousands of scientific studies conclude that meaning is the combination of motivation, values, understanding of our place in the world, setting goals and flexibly committing to them, self-worth, and coping with challenges in life (see reviews in Vos, 2017, 2016, 2016a). Motivation means that we are moving (*movere* in Latin) in a general direction since humans are directional beings with patterns or structures in their behaviour. Being directional helps people not to reinvent the wheel each day and not spend a long time reflecting on what they want because it gives stability, rules-of-thumb and efficient use of resources. Values describe what we find important or worthy about certain goals and the road towards these goals, such as the values of modesty or altruism. Understanding is about our awareness of our unique situation and life-world, knowing our place, our possibilities and impossibilities, such as understanding that I live in a market economy where I need to compete with others to make a living. Self-worth is involved since I find myself worthy enough to take my own values seriously and not merely conform to traditional values that others have imposed on me. Goal regulation is about knowing how to regulate our meaning in daily life and knowing how to realise our goals. Meaning without commitment to action is mere imagination and symbols; thus, we need to be committed to bringing meaning into reality. Finally, we need to know how to cope with existential challenges that we will undoubtedly encounter, such as being flexible and able to tolerate frustration, anxiety, and recognizing that we are a limited being. These six characteristics often come together, and their combination is what we call 'meaning'; better formulated as adjectives, they describe the way we are living a meaningful life.

The Capitalist Life Syndrome

The spirit of our modern economic system is in crisis, wrote Paul Valery in 1919 in *La Crise de L'Esprit*. His words could not be more applicable now, precisely a century later. Systematic research shows that many individuals struggle with living a meaningful life in capitalist societies, more than in the past and in less capitalist countries. These meaning-centred struggles lead to other problems such as the large mental health crisis in Western countries. For example, never have so many individuals experienced psychological problems as now in Western countries such as the United States and the United Kingdom, and this seems to be due to the lack of living an authentically meaningful life (see reviews in Vos, Roberts, & Davies, 2019). This widespread crisis in meaning-making and mental health seems to be caused by the capitalist system that they live in, where meaning is approached in a unique and often mentally unhealthy way.

This unique capitalist spirit that individuals suffer from may be called *The Capitalist Life Syndrome*, a name derived from a pseudo-psychological diagnosis called the Stockholm Syndrome. The first time Stockholm Syndrome was described was in a psychological analysis of the positive feelings that hostages felt towards their captors during a violent bank robbery in Stockholm in 1973. The Stockholm Syndrome causes hostages to develop a psychological alliance with their captors. Despite the actual danger that the captors are to their well-being, hostages develop positive feelings towards their captors and even refuse to cooperate with the police or the legal system. The hostages believe in the humanity of their hostage-takers and believe that they hold the same values.

Similarly, the lives of individuals in Western countries seem to be taken over by capitalism, and particularly by the manipulation of their mindset. Although capitalism may offer them different values than they initially experience, they will buy into the system and start to believe that the capitalist lifestyle will help them personally to live a meaningful life. They may even passionately defend the capitalist system, even when this does not actually help them to realise what they experience as truly meaningful in life. Thus, the problem is not merely the fact that they live in a physical system that is dominated by capitalist institutions and regulations, but that their spirit is taken over. They do not see, or do not want to see, the violence and manipulation of their perception and values. They believe that they have freely chosen this capitalist lifestyle themselves even as governments and companies impose their capitalist meanings ingeniously onto citizens (Foucault, 2001/2008,1988). Instead of directly ordering 'thou must buy' or 'thou shall work', governments tell citizens to govern themselves. That is, we are officially free, but we live in a market full of external influences such as marketing campaigns, while many of us are desperate to receive any guidance as we lack the clear direction of a religion or a belief system. Consequently, many individuals voluntarily adopt these superficial and functionalist meanings, and by buying and working on the market they contribute to the system (Part II will give empirical evidence for all these statements).

Thus, individuals seem to think that they have chosen in all freedom to live a capitalist life, and subsequently feel that they have only themselves to blame for any problems or lack of satisfaction in life (cf. Verhaeghe, 2012). This creates the paradoxical feeling of fatalism and helplessness, on the one hand, and identification with this lifestyle, on the other hand. Like the elderly man who felt tricked into his lifestyle, only retrospectively do individuals seem able to acknowledge the source of this paradox; only afterwards do they see how they have identified themselves with a political-economic system that they have not consciously chosen and which may not have helped them to realise what is truly meaningful.

How does meaning in this cultural pseudo-diagnosis of the Capitalist Life Syndrome look like? Chapter 3 will introduce ten questions or perspectives on how we can analyse meaning. In contrast with the works of other authors such as Oliver James (2007, 2008), who focus mainly at a single criterion at a time—such as his term 'Affluenza'—this book shows that it is the interlocking combination of these ten perspectives that makes the Capitalist Life Syndrome so detrimental to mental health and ultimately for socio-economic prosperity. Chapter 7 will show empirical evidence for this model in tens of thousands of people, and the chapters following will provide systematic empirical evidence for each of these criteria. Capitalism is like a forced package deal, where you cannot only buy one product but are forced to buy all products at once.

The following is a brief outline, but in Part II each perspective will be elaborated. It is important not to interpret this outline as a formal diagnosis that we can impose on people—like telling a patient that he or she has cancer in the terminal stage. The Capitalist Life Syndrome is a pragmatic rule-of-thumb that makes the intertwining of ten perspectives easier to understand.

Name
Individuals suffering from the Capitalist Life Syndrome either live in a country with a dominantly capitalist economy and/or personally value capitalist ideas. In the next chapter, capitalism will be defined as the economic system that functions in such a way that individuals attempt to maximize their private material wealth by using and increasing their capital—albeit natural, machinal, social, financial, informational, symbolic, or imaginary capital. Of course, capitalism is not a monolithic phenomenon (Hancke, 2009), but this book primarily focuses on the neoliberal ideology and politics that seem to currently dominate Western countries.

Status
Capitalism is imagined, symbolic and real at the same time. For example, Adam Smith imagined an Invisible Hand that would create a perfect balance between supply and demand, and Milton Friedman imagined that a small state, a free market, and private companies would benefit all. This image of the free market is more than merely an imagination; it is a powerful symbol that has led people to revolutions, such as people dancing on the Berlin Wall in November 1989 and shouting 'freedom!' Thus, capitalism imagines and symbolises how we can live our lives, and these images and symbols are powerful influences on the actual social relationships between individuals and how they see themselves and their lives. For example, people are bombarded with the image from childhood onwards that they need to live life to the max, optimise their economic function, and achieve the highest possible education, career, salary, family life, housing, luxury goods such as cars, etc. Becoming yourself, contributing to the well-being of others, or fighting for justice have relatively little value in this model. Instead, we are told self-interest and competition are the cornerstones of economic

prosperity, and we should compete to achieve the highest level possible. Capitalism is not value-neutral but inherently prescribes how we should imagine and symbolise our lives and act on these imaginations and symbols. But capitalism is also a physical reality in daily life, describing how citizens interact, the regulations that governments set, and the ways that companies develop. Margaret Thatcher's decrease in benefits in the name of the free market has impacted the daily lives of many citizens (Chapter 10). Thus, capitalism is imagined, symbolic, and real.

Type of Meaning
Viewed across countries and time, individuals differ in what they experience as meaningful (Chapter 10). Research involving more than 45,000 individuals worldwide shows that people often experience six types of meaning: materialist, hedonist, self-oriented, social, larger, and existential–philosophical meanings (Vos, 2019, 2018, 2016). Individuals suffering from Capitalist Life Syndrome focus mainly on superficial types of meanings. For example, they attempt to find meaning in materialism, hedonism, or themselves. They concentrate on buying things, success in their careers, improving their social status, having the most fun possible, or developing themselves to the max. In contrast, they focus less on social connections, altruism, or higher purposes such as creating a just society or following a religious calling.

Approach to Meaning
Capitalists often have a functionalist approach to their lives (Chapter 11). They believe they can simply demand or buy meaning in life, like any materialist product on the market. They believe that their desire for meaning will be quickly fulfilled, like buying a Burger McMeaning (Vos, 2018). They may stereotypically expect that exotic holidays, binge drinking, or drug taking bring life fulfillment. Although these McMeanings could give temporary satisfaction, they do not provide a deeper sense of meaningfulness.

Relationship Between Individual and Society
Individuals identify themselves with their capitalist lifestyle, consciously or unconsciously (Chapter 12). For example, they believe that this lifestyle is the best they could achieve in life. Or they do not reflect on how they live but simply show-till-they-drop. This belief could be due to a lack of criticism or reflexivity. This makes them vulnerable to mind manipulation by mass media, marketing, and managers.

Development Over Time
Many capitalists imagine human history as a story about materialistic progress—a linear line from poverty and ignorance to richness and wisdom for all (Chapter 13). This development is seen as a materialist and self-oriented function: When people are free enough to follow their own materialist goals, they will be able to improve

themselves, and with their self-improvement, the wealth of the nation will improve in its totality.

Emergence of Individual Meaning

Some sociologists have been obsessed with the question of whether the egg or the chicken came first, or in economic terms whether the individual agent determines society or whether the societal structure determines the individual (Chapter 13). The most popular answer nowadays is that we need both the chicken and the egg: Individuals and their socio-economic system are involved in a complex dynamic interaction (Giddens, 1971). In Chapter 3, we will show that economics is even more than this complexity, as a third factor mediates between agent and structure: meaning. We can only understand the relationship between both when we take meaning into account. However, capitalism gives us the illusion that we are unique individuals who can freely choose our own meaning. The way in which our meanings are manipulated by commercials and social media is hidden behind a curtain of socio-economic ignorance.

Sense of Freedom

Many individuals in capitalist countries seem to suffer from capitalistic (chapters 9 and 13). They feel stuck in their lives and see no alternative, even though they may theoretically acknowledge the limitations of their capitalist lifestyle. Their helplessness, hopelessness, and nihilism about their personal life are in sharp contrast to the capitalist imagination of the free market. People are told that they are free to choose their own lifestyle, but economic studies clearly show that full freedom may only be achievable by the rich and powerful few at the top (see chapters 8 and 12 for evidence).

Existential Well-Being

The capitalist lifestyle is also associated with structural existential worries (Chapter 12). For example, individuals feel fundamentally anxious and uncertain about life, face ever higher productivity goals, suffer from indecision, feel inauthentic, and are driven by the existential urgency to get the most out of life. The lack of freedom cannot only lead to anxiety but also to anger.

Impact on Daily Life

Individuals who suffer from the Capitalist Life Syndrome report many psychological, social, and professional concerns (Chapter 12). This does not necessarily mean that they have clinical depression or anxiety, but they feel a structural sense of emotional discomfort, unhappiness, or lack of satisfaction in life. They often describe a vague discomfort or dissatisfaction in life: 'I cannot put my finger on it, but...' This ambiguous discomfort may grow and lead to more serious psychological stress or disorders. Consequently, Western countries have never seen a larger-scale mental health crisis, and many mental health problems are often directly related to the socio-economic situation and lifestyle (Vos, Roberts, & Davies, 2019). Research in Chapter 7 will show that the more individuals live a capitalist lifestyle, the more grievous their mental health problems are.

Summary
The Capitalist Life Syndrome can be defined as that perspective on economics—whether a reality, symbol, or imagined model—which focuses on materialist, hedonist, and self-oriented types of meaning from a functionalist perspective; which sees individuals and history as a functionalist process predominantly determined by materialist factors; which makes individuals feel unfree despite the capitalist imagination of freedom; and which leads to a crisis in the existential, psychological and overall well-being of individuals.

Looking back at the story of the elderly man, it seems that this is what he was describing. It was more than just description; it seems as if he gave me his story as a riddle: What is the meaning of economics, and how can ordinary citizens and consumers be enabled to live a free and meaningful life again? This book is the legacy of that conversation. The next sections will further explain the importance of having a meaning-oriented perspective in economics and will show that the Capitalist Life Syndrome is not the only answer to the capitalist system. Since the turn of the millennium, an increasing number of individuals are steering away from the Capitalist Life Syndrome, developing a meaning-oriented perspective on economics.

Table 1.1. Ten Perspectives of the Capitalist Life Syndrome

Question	Perspective	Capitalist Life Syndrome
Name?	Name of system	Capitalism
Status?	Ontological status	Reality, symbol, and imagination
What?	Type of meaning	Materialistic Hedonistic Self-oriented
How?	Approach to meaning	Functionalistic
Where?	Relationship between individual and society	Social and individual determinism
When?	Development over time	Historicism
Who?	Emergence of individual meaning	Individual & mass psychology Meaning manipulation ('mind mafia')
Whose?	Sense of freedom	-Negative freedom in the imagination of a free market; - Inequality in the ability to use freedom; - Individual fatalism, helplessness. and hopelessness
Why?	Existential ground	Existential questions and concerns
Which?	Impact on daily life	Mental health problems, low quality of life, low life satisfaction

All Economics is About Meaning

Many modern economists claim that they do not describe or prescribe any meanings to individuals and that they merely give a functional description of the economy. They would frown at the inclusion of 'exogenous' variables such as meaning in a book on economics and see human behaviour as rational and predictable by economic mechanisms such as supply and demand. They argue that products and services are sold because people prefer them for their utility and that the price is mainly determined by the number of available products and the demand for these products. Similarly, individuals put their labour on the market, are employed where their skills are needed, and are paid relative to their contribution or utility to the production process. *Give me an individual at the age of five and I will tell you how they will live their life.* This view of an individual as a *Homo calculus* has led economists such as Samuelson and Becker to completely mathematise economic behaviour. This maths mindset has to some extent been beneficial as it seems to have helped better understand and guide some economic behaviour. However, this mindset has also limited the freedom and capability of individuals to self-determine and live a fully meaningful life.

Chapter 3 will use the fairy tale of the naked emperor to argue that economics is not naked and value-neutral, but it has been wearing many layers of clothes all along. This is not the first book investigating the meanings that the economic rhetoric attempts to hide. Many other voices can be heard in this crowd, including neo-Marxists, the Frankfurt School of Critical Theory, and French post-structuralist philosophers. For example, Schumacher asks in *Small is beautiful* (1974) about the limitations of this value-neutral paradigm, although his book was initially disregarded as heretical. Similarly, economists and government advisors seemed to ignore critical theorists and humanists such as Erich Fromm and Herbert Marcuse. The call from these humanists seemed too radical; they wanted a full transformation of the acquisitive society of having-having-having to an economy of being, which instead centres around topics such as justice and sharing communities. However, since the turn of the millennium, a silent paradigm shift has become visible. The economic maths mindset is more and more joined by a humanist mindset as increasing numbers of authors describe how economics is inherently about how people live their lives and how they give meaning to their behaviour.

Two Nobel Prize winners, George Acerola and Robert Shiller, summarised this recent trend (2009, p.1): 'To understand how economies work and how we can manage them and proposer, we could pay attention to the thought patterns that animate people's feelings, their *animal spirits.* We will never really understand important economic events unless we confront the fact that their causes are largely mental in nature.' Akerlof and Shiller (2010) borrowed the term *animal spirits* from John Maynard Keynes, who used this term to describe the unpredictable and irrational events in economics. Many psychologists have analysed such animalistic behaviour and brought spirit back to economics. For instance, Daniel Kahneman (2011) and Nasim Taleb (2011, 2005) have shown how consumers, producers and investors make decisions by cognitive biases and fallacies, such as black-or-white reasoning, which traditional economic models could not explain. These cognitive factors have now become a standard part of advanced market analysis and financial risk management (see Chapter 7). However, the paradigm shifts in economics evolved further and refocused attention from cold cognitions to hot emotions, passions, and values. For example, even when individuals know they are biased, their passion can lead them to pursue what they believe in, such as investors buying packages of high-risk mortgages before the 2008 housing market crash. These passions have to do with deeper feelings such as confidence and belief in the fairness of the market. Thus, increasing numbers of studies explain economic behaviour in terms of the beliefs and values of individuals instead of in rational terms.

What could explain this paradigm shift towards more humanist economics? Some hypotheses follow.

First, economic models have shown to fail at predicting economic developments (see Chapter 7). The 2007–2008 sub-prime mortgage crisis and the subsequent litany of banking, stock market, and monetary crises revealed fundamental flaws in neoliberal models. Several authors have attributed the failure of these models and the subsequent inefficient government responses to the lack of attention to *animal spirits* (Skidelsky & Skidelsky, 2012). For example, cognitive biases and irrational reasoning appear better predictors than statistical forecasts (Kahneman, 2016). Thus, we need to give attention to how companies, investors, and governments give meaning to the economic processes. Part II will elaborate how ignoring meaning-making in the economic process has contributed to the crisis.

Second, the mantra of economic growth has been challenged for a long time, from the Club of Rome in the 1970s to environmental activists such as Extinction Rebellion. These challengers have argued that when markets are left free, they will not perfectly regulate themselves, at least from the perspective of the natural and human environment. It is, for instance, not in the interest of the industry to regulate its own pollution in the short term, although in the long-term it will undermine itself by destroying the natural resources it needs. Left-wing thinkers and politicians ranging from Noam Chomsky to Bernie Sanders and Jeremy Corbyn have argued that markets will not create the safety net that unemployed or sick individuals need for their survival. Thus, the rational economic formulas focused in the past on materialistic meanings, but they may have lacked ecological and humanist meaning; consequently, the public support for this narrow view of the economy seems to be rapidly decreasing, while the support for sustainable economics is increasing (Chapter 7). Furthermore, companies and governments are put under pressure to give attention to ecological and human values, as they do not want to lose the support from consumers, lobbyists, and voters that is of existential importance in this digital era in which one negative review online or a tweet from the American president can bankrupt a business.

Third, the personal lives of many individuals in Western countries have been affected by the financial crisis and austerity measures of the last decade. For example, socio-economic inequality has never been so large in the West, and the impact of this inequality can be felt at a personal level (Pikkety, 2014). In the United Kingdom, approximately half a million individuals are homeless and one million need support from the foodbank for their survival (Foodbanks UK, 2018). The International Monetary Fund (2016) has also concluded in its reports that austerity measures have disproportionally impacted the lives of poor individuals. Due to this personal impact, economic topics are not merely relevant to and debated by a small academic and political elite, but their consequences can be felt in daily life by the general population, which has started to publicly criticise capitalist ideas. This can, for instance, be seen in the public mistrust in traditional academic economic research and politics in general and in the rise of political parties that promote themselves as being outside or against the economic-political establishment, as a Gallup poll showed in 2016. Consequently, bookstores seem to be flooded by populist publications on economics, and public political–economic debates have not been so well attended since the 1970s. Thus, there seems to be a growing gap between the obsession of economists and governments with economic growth and the daily life experience of ordinary people that wealth is not and should not be an end but merely a means to 'the good life' (Skidelsky & Skidelsky, 2012).

Fourth, economists in the so-called Chicago School of Economics have described economics as a value-neutral analysis of individuals and markets (see Chapter 4). However, a flurry of recent publications suggests that the opposite is true. For example, Robert Nelson's book *Economics as Religion* (2001) shows how the ideas from modern economics are loaded with values about the free market, privatization, and a focus on rational behaviour and the utility of products and services. Similarly, Tomas Sedlacek describes in *Economics of Good and Evil* (2011) how economic models are implicitly or explicitly based on religious and philosophical concepts of good and evil, such as the need for self-interest, freedom, hedonism, private ownership, and the benevolence of markets. Several others have critically retraced the value-loaded roots of economics and have shown how even the godfather of liberalism, Adam Smith (1759/2010), proposed the inclusion of moral sentiments in market analyses. Similarly, even mathematical models in economics, which may appear objective, have been shown to be based on hypothetical philosophical assumptions (Hausman, McPherson, & Satz, 2017). This book stands in this tradition.

Functionalist Approaches

The preliminary definition of the Capitalist Life Syndrome above will become clearer in the following chapters. However, it is important to underline one crucial aspect that is often overlooked: the functionalist approach to life that underlies capitalism (this will be elaborated in Chapter 9). The clearest example of functionalism can be found in Gary Becker (1976), who writes that all economic behaviour can be explained by the individual's ability to increase the economic utility or efficiency. This includes love—which, according to him, means that individuals derive utility from the utility from each other: 'It can be said that Mi [Man i] loves Fj [Female j] if her welfare enters his utility function, and perhaps also if Mi values emotional and physical contact with Fj'. In other words, Becker writes that meaning is about a relationship that increases each other's well-being. This would imply that love would disappear if one partner would no longer be completely able to increase the well-being of the other—for instance, due to physical or mental health problems. This utilitarian approach has made love vulnerable to manipulation and commercial exploitation (Armstrong, 2002). For example, Hollywood movies and greeting card companies thrive on marketing love, and the invention of Valentine's Day gives companies in the United States alone approximately £20 billion extra annual income. Television series on dating and sexual coupling yield big revenues: 'Big Brother' provides nearly 25% of the annual revenues of Channel 4, and 'The Bachelorette' brings in approximately £250 million per year for ABC. Meanwhile, this marketization of love gives the idea that true love can be easily demanded and achieved—like ordering a 'Burger McLove' or buying Valentine gifts or going on a television show.

However, research shows that many couples remain together and express feelings of love even if this may not directly improve their mutual well-being. For most people, love is not a calculation about 'from whom will I benefit most', but about meanings that transcend the functionality of the relationship (Bruckner, 2012). Romantic love is irrational and blind, guided by passion and not reason (Silverman, 2009). Most people love someone for the sake of love. Consequently, psychologists would see a one-dimensional functionalist approach to relationships, such as Becker's, as symptoms of autism, narcissism, or even psychopathy.

This example shows how different individuals approach the meanings of love in different ways, from something you can demand and that is about utility to love for the sake of love. Historically, this difference goes back to the Middle Ages, when ordinary citizens usually had relationships for practical reasons and not for the sake of love. People mainly married for pragmatic reasons, such as getting children to provide future income, or marrying into rich families (Taylor, 2002). This functionalist concept of love started to change in cities in the 16th century when their increasing wealth gave the new middle class the option to search for love not merely for the sake of survival but also for the sake of authentic love (Berman, 2004).

In general, the end of the Middle Ages showed a transformation from functionalist meanings to authentic meanings (Vos, 2018). Even the etymology of the term 'meaning' reveals this. The term comes from the Old German *meinung*, which started as 'opinion' in late German and other European languages, something rational and vulgar that can change and be manipulated. However, at the end of the Middle Ages, religious authors such as Meister Eckhart and Martin Luther popularised the term *sinn* as a replacement for the functionalist term *meinung*. The word 'sinn' is derived from the Latin *sentire*, which means 'perceiving with all senses'. Instead of imposing our predetermined ideas *on* relationships, we listen to what our feelings and intuitions tell about what we experience as meaningful in relationships. We do not buy a product merely because of its functionality but because we love it. I will not be able to randomly exchange this product for another product because it has an irreducible meaning for me, just as I cannot simply exchange my partner and expect to feel the same love for any other random partner. All European and Slavic languages have developed a similar term to speak in an experiential way about meaning in life except for English, which still uses the term 'meaning' (Vos, 2018).

Classical economics is often based on utilitarian approaches to meaning, as popularised by authors such as Mill and Bentham. Adam Smith used the terms 'interest' and 'preference' to describe the functional utility that individuals attributed to products, services, jobs, and other economic phenomena. This focus on functionalist utility seems to appropriately describe how individuals experienced meaning until the end of the Middle Ages, after which many individuals experienced meaning in more experiential ways. However, this medieval functionalism still seems to dominate the most influential economic theories, such as those from Friedrich Hayek and Milton Friedman and the government policies inspired by them. For example, Friedman (1988) proposed a functionalist approach to the housing market, which he described as mere financial assets. He did not include the deep emotional meanings that living in a home can have for individuals. Consumers have been willing to buy a house they could not afford as they did not make this decision with a rational functionalist approach but with an intuitive love and emotional attachment to the house. However, banks and investors have approached housing in functionalist ways. When they offered risky mortgages, they did not take the emotional and existential impact of the housing bubble into account. The crash of the housing market was, therefore, not only a financial crisis but an existential crisis for many house owners, which was caused by a totally different approach to meaning than their daily life experience. Economists assume that people randomly buy and live in houses and sell them without emotion, but the reality is that a house offers the meaning of a psychological and existential home. Thus, the functionalist economic approach does not only inaccurately describe the psychological reality of the economic market but has also created a severe psychological and existential crisis for many home owners.

From Capitalist Life Syndrome to Meaning-Oriented Economy

This chapter already preluded the socio-economic trend during the first decades of the 21st century away from the Capitalist Life Syndrome to a more Meaning-Oriented Economy. This trend is characterised by the opposites of the Capitalist Life Syndrome.

The values and behaviour of these individuals do not orient towards capitalism but towards moral or ecological economics, which includes a wide range of meanings with a dominant focus on social and larger types of meanings in life. Their approach to meaning is not functionalist but intuitive and critical (also called phenomenological). Individuals feel both free and responsible at the same time towards their life situation, while they keep a realistic sense of their limitations. They live a meaningful and satisfying life despite life's challenges and experience positive well-being.

Chapter 13 will discuss why this transition is happening. This will centre around the hypothesis that the Capitalist Life Syndrome creates internal pressure that stimulates individuals to start asking what really matters in life and begin focusing on the most meaningful in their personal life, the economy, and society in general. This follows Karl Marx's comment (1850) that capitalism 'will carry within it the seeds of its own destruction', and these seeds can be found in the Capitalist Life Syndrome.

Table 1.2. Ten Perspectives on the Meaning-Oriented Perspective on the Economy

Question	Perspective	Meaning-Orientated Perspective
Name?	Name of system	Meaning-Oriented Economy
Status?	Ontological status	Reality, symbol & imagination
What?	Type of meaning	All types of meaning, but dominant focus on social and larger types
How?	Approach to meaning	Phenomenological, also called critical–intuitive
Where?	Relationship between individual and society	Interaction
When?	Development over time	Historiographic
Who?	Emergence of individual meaning	Complex, pluralistic psychology
Whose?	Sense of freedom	Realistic sense of freedom
Why?	Existential ground	Sense of living a meaningful life despite the socio-economic situation
Which?	Impact on daily life	Positive mental health, high quality of life, high life satisfaction

About this Book

The overall aim of this book is to describe the relationship between economics and meaning in life. Its first sub-aim is to describe the socio-economic transition from the Capitalist Life Syndrome to the Meaning-Oriented Economy. This book will specifically focus on the role of meaning in this transition, and how this transition can be stimulated by individuals, companies, and governments.

The second sub-aim of this book is to offer an alternative to the meaningless economic theories and to lay the foundations of a new sub-discipline called 'the economics of meaning in life'. This will show how the economics profession has ignored the topic of meaning, even though meaning is inherent to all economic theories, models, and political applications. Existing research and examples of the economics of meaning in life will be described.

Part I of this book will give an overview of the Economics of Meaning in Life. Chapter 2 describes the meanings that are usually hidden in capitalism, and Chapter 3 lays the scientific foundations for the economics of meaning in life (readers less interested in science could skip this chapter). Chapters 4–6 describe how meaning has been addressed in different historical periods, starting with social economics, followed by both capitalism and Marxism, and finalised by post-materialist economies. Part II starts with an overview of research on the Capitalist Life Syndrome (this could be skipped by those with less scientific interests). Each of the following chapters describes one of the ten perspectives on the Capitalist Life Syndrome, and its support by research evidence. Part III offers an overview of meaning-oriented economics, starting with an overview of research. The last chapters describe examples of how people can develop a meaning-oriented perspective within, outside, against, or beyond capitalism.

> *This book is adorned with case studies and personal reflections, such as the story of the elderly man that appeared in this chapter—usually formulated in the first person and printed in italics. As the feminist movement in the 1960s touted: 'the personal is political'. Personal examples can sometimes illustrate a complex phenomenon in few words. Furthermore, reflexivity is a methodological part of any serious exploration of meaning in life (Vos, 2018). These examples contribute to the exploration of the plurality of empirical evidence that follows from the pragmatic phenomenology described in Chapter 3. Naturally, these examples should only be regarded as one of the many sources of data in the mixed methods that I use in this book, and not too much weight should be given to these examples to prevent any induction bias. In these examples, my personal and professional voices will join each other to phenomenologically explore what is meaningful to myself and to others, such as to the elderly man.*

Key Points

1. There is no such thing as neutral economics. All economic theories, models, and symbols explicitly or implicitly describe meaning.
2. The Capitalist Life Syndrome is that perspective on economics—albeit economics as a reality, symbol, or imagined model—which focuses on materialist, hedonist, and self-oriented types of meaning from a functionalist perspective. This perspective sees individuals and history as a functionalist process predominantly determined by materialist factors that make individuals feel unfree despite the capitalist imagination of freedom, and that lead to a crisis in the existential, psychological, and overall well-being of

individuals. This syndrome is reinforced by the mind- manipulation techniques that manipulate the meanings of citizens and consumers.

3. Since the end of the 20th century, fewer individuals seem to focus on capitalism and more on the Meaning-Oriented Economy. The latter is an intuitive, critical (phenomenological) perspective on economics, which is oriented around a wide range of meanings, with a dominant focus on social and larger meanings where individuals feel free and responsible towards their life situation while keeping a realistic sense of their limitations. They live a meaningful and satisfying life despite life's challenges and experience positive well-being.

4. This book aims to describe the transition towards the Meaning-Oriented Economy, as well as describing how meaning in life can be studied in economics. The next chapter introduces the methodology of this new sub-discipline of the economics of meaning in life, which will be applied to the history of economics in the subsequent chapters. Part II of this book describes the Capitalist Life Syndrome, and Part III describes the Meaning-Oriented Economy.

Part I

The Economics
of Meaning in Life

Chapter 2

The Multiple Meanings
of Capitalism

[Capitalism is] a purely cultic religion, perhaps the most extremely cultic that ever existed. Within it, nothing has meaning that is not immediately related to the cult; it has no specific dogma or theology. Utilitarianism acquires in it, from this viewpoint, its religious colouration. (Walter Benjamin, 2001, p. 19 in Lowy, 2009)

The Multiple Meanings of the Baker

It is not from the benevolence of the butcher, the brewer, or the baker that we expect our dinner, but from their regard to their own interest. We address ourselves, not to their humanity but to their self-love, and never talk to them of our own necessities but of their advantages. [The baker] generally, indeed, neither intends to promote the public interest nor knows how much he is promoting it. By preferring the support of domestic to that of foreign industry, he intends only his own security; and by directing that industry in such a manner as its produce may be of the greatest value, he intends only his own gain, and he is in this, as in many other cases, led by an invisible hand to promote an end which was no part of his intention. By pursuing his own interest, he frequently promotes that of the society more effectually than when he really intends to promote it.

This is the classic citation in Adam Smith's *The Wealth of Nations* (1776/2010, p.32). Neoliberal economists such as Friedman (1977) and Hayek (1960/2013, 1944/2014) ascribe much meaning to these symbols of the invisible hand, free market, and self-interest. They interpret this text as saying that individuals like the baker are primarily driven by their wish for their own financial gains. Thanks to the fact that the baker follows his self-oriented materialistc meanings, he contributes to the productivity and growth of national wealth.

Mandeville (1705) went further than Smith by suggesting in *The Fable of the Bees* that if individuals would focus on social values and a just world, people would lose their jobs. Blacksmiths would lose their jobs because the bars and ironwork on windows and doors they had been creating against thieves, judges, and bureaucrats would be unnecessary to oversee the law; farmers and servants would lose their jobs due to a decreased demand for luxury products and services; and the army would become obsolete. Thus, Mandeville argued that economic prosperity needs economic agents to be driven by self-oriented materialistic meanings. Similar Mandevillian ideas seem to form the cornerstone of what has been called neoliberalism, and particularly the Chicago School of Economics in the 20th century. For instance, according to Gary Becker (1976), crime can be regarded as mere economic redistribution, driven by economic motivations. To be able to justify this bold statement, Becker had to ignore the impact that the experience of being a thief and being robbed have on the identity, mental health, and economic functioning of individuals. For example, the robbed family may feel so traumatised that their productivity decreases, or the thief may have broken so much that he has not primarily redistributed but destroyed materialistic wealth.

As the previous chapter preluded, all economic behaviour involves meaning, even if the meaning may not be directly visible. For centuries, authors have tried to hide how meaning was imposed on people. However, in the 20th century, meaning has received a more central role in economic texts. The manipulation of meaning has even become a crucial tool in promoting the capitalist life. That is, there has been a gradual shift towards an economic system that focuses on the manipulation of what individuals experience as meaningful in life. This shift can be shown by a range of examples, as will be described in the next paragraphs. Meaning manipulation seems to be the core mechanism to create public support for capitalism (as will be elaborated in Chapter 9), even though it may not always be in the best interest for the public to give their backing. Without manipulating personal meanings, the capitalist system may collapse.

The Meanings of the Baker

Adam Smith did not promote selfishness but had a nuanced ethical perspective (Forman-Barzilai, 2010; Bassiry & Jones, 1993; Waszek, 1984) and warned against alienation in the economic system (Ten Houten, 2016; Drosos, 1996; West, 1969). For example, in his book *The Theory of Moral Sentiments*, Smith explicitly denounced egoism (see Chapter 5, which elaborates this point). Many other types of meaning, which he called 'passions', are important for the economy, such as morality. Thus, following one's own interest' does not contradict these other meanings, as Smith has a pluralist model: Individuals are motivated by multiple types of meaning in life and can have multiple meanings next to each other, such as self-oriented and social types of meaning (Wilson & Dixon, 2015; Schoene, 2015; Montes, 2003).

In the 20th century, the pluralism of economic motivations was underlined by the studies from critical theorists. Deleuze and Guattari (1988) argued, for instance, that individuals are not only driven by the desire for material acquisition but also by the relational process of producing or by extra-economic desires. Individuals may have a multiplicity of socially embedded meanings motivating their economic behaviour. Thus, this economic reality seems very different from Mandeville's fictional fable, as will be shown in detail in Chapter 5.

What motivations other than getting money for himself could the baker have had to work in the bakery? To answer this question, this book will centre around six types and 25 sub-types of meaning that individuals could experience in life. This sextet of meanings has been developed on the basis of answers of more than 45.000 individuals in a review of 107 research studies worldwide about how they experience meaning in life (Vos, 2018). They reveal that they find meaning in materialist, hedonist, self-oriented, social, larger, and existential–philosophical types of meaning. For instance, the baker may have liked this job because he enjoys being successful and creative in manually making products (materialistic meanings). He may have enjoyed the kneading of the dough, seeing the bread rise, and having fun with his colleagues (hedonist meanings). The job could also have meant that he could be proud of his perseverance, mastery, and flexibility in overcoming challenges such as coping with the fluctuating quality of the wheat and the competition from other bakers. It could have also given him a sense of identity and autonomy (self-oriented meanings). He also could have experienced a sense of belonging to the bakers' guild and wanted to socialise with colleagues and customers. Possibly his only motivation was to be able to care for his wife and children. He may also have had altruist or larger purposes— for instance, to make healthy bread to feed people (social meanings). This job could also have been about developing his skills and fulfilling his personal potential. The bakery could have been a family business so that he could feel connected with the generations before him and wanted to hand over the business to his children. The job could have given him the idea that he is fulfilling a role in the larger plan or kingdom of God (larger meanings). Possibly the baker was not interested in the job, but he was grateful to find any job and be able to survive and do something responsible (existential–philosophical meanings).

Innovation
Thus, work can have many different meanings for different individuals, and individuals can experience multiple meanings in one job. All these different meanings can drive individuals to join the labour market and thus indirectly contribute to the gross national product and the wealth of the country. The social and larger meanings could even have motivated the baker to excel and be innovative.

To stay with Smith's example of bakers, one baker in the 19th century, my great-grandfather, Marius Vos, saw the wider social importance of bread. The quality of the bread often fluctuated, and the grain could not be stored for a long time as it started rotting; consequently, bread was known to cause diseases, particularly in wintertime when there was no fresh grain. Therefore, he started to experiment with improving the quality, and he discovered a way to create bread with guaranteed quality in factories; by burning the grains slightly, he killed most bacteria. He marketed this invention with the slogan 'your baker, your doctor'. Marius Vos may not have gained very great personal material wealth from his invention as he focused primarily on the social meaning of his bread. Thus, one of the main innovations in the Dutch history of bread did not merely come from the self-oriented materialist meanings of the baker but from social and larger meanings. We may generalise this finding and hypothesize that the economy would possibly not flourish if individuals were only motivated by short-term, self-oriented materialist meanings. Similarly, research indicates that scientific revolutions and product innovations are led by individuals who were driven by larger meanings, and not by individuals who are only going after self-oriented materialist meanings (Kuhn, 2012; Popper, 2012). Thus, economic growth requires social and larger meanings, but classical economic models do not include these types of meanings.

Human Resource Management

The idea that employees can have plural reasons to work has been taken up by Human Resource Managers (HRM) during the last decade. The HRM field has been transforming from a functionalist to a more meaning-oriented approach. Stereotypically, in the past, human resources had to be managed efficiently like natural resources, ensuring that these 'things'—human beings—functioned in the way that they were expected to. The primary focus was aligning employees to their role in the organisational machine. Thus, the company determined the employee's meaning. However, HRM has moved towards an employee-centred approach, with the individual meanings of the employee at its heart (e.g. Ullrich, 2011). This employee-centred revolution in HR was stimulated by psychological research in the '80s and '90s, which showed that employees are more productive when they have a larger sense of autonomy and control, enough breaks, etc. (e.g., Dik, Byrne, & Steger, 2017). Initially, HRM implemented these research findings directly for all employees in general, but this did not always do the magic because some individuals would indeed like to have more autonomy while others would not. Thus, HR managers started to listen to the individual meanings that employees prefer in their job, and they facilitated them in realising these personal meanings so that the employee would function optimally: *What do you need to make a meaningful contribution to this company?* This led to the idea of personal plans, tenureships, flexible working, flexible parental leave, and holiday time.

This meaning-oriented revolution of HRM is possibly most visible in the creative and IT sectors, where a functionalist focus seems particularly counterproductive. For example, Google has created a home atmosphere in their buildings, with many options—even gaming rooms and masseurs—for employees to experience many meanings. To improve the input from individual employees, several companies have flattened the organisational structure, created self-run units, and include employees in management conversations. Several company owners such as Ricardo Semler (2003, 2001) have described how the bottom-up input from employees is crucial for a flourishing business, as employees know from their experience what the core problems are and where the production or service processes could be streamlined to become more meaningful to the employees, clients, productivity, sales, and the company—and to the economy in general.

Thus, the new HRM field seems to be defined by the assumption that the more narrowly focused labourers are on their materialist functionality, the less productive and the less satisfied they are in their jobs. Research indicates that meaning-centred interventions improve the job satisfaction and productivity of employees. Workers who feel that their jobs are meaningful seem more dedicated and productive (Dik, Byrne, & Steger, 2017).

Consumption

Products and services are increasingly sold not merely for their materialist functionality but for a multiplicity of meanings. This does not necessarily mean that consumers buy more luxury products, but it implies that whatever they buy, it needs to mean more to them than mere functionality (like Lacanian 'surplus'). The philosopher Hegel (1807) already saw the increasing influence of personal taste in the marketplace in his time. This trend has progressed exponentially since Hegel's era, and we may conclude that we live now in a Meaning-Oriented Economy focused around the subjective selection of products and services based on the meanings they offer (Visser, 1998).

For example, any car from any respectable manufacturer can take you from A to B. Despite this, consumers often swear by specific brands. They buy cars for meanings other than their mere material functionality. Which other meanings could motivate buyers to purchase a specific car, according to the meanings sextet? Of course, there are different functions that individuals would like a car to have. For example, someone living in a mountainous area might prefer a stronger motor, whereas a city car should be small for lack of parking spaces (materialist meanings). Cars can also be bought for leisure time and fun, to be able to go into nature and cities or engage in car shows (hedonist meanings). The psychoanalyst Freud suggested that individuals may buy a car to get a sense of self or to compensate for feelings of sexual incompetence. Cars could also be used to develop a sense of psychological hardiness, for instance, by engaging in challenging experiences such as car rallies or far trips in difficult terrains. This could also give a sense of self-efficacy, self-control, and autonomy. Cars are also often seen as status symbols, to show off to others or to communicate social status (self-oriented meanings). Cars could also help community building, by taking you places with family or friends (social meanings). Consumers may also decide to buy an electric or emission-minimising car, and thus follow their ecological values and contribute to a better world. Consumers could also decide to buy a car from a company in which employees are treated ethically (larger meanings). Finally, cars could also have an existential meaning for individuals, giving them a fundamental sense of freedom or a connection with places they could not reach before (existential–philosophical meanings).

The transformation from materialist functionalism to meaning-centred consumption has had a drastic impact on the organisation and growth of the economy. For instance, this transformation made the forecasts of several economists at the start of the 20th century fail. Maynard Keynes believed that within 100 years 'the economic problem may be solved, or at least within sight of solution' (Keynes, 1928). He meant that humanity would be able to satisfy all their material needs with minimum effort (Skidelsky & Skidelsky, 2012). Keynes has been shown wrong: the number of hours that individuals work has only marginally decreased, while the economic productivity has significantly increased, and the average happiness and life satisfaction have not increased much. Keynes' prediction failed because he only focused on the materialist functionality of labour and consumption. He did not realise that, as described above, individuals do not only work to survive but can find multiple meanings in their job. Products and services are also not merely sold for their functionality but for a multiplicity of meanings. Companies make profit by adding meaning to the products, and their sales increase by manipulating the meanings that potential buyers may experience.

A century ago, consumers may have mainly looked at the material functionality of a product, but they look now much more explicitly at the different possible meanings. Social research indicates that the proportion of the average price that is directly related to the functionality of products (the marginal price curve) has been decreasing during the last decades. Individuals can choose between different products because there are more options to choose from: The material abundance enables them to select between different products on the basis of different meanings for different buyers. Consequently, for their financial survival, manufacturers need either to offer products with a significantly larger functionality or products that are perceived as much more meaningful than those of their competitors, even if these perceptions are merely psychological (the latest iPhone is not much better in functionality than the previous version or phones from their competitors Samsung or HTC.

Selling products for their meaning in addition to the material functionality assumes that producers are based in a relatively free market with multiple producers.

For example, Apple would not need to release a new iPhone with limited new functionality if there were no competitors because the old phones would be selling. In contrast, in former communist countries, industry primarily focused on making functional products. (The famous example of this is the Trabant, which became the face of the former DDR industry. Everyone could afford to buy this car, although the Trabant, a basic car that brought customers from A to B, did not offer many luxury options or other meanings.) Furthermore, the internet revolution has enabled consumers to get in touch with manufacturers and service providers worldwide who could offer them more meaningful experiences than their local companies. Thus, products nowadays are sold more because of the perceived likelihood that they will increase the sense of meaningfulness in life than merely based on their material functionality like in the DDR. This added meaning is an essential mechanism by which capitalism thrives.

Marketing
An important reason why consumers now look at more than merely material functionality is because of the role of marketing. Chapter 10 will describe how Bernard Bernays invented the discipline of 'public relationships', and how this has totally transformed the economic system. Bernays developed the idea that products and services could be sold by creating the expectation that this will help buyers to realise what they find meaningful in life. His marketing technique was simple: Look at what potential customers find meaningful in life and subsequently create the expectation that this product will help to realise this meaning. For example, if you want to sell pianos, create advertising that tells how a piano helps you to reach your highest potential creativity in life. If this strategy does not work, create a need by telling people that they are missing out on life if they do not achieve for this meaning. The more meaningful a product is for more people, the larger the demand and the selling price.

This implies that companies need to focus on the most important meanings for potential customers—the social and larger meanings instead of mere materialistic and hedonistic meanings. Instead of saying 'you will enjoy the nice taste of this coke', the slogan of Pepsi Max is 'live life to the Max'. A nice taste may not be enough to sell cola as a taste is brief; therefore, the industry must give cola a longer lasting and more important meaning than the taste, even if this meaning is unrelated to the actual material functionality of the product. Products are touted as helping us reach our highest potential: Red Bull 'gives you wings', Panasonic cameras give 'ideas for life', Skittles helps you to 'taste the rainbow', and Zurich Insurance helps us to be realist 'because change happens'. While Nike says 'just do it', Adidas aims for the lofty thought that by saying 'impossible is nothing'. Brands even call on us to be good humans, such as Google's asks us 'don't be evil', as if anyone would sincerely consider doing evil. Customers can also get a sense of community: Nokia helps by 'connecting people', and we can achieve self-worth by using L'Oreal, 'because you're worth it'. These slogans often have no direct connection with the product or service: How could a drink help you live life to the maximum, and how could a camera give ideas for life? Broad slogans work particularly well because advertisements need to appeal to the largest number of customers, and the largest number of individuals should be able to identify their own meaning in the product. This public relations industry is the mind manipulation that is the cornerstone of modern capitalism.

Governments & Army

Not only commercial companies but also governments and armies use mind manipulation. For example, in 2016 the Dutch army decided to sell all their tanks, while simultaneously posting vacancies for 900 social scientists. A Dutch general explained this decision by saying that modern wars are not won by material force but by manipulating public opinion. The Vietnam War had, for instance, failed due to live broadcasting on the battlefield; apparently, the audience did not like to see the physical reality of the war (Streatfield, 2008; Taylor, 2006; Winn, 2000; Hallin, 1989). 'It does not matter whether we physically win a war, it matters whether we win it in social media' (anonymised personal communication, 2016)

This general followed by describing how fake news and alternative facts in social media have started to dominate international politics and foreign relations. For example, in 2016 Trump was elected president with a political campaign based on twice as many falsehoods as his political opponents. The United Kingdom decided to leave the European Union, as the political campaign on Brexit added such false facts as saying that £350 million per week would be reallocated from EU spending to the national health services and stirring up unrealistic fears about immigration (Kirk, 2017; FactCheck.com, 2016). Politicians appeal to existential threats and injustices to sell their political ideology, even if there is no actual danger or injustice. During the last decades, the role of meaning manipulation has exponentially increased in politics. For example, Israel and the United States are the two countries that invest the largest amount of money per capita on psychological research about community management and nation branding, and this has doubled during the last two decades (Shennan, 2013). Empirical evidence for this will be elaborated in Chapter 10.

Social Sciences

The previous paragraphs show how the scientific insights from psychology and psychiatry have been used to sell commercial products and services, as well as political and military ideologies. However, these disciplines have also become infused with capitalist ideologies themselves (Roberts, 2017, 2015). For example, philosopher Michel Foucault showed how mental health is a normative concept that tells possibly more about societal norms than about an individual's actual mental problems. The diagnosis and treatment for so-called 'psychopathology' can be used to realign non-fitting individuals with capitalist meanings. Psychotherapy can give individuals the message that they are the cause of their psychological problems, while their problems may really have been caused by the socio-economic system. For example, unemployed individuals in the United Kingdom are forced to undergo psychotherapy in the job centre, even though they may not have mental health problems. In this case, psychotherapy is used to manipulate their minds until they fit the work process (Vos, Roberts, & Davies, 2019).

Critical psychology and psychiatry give attention to the wider socio-economic context of mental health. Instead of individualising problems—*you are the cause of your own problems!*—they show how the social context influences our experiences and well-being. For example, the British Psychological Society released several reports in 2017 showing how difficult socio-economic life circumstances, such as the personal meaning of benefit cuts, are an important cause of mental health problems. They suggest that instead of treating the individuals, society should be treated, as it is the socio-economic context that created their problems.

Psychiatrist Ronnie Laing (1972) argued that instead of setting individuals aside from society with a clinical diagnosis and a standardised treatment, we should try to understand the personal meanings of their lived experience. He showed for instance that the experiences of schizophrenic individuals make sense when psychiatrists give close attention to what clients say. This assumes a different approach to mental health care than the usual functionalist diagnoses and standardised treatments. Instead, the subjective world of meanings can only be understood from within the client's lived experience. This critical approach in mental health care seems desperately needed if we want individuals to live a truly meaningful life under capitalism.

Summary

This brief overview has introduced the main hypothesis: that economic behaviour often involves a plurality of personal meanings. Capitalist economists have been imposing their specific meanings on the public debate and government policies, and marketers have been manipulating the meanings of customers. Ignoring or limiting the multiplicity of possible individual meanings makes the economy more volatile and vulnerable to crisis. Imposing specific types of meanings on individuals will make them less creative and less dedicated to the delivery of a good product or service. Most of all, meaning manipulation can lead to mental health problems and, in particular, to the Capitalist Life Syndrome (Part II will give systematic empirical evidence for these bold statements).

A Meaning-Oriented Definition of Capitalism

The previous section has suggested that capitalism and meaning are intertwined. But what is capitalism? Karl Marx was possibly one of the first to popularise the term 'capitalism' to describe the ideas of some of his historic antagonists. Nowadays, economists who use the term capitalism to describe their own position, such as Von Mises (1947) and Friedman (1972), advise that this is a complex and dynamic term that should not be treated as a monolithic concept (Hancke, 2009) like some left-wing activists seem to use it—as a straw man to attribute everything to that is wrong in society. Consequently, many different capitalist variations exist, such as classical liberalism, welfare and state capitalism, neoliberalism, neoconservatism, etc.

Regarded from an historical–etymological perspective, the term capitalism is already loaded with meaning. Until the Middle Ages, most farms were relatively small and, consequently, animal farmers most likely knew each of their individual animals, including their character and their relationships. Imagine that the peasant Godwin Rolfe had a cow that he had called Bella. Bella was born on his parents' farm when Godwin was a young boy. Bella provided the family milk and gave birth to many calves, some of which were killed for food. Bella had a complex set of meanings for Godwin, being both an animal with her own character and relationships but also a potential source of food. She had a unique meaning to Godwin. He would never sell or kill Bella on a whim—for example, just to have food on the table for some weeks—but he would intuit the complexity of the social situation if she became too sick or too old or if his family would starve if he did not slaughter Bella. Animals were to some extent respected in their own meaningfulness, like pets in modern society. However, in the 12th century, the term and concept of capitalism emerged, derived from the Latin word *caput*, meaning 'head', and used to refer to movable property including livestock. The word 'capital' meant that a peasant could count multiple heads of cattle as his own: this cow, those sheep, etc. Thus, the accent lay on the personal ownership and control of moving the object. Bella became reduced to being an asset—an object Godwin owned and whose meaning, life, and death he controlled—instead of Godwin intuitive attuning to her meaningfulness in their complex relationship.

Capital did not only mean possessing something but owning something that has a potential for accumulation. This meant not only that you owned a cow but that you had a possible future source of income from their milk, wool, meat ,and skin; even better, if you treated the animals well, they could give milk or even birth, and your capital would increase. Thus, capital is your potential for development, 'a step forward on the road to a more plentiful existence', as Von Mises (1947) called such assets (although he used this explanation for capital goods). This concept means that an asset is not merely an object, but it is an object plus the imagination that the object can grow. Bella is not merely Bella the cow, but an abstract Material object (M) with a Potential (M+P). This potential can serve many aims of a 'plentiful existence', such as financial survival, wealth accumulation, etc. Regardless of the meaning that the potential has for the individual, it has brought Bella into an abstract function (functionalisation): Bella plus her potential can lead to Plentiful Existence (M+P→PE). However, for the potential to be used, this assumes specific Actions, such as the farmer introducing Bella to a bull to impregnate her, within specific Circumstances such as a market where bulls can be rented or bought (M+P+C+A→PE).

Thus, Bella lost her prior embedding in an intuitive network of meaningfulness in the daily life-world and became reduced to a factor in an abstract function, which is even more poignant in the modern meat industry where cows do not have a name but only an ear tag. It seems that this etymology of the word capitalism includes the functionalisation and materialisation of the life-world. Capitalism depends on an imaginary or symbolic surplus that is added to the immediate reality of our life-world, just as Bella was abstracted from her individual being to being one instance of an aggregated type of material object (M_1) with a potential for a plentiful-existence (P_1). For the Individual (I_1), such as Godwin, this also meant a functionalisation: He became the individual owner of multiple material objects with potential capital that he could use by acting under the right circumstances ($I_{x=}M_x+P_x+A_x+C_x$).

The next sub-sections will elaborate on several other aspects of this historically unique concept of capitalism, with a specific focus on the imaginary and symbolic surplus that each aspect assumes.

Private Ownership
The concept of private property already existed in Sumerian times and was stipulated in Roman Law, but its applications were limited because only a few individuals could own property; women, slaves, and children were, for example, excluded. This concept became widespread at the end of the Middle Ages, with John Locke (1689/2014) as one of the first to analyse this. Before this time, products and services were often shared, and land did not have clear boundaries. In addition, land was not sellable; it was inherited. In contrast, in collectivist and hierarchical cultures, capital is often shared (see Chapter 5). Capitalists often promote governments to be as small as possible by privatising as many public services and industries as possible (see Chapter 6). Whatever the potential of the capital is used for, it is the individual owner of the capital that makes the decision how the potential is used. This is where Adam Smith introduced the term 'self-interest', not as a specific type of meaning but as a meta-term to describe who makes the decision of which meaning the potential is used for, almost synonymous with speaking about private ownership (Chapter 5 shows that for Smith this may have meant an intuitive attuning to the pluralistic life-world). The privatisation of meaning was a unique step in history, as meaningfulness had been a social process between beings (*inter-esse*) until then. The cosmocentrist perspective, which regarding individuals, community, and nature in harmony with one another, was replaced by an anthropocentric perspective that disconnected individuals from their cosmic–social embedding (Chapter 14). According to Pierre-Joseph Proudhon (1876), the idea of property symbolises a sovereign right for owners to use and abuse their property as they please, even if this negatively impacts other people and the wider cosmos—such as depleting natural resources, polluting, and exploiting workers. Furthermore, Proudhon argued that the accumulation of property, exclusion, and encroachment, inherently led to conflicts and wars.

Specific Types of Meaning

The etymology of the word capitalism tells us that the potential of material objects is used for plentiful existence; it does not specify what this 'plenty' is about. Research shows that there are many possible goals that individuals could aim for with this potential, such as materialist, hedonist, self-oriented, social, larger, and existential–philosophical meanings (Vos, 2018, 2016). Thus, while the definition of capitalism does not necessarily imply materialist, hedonist, or self-oriented types of meaning, it often conveys this meaning to economists and politicians, as we will see in Chapter 6. This implies a narrowing of the potential, which loses its social, larger, and existential–philosophical options.

Means Towards Goals

We could imagine that the first humans (*Homo erectus*) did not regard all animals as potential food, and particularly not as investment for the future, such as getting milk next week or next year or selling it to the milk industry. The first humans simply did not have the cognitive ability and the neurological structures to be able to add imagination and symbols to their immediate reality (e.g., Lewis-Williams, 2002). Animals were simply other beings that they encountered. A cow is a cow, a being in itself, and animals were not a means to an end—food, sales, investment. However, capital is always about the potential to progress towards a goal, or 'functionalism': *I only approach Bella for the function that she has for me. Bella helps me to reach my goals, whereas Bella has lost the potential for my regarding her as a sentient-being with whom humans share a significant percentage of DNA.* This functionalist approach became more popular at the end of the Middle Ages, and this trend has particularly been associated with the nascent idea of what Adam Smith started to call the rational *Homo economicus:* everything can be calculated and demanded towards a larger goal.

Progress

A means towards a goal does not necessarily imply progress. I could, for instance, use my potential in an inefficient way or waste it, like the Biblical metaphor of wasted talents. However, in capitalism the focus lies on the expected progress, ultimately on macro-economic-level GNP growth. We are expected to multiply or profit from our capital. Progress is a key value in capitalism. To modern people in Western countries it may seem unthinkable that individuals would not be oriented towards progress, and that they would, for instance, not look at their livestock and think about the possibility of using them for sales or future investment. Until the late Middle Ages, this idea of progress seemed relatively absent, and nowadays in some non-capitalist countries people do not have a strong progress mindset (Nisbett, 2009; Spadafora, 1990). *Whatever you do, do it to the max!*

Efficiency

Progress describes our forward direction. However, in capitalism we are not only expected to move at any tempo but as fast as possible with the smallest use of resources possible so that we can maximise our capital. Efficiency is about progressing with a clear organisation, plan, and structure. In technology, efficiency can be expressed as the ratio of the amount of useful work performed by a machine or in a process to the total energy expended or heat taken in (e.g., 'the boiler has an efficiency of 35 per cent'). Capitalism 'ratio-nalises' the use of our potential; that is, we make the process towards the goals more efficiently, for instance, by 'freeing' superfluous personnel or equipment. The rationalisation of economic behaviour emerged in the 16th century and was accelerated by the Industrial Revolution. This is in stark contrast with collectivist cultures, where the social process is often regarded as more important—for instance, a stereotypic image of multiple mechanics involved with the repair of a broken car in a garage in India versus this work being done by only one person in a Western country. This social aspect may seem inefficient in modern Western eyes, but from a non-Western perspective it may be difficult to understand how social relations can be ignored.

Abstracted Aggregates

Economists are not necessarily interested in individual objects, such as Bella, but they *imagine* abstract aggregate functions. For example, the efficiency of the free competitive market is assumed to be the result of the aggregate of individual rationalised behaviour. This is a cornerstone of econometrics, with aggregate indexes such as Gross National Product (GNP) or a stock index (the Dow). The image of the market, or market segments, is abstracted from the sum of individuals. This abstract imagination flattens out the statistical variation between individuals and even ignores the unique personal meanings that individual economic agents experience; this comes at the cost of reduced explanatory and predictive accuracy. In contrast, one of the founders of the Austrian school of neoliberalism, Ludwig Von Mises, takes the unpredictability and the subjective meanings as starting point of his work. Economic concepts like prices, costs, money, exchange rates, expenditures, and savings have no importance to individuals except in terms of their subjective meaning and subsequent actions; economics should start with human values and purposes, not with aggregates (Von Mises, 2002).

Small Social Context

Capital is always embedded in a network of relations. More particularly, capitalists focus on the economic exchange between individuals in the 'market'. This can be a physical market but is more likely the symbolic and imaginary aggregate relations between buyers and seller, supply and demand. The market itself is part of a wider network of influences, such as other markets and governments. Capitalists imagine that the market functions most efficiently with as little influence from the social context as possible, such as few government regulations and interventions, unlimited trade without national borders, etc. Naturally, this is a highly individualist image of the economy, which is in stark contrast with political systems in most of human history's collectivist and hierarchical cultures.

Competition

In the economic market, individuals meet other individuals with their own capital: capital meets capital. Capitalists sketch the image that the most efficient way for the market to function is by individuals competing and progressing towards their own self-interest as a goal. Historians suggest that competition has been a very ambiguous concept in history (McNulty, 1968, p. 641) and only seems to have achieved its relatively clear meaning with the liberal philosophers in the 16th century: 'Competition can be seen to be both equilibrating and disequilibrating in its tendencies, comprising both innovative and adaptive patterns of behaviour, and is both freeing and constraining in its effects, entailing as it does not only deliberate and conscious striving (or the exercise of free will) but as well the clash of opposing interests, or contention between two or more persons' (Dennis, 1975).

This ambiguity is surprising as competition seems to be a fundamental premise of the national economies of many governments and of international development organisations such as the World Bank and the International Monetary Fund (Cook, 2002). Systematic reviews of international economic growth indicate that competition is neither always efficient nor always leads to the largest growth (Aghion & Griffith, 2008). To identify which type of competition works best for whom in which social context, a multiplicity of theoretical and statistical models is needed (Aghion, Akcigit & Howitt, 2014; Baumol, Litan, & Schramm, 2007). For instance, companies seem to benefit from belonging to a geographic cluster of other companies, whereas competition outside their own cluster on the global domain seems less efficient (Porter, 2000). The research also shows that competition does not work efficiently in countries without a long history of capitalism and may not fit collectivist and hierarchical cultures very well. It has been suggested that the only way capitalism may work in these countries is enforcing capitalism via international political and/or military interventions (Klein, 2007).

Thus, one size does not fit all; competition does not fit all social contexts. What seems required is a larger pluralism of economic models based on local meanings: greater policy autonomy for developing countries and at the same time a more stringent framework for dealing with mammoth multinational companies and their endless appetite for overseas expansion often through mergers and takeovers' (Singh, 2004, p.15). Thus, competition seems to be a unique symbolic and imaginary concept in capitalism that has been imposed as a monolith on economic agents and countries where the concept does not always seem fit economically and culturally.

Market-Set Prices and Wages
What is the imagined and symbolic efficiency of the market about? Each textbook on economics shows the function of the amount of supply and demand, on the one hand, and the price, on the other hand. For example, for a price of £10, few customers would buy a cup of coffee, but for a price of £1 many would. A wage function could tell that for a wage of £5,000 per hour, many people would like to work but few companies would be able to afford this. Whatever the function is about, it translates relationships between individual economic agents and societal structures into money, a price, or wage. This translation is imaginary and symbolic in nature, as a pound coin is merely a social convention about how much could be potentially bought with this pound, an 'IOU' (financial potential). This convention can change, as inflation exemplifies. In addition to the financial functionalisation of producer–consumer relationships and employer–employee relationships, many complex financial products have been imagined, the meaning of some even too complex to grasp in their totality by financial experts. It has been argued that the creation of these complex financial 'bubbles' led to the crash of 2007–2008, but with it the financial functionalisation of our life-world came under attack, which seems to have led to the emergence of post-materialist economics (e.g. Tooze, 2018; Whitham, 2018; Sornette, 2017).

Multiple Means
We have already seen that animals can be capital. What else could be capital? Economists have had many debates about this. Some distinguish capital goods that have already been produced and/or are durable—such as machines, unused stock, etc.—from financial capital such as savings and shares. Land is sometimes not regarded as capital because it cannot be increased by human labour. Social capital has been described as the goodwill or brand value of an enterprise; generally, this is anything that influences the functioning of social groups such as identity, norms, values, trust, and cooperation. Chapter 6 will show how modern identity economics is strongly focused on this. Similarly, intellectual capital is also quickly growing in importance in our internet era; Silicon Valley is one of the biggest owners and producers of this type of capital. Human capital is the domain of psychologists and human resources, and focuses on the potential of stakeholders in an enterprise, such as skills, knowledge, habits, personality, etc. Ecological capital describes the dependence on natural resources, and the impact on local nature and global climate.

In addition to these traditional types of capital, the concepts of symbolic and imaginary capital may be identified. As defined earlier, the terms 'symbolic' and 'imaginary' are derived from psychoanalyst Jacques Lacan (2001; Fotaki, 2009; Valente, 2003; Stavrakakis, 2000; Zizek, 1989). Lacan distinguishes the symbolic and imaginary orders from reality. That is, people do not always have direct access or accurate understanding of what is really going in in the economy, because for ordinary citizens and customers, and also many politicians and companies, the economy is fundamentally too complex to totally understand. Instead, people have symbolic interpretations such as stories, cultures, rituals, etc.

Symbolic capital is the potential that an individual or a company has in terms of symbolic meaning; that is, what stories do people associate with a company and what rituals do companies offer? For example, the golden arches of the yellow M are the symbol of the fast-food chain McDonald's, which has become a cultural symbol of the strength of consumerism, a bellwether for the condition of labour in a globalised economy, and often a powerful educational tool that defines the culture of people (Kincheloe, 2002). Nobody was better at creating cultural symbols than Walt Disney, although some have argued that under the symbolic cloak of innocence and entertainment, Disney Corporation has become a political force in shaping public memory, producing children as consuming subjects and legitimising conservative views (Giroux, 2010). It has been argued that money and all its financial derivatives—such as IOUs, loans, stocks, etc.—are primarily symbolic. This symbolic capital is the primary focus of our experience economy (Chapter 7).

The Lacanian imaginary order regards the individual images we create of our self, world and people around us: What is the image that we see in the mirror? We imagine, for instance, how the economy is organised and what our role in it is. The imaginary often involves alienation, according to Lacan, as this is about our *imaginations*, set aside from reality; this is also the domain of the Marxist concept of alienation (Ollman & Bertell, 1976). Imaginary capital is the potential of images that enterprises, consumers, and citizens have about themselves in the wider economy. For example, consumers often have the image of themselves as being free and non-manipulated in the purchase of products and services; however, marketing techniques often subliminally direct their choices. Many individuals feel that they are conscientious in what they share on social media, but this self-image is often inaccurate—for example, the 'know-it-alls' like Facebook often know sooner than the partner when someone is pregnant (Cohen, 2018). People who work in Silicon Valley may see their work as creative, free, and alternative, but the reality is that most of them work long hours on top-down delegated projects (Foer, 2017). Neoliberals such as Milton Friedman and Ronald Reagan shared the image of the free market, but many studies have shown that their neoliberal policies have created the opposite—high government spending, regulations, and interventions (Rayack, 1987). Liberal and neoliberal ideologies are founded on romantic imaginations (Bronk, 2009).

In sum, the symbolic and imaginary capital consists of the unique domains of meanings–the topic of this book—and they are also the domains that are often manipulated in the economic process.

Conclusions

Capitalism can be defined as the imaginations and symbols of an economic system that functions in such a way that individuals attempt to rationally and financially maximize their personal material wealth by efficiently using and increasing their capital in an imagined free and competitive market. This system is strongly based on symbolism and imaginations; thus, it may not reflect the actual economy but merely exist in subjective interpretations. For example, the economy in the United States and the United Kingdom are often presented as free markets, while research indicates that these economies are regulated by oligarchies (Mount, 2012). Furthermore, China presents its economy as non-capitalist but has many characteristics of capitalism (Gunthrie, 2012). The research in Chapter 7 also shows only moderate correlations between how capitalist a country is and how capitalist an individual is within that country. This indicates that capitalism may be telling more about people's symbolic and imaginary representation of the economy than objective facts about the economy. People have some individual freedom within the capitalist system to have different ideas about what they find personally meaningful.

Capitalism has transformed nature into anonymous objects with a potential ready to be used ($M_y+P_y+C_y+A_y \rightarrow PE_{xy}$), and it has subsequently specified individuals as anonymous objects with a potential ready to be used ($I_{x=}M_x+P_x+A_x+C_x$). This seems to reflect what Heidegger (1954/1977) suggested, that the modern system (*Gestell*) has an empty core: It consists of symbols and imaginations and only becomes a reality when individuals decide to act on the basis of their potential that is lying ready to be used (see also Chapter 8). There is no secret master puppeteer pulling the strings of the billions of people living in capitalist countries, except when you believe in conspiracy theories about Illuminati, Masons, Jews, or the Bildenberg Group. Despite its empty core, the capitalist system offers us a socialisation with capitalist symbols and imaginations that give meaning to our personal and social lives. By internalising and acting on these meanings, we influence one another's realities, symbols, and imaginations, and thus reinforce the system as such. It is these imaginations, symbols, internalisations, and actions that are studied by 'the economics of meaning in life'.

Key Points

1. Capitalism offers an historically and culturally unique perspective on economics, which can be defined as the imagination and symbol of an economic system that functions in such a way that individuals attempt to rationally and financially maximize their personal material wealth by efficiently using and increasing their capital in an imagined free and competitive market.
2. These imaginations and symbols within capitalist economics could be analysed via 'the economics of meaning in life'.
3. The philosophers and the economists were wrong to ask whether capitalism, communism, or anarchism functions best for everyone. The question should

not be what is universally true, but which socio-economic conditions are meaningful at which moment in which situation for whom.

Chapter 3

Methodology, or How to Analyse the Clothes of Economists

In our vital needs, this science has nothing to say to us. It excludes precisely the questions which man, given over in our unhappy times to the most portentous upheavals, find the most burning: questions of the meaning or meaninglessness of the whole of the human existence. (Husserl, 1934/1970, p.6)

Long Live the Naked King of Economics

Once upon a time, an emperor believed that he was the most beautiful human being. He decided to throw off all his clothes and walk around naked in his palace, to the embarrassment of his ministers. They had subtly advised him to put on some clothes, but anyone suggesting this was immediately imprisoned. Until one day two clever tailors found a solution. They asked the emperor whether he ever felt cold. Yes, he did. The tailors told him that they had a solution that didn't involve covering his beautiful body: an invisible cloak which only the emperor could see. The emperor was curious and tried on the cloak that he thought was invisible to others, even though everyone could see it. He loved the garment and started walking around, shouting to his citizens 'Look how beautiful my naked body is!' The citizens were afraid to get jailed and thus they confirmed the emperor by chanting 'Long live the naked king'. Many economists seem to personalise this inverted story of 'The Emperor's New Clothes', originally written by Hans Christian Andersen. The emperor symbolises those stereotypical economists who claim that their theories are value-free.

The exclusion of meaning from economics is unique in history. The term economics has been derived from the Ancient Greek word *oikonomia*, meaning the whole house (*oikos*) and convention, social habit, or norms (*nomos*); a very loose translation of *oikonomia* would be the 'household of all our habits/norms in life'. These habits can only be understood from their meaningfulness (*logos*) to individuals; thus, *oikonomia* ultimately referred to 'household of all meanings in life'. The first authors on economics, Xenophon and Aristotle, described the habits of the household in the context of social and larger types of meanings such as virtues and purposes. In the *Politeia*, Aristotle (unknown/2019) described how *oikonomia* is different from *chremestika*—money—which lacked inherent meaningfulness. Thus, for these early authors, economics is about the meaningful organisation of daily life and not about money or business behaviour. Similarly, the position at the university of one of the founders of modern economics, Adam Smith, was not about money, but about 'moral philosophy', which he called 'political economics' (1759/2010).

However, ignoring this association with moral meanings, influential capitalist thinkers have described their economic ideas as 'objective' and 'rational' (Hayek, 1945). Paul Samuelson (1948) described economics as an 'analytical science' using maths; his follower Gary Becker (1966) even described any 'tastes'—including love, values, culture, and tradition—in mathematical functions. They pretend that they are merely neutral calculators: *Don't shoot me; I am just the statistician!* By simulating scientific detachment, they seem to communicate that we should not treat these economic ideas as a religion or human science, but like formal logics stating universal truths such as 2+2=4, even though both the numbers and use of the functions themselves may be incorrect.

This bubble of objectivity has been punctured by a recent flood of academic and popular publications. The following book titles are self-explanatory: *The Econocracy: On the Perils of Leaving Economics to the Experts* (Earle, Moran, & Ward-Perkins, 2017), *Economics as Religion* (Nelson, 2014), *The Values of Economics* (Van Staveren, 2013), *Economics of Good and Evil* (Sedlacek, 2011), *The Worldly Philosophers* (Heilbroner, 2011), *The Utopia of the Free Market* (Achterhuis, 2010), *Adam's Fallacy: A Guide to Economic Theology* (Foley, 2009), *The Gods That Failed* (Atkinson & Elliott, 2008), *One Market Under God* (Frank, 2001), *The Rhetoric of Economics* (McCloskey, 1998/1985) and *The Economics of Imagination* (Heinzelman, 1980). According to these authors, we need to look beyond 'the vanity of rigour' (Cartwright, 2007) and the 'autistic economics' (Fullbrook, 2003). Michael Hudson calls the mantra of neutrality a deception, which he describes as a deliberate attempt to veil the failure of the economic models that have created a 'junk economics' of outer-world hypotheses and as-ifs (Hudson, 2017). There is a clear difference between the imagination that the public has been fed by economists and economic reality. For example, the symbolic freedom in neoliberal theory has in practice devolved into countless numbers of paternalist regulations and imperialist endeavours of governments in the name of freedom, but with the names of powerful corporate sponsors on their T-shirts. All economies are political, and all economies are about meaning.

The Economics of Meaning in Life

This chapter describes the methodology of how we can discover the hidden meanings in economics. Although many behavioural economists and economic sociologists, such as the before-mentioned authors, have described many facets of these meanings, there is no subdiscipline in economics that systematically examines the relationship between economics and meaning. Therefore, we may want a new subdiscipline called 'economics of meaning in life', which is the study that systematically explores the meaning of economic imaginations, symbols, and realities in critical, systematic, evidence-based, reflexive, and pluralistic ways.

Critical
In line with the Frankfurt School of Critical Theory, the word 'critical' means, first, offering a thorough analysis of the content and form of economics, as a critique in literary criticism. Second, critical means revealing the processes that make individuals become enslaved or enslave themselves, such as in the Capitalist Life Syndrome that aims to 'liberate human beings from the circumstances that enslave them.' (Horkheimer, 1982, p.244). Third, critical refers to the critical moment in time in which we live, and in which a shift in economic perspectives seems to be occurring.

Systematic & Evidence Based
The economics of meaning in life is systematic; it does not merely express the opinion from one individual but mixes methods from multiple disciplines such as psychology, sociology, and economics. Evidence is found in multiple ways, including in-depth analyses from interview studies as well as generalisable quantitative data from questionnaires and econometrics. The next section provides an example of such a systematic method: ten questions and perspectives.

Reflexive
One of the perspectives explicitly examined is the role of the researcher. There is no such thing as an objective description of economics: All economic studies explicitly or implicitly reveal the author's meanings. Instead of pretending neutrality, the author explicates their unique position in the history of economics, called 'reflexivity'.

Pluralistic
The collected evidence should do justice to the complexity and plurality of perspectives, instead of providing an all-explaining theory in which outliers, differences, and paradoxes have no place. The question about meaning is inherently a question about pluralism: What is meaningful to you may not be meaningful to me. Pluralism gained momentum in economics around 2000 when series of petitions from students in France, the United Kingdom, and the United States called for more open economics, based on a pluralism 'which regards different schools of economics as offering different windows on economic reality, each bringing into view different subsets of economic phenomena (...) And rejects the idea that any school could possess final or total solutions, but accepts all as possible means for understanding real-life economic problems' (Fullbrook, 2003, pp. 8–9) Alternatively formulated, these students asked for pluralistic heterodox economics to bring mathematical

'autism' of economism back to the real life-world of people (Garnett, Olsen & Starr, 2010). This call for pluralism in economics is not only a subjective opinion of these critical studies, but this is also supported by many anthropological studies showing how different socio-economic systems evolve in different ways and thus suggesting that the usual one-size-fits-all approach does not apply (Caldararo, 2014). A pluralistic perspective is needed to examine the unique meanings of the unique socio-economic situation.

Economics as a Deductive Science

During the *Methodenstreit* of the Austrian school at the beginning of the 20th century, the foundations were laid for the dominant methodological approaches in economics (Coats, 2005, 2003; Boylan & O'Gorman, 1995).

Von Mises described economics as a deductive science, similar to geometrics: 'all geometrical theorems are already implied in the axioms; the concept of a rectangular triangle already implies the theorem of Pythagoras. This theorem is a tautology, its deduction results in an analytic judgment'. Similarly, 'in the concept of money all the theorems of monetary theory are already implied' and economic theory 'transforms, develops, and unfolds; it only analyzes and is therefore tautological like the theorem of Pythagoras in relation to the concept of the rectangular triangle' (Von Mises, 1948). However, Von Mises acknowledged that in contrast with geometrics, deductive theoretical knowledge cannot provide 'the totality of factual knowledge about all things (...) Experience concerning human action differs from that concerning natural phenomena in that it requires and presupposes praxeological knowledge.' That is, to explain human behaviour it is not enough to know a set of axioms; what is required is analyses of meanings, human motivation, and ultimately 'reflection about the essence of action'.

For Von Mises, analysis of individual subjective meanings is the first step towards uncovering more fundamental underlying categories. He believed that 'economics is a deductive science; its principles can be derived logically from the very existence and nature of human purposes and actions' (Butler, 2012). He searches for 'essences', a priori laws in human behaviour, or as he calls this 'praxeological categories': 'There is no action in which the praxeological categories do not appear fully and perfectly. There is no mode of action thinkable in which means and ends or costs and proceeds cannot be clearly distinguished and precisely separated.' These essential a priori categories do not only underlie our actions but also our reflections: 'If we had not in our mind the schemes provided by praxeological reasoning, we should never be in a position to discern and to grasp any action'. Our actions are not inherently meaningful in and of themselves. They derive their meaningfulness from this praxeological schema that economic agents have in their mind. Thus, by analysing human behaviour, economists may discover some fundamental categories that people share (although Von Mises does not claim that researchers will ultimately discover one ultimate truth).

Von Mises' deductive essentialism was later criticised by philosophers of science, such as Popper, who argued that deductive essentialism is not empirically verifiable and thus scientifically not justifiable (Taleb, 2011, 2005). For example, with the essentialist method, any essence may be identified in behaviour even though in reality this essence may not exist. This can lead to a self-fulfilling prophecy and a self-serving bias, like seeing everything in pink when wearing rose-tinted glasses. When you assume that you will find an essence, you will see an essence, and you will pay relatively less attention to pluralities, paradoxes, and inconsistencies.

Wary of Von Mises' radical deductive methodology, Friedman agreed with Popper's criticism in his 1953 essay *The Methodology of Positive Economics,* in which he wrote that 'Laymen and experts alike are inevitably tempted to shape positive conclusions to fit strongly held normative preconceptions and to reject positive conclusions if their normative, implications -or what are said to be their normative implications- are unpalatable'. Compared to physical sciences, in economics there is a 'closer interaction between the observer and the process observed', which needs to be critically taken into account: 'the fact that economics deals with the interrelations of human beings, and that the investigator is himself part of the subject matter being investigated in a more intimate sense than in the physical sciences, raises special difficulties in achieving objectivity at the same time that it provides the social scientist with a class of data not available to the physical scientist'. Consequently, empirical research cannot definitely confirm the fundamental laws of economics: It can never prove a hypothesis but can only fail to disprove it.

However, Friedman (1953, pp. 3) believed that positive economics is possible, independent of any particular ethical position or normative judgments:

> Its task is to provide a system of generalizations that can be used to make correct predictions about the consequences of any change in circumstances. Its performance is to be judged by the precision, scope, and conformity with experience of the predictions it yields. In short, positive economics is, or can be, an 'objective' science, in precisely the same sense as any of the physical sciences.(…) The ultimate goal of a positive science is the development of a 'theory' or 'hypothesis' that yields valid and meaningful (i.e., not truistic) predictions about phenomena not yet observed.

Thus, the validity of economic hypotheses is determined by their predictive capacity. Although a definitive truth may never be found as there may be multiple hypothetical explanations for the same empirical phenomenon, including the variation and the conditions of the economic experiments. Consequently, Friedman argued that we should not search for truisms but for hypotheses that can survive many opportunities for contradiction and thus have 'greater confidence'. In contrast, hypotheses that are contradicted more often than alternative hypotheses should be discarded. Thus, the danger from deductive essentialist methodology, such as the stereotypical sketch of Von Mises' theory above has suggested, is an increased risk to self-serving bias and deduction fallacy.

Although Friedman does not aim to find and prove true essences, his methodology does not seem to systematically reflect on the interaction between observer and observed. Consequently, his methods remain relatively bound to the limitations of a deductive science. That is, his starting point is the formulation of hypotheses, usually on the basis of theory as in positive sciences. This implies that the researcher pre-selects the field from which the hypotheses will be derived; for example, the researcher may want to derive hypotheses from the field of monetary theory, which they will subsequently test. If this field does not already include a phenomenon such as meaning in life, this phenomenon will most likely neither be tested nor found in the research. Subsequently, when a hypothesis has not been contradicted by evidence in this particular field, it can be generalised and tested in other fields.

For example, Gary Becker started his functional analyses of human behaviour with testing functionalist hypotheses about consumption, and he later extended this to other experiences such as love. However, because Becker's hypothesis of love started in a functionalistic field, while assuming that other factors remain the same—*ceterus paribus*—of course he found evidence for the functionality of love. The limitation of this deductive approach has been proven by systematic research from other fields: In contrast to Becker's hypothesis that love is fuctionalistic, many psychological and sociological studies have shown that love is more than mere functionality (Bruckner, 2012; Silverman, 2009; Armstrong, 2002). Thus, Becker's economic hypothesis can only be confirmed under specific conditions in specific fields.

Popper wrote that hypotheses should not be tested by searching for evidence in the same field but by searching for counter-evidence in other fields (verificationism). For example, instead of searching for white swans only in the United Kingdom to confirm the hypothesis that all swans are white, a researcher should search for black swans, for example, in Australia where they actually live. Similarly, Friedman's hypothesis that economic freedom is a prerequisite for political freedom is disproven by research from other fields (Schwartz, 2007; Kasser, Cohen, Kanner, & Ryan, 2007). Competition only seems to be effective in capitalist contexts and can be counter-effective when introduced to traditionally less capitalist countries (Aghion & Griffith, 2008; Aghion, Akcigit, & Howitt, 2014; Baumol, Litan, & Schramm, 2007; Singh, 2004; Porter, 2000). Likewise, the hypothesis that the market fulfills fundamental human needs is disproven: psychological studies have shown that fulfillment of material needs are only important for people's happiness and life satisfaction in capitalist countries, but not in less-capitalist and collectivist cultures (Bouzenita, 2016; Wachter, 2003; Gambrell & Cianci, 2003; Wahba & Bridwell, 1976). These studies do not imply, for example, that love is never functional and that material conditions and the free market *never* contribute to human happiness. They just show that multiple perspectives and hypotheses need to be derived from different fields to understand complex human experiences and meaning in life in different contexts. One size does not fit all.

Thus, similar to Von Mises' deductive methodology, Friedman's idea of economics as a positive science may include a risk of self-confirmation bias, as long as only narrow hypotheses are formulated and tested in specialised fields like Becker did (although some authors have argued that Von Mises and Friedman would agree with Popper's idea of verificationism). This economic deductive methodology implies a pre-determined area of research instead of casting pluralistic lights on the economic reality from as many fields and perspectives as possible to gaining a 360-degree picture.

Heterodox economists have criticised this deductive methodology and they attempt to do justice to the complexity and plurality of economic experiences, which require different methodologies (Cronin, 2016; Lee, 2009). Similarly, the pragmatic phenomenological methodology in this book starts with a systematic reflection on what Friedman described as 'the interaction between the observer and the process observed', and on the fact that different observers may see different processes due to their subjective biases. Instead of regarding the lack of one essential truth as negative, the plurality and hermeneutics in research observations are regarded as opportunities to uncover a plurality of meanings.

Economics as a Positivist Science

Von Mises and Friedman responded to the dominant mathematical methods that authors such as Marshall (2009) taught to students. These methods are based on a realist ontology and positivist epistemology—ontology describes our understanding of reality, and epistemology describes our perspective on how we can develop knowledge and truth about this reality (Dos Santos, 2009, Fullbrook, 2008; Knuutilla, 2008; Coats, 2005, 2003; Boylan & O'Gorman, 1995). These realists and positivists assume that there is an absolute reality that we can directly observe and measure with our instruments, such as behavioural observation or questionnaires. Economic methods are assumed to function as a thermometer, directly measuring the temperature of the economy. However, this positivist epistemology does not give an in-depth understanding of the meaning of this temperature: Is it likely to be feverish or to be healthy? What are the other symptoms and what is the underlying disease? This difference has been described as the difference between *explaining* and *understanding* a phenomenon (Dilthey, 1898/2010). The inability to understand meaning from a positivist perspective may be compared with our lack of understanding the meaning of a sentence, even though we may be able to explain the grammar and spelling perfectly. Similarly, meaning transcends mathematical economic functions. Economic functions are neither sufficient nor necessary for meaning to emerge.

For example, an economist could describe the price that most people are willing to pay for a loaf of bread, and for what price the baker is willing to sell the loaf. The economist's model tells the price and the likelihood of selling and buying, but this does not say anything about the meaning of the product. For example, the buying experience of bread in an anonymously large supermarket is different from the experience of buying from a befriended baker in the local market. In economics, the complexity of our subjectively lived experience of our life-world is reduced to economic materialism and mathematical functions; thus, economics leads to an 'oblivion of the life-world' (*Lebenswelt-vergessenheit*) and 'a loss of its meaning for life' (Husserl,1934/1970, vol.1, p. 3).

The neutralisation and mathematization of economics 'represent a rupture since it liberates the economist from the burden of negotiating the meaning of economic theory. It frees economics from its *weight of meaning*. Formalism is inherent in economic theory, and the anonymity of markets, accordingly, is not merely an epistemic deficit but the very condition of economic knowledge.' (Duppe, 2011, p. 75). That is, seen through a positivist lens economic knowledge inherently reduces the complexity of meaning into the formal functions between material objects and hedonist, self-oriented agents. The positivist nature of economic knowledge is such that it ignores the meanings of our life-world (cf. Dos Santos, 2009; Fullbrook, 2008; Knuutilla, 2008).

Our understanding of meaning in economics needs to be based on a different ontology and epistemology. Like the meaning of a sentence needs spelling and grammar to be expressed, the meanings of economics need people, behaviour, and a material world to be understood. There is no economy without individuals who understand, share and experience emerging meanings. Meaning transactions happen for the economist behind an invisible screen, similar to the way meaning transactions happen hidden from the linguist. Just as the meaning of language can only be understood in a social context in which two communicators have a similar frame of reference that helps them understand the meaning of words (e.g. speaking the same language), individuals in economies often have a shared sense of meaning; they speak the same language of economic meanings. This does not imply that these individuals are completely determined by their social context similar to individuals having the ability to learn multiple languages, but it means that they share an understanding of the meaning of the economy, and they contribute to this shared understanding.

Before we can understand the meaning of a sentence, we already know the language. For example, without first learning Chinese, the linguistic characters do not make sense. Before we can understand the meaning, we are already part of a social context in which we share certain meanings, such as the meaning of characters. Phenomenologist Edmund Husserl wrote that the life-world is pre-given before we can, for example, identify the themes or types of meaning (e.g., materialist, hedonist, self-oriented) and before we can identify its functions. This is the lived world of the individual. We do not need economic science to understand what it means when I pay the baker for a loaf of bread; these interactions are already pre-given before any theorising. Before Adam Smith described in The *Wealth of Nations* how supply and demand meet each other in the market, people had already been meeting each other for thousands of years in markets. These markets already meant something to them, and they did not need an economist to explain these meanings. However, mathematical formulas give the illusion of understanding these daily life phenomena: 'We must indeed when engaged in this type of mathematical investigation remember always that it is a second-rate affair, prolegomena to economics, not economics itself, not real ballistics' (Pigou, 1941, p.278). Thus, our intuitively lived meanings of the life-world come first, and the economic formulas come second, attempting to force the complexities, pluralities, and paradoxes of our life-world into simplified formulas. Before we can theoretically identify the themes, categories, or essence of economics, we already exist in a world full of meaningful relations: 'existence precedes essence' (Sartre, 1967). And our daily-life existence is often full of pluralities, aporias, and paradoxes.

An individual's sense of personal meaning is the expression of their intuitive experience of being embedded and actively positioning themselves in a socio-economic context, and, as such, describes the complexities, changes, and fluidity of our daily life-world. That is, most individuals do not merely have one big meaning in life. They have multiple meanings, some of which are more important than others. Some meanings can be large, such as wanting to give birth and raise multiple children; other meanings can be smaller, such as enjoying nature—like listening in the here-and-now to a bird in the park can already be a meaningful moment. For example, both a successful career as well as a family life can be important for individuals. Research indicates that people are more resilient if they have multiple meanings in life with different levels of importance—as, for instance, when one cannot succeed in their career, one still can have a family life that gives a sense of meaning. When individuals dominantly focus on one specific type of meaning, this makes the likelihood of frustration and failure more probable and may lead to severe psychological problems and even suicidal ideation if that one meaning fails. During our lifetime, our experiences of what is meaningful can change; for instance, few adults actually want to realise their childhood dreams such as becoming a fireman. Meaning is unique to the individual, and only the individual can decide what is meaningful and what is not. Others can help individuals discover what is meaningful, psychotherapists can act like a midwife helping to give birth, but it is the client who is responsible for giving birth (Vos, 2018).

Economics as a Relativist Science

What alternatives are there for positivism? Several authors have described economics as an interpretative science: Economics do not objectively observe human behaviour like a thermometer but interpret behaviour like a writer or painter. For example, philosopher Jacques Derrida described how public discourses are based on implicit assumptions and leave out important information; therefore, we should try via linguistic analysis to deconstruct how meaning emerges in public discourses. The Frankfurt School has particularly analysed hidden meanings in our current economic systems, such as Adorno and Horkheimer questioning the idea of continuous economic progress in their book *Dialectics of Enlightenment* (1944/1997). Others, including Lacan (1977/2006) and Zizek (2010), have used a psychoanalytic lens to describe how citizens and customers develop their sense of subjectivity and meaning, and how the meanings that individuals experience may merely symbolise the societal influences rather than what they authentically experience as meaningful. For example, individuals may even believe and imagine the meanings that advertisements impose onto them. *I felt that I simply had to buy the newest iPhone; I did not ask myself whether I really needed it or had the money for it.* We are not the sole author of our own thoughts and feelings but are always influenced by the society and economy around us.

These authors stand in a tradition that aims to uncover the hidden discourse in capitalism and deconstruct how individuals give meaning to their individual lives within their socio-economic–political context. Some postmodernist authors go further by not only saying that our thoughts and feelings are continuously manipulated but by claiming we can fundamentally never know what is truly meaningful for us. For example, on an average day, each individual in the United Kingdom sees approximately 4000 brand names and advertisements, which explicitly or subliminally influence their preferences. How can we make an objective decision whether we really want to buy the newest iPhone when we are bombarded by so many ads and social expectations? We seem unable to completely transcend this manipulation process as we live in this manipulative life-world. We are hostages of the system (see Chapter 11 where this point will be proven and elaborated).

How do we respond to this mental hijack? Some postmodernist philosophers have developed a relativist stance to meaning. We cannot abstract ourselves from the manipulating system and cannot know what is authentic and what is manipulated; the full idea of authenticity is corrupted (Adorno 1964/2002). This relativist argument comes from the premise that individuals cannot know their real meanings, that individuals have no valid reason to prefer one option over another. There is no valid reason why we would prefer one meaning over another meaning. If we cannot objectively know what is most meaningful, we can randomly pick and follow any meanings that just feel good. Thus, according to these relativists, the capitalist adage of *laissez-faire* applies not only to our economic behaviour but also to our personal lives (MacIntyre, 1981).

Economics as a Pragmatic-Phenomenological Science

Is there an alternative to either positivism or relativism in the economics of meaning in life? How can we do justice to the meanings in our life-world without either reducing meanings to materialist functions or being unable to communicate anything at all as relativism does not offer a common ground to share meaning? We will need to take a step back to understand how we have come to make sense of our world.

For example, one may argue that in the capitalist country in which I grew up, I may have learned to focus on materialist functions via endless forms of socialisation, reinforcing parents and teachers, and later in my life, many others who may have manipulated my mind. I have started to confuse this manipulated world of ideologies, social media, and commercials with the real life-world. For instance, I may start to think that to live a meaningful life I may need to buy the latest iPhone, live from kick to kick, and go on adventurous holidays and hipster mindfulness retreats. Naturally, the process of getting sucked into the capitalist lifestyle is more subtle than this example, but research is clear about this hermeneutic embedding of the individual in the socio-economic context (e.g. Lavoie, 2005; Berger, 1998). Thus, mind manipulators continuously influence us (see chapter 11).

In Part III, I will attempt to set these manipulated world views aside (Husserl called this 'bracketing of assumptions') to return to the immediately experienced meanings of the life-world prior to the influences from economists and mind manipulators (as far as we are able to do this). When we have bracketed our assumptions, we open ourselves to find possible new answers to the many questions that the phenomena under investigation are asking. This implies that this meaning-oriented philosophy of economics 'is not a disengaged, contemplative, a neutral reception of objects but rather the practice of an interested, projected and active possibility' (Vattimo & Zabala, 2011, p.14).

This book stands in the line of post-postmodernism, sometimes called 'critical realism', which posits the idea that although absolute truths may not exist, individuals can experience differences between what is meaningful and what is less meaningful for themselves in their life situation (Vos, 2018; cf. Dreyfus & Taylor, 2015). Individuals can, to some extent, discover what is relatively more meaningful and what is less meaningful. They can do this by reflecting on the influences from their socio-economic context. Thus, this book avoids the complete relativist stance that *any meaning goes* while avoiding an endless metaphysical debate on the essence of meaning. Instead, a pragmatic phenomenological perspective will be used. This starts with the idea that for ordinary individuals, these metaphysical questions are not relevant in daily life. Nobody starts by questioning how they are being manipulated and debating what truth is before they go grocery shopping. From the psychological perspective of daily life, these fundamental questions are irrelevant. Therefore, this book focuses on the practices of individuals living a meaningful daily life. Naturally, this does not mean that the process of deconstructing is totally irrelevant for these daily meaning practices. For instance, it can help shoppers to be aware of how they are tricked into buying this type of cola because the commercials give them the idea that it offers something more than a brief nice taste.

Elsewhere, I have called this method *pragmatic phenomenology* or *a critical–intuitive attitude* (Vos, 2018). Phenomenology is the study of how individuals experience phenomena. Phenomenology and deconstruction philosophy have in common that they try to unpeel the layers that are covering our meanings. Philosophers often debate the underlying ontological question of whether there is anything left after the unpeeling process. Some authors claim that we can find some truly authentic meanings, like the core of a mango, while others say that there are no true meanings but only manipulations of our meanings, like an onion has no core, only layers. This debate itself serves the hegemony of capitalism. From the pragmatic phenomenological perspective in this book, the benefits of the process of deconstruction for individuals will be shown, without claiming that all individuals will end up finding an absolute true meaning (although some may feel they do). Therefore, this book only briefly touches on these critical-theoretical debates—which happen in the cultural background of the daily life of ordinary citizens—whose focus lie in describing social-empirical research on how individuals live a meaningful daily life under capitalism. The pragmatic focus on the daily life-world may also avoid unhelpful metaphysical discussions. Although internal debates can be inspiring and improve the quality of their theories, rigidly relativist or (neo-)Marxist publications seem primarily internally referential by predominantly critiquing peers and consequently reinforcing the emergence of an intellectual world separate from the reality of daily life. (This section is inspired by research on phenomenology in economics as described by Galbacs, 2016; Duppe, 2011; Fast & Clark, 2008; Lavoie, 2005; Rubin, 1998; Madison, 1994.)

Methodology: Ten Questions and Perspectives on Meaning

The previous sections have suggested that the totality of our life-world is treated with justice in dominant rationalistic economics. Economic models assume that our world is calculable, categorizable in economic essences, and generalisable across fields (see Chapter 10). Even though this calculability and categorisability are only a learned secondary approach to life compared to when we were children, the secondary world pretends to be primary. This inversion is also reflected in the fact that our study of *oikonomia* predominantly concerns itself with *chremestika*, money, whereas for Aristotle (unknown/2019) *oikonomia* was a holistic concept that included the *whole* house and not only its finances. If our focus is limited, what lies beyond our horizon?

Which questions do we not ask? What else is included in the totality of our meaning besides our habitual economical and capitalist answers?

Sometimes meaning is translated as 'why' questions: Why do we live? Why do we work hard? Why do we consume? Aristotle (unknown/2019) wrote that questioning why always includes four sub-questions, which will give four causal explanations (*aitia*, traditionally translated as 'causes', our understanding of which is different than in Aristotle's time; therefore 'questions' is a more neutral translation; Hankinson, 1998). By asking these four questions about a phenomenon, we may understand its meaning. The first question, 'what', is about the matter or material of something (hyle), such as wood can be the material of a table or the theoretical nature of an economic model—such as a model of-reality and not reality. The second question, 'how', is about form, shape, or appearance (eidos), such as the round shape and the legs of the table or the idea of the free market, even though this ideal may never be materialised. The third question, 'who', is about the agent that created the phenomenon—the efficient or moving cause (kinoun)—such as the carpenter who made the table or the CEO of a company who paid for a PR campaign that planted the ideal of the product in the mind of potential customers. The fourth question, is 'for what', is the sake for which something is what it is (telos), which we sometimes translate as 'goal' or 'purpose'—such as the table is used to sit at and serve our dinner on, or the telos of a seed is becoming an adult plant. We need answers to all four of these questions—what, how, who, what for—to understand the meaning of any phenomenon, such as an economic phenomenon or our life's meaning.

Philosopher Martin Heidegger (1921/1995) describes that in our modern era, which followed the Middle Ages, many people do not do justice to the totality of these four questions. We mainly focus on the material (what/hyle) and the functional efficiency (who/kinoun) of phenomena. The other questions (how/eidos, what-for/telos) are answered in these functionalist–materialist terms. For example, when we think about how we do things, we look at this from a perspective of efficiency and functionality: What is the most efficient way to achieve our material goal of profit? When we think nowadays about the purpose of something or even the purpose of life (telos), we often interpret this with a functionalist focus on materialist goals. For example, people see life as a box-ticking exercise with self-chosen specific goals such as successful career, family life, children, etc. Whereas, for Aristotle, telos meant the realisation of our full potential as a human being, like the telos of a seed becoming a full-grown plant. Becoming our full self may or may not include such goals as career and family, but these goals are not necessarily self-chosen, like the seed that did not choose to become full grown. Becoming full grown implies the involvement of the other *aitia*, which are not included in the modern understanding of meaning in life as setting self-chosen goals that we will move forward in a linear path.

Individuals may think that all people in all eras have asked questions about life in a similar manner, but that is most likely a myth: The rational quest for meaning is an invention of modern time (Vos, 2018). Our functionalist–materialist focus towards life has only been popular in Western countries since the 17th century; before that and still in many non-Western countries, people do not reduce the totality of meaning to materialist functionalism. Heidegger seems to connect the emergence of the functionalist–materialist questions about life with the spirit of modern economics, which he calls 'calculative thinking' (*rechnendes denken*) that is turning everything into a calculation and a theory instead of being engaged in the meaningful totality of our life-world (Heidegger, 1954/1977). Thus, the totality of our Being is not done justice to in the current economic and capitalist perspectives because we forget to ask fundamental questions about what is meaningful.

What happens when we forget to ask questions and the totality of Being is not done justice? Traditionally, we would use the word 'conscience' for what happens then: our conscience will tell us something is wrong. For example, many see reducing individuals to a mere number or object (materialism and functionalism), such as Hitler's final solution of killing all Jews, as unethical and believe that individuals should be treated as meaningful in themselves. Heidegger (1927/1996) writes that, seen from an existential perspective, a call from our conscience is the self that calls the self back to the self. The self—that is, the totality of our Being in all its potentiality—is thus seen from all possible perspectives by asking all possible questions. This means that instead of having one narrow-minded focus, we become aware of our potentiality of perspectives. We understand, for example, that our functionalist–materialist perspective is limited and that other perspectives are possible. Heidegger is not clear how this call develops psychologically, but based on research and clinical experience, we could say that this call is translated in existential questions and existential moods. It is like a pressure that builds up inside the individual and in communities (Vos, 2018). When our potentiality is not done justice for a long time—for example, because we have a narrow perspective or forget to ask fundamental questions—an existential, social and/or psychological pressure can build up inside individuals and societies, which can lead to a call for change, action, and revolution. When many people focus for a long time in an extreme manner on materialism and functionalism, they will start to experience discomfort and dissatisfaction about life, question life's meaningfulness, and succumb to an existential crisis or a mental health crisis. Such a crisis can be a sign of pressure caused by the narrowness of our perspectives on life. This crisis calls for us to widen our perspective (Heidegger, 1927/1996).

In this book, we use the words 'questions' and 'perspectives' as synonyms as each question addresses a different perspective on meaning in economics. Looking from different perspectives at the same phenomenon means that we move around the object by looking at it from different angles. However, the hermeneutic tradition tells us that a perspective is never passive; it is active and we need to walk around the object to see it from multiple angles. We may never be able to grasp the totality of the diamond, but by changing perspectives we may see as many facets as possible. For example, 'type of meaning' and 'approach to meaning' are two different perspectives. Thus, we can look at capitalism from the angle of the type of meaning (materialist) or from the angle of the approach to meaning (functionalist). When we look systematically at a diamond from different perspectives, we can start to understand the complexity of this diamond. It is this emerging meaning, the totality of the being of the phenomenon, that we may grasp after systematic variation of our perspectives in the economics of meaning in life. (This simplistic explanation of phenomenology is based on Heidegger, 1927/1996, 1914 and Husserl, 1897).

What questions could we ask? Which layers can we unpeel from the superficial economic ideas? Aristotle already identified four questions: what, how, who and what for? In the fields of phenomenology and anthropology, many more questions have been identified over the years. Therefore, in this book, we will focus on unpeeling economics from ten layers that obstruct seeing its underlying meanings, although undoubtedly many more questions could be posed. The ten questions/perspectives include: Name? Status? What? How? Where? When? Who? Whose? Why? Which? The paragraphs below and Table 3.1. provide an overview of these ten questions or perspectives.

1. Name?

When someone systematically and critically studies the meaning of economic ideas, a complex, rich. and lively picture can arise. We can give this emergent picture a name, such as 'The Capitalist Life Syndrome' or 'The Communist Life Syndrome'. A syndrome is like a package deal where you get multiple products together (Vos, 2018). For example, someone's life is not only meaningful to them because of their successful career, or their children, or their wealth; for them, all of these are meaningful. The identification of multiple perspectives as one connected phenomenon is based on the convergence of findings by multiple research methods.

2. Status?

What is the status of the economic phenomenon that we are describing? Is this a real economic phenomenon, or just an imaginary theory or symbolic model? That is, the lived experience of a real economic situation (and politics) may be different from a theoretical vision about the economy (and politics). For example, politicians may tell their voters that austerity measures such as benefit cuts can reduce the government deficit and lift the economy out of depression, but this theory does not do justice to the harsh reality and pains that benefit cuts can have in individual lives. People use language and symbols to make sense of their lived reality, and these symbols can become manipulated by 'mind mafia', such as populist newspapers that may equate benefit seekers with scoundrels, a symbol that is often disastrously powerful in public debates. This triptych of real–imaginary–symbolic is loosely derived from Jacques Lacan's three psychoanalytic orders, which he developed during a series of lectures in the 1950s, and which others such as Slavoj Zizek have further evolved. Often, it is difficult to precisely identify the real, imaginary. and symbolic aspects of an economic phenomenon because they are intertwined.

The *Real* is something we will never be able to understand or represent completely. I may look at the family's bank account to see their factual financial status, but I do not know whether they have hidden the money somewhere. Even more, money does not exist without its symbolic meaning: We have agreed with one another that these sheets of paper and these numbers on the bank account mean the amount of financial capital that I possess. However, if all of us decide to give up money and start e trading natural products—I give you a product I made, and in exchange you give me a product that you made—money would become meaningless, and we would not have grasped what the financial situation of this family really is. Thus, we may never know absolute reality. When we speak in economics about reality, we refer to our understanding of a phenomenon seen within our social conventions. Most neoclassical economics happen in the positivist domain of the Real, ignoring the fact that it depends on the shared symbolic meanings of our life-world.

The *Imaginary* describes the theoretical and abstract steps in economic models. Whereas the Real may never be completely understood in its totality, complexity, and plurality, the imagination tries to create an ideal image of coherence and simplicity rather than fragmentation. For example, 'the free market' often does not exist as a physical place where buyers and sellers meet in modern societies. The term helps us to understand the complex reality, that 'free markets' consist of countless numbers of people, all with unique behaviours and meanings. Often, economic models combine imagination and reality. For example, econometrics combines an abstract mathematical function with data from behavioural observations, while the function is based on many assumptions such as linear or non-linear relationships between variables, and excluding variables, *ceteris paribus*.

The *Symbolic* describes the endless web of symbols that we use to understand our world and ourselves, such as the use of language and other signifiers. Symbols often have both conscious and unconscious aspects. For example, the symbol of money has a strong unconscious power over people; many individuals dedicate their entire life to acquiring more of this symbolic phenomenon and connect their personal well-being with their success or failure at attaining this symbolic wealth. Thus, symbols are powerful images formulated as 'X stands for Y', where Y has a larger significance for the individual (money stands for happiness, and happiness is the highest goal in life for this person). We think, feel, interact, speak, and live in symbols that we share in our life-world. The Symbolic Order shows how our inner life is organized and how we can access and show our psyche. Economic phenomena such as the 2008 financial crisis may be interpreted as symbolic events, where the application of capitalist archetypes have failed: The symbolic order that the capitalist model promotes did not fit reality, and the crisis revealed this structural misfit (Hageback, 2017, 2014).

3. What? Types of Meaning
Psychoanalyst Sigmund Freud said that a good life is about love and work. Are these all our options, or can we have more types of meaning? At least 107 studies including 45,710 participants in 49 countries have tried to answer these questions. A systematic literature review of these studies identified six overarching types and 29 sub-types of meaning, and this categorisation was validated in the Worldwide Survey of Meaning (WSM): materialist, hedonist, self-oriented, social, larger, and existential–philosophical (Chapter 7).

4. How? Approach to Meaning
Many philosophers and sociologists have argued that capitalism has a unique approach to meaning in life. Weber called this 'rationalisation', Heidegger 'technology', and Durkheim 'disenchantment of the world' (Chapter 9). As an umbrella term for all these phenomena, I use the term 'functionalism'. In contrast, non-capitalist approaches to life are traditional or critical–intuitive. This rationalisation/technology/disenchantment trio was identified in a systematic analysis of the world history of meaning in life (Vos, 2018), and empirically validated in the Meaning Approach Scale (WSM in Chapter 7).

A *traditional approach to meaning* focuses on 'doing what others do', such as believing in One Big Absolute Meaning of Life, holy books, conformism or conservatism. Research shows that individuals with a traditional approach focus on their meaning when they make decisions in daily life, and they experience a relatively lower life satisfaction and more negative moods than people with a critical–intuitive approach (Vos, 2019). This approach is particularly dominant in religious and communist countries, such as Iran and Cuba.

A *functionalist approach to meaning* may be summarised as 'demanding random meanings from life'. This includes the belief that people can create their own meaning in life, that money or hard work will lead to a meaningful life, and that people can pick any random meaning (all meanings are equally important). In their decisions in daily life, they do not focus much on their meanings, which often implies that people quickly change their meanings, and live from kick to kick. Functionalist individuals experience relatively high anxiety and frustration and experience more negative moods than critical–intuitive individuals. This approach is particularly dominant in capitalist countries, such as the United States and the United Kingdom.

A *critical–intuitive approach to meaning* is also called a phenomenological approach and may be summarised as 'critically listening to intuition'. This implies that individuals listen to their intuition to understand what is meaningful (perceptive/receptive attitude) while remaining critical about possible influences from others and about their own motivations (is this truly meaningful?). They use self-insight and creativity. When critical–intuitive individuals need to make decisions in daily life, they often consult their intuition. This approach to meaning is correlated with better life satisfaction, more positive and less negative moods than traditional and functionalist approaches. This approach is becoming increasingly important in post-materialist countries such as the Netherlands and Scandinavia.

5. Where? Relationship Between Individual and Society

The question 'where is meaning' regards the chicken–egg debate in social science. Is human behaviour primarily shaped by individual agency or by societal structure? Agency is the capacity of individuals to act independently and make their own free decisions. Structure is the 'recurrent patterned arrangements which influence or limit the choices and opportunities available' (Barker, 2005), such as the norms, traditions, customs and institutions in a society. For example, do I choose to buy at this supermarket because I want to or because the marketing has made me do so?

Structuralism. In line with positivist researcher Comte, neoclassical economics see the individual as the result of their circumstances, just as the functioning of individual organs depends on the totality of the body (structural functionalism). Everything I do can be explained by my role in society. My behaviour, thoughts, and feelings are determined by the rules and resources of the societal structures in which I am embedded. In the historical–materialist perspective of some Marxists, the material conditions and class conflict structure the daily life of workers and the individual struggle as societal adaptation and a motor of historical change.

Individualism. The opposite view can be found with existentialist authors, who accentuate the freedom of individuals to determine their own lives independently from their context. From this individualist perspective, a societal structure needs to be interpreted and actively acted upon by individuals: If individuals refuse to participate, the structure collapses. People attempted to reclaim this sense of freedom during the student revolution in 1968, the Flower Power movement in the United States and later the punk movement in the United Kingdom, in their rebellion against the system.

Interactionism. Sociologist Anthony Giddens has proposed a third way in *The Constitution of Society* (1993). Neither micro nor macro processes alone are sufficient as there is an inseparable intersection of structures and agents. Giddens sees societal structures not 'as a mechanical outcome, [but] rather ... as an active constituting process, accomplished by, and consisting in, the doings of active subjects' (Giddens, 1993, p.121). Individuals are active participants in the productive processes as well as in viewing the structure through their use of language and symbols. Whereas Giddens used the term 'structuration' to describe this active interactional process, McLennan called this 'the duality of structure and agency' as both aspects are involved in using and producing social actions. This duality is a feedback–feedforward process, with agents and structures mutually enacting social systems that, subsequently, become part of this duality. This interactionist position seems to be based on a critical realist epistemology:

Critical realists strive to find a middle way between the reductionist extremes of voluntarism [i.e. individualism] and determinism [structuralism]. Instead of regarding social structure as being ontologically reducible to human agency, or vice versa, critical realists subscribe to a transformational model of social activity according to which structure and agency are recursively related; each is both a precondition for and a consequence of the other. Social structures are a necessary condition for individual acts, but it is only through (the totality of) the actions of individuals that they persist over time. Social structures should never be regarded as permanently fixed—they should never be reified—because, given the dependency on (potentially creative and transformative) intentional agency, the scope for change is ever-present. (Lewis, 2004, pp. 4, 9)

Phenomenology. A phenomenological perspective starts with the question of why researchers have made a distinction between individual agency and social structures in the first place. As in our embodied experiences of our daily life-world, this duality does not exist (Chapter 13). The crucial question is how this Cartesian split came into existence and how this has impacted our relationships to ourselves and others. Another phenomenological question is how individuals concretely experience Giddensian structuration in daily life. Instead of speaking in terms of generic rules, phenomenologists analyse the concrete lived-experience and meanings of individuals. For example, different individuals have developed different meanings in different contexts with a different resource.

As critical realists say, individual meaning does not exist in a cultural vacuum, as we are continuously influenced by and we influence others, even though we may usually not be aware of how we are influenced (cf. Sewell, Bourdieu). There are individuals and institutions who actively try to influence the meanings of others whom I have dubbed 'after mind mafia, which includes marketing, public relations, and social media. Instead of speaking *in abstracto* about the influence of socio-cultural structures on individuals, seen from a phenomenological perspective, it is important to pinpoint how people are manipulated, and how mind manipulation structures individual agency. Therefore, I will focus in this book much on how mind manipulation influences individual meanings.

6. When? Development Over Time

Historiography. Individual and cultural meanings are not fixed but change over time. Traditional historical approaches create a timeline of events and actors and show how event X led to event Y. This history consists of a mere assemblage of facts and sequences of events constituted self-evidently as historical knowledge. This type of history is usually taught in schools and shapes the functionalist expectations and meanings that young people have about their identity, life, and society. For example, this linear way of looking at history can make pupils see their own life also as a linear process in which deliberate decisions will lead to successfully achieving their goals. This type of history stimulates individuals to control and govern their own lives instead of seeing the complexity and dynamic interaction between individual agency and societal structure.

Historiology. Martin Heidegger (1954) distinguishes historiography from historiology, which includes a role for interpretation. History is not merely a factual account but an interpretation of events. For example, there is much evidence behind the saying that 'the conqueror writes the history books' (Popper, 2013); for example, the atrocities done by Allied Forces in WWII are seldom spoken about and the focus is only on Nazi cruelty. As such, this interpretation of history is a result of historical processes: It is the product and producer of meaning. This is particularly important when we examine the history of meaning. How we speak about meaning is a result of our own sense of meaning. For example, whereas capitalism dominates our culture, we cannot assume that capitalism is the logical end-stage of the history of man (Fukuyama, 2006). Our very conception of economics is shaped by our unique interpretations; the meaning of what we mean by 'economics' and 'capitalism' would be unintelligible outside capitalism. For example, in recent years neoliberals have re-popularized Ancient Greek philosophy, such as Aristotle's virtue economics. However, we should not forget that these ancient philosophers wrote their texts as middle-age men living in relative wealth, in an era when women and individuals were without material possessions (most citizens were not allowed to participate in the direct democracy of the city-state), which does not seem so romantic to our modern standards. These authors were a privileged few, and these manuscripts do not reflect the daily life-world of the many. Therefore, we need to search for the gaps, paradoxes, and aporias in these narratives, try to understand which perspectives dominate the historical discourse, and see how the totality of the story is not done justice. We need to reconstruct history and conduct a genealogy of our knowledge (Foucault, 1965/2013).

Phenomenology. In line with critical realism, it would be too simplistic to conclude from the interpretive turn in history that we cannot say anything about history at all. The main conclusion is that we should systematically, critically, and reflexively analyse the historical narrative, and look below the surface. We may never know exactly what happened and why events happened as long as time machines only exist in movies; but in the phenomenological–genealogical process we may be able to distinguish the more meaningful history from the less meaningful history. Thus, it is important to distinguish the so-called 'neutral academic narratives from daily life. This implies that in our examinations of meaning in economics, we should not blindly follow economic theories but should verify these with a systematic, critical, and reflexive methodology.

7.Who? Emergence of Individual Meaning
The previous questions/perspectives described the influence of large-scale societal processes on individual meaning. However, there is a level in between, which describes how personal experiences and institutions have shaped individual meanings. For example, Sigmund Freud analysed how early experiences in life with our primary care-givers shape our expectations about life. Eric Berne (1952) called such early experiences 'life-scripts' that can influence our later relationships with others and with ourselves. These life-scripts describe the perspective on meaning that we learn, often in the interaction between our immediate social context and our own individual decisions. Although these psychological models may appear deterministic on the surface, they all keep some space for our decisions during life and for the option to actively reinterpret or take a stand against our past. Depth-psychologists help clients to gain insights into how they have developed their limiting perspectives on life and regain the freedom to actively redecide their life-script. Psychology offers countless examples of how life-scripts are formed, some of which will be described in Chapter 11.

8. Whose? Sense of Freedom
Freedom is possibly one of the most important and most complex phenomena in modern economics. Freedom can be viewed from many different perspectives.

Symbolic versus real freedom. The quest for freedom became popular during the Enlightenment in the 17th century, when philosophers wanted to liberate themselves from the limiting structures of the church, state, guilds, and societal conformism. *Sapere aude*, think for yourself, was their slogan. Freedom is possibly the most popular symbol in modern history, which has led to many wars and empowerment and emancipation movements. The freedom fight was taken over by moral economists such as Adam Smith, who promoted the idea of following our self-interest, not as a form of egoism but as a response to the restrictive societal structures of his time. However, the power of the symbol of freedom should not be conflated with real freedom. For example, Adolf Hitler used the term freedom in the context of the Arian race, while he simultaneously led a fascist regime.

Negative versus positive freedom. The French physiocrats added the idea of the *free* market. Freedom meant for them laissez-faire, let the market do its own work without any interventions or regulations from the state. Thus, they focused on a negative *freedom-from* interventions. Isaiah Berlin (1958/2017) differentiated negative freedom from positive freedom. Negative freedom describes how restrictions—such as government regulations—are removed, whereas positive freedom describes how individuals are actively supported to use their potential—for instance, by giving them education, health care, or basic income. Karl Marx showed in his work how laissez-faire often means in economics that some individuals get very powerful and others get oppressed. Negative freedom does not suffice to create freedom for all but only for the few. Therefore, the means of production and oppression should be actively shared with all to give freedom to the many, according to Marx. Reformists and socio-democrats described this as 'creating opportunities'—such as a welfare state—to enable people to actively use their freedom in contrast with merely 'creating possibilities', which rise from capitalist negative freedom.

Structural versus individual freedom. Similar to Marxists, neoliberalists such as Walter Lippmann and Friedrich Hayek argue that negative freedom is not enough and that government interventions are needed to keep the freedom mechanisms of the market free. However, they do not add a positive freedom perspective, as they imagine that as long as the market is free enough most individuals will flourish economically. They imagine that actively offering resources such as income distribution is an impingement of individual freedom. Thus, they contrast social/structural freedom with individual freedom.

9. Why? Existential Impact

Existential questions regard our human condition and our individual existence. These questions differ from psychological questions because they are about our life in general. For example, existential anxiety is a fundamental fear about our finitude and about the contingency of our meanings and endeavours in life. Existentialism lies at the foundations of economics; it does not merely describe our material transactions with others but our fundamental attitude to existence.

Existential questions and moods. Individuals could ask existential questions such as: Why am I here? and Why am I engaging in economic transactions at all? How can I survive in this world? How can I be me and define my own meaning? The answers to these existential questions are often not conscious but reveal themselves in a general mood or attitude towards life. For example, individuals find it difficult to make decisions or feel overwhelmed by the choice overload. There are many other examples of existential moods and concerns that people can have in relation to their socio-economic situation (Vos, 2018).

Living a meaningful and satisfying life despite socio-economic limitations. Asking existential questions is normal; everyone asks existential questions from time to time. However, instead of getting stuck in feeling overwhelmed or apathetic, individuals can find ways to live a meaningful and satisfying life despite their questions, limitations, and struggles. This is a dual attitude towards life, which combines two positions (Vos, 2014). On the one hand, individuals have a sense of realism about their limitations—for example, realising that life will never be perfect, that we will never have a complete understanding of ourselves and the world around us, and that we will never be totally in control of our socio-economic circumstances. On the other hand, these individuals see ways to live a life that feels meaningful and satisfying to them, even realizing that this meaningfulness is not as pretentious as the absolute meaning of life.

10. Which? Impact on Mental Health
Countless studies have shown that socio-economic circumstances can influence mental health problems among women, individuals with a lower socio-economic status, Black, Asian and other ethnic minority groups, LGBTQI+, and individuals suffering from a chronic or life-threatening physical or mental problem. Individuals in these groups often struggle with their socio-economic circumstances and may consequently experience stigma, fear, distrust, humiliation, shame, instability, insecurity, loneliness, and feeling trapped and helpless. Research indicates that there is both a crisis in mental health as well in mental health care. Never have so many people reported so many serious mental health problems (Vos, Roberts, & Davies, 2019).

Conclusions

In sum, if we want to understand the meaning of economics in its totality, we need to systematically ask multiple questions that go some layers deeper and not be satisfied with our habitual superficial answers. We should not feel satisfied with answers about essential economic categories or laws, or with evidence found in only one field. This questioning method is at the heart of the economics of meaning in life. We ask questions until we start to understand meaning more and more in its totality. Asking a question is like unpeeling a layer from a piece of fruit such as a mango. Systematically asking questions means that we unpeel many layers to go further away from the superficial surface and come closer to the core. We start to understand more and more the totality of the phenomenon. However, in pragmatic phenomenology, we do not know whether there is a core or an endpoint to the unpeeling process. Possibly there is an essence or universal law in economics, but we do not know whether we are unpeeling a mango, which has a core, or an onion, which does not have a core. What matters is that the unpeeling process differentiates the less meaningful answers from the more meaningful answers without claiming that the more meaningful is the absolute meaning of life. Thus, we ask questions, and each answer helps us to develop a better understanding of what is meaningful, although we do not necessarily find a final answer.

This book will explicitly examine these ten questions. The next chapters in Part I apply these ten questions to a brief overview of economic history. Part II systematically answers each of these questions for the Capitalist Life Syndrome. Part III investigates these ten perspectives for the Meaning-Oriented Economy.

Key Points

1. An increasing number of researchers show that economics is not a neutral science but is interwoven with unique perspectives on meaning in life.

2. The economics of meaning in life is the study that systematically explores the meaning of economic imaginations, symbols, and realities in critical, systematic, evidence-based, reflexive, and pluralistic ways.
3. Meaning cannot be understood via deductive, positivist–empiricist or relativist approaches alone.
4. The economics of meaning in life is based on a pragmatic phenomenological approach that critically and systematically distinguishes the more meaningful from the less meaningful without claiming to identify an absolute unchangeable essence or meaning of life.
5. Meaning in economic realities, symbols, and imaginations can be studied by asking ten questions, or casting light from ten different perspectives: Name? Status? What? How? Where? When? Who? Whose? Why? Which?

Table 3.1. Ten Questions and Perspectives about the Economics of Meaning in Life

	Name of perspective	Examples
Name?	Overall name of economic model	
Status?	Ontological status	Reality Symbol Imagination
What?	Type of meaning	Materialistic Hedonistic Self-oriented Social Larger Existential–philosophical
How?	Approach to meaning	Traditional Functionalistic Critical–intuitive (also called phenomenological)
Where?	Relationship between individual and society	Social determinism Social-individual interactionism Individual determinism
When?	Development over time	Historiography Historiology
Who?	Emergence of individual meaning (individual history)	Psychology Pedagogy Anthropology
Whose?	Sense of freedom	Symbolic vs. realised freedom Negative vs. positive freedom Individual vs. structural freedom
Why?	Existential well-being	Existential questions and concerns Realistic sense of freedom and limitations
Which?	Impact on daily life	Many mental health problems, low quality of life, and low life satisfaction Few mental health problems, large quality of life, and large life satisfaction

Chapter 4

A History of Meaning in Social Economies

Competition is the law of the jungle, but cooperation is the law of civilisation. (Kropotkin, 1902/2012, p. 56)

Evolutionary Economies

This chapter describes the meaning-oriented history of social economies, ranging from evolutionary economics and survival economies to collectivist and religious economies. These economic perspectives have in common a relatively greater focus on social meanings and a relatively more critical–intuitive than functionalist approach to life (see Nelson, 2014; Sedlacek, 2011).

Our first stop on the historical tour of social economies is the animal realm. We may better understand ourselves as biological beings when we understand animals first. We may also be able to test statements of some (neo)liberal economists about the hypothesized 'natural state' of the market, and the 'self-interested nature of people'. If there is a state dictated by nature, is it a neoliberal state of negative freedom, with stereotypic 'animalist' characteristics such as competition and survival of the fittest? Or are other motivations such as helping others equally important?

The idea that human behaviour follows and should follow nature was trending in the Romantic era of the 18th and 19th century, particularly among economists (Bronk, 2009; Heinzelman, 1980). This idea is still reinforced by the flooding of our culture with anthropomorphic fairy tales such as the wolf in Red Riding Hood as well as television cartoons and entertainment parks showing us the unalterable socio-economic discrepancy between the Scrooge McDucks and the Donald Ducks (cf. Giroux, 2010). This naturalist fallacy of deriving norms from nature has been going on since the Renaissance (De Waal, 2010, 1996), even though it appears that we are not so much deriving norms from real nature as projecting our own ideas on nature and subsequently identifying ourselves with this projected idea (psychodynamic theorists call this 'projective identification').

Philosopher Thomas Hobbes (1651/2016) compared human behaviour with wolf behaviour (*Homo homini lupus*). Nobody will deny that animals, including human beings, have a selfish drive. Animals need to survive, either by fighting over limited resources of food and shelter, or by killing and eating prey. Charles Darwin was one of the first biologists to describe the benefits of survival skills, as evolutionary theory tells that the better skills you have for your own survival, the more likely it is that you will survive, procreate, and be more likely to pass on your genes to succeeding generations. Thus, it is not from the benevolence of the gazelle that we expect the lion to be fed, but from the lion's own interest—although the lion does not intend to promote the interest of his species or know how much he is promoting it; the lion contributes to the wealth of his species and possibly even to the full ecology, as if by an invisible hand. Of course, this reminds us of Adam Smith's economic model (1817). Smith does not explicitly connect biology with economics, but Herbert Spencer does (Offer, 2000). Economics is like the animal kingdom, and as animals are ultimately free, it is merely human interventions that interfere with this natural state, which should be forbidden if we want to achieve natural freedom. 'Social Darwinism is all about what Gordon Gekko called the evolutionary spirit [in the movie *The Wolf of Wall Street*]. It depicts life as a struggle in which those who make it shouldn't let themselves be dragged down by those who don't.' (De Waal, 2010, 1996). Animals and humans fight over scarce resources to save their own life, and it is in the interest of the species/markets that only individuals with the best survival skills procreate. Thus says the theory (Achterhuis, 2010, 1988).

There is a fundamental flaw in this Romantic ideal of social Darwinism: survival of the fittest is only one part of the full story of animal behaviour. Similarly, the human economic market is more than mere competition based on individual self-interest. In the quickly expanding field of psychobiology (Gazzaniga, 2012), there are countless stories and systematic research studies about prosocial and altruistic behaviour in animals (Bowles & Gintis, 2011; De Waal, 2010, 1996; Alexander, 2017). In response to threats, animals as well as human beings do not only show the evolutionary stress mechanisms of fighting, fleeing, or freezing but also of feeding, that is of helping and supporting others—a behaviour that is particularly seen in females (Pribram, 1958). Such stress mechanisms happen automatically when individuals feel their existence threatened. Thus, Hobbes was right but not for the reason he imagined: Humans are like wolves not because they always fight one another, but because troupes of wolves have social norms.

Like animals, 'people cooperate not only for self-interested reasons but also because they are genuinely concerned about the well-being of others, try to uphold social norms, and value behaving ethically for its own sake. People punish those who exploit the cooperative behaviour of others for the same reason.' (Bowles & Gintis, 2010, p.1). Neuropsychological research has shown that empathy and altruism are biologically built in via so-called mirror-neurons that let us feel what someone else feels (Iacobini, 2009). The most famous political author in this field, Kropotkin (1902/2012), shows how not only animals but also human beings benefit from cooperation, such as guilds in the medieval era and unions in modern times. Liberal philosophers such as Adam Smith did not totally ignore the existence of moral drives, as they are sometimes inaccurately depicted by neoliberal authors. Smith described, for example, our human inclination to look at ourselves from a moral distance like an impartial spectator. He explicitly described both these moral sentiments (2010) and following our self-interests in the economic market (1817). Although, evolutionary speaking, Smith's duality of survival of the fittest and mutual aid was accurate, history mainly remembers Smith for his texts about the importance of bakers following their self-interest, possibly fed by the neoliberal mind manipulators rewriting the history of economics. Thus, the set characteristics of the neoliberal market such as pure self-interested competition and private property have nothing to do with real 'natural states', but everything to do with an outdated mechanist model of human motivation. Economists who plea for merely following our own interests want to create an imaginary economy which strips us of what makes us human and part of the natural realm: our empathy and altruism, as well as social and larger types of meaning.

Some economists have argued that the moral reasoning of animals may be explained as evolutionarily beneficial: the trait to help others is beneficial for the survival of the species. This argument may be criticised for its lack of Popperian verificationism (i.e., everything can be reduced to Darwinism, and there is no way to reject the hypothesis of survival of the fittest). This argument does not reject the fact that social and behavioural sciences, including economics, should pay attention to the benefits of morality and social behaviour for the species and the individual *in addition* to individual competition.

What does this tell us about meaning in life? Of course, animals do not ask themselves rationally what the meaning of their life is. Neuropsychologists assume that the ability to reflect on ourselves, to question and determine our life course is a function of the neocortex, which is the part of the mammalian brain that seems to distinguish human beings from other animal species. However, when we look beyond the Aristotelean myth that humans are *animals rationales* and realise that meaning is more than cognitive self-reflection, we can see that the social codes in higher primates already show an intuitive understanding of what is meaningful and what is less meaningful (Bekoff, 2000). Like these higher primates, humans already have an intuitive understanding of what is meaningful, as well as that they can be critical about these meanings, thanks to the prefrontal neocortex that the latest stages of evolution have endowed them with. Thus, human beings may both combine their intuitive understanding of meaning, as well as critically reflect on this. That is, human beings have the unique capacity to gain a critical–intuitive understanding of meaning in life. This implies that the solution to people allegedly 'behaving like animals' is possibly not to become less like animals but to follow more our animalistic sense of social belonging and helping others inside and outside our herd, and subsequently add a bit of our reflective capacities.

Collectivist Economies

We know little about the economy of *Homo erectus* and the first *Homo sapiens*. We can only speculate on the basis of archaeological findings and extrapolate our experiences from contemporary nomadic people (e.g., Nelson, 2014; Smith, 2013; Sedlacek, 2011). The first humans lived most likely as hunter–gatherers, collecting wild plants and pursuing wild animals. Because food supplies can run out in any one location, they were often nomadic. They lived in small groups of extended families, and the group structure was egalitarian, which Karl Marx called 'primitive communism'; if one subgroup would feel oppressed, they could simply leave. Some tasks may have been specialised with a basic division of labour, based on individual differences; for example, women often focused on plant gathering and family care, whereas men would hunt. However, many exceptions have been found in archaeological and anthropological studies, showing how roles were less rigidly divided, for example, in early native Americans. Because of their nomadic lifestyle, nomadic people may not have had much property; possibly they built some temporary shelters that they left behind when moving to another location. Many people still do not have a Western concept of private property; for example, the Cherokee Constitution states that all lands are common property (Thurnwald, 2018).

The basis of early economies most likely focused on mutual exchange and sharing of resources such as meat and gifts (Mauss, 2002), with generosity as a key virtue (Kiefer, 2002). Thus, the first humans seemed primarily oriented towards social types of meaning, whereas materialist and self-oriented meaning received less attention. Some groups may have also focused on spiritual meanings, as religious objects in archaeological digs indicate. Most likely, individuals did not have a functionalist approach to the world, others, and themselves because they lived in the non-Cartesian dualistic immediacy of nature (which will be elaborated on in Chapter 13). The early *Homo sapiens* may also have been unable to reflect on a very abstract level due to the lack of a fully evolved neocortex (Lewis-Williams, 2004). Thomas Hobbes imagined that their lives were 'solitary, poor, nasty, brutal' (1651), but anthropological research questions this (Lee & Devore, 1968). Although they faced direct dangers and die relatively young, they worked far fewer hours and enjoyed more leisure than individuals in industrial societies. Most likely, they also felt satisfied with very little material wealth and felt connected with their community (Sackett, 1996).

The transition from nomadic hunter–gatherer societies to agricultural settlements was most likely gradual, as people learned how to cultivate and grow crops, and make tools. This was possibly a more planned type of economy, with a clearer division of tasks and a more distinct sense of individual responsibility (Nelson, 2014; Smith, 2013; Sedlacek, 2011; Oysterman, Coon & Kemmelmeier, 2002; Kagitcibasi, 1997). Social structures became more stable as individuals remained in one location for longer periods of time. It may have been that the increased specialisation of roles and stable social structures led to social stratification, with more powerful leaders and followers.

Individuals may have developed some sense of individual property as material wealth increased and the stable location enabled wealth collection. More formal forms of trade emerged between and within tribes, which developed from gifting, to mutual exchange, and trade via the use of proto-money such as precious shells or metals (Ferguson, 2008). These developments may have implied a larger focus on materialist, hedonist, or self-oriented types of meaning in addition to the continued importance of social and larger meanings. Individuals started living less in the immediacy of nature, although most people were still in physical contact with nature via manual labour. We do not know whether individuals had a functionalist approach to life, but most likely this was more than the hunter–gatherers as the development of tools created a sense of using something as a means to an end (cf. Nelson, 2014; Sedlacek, 2011; Lewis-Williams, 2004). Whatever their approach to life, they did not have the strong functionalism that existed in industrial societies because of their primary focus on agriculture and the small size and tribal nature of their communities. Some individuals may have had a sense of fatalism, of feeling stuck in their role and community, although this was most likely small due to the relative lack of comparison with other groups because of limited inter-tribal interactions. Consequently, research suggests that individuals in tribal cultures experienced relatively low levels of psychological stress (Abdullah & Brown, 2011).

The first human communities and societies are characterised by a collectivist instead of an individualist nature (Kagitcibasi, 1997). It was in their own interest of survival to experience strong social bonds and cohesion and to foster the sharing of products and tasks. People had strong values around social belonging, sharing, care, and a social definition of their self (Sedlacek, 2011; Oysterman, Coon & Kemmelmeier, 2002). Collectivist economies are very distinct from individualist economies, for instance, with a limited sense of private property and fair sharing of products and tasks (Smith, 2013; De Jong, 2009; Triandis, 1995). Land, machines and harvests are shared. Self-interest and opportunism have no role in economic transactions, and it is more important that there is a fair exchange (Chen, Peng & Saparito, 2002). The social structure is relatively egalitarian, and organisational structures are relatively flat, with little bureaucracy (Sedlacek, 2011; Rothschild-Whitt, 1979).

We now will make a large historical jump, from early collectivist to modern collectivist cultures. Of course, there are many different forms of collectivist societies, ranging from small anarchist communities to state economies. Some have also argued that our modern global online network is a collectivist global society. What these have in common is a clear focus on social meanings: the community always prevails over materialist or personal interests (Smith, 2013; De Jong, 2009; Triandis, 1995). This also implies a predominantly non-functionalist approach since production and social relationships are regarded as an end in themselves and not as a means to another self-oriented or materialist goal. However, in practice this may not always be the case, as highly cohesive groups may become socially rigid and not do justice to the potential of individuals, creating social stress and suppressing socio-emotional expressions. An example is the Japanese concept of *Ikigai*, translated as 'a reason for being' or 'a reason to get up in the morning' (Mitsuhashi, 2018). Ikigai is explained as the interaction between what you love, what you are good at, what the world needs, and what you can be paid for; in ikigai, passion, mission, profession, and vocation coincide.

A practical example are longhouse communities on Sarawak, Malaysia, which can also be found in other Southeast Asian cultures and in Latin America. Multiple families live in houses alongside a long, shared corridor where communal activities happen. The common space stimulates families to share resources such as food and look after one another's children and help them do homework together. Similar small-scale community–economies can be found in the popular cohousing trend in Western countries, as will be discussed in Part III.

Physical markets are another good example of economic meanings in collectivist cultures, in such contexts as 'the market system is not just a means of exchanging goods; it is a mechanism for sustaining and maintaining an entire society' (Heilbroner, 1953, p.22). Markets have formed when settlements started to grow, the interactions between communities increased, and the production of food and products was more than what a community needed for its own direct survival (Bintliff, 2002). Initially, products were exchanged against other products, and money was only introduced at a later stage, most likely in temples as a religious offering (Davies, 2010). Demand and supply did often not meet, as the products that were for sale often consisted of what the sellers did not need for themselves (random surplus); thus, the supply depended on individual needs (such as amount of food they consumed) and productive circumstances (such as having a good or a bad harvest). The small range of products meant that customers could not always buy precisely the product they wanted and that there were not many competitive products with which they could compare the quality and price.

Buyers did not necessarily get products on the basis of their personal taste, but they had a holistic perspective that did not only consider their own demands but took the perspectives of multiple stakeholders into account, including that of the seller (Schrank & Running, 2018). The just price balances the individual, social and universal inter-esses/interests ('cosmocentrism', as will be elaborated in Chapter 13). The collective meaning of a product exchange is seen as most important; consumers may be concerned about how others would look at their purchase (Eckhardt & Houston, 1998). Sellers do not exchange their products for the largest profit but with an explicit awareness of the needs of the customer and the wider community. Thus, the market in collectivist cultures is not merely a place for negotiating and hassling, but also a place of genuinely meeting and even helping one another, albeit out of habit or direct kinship. Fairness of exchange often depends on tradition and custom in collectivist markets. Research shows that these communities strongly disapprove of inequality and unfairness, and desire to police the market for the good of the group or society in general (Price, Feick & Guskey, 1995). This may not only indicate a sense of realised freedom, but also a combination of negative and positive freedom, individual and structural freedom.

> *The difference between individualist and collectivist markets become very clear for me when I, a white Western young man, visited a local farmer's market in the countryside of Ghana in 2008, which had rarely been visited by foreigners before. When I spoke with the sellers, they told me that they were selling the crops that they had grown and that they did not need as food for themselves (random surplus). Most stores were selling mangoes, as the mango harvest had just finished. The price was relatively fixed; thus there was no negotiation, and the price was low for me but seemed sufficient and just for the locals. When I returned a week later and wanted to buy the same product, the cost had doubled. Another week later, the amount had quadrupled. The first time the sellers were not explicitly competing with each other, but the last time they asked me the price that their competitors had offered and said they would sell it for slightly less.*
>
> *My local friend asked the salespeople why they had started raising the price and competing. What he learned is that products usually have a relatively fixed price among all sellers, as I experienced during my first visit. However, my—assumed—financial wealth had made them ask more, and they assumed that I would be haggling and trying to pay a price that was unfair to them. Consequently, they started to treat me in the way they expected me to treat them, and thus they also started to compete. Their competition was the result of what psychodynamic authors call the process of 'projective identification' whereby individuals project their own idea onto others, and both they and the others may identify with this projection; this led to the self-fulfilling prophecy of me starting to haggle. My local friends added that they found this very unfair to me. I felt ashamed, as I had non-deliberately introduced an inequality on the market that had changed the system of exchange values and replaced the social meaning of the exchange with a materialist self-interest.*

This example contradicts traditional economic theories, which state that markets are the cause of materialist (in)equality and not the other way around. Both processes can coincide and escalate: The introduction of socio-economic inequality can cause the commercialisation of the market and the emergence of self-oriented materialistic competition via the process of symbolisation and imagination. What I experienced was not the normal functioning of this local market but the effects of the introduction of a tourist symbolising capitalist self-interests and triggering the salespeople's imaginations.

Thus, in undisturbed collectivist markets, it is from the benevolence of the butcher, the brewer, or the baker that we expect our dinner, and not from their regard of their self-interest. They address our shared humanity and do not intend to take advantage of others. The baker explicitly intends to promote the public interest, albeit that of his closest community; he would never consider over-selling his products to friends and family, although he may do that to a stranger like me. Sellers and customers meet each other in the local market as if guided by an invisible hand to promote the humanity that they were already aware of. By pursuing their communal interests, they promote the interest of the society, as long as they remain undisturbed by the functionalist–materialist symbolisation and imagination of global capitalism. Whereas Adam Smith had to invent the complex concept of an invisible hand that forges the disjointed self-interests in his unique individualist society, there is a direct connection between individual behaviour and the community in collectivist societies that are non-functionalistically oriented towards social and larger meanings.

Social-Hierarchical Economies

As the previous section showed, the hunter–gatherer societies had a relatively high level of social equality and cooperation, but this started to change with the first settlements. It seems that the socio-economic stratification was formed during a brief period, which some have called the Axial Age (c. 800 BC to 300 AC). Worldwide, this period is characterised by the establishment of larger settlements and civilisations such as the Egyptians, Ancient Greeks, and Romans. During most of the Middle Ages, societies were socially hierarchical (Pounds, 2014): peasants occupied low rungs on the social–cosmic–divine ladder, and clergy and kings the higher rungs of this great chain of being (Lovejoy, 2017):

> Imagine the medieval peasant Godwin Rolfe. He was born in a wood-and-mud house in the manor of Lord Montagu. From early childhood, like all family and friends, Godwin ploughed the fields, sowing and harvesting, day in and day out, season after season. As expected in his time, his eldest brother had become a priest; his second brother had inherited the farm, and Godwin was working on his brother's farm. His sisters had wedded local farmers and one married a shop owner; love was not involved—love for the sake of love did not exist, the partnership meant nothing other than a practical arrangement and if they were lucky, they may have experienced occasional moments of love. There was not one second when Godwin doubted this societal system, as he knew that any doubt implied ex-communication and hell, and he also had no reason to doubt as this system was all he knew.
>
> Imagine anachronistically, that Godwin met a meaning-centred practitioner who asked him the question: 'What is the meaning in your life?' Godwin would not know how to reply. Perhaps he would have answered: 'I

simply live my life, do my duty, pay my rent and taxes, marry a wife to have children with, and that is it.' The medieval mystic Meister Eckhart wrote that individuals in his time usually understood the meaning of their life as being in service to the community, doing their duty and simply knowing their place (Eckhart, unknown/1979, Sermon 9). It seems anachronist to call this 'meaningful', as this was simply the way in which they lived their lives, and most people did not seem to have a sense of individuality or freedom of choice. The explicit quest for meaning is an invention of modern western society. The individual and societal order were apparently closely connected. The meaning for the individual was about fulfilling their place in the societal order, thus individual and social meaning were the same. As the societal order was decreed by God, this order was also a cosmic and divine one: 'human agents were embedded in society, society in the cosmos, and the cosmos incorporates the divine' (Taylor, 2007, p.152). This societal–cosmic–divine order was communicated through a person's life and work. (Vos, 2018, p. 3–5)

Simultaneous with the emergence of socially hierarchical societies, large world religions developed, such as Confucianism, Hinduism, Buddhism, Judaism, Christianity, and Islam (Voegelin, 1985/2000; Armstrong, 2006; Jaspers, 1949/2011). Most religious texts prescribe explicit norms and values about daily life, including economic behaviour, and justifications of the social structures. The development of civilisations and religion seemed to go hand in hand with leaders explicitly justifying their actions with religious motives, such as Pharaohs claiming their power by their status as a god. Thus, the order in the societal, cosmic, and divine realms seemed to fit perfectly in each other, like Russian matryoshka dolls:

Meaning for individuals was about fulfilling their role in the societal–cosmic–divine order, and few would question this as there was no place outside this system. When individuals were unable to fulfill their role in society—for instance, owing to diseases such as leprosy—or when they deliberately decided to leave this order—as in the case of vagabonds—their lives were literally considered meaningless. They did not fit into the system and the divine was not communicated through them. This narrow sense of meaning as fulfilling a successful position meant that such individuals were socially treated in what we would call nowadays an inhumane way; they were cast out from society to colonies or even burnt at the stake, and this was regarded as normal because their lives, meaningless, relegated them to a position akin to that designated to animals and lower on the societal cosmic ladder. Some human lives were also regarded as more meaningful than others if they were deemed higher on the societal ladder. Consequently, those higher in status expected to be served by peasants, women, slaves, and ethnic and religious minorities. These powerholders were within their rights to treat their servants poorly as they were considered less meaningful. (Vos, 2018, p.5–6)

In Europe, the Church fulfilled an important role in the organisation of society. The social hierarchy was justified by the divine–cosmic order that the clergy preached, and any immoral behaviour could be punished by the bishop with ex-communication or even burning or hanging for witchcraft as ultimate punishment. The nobility offered a firm hand to prevent ordinary people from doing evil as Aquinas had argued, but they did not seem to be actively trying to create a class conflict as they often had similar interests as their workers and depended on their labour. Workers were usually offered their own plot of land near the noble's house and could also use the common land meant for commoners' own sustenance and additional income in the market.

Thus, there was not a clear distinction of who owned what because there were no absolute boundaries between plots of land, people shared agricultural tools, and they helped one another during harvests. The concept of 'land for sale' did not exist. Like their land, labour until then had not been saleable. Peasants lived on the lord's estate, baked in their oven, ground grain at the lord's mill, tilled the lord's fields—for which they sometimes needed to pay rent—and served the lord in war. Until the late Middle Ages, they usually were not paid for their work and duties and did not negotiate over these tasks, as these were their duties as *serfs* rather than a freely contracting agent (Heilbroner, 1953). Because farming was a seasonal activity, in summer and wintertime peasants did manual labour in their own houses, such as weaving, pottery and basket making. Villages and cities were small and connected by an intricate network of roads that were usually built on crossroads around the church and the marketplace. Urban centres were quickly becoming a place of crafts and technological advancements. The craftsmen were often organised in guilds and shared their tools and expertise. Many young people would become servants in their teenage years, serve lords or masters to learn a craft, possibly even travel around as a journeyman to learn skills from several experts, and gather enough wealth before they could marry (Laslett, 1965).

Products in the market consisted of craftwork that had common prices set by the guilds, and of the food and products that peasants did not need for their own personal survival. The trade in the market was thus built on collectivist values, and people did not follow their self-interest or the maximum material profit. Marketing was even forbidden since the price was set by the guilds; thus, people followed their community traditions and norms. Like previous societies, economic relations were embedded and submerged in the non-economic realm of kinship, communal, religious, and political relationships (Polanyi, 1944). Companies could not set their own prices or introduce their own products or services in the market, without a thorough social embedding. Our modern idea of a market outside this social domain was unthinkable.

Thus, it may be argued that individuals were not so much focused on materialist, hedonist, or self-oriented meanings but relatively more on having enough for their survival and fulfilling their social duties. By doing their work, they contributed to the kingdom of God. On first sight, we may have seen their physical activities, but if we looked closer we would see that it was God who was present and active in their service to society. Thus, their individual face was merely a mask of God; for example, according to Luther, God milks the cows through the vocation of the milkmaid (Wingren, 1957; Billing, 1964). People did not question this functionalist divine–cosmic–social order and the function they fulfilled. However, when their place in the order was unfulfilling, they may have felt existentially threatened and psychologically stressed, which may have led to them supporting the growing social revolutions. In social–hierarchical societies, individuals focus on a plurality of meanings, but ultimately all meanings are determined by the larger meanings of clergy and nobility. This hierarchical structure in society implied a lack of freedom and a relatively functionalist approach for ordinary citizens. Individuals were often trapped inside their role in this system, and when they were unable to fulfill their prescribed economic role, they may have felt existential and psychological stress, even though these are anachronistic concepts. (This section is based on e.g. Polanyi, 1964; Epstein, 2009; Wood, 2002; Pound, 1994.)

Religious Economies

The emergence of religion seems to have stimulated social organisation and productivity. Empirical research shows that religious beliefs, particularly those in punishment in hell and reward in heaven, often go hand in hand with economic growth (Barro & McCleary, 2003; Guiso, Sapienza & Zingales, 2003). Religion has been particularly economically beneficial, fostering a sense of belonging, planning, responsibility, bequest motivation, literacy, and other social and larger types of meaning that stimulate economic productivity (Renneboog & Spaenjers, 2012). However, this may have come at the cost of individual freedom as people in religious countries in the past were expected to fit in a pre-given divine–cosmic–social order.

The next paragraphs provide some examples of religious economies (texts on Islam and Asian religions can be found in Part III). This shows how religions offer symbolic and imaginary economic theories, which often focus on social and larger types of meaning, frequently with a traditional or functionalist approach—although Eastern and mystic traditions suggest critical–intuitive approaches. Many old religions seem to expect the submission of the individual to a larger Being or to certain holy individuals and institutions. However, in younger religious developments such as the Islamic Enlightenment and Protestant Reformation, individuals are not completely determined by their submissive position; instead, the freedom of the individual became central to these religions. Countless studies show that oppressive-deterministic religions often lead to many existential questions and psychological problems in their followers, whereas freedom-oriented religions are associated with more positive well-being (Chapter 12). This freedom revolution meant a completely different understanding of freedom and meaning in life (Vos, 2018).

Vedic Religions

Some of the oldest manuscripts mankind has preserved concern Vedic religions, such as the *Upanishads*, the *Brahma Sutras* and the *Bhagavad Gita*. Central to these texts is the fourfold system of *dharma* (a moral way of living, following duties and laws), *artha* (finding meaning in means of life such as food, shelter, and wealth), *kama* (finding meaning in experiences such as pleasure, desire, sex, and love), and *moksha* (spiritual meaning, liberation from the life–rebirth cycle, or self-realisation in this life). The dynamic totality of this fourfold system tells what is meaningful in our personal life and economic interactions (Agarwal, 2015). In these Vedic texts, physical, mental, and spiritual practices are intertwined, and meanings can be realised via a complex system of yoga. This cosmocentrist fourfold system seems similar to Aristotle's holistic perspective of the four *aitia*, and in general to the plural nature of meaning in life in many early religions and philosophies.

Examples of all types of meaning can be found in these Vedic texts, ranging from securing our material well-being (*artha*), hedonism (*kama*) to social (*dharma*) and larger meanings (*moksha*). However, the ultimate weight lies in the larger meanings, as we are urged to realise that there is no world or self. The *mayan* (mundane) world and individuality (*atman*) that we perceive in our daily life are already one with *Brahman*, the One Ultimate Reality. Thus, in their personal and economic life, individuals learn to balance and transcend their materialist, hedonist, and self-oriented meanings. Individuals should not merely identify with their socio-economic situation but should experience the freedom of larger meanings. Brahman is like the invisible hand bringing people together. Early Vedic texts breathe a non-functionalist approach that asks us not merely to treat people based on their position or looks but to see their potential, freedom, and the Brahman that shows in them. For example, the Epic of Gilgamesh is one big fight against the tendency to treat people like animals, and an appeal to treat them for who they are as human inviduals (Sedlacek, 2011). However, later religious leaders have re-interpreted the Vedic texts as revealing a societal–cosmic–divine hierarchy. This functionalist and fatalist interpretation forms the cornerstone of the caste system, meaning that at birth individuals are born into a caste, prescribing all meanings in their life—including their occupation, ritual status, and customary social interactions and exclusions (Smith, 2000).

Judaism

Judeo-Christian religions form the cornerstone of modern economics. Several key ideas from modern economists have developed in the petri dish of these religions. The Torah starts with a strong work ethic, stating that God had put man in the garden of Eden to cultivate it. Whereas man starts in the cosmocentrist balance between all different types of meaning—work is pleasure and a social and holy task at the same time—due to the Fall man is doomed to painful labour and eating his food through the sweat of his brow, with a disdain for anything material and physical that has lost its shine after Eden. Genesis predicates hard work as an inescapable duty and virtue.

In our work, we continuously make conscious decisions for good or evil, like Adam. Adherence to the moral rules of the Commandments will stimulate the well-being of the community and will particularly pay off well for people materially. That is, people are rewarded for their work, and their wealth does not merely depend on holy grace. This lays the cornerstone for modern economics by advising that individual work will lead to progress. In the background of this idea of progress is the fundamentally Judaic new world view of historical progress—expecting growth—by looking forward to the coming of the Messiah, which breaks the fatalist view of man's hard labour. However, this does not necessarily imply that we should primarily follow materialistic self-interests; like Moses, our Exodus—freedom from oppression by tyrants like the Pharaoh—is more important than our material stability. We cannot take our possessions with us on our nomadic journeys through life, and we should not worship the Golden Cow or ask interests on loans; instead, we are urged to material asceticism. More important than physical wealth is our social duty, like supporting our neighbours and the Jubilee year when all debts are forgiven (Hudson, 2017). Work is also not an end in itself, as the rest day of the Sabbath shows that the meaning of God's Creation is not merely working but also resting and belonging to a community. Thus, although Judaism does respect materialist, hedonist, and self-oriented types of meaning, it ultimately focuses on social and larger meanings. The focus on doing our duty and having a rational work ethic seems functionalist, although the Sabbath and Jubilee year ask for frequent breaks from the almost fatalist work ethos.

Ancient World
Many Ancient Greek myths and philosophies have formed the foundations of modern economic models. For example, the hedonism of Epicurus inspired Bentham and Mill in their idea that we should try to maximise happiness and minimise pain for the largest number of people possible. The Stoics told that we must follow rules, although this may not always work out in the way we like; it is our intention of utility maximisation that matters, not the real outcome.

Xenophon urged the Greek state to maximise its income by increasing trade with foreigners. He also mentioned that we should take the motivation of our trade partners into account—for example, by building homes for immigrants. Thus, trade is not neutral but follows subjective meanings, and we can manipulate these meanings to our benefit. This also shows the difference between the value in use of products and the value in exchange; that is, products or services are not merely sold for the value of their direct use but also for how much others are willing to pay for them. This creates the possibility of profit, which is a sharp contrast with the pre-Ancient world where economic exchange was immediate and primarily based on use-value.

However, the economy is not merely focused on materialistic self-interests; we are influenced by 'animal spirits' and we should consult the gods about the larger perspectives. Individuals stand in a larger hierarchical order, which Plato exemplified with the Cave Myth, showing that most individuals are akin to being chained in a cave where only shadows are visible, but some people are able to free themselves and go above ground where they find stable, invariable truth. It is these larger essences, or Platonic *ideas,* which give our physical world and our economic actions their meaning. The cave myth has influenced the call of many philosophers in Ancient Greece, Rome, and Christianity to release us from our ignorance and from our earthly body, with its materialist, hedonist, and self-oriented demands. Instead, we should focus on social and larger meanings.

This is the larger purpose (telos) of human meanings, according to Aristotle: We should strive towards realising our larger potential. Private interests are only good when they are also good for society as a whole. In Chapter 3 we have explored Aristotle's teleological perspective in more detail, as this forms a cornerstone of modern economics. It suffices here to say that we commit to our actions 'for its own sake... which is the good and the chief good' (Aristotle, unknown/2019a); our actions are the telos in itself and not a functionalist means to something else. What matters is not merely the functionalist use-value, but the exchange value in the economy. Other people are not instruments for realising our self-interests. For example, justice and care are important values in their own right, and we realise these values by genuine commitment to virtues such as modesty and courage (Schoene, 2015; Van Staveren, 2001). What matters is deliberation, not calculation. Thus, the Ancient Greeks described a wide variety of meanings, but social and larger meanings seemed the most important. They offered a non-functionalist approach, although a hierarchical way of thinking was introduced that was later taken over by Christianity and influenced the medieval divine–cosmic–social hierarchy.

Christianity
Christian economics integrates many Greek, Jewish, and Vedic ideas and follows the divine–cosmic–social hierarchical world view. We may summarise their economic ethics with Jesus' saying that man does not live on bread alone, like Adam Smith's baker did not merely focus on his bread but also on social and larger meanings. The Bible portrayed Jesus as a rebel who chased tradesmen out of the temple who were mixing the sacred with the profane, who asked for radical forgiveness and debt release, and who turned away rich people who refused to sell their possessions and give to the poor as 'it is easier for a camel to go through the eye of a needle than for a rich man to enter the kingdom of God' (Dear, 2000).

Jesus was regarded as a threat to Jewish belief. His idea of the kingdom of God was more reflective of a Platonic scheme and has more in common with Vedic and Germanic religions than with Judaism which lacks an elaborated concept of a world beyond. Augustine elaborated this idea and presented human history as a conflict between 'the Earthly City' and 'the City of God'. The latter is populated by people who forego earthly pleasures to dedicate themselves to the eternal truths of God rather than by those earthly individuals who have immersed themselves in the cares and pleasures of the present, passing world. Aquinas radicalised this by saying that for the soul to be happy it needs to be severed from everything corporeal. This idea broke with the Judaic idea of following rules for the sake of rules -as 'the ultimate end of the whole man and of all his actions and desires is to know the first truth; namely, God.' (Aquinas, 1988, p.6-7) Do not love thy neighbour because you are told to do so but love him as yourself. *Charitas* (love) and *agape* (divine love) are key Christian values that put the interests of the other central and, thus, need to be distinguished from functionalist emotions such as *eros* (sexual love, attraction), *stergein* (family love) and *filia* (friendly love) (Lewis, 1991). Jesus replaced the stereotypic Judaic functionalism of following commandments and rules with the sole commandment of love. But love is not merely following a command—behaving in a loving way; it is about love from 'a pure heart, and a good conscience and a sincere faith'—being in love (1 Timothy 1:5). Love for the sake of love.

However, while we are in our earthly life, we live after the Fall of Man. And it is our responsibility to work through the sweat of our brow because 'if a man will not work, man will not eat' (2 Thessalonians 3:10). We also need to acknowledge the reality of evil. People are inclined to do evil as the flesh is weak. According to Aquinas, this is like an invisible hand: There can be no good if evil did not exist; the temptations challenge us to show our good intentions (Sedlacek, 2011). Therefore, people need a firm ruler, and we need laws to guide people. Private property can also stimulate social order, as Aquinas argues that stealing would be propagated if there would be no clear rules about what is mine and what is thine. This does not mean that for Aquinas acquisition of more and more property for self-interest is man's purpose. This would undermine God's Creation, and we should realise that all land and natural resources are given to all mankind as a common good.

In sum, many Christian thinkers focus on social and larger meanings from a non-functionalist approach. Simultaneously they acknowledge the pragmatic need for economic rules and societal hierarchies in our earthly life. We may suffer from existential and psychological stress during our life in the post-Eden world that we have been born into, but there is hope for liberation in the afterlife, the City of God.

Reformation
Until the Middle Ages, many religions seemed to offer a package deal in which religious hierarchy was combined with social stratification and its associated socio-economic inequalities. This package deal started to break in 1517 when Martin Luther sent his *Ninety-Five Theses on the Power and Efficacy of Indulgences* to the Archbishop of Mainz (historians question the myth that he nailed these on the door of a church). He criticised the Church and the papacy for the misuse of their hierarchical position in

society as well as the weakness of the theoretical justifications of the divine–cosmic–social order. In particular, Luther critiqued the selling of indulgences and the doctrines about purgatory, judgment, and the pope's authority. In later works he concentrated on the intercession and devotion to the saints, clerical celibacy, the sacraments, and the relationship between the Church and secular law. He said that these have no foundation in the Bible. As an alternative, Luther proposed a Christianity that was not based on the social hierarchy but that laid the freedom and responsibility of faith with the individual Christian. The individual does not need mediation from the clergy to be religious. The protestant movement in Germany quickly diversified, with reformers such as Calvin and Zwingli. As the social power of the Catholic Church started to disintegrate, the Counter-Reformation was started, which aimed at re-confirming their societal powers and their theological embedding in the divine–cosmic order.

The protestant fight against the Catholic Church was more than theological; a deep economic conflict of interests was underlying the Reformation and the Counter-Reformation (Eaton, 2013; Rossner, 2013). Luther condemned the financial exploitation of ordinary people, not only by the Church but by any merchants selling goods for the highest price possible and taking advantage of the needs of others; he argued against economic coercion, collusion, and monopolies (Langholm, 2009). He felt that while commerce for the exchange of necessities was legitimate, other trade had 'no useful purpose' and drained 'away the money of people and land' (Luther's Works, 1962, Vol.45, p.246). The financialisation of the economy, such as asking for interest, is mere greed and avarice. Instead, workers should get a fair salary in return for their time and energy commitment, and products should be sold for a fair price. To guarantee socio-economic equity, governments should regulate the market. The fact that Luther rejected the social dominance of the Church did not undermine his belief in the divine–cosmic order. He believed that although people should not treat one another as objects, God approaches individuals almost in a functionalist way by communicating—calling- through the work of people (the German word for work, *beruf*, literally means 'calling') (Rossner, 2013). Individuals can experience a divine calling and service to God in their work, just as work was a blessing for Adam and Eve in Paradise before the Fall. This idea was quickly followed by those of other reformers such as Calvin, who promoted a hard-work ethos that could reflect the grace of God (Weber, 2013).

Conclusions

Table 4.1. shows the diversity of meaning in social economies. Most of these have a non-functionalist focus on social types of meaning, and they are based on a cosmocentrist model of the universe, in which the individual, social, and cosmic interests are balanced (Chapter 13). The symbols and imagination of religion radically moved the perspective on meaning in life in the direction of functionalisation, which would get a high flight after the Middle Ages, as the next chapter will explain.

However, compared to functionalist–materialist economies, social economies are less oriented around materialist types of meaning and offer relatively greater freedom and existential and psychological well-being.

Key Points

1. Animalistic, collectivist, social-hierarchical, and religious economies focus on social types of meaning, often from a non-functionalist perspective.
2. In early religious economies, individuals were often seen as being determined by their submissive position, which possibly brought a sense of lack of freedom, existential questions, and low well-being.
3. The non-functionalist social perspective disappeared during the Enlightenment, when secularisation, technological advancements, the industrial revolution, and Cartesian dualism introduced a materialist and functionalist perspective on meaning in life.

Table 4.1. Overview of Ten Perspectives on Social Economies

Name of question	Formal name of perspective	Animalistic & evolutionary economies	Collectivist economies	Social-hierarchical economies	Religious economies
Status?	Ontological status	Reality	Reality Symbol Imagination	Reality Symbol Imagination	Symbol Imagination
What?	Type of meaning	Materialistic Hedonistic Self-oriented Social?	Materialistic Hedonistic Self-oriented Social Larger	Materialistic Social Larger	Social Larger Existential–philosophical
How?	Approach to meaning	Traditional? Functionalistic	Traditional Functionalistic?	Traditional Functionalistic	Traditional
Where?	Relationship between individual and society	Interactionism	Interactionism	Social determinism	Social determinism
When?	Development over time	Historiography	Historiography	Historiography	Historiography
Who?	Emergence of individual meaning	Ethology	Anthropology	Anthropology	Theology Anthropology
Whose?	Sense of freedom	Realised freedom Negative and positive freedom? Individual and structural freedom?	Realised freedom Negative and positive freedom Individual and structural freedom	Symbolic and imagined freedom Negative freedom (fatalism) Structural freedom	Symbolic and imagined freedom Negative freedom (fatalism) Structural freedom
Why?	Existential well-being	Unknown	Realistic sense of freedom and limitations?	Existential questions and concerns	Existential questions and concerns
Which?	Impact on daily life	Unknown	Few mental health problems, large quality of life, and large life satisfaction	Many mental health problems, low quality of life, and low life satisfaction	Dependent on (sub)type of religion: No Many mental health problems, low-high quality of life, and low–high life satisfaction

Chapter 5

A History of Meaning in Functionalist–Materialist Liberalism and Neoliberalism

Advocates of capitalism are very apt to appeal to the sacred principles of liberty, which are embodied in one maxim: the fortunate must not be restrained in the exercise of tyranny over the unfortunate. (Quote attributed to Bertrand Russell)

Economic Transformations

The previous chapter described how until the end of the Middle Ages most economies centred predominantly around social types of meaning, where the inherent meaningfulness of the community mattered and individuals were not usually reduced to variables in the function of an entrepreneur or political strategist (Nelson, 2014; Smith, 2013; Epstein, 2009; Sedlacek, 2011; Wood, 2002; Oysterman, Coon & Kemmelmeier, 2002; Kagitcibasi, 1997; Pound, 1994; Polanyi, 1964). This changed radically at the end of the Middle Ages, creating a fertile breeding ground for functionalist–materialist approaches to the economy. The following is an overview of economic transformations, explained via the types of meaning. Of course, these are only generic societal trends, and most likely there were many individual exceptions.

Materialist Meanings
Unemployment grew quickly. Many theories explain its causes, such as agricultural innovations replacing workers and land enclosures as landlords put borders around their land and forced individual workers off their land. Work also became more specialised, as individuals dedicated themselves to one craft. The Industrial Revolution also started to replace manual labour with machines. Parallel to the demise in agricultural employment, work opportunities grew in the factories and in related sectors such as mining. The new workforce in factories also included women, although their lives had previously mainly centred around family life and homework (Postan, 1973). Consequently, the change in home life was at the heart of the revolutionary changes, as for the first time a difference emerged between 'home' and 'work'.

Hedonist Meanings

The growing wealth of the middle class paralleled a shift in what they experienced as meaningful as they started to focus on materialist and hedonist meanings, such as having a cosy house or looking good in nice clothes (Sennett, 2017).

Self-Oriented Meanings

The largest revolution was possibly the emergence of the idea of private property, as for instance, John Locke (1689/2014) described. Until then, land had been open, tools were shared, and workers had helped each other. Locke called private property a human right, which did not merely justify private ownership of property but also its exclusive rights of use -in stark contrast with Aquinas and the medieval practices of open land and commons. Suddenly, everything became for sale for a financial price instead of being embedded in a social community. Workers lost their sources of self-sustenance and had to search for employment, and labour itself became commodified as workers could no longer offer their labour as their duty but for a wage -for instance in factories, and a functionalist approach to life emerged.

Social Meanings

Until the end of the Middle Ages, economic life was strongly determined by one's socio-economic position at birth—e.g., peasants would serve their unpaid duty to their lords. Society was organised in a social hierarchy, with peasants below nobility and clergy, and angels and God at the top. This social order was justified by the story that people heard in the church about God allocating them to this place in the divine–cosmic–social order. Of course, there had been some exceptions, such as the rich and powerful elite. Similarly, philosophers, such as Ancient Greek philosophers who had promoted the theoretical ideas of freedom, usually belonged to a relatively wealthy elite and had relatively little impact on ordinary illiterate citizens. Often, their philosophies seemed to justify the divine–cosmic–social order of their era, from which the wealthy establishment benefited; thus, philosophy initially emerged as an elitist movement for and by the establishment.

The enclosures of agricultural land in countries such as England meant quick urbanisation. The enclosures meant that whereas in the past landlords had expected duty from their workers, they started to demand rent. With their sudden wealth, a new class of landlords and property owners was created, becoming a power that still dominates today (Hudson, 2017). In the cities, guilds were dismantled, and former masters who had aligned their workshops with the guild rules in the past became sole traders with their own interests at heart. The increasing wealth led to an upcoming middle class whose members received their wealth from their own work instead of from inheritance like the medieval establishment of landlords and nobility. Whereas prior society had been focused on relatively balanced communities with common aims, different groups started to fight one another for their own survival: the establishment of landlords felt threatened by the growing bourgeoisie, the workers felt maltreated by the bourgeois, and the middle class had to fight the powers of the nobility and landlords. This transformative social context gave rise to Thomas Hobbes crying aloud: *Homo homini lupus!* (Achterhuis, 2010).

Thomas Hobbes and Jean-Jacques Rousseau recommended that we should have a strong state or social contract to meld all these interests and give power to higher authorities as an Aquinal solution to prevent the masses from annihilating one another. Immanuel Kant returned to the Judaic idea of following rules ('deontology'), with the ultimate law of 'act only according to that maxim whereby you can, at the same time, will that it should become a universal law' ('categorical imperative'), a more complex version of the Golden Rule that says 'treat others how you wish to be treated'. Similarly, Adam Smith struggled in *Theory of Moral Sentiments* with the same question: How can we have morality despite self-interests? Individuals are driven by a wide range of 'passions' with materialist, hedonist, and self-oriented aims, but they are also driven by moral motivations. Smith developed the idea of the impartial observer, which means that instead of directly following our unlimited self-interest we should look at ourselves and our social context from a larger perspective and make a decision from this helicopter view: 'If anyone were, in respect of *x* and *y*, fully informed and vividly imaginative, impartial, in a calm frame of mind and otherwise normal, he would *prefer x* to *y*' (Campbell, 2014). Thus, the conflict of economic interests is solved by asking all economic agents to imagine the interests, norms, and values of their larger context, which seems to imply a critical–intuitive balancing of a plurality of possible meanings.

Larger Meanings
An increasing opposition developed against the authority of the Church. Individuals became skeptical about the theological doctrine, possibly in response to the growing scientific, skeptical mindset; the mechanical world view of the Enlightenment; the increasing education; and resistance against corruption in the church. This sentiment was summarised in Immanuel Kant's imperative *Sapere Aude*: think for yourself! With the demise of the divine–cosmic order, the social order also seemed to collapse: the traditional hierarchies of the inherited aristocracy were questioned, and multiple uprisings against the misuse of power occurred, culminating in the French Revolution and the American Civil War. On an existential level, this meant that individuals started to question the traditional societal roles and meanings. As they assumed that there was no absolute religious power or community anymore, they questioned who could tell then what their individual meaning in life was. This was possibly the most significant change in this era: individuals starting to ask questions about their personal meaning in life. Prior to the Reformation, individuals most likely did not ask such questions as 'what is the meaning of *my* life?' They had simply fulfilled their traditional role in the divine–cosmic–social order like the hand serves the head. This subjectification of meaning was fueled further by Romanticism. Georg Wilhelm

Friedrich Hegel observed, for instance, that individuals in his time started to live their lives according to the uniqueness of their own experiences and taste (*'besonderheit der empfindung'*).

Thus, we see that around 1500 a period of religious, cultural, and economic transformation emerged in response to scientific and economic developments such as the Industrial Revolution, but also as an answer to the rigid socio-economic hierarchies of the past. These existential challenges gave rise to a wide sense of fatalism, existential angst, and mental health problems, reflected in the tragic moods of Romanticism. Whereas the Church had guaranteed the social order, the demise of the religious order meant that that the social structure had also lost its fundaments. Consequently, philosophers like Hobbes described how interests of different people conflicted. As a solution, Rousseau promoted an implicit social contract as the new societal foundation, and moral philosophers such as Kant found this foundation in universal moral rules. In sum, the rational liberal economists faced unique historic challenges that offered fertile soil for the emergence of materialist–functionalist economic ideas ranging from liberalism to Marxism. (This section is based on many studies on the history of economics, including Wood, 2017; Heilbroner & Milberg, 2009; Nisbett, 2009; McCloskey, 2006; Laslett, 2000; Cameron, 1997; Galbraith, 1987; Spadafora, 1990; Cassirer, Kristeller & Randall, 1956; Bury, 1932).

Rational Liberalism

In the spirit of the Enlightenment, many rational liberal economists searched for universal laws to explain socio-economic mechanisms, as they believed that society functions as mechanics do, like the modern invention of the clock. They were strongly influenced by the philosopher Descartes, who had introduced the idea of the man-machine: 'I should like you to consider that these functions (including passion, memory, and imagination) follow from the mere arrangement of the machine's organs every bit as naturally as the movements of a clock or other automaton follow from the arrangement of its counter-weights and wheels' (Descartes, 1629/2003). When we use our method of critical thinking well, we may be able to find the mechanisms behind any human behaviour, including moral and economic behaviour. Although Descartes had few economic publications, his idea of man as a machine has strongly influenced authors on the economy. The rational economists introduced a functionalist approach to social theories, as individuals and communities were no longer seen as an end in themselves but as capital—means to larger ends—in the market.

The rational economists did not have access to systematic empirical studies as we have nowadays; thus, most of their work was based on theoretical speculation, although some economists argued that their deductive–philosophical method was preferable to making overgenerous inductions (Von Mises, 1929). For example, Adam Smith contended that a small government is the best for the economy overall, but he offered little empirical evidence, for instance when comparing the effectiveness of small and large governments. In contrast, we know from economic research nowadays, that striving for a small government is paradoxical as a relatively strong government is needed to guarantee the rules and the freedom of the market. We also know from numerous empirical studies in many countries that one size does not fit all (this will be elaborated on and proven in Chapter 7). Thus, Adam Smith's appeal for a small government seems more indicative of an abstract Platonic essential truth than of the complex reality of ordinary people.

Utilitarianism

John Mill (1859/1966) started his famous book *Utilitarianism* by asking what the highest good is. He was not interested in how people actually made decisions, but in the moral foundations—that is, the Platonic idea of principles by which we *should* live. He was not interested in following the answers in terms of a God-given moral order imposed by the Church or by social pressure, not regarding such morality as a means to a higher goal such as God or conformism; rather, Mill searched for a *summum bonum* that is desirable for its own sake (Mulgan, 2014; Farina, Hahn & Vannucci, 1996).

Jeremy Bentham (1789/1970) argued that Nature had only placed mankind under the governance of two sovereign masters—pain and pleasure—and 'it is for them alone to point out what we ought to do'. Happiness, nowadays more generally called 'well-being', is intended pleasure and the absence of pain; unhappiness is pain and the privation of pleasure. Since all individuals desire their own well-being, it must follow that all of us desire the well-being of everyone; consequently, an action that results in the greatest well-being for the greatest number of people is the best action. Individuals should not follow their own interest over the public good, as this runs counter to this deep-seated natural impulse. Mill's utilitarianism meant a subjectivist turn in ethics, which puts the weight on individuals as knowledgeable of what is moral, without needing others to tell them what is right and wrong; therefore, governments should trust individual ethics by giving individuals maximum freedom.

Following Bentham and Mill's work, different versions of utilitarianism, as well as criticism, have emerged. For example, Chapter 4 showed how in nature, animals—and humans—do not only follow what gives them pleasure and avoids pain; this selfish survival instinct is sided by a moral instinct that takes the well-being of others as its highest end, even if this comes at the cost of their own pleasure and pain. More in general, it is has been argued that happiness is not the sole intrinsic good, as there are a variety of meanings that people may consider in ethical decision making; therefore, it has been argued that it is more appropriate to use the general term 'well-being', as described above, because not every individual may always be interested in personal pleasure (Scarre, 1996).

What has remained influential in utilitarianism is the concept of utility and its modern formulations in terms of 'preference'. The word 'utility' means approximately what we call nowadays well-being. Jeremy Bentham described utility as the sum of all pleasure that results from an action, minus the suffering of anyone involved in the action.

Prior to Bentham and Mill, the philosopher Hutcheson had developed algorithms for calculating the greatest well-being, although the author had removed them because his readers found them objectionable. However, such calculations have become a cornerstone of modern economics. Consider an individual facing a set of alternatives, over which the individual has a preference order. A utility function represents these preferences. A number is given to each alternative; for example, if alternative 'a' is given the number '5' and alternative 'b' the number '2', this would mean that the individual prefers alternative 'a' over 'b'. However, some economists have argued that individuals are often unconscious of the number ordering of their preferences, and it would also be very time-consuming to ask each consumer or citizen about all their preferences. Instead, economists often infer underlying relative utilities from observed choice; for instance, when a product is sold 1000 times at the price of £10 and only sold 500 times for £15, they assume that this shows the willingness of customers to pay £10 for the fulfillment or satisfaction of their desire, indicating their underlying utility (Marshall, 1921/1961). Thus, revealed, rather than abstract, preferences have become the focus of economic calculations. In many economic sub-disciplines, functions have been evolved such as expected utility or prisoner's dilemmas.

Mill's search for the *summum bonum*—principles that we want as an end in themselves—has become functionalist in the hands of modern economists. However, Mill wrote that utility not only includes quantitative components—the amount of pleasure or pain that we might measure with a psychological questionnaire—but also such qualitative components as the subjective meaning of experience—e.g., masochists preferring pain. Some economists, including Gary Becker (1992), have tried to quantify such qualitative experiences by, for example, including 'love' as a variable in the function. Similarly, psychologists have developed questionnaires about countless topics. However, it seems inaccurate to include both apples and oranges in one function; for example, while love for the sake of love could be given a different weight in the function than sexual attraction, they are phenomena on different dimensions that cannot be balanced, subtracted, or summed up. This is like the difference between the grammar and the spelling of a sentence, on the one hand, and the meaning of the sentence, on the other hand. However, we will see later that this functionalism has become a key characteristic of neoliberalism.

The Invisible Hand
Utilitarianists have shown how individuals may act to improve their own well-being, assuming that they do not follow the evolutionary moral drive (Chapter 4). What

happens if multiple individuals, each with their own preferences, meet one another, particularly if they have conflicting interests, such as the seller wanting to get the highest price and the buyer wanting to offer the lowest price? How do supply and demand meet?

The French Physiocrats—also called Natural Philosophers—believed that there was a natural order that connected people with 'invisible chains' or an 'invisible hand,' according to Joseph Glanville (1661, in Rothbard, 1995). Belesbat stated that God had woven all peoples into an interdependent network of reciprocal advantage by means of trade and specialization: 'There is nothing that one [country] lacks which the others do not produce.... God... having created men for society, has so well divided them that they cannot do without one another' (Rothbard, 1995). As long as we do not interfere with the natural order, trying to maximise our own well-being will maximise everybody's well-being in the long term. Thus, individuals do not aim at well-being as the ultimate end but at their own self-interest, their private utility. Thus, there was a balance between individuals' belief in a perfect cosmic–social order, and government's belief that it should not try to regulate this order: 'Nature or Providence [had]... so ordered the business of life that (...) everything works out all right provided that nature is left alone (*on laisse faire la nature*)... [i.e.,] provided that it is left free and that no one meddles with this business save to grant protection in it to all and to prevent violence' (Boisguilbert in Rothbard, 1995). The wealth of nations is the result of individuals following their own interest. This symbol of the Invisible Hand was later taken over by Adam Smith, radicalised by Bernard Mandeville, and popularised by neoliberalism.

Laissez-faire

The concept of *laissez-faire*, let it be, was popularised by the physiocrat Quesnay, being an (inaccurate) translation of the term *Wu Wei* in Taoism and Chinese Daoism (Baghdiantz McCabe, 2008). *Laissez-faire* means that the government intervenes or regulates only minimally in the interactions between their citizens, as they trust the order and process of 'Nature'. This concept of nature is a romantic or even mystic concept that seems beyond criticism for many economists, an example of imagination in economics. Possibly, some of the reasoning may be better explained as being more naïve than romantic, such as Marshall's belief that free economics would bring about a spirit of honesty and, therefore, we do not need additional regulation or moral principles as Nature provides everything for a moral society (Bronk, 2009; Heinzelman, 1980). The crash of the banks in 2008 shockingly revealed the blatant naivety of this illusionary belief in the natural goodness of *laissez-faire.* The next chapter will show how countless empirical studies have disproven the rationality of the so-called 'free market'.

Similar concepts such as *Wu Wei* can be found in Western philosophy, such as the medieval mystic Meister Eckhart who inspired 20th century philosopher Martin

Heidegger, who used the term *gelassenheit*, let it be (Vos, 2014; Visser, 2008). Although their underlying phenomenological method means giving space to individual meanings to reveal themselves, it does not seem to imply a mythical nature but, rather, critical analyses of what is meaningful and what is not meaningful, what meanings are manipulated and which are not, and what the real relationships are in our current specific socio-economic context. Heidegger wrote that what hinders this freedom is our approach of calculating everything, the functionalist perspective. Thus, a true *laissez-faire* government would imply that economists and politics would have a non-functionalist approach (see Part III; Bronk, 2009; Heinzelman, 1980). Even Alan Greenspan, the longtime head of the American Federal Reserve, said in 2008 that his previously free-market thinking was erroneous because all models are imperfect and human behaviour cannot be put in equations in full (Knowlton & Grynbaum, 2008). Freedom cannot be found in so-called 'rational' economics because of its irrationality.

In sum, rational economists predominantly focused on materialist, hedonist, and self-oriented meanings. Although the authors mentioned not wanting to oppress the freedom of individuals, their approach seemed functionalist because it reduced people to means to an end and meaning in life to manipulated and manipulatable functions.

Moral Liberalism

Can Adam Smith's texts on the invisible hand be used by rational and neoliberal economists and politicians to evangelise their belief in the free market, selfishness and competition? No! (Ten Houten, 2016; Forman-Barzilai, 2010; Drosos, 1996; Bassiry & Jones, 1993; Waszek, 1984; West, 1969). The meanings of their rational liberalism and Smith's moral liberalism need to be distinguished, which is the difference between neoliberal materialism–functionalism and Smithian critical–intuitive pluralism. This explanation follows the research from recent studies on *Das Smith Problem* (Wilson & Dixon, 2015; Schoene, 2015; Montes, 2003).

Smith wrote in his *Theory of Moral Sentiments* (1851) that individuals are not only driven by materialist and self-interested meanings but also by kindness, although Smith seems to assume that 'trade for the public good' is a less strong drive than self-love. He even fulminated against Mandeville's work: greed is avarice. This is known as *Das Smith Problem*: How can we marry self-oriented and social meanings? Some have argued that *The Moral Sentiments* was written several decades before the *Wealth of Nations* and that in the period between Smith evolved from a socialist to a capitalist, possibly due to reading the works of the physiocrats. This is unlikely as Smith continued speaking about morality in the *Wealth* and he is not the liberal poster boy that some neoliberals have tried to make him. He continued seeing an important role for the government to safeguard the basic trust in the market—for instance, by guaranteeing law, defence, public works, and institutions facilitating commerce and preventing monopolies, as well as empowering socio-economically disenfranchised individuals. Smith is also clear in explaining why money will not save us from existential limitations like fear, sorrow, and death; thinking that our wealth can transcend these is vanity, and we need to be realistic instead of fetishizing our economic symbols and illusions. Even before Karl Marx, Smith described how workers could become alienated in the economy (Drosos, 1996; West, 1969).

Das Smith Problem only exists if we assume that individuals can be driven solely by one meaning in life—that is, either by their own interest or the interests of others (Wilson & Dixon, 2015). In *The Moral Sentiments*, Smith writes about a large number of passions that individuals may have in life, depending on the social context, and sometimes even multiple passions at the same time, like the evidence-based-meaning sextet (Keppler, 2020; Ten Houten, 2016). This shows that Smith had a pluralist view of economic actions, which was later replaced by the monist view of neoliberal theorists—that individuals have only one drive, which is self-interest. The citation of the baker and the invisible hand was embedded in the context of Smith explicitly asking about the 'meaning' of economic transactions. In hundreds of places in *The Wealth of Nations*, he uses this term 'meaning' and argues how the same economic transaction can have different meanings for different individuals (he used the word 'meaning' or 'meaningful' 246 times and the word 'interest' 345 times). Thus, it is not the self-interest per se, but the meaning of the self-interest that matters (Hirschman, 1977/2013).

The meaning of economic transactions is determined in *The Moral Sentiments* by our subjective passions, what Hegel later called 'subjective taste' (*besonderheit der empfindung*). Some decades later, in *The Wealth of Nations,* Smith replaced the term 'passion' for 'interest' and in several places uses these terms indistinguishably. This linguist transformation is intriguing. The term *interesse* means 'importance' in Latin and simultaneously describes the relationship between individuals as the term interesse is etymologically derived from inter-, meaning in-between, and -esse, being. In Smith's time, the term *interest* was usually used in economic texts to refer to the possession of a share or right to something, or the compensation for a debtor's defaulting. Thus, by changing from using the individualist term 'passion' to 'interest', Smith focused less on solipsist meanings and more on the emergence of meanings in the relational dynamics of the market and the share that individuals have in the market. In his time, the word *interesse* meant something like prudence in Ancient Greece with Aristotelean virtues such as justice and beneficence; what matters is not following general rules but fostering individual judgment. This relational interpretation is strongly supported by many systematic analyses that have clearly shown how Smith was influenced by Stoic ethics, and how it seems that his concepts should be interpreted in this moral context (Force, 2003; Vivenza, 2001; Waszek, 1984).

Thus, self-interest seems to automatically include morality, and as morality is natural to everyone, we can trust that individuals follow their self-interest; this is why there is an invisible hand, as it is guided by moral deliberation and relational ethics. Giving attention to our own relational share in the market dynamics does not imply selfishness but critical reflexivity regarding our own position or, as Smith calls this, 'the regard' towards ourselves, which entails 'paying critical attention', like a guard on watch (cf. 'critical intuition'). In contrast with dogs, who merely follow their passion, humans should deliberate, wrote Smith in the same section as the invisible hand in The *Wealth of Nations*. In his *Sentiments*, he described this as imagining that we look from the perspective of an independent spectator at our situation, ourselves and others, and all our interests, however diverging these may be (Heath, 2013). Thus, the metaphor of the invisible hand describes the critical analyses of the multiple meanings that the market may have and not to plea for selfishness. The invisible hand describes how economic transactions can have different meanings for different individuals, and how critical reflexivity can help individuals to meet one another (like the baker critically examining his own local place in the market), balance their interests; it also describes how this process can stimulate the wealth of the nation, which is possibly more in line with the practice of the invisible hand in collectivist societies than in modern individualism. We can find many examples of this in Smith's later works.

As Chapter 4 described, until the end of the Middle Ages, individuals had not asked themselves questions such as 'What is the meaning of my life'?, 'What do I want'?, or 'What is the meaning of this interaction'? Individuals were part of a pre-given social order, which was in turn embedded in a larger divine–cosmic order with nobility, clergy, angels, and God higher on the ladder of importance. Individuals did not reflect on themselves but merely fulfilled their role (as the baker 'merely' baked the bread because he was the son of a baker and had inherited the bakery); people did not have the cognitive distance towards the immediacy of their economic behaviour. Similarly, Smith wondered how individuals could be let free to follow their own range of meanings instead of having societal meanings imposed on them by birth, church, or nobility, or having governments strictly organising the economic activities of all economic agents with planned economies, like the mercantilist governments, exporting many products. Thus, Smith seemed to believe that if individuals would live their lives in ways that are meaningful *to them*, including the meaningfulness of morality, the overall wealth of the nation would improve (Von Mises, 1947).

In Smith's time, the market was a physical place with strong collectivist characteristics where people meet and knew one another. Most likely, there was still a strong collectivist culture in small villages such as Kirkcaldy in Scotland where Smith grew up, or Glasgow and Edinburgh, which kept possibly more collectivist cultures than the rapidly individualising cities in the south of the United Kingdom. Of course, Smith knew that the *idea* of the market was changing; he was, for example, aware of the tulip mania at the stock exchange in Amsterdam at 1637, but even that stock exchange was a physical place, where sellers and buyers could look one another in the eyes. However, the idea of the market was not totally imaginary and symbolic; it had a physical location. It was the lack of immediate relational contacts in the emerging impersonal markets that triggered Smith to warn against greed. Smith seemed more concerned with the real life-world of common workers than with abstract markets—for example labourers in pin-making factories. The freedom of the market implied a *real* freedom, both negative and positive, based on a social understanding of physical markets. It was only with the introduction of electronic stock exchanges in the 20th century that the market lost its physical embodiment and became a symbol and place of imagination. Therefore, applying Smith's concept of the free market to the modern markets of digital stock exchanges or mega-chain supermarkets is a historiological fallacy, as nowadays markets have lost the physical immediacy of the social relationships in Smith's collectivist culture. Freedom of the modern market is impersonal freedom, which inherently leaves morality outside, with automatic trade as its culmination point. If he were still alive, Adam Smith would most likely appeal against the neoliberal misuse of his ideas.

Early Austrian School & Marginalists

While Marxist ideas became popular among political activists, rational liberalism dominated the universities at the end of the 19th century. Benefiting from the popularity of positivism, they believed that everything can be measured in concrete empirical terms. For example, Marshall's handbook, *Principles of Economics* (2009), was full of functions and became the standard introductory text for generations of students. However, rational liberals received much criticism from the beginning. For example, economist Friedrich Hayek criticised this approach in his 1941 essay *The Counter-Revolution of Science*, as he described that

> the persistent effort of modern Science has been to get down to 'objective facts', to cease studying what men thought about nature or regarding the given concepts as true images of the real world, and, above all, to discard all theories which pretended to explain phenomena by imputing to them a directing mind like our own. Instead, its main task became to revise and reconstruct the concepts formed from ordinary experience on the basis of systematic testing of the phenomena, so as to be better able to recognize the particular as an instance of a general rule.

Instead, Hayek argued that economics is more like a moral science

> concerned with man's conscious or reflected action, actions where a person can be said to choose between various courses open to him, and here the situation is essentially different. The external stimulus which may be said to cause or occasion such actions can of course also be defined in purely physical

terms. But if we tried to do so for the purposes of explaining human action, we would confine ourselves to less than we know about the situation.

Hayek's critique of rationalised economics followed the so-called Austrian school of economic thought. Instead of focusing on aggregated functions of masses, they focused more on methodological individualism (Von Mises, 1949). They argued that generalised statistical functions do not do justice to the meanings that individuals attach to their economic actions. Humans are purpose-driven, and products and services have unique meanings to them.

Similarly, the marginal value theory states that the actual value of a product depends on the product's utility in its least important use (Von Mises, 1912). For example, water is much more valuable than diamonds for survival. However, as water is plentiful and diamonds are scarce, the marginal value of a pound of diamonds is more than the marginal value of a pound of water. Individual consumers often buy products based on 'opportunity costs': the opportunity of buying a new washing machine could, for instance, imply that someone does not have the money to go on holiday or buy DVDs they wanted. Similarly, an increase of £1000 in taxes means more for an individual with a small salary than someone with large savings; thus, the same economic phenomenon has different meanings for different individuals in different situations. Hayek also described how consumers and producers prefer products and production processes that give immediate gratification instead of investing for the long term, except when there is a large likelihood of yielding a greater return than investing for a shorter time; thus, time has an important meaning for both consumers and producers. The marginal difference reflects both their situation—such as the scarcity of the product, their socio-economic situation, or their lifespan—as well as subjective values and fundamental ideas on meaning in life.

Thus, the early Austrian School and the Marginalists brought meaning into the economic field, albeit in terms of preferences and marginalism, and based on an essentialist–deductive method (see Chapter 4). Consumers and producers are assumed to be implicitly or explicitly comparing the meanings of products or services, and they create inner hierarchies of meanings—for instance, concluding that the washing machine is more important than going on vacation. Extensive psychological research on meaning in life has confirmed that individuals indeed seem to create such hierarchies of meaning and that this determines their decisions and behaviour (Vos, 2018). However, research revealed in Part II undermines the Austrian idea that individuals are rational in this hierarchy creation, and that scarcity impacts their perceived meaning. The solution to material scarcity is not to increase material productivity, and continue feeding our materialist tastes, but to give up materialism and develop post-materialist tastes.

Neoliberal Economists

At the start of the 20th century, neo-Marxist, Keynesian, communist, and Austrian economic ideas were on the rise, while the popularity of rational liberalism and moral liberalism was declining. As will be described in Chapter 9, this development raised serious concerns among liberal economists. Therefore, in 1938, a group of liberals came together to discuss the crisis of liberalism during the Walter Lippmann Colloquium in Paris (Reinhoudt & Audier, 2018), which was followed a decade later with the Mont Pelerin Society in Switzerland (Mirowski & Plehwe, 2009/2015; Hartwell, 1995). These two events are often interpreted as the revival of liberalism, which came to be known as neoliberalism. It is hard to define neoliberalism, as different people have different interpretations. A working definition is that neoliberalism is the imaginary and symbolic opposition to a large state, and the protection of the negative freedom of the market by any means, including the use of political technologies, interventions from a strong but small state, and sacrifice of the sense of individual freedom. Part II will elaborate this in detail, but to get a flavour, the ideas from the influential neoliberal economists Hayek and Friedman will now be explained, followed by those of the neoliberal politicians Reagan and Thatcher in the next section (Jones, 2012).

Friedrich von Hayek

Hayek started his career in the Austrian School. Based on the idea that market prices depend on subjective meanings, he concluded that governments can never have complete information for centralised planning, and therefore argued that a complex economy cannot be rationally planned. As markets are not transparent for any economic agent, nobody should control markets, including government interventions (Jones, 2012). Subsequently, Hayek used the romantic imagination of rational economists—that we should trust the price mechanisms of free markets to maintain efficient exchange and use of resources (Bronk, 2009; Heinzelman, 1980). Hayek's work has been widely criticised for being 'ideological', as even his co-winner of the Nobel Prize for Economics, Myrdal, described it. Hayek idealised freedom of the market as the foundation for political freedom and ultimately as the condition for living a meaningful life: 'Economic control is not merely control of a sector of human life which can be separated from the rest; it is the control of the means for all our ends' (Hayek, 1944/2014, p.95). Other economists have criticised Hayek for not being evidence-based enough about mistrusting governments and instead trusting private enterprises since research indicates that free private interests tend to become monopolies.

Hayek seemed to ignore the role of meaning in life (e.g., Nelson, 2014; Sedlacek, 2011). He used the metaphor of his trust in language for his trust in the market (2014): Just as individuals use and create language without anyone deliberately controlling language development, states should not intervene in the economic interactions between individuals. However, Hayek's limited view of language seems to mirror his limited view of economics. Language is more than linguist functions—spelling, grammar, the sounds of letters and words—and Hayek left out the meaning that language expresses. For example, the sentence 'I love you' is more than a randomly evolved string of letters, sounds, and grammar. Although people may be free in the spelling and grammar they use, certain meanings may be preferable over those of other languages, as Hayek rejected the ideas of national-socialism or communism. Thus, there is a meaning-oriented dimension in economics that Hayek restricts, even though he presents himself as promoting freedom.

Similarly, his vision of the economy focused predominantly on its materialist functions, even though he did not use mathematical functions (Nelson, 2014; Sedlacek, 2011). Hayek's concept of the free market was limited by his limited concept of human meanings; for example, when he spoke about the freedom of the market, he imagined that individuals could optimise their materialist, hedonist, and self-oriented meanings. In his book *The Mirage of Social Justice* (1976, Ch.10), he disapproved of social and larger meanings such as the notion of 'social justice'; he compared the market to a game in which 'there is no point in calling the outcome just or unjust' and argued that 'social justice is an empty phrase with no determinable content'; he also argued that 'the results of the individual's efforts are necessarily unpredictable, and the question as to whether the resulting distribution of incomes is just has no meaning' (see Chapter 7). By excluding the meaning of suffering and social justice from his philosophy, Hayek defended liberal dictatorship, such as Pinochet in Chile, as a temporary means towards full liberalism. Not only have many economists and ethicists called his stance unethical and paradoxical, Hayek's limited focus on materialist, hedonist, and self-oriented meanings have been contradicted by countless empirical research showing that social and larger meanings drive human motivation and that these are often more powerful predictors of human action than any other types of meanings. By excluding these fundamental facts, Hayek has created an imaginary account of the market stripped of its soul of social meaning and justice, which seem to have influenced many politicians (Jones, 2012).

Later in his life, Hayek left Vienna for Chicago, after a decade detour at the London School of Economics. He worked at the Institute of Economics in Chicago, founded by John Rockefeller, whose oil emporium owned 90% of the American oil and petrol industry and who was fighting in court against antitrust laws. In the spirit of Rockefeller, the school of economics would attempt to provide academic credibility to Rockefeller's ideology of the free market with free play for all private parties and no role for government regulations, with the exception of a central bank crucial for money supply (although even central banks would be privatised, and 'advise' governments to borrow more and more money from them). Their school has been one of the most influential schools of the economy—together with the Virginia and London Schools—determining political history in many countries.

Milton Friedman

Friedman, one of the most popular faces of the Chicago School, commented that the centralised control of economic activities is always accompanied by political repression. Thus ultimately, for him economic freedom implied political and individual freedom, even though research has disproved this (see Part II; Jones, 2012). Friedman argued that competitive capitalism is particularly important for minority groups, such as LGBTQI individuals, to realise what is meaningful for them as he believed that impersonal market forces would protect people from discrimination for reasons unrelated to their productivity. Friedman seemed to sketch a black-or-white world view: either you are democratic and stimulate freedom by unregulated economic markets, or you are totalitarian and undemocratic. Other scholars have proved this argument to be a fallacy as many markets are non-democratic yet market-liberal regimes, and many forces such as media monopolies impinge the freedom of consumers and employees (Guilhot, 2005). The main meaning-oriented argument against Friedman and his Chicago peers is that the market does not follow rational rules, and, for instance, government regulation and critical pedagogy in education are required to enable individuals to freely examine what they experience as meaningful (Vos, Roberts, & Davies, 2019).

Furthermore, for Friedman materialist—or even more strictly, monetary—freedom seemed to suffice for economic progress; this is reflected in his focus on monetary economics, which accentuated the meaning of money supply in determining consumption and production (Schwartz, 2007; Kasser, Cohen, Kanner and Ryan, 2007). Consequently, he ignored social and larger types of meaning, such as the importance that love, families, and social justice have for individuals. For example, Friedman argued that Keynes was wrong in stimulating government spending as this increased money supply and led to devaluation and further worsening of the depression of the 1930s; he argued that the same amount of money meant less to people when more money was available. Thus, Friedman argued that individuals have a rational understanding of money, ignoring the symbolic and imaginary meanings that money has for individuals as well as that individual behaviour could be led by irrational and non-materialistic motivations.

Since the financial crisis of 2007/2008, Friedman's restrictive financial philosophy has influenced many Western governments such as the United Kingdom and the United States to administer strong austerity policies; it was argued that by limiting the government deficits and restricting the money flow, the economy would be made stronger and more resilient. However, the social and larger meanings of austerity were underestimated, as the public narrative of crisis and austerity led consumers and producers to worry about their financial future; thus they started saving their money instead of consuming or investing, as future security had become an important value in the public debate. The austerity measures also decreased the actual and marginal material wealth of individuals with lower incomes—for instance due to stricter benefit policies—which further put a brake on economic progress. Furthermore, austerity also shifted the nature of government expenses as, for instance unemployment and job-related psychological stress increased costs for unemployment and sickness benefits. Consequently, based on empirical research, the International Monetary Fund has concluded that the austerity measures actually stagnated the recovery after the 2007/2008 crisis due to the adverse meaning for consumers and producers (Ostry, Lungani & Furcery, 2016). In sum, the Friedmanian obsession with monetary policies ignored the multiplicity of subjective meanings and led to an exacerbation of the crisis.

Conclusion

Neoliberals such as Hayek and Friedman seem to focus on materialist and self-oriented meanings with a functionalist approach. Their focus moved from the moral-liberal focus of the freedom of the individual to the freedom of the market, and they promoted the idea that states should fulfill a small role, whereas the private sector should play a large role.

As described in Chapter 3, neoliberal research is often deductive in nature. This means that researchers derive hypotheses from their imaginary and symbolic model and subsequently try to find evidence for these hypotheses; this raises the risk of self-affirming bias and of missing important variables that they regard as 'exogenous' to their model. In practice, this means that econometrists start by setting out the assumptions of their model and deciding which variables they will leave out. The neoliberal model seems to work well when the ideal conditions of their models are met; for example, competition may benefit the overall productivity within small free markets but not in countries where there is not a totally free market. To make their models work in situations outside their original scope of research, they either used mind manipulation to manipulate the ideas that people have about the situation (Chapter 11), or they use political–military force to transform the market conditions in their favour. For example, the United States intervened in Chile and Guatemala to impose an economy in which American companies could flourish, although the formal diplomatic language is 'humanitarian interventions' (Klein, 2007). Thus, neoliberal politicians help to create the socio-economic conditions in which neoliberal meanings can flourish.

Neoliberal Politics

The Chicago, Virginia, and London Schools inspired a wave of neoliberal governments in the 1980s, ranging from Reaganomics in the United States to economic rationalism in Australia and Rogernomics in New Zealand. However, politicians are not necessarily economists (Jones, 2012). Politicians present visions—imaginations and symbols—of the ideal economy and, subsequently, try to apply this in societal reality. In this realisation process, they have to deal with the complex reality of the civil service, party politics, voters' expectations, etc. This often means that they need to water their wine—or sometimes their best is to only put some drips of wine in the ocean. Therefore, the reality of political policies is often far from the economic visions developed in the safe haven of academic economics.

Can we call neoliberal politics 'neoliberal'? An often-used argument of neoliberal economists is that politicians such as Thatcher and Reagan were not 'really neoliberal', and thus the ideal of neoliberalism should not be dismissed on the basis of their political failures; instead, a more extreme version should be used to prove the truth of neoliberalism. Thus, the failure of Thatcherism and Reaganism is used for neoliberal extremism. This is a clear logical fallacy of self-serving bias: failures need to be attributed to others, success to yourself. The philosopher Popper would also shiver due to the failure of verificationism: This argument can always be used to dismiss any failures of your model. Whether neoliberal politics can be called 'neoliberal' or not, the many failures clearly show that at least one part of neoliberal imagination and symbols fails: the translation from theory into practice. The gap between theory and practice is not surprising; as neoliberal theory is more deductive than inductive in nature and thus is bound for error in its practical realisation.

Thatcherism
One of the most famous neoliberal politicians was British Prime Minister Margaret Thatcher. She has been said to have carried a copy of Hayek's *The Constitution of Liberty* in her handbag, which she described as the philosophy of her government (Jones, 2012). However, the reality is that her first government did not offer a clear break from Keynesian politics. Her politics only turned neoliberal after a slurry of white papers from her adviser and education minister, Sir Keith Joseph, and after lobbying by Hayek as well as other advisers from the early neoliberal school. This later political philosophy, branded Thatcherism, was summarised by Nigel Lawson, Thatcher's Chancellor of the Exchequer from 1983 to 1989, as 'free markets, financial discipline, firm control over public expenditure, tax cuts, nationalism, Victorian values of the Samuel Smiles' self-help variety, privatisation and a dash of populism' (Lawson, 1992, p.64). Thus, in line with the 'Chicago Boys' (Jones, 2012), Thatcher attempted to realise a free market, via deregulation and privatisation; lower taxes; create a flexible workforce, by reducing rights of labourers and labour unions; decrease government expenditure, by decreasing benefits and council housing; and assume tight control of the money supply particularly via inflation control, even at the cost of unemployment. In contrast with neoliberal academics, but in line with other neoliberal politicians, Thatcher developed a centralised and strong government role as well as an authoritarian approach as Prime Minister—for instance, by overruling government committees—which popularised her nickname as the 'Iron Lady' and which her Foreign Affairs Private Secretary, Sir Charles Powell, even compared with outright Leninism (Hennessy, 2001).

Reaganomics

Thatcher was a close ally of the American president, Ronald Reagan, and both had many economic advisers in common (Mirowski & Plehwe, 2015). The four pillars of Reagan's economic policy included reduced government expenditure, lower federal income tax and capital gains tax, cuts to government regulations, and tight money supply to reduce inflation. Reagan based this policy on the idea of bringing back free enterprise principles and a free-market economy as it existed before the depression of the 1930s and the New Deal (Jones, 2012).

Through lower tax rates and less regulation, Reagan had hoped to increase the incentive for enterprises to invest (in line with the so-called Laffer curve, a theory that was trending in his time). Additionally, the tax rate for the richest echelons decreased from 70.1% to 28.4%. Reagan justified this with his belief in what his opponents called the trickle-down effect (formally called 'supply-side economics'). This is the idea that the nation as a whole benefits from increasing the wealth of the wealthiest, as larger net income and savings will increase investments that could increase employment and the income of smaller companies and employees. Many systematic studies have rejected this hypothesis since it has been shown that only a small amount of the wealth at the top trickles down (Dabla-Norris, 2015; Tcherneva, 2015; Sowell, 2013). Because that wealth has subjective marginal meanings, an increase in wealth at the top has a smaller effect on investments than a similar increase in wealth for individuals with lower incomes. Prosperous individuals are less likely to invest their marginal wealth in actual products or services—there is a limit to the number of houses of yachts they can buy or staff they could pay—than in financial assets that are more likely to be used for risks such as investing in mortgages, which contributed to the burst of housing market bubble in 2007/2008. The trickle-down effect has been described as an ideological imagination that deviates from the ideas of classical economists such as Adam Smith (Herzog, 2016). At the heart of the failure of the myth is the diversity of meanings of the trickle-down effect.

The Reagan period led to historically unseen increases in the financial market, socio-economic inequality, and social mobility, which reduced the diversity of meanings that ordinary citizens focused on as financial and other monetary/ materialist meanings determined the market. Meanwhile, the GNP only rose by half a per cent compared to previous governments, unemployment temporarily peaked and returned at its best to the pre-Reagan era. Reaganomics meant slow growth of inflation but at the cost of government spending reaching a historic height, particularly due to Reagan's investments in the army and government–private business deals (e.g., Federal Reserve Bank of Saint Louis, 2018, 2018a; Hudson, 2015; Kocieniewski, 2012; Krugman, 2007; Mitchell, 1996). This seems to suggest that Reaganomics did not achieve the promised economic aims, although his supporters claim there were some significant technical effects such as reduced inflation growth, and that any failures were due to external factors such as Congress blocking and modifying his bills (D'Souza, 1997). This policy did not help ordinary citizens to live a self-determined meaningful life; it reduced their opportunities and created a materialist, hedonist, and self-oriented focus in societal narratives about the economy.

Military–Economic Interventions
At this moment of writing in 2019, there is a public outcry about the role of the United States, and other Western nations, in intervening in Venezuelan politics. Some critics argue that Americans are there to protect their economic interests, including the desire for privatisation of the oil and the pharmaceutical industries. The proponents of the American role are claiming that the Venezuelan president is responsible for a humanitarian crisis. However, a United Nations report (2019) indicates that the economic hardships of Venezuelan citizens have mainly been caused by the long-term economic sanctions by the United States. For ordinary citizens, it is difficult to conclude what is going on behind the screens of the media.

Several politicians have compared the situation with similar American interventions in other countries for financial profit. Naomi Klein (2007) has called this 'disaster capitalism'. Klein argues in her book *The Shock Doctrine* how neoliberal free-market policies, as promoted by 'The Chicago Boys' (Jones, 2012), have developed in several countries due to a deliberate strategy of economic shock therapy. This means that a national crisis is used to push through controversial policies while citizens are too emotionally and physically distracted by disasters or upheavals to mount an effective resistance. Klein attributes many international military and economic interventions since the 1970s to this shock doctrine—such as the wars in Iraq, Falklands, and Bolivia. Her strongest examples are about the use of the shock doctrine to transform South American economies in the 1970s, particularly the 1973 coup in Chile led by General Augusto Pinochet and directly supported by economists who were trained at the University of Chicago's School of Economics, were advised by Milton Friedman, and received funding from the CIA. After the fall of the Iron Curtain, 'The Chicago Boys' were involved in the creation of radical economic changes in Eastern Europe countries such as Poland and Russia. The financial crisis of 1997 was allegedly used to further neoliberal interests. Klein argues that this shock doctrine is structurally supported by neoliberal economic institutions such as the World Bank and the IMF.

One criticism that neoliberal authors express against Klein's *Shock Doctrine* is that she 'conflates free-market orthodoxy with predatory corporate behaviour' (Holmes, 2008). Similarly, Zingales (2012) argues that nowadays we mainly see 'business capitalism' that contradicts the initial ideology of capitalism, which may be described as a capitalism 'for the people'. We saw a similar argument by economists defending Reaganomics whose failure to achieve all its aims were attributed to Congress blocking Reagan's economic bills (D'Souza, 1997). They try to rescue the imagined and symbolic capitalism from its examples of failure in reality. Thus, they separate the Platonic Ideal from the mundane cave where we can only see shadows of the Goodness of the True Free Market. This seems to be deductive economics at its worst.

Several defenders of neoliberalism assume that the economic ideology and political practice of neoliberalism can be separated. This argument smells of self-serving bias and verification fallacy. Instead, empirical research indicates that neoliberal politics are in line with the economic ideas of a small neoliberal elite. A systematic review of nearly 1,800 US policies between 1981 and 2002 showed that federal and national policies reflect the interests of a small business oligarchy, particularly the richest 10%, many times more than the interests of the average Americans (Gilens & Page, 2014): 'The central point that emerges from our research is that economic elites and organized groups representing business interests have substantial independent impacts on US government policy, while mass-based interest groups and average citizens have little or no independent influence.' However, despite the fact that government policies rarely align with the preferences of most Americans, the political system seems skewed: 'When a majority of citizens disagrees with economic elites and/or with organized interests, they generally lose. Moreover, because of the strong status quo bias built into the US political system, even when fairly large majorities of Americans favour policy change, they generally do not get it.' It seems that an oligarchy has used the symbolic image of the free market and the rational citizen in their arguments to promote their own interests.

Furthermore, how is it ethically and psychologically possible to ignore the reality of pain and suffering of real people in the real economy when theorising from the armchair about the best romantic imagination of economy? This is like Karl Marx's appeal to focus on the lived experience of real people and not on theoretical economics. This is 'the fiction of a thinkable world', an idea which emerged in the 16th century with Descartes, and which is not supported by the experiences of people in non-Western countries, who see no strict distinction between thinking, feeling, and behaving (Steinberg, 2005). The neoliberal critics seem to separate form and content. The form regards the ideal functioning of the economy, and the content is about the meaning that the real economy has for real people. This is what meaning-oriented economics is about: acknowledging the meaning that the daily life economy has for individuals, how they shape the economy, and how they make sense of it.

Summary

This section described neoliberalism as promoted by economists from the Austrian and Chicago schools, which has inspired politicians such as Thatcher, Reagan, Bush, and Trump. They focus strongly on materialist, hedonist, and self-oriented types of meanings from a functionalist perspective. Individuals are expected to govern their own lives, in line with Thatcherian self-help, and only they are to blame when they fail, even if they do not succeed due to their socio-economic circumstances or unexpected life events. As Chapter 11 will show, neoliberalism seems to lead to a sense of fatalism, existential concerns, and psychological stress in many individuals.

Conclusions

Let us zoom out. This chapter showed how (neo)liberalism emerged in response to socio-economic transformations at the end of the Middle Ages. The next chapter will show how, not much later, Marxism emerged. Traditional interpretations of liberalism and Marxism have a strong focus on functionalism and materialism in common. A large difference is the importance of self-oriented types of meaning in neoliberalism. The neoliberal focus towards the self also implies the emergence of political technics, mind manipulation, and military interventions to share or impose neoliberal ideas, as will be further explained in Part II. Whereas moral liberals such as Adam Smith focused on the freedom of individuals to determine their own lives, neoliberals shifted the focus towards the freedom of the market, even if this would come at the cost of individual freedom. This seems to have created the paradox of the Capitalist Life Syndrome: On the one hand individuals are told they are free but, on the other hand, many implicit and explicit demands are imposed on them. This seems to lead to existential and psychological crises. Consequently, the Capitalist Life Syndrome gradually evolved over the last centuries, as Part II will prove in detail.

Key Points

1. Since the end of the Middle Ages, many transitions have occurred in materialist and social relationships, which have led to the emergence of the functionalist–materialist philosophies of (neo)liberalism and (neo)Marxism.
2. The popularity of positivism and Marxism led to a sense of crisis in liberalism at the start of the 20th century. Neoliberal economists revived the ideal of liberalism with a strong functionalist perspective, where the freedom of the market becomes more important than the freedom of the individual.
3. The deductive method underlying neoliberalism leads to a self-serving bias and structural ignoring of other meaningful 'exogenous' topics. To impose neoliberal ideas on non-fitting socio-economic realities, mind manipulation and political–military interventions have attempted to change either the perceptions or the political–economic system.

Table 5.1. Overview of Ten Questions and Perspectives on Liberal and Neoliberal Economies

Name of question	Formal name of perspective	Rational liberalism	Moral liberalism	Early Neoliberalism	Early Austrian School & Marginalists	Late Austrian School & Chicago School	Neoliberal politics
Status?	Ontological status	Reality Symbol Imagination	Reality Symbol Imagination	Reality Symbol Imagination	Symbol Imagination	Symbol Imagination	Reality
What?	Type of meaning	Materialistic Hedonistic	Materialistic Hedonistic Social Larger	Materialistic Hedonistic Self-oriented	Materialistic Hedonistic Self-oriented	Materialistic Hedonistic Self-oriented	Materialistic Self-oriented
How?	Approach to meaning	Functionalistic	Critical–intuitive	Functionalistic	Functionalistic	Functionalistic	Functionalistic
Where?	Relationship between individual and society	Individual determinism	Social determinism	Individual determinism	interactionism	Individual determinism	Individual determinism
When?	Development over time	Historiography	Historiography	Historiography	Historiography	Historiography	Historiography
Who?	Emergence of individual meaning	Psychology	Ethics	Psychology	Psychology	Psychology	Psychology
Whose?	Sense of freedom	-Symbolic and imagined freedom -Negative freedom -Individual freedom	Symbolic and imagined freedom -Negative and positive freedom -Individual and structural freedom	Negative freedom -Imagined structural freedom vs. real individual lack of freedom (fatalism)	Symbolic and imagined freedom Negative and positive freedom Individual and structural freedom	Symbolic and imagined freedom Negative freedom Imagined structural freedom vs. real individual lack of freedom (fatalism)	Symbolic and imagined freedom Negative freedom Imagined structural freedom vs. real individual lack of freedom (fatalism)
Why?	Existential well-being	Existential questions and concerns	Realistic sense of freedom and limitations	Existential questions and concerns	Existential questions and concerns	Existential questions and concerns	Existential questions and concerns
Which?	Impact on daily life	Many mental health problems, low quality of life, and low life satisfaction	Few mental health problems, large quality of life, and large life satisfaction	Many mental health problems, low quality of life, and low life satisfaction	Many mental health problems, low quality of life, and low life satisfaction	Many mental health problems, low quality of life, and low life satisfaction	Many mental health problems, low quality of life, and low life satisfaction

Chapter 6

A History of Meaning in Functionalist–Materialist Marxism

> The only intelligible language in which we converse with one another consists of our objects in their relation to each other. We would not understand a human language and it would remain without effect. By one side it would be recognised and felt as being a request, an entreaty, and therefore a *humiliation. (*Marx, 1844/1975, p. 102)

Marxist Functionalist Materialism

Three decades after Adam Smith's death, Karl Marx was born. He wrote his first texts at the beginning of the 19th century, an era of many socio-economic transformations and an increasing loss of the collectivist culture during the Industrial Revolution. Although Marx has become renowned for his pleas for morality and unification of workers over the world, in his early works he criticised one aspect of the collectivist culture: the divine–cosmic–social order from the Middle Ages. For example, he criticised the role of religion that had determined how individuals should live their lives. Thus, like liberal philosophers, Marx was fighting for the freedom of individuals to live their lives in ways that are meaningful to themselves instead of being told by a church or king how to live their lives. However, in his early works, Marx noted that the divine–cosmic–social order was gradually being replaced by a new social hierarchy since the end of the Middle Ages, justified by rational economists and promoted by governments. The idea of *laissez-faire* had given freedom to the bourgeoisie to develop monopolies and exploit the class of people with fewer socio-economic resources as cheap labour and as consumers emptying their wallets for the profits of entrepreneurs. In this new order, it was not nobility, clergy, and religious beings such as God at the top but the emergence of the bourgeoisie. During the Middle Ages, the bourgeois was usually a self-employed businessman such as a baker, merchant, or entrepreneur. The fall of feudalism combined with the industrial revolution transformed this position into an economic ruling class that owned the means of production (capital and land), and controlled the means of coercion (armed forces and legal system, police force, and prison system).

On a superficial reading, Utilitarians and Marxists seem to have the same aim of striving for the well-being of the masses, but their methods fundamentally differ due to a different idea about human nature. Rational economists focused on individuals, and they imagined that the nature of interactions between individuals could be trusted in such a way that, with minimum government intervention, when individuals follow their own interest they will contribute to the overall well-being of society. Society is the sum of individuals. However, Marx rejected the Bentham–Mill idea of society as the sum of individual utilities. He wrote that 'society does not consist of individuals, but expresses the sum of interrelations, the relations within which these individuals stand' (Marx, 1939/2005, p. 265). The rational economists seem to view the functionalist combination of individuals as an inorganic mechanism, like the combination of individual grains of sand making up a sand beach without interaction, whereas Marx sketched relationships as non-functionalist dynamic relationships between complex beings, like the relationships between cells or organs in a body. Individuals may perceive themselves as independent beings, but in economic reality they participate in a complex dynamic society, like in collectivist economies. Thus, according to Marx, rational economists seem to have thrown away the baby—social relationships and a sense of community—with the bathwater when they criticised the divine–cosmic–social order and created a functionalist individualist ideology. Marx seems to want to bring back some aspects of social/collectivist economies but without divine–cosmic–social hierarchies.

The return to the social dimension in economics should be interpreted in the light of the wider fight of Marx against the theoretical nature of philosophers of his time. In his early work, Marx criticised the speculative nature of philosophies, equating metaphysics with ideology. For example, he had a love–hate relationship with the philosopher Hegel, who had described how an abstract Spirit influenced the development of society (Hook, 1994; Fraser, 1998). Marx complained that such texts were too theoretical and, instead, pleaded for taking the daily life and needs of ordinary people as a starting point. For example, the symbol of the invisible hand was far away from the daily reality of ordinary factory workers. Individuals such as Mill were moral philosophers who were interested in the Platonic idea of how society *should* function, but they seemed less interested in searching for systematic empirical evidence for their ideas. The theory that society may benefit from individuals following their self-interest may sound great, but what does this mean to the child labourer who works more than ten hours a day in a factory for a minimum salary? Should we ignore their pain and focus on the abstract Platonic idea of pleasure and pain? Their phenomenological life-world demands to be done justice. The symbol and imagination of the free market may sound nice on paper to some but, in reality, this means that manufacturers have free rein to do whatever they want and oppress the meaning of individuals and thus hinder the wealth of the nation.

For example, Marx described how human nature should be seen as species because we do not merely live as independent individuals but belong to a social species ('*gattungswesen*'), as evolutionary biologists have shown. A human is a 'natural, corporeal, sensuous objective being who is a suffering, conditioned and limited creature, like animals and plants' (Marx, 1939/2005). In contrast with animals and plants, humans are also conditioned by their social relations, which are intertwined with materialist conditions, as will be explained below (Marx's idea that animals are not socially conditioned is in contrast to the 21st century discovery of animal morality, as we saw in Chapter 4).

However, humans are also more than animal plus socialisation: '[man] is (...) endowed with natural powers, vital powers—he is an active natural being. These forces exist in him as tendencies and abilities—as instincts' (Marx, 1939/2005, p.67). Humans distinguish themselves from animals as soon as they begin to produce their means of subsistence. A real human being is a combination of the actuality of social–material conditions and potentiality, which Marx called 'the rich human being'. Human progress means that people have started to recognise their dual nature of possessing both actual and potential selves. When individuals starts to realise the restrictions in their social-material conditions, they may render their potential as a subjective creative agent in moulding nature in ways that they desire, according to their physical need or following their sense of beauty (Marx, 1867/1990). Most important, though, human production is *purposive* and *planned*, as they make plans for their future activity and attempt to exercise their production and lifestyle according to them.

Thus, humans have a large potential of designing and living their lives in such a way that they can realise what they experience as meaningful. However, Marx describes how this potential of meanings can be reduced to a functionalist selection of materialist meanings by the capitalist system. Individuals can become estranged from aspects of their species-being, as a consequence of the socio-economic constellation of the capitalist modes of production and of the society being socially stratified in social classes. That is, material and social conditions treat us as a materialist function, and we may also start perceiving ourselves merely in materialist and functionalist terms and feel limited by our socio-economic situation (Wendling, 2009; Mészáros, 2006).

Marx describes multiple forms of alienation. Individuals may alienate from the product they are making. Whereas the individual baker would decide which bread to make, in modern economic relations this is decided by the management in distant headquarters. The engineer and the industrial designer create products to shape the taste of consumers to sell for maximum profit. The worker is alienated from the production process. Whereas in the past, the craftsman was involved directly or indirectly in all parts of the production of a product, in modern work, individuals only create one part of the work process (Sennett, 2008). In factories, this often means an endless sequence of discrete, repetitive motions that offer the worker little psychological satisfaction. Individual workers have little to say over the content of work, and they are reduced to a cog in the production process that can be replaced by another worker or technological innovation. Workers alienate from co-workers as their role can be exchanged for that of any other worker, and they have to compete with each other for work.

Thus, the capitalist system renders each individual a mechanical part of an industrialized system of production, rather than a person capable of defining their own meaning through direct, purposeful activity. The worker loses the ability to determine life when deprived of the right to conceive of themselves as the director of their own actions. Individuals lose the freedom of their will to impose internal demands they have made on themselves by their imagination because of the external demands and symbolic actions from more powerful individuals in the capitalist system. The near-total mechanization allows the capital-owners the possibility to exploit the working class almost to the degree that the meaning obtained from their labour diminishes the ability of the worker to materially survive. This is commodity fetishism: The large potential of subjective meanings is reduced to a small range of materialist meanings (Marx & Engels, 1965).

The texts on alienation reveal Marx's idea that there is a close interaction between the materialist and social domains of our life or, in Marxist terms, there is a union of society's means of production (such as tools, machines, land, raw materials) and the social relations of production (such as the social stratification of the working class and the bourgeoisie who own the means of production). These interwoven materialist–social conditions determine all aspects of society that do not directly have to do with the means of production, such as art, family, culture, religion, philosophy, law, and politics. Marx calls the first 'the base' and the latter 'the superstructure'. The base shapes and maintains the superstructure, but the superstructure also shapes and maintains the base (Marx & Engels, 1965), which leads to statements such as: 'The ruling ideas are nothing more than the ideal expression of the dominant material relations, the dominant material relations grasped as ideas' (Marx & Engels, 1846/2011, p. 59). This theory has come to be known as 'historical materialism', which looks for the causes of developments and changes in society in the means by which humans collectively produce the necessities of life. Humans are thrown into the world with pre-determined materialist and relational conditions, and first and foremost they participate in this life-world.

In Marxist formulations, individuals are never on their own: They stand in a web of interrelations and of materialistic circumstances. The collective is often formulated in functionalist and materialist terms, such as: 'the organisation of communism is essentially economic, the material production of the conditions of (...) the free association of individuals' (Marx & Engels, 1846/2011, p.70). Thus, Marx and Engels base their work on the bold ontological assumption that 'in direct contrast with

German philosophy which descends from heaven to earth, here we ascend from earth to heaven'.

What does this practically mean for workers? They will not be able to use their potential to live a free life according to self-determined meanings as long as they are locked in the class struggle. To be able to freely determine their own meanings in life, they first need to free themselves from the materialistic circumstances that enslave them. More specifically, the workers need to overthrow the class system and by this liberate themselves from the constraints in their life. Thus, crudely speaking, the class struggle comes prior to a meaningful life, as in a capitalist society individuals only function as part of the means of production—and its associated production relations—and, therefore, cannot fulfill their full individual potential (Irwin, 2015; Hemming, 2013; Stahl, 2010; Axelos, 2009; Marcuse, 2005; Sartre, 1974).

Martin Buber (1949) sharply characterises the tendency in Marxist formulations to reduce individuals and historical movements to materialist functions:

> Of the three modes of thinking in public matters—the economic, the social and the political—Marx exercised the first with methodical mastery, devoted himself with passion to the third, but—absurd as it may sound in the ears of the unqualified Marxist—only very seldom did he come into more intimate contact with the second, and it never became a deciding factor for him. (p. 76)

Marxist Phenomenology

Although Marx and Engels used functionalistic and materialistic terms to describe capitalism and the workers' revolution, they also fought the functionalistic and materialistic trend in capitalism. They may not have elaborated 'the social' in detail, as Buber argued, their aim was a social utopia. They could even be seen as phenomenologists *avant la lettre,* who wanted to do justice to the meaning potential of individuals (Hemming, 2013; Eldred, 2005; Marcuse, 2005), like the neo-Marxist Antonio Gramsci (1994) argued:

> The claim (presented as an essential postulate of historical materialism) that every fluctuation of politics and ideology can be presented and expounded as an immediate expression of the structure, must be contested in theory as primitive infantilism, and combated in practice with the authentic testimony of Marx, the author of concrete political and historical works.

What did Marx and his companion Engels 'authentically' write? The following paragraphs will show how they seemed to envisage how we live currently in a materialistic–functionalistic system, which will one day be replaced by a meaning-oriented society.

As previously described, Marx and Engels believed that individuals are not completely determined by their circumstances. Individuals are more than functions of nature or social Darwinist processes: their potential reaches beyond their actual situation. Individuals can feel a tension between their actuality and their potentiality and become conscious of their alienation, like labourers can become aware of the limitations of their position in the workplace. This increasing awareness can stimulate individuals to demand a transformation of their circumstances—the creation of a situation in which they can fulfill their potential. Or better formulated: they have the potential to demand a situation in which they can use their potential to a larger extent than in their current situation, albeit no human being will never be able to completely transcend all their materialistic circumstances.

Thus, Marx and Engels define human beings as self-mediated beings who are both the result and the transformers of their own circumstances, although their transformative process starts with their circumstances, which may never be completely overcome (Marx & Engels, 1965). Whereas capitalism tries to reduce individuals to functionalistic utilities and cogs in the big economic machine, Marx and Engels wanted to transcend this functionalistic determinism and return to 'the human world and man himself' (Marx, 1975). As Marx writes in his *Third Thesis on Feuerbach*, 'The materialist doctrine concerning the changing of circumstances and upbringing forgets that circumstances are changed by men and that it is essential to educate the educator himself.'

In Marx's post-capitalist society, the human potential of labour and of man-made products also changes. That is, Marx described how capitalism had made a distinction between the use-value and exchange-value of man-made products. For example, a hammer is not merely a material object (M) that can be used for hammering (H), but under capitalism it also has an extra value when it is Exchanged (E), for example, for money in a store (M+H$\rightarrow$M+H+E). In the case of the financial market, the hammer does not need to be used at all and can become a mere object of exchange because only the stocks and options matter (M+H$\rightarrow$E). Similarly, in the eyes of the capital-owners, labourers are not merely the makers of hammers (M) but also the creators of products that can be exchanged (E) for financial profit (M$\rightarrow$E). Simultaneously, in their own eyes, workers became wage-slaves (W), feeling alienated from the production process and their products (M+H$\rightarrow$W): 'In the wage of labour, the labourer does not appear as an end in itself but as the servant of the wage'. Thus, capitalism has robbed workers and the products of their work of their concrete meanings and replaced them with abstract meanings. Work has become a means to an end; as Genesis says, 'in the sweat of thy brow shalt thou eat bread till thou return unto the ground'.

In Marx's post-capitalist utopia, people may still need to work for their subsistence, but they do not need to spend more time than that, as individuals will work 'from each according to his ability, to each according to his needs'. In other words, the revolution aims to liberate the meaning potential of individuals by removing the material obstacles to fulfilling their meanings; the life of each individual will be their own creation (Kolakowski, 2005). The work of labourers will be *their* work and no longer the object of profit-making for their bosses. Work will not be merely about getting a wage anymore, as there will be no wages. Therefore, according to Marx, the slogan for the workers' movement should not be 'a fair day's pay for a fair day's work' but 'abolish the wage system'. In utopia, labour is no longer *abstract labour*—working to get a bigger number in the bank account and creating a profit for shareholders—but *concrete labour*. Workers are no longer indifferent to the content of our work, but work becomes meaningful in itself: 'I would now enjoy my activity as well as its products, since the products would express the specific character of my individuality.'

Marx (1844/2014b) writes that our work would not only help us to fulfill a narrow number of materialistic or hedonistic desires, but it would enable us to 'develop a totality of desires'. Here, Marx seems to suggest that we would not only follow our materialistic or hedonistic types of meaning, but also personal, social, and larger types of meaning. Thus, our work becomes oriented towards fulfilling our meaning potential in life: 'my work would be a free manifestation of life, as would yours' (Marx, 1844/1975). We will do justice to the meaning potential of ourselves and of our fellow citizens instead of being stuck in one identity or social role that the capitalistic division of labour has put us in: 'In communist society, where nobody has one exclusive sphere of activity but each can become accomplished in any branch he wishes, society regulates the general production and thus makes it possible for me to do one thing in the morning, fish in the afternoon, rear cattle in the evening, criticize after dinner, just as I have a mind, without ever becoming a hunter, fisherman, shepherd or critic' (Marx & Engels, 1846/2011, p. 47).

Thus, Marx the philosopher seemed to despise materialism as the sole meaning in life (Hudis, 2012; Megill, 2001; Kline, 1988). He also seemed despise materialist interests as a private person when he wrote: 'In the year 1842–43, as editor of the *Rheinische Zeitung*, I first found myself in the embarrassing position of having to discuss what is known as material interests' (Marx, 1844/1975, p. 20). In Marx's post-capitalist utopia, all objects, animals, and nature will no longer appear to us as a capitalist–materialist function; they do not have the mere function of standing ready to be used for profit-making, but their full potential pre-capitalist meanings are respected (Heidegger, 1954/1977). There would still be exchanges between people, but these exchanges would be for their own sake: 'love only for love, trust for trust, etc.'; these will all be 'expressions of real life' (Marx, 1844/2014a*)*.

Some interpreters have also argued that in a Marxist utopia, animals, and nature would also no longer be reduced to capitalist functions but have meaning in themselves. For example, I would no longer see the mountain there in front of me as a mining opportunity that I can own, but as nature with inherent value and potential for everyone—such as enjoying my hikes with others and sharing the space on the mountain with grazing sheep. Thus, our relationships with other people, animals, nature, and objects change as we approach them as 'manifestations of life' with their full meaning potential, and not merely as economic abstractions. Consequently, this post-capitalist society would be materialistically self-sufficient: People would produce and consume what is meaningful for them, and not what their bosses or marketing tell them to produce, exchange, and consume (Hudis, 2012).

Playing devil's advocate, one could argue that although Marx wanted to build a society beyond functionalism and materialism, most of his work was about capitalism. Thus, in most texts he had to use functionalist and materialist formulations to describe this functionalist–materialist situation. He also did not elaborate in much detail how he envisioned the post-materialist and post-functionalist utopia, as he did not want to impose his ideas on the future of people but wanted utopia to emerge from the needs and skills of people themselves (Hudis, 2012). Furthermore, on first reading, Marx's description of how the revolution towards the post-capitalist society should happen seemed to focus on functionalist and materialist processes: 'The weapon of criticism cannot, of course, replace criticism of the weapon; material force must be overthrown by material force'. One may argue that in Marx's eyes, the revolution towards a post-materialist/post-functionalist society is materialist/functionalist itself by uniting 'workers of the world' to take over the means of mass production from individual capital-owners.

However, for Marx the revolution does not merely start with the materialistic deprivation of the working class but with their awareness of this situation. For example, it is not the fact that someone belongs to a class per se that makes them a revolutionary but the meaning that this sense of belonging has for them: 'The separate individuals form a class *only* insofar as they have to carry on a common battle against another class; in other respects, they are on hostile terms with each other as competitors' (Marx & Engels, 1846/2011, p. 77; my italics). To show this distinction, Marx differentiates the concept of 'the working class *in itself*', which means that the working class is organised to sell its labour within the materialist and functionalist structure of capitalist society, and 'the working class *in and for itself*', which means that people are conscious of the social and larger meanings of the class and are organised to struggle against the injustice in society. The dire materialist and social circumstances of the class in itself do not inevitably lead to class consciousness; classes are a political category, not merely economic.

> Insofar as millions of families live under economic conditions of existence that separate their mode of life, their interests and their cultural formation from those of other classes, they form a class. Insofar as these small peasant properties are merely connected on a local basis, and the identity of their interests fails to produce a feeling of community, national links, or a political organisation, they do not form a class. (Marx, 1974, p. 239)

Marx calls his alternative to capitalism a 'positive humanism, beginning from itself'. It is actively self-determined, and does not depend on others to tell what is meaningful for them. He also writes that his idea of utopia is not merely a negative picture of capitalism, like 'vulgar communism', where, for example, money and industry ownership change hands from the capitalist elite to the workers as this would only create 'a sham universality' and 'wanting capitalism without capitalists'. There is no real liberation as long as workers still have to work for a wage and use their income to buy and own products that they do not really need. Marx suggests in his notes on Hegel's *Phenomenology of the Spirit* (1975) that the alternative society is also not a negation of the negation of capitalism; it is a new 'positive' beginning that posits its own meanings. Thus, the starting point of the post-capitalistic society is 'a totality of human manifestations of life'–man's full potential of meanings.

Revolution, therefore, requires *all* types of meaning as it starts with an amalgam of materialist, personal, social, and larger types of meaning. For example, taking over the means of mass production is only done for the sake of social and larger purposes, not for self-enrichment. Revolution is also only temporary, after capitalism and before positive humanism can be achieved; thus, insofar as revolution is functionalist and materialist, this is only a temporary necessity before a post-functionalist/post-materialist society is reached. Here, Marx's ideas come remarkably close to Adam Smith' pluralism of meanings. However, these descriptions can only be understood when we interpret their work as post-functionalist and post-materialist, and do not let ourselves be brainwashed into reading their work as functionalist and materialist.

Communist Life Syndrome

The consequence of the ambiguity about functionalism and materialism in Marx's works is that many people have interpreted and applied him in functionalist and materialist ways (Irwin, 2015; Hemming, 2013; Stahl, 2010; Axelos, 2009; Marcuse, 2005; Sartre, 1974). The clearest example is the communist state, as described and realised by Stalin and Mao.

Communism has traditionally been sketched as an alternative to neoliberalism. However, it may not be as 'alternative' as one may suspect. Due to a history of propaganda and McCarthyism, the differences between communism and capitalism may have been exaggerated while their overlap may have been minimised (Lippmann, 2018). Communism is often used as a strawman or slippery-slope argument, despite its similarities with neoliberalism.

Both sides of the ocean, both communism and capitalism, use strong rhetoric and symbols, have a functionalist focus on materialism, use words of historical progress in their propaganda, expect obedience, and apply intricate mind- manipulation systems. Although the mind manipulation seemed to be more explicitly organised by the communist state than under capitalism, with explicit control mechanisms. Individuals lived with the fear that any of their friends could be Stasi and betray them. Consequently, in the USSR, citizens felt unfree and fatalistic, sometimes leading to large existential and mental health problems. This combination may be called The Communist Life Syndrome. (This section is based on O'Connor, 2016; Dimitrov, 2013; Klicperova, Feierabend & Hofstetter, 1998; Sloutsky & Searle-White, 1993; Farland & Agayev, 1992).

The Communist Life Syndrome seems far away from the early ideology of the Russian Revolution (Faulkner, 2017), which started with a call from workers to take democratic control and ownership of their factory and from landless peasants to own a piece of land.

> The Russian Revolution was an explosion of democracy and activity from below. It transformed the millions of people who took part in it and inspired tens of millions who watched. It offered a tantalising glimpse of a radically different world—a world without bosses and police, a world of democracy, equality and peace. But sadly, only a glimpse. The revolutionaries were not strong enough to win from the forces defending the system—the millionaires, the statesmen, the generals, the churches, the tabloid press, the fascist squads, the fake socialists in red ties, the sell-out union bureaucrats—these forces, across most of Europe, proved too powerful. (Faulkner, 2017, p. 1)

The Bolshevik Party started as a mass democratic movement, which was later taken over and destroyed by Stalinism. It was never the aim of the original rebels to put a dictator in place. The opposite is true; they wanted democratic self-determination and equality, but Moscow sent their representatives to the work floor so that workers would not vote against the government interests.

Why did the Iron Curtain fall in 1989? Historians often explain the emergence of *glasnost*, openness and transparency, and *perestroika*, reform of the communist party, as an economic necessity (Faulkner, 2017). They describe the economy as stagnant and traditional, based on artificial full employment, even when this meant production for the sake of giving workers a job instead of the demand from consumers, exemplified by periods of over-production. The economic stagnation meant that the dominant meaning of materialism remained unfulfilled. At the same time, other types of meaning were structurally undermined, as self-development and communities were mistrusted along with as religion and creative self-expression. Of course, there were underground churches and people found meaning in daily life experiences and family relationships, but this was often entangled with mistrust and fear. Ultimately, the only meaning that really mattered was the role people played for the state, being well-behaving cogs in the functionalist machinery of five-year plans and Stasi-control. This political oppression seems to have led to frustration about their unfulfilled meaning in life, low life satisfaction, and poor well-being. Thus, the USSR seemed to suffer both from a crisis in the economy as well as a wide-scale crisis of meaning in life.

Fast forward to the 21st century: Many individuals in former communist countries still focus on materialist meanings, albeit more in terms of career and possessions. Surprisingly, religion plays an important role for many. Research also shows that many people feel frustrated with the slow economic progress and with the complexity of democracy, which evokes a nostalgia for the communist era. For example, in 1999 only Poland, of all former communist countries, had a better GNP than in 1989; in Russia, a small oligarchy had created monopolies after they bought former state enterprises at a value of less than 10% of the real value (Kagarlitsky, 2002). People in the former East bloc are also supportive of authoritarian governments, possibly as the inter-generational legacy of communist authoritarianism, as exemplified by widespread negative attitudes about minorities and an idealisation of strong leaders and punishment (European Commission, 2014).

China's development is different from that of the USSR, even though both were communist in name. Additionally, China is also an immense country with large internal differences between provinces (Chow, 2015; White, 1988). The Communist Life Syndrome is also supported by traditional Chinese ideas, such as fatalistic cyclical ideas of time and space. Chinese cultural values also seem to focus much on harmony and balance, such as the old spiritual texts about *Yi Jing*, which sketch the universe as the opposites between chaos and stability and which cannot be translated as the Judaeo-Christian battle between good and evil. This implies that conformity and preventing loss of face are important. The family and loyalties are more important than self-expression, which can give a sense of belonging and altruism.

The Confucian conflict between status projection and self-protection leads to continuous conflict between personal ambition and the rigid regimentation by the government and top-down organised corporations. Additionally, 'capitalist' consumerism and individual rights have seen a gradual increase with the market reforms set in motion by the Communist Party under Deng Xiaoping in 1978. This led to some autonomy of state enterprises and private companies. However, many sinologists interpret these changes as experiments or slight adjustments and not as a full reform of the economic system. As China has at the same time perfected its mind manipulation, for example with 're-education' camps for religious people, which criticasters have branded concentration camps for organ harvesting. The lack of political freedom limits the opportunities for individuals to determine and express their own meaning in life. Thus, whereas the meaning crisis contributed to the fall of the USSR, China seems to respond to the crisis in meaning by offering some freedom in economic areas while increasing their mind manipulation and functionalisation of the state.

Conclusions

This chapter has shown that Marx was not merely the functionalist materialist that he is often seen as. This traditional interpretation may have been the result of state propaganda by people such as Lenin, Stalin, and Mao, who reinterpreted Marx for their own functionalist–materialist goals. However, their Communist Life Syndrome seems to be precisely what Marx would have called 'a sham universality' and 'capitalism without capitalists'. They reinforced the functionalisation and materialisation of society, whereas Marx aimed for a post-functionalist/post-materialist utopia, which seems closer to Adam Smith than these communist state ideologies. Historic materialism described the historic stages only until the revolution; the post-capitalistic situation is neither materialistic nor functionalistic.

Some Marxists seemed to describe the revolution towards the non-materialist/non-functionalist utopia with materialist and functionalist means. However, Chapter 11 will elaborate why these materialist and functionalist revolutions failed, according to some neo-Marxists: If people want to achieve a post-capitalist society, they need a post-functionalist/post-materialist revolution. If we want to fight functionalistic materialism, we should not use functionalist and materialist tools. Subsequently, Part III will describe empirical research on social movements and revolutions, which indicate that we are now living in an era of revolutions via post-materialist/post-functionalist means, and that we are slowly moving towards the meaning-oriented utopia that both Adam Smith and Karl Marx seemed to imagine.

Key Points

1. This chapter has shown two different interpretations of Marx, from a functionalist–materialist and a phenomenological perspective.
2. Although Marx seemed to idealise a phenomenological approach and pluralistic meanings for the communist utopia, he used functionalist and materialist terms to describe both the current situation of capitalism and the revolution away from capitalism.
3. The Communist Life Syndrome is based on a functionalist and materialist interpretation of Karl Marx, which has many characteristics in common with the Capitalist Life Syndrome. Karl Marx's phenomenology is closer to Adam Smith's philosophy than are many social movements and revolutions conducted in Marx's name. The difference between Marx and Smith is fueled by state propaganda from both capitalist and communist countries.

Table 6.1. Overview of Ten Questions and Perspectives on Marxist Economics

Name of question	Formal name of perspective	Functionalist–materialist Marxism	Phenomenological Marxism	Communism
Status?	Ontological status	Reality Symbol Imagination	Reality Symbol Imagination	Reality Symbol Imagination
What?	Type of meaning	Materialistic Hedonistic Social Larger	Materialistic Hedonistic Social Larger	Materialistic Social (enforced social meaning)
How?	Approach to meaning	Traditional Functionalistic	Phenomenology	Functionalistic
Where?	Relationship between individual and society	Interactionism	Interactionism	Social and individual determinism
When?	Development over time	Historiology	Historiology	Historicism
Who?	Emergence of individual meaning	Sociology	Sociology	Individual & mass psychology Meaning manipulation ('mind mafia')
Whose?	Sense of freedom	Symbolic, imagined and realised freedom; Negative freedom; Structural freedom	Symbolic, imagined and realised freedom Positive freedom Individual and structural freedom	-Negative freedom -Inequality in the ability to use freedom -Individual fatalism, helplessness and hopelessness
Why?	Existential well-being	Existential questions and concerns	No existential questions and concerns	Existential questions and concerns
Which?	Impact on daily life	Many mental health problems, low quality of life, and low life satisfaction	Few mental health problems, high quality of life, and high life satisfaction	Mental health problems, low quality of life, low life satisfaction

Chapter 7

A History of Meaning
in Post-Materialist Economies

Without work, all life goes rotten, but when work is soulless, life stifles and dies. (Camus, 1951/2012)

The Post-Industrial Economy

I met Robert in his office on the 35th floor after his secretary had brought me in. Behind him, I could see the skyline of London and beyond. While I was still adjusting to this overwhelming view, Robert loosened his tie, sighed, and started a passionate monologue. 'I own everything I ever wanted to buy. I have the career that everyone is jealous of. After our session, I will go home to my wife and two kids: the perfect picture. But something is missing. Is this it? Is this what life is about? I am living the life that I have always wanted, but is this what I really want? Or is this merely how I have been told I should live?' Robert had a desperate look in his eyes, seemingly clasping me to provide a quick solution.

This would become the first of several sessions in his office. Robert told me that he had tried many therapists and what he called 'hipster retreats in exotic resorts', which could 'only give some nice experiences but no structural change in life'. He had tried to find new 'hobbies and buddies', and 'although they looked cool there was still something missing'. Robert concluded: 'I feel so frustrated as for the first time in my life, I am not able to get what I want; I cannot buy real happiness.' The cause of his mental health problems did not lie in bad psychological habits or horrible life situations, but in his expectations of life, which had triggered this existential crisis.

Robert is one of many clients whose primary problems lie in being estranged from what they personally intuit as meaningful. Robert had grown up in a privileged family with the expectation that he would become rich and successful, and greed was taught as a vice. However, he had not learned to listen to what he finds meaningful for himself beyond the perfect picture that others had cast for him. In our era of intrusive social media and continuous commercials, it seems that we are surrounded by many voices but little silence in which to listen to ourselves. I helped Robert to make time for himself, and to differentiate between what he finds meaningful and what others tell him he should find meaningful. Robert was privileged enough to be able to free time in his diary to follow his heart, which meant spending more time with his family and doing charity work.

Neoliberalism is quickly fading in popularity both among the general population and economists (Ostry, Loungani & Furcery, 2016; Bowman & Rugg, 2010, 2010a; Elliott & Atkinson, 2008). Robert's case gives one example of why. His economics degree and his successful career had put him on a functionalist path of unsatisfiable materialist, hedonist, and self-oriented goals. However, he realised that these goals were not giving deep happiness and that a functionalist approach did not help him to control this. Robert's solution was to search for meaning beyond his capitalist life. This chapter will describe several post-capitalist economies: irrational, experience, moral, and meaning-oriented economies. Although these economies differ on many points, they have in common that they do not longer believe in functionalist materialism.

The Irrational Economy

Sir, Paul Krugman has compared our GDP figures to 'leprechaun economics'. How ludicrous. Get with your times, Prof Krugman. Nobody believes in economics anymore. (O'Riorda, Letter in the *Irish Times*, 18 July 2016).

At the end of the 20th century, the rational *Homo calculus*, on which many capitalist ideas are based, tumbled from its pedestal. That is, countless research studies have shown that individuals are irrational and uncertain, trying to find meaning in complex socio-economic processes. Let me summarise the key research findings.

Irrationality

Citizens, consumers, and entrepreneurs often act irrational, as countless studies in the exponentially growing field of economic psychology show (Akerlof & Shiller, 2010; Lewis, 2008; Webley et al., 2002). Theories about rational agents and utilities make assumptions about economic rationality that do not reflect people's actual choices and do not consider cognitive biases (Kahneman & Tversky, 2013). For example, based on decades of research, often together with his colleague Amos Tversky, Daniel Kahneman (2011) writes how the idea of the rational agent is only one of two modes of thinking: System 1 is fast, automatic, emotional, stereotypic, and unconscious; System 2 is slow, effortful, infrequent, logical, calculating, and conscious. Many economists have focused their models on the assumption that System 2 dominates our actions, and politicians like Thatcher promoted this rational type of the calculating 'self-help citizen'. However, often System 1 dominates our economic actions in daily life, even though we may try to act rationally. Instead of taking the time to use a rational approach and look at the situation with a critical eye, we use heuristics to make fast decisions; that is, we associate new information with existing patterns (Tversky & Kahneman, 1974). Kahneman and Tversky have shown this with countless examples of cognitive biases, such as people making decisions to prevent potential future loss.

Uncertainty

Often, individuals see in hindsight what would have been the best option, but they cannot accurately predict what will be the best option in the future. The reason is that in many situations people have too much information and need to regard many options and external influences while some information may still be undisclosed or may look unimportant at first glance even though it is actually crucial. In such overwhelming, uncertain, and time-limited contexts, individuals use heuristics (Taleb, 2015). We can learn to use our logical thinking more often, but we will never be able to get completely rid of our biases. The best we can do is become 'antifragile' (the opposite of fragile, beyond resilience, and resistant to shock)—that is, considering in our individual economic actions and in the macro-economic models factors such as volatility, randomness, disorder, stressors, love, adventure, risk, and uncertainties (Taleb, 2011). We live in a society in which we are aware of many risks, and this has become a fundamental characteristic of modern economic behaviour: decision-making despite risks and uncertainty (Beck, 1992). We do not believe in pre-given cosmic–divine–social hierarchies, and we need to discover our own goals (*telos*) in life; we have no clear distinctions between good and wrong, and we are in continuous change: modernity is liquid and not a fixed state (Bauman, 2013). Thus, our economy seems to be a complex dynamic system with an unlimited number of variables and interactions that no human being or computer could perfectly calculate (Keen, 2011).

Process

What economic functions see as impersonal is ultimately constituted by individual action, with millions of individuals making decisions in uncertain situations (O'Driscoll & Rizzo, 2015). Therefore, it has been argued that we should focus on understanding the economic *process* instead of fixed end-states: 'In the usual presentations of equilibrium it is generally made to appear as if these questions of *how the equilibrium comes about* were solved. If we look closer, it soon becomes evident that these apparent demonstrations amount to no more than the apparent proof of *what is already assumed*' (Hayek, 1948, p. 45). In neoclassical economics 'the outcome is confused with *the process* that leads to the outcome. Human action and choices are squeezed from the model, and hence, from the economist notion of price competition' (Boudreaux, 1994, p. 54).

Complexity

Many models assume that the economy can be viewed as being at or near equilibrium, but Steve Keen (2011) described this as an oversimplification of the way that the real economy behaves. Many formulas include aggregates of statistical estimations, such as the average price of a cup of coffee in a take-away shop is determined by the willingness of coffee-sellers to sell their coffee and the willingness of customers to buy it. The coffee company will set its price by looking at the prices of their competitors and at their experience of what their customers are willing to pay. However, such a formula disregards the individual variation and the so-called outliers from the average function; this implies the loss of data and explanatory power, as, for instance, when the customer who is willing to pay much more than average is not considered.

It is impossible to define Pareto optimality—the point where supply and demand perfectly meet each other—as it is unfeasible to know all factors determining this optimum (Von Mises, 1948). Naturally, Pareto assumed supply and demand always fluctuate, but this assumption limited the applications of his theory. Each individual point in equilibrium is an aggregate of other economic equilibria, and it is this chain of equilibria, the reality of the phenomenological life-world, that needs to be understood. For example, the price that an individual pays for a cup of coffee is determined not only by the price of the coffee but also by the amount of money they have, which depends on the salary they earn, the amount of which may also be calculated in another equilibrium. In this Chaos Theory of Economics, a butterfly flying in a park in Japan could via a chain of reactions lead to a sudden rise of prices at my local coffee shop. This is also how the financial crash of 2007/2008 has often been explained, as a chain of action–reaction, accelerated by automatic trade (Kiel & Elliott, 1996). Instead of assuming linear models where we discard of outliers, we should start with complex models that regard outliers as part of the model and that factors in the role of uncertainty and not-knowing. Not only does this imply different statistical models (nonlinear differential equations) and an awareness of their limitations, but also a different role for narratives and meaning-making (Jo, Chester & D'Ippoliti, 2017; Cronin, 2016). If each economic model focuses only on a relatively small selection of variables, we may need multiple co-existing economic models and narratives to make sense of the economic complexities instead of having one big narrative such as neoliberalism.

Meaning

Thus, all economic agents seem to be playing economic chess at multiple boards simultaneously, and there is even an interaction between the boards because the sets on one board may influence the sets on other boards. And due to the enormous amount of games people play and the many opportunities they may have to engage in sets, they use heuristic rules of thumb and make cognitive errors. Or are they not errors? Could this be a meaningful strategy? Could people base their sets on what they find meaningful, or do the sets create new meaningful patterns? Economists often look at the fixed outcome of the chess game, such as the Pareto optimum, but not at the individual strategies and the personal meaning of the economic process. Buying and drinking a cup of coffee is more than getting a shot of caffeine on the run; it is part of a pattern of multiple meanings in life, such as wanting to take care of oneself by having something warm and nice to drink (self-oriented meaning) or wanting to be awake to perform well at the job or be able to make money (materialist meaning). It is this symbolising and imagining of coffee that determines the real price that an individual is willing to pay for a cup of coffee, as will later be explained as part of the Meaning-Oriented Economy. It could be these deep feelings associated with the meaning of products and services that determine economic behaviour. Meaning can play an important role in addition to common theories about human economic behaviour, and it has been argued that there is relatively little attention to emotions and meanings in the afore-mentioned psychological and complex systems models of authors such as Kahneman (Newell et al., 2007). The cognitive models are too simplistic and have less predictive power in several situations than models that focus on meaning in life; meaning in life seems to function as a super-heuristic that determines the biases and strategies we may use in the complex interactions of daily life (Vos, 2011).

In sum, countless studies—and the reality of the 2017/2018 crash—have shown that the rational *Homo economicus* is a crude oversimplification of economic reality.

The Experience Economy

> Experiences are as distinct from services as services are from goods.
> (Pine & Gilmore, 1999, p. 3)

In 1970, Alvin Toffler wrote in his futurist novel *Future Shock* how the economy underwent a fundamental structural change from the service economy that had followed from the industrial economy and the agrarian economy. He described the emergence of a fourth economic sector, the 'experiential industry': 'people in the future are willing to allocate high percentages of their salaries to live amazing experiences'. People do not merely want to buy products or services for the sake of their material functionality but for the sake of the psychological gratification they can acquire from it. This experience society emerges together with the limitless availability of technology and information, which leads to 'information overloads' and 'shattering stress and disorientation', or what Toffler calls 'future shock' defined as 'too much change in too short time'. Toffler could not have been more correct in his predictions: consumption and production have quickly become more and more focused on creating nice experiences (Holbrook & Hirschman, 1982).

Pine and Gilmore (1998) argued that products can be placed on a continuum from undifferentiated commodities to highly differentiated, which means that they are strongly focused on giving positive experiences. They use this continuum to describe the stages that businesses go through. A commodity business charges for undifferentiated products, a goods business for distinctive tangible products, a service business for activities that they perform, an experience business for the feeling customers get by engaging it, and a transformation business for the benefit that customers or 'guests' receive by spending time there. Pine and Gilmore (1999) described how experiences differ from services, goods, and commodities as they function like a stage in a theatre to offer a nice experience. These experiences are memorable, personal, revealed over time, and offered by a stager to a guest as sensations.

Experience businesses focus on the experience of flow (Csikszentmihalyi, 2004) and of us*ing* the good or service, with an emphasis on the suffix '-ing.' Customers can absorb or immerse themselves in actively experienc*ing*, for instance, in the form of 'themes' such as theme entertainment parks like Disneyworld. The price point is a function of the value of remembering the experience, which subsequently depends on the extent to which the experience is sensorial. To sell products as experiences, they first need to be customised to the customers—albeit sometimes through mass customisation like Nike's, which offers customers the opportunity to design their own shoes. This also implies tailoring to the unique individual so the individual customer does need to sift through many options; the business does this for them. Customers do not want choice; they just want exactly what they want. Although in reality clients are often unaware of what they want, and companies need to either remind them or imagine for them what they want. This customisation of products and services can take any form (collaborative, adaptive, cosmetic, or transparent), as long as the business tailors its offering to the unique wants of the customer.

Countless studies have validated the thesis from Pine and Gilmore that experience has become an important factor in the economy (Boswijk & Peelen, 2003; Sundbo & Sorensen). Businesses have begun charging for the value of the transformation that experience offers, a value over and above its inputs. Even before the work of Pine and Gilmore, Gerhard Schulze (1992) described, for example, how inhabitants of the German city Nürnberg showed a new way of living where basic needs were covered and people merely were striving for a nice way of living (*'schönes leben'*), experiencing life (*'er-leben'*). Schulze describes how products are no longer bought for their general usefulness or functionality but to deliver an individual experience. People buy products merely for their aesthetics; for example, the latest iPhone differs little in functionality from the previous version but offers a nice new design. Schulze shows how individuals do not merely buy products or services for the random meaning they supply, as they have pre-determined experiential schemas. That is, individuals often tend to follow specific types of lifestyles and aesthetics in their life. For instance, individuals who identify themselves as punks follow a specific style of clothing, ethics, and relating to peers and authorities (Vos, 2016). Demand for and supply of such experiences meet at the *'Experience Market'* (*'Erlebnismarkt'*).

Example

The experience economy seems to particularly apply to the generation born after 1984, the so-called 'Millennials'. Their style of consumption is characterised by materialist minimalism and investments in satisfying experiences such as vacations, adventure, education, volunteering, live concert and theatre performances, and sports (How & Strauss, 2000). Their self-orientation has taken over the dominant role from materialist types of meaning, with social media playing a crucial role (Arnold, 2017). Their work style may be characterised by the increasingly popular concept of 'the gig economy', which describes a labour market focused on short-term contracts or freelance work. Millennials are often self-employed or semi-semi-employed in workers' collectives such as Uber drivers, take-away couriers for Deliveroo, and renting out spare bedrooms via Airbnb. The flexibility of such work offers the opportunity to tailor work around other priorities in life, and it can respond quickly to social trends. However, the gig economy has been criticised for lack of stability and uncertainty, loneliness, and the requirement of continuous adjustment to changing circumstances—Toffler's 'future shock'.

Intensity & Flow

In the experience economy, the intensity of experiences seems to matter. Instead of the monotonous rhythm of work–sleep–work in the neoliberal economy, individuals feel the urge for a life that feels intense and happy, something real where they can forge the here-and-now and experience a larger perspective. Garcia (2016) argues that any intense experiences are good enough, even negative experiences. People want to feel alive and feel connected with reality and their physical being—similar to what Wilhelm Dilthey (1898/2010) wrote: that in the intensity of physical resistance, for instance in sports, we feel alive and connected with the totality of our life—past, present and future. People search for immediacy in their experiences, not merely a theoretical experience or a rational plan to life. Similarly, Csikszentmihalyi (1997, 2004) wrote that people are nowadays searching for flow, which is the mental state of an individual who is fully immersed in experiencing something in the here and now, with an energized focus, full involvement and enjoyment, and loss of one's sense of space and time. Danish researcher Rolf Jensen (1996) went one step further by describing a 'dream economy': 'In 25 years, what people buy will be mostly stories, legends, emotion, and lifestyle.' As long as it is real, not merely imagined stories.

A specific trend is what has been called 'downshifting', which means that people 'seek more meaningful lives by decreasing the amount of time they devote to work, leaving more time for the valuable goods of friendship, family, and personal development' (Levy, 2005). Similarly, others have observed the development of a 'slow movement' that intends a cultural shift away from the quick-eating culture of fast food chains toward slowing down life's pace and doing things 'at the right speed', particularly around eating, shopping, sex and traveling (Honore, 2005). However, merely having more social and personal time does not necessarily imply deep, authentic connections or finding meaning in a self-transcending act such as altruism and morality. The relationship can remain superficial and functional as a means towards social enjoyment (hedonism), and self-development can be a narcissistic obsession with the self (self-oriented meaning).

Care for Experiences
Intense emotions have also entered the workplace. Roughly one-third of American men and one-half of American women hold jobs that call for substantial emotional labour (Hochschild, 1983/2012). They are expected to use techniques of emotional management that serve the company's commercial purpose, ranging from the smiles of the receptionist to the team spirit of employees. Thus, human feelings are commodified and commercialised; they become a functional tool in the production process. Emotional labour is often not recognised and does not receive large financial rewards. The psychological costs of emotional labour can be large, as individuals are, for instance, expected to show a false self and hide their authentic feelings: the customer is always king, even when they treat you unfairly.

Information Economics
Futurist Toffler predicted that our economy would combine experiences and information. Regarding the latter, he explained that technology would evolve in such a way that it would offer limitless information to consumers. It is not information per se that determines this experience economy, but the experiential meaning of the information, and information about people's experiences and potential experiences. Although the invention of the Worldwide Web needed two more decades to emerge and social media was not even conceptualised, Toffler seems to have perfectly described our society in which information and online experiences have become key currencies in our economy. Many economists have called our modern era an 'information economy'; however, this term only focuses on the function of the information, random zeros and ones on a computer screen, not on how people experience this information or that the most expensive information nowadays is information about people's experiences—for instance, in the form of information on their social media profile (like the costly data Cambridge Analytica used during the Brexit Campaign in the United Kingdom and the presidential election campaign of Donald Trump; Kirk, 2017).

Identity
Identity and experience are close phenomena. However, the difference is that identity is about someone's self-expression in the social domain, whereas someone can merely have nice experiences in their own room without anyone observing. Thus, identity may be regarded as a specific type of experience. The identity economy

captures the idea that people make economic decisions oriented around their identity. For example, people will avoid actions that conflict with their self-concept (Akerlof & Kranton, 2010, 2000). Particularly in the contexts of work and school, identity preservation has been shown to be an important motivator, such as the feeling of being an 'insider' or a part of the in-group. This can often be seen in statements such as 'I am not a person who....' The importance of a positive social identity shows that the capitalist self-interested view of human identity is plainly false. People define their identity and their wider experiences in life in a social context. For example, in our globalised society, personal or regional identity has become more important than national identity. People connect on the internet with others with similar hobbies and interests on the other side of the world, while they feel disconnected from their neighbour who lives only meters away. Subcultures are becoming more important, defined by symbols such as clothing and music style. Similarly, regional cultures are increasingly crucial, and can even lead to protest or violence, as was seen in the former countries of the USSR and Yugoslavia, Catalonia and Basques in Spain, and Palestinian Arabs (Sen, 2007). People hold to a romantic imagination of identity.

Political Populism
Another example of the experience economy that is intertwined with identity and information economics is political populism. This is a type of politics that appeals to the immediate emotions of voters and presents a strong identity. Often, populists appeal to threats to the national identity and national interests which they want to protect with strong measures, such as closing the borders for immigrants (see Chapter 9 on neoconservatism and Chapter 12 on authoritarianism). Often the ideology of the free national market is used to promote regulating the market against threats, such as immigrants, foreign trade, or influence from the European Union. Examples of populist movements since 2010 are the rise of the alt-right movement, the Tea party, and the political campaign of Donald Trump. In other countries, examples include Hungarian president Urban, Brazilian president Bolsano, and some campaigners such as Nigel Farage in the Brexit campaign. Based on systematic research, some historians have compared these trends with the rise of fascism in 1930s (Faulkner & Dhati, 2017).

Scientists have tried to give many explanations for the rise of populism. One relevant explanation is that psychological experiments have shown that in response to feeling existentially threatened, individuals become more nationalistic and conservative (Pysczsinski, Greenberg, & Koole, 2014). For example, when New Yorkers were subliminally shown pictures of 9-11, many of them immediately became more chauvinistic and paid attention to family and work values. Evolutionary speaking, this way to manage existential terror is understandable as individuals start to prepare for self-defence against threats. However, it may be argued that in a neoliberal culture, many individuals feel chronically under threat both physically and psychologically and report high stress levels. These levels were further heightened and brought to public consciousness after the 2007/2008 financial crash and the subsequent austerity measures. Thus, it is not surprising that in this period populist politics—with their manipulation of experiences, identity and information—are quickly on the rise in many neoliberal economies. Naomi Klein (2007) has described this process as disaster capitalism and a shock doctrine, where politicians and economists deliberately create a culture of fear that either provides electoral support for or divides attention away from radical economic and political measures. However, a shortcoming of these studies is that they seem based on the assumption of the evolutionary survival of the fittest which merely triggers stress responses of fighting, fleeing, and freezing; in contrast, Chapter 4 has shown how existential threats could also trigger mutual aid, and it is this response mechanism that may be seen in the rise of the moral economy and the Meaning-Oriented Economy.

Happiness
One specific type of experience has received specific attention: happiness (Frey, 2008). The reason behind this focus on happiness is an understandable response to the over-rationalised *Homo calculus.* Not only have the previously cited studies shown that people often do not act rationally, but market economies are also associated with a structural loss of happiness (Lane, 2000). William Davies (2015) states that our modern obsession with happiness started with Bentham's utilitarianism, which had reaching pleasure and avoiding pain as its aim. Davies gives many examples of how the creation of happiness has become profitable. Clear examples are in the entertainment industry such as Disney (Giroux & Pollock, 2010) or companies with recognisable symbols such as McDonald's (Kincheloe, 2002). The entertainment industry has become a core industry (Wolf, 1999). Thus, happiness equals profit.

However, happiness is not always meaningful. Imagine that you have two options: a happy but meaningless life, or a meaningful and unhappy life. Which one would you choose? Many people choose a meaningful life (Vos, 2018, 2019). This is a decision that we often need to make in daily life. Therefore, 'quick happiness', as can be found in the experience economy—can be distinguished from 'slow happiness'—as can be found in the Meaning-Oriented Economy (Vos, 2018, pp. 78–80):

> Meaning does not necessarily offer quick happiness, but it can foster a sense of slow happiness. Many studies found only a small relationship between meaningfulness and happiness measured as a state of positive emotions or hedonist pleasure. This is possibly most obvious in the repeated study finding that raising children does not make people happier, although they often experience taking care of children as meaningful. This lack of happiness has been explained by the fact that taking care of children often involves a busier life, a child-centred focus which shifts the attention from other meaningful aspects in life and worries about the development of the child. However,

raising children is also experienced as providing a different type of happiness in the long term, which results from a long-term commitment to the value of raising children, which raises someone's self-worth as a parent, educator or caregiver.

This type of happiness is like the deep currents in the ocean, while quick happiness or busyness are superficial waves. Such deep currents are experienced as slower, like a state of tranquility or harmony below the surface. The slowness of this type of happiness has been given different names by different traditions, for example, ataraxia in ancient Greece, sukkah in Buddhism and oikeion in Roman stoa. I call this kind of happiness based on phenomenological meanings slow happiness. Quick happiness, in contrast, is often about functional meanings and temporary states, which do not require a commitment to values but can even be artificially created by drugs or alcohol. Quick happiness is about fulfilling one's own needs and desires that one demands from reality; slow happiness is about being immersed in reality. That is, slow happiness is about connecting with the real world and being inside the flow of experiencing the here and now, but quick happiness can even be artificially manipulated in a state detached from the world.

Many studies show that striving for happiness is self-defeating [i.e., functionalism], as it makes people unhappier and lonelier. The quest for happiness can even lead to depression. Research also indicates that materialist–hedonist and self-oriented types of meaning are experienced as less meaningful and satisfying, and are correlated with lower long-term well-being, while social and larger values are associated with better well-being. This is also called the happiness paradox: constant pleasure-seeking does not yield the most happiness in the long run. Thus, focusing on quick happiness may not necessarily provide a long-term sense of meaningfulness and slow happiness. Although researchers know these facts, the '(quick) happiness industry' is flourishing.

Conclusion

The experience economy differs in many aspects from neoliberal economics, particularly by not assuming a rational *Homo calculus.* However, many of the aforementioned studies present a functionalist approach to (hedonist and self-oriented) experiences, where people deliberately create a stage for positive experiences. Pine and Gilmore argue that in the experience economy it does not matter whether an experience is authentic or not. They describe the role of businesses as actors who pretend 'as if' they care for the customer, and they describe that this 'as if' is at the heart of the characterising role. Pine and Gilmore even go further by describing the cast, roles, characters, ensemble, and theatre stage that businesses offer in the experience economy—or, in economic terms, responsibilities, representations, organisations, and workplace. Many authors have written guidelines on how companies could manipulate the experiences of their customers, particularly to give happiness and sell more (Hsieh, 2010, Bok, 2010). Thus, the experience economy seems to be the apotheosis of neoliberalism, where subjective experiences are the ultimate individual freedom. It offers a society of self-help citizens in which individuals determine their own lives according to their own taste, and where media present political–military interventions of their government as entertaining experiences. However, experiences can both be 'domains of undergoing and of overgoing' (Visser, 1998). The awareness for our experiences can also open us for moral and meaning-oriented economics.

Moral Economics

Overview
Pine and Gilmore (1998) predicted how the experience economy would be followed by 'transformational economics', which gives buyers a sense of transformation. Products or services are, for instance, not merely sold to provide nice experiences—like the experience of coffee drinkers going into a coffee-store, which includes both the taste of the coffee and also the full experience of the economic exchange that ranges from the interaction with the barista to the colourful packaging of products. Nowadays, having a nice hedonistic and self-oriented experience is not enough; the experience needs to contribute to the positive development of the self, others, nature, or society. In other words, the economic experience must be authentic and moral. The coffee beans must be ecologically grown and transported, and the coffee farmers, factory workers, and transport workers should get a good wage. On a superficial level, one may say that morality is an experience and should, therefore, be discussed as part of experience economics. However, moral economics is a separate type of economics because morality concerns a social or a larger type of meaning and not merely a materialist, hedonist, or self-oriented type of meaning. Moral economics often has a non-functionalist approach, whereas experience economics often seem functionalist.

The 2007/2008 financial crash has triggered a moral self-investigation. For example, the World Economic Forum launched the Global Agenda Council on Faith and Values to address the ethical deficits that led to the collapse of financial institutions and housing markets. The conference in Davos was attended by the Archbishop of Dublin, a founder of a Buddhist Centre, and an Evangelical Minister, and morning sessions were started by guided meditation. Furthermore, an explosion of books on moral economics occurred, describing how neoliberalism lacks morality and how morality should be included in economics. Topics include compassion, emotion, and authenticity in the economy (Hirschberger, 2015; Hoffman & McNulty, 2012; Schwartz et al., 2009). It seems as if there is an increasing awareness that the moral costs of neoliberalism are too high, led by fears such as jobless growth, climate change and mass migration (Drewell & Larsson, 2017). As described in the first section of this chapter, we live in a Volatile, Uncertain, Complex and Ambiguous (VUCA) world, and awareness of this may lead to a desire for a moral compass, structure, and stability. The large-scale loneliness that resulted from the Thatcherite self-help culture becomes fertile soil for the deep desire for authentic connectedness, sharing, and community.

Critical Theory

Of course, these authors are not the first to include morality in economics. The previous chapter described how liberal economists started as 'moral philosophers'— for example, Adam Smith wrote about 'moral sentiments' and Marx demanded economic equity. However, morality was often intertwined with materialist conditions or even functionalist approaches, such as Marx's call for the working class of the world to unite to take over the means of mass production. It is this underlying materialism and functionalism that came under criticism in the 1950s Frankfurt School of Critical Theory by such as Herbert Marcuse, Theodor Adorno, Max Horkheimer, Walter Benjamin, and Erich Fromm. They are critical insofar as they sought 'to liberate human beings from the circumstances that enslave them' (Horkheimer 1982, p.244), which included criticism of both neoliberalism as well as covert positivism and authoritarianism in Marxism and Communism. They particularly critiqued the functionalism, or as they called it 'instrumental rationality', of neoliberalism, and instead pleaded for 'value rationality'—that is putting ethics and spiritual interests central. Modernist critical theory concerns itself with 'forms of authority and injustice that accompanied the evolution of industrial and corporate capitalism as a political-economic system', whereas postmodern critical theory looks at social problems 'by situating them in historical and cultural contexts, to implicate themselves in the process of collecting and analysing data, and to relativize their findings' (Lindlof & Taylor, 2002). In line with critical theorists, feminist and queer critiques have shown how voices of diversity are muted in neoliberal cultures, even though these could be very meaningful voices (Butler, 2002). All these critical voices have in common that they demand more attention to the moral dimension in economics and politics. The following is a selection of examples.

Neo-Collectivism

Chapter 4 started the history of economics with a description of morality in the animal realm and collectivist economics. Most of these publications have been published in the last decade and seem to lay the foundations of new collectivist economics. This type of economics focuses on the interest of the community and not merely on the survival of the fittest individual. Social and larger types of meaning are crucial, but without the oppression of the divine–cosmic–social hierarchy like in the Middle Ages. Neo-collectivism follows logically from experience economics, with the addition of a conscience. Many neo-Marxist ideas can be found here but without the materialist reductionism and authoritarianism of traditional Marxists. Examples include ideas about sharing economics, gift-based economics, mutualism, humanistic economics, and caring democracy (Tronto, 2003). Part III gives more examples.

Varieties of Welfare Capitalism

Many economists have argued for conscious capitalism (Mackey & Sisodia, 2013; Schwerin, 1998), a form of neoliberalism without the worst consequences for humans and nature. This economic model combines free-market capitalism with social policies to establish fair competition within the market as well as a welfare state; therefore, this is sometimes called a coordinated market economy. The Swiss-German economist Röpke called this 'the third way' to build 'a humane economy', as will be explained in Chapter 14.

Ecological Capitalism

The previous examples focused on the social domain of moral economics. Additionally, the climate crisis has an immediate appeal on our morality. Increasing numbers of authors are writing about the role of economics in climate change, such as consumerism and pollution. The relationship between consumerism and climate change seems beyond doubt since mere consumption without climate consciousness, such as buying climate-neutral products, seems to have a large negative impact on the environment. Consequently, many economic schools have evolved, such as the degrowth movement and green economics, all of which ask for immediate reduction of polluting economic activities and financial support for climate-friendly activities such as buying solar panels and recycling. There is a clear trend of more customers and companies turning green (Tkachenko, 2018; Isaak, 2016).

Summary

Naturally, neither one type of morality nor one type of moral economics exists. Sometimes, moral intentions clash, as when the ecological transformation of the economy can come at the short-term cost of small and medium enterprises, which find it more difficult to catch up with the ecological demands from the market. However, what all these moral economies have in common is that they reject neoliberalism in its pure form. They argue for more collectivist types of economics but without the divine–cosmic–social hierarchy of medieval economics. They focus on social and/or larger types of meaning and strongly reject economies that merely focus on materialist, hedonist, and self-oriented types of meaning. Although many moral economists are non-functionalist in nature—for example, they fight for nature for nature's sake and for workers as an end in themselves rather than a means to a larger purpose—some economists and businesses have used climate change to better market their own products commercially. Almost all the texts on moral economics start with a fatalistic sketch of economic, existential and psychological disaster if neoliberalism continues in the way it is; however, they argue that they offer hope and existential and psychological well-being, as indicated by the very positive quality-of-life outcomes of some moral economies (Chapter 7).

Moral economics is an example of meaning-oriented economics, although meaning-oriented economics has a larger meta-perspective. The publications on moral economics often focus on only one specific meaning at a time—e.g., climate change or social equality—but seldom both. The specific focus can lead to functionalist misuse of a topic to make a profit, such as companies making a profit by selling climate-neutral products. There is also a danger of functionalistically rendering employees and customers into either climate-changers (devilish carnivores with petrol cars) or climate-defenders (holy vegans on public-transport). Many books on moral economics justify their purpose by explaining that the company will function better or make more profit by being moral. Thus, they make morality a functionalist means towards a larger end and not an aim in itself. Furthermore, there is a risk of paternalism and neo-colonialism when economists advise what is 'moral' and what is 'immoral'—for example, cutting down of the rainforest could imply ecological disaster, on the one hand, but it could also mean the creation of new farmland that gives work to a previously poor farmer, on the other hand. In sum, moral economics seems to suffer from the fact that it does not speak on a meta-level about what is meaningful but immediately assumes what is meaningful for everyone. This is where the Meaning-Oriented Economy enters the stage.

Meaning-Oriented Economy

> For too long we have been dreaming a dream from which we are now waking up: the dream that if we just improve the socio-economic situation of people everything will be okay, people will become happy. The truth is that as the struggle for survival has subsided, the question has emerged: survival for what? Evermore people today have the means to live, but no meaning to live for. (Frankl, 1977, p. 98)

Definition
The 'Meaning-Oriented Economy' is an overarching term for an economy that aims to stimulate the meaningful lives for all stakeholders in the economy, including nature, animals, and unborn generations. This includes and integrates examples of moral and experiential economics, as will be explained below. Hurst (2017) defined the Meaning-Oriented Economy by its focus on personal growth, social relationships, and meaning for the wider society (in my terms: self-oriented, social, and larger types of meaning). Similarly, Drewell and Larsson (2017) define the meaningful economy as an economy in which economic choices are based on a preference for actions informed by a 'sense

of higher purpose' (i.e., social and larger types of meaning, positive values that we share as human beings and make a contribution towards building a global caring society (i.e., moral economics), while providing a basis for creating a sense of well-being and fulfillment in our individual lives. However, these definitions merely focus on the change in content of our economic activities but not on the transformation of our functionalist attitude and the associated existential and psychological impact. However, without a non-functionalist attitude, meaning remains a means to a larger end and is not inherently meaningful. Similarly, these definitions focus predominantly on social and larger meanings; but, although there is a stronger focus on these types of meaning, this seems to exclude the plurality of interests and meanings, including the role that materialist circumstances can play beside moral intentions.

Therefore, the Meaning-Oriented Economy can be defined as a combination of the following perspectives:

1. Visionary (imagination and symbolic) as well as realistic;
2. A plurality of meanings (materialist, hedonist, self-oriented, social, larger types of meaning, but with main focus on social and larger meanings);
3. A non-functionalist approach (main focus on critical–intuitive approach);
4. Individuals critical of themselves and others, and particularly of mind manipulation and governments trying to impose their ideas on them;
5. Historical change as a complex, non-functionalist interaction between individuals and society, with a plurality of meanings;
6. Individuals developing their personal sense of meaning in a critical–intuitive interaction with their social context;
7. Individuals with a realistic sense of freedom and responsibility;
8. Individuals with a sense of living a meaningful life despite the socio-economic situation;
9. Individuals experiencing positive mental health, high quality of life, high life satisfaction.

These characteristics of the Meaning-Oriented Economy create a stark contrast with older economic models. Therefore, the next paragraphs will elaborate on its unique characteristics.

Beyond Capitalist Life Syndrome

The Meaning-Oriented Economy seems to result from the Capitalist Life Syndrome as the fatalistic, existential, and psychological impact of capitalism seems to ultimately lead to individuals questioning the economic system that is causing these symptoms. Drewell and Larsson (2017) mention that our experience of a Volatile, Uncertain, Complex and Ambiguous (VUCA) world leads to worries about jobless growth, climate change, and mass migration, and that these worries are drivers of the economic shift towards a meaning-orientation.

Beyond Utilitarianism
Classical utilitarians focus traditionally on happiness and pain, but this only regards one specific type of meaning: hedonism. In the utilitarian theory, individuals care for others as a generalisation of the desire for their own well-being; since each individual desires his or her own well-being, it must follow that all of us desire the well-being of everyone (Mulgan, 2014; Farina, Hahn & Vannucci, 1996). However, in a Meaning-Oriented Economy, others are meaningful in themselves, and their meaningfulness does not depend on my subjective desire. Meaning is also more than mere 'preference,' like a selection of one option from a range of options—buying product A instead of product B; in an individual's phenomenological experience all options already have meaning and are pre-shaped by their complex meaning-oriented context. For example, the meaning-loaded context of product A includes the fact that this is made by a company that treats its customers unethically and that pollutes the environment, whereas product B is made by a company with high social and ecological standards. Utilities assume that the options can be compared on a common measure, like the score on a questionnaire. However, from a meaning-oriented perspective, there is no commonality between the unique options, and thus there is also nothing to be preferred; there are only meanings. The question is in which meaningful context individuals put themselves and how they relate to this.

Beyond Romantic Imagination
Liberal/neoliberal ideologies are based on the Romantic image of the free market and of magical harmony between differing interests (Bronk, 2010; Heinzelman, 1980). The moral philosophers and the Austrian school of economics were theoretical–deductive in nature, and Karl Marx complained that economists did not do sufficient justice to the lived experience of real individuals. Stockinger (2016, p.3) describes that the Meaning-Oriented Economy 'has its roots in the principle of sensible and perceptible word of data forming a signifying text-scape which stages the inner (mental, emotional...) world of a person or a collective agent'. In contrast with the Romantic symbolism and imagination from economists, the lived experience of what is meaningful for individuals is taken as a starting point in meaning-oriented economics. This implies, for instance, that the functionalist approach is replaced by a phenomenological approach that focuses on perceived meanings. These perceptions do not exist independently from a social context but are embedded in social and cultural ecosystems.

Beyond Laissez-Faire
As chapter 5 described, the physiocrat Quesnay had developed the concept of laissez-faire as a materialist and functionalist translation of the Daoist concept *Wu Wei*. However, Daoists seem to use this concept to describe a non-functionalist approach to life; thus, governments should *not* treat its citizens in a functionalist way but

facilitate individuals to fulfill their meaning in life as they are inherently meaningful individuals. Similarly, in a Meaning-Oriented Economy, the focus does not lie in the size of the state or the extent that it intervenes but on the meaningfulness of its citizens. This implies that governments do not tell citizens what is meaningful to them but they let citizens determine their own meaningfulness in line with classic moral liberals. But this may also imply that governments may actively support citizens to become aware of what is meaningful for them, including strict regulations for mind manipulation, and teaching critical thinking skills. This may also imply offering the material conditions for citizens to develop a meaningful life—for instance, with a universal basic income, a personal development grant, micro-credits, and supportive life coaches, counsellors, and psychotherapists. This means that individuals are offered real opportunities and hope instead of the fatalism of capitalism (see Part III in which this will be elaborated).

Beyond Self-Aggrandisement
The neoliberal idea of liberating markets seems to have led to monopolies and oligarchies (Guilhot, 2005). In a Meaning-Oriented Economy, this is seen as immoral because the meanings of the few are prioritised. Instead, a Meaning-Oriented Economy stimulates caring relationships among colleagues, with customers, and in communities. Tronto (2013) argues that this concept of a caring economy goes beyond the individualist and functionalist masculine relationships fostered by capitalism, such as the Thatcherite stimulation of the self-help citizen. This does not merely include caring about, caring for, care giving and care receiving, which can all still be functionalist forms of caring (Heidegger, 1927/1996). Caring with is 'the final phase of care [which] requires that caring needs and the ways in which they are met need to be consistent with democratic commitments to justice, equality and freedom for all' (Tronto, 2013, p. 23). This is based on values of pluralism, trust, respect, and solidarity, descriptions of the *relationships* between people and not of the skills or activities of a single individual. This implies that economic processes are regarded as inherently *relational processes*. For instance, in the production process, multiple relationships are produced—with colleagues, customers, non-customers, nature, and unborn future generations. These relationships are neither functionalist ('I use you as a means to my end') nor rule-based ('do this and do not do that') but attempt to do justice to the meaning of the dynamic and always evolving relationship between all stakeholders. The meaning-oriented invisible hand on socio-economic markets thus describes dynamic relationships in a complex web of interactions, transactions, and negotiations, where the meanings of all meet one another and are continuously evaluated and renegotiated instead of being fixed by a dominant partner at one stable price.

Beyond False Self

A Meaning-Oriented Economy does not focus on functionalist and superficial identities and relationships but gives an important role to authenticity (Gilmore & Pine, 2007). This contrasts with the experience economy, where the development of a false self is stimulated and used for profit. Trilling (1972) showed in his classic work *Sincerity and Authenticity* how sincerity became popular at the end of the Middle Ages, possibly in response to the disappearance of the divine–cosmic–social hierarchy that had expected people to behave according to their pre-given role. The social concept of sincerity started to transform into the more individualistic concept of authenticity during the Romantic period, which focused on individuals accepting, exploring, and expressing their 'natural' and spontaneous feelings, like the Noble Savage. During the Industrial Revolution, there was little place for authentic expression by ordinary labourers oppressed by the factory owners, later followed by neoliberal politicians suppressing the voices of unions. Workers were expected to suppress their emotions. In the experience economy, workers may even be expected to offer emotional labour for no or low wages but a large profit for the company owners (Hochschild, 1983/2012). In the Meaning-Oriented Economy, workers are stimulated to show their true self and be authentic in communication with colleagues and customers alike, and governments and companies actively work together to prevent employees, customers, and citizens from experiencing alienation.

Beyond Functionalist Experiences

Individuals can become aware of their meanings via their lived experiences, but their meanings are also more than mere experiences. Many philosophers have reflected on this double nature of experiences (Heidegger, 1914). For example, Dilthey wanted to *understand* life from within—that is, let meanings reveal themselves instead of using our manipulated meanings, our rational thinking, or our meaning-loaded symbolic language, thus experiencing without the (neo)liberal exploitation. This is where Dilthey and Heidegger used the German term *erlebnis*—which includes the word 'life' ('leben') and is often translated as 'lived experience'—in contrast with emotions that are manipulated by others or non-lived experiences that result from rationalisation and intellectualisation from our rational mind. Before the 18th century, the term *erlebnis* did not exist in German, and it seems to have emerged in response to the concept of the rational *Homo calculus*, as our rational calculations cannot do total justice to the liveliness of our experiences (Visser, 1998). Philosopher Friedrich Nietzsche described how in the functionalist context of meaning-less experiences, individuals can start to feel an internal pressure demanding a change; similarly, Martin Heidegger said that individuals heard a call of their conscience. That is, individuals can start intuiting that a fundamental part of themselves is not done justice in their societal, professional, and private context and not even in their self-experience. They feel something meaningful is missing because they have only been listening to the meanings of others rather than to *their own unique meanings*. Applied to the situation of capitalism, the Capitalist Life Syndrome can create internal pressure on individuals to break the chains of their syndrome and start listening to what is meaningful to *themselves* in *their* context. Under this experiential pressure, the superficial functionalist–experience economy can transform into a Meaning-Oriented Economy.

Beyond Single-Issue Morality
Although meaning is a subjective–intuitive experience, it does not imply selfishness but rather its opposite. Individuals can intuit the inherent meaningfulness of other people, past and future generations, animals, and nature. This implies a pluralistic perspective that goes beyond single-issue morality and instead stimulates intersectional approaches where, for instance, social and ecologies ideals merge. In the complexities of daily life, individuals often use heuristic meanings, rules of thumb about what is meaningful and what is not meaningful, such as religious world views or subcultural norms giving clear sets of rules about meaning. However, in a Meaning-Oriented Economy, individuals are open for correction when their heuristics fail, and for enlarging their perspectives. Thus, individuals follow the call 'you must change yourself' (Sloterdijk, 2010). This continuous reflexivity and moral self-improvement originate in a new perspective on the capitalist adage of progress, although this is not mere functionalist progress oriented towards materialist self-enlargement. Instead, this is about new ethics that have evolved and are already visible in the practices of many government bureaucracies and companies that put human fulfillment of self and others at its heart (Rubin, 2016). Formulated in terms of meaning, this signals that although individuals should be allowed to follow any types of meaning, the highest morality in our society centres around social and larger types of meaning such as self-realisation and social justice. Thus, we live according to a new morality of self-fulfillment, which encourages people to a meaningful and rewarding life-path. It demands people respect one another's choices, mutuality of interactions, public positions allocated according to merit, and fulfillment of everyone's basic needs.

Conclusions

This chapter has shown how several post-capitalist approaches to economics have emerged since the end of the 20th century, a development that has been accelerating since the 2007/2008 financial crisis. In response to the reductionism of the rational Homo calculus in (neo)liberal economies, the experience economy emerged, which puts experiences, and the manipulation and market of experiences, central. However, this did not do justice to the lived experiences of many individuals, and moral economics developed, which went beyond mere functionalist approaches to materialist, hedonist, and self-oriented meanings. The simultaneous emergence of the experience and moral economies seem to have given rise to the Meaning-Oriented Economy, which integrates and transcends these previous economies. The

Meaning-Oriented Economy focuses on a plurality of meanings, with a non-functionalist approach in which individuals no longer self-identify with an imposed economic–political system; instead it offers a perspective of realistic opportunities and positive hopeful symbols and images with a continuous balancing between freedom and responsibility, promoting physical, psychological, existential, and spiritual well-being of people.

However strong the meaning-oriented trend may be, meaning can also be misused in a functionalist, self-oriented way. Many studies show how easy it is to manipulate meaning via advertising and social networks (Jhally, 2014; Green & Jenkins, 2011). Companies and governments could, for example, use the insights in meaning-oriented economics to manipulate the meanings of customers, employees, and citizens for their own interests. This is already visible, as research of the Fortune 500 indicates that meaning-oriented businesses are four times more profitable than traditional businesses (Sisodia, Wolfe & Sheth, 2003). The profitability of meaning-oriented work may stimulate the popularity of meaning-oriented economics, but this may also keep the trend functionalist, as Ulrich and Ulrich (2010) wrote: 'meaning has market value'. However, the uniqueness of meaning-oriented economics is that it does *not* focus on market values. Profit can be a welcome side effect to meaningful work, but people commit themselves to these meanings for the sake of these meanings. This is reminiscent of Aristotle, who wrote that *eudaimonia*, flourishing, is a byproduct and a gift from the gods after good work. Therefore, meaning-oriented economists continuously ask critical questions. How meaningful is the meaning-oriented change in the economy? Should we believe the authenticity of the words from the CEO from Pepsi, Indra Noyi, who described that 'the northern star of the company is to perform with purpose' and to stimulate 'healthy eats'? Should we believe Deloitte's call for an internal meaning-oriented organisation culture? Is cause-based marketing immoral and functionalist, such as fashion brand Gucci supporting UNICEF?

Key Points

1. Increasing numbers of people no longer support capitalist values, and particularly neoliberalism, since the 2007/2008 crash.
2. Psychological research has disproven the illusion of the rational *Homo calculus* on which neoliberalism is based.
3. Several post-materialist economic models have emerged that can be categorised in three groups: the experience economy, the moral economy, and the Meaning-Oriented Economy.
4. A Meaning-Oriented Economy has a predominantly non-functionalist approach towards social or larger meanings, seen from complex interaction between individuals and society, with a plurality of meanings; individuals

with a meaning-oriented perspective on the economy have better existential, social, psychological, and physical well-being.

5. The Meaning-Oriented Economy has ideas that contrast with the Capitalist Life Syndrome, utilitarianism, Romantic imagination, laissez-faire, self-aggrandisement, false self, functionalist experiences, and single-issue morality.

Table 7.1. Overview of Ten Questions and Perspectives on Post-Materialistic Economies

Name of question	Formal name of perspective	Irrational economics	Experience economics	Moral economics	Meaning-oriented economics
Status?	Ontological status	Symbol Imagination	Reality Symbol Imagination	Symbol Imagination	Reality Symbol Imagination
What?	Type of meaning	Materialistic Hedonistic	Materialistic Hedonistic	Social Larger	Materialistic Hedonistic Self-oriented Social Larger Existential-philosophical
How?	Approach to meaning	Critical–intuitive	Functional-istic or Critical–intuitive	Critical–intuitive	Critical–intuitive
Where?	Relationship between individual and society	Individual determinism	Individual determinism	Interaction-ism	Interactionism
When?	Development over time	Historiology	Historiology	Historiology	Historiology
Who?	Emergence of individual meaning	Psychology	Psychology Sociology	Ethics	Human sciences Social sciences
Whose?	Sense of freedom	Symbolic and imagined freedom; Negative freedom; Individual freedom	Symbolic and imagined freedom; Negative and positive freedom; Individual freedom	Symbolic, imagined and realised freedom; Negative and positive freedom; Individual and structural freedom	Symbolic, imagined and realised freedom; Negative and positive freedom; Individual and structural freedom
Why?	Existential well-being	Existential questions and concerns	Realistic sense of freedom and limitations	Realistic sense of freedom and limitations	Realistic sense of freedom and limitations
Which?	Impact on daily life	Many mental health problems, low quality of life, and low life satisfaction	Some mental health problems, moderately high quality of life, and moderately high life satisfaction	Few mental health problems, high quality of life, and high life satisfaction	Few mental health problems, high quality of life, and high life satisfaction

Part II

The Capitalist Life Syndrome

Chapter 8

Overview of Research
on the Capitalist Life Syndrome

One of the greatest gains of capitalism is that even the proletarian slave feels like a master. He believes he has the power to change his life. We are propelled by the ideology of the self-made man: we work more, we consume more, and, in the end, we consume ourselves. The consequences are burnout, bulimia, and other lifestyle diseases. (Renata Salecl, 1994)

Standing on Giants' Shoulders

Anyone wanting to look far needs to stand on the shoulders of giants. This is what we did in Part I by describing how all economic theories cast unique perspectives on meaning in life, and that we live in a period of transformation from capitalism to a Meaning-Oriented Economy. However, Part I depicted large historical trends and did not zoom into the specific aspects of the Capitalist Life Syndrome. The cited literature was also predominantly historical in nature and, for example, did not include empirical psychological studies and population surveys. Therefore, Part II of this book will elaborate on each of the ten perspectives that constitute this syndrome. This chapter will start with an overview of research on the Capitalist Life Syndrome. The following sections will delineate a systematic literature review, a meta-analysis, an interview study, and a worldwide survey. Together, they provide evidence for the Capitalist Life Syndrome. Anyone less interested in research can jump to the next chapter.

Systematic Literature Review

We conducted a systematic literature review to find any empirical literature on the relationship between capitalism and meaning in life (see Appendices for methodology and findings). Approximately 60% of these studies were published after the 2007/2008 crash, which confirms the trend of an increased interest in the economics of meaning in life. All publications are categorised according to the ten perspectives of the Capitalist Life Syndrome. Details will be included in the following chapters, which elaborate each perspective.

Ontological Status

There were 127 publications offering a philosophical perspective on the meaning of capitalism. Most of these publications were written from an existential, Marxist, Foucauldian, or critical theory perspective. Although the philosophies were divergent in nature, overall the authors described how the wider socio–politico–economic system influences individual lives. Individual meaning in life is influenced by governments, companies, oligarchies, or the dominant group dynamics and values in a country. Reality, symbol, and imagination become intertwined in capitalism. Many of these studies have already been described in Part I.

Type of meaning. Seventy-four empirical and conceptual studies described how capitalism focuses on materialist, hedonist, and self-oriented types of meaning. These include empirical studies on consumerism (51 studies) and on the experience economy (23 studies). Sixty studies describe how capitalism is associated with a self-oriented focus such as self-promotion, narcissism, personal identity, greed, and psychopathy. Several large-scale studies, such as the World Values Survey (Inglehart et al., 2018) and Gallup Polls (www.gallup.com), showed a gradual shift from these types of meaning towards social and larger types of meaning.

Approach. The functionalist approach was described by 29 empirical studies on meaning and capitalism. Examples include studies showing how individuals feel overwhelmed by a choice overload in capitalist countries and by a controlling and demanding approach to life. Seven studies indicated that individuals experience meaning as changeable, flexible, and to some extent random in life. Several studies particularly focused on the flexibility of meaning in the 'gig economy'.

Individual society. Fourteen empirical studies described how lifestyle and life decisions are systematically manipulated by others—for instance, via advertising, journalism, social media, and entertainment. Research indicates that individual meaning and well-being in life do not depend on economic freedom but on political freedom. Thus, the material conditions for living a meaningful life may be less relevant for one's sense of meaning than the political conditions such as freedom of expression and the right to vote. This is also reflected in the research on the income–happiness paradox: A larger income increases an individual's happiness but not their sense of life fulfillment or meaningfulness of life. Income is not a necessary and sufficient condition for meaning; instead, several studies indicate that individuals living in poorer countries have greater life satisfaction. Furthermore, 60 studies show that for life fulfillment, social resources are more important than material conditions. For example, individuals live a more meaningful life when they have many relatives and friends. A strong social network not only provides a social type of meaning, but friends and family can also offer opportunities such as work or hobbies. Therefore, it is not surprising that socio-economic inequality and bad neighbourhoods lead to less life satisfaction. This has been called a poverty trap: The social context offers few opportunities to fulfill meaning.

History. Ninety-five empirical studies described the relationship between individual meaning and socio-economic–political transitions. For example, research shows how having a sense of meaningfulness in life is an important source of resilience in times of nationwide natural disasters or economic crises. Furthermore, a change in the political and economic system does not immediately lead to new individual meaning in life. For example, several decades after the fall of communism in Eastern Europe, many individuals still have different priorities and expectations in life than individuals in capitalist countries. Individuals who experience a strong sense of social or larger meaning are better able to cope with the post-communism disappointments about capitalism. Thus, it is important not to describe world history merely from a political or economic perspective, as this may not reflect the actual changes that people experience in what they find meaningful in life. Research indicates that radical societal changes—revolutions—may depend more on people's individual meaning than on their actual political and economic situation.

Individual meaning. Many empirical studies (315) describe how individuals develop their sense of personal meaning within their social context). Most studies focus on the sense of meaning in vulnerable populations in capitalist countries, such as physically ill individuals, immigrants and refugees, ethnic minorities, addicted individuals, very young and very old people, homeless, unemployed and low-waged individuals, women, and LGBTQI+ individuals. These studies prove that their vulnerability makes it more difficult for them to experience life as meaningful. However, individuals who live a meaningful life despite life's tragedies experience better physical and mental well-being. The sense of meaning provides a psychological buffer that makes individuals more resilient and better able to cope with these liminal conditions.

Freedom. There are 31 empirical studies showing how capitalism is correlated with a sense of helplessness, hopelessness, and nihilism. Many studies cite the 'TINA syndrome' (There Is No Alternative). The percentage of the capitalist population that experiences a lack of freedom and hope differs per study, ranging between 6% and 68% depending on the type of measurement.

Existential impact. Thirty-seven interview studies and small surveys describe the existential impact that capitalism can have on individuals. This includes existential anxiety, loneliness, and guilt.

Daily life impact. Countless empirical studies describe how capitalism correlates with worse mental health and lower quality of life. Several studies also provide some evidence that capitalism *causes* these conditions (e.g.,Vos, Roberts, & Davies, 2019).

Conclusion. The existing scientific literature seems to confirm that capitalism is associated with the ten unique perspectives on meaning summarised as The Capitalist Life Syndrome. However, these studies looked at one single perspective at a time and did not systematically examine the relationship between these perspectives. Therefore, new research is needed to prove the existence of the Capitalist Life Syndrome.

Table 8.1. Systematic Empirical and Conceptual Publications on the Capitalist Life Syndrome

Name of question	Formal name of perspective	Capitalist Life Syndrome	Number of research studies
Name?	Name of system	Capitalism	
Status?	Ontological status	Reality, symbol & imagination	127
What?	Type of meaning	Materialistic Hedonistic Self-oriented	74
How?	Approach to meaning	Functionalistic	29
Where?	Relationship between individual and society	Social and individual determinism	14
When?	Development over time	Historicism	95
Who?	Emergence of individual meaning	Individual psychology	315
Whose?	Sense of freedom	Three components: I. Negative freedom in the imagination of a free market; II. Inequality in the ability to use freedom; III. Individual fatalism, helplessness and hopelessness IV. Mind mafia	31
Why?	Existential ground	Existential questions and concerns	37
Which?	Impact on daily life	Many mental health problems, low quality of life, and low life satisfaction	Many (e.g., Vos, Roberts, & Davies, 2019)

Meta-Analysis of Types of Meaning

A previous systematic literature review included 45,710 participants from 107 studies worldwide who answered the question: What is meaningful, valuable, or important in life (Vos, 2018, 2016). Their answers were categorised, which led to the differentiation of six types of meaning (materialist, hedonist, self-oriented, larger, and existential–philosophical). The studies did not include any economic variables. However, by adding national economic data about the country in which each of the 107 studies had been conducted, hypotheses could be tested about the relationships between these national economic variables and the answers that people gave. These economic variables included core characteristics of capitalism as described in Chapter 2, such as private property, self-interest, competition, capital accumulation, wage labour, market-set prices, freedom to choose consumption production and investment, and a small government. These data were used to conduct meta-analyses (i.e., statistical analyses of a collection of studies; see Appendices for detailed findings).

Hypothesis 1: Capitalism and Types of Meaning
The more capitalist a country is, the more citizens focus on materialistic, hedonistic, and self-oriented types of meaning, and the less they focus on social and larger types of meaning. This was the first hypothesis that my meta-analyses confirmed with significant moderately strong effect sizes. The findings were present for all capitalist characteristics.

Hypothesis 2: Capitalism and Mental Health
Previous studies have shown that materialist, hedonist, and self-oriented meanings are correlated with worse psychological well-being, and social and larger meanings with better well-being (Vos, 2018, 2016a). Therefore, the second hypothesis of my meta-analyses was that the more capitalist a country is, the worse the average level of mental health of the population is *because* individuals focus on these types of meaning. A broad range of characteristics of national mental health was included in the regression mediation analyses, along with mental health characteristics from the included studies. The findings showed that the more capitalist a country is, the worse the average mental health is. However, this was not a very strong relationship, and political freedom and social freedom better predicted mental health. Materialist, hedonist, and self-oriented types of meaning strongly predicted worse mental health, and social and larger types of meaning predicted better mental health. Finally, via the complete or partial mediation of meaning, capitalism strongly predicted mental health. This means that the more capitalist a country is, the worse the average mental health of its citizens is *because* these citizens focus more on materialist, hedonist, and self-oriented meanings. These mediation effects are significant and moderately strong. Thus, capitalism has an indirect influence on mental health via its focus on capitalist types of meanings. Capitalism leads to individuals predominantly focusing on materialist, hedonist, or self-oriented meaning in life, and these types of meaning lead to worse mental health. Although it is important to mention that this is not a perfect explanation, as there are individuals in capitalist countries who instead focus predominantly on social and larger types of meaning and consequently experience better mental health.

Hypothesis 3: Capitalism Overrules Other Variables
My third hypothesis was that other variables, such as characteristics of the study and the culture of the country, do not significantly correlate with meaning in life. Indeed, neither culture nor study characteristics correlated with meaning in life, capitalism, or their relationship. Political freedom and social mobility did not correlate with economic freedom and other capitalistic characteristics, but they did correlate

strongly with social and larger types of meaning and positive mental health. Financial characteristics and productivity were unrelated to all other variables. There were some statistical trends that were almost statistically significant, suggesting that collectivist countries may have a larger focus on social and larger types of meaning in life.

Summary

This study shows that the dominant economic system of a country predicts the types of meaning that citizens experience. Individuals in relatively capitalist countries focus relatively more on materialist, hedonist, and self-oriented types of meaning than individuals in less capitalist countries, whereas the latter focus more on authenticity, social, and larger types of meaning. Furthermore, the mediation findings indicate that capitalism is bad for mental health because it stimulates a focus on materialist, hedonist, and self-oriented types of meaning instead of on social and larger meanings. The nature of causation may be debated, whether capitalism stimulates people to focus on these specific types of meaning or vice versa; however, longitudinal and experimental studies indicate this causality (Vos, 2018, 2016).

These findings are in line with previous studies (Schwartz, 2007; Kasser, Cohen, Kanner and Ryan, 2007). Similarly, Skidelsky (1996) argued that the economist Keynes was wrong in his prediction that by the end of the 20th century people would work less with better overall well-being, because Keynes did not include the fact that capitalism has stimulated people to spend more money on acquiring material wealth and hedonistic experiences than in his time. In meaning-oriented terms: Keynes was wrong in his prediction that we would have better well-being because of the increased focus on materialist, hedonist, and self-oriented meanings and an erosion of social and larger types of meaning. This shift in meanings could subsequently also explain the large 'mental health crisis' in modern Western countries, which particularly affects individuals in difficult socio-economic circumstances (Vos, Roberts, & Davies, 2019).

Political freedom and social mobility were not correlated with other characteristics of capitalism, which refutes the neoliberal hypothesis that capitalism fosters political freedom and social mobility (Schwartz, 2007). However, political freedom and social mobility were correlated with a larger focus on social and larger types of meaning in life, which is understandable as it may be argued that freedom and mobility are founded on social and ethical values (i.e., social and larger meanings). Political freedom and social mobility also predicted better mental health, albeit partially mediated by these types of meaning. Thus, political freedom and social mobility seem to be good for mental health for their own sake, but also because they are associated with a larger focus on social and larger meanings in life.

Interview Study

The meta-analysis was based on questionnaire surveys. Although such surveys can tell much about people's general attitudes, they do not give an in-depth picture of their lived experience. How do individuals experience the relationship between capitalism and meaning? To answer this question, 8 individuals were interviewed, who identify themselves as supportive of capitalist values and another 8 individuals who identify themselves as anti-capitalist (see Appendices).

Both capitalists and anti-capitalists mentioned all six types of meaning. However, capitalists more often mentioned materialist, hedonist, and self-oriented meanings, and anti-capitalists reported more social, larger, and existential–philosophical meanings. Most capitalists described meaning in life as a random experience that can be controlled and replaced with any other type of meaning, whereas most anti-capitalists described that they used both their intuition and their critical skills to discover a sense of an absolute meaning in life. Some capitalists and some anti-capitalists used religion or spirituality as guidance to meaning in life.

Capitalists mentioned that capitalism can socially limit their lives, particularly regarding a bad life/work balance. Anti-capitalists mentioned that capitalism makes many people powerless, disrupts social life and communities, and causes an ecological and climate crisis. Capitalists mentioned that capitalism has positive effects on their mood such as happiness, but they also mentioned negative experiences such as a lack of life fulfillment, irritability and burnout, and uncertainty. Anti-capitalists did not report any positive effects of capitalism on their mood and instead mentioned uncertainty, anxiety, helplessness, depression, emptiness, and loneliness. The majority of both groups thought that the impact of capitalism on their lives could not be completely overcome, as capitalism is too large for individuals to change. Some individuals in both groups mentioned development of themselves and their skills as a solution, and anti-capitalists also mentioned the role of anti-capitalist struggle. In sum, these findings seemed to confirm the existence of the Capitalist Life Syndrome, although capitalists and non-capitalists obviously have different perspectives.

Worldwide Survey of Meaning in Life

Previous research studies have discussed each of the perspectives of the Capitalist Life Syndrome, but they usually did so by discussing one perspective at a time. However, I hypothesize that all ten characteristics occur together as a package deal: The Capitalist Life Syndrome. Therefore, I developed the Worldwide Survey of Meaning in Life, which consisted of a combination of valid and reliable questionnaires (see Appendices). I received 1,871 surveys, 590 of which had to be discarded as these were filled in less than 50%. In total, surveys from 1,281 participants from 49 countries in all inhabited continents were included. There were significantly more Europeans and

North Americans in the sample than individuals from Africa or Southeast Asia. Furthermore, this sample seemed slightly biased as compared to the average population of the included countries; the participants seemed to have studied longer, had a higher income, and were more likely to be a student or single, which is not uncommon for surveys.

Hypothesis 1: Capitalist Life Syndrome
To statistically test the hypothesis that all perspectives of the Capitalist Life Syndrome are part of the same phenomenon, statistical techniques were used which test full models at once (multi-level structural-equation-modelling). The findings confirmed that all perspectives of the Capitalist Life Syndrome were highly correlated. Furthermore, the more capitalist a country was, the more likely it was that individuals simultaneously experienced these perspectives. Both the capitalist characteristics of the country and the individual's subjective capitalist values explained their experience of the Capitalist Life Syndrome. Thus, the system of capitalism influences how individuals experience meaning in life, but they are not totally determined by this system as they can change their own subjective perspectives.

Hypothesis 2: Unfulfilled Meaning in Life Matters
The second hypothesis in the Worldwide Survey of Meaning in Life followed from the statement by one participant in the interview study, who said: 'It does not matter what I find important in life; it depends on the economy what will become of my life. It is this dependence on the economy that is uncertain and frustrating.' Thus, we could hypothesize that there is a difference between how important, for example, material wealth is for an individual ('imagined meaning'), although the individual could actually have little material wealth ('realised meaning'). This hypothesis was confirmed with statistical large effects (t-tests, Pearson's correlations, structural equation modeling). There was a significant difference between imagined and realised meaning in life, implying that individuals experienced a lack of fulfilled meaning in life. The realisation of materialist and hedonist meanings correlated strongly with individual income level, and moderately with GNP, social mobility, political freedom, and socio-economic equality, but *not* with other variables. The findings indicate that positive material and political circumstances are to some extent important for realising materialistic and self-oriented meanings, but that social, larger, and existential–philosophical types of meaning do *not* depend on material and political circumstances. The average fulfillment of meaning (i.e., the average difference between imagined and realised meaning) correlated strongly with the average mental well-being, indicating that the extent to which one's meanings in life remains unfulfilled predicts one's overall well-being. There were some statistical indications that the imagination of meaning is more important than its realisation, but this requires further research.

In sum, because of material circumstances, individuals may experience that they cannot fulfill their imagined meaning in life, and this lack of fulfillment can lead to psychological stress and lower quality of life. However, it seems that the imagination is more important than the realisation of meaning in life, possibly because it may be easier for individuals to change their imagination than their actual socio-economic circumstances (e.g., lower goals when you cannot reach them). These findings were not correlated with any other variables or relationships between variables in this survey.

Conclusion
This survey shows that the different perspectives of the Capitalist Life Syndrome come together as a package deal. The study included both individual and nation-specific estimations of capitalism, which both yielded similar results. However, individual and country-specific variables only correlated moderately with one another. This seems to indicate that individuals can have different economic perspectives than the economic system of their country. For example, not all citizens in a predominantly capitalist country like the United States support capitalism, and some citizens in a predominantly anti-capitalist country like Venezuela may support capitalism.

This is the first study ever to test the difference between the imagination and the realisation of meaning in life. This seems particularly important to understanding the impact of a 'frustrated will to meaning' (Frankl, 1948) on one's mental health. The findings show that when you desire a certain meaning in life and achieve it, this can give a sense of fulfillment and mental health. When you desire something, and you do not achieve this, you can feel unfulfilled. When you cannot fulfill many of your desires for a long time, this could lead to poor mental health. This seems to be particularly the case for individuals with a small income and/or who live in a poor country with limited social mobility and great socio-economic inequality, as they may have fewer resources to realise their desired materialist, hedonist, and self-oriented types of meaning. However, the realisation of social and larger types of meaning does not seem to depend on the socio-economic situation of individuals, indicating that material and political conditions are neither necessary nor sufficient to experience social or larger types of meaning.

Conclusion

These four studies have shown that capitalism is not a neutral ideology but is associated with a narrow functionalist focus on materialist, hedonist, and self-oriented types of meaning in life. Supporters of capitalism seem to identify themselves with an economic system that may not be good for their sense of fulfillment in life and for their mental health. They experience fatalism and lack of control, like hostages. In contrast, other individuals have a meaning-oriented approach towards the economy that follows their critical intuition for social and larger types of meaning in life.

Thus, scientific research confirms the existence of the Capitalist Life Syndrome and the Meaning-Oriented Economy. The next chapters will elaborate on each of the ten perspectives, using the literature in this chapter.

Key Points

1. A systematic review of all scientific literature yielded empirical and conceptual evidence for the existence of the Capitalist Life Syndrome.
2. Meta-analyses of 107 studies with 45,710 individuals worldwide showed that the more capitalist a country is, the more individuals focus on materialist, hedonist, and self-oriented types of meaning and less on social and larger types of meaning.
3. These meta-analyses also showed that the more capitalist a country is, the lower the average mental health of its citizens; this stems from the fact that these citizens focus more on materialist, hedonist, and self-oriented types of meaning.
4. The Worldwide Survey of Meaning in Life (WSM) showed that the more capitalist a country is, the more its citizens focus on the unique capitalistic perspectives on meaning in life.
5. The WSM also showed that the national economic system influences how individuals experience meaning in life, but does not completely determine their sense of meaning. Thus, regardless of their socio-economic situation, individuals have some individual freedom to decide their own perspectives on life.
6. In addition, the WSM showed that socio-economic circumstances can make individuals feel that they cannot fulfill their imagined meaning in life, and this lack of fulfillment can lead to psychological stress and lower quality of life. However, it seems that imagination is more important than the realisation of meaning in life, possibly because it may be easier for individuals to change their imagination than their actual socio-economic circumstances.

Chapter 9

Capitalist Types of Meaning:
Materialist, Hedonist, and Self-Oriented

Sorry, the lifestyle you ordered is currently out of stock. (Banksy, graffiti)

Definitions

Often, when people speak about meaning, they use abstract terms such as 'The Meaning of Life', and they give examples of exceptional moments in life such as marriage or ecstatic holidays. This hides the fact that our actions and experiences in our daily life already reveal what is meaningful to individuals, albeit non-reflected and involving more mundane activities (Vos, 2016). For example, what made you read this book? Most likely you did not spend a long time soul searching to find out what your meaning in life is and whether reading this book fits into your hierarchies of meaning in life. Instead of reading this, you may have gone shopping or partying, but apparently, at this moment that feels less meaningful to you. We are often led by the voiceless voice of our intuition telling us what is meaningful and what is not (Vos, 2017).

We intuitively prefer certain types of meaning over others. For example, if you often read books like this, that may reflect the general trend in your life that self-education and critical thinking are important to you. These patterns can be called 'types of meaning'. The table below gives an overview of all types and sub-types of meaning in life (based on the meta-analysis of 107 previous studies and validation in, for example, the Worldwide Survey of Meaning in Life, which is presented in Chapter 7).

When we closely analyse our daily life, we will discover multiple simultaneous meanings. Meanings are not necessarily mutually exclusive, and sometimes people have conflicting meanings. For example, a reader could love both self-education via reading as well as going out, and although these activities may clash in the short term—reading in a nightclub may be difficult—they can fulfill the different meanings at different moments in life. In the long term, we can describe our household of meanings ('*oikonomia*' in Aristotelian terms), where certain meanings are prioritised over others at certain times. The next sections will elaborate the types of meaning in capitalism, including summaries of previous publications (Vos, 2017, 2016a, 2016).

Table 9.1. Overview of Types and Sub-Types of Meaning in Life (Based on Vos, 2019, 2018, 2016)

I. MATERIALISTIC TYPE OF MEANINGS
Underlying value: the value of having material goods or visible success
  A. Material conditions
        Finances, housing, possessions, practical activities, physical survival
  B. General and social success
        General success, social status, power
  C. Educational success
        Success in educational achievements
  D. Professional success
        Success in career and profession

II. HEDONISTIC TYPE OF MEANING
Underlying value: the value of the self
  A. Hedonistic–experiential activities
        Hedonism, fun, leisure, and joyful activities, enjoying beauty (music, art, eating, drinking, etc.), peak experiences, pain avoidance
  B. Enjoyment in nature and with animals
  C. Enjoyment of the body
        Being healthy, healthy lifestyle, sports, sex

III. SELF-ORIENTED TYPE OF MEANING
Underlying value: the value of the self
  A. Resilience (coping successfully with difficult life situations)
        Flexibility, perseverance, and hardiness, acceptance of challenges, effective coping skills, positive and hopeful perspective
  B. Self-efficacy
        Effective actions in daily life (setting specific activities or goals, planning, organising, discipline, evaluating and adjusting daily life, activities, or goals), being in control
  C. Self-acceptance
        Self-insight, self-acceptance, self-worth, self-esteem
  E. Autonomy
        Self-reliance, non-selfish balance with social context
  F. Creative self-expression
  G. Self-care

IV. SOCIAL TYPE OF MEANING
Underlying value: the value of being connected with others, belonging to a specific community and improving the well-being of others. and children in particular
- A. Feeling socially connected
    - Sociability, friends, family, intimate relationships/partner
- B. Belonging to a specific community
    - Family, community, history, and society
- C. Following social expectations
    - Doing what is socially expected, following social virtues, conformism, tradition
- D. Altruism
- E. Giving birth and taking care of children

V. LARGER TYPE OF MEANING
Underlying value: values of something bigger than their materialistic–hedonistic experiences, themselves and other human beings, merely for the sake of that larger value.
- A. Purposes
    - Specific higher goals, purposes, aims or dreams in life
- B. Authenticity
    - Following the perceived true self
- C. Personal growth
    - Self-development, self-transcendence, self-realisation, fulfilling one's potential, authenticity, wisdom
- D. Temporality
    - Sense of coherence, future oriented, reflection on the past, legacy, after-life, position in life span, little time or resources left
- E. Justice & ethics
    - Following ethical standards, being treated in a just way, contributing to a just world
- F. Spirituality and religion
    - Spirituality and religion, beliefs, worship and religious practices, insight into cosmic meaning, spiritual union, peace, harmony and balance, Platonic Ideal or Highest Good

VI. EXISTENTIAL–PHILOSOPHICAL TYPE OF MEANING
Underlying value: the value of life as such. This type of meaning does not have a specific content like the other types of meaning but is more abstract; the mere fact that someone is breathing and is able to make unique decisions within freedom is a gift for which one may feel grateful and may want to respond to with responsible decisions.
- A. Being alive:
    - Being born, feeling alive, being until death
- B. Uniqueness:
    - The unique individuality of one's own experiences, own life, own world. and own self

C. Connectedness with the world and others
>   Being in the world, being in context, being in relationships

D. Individual freedom:
>   Freedom of decision, freedom to decide one's attitude towards a limitation situation in life, the possibility to leave a legacy

E. Gratitude to life as a gift:
>   Experiencing the mere fact of being born as a gift or miracle that one did not ask for but that one regards as highly precious and special, and to which one responds with gratitude

F. Responsibility:
>   Individual responsibility for oneself to live a meaningful life according to one's highest values

Materialistic Meanings

> Materialism is the philosophy of the subject who forgets to take account of himself. (Schopenhauer, 1851/2000, p. 76)

Materialist meanings are about the value that people attach to material goods and personal success. Individuals can find it important to have financial security, earn a great deal of money, buy a good house, have an aesthetic house interior, buy the latest phone, etc. This value can stretch from obsessively focusing on your survival when you are struggling to make ends meet, to buying the latest Maserati. This type of materialist meaning also includes recognised success in the physical world, such as having high social status and power, getting a PhD or being voted the most influential businessman of London City. Of course, these examples could have other meanings at the same time: getting your PhD may not only have a materialist meaning but also a meaning for self-esteem or trying to improve the world with your research, etc.

Countless authors have described how people in capitalist countries tend to attach much value to money, house ownership, and being seen as successful. For example, the Frankfurt School combined Marxist critique with psychoanalysis to describe how people focus more on 'having' than on 'being' (Fromm, 1976/2013). Marcuse (2013) described how 'man' has become 'one-dimensional', and Baudrillard (1998) described consumerism as our modern human condition. Questions about the good life beyond material success have disappeared into the background, according to the Skidelskys (2012).

Some philosophers have argued that a materialist or hedonist focus has nothing to do with meaning, as they only regard social or larger types as truly meaningful. Most likely this tells much about their own perspective because in the general population many people do find meaning in materialist experiences, albeit this type of meaning is less satisfying than social or larger meanings. With the philosopher Aristotle, we may argue that focusing on materialist or hedonistic meanings is not problematic per se, as long as people do not always and only focus on these meanings;

living a good life (*eudaimonia*) is the result of a meaning household (*oikonomia*) that includes a wide array of meanings. For Aristotle, there is a problem when materialism or hedonism are combined with selfishness and obsession, such as greed (a general, intense, selfish materialist desire), avarice (intense desire for monetary and materialist wealth), and gluttony (lack of self-control). Therefore, he recommended the virtue of temperance (self-control and restraint). Several religions, including Buddhism, Confucianism and Daoism, do not regard materialism as problematic in itself but see our dependent–obsessive relationship with it as problematic. These religions seem psychologically accurate, as countless studies show that a structural and complete focus on materialist meanings lead to the long-term lack of life satisfaction (Vos, 2018, 2019).

Why do some individuals focus obsessively on materialist, hedonist, and self-oriented meanings? In Chapter 11, we will look at the individual psychology of greed, and particularly how this is related to inherited social power structures and authoritarianism. Another aspect is that people are continuously told via commercials, education, and culture that a meaningful life can be found in achieving material goals (Chapter 11). When you buy a product or a service, you do not merely buy one thing but may buy into the materialist life-world, or as Horkheimer (2014) writes in line with Marx: 'the ultimate condition for production is *the reproduction of the conditions of production*'. The relationships of power and ownership of the industry are reproduced. For example, when you buy a product, your money gives income to the factory owner and, as such, you contribute to the system in which the owner can invest his income to become richer and more powerful. By buying products, we further materialise our life-world: our social relationships and meaning in life become more focused on material ends, instead of regarding the material world as means to social or larger ends. The best example of this is the vicious cycle of chronically unfulfilled materialistic desires, as Lacan describes, where people start shopping with the hope that this will provide a sense of fulfillment in life; but since materialistic success rarely gives a long-term sense of satisfaction (Vos, 2019), people will need to go on shopping more, hoping that their new materialist 'fix' will satisfy them. Metaphorically described, this is like drug addicts who start craving for more drugs and who need larger and larger dosages to experience a sense of satisfaction. By buying and selling, we reinforce the commodification of our relationships with our life-world, others, and ourselves. However, entrepreneurs and investors need this chronically unfulfilled desire for materialistic meanings; otherwise they cannot sell their products and services. The biggest hidden truth of consumerist culture is that one sale may satisfy one specific *want*, but consumerism will never fulfill the fundamental *desire* in life.

An extreme example of materialism is avarice: a self-oriented, limitless striving towards acquiring more and more material wealth or success for *oneself* rather than for the community. Several authors have identified greed as the root of the financial crisis of 2007/2008. Unrestrained greed has 'corrupted a dream, shattered global markets and unleashed a catastrophe' (Tett, 2009). Companies like Enron had their dreams shattered due to their accounting tricks, insider stock trades, fraudulent partnerships, and coverups by company propaganda, all of which contributed to a company culture of greed (Cruver, 2002). Banks sold their risky financial products with advertisements hyping a life of material success. The 1990 advertisement from Lehman Brothers started with a deep male voice asking, 'Where do you want to be in five years?', and a layman with whom the general audience could identify described his dreams of paying for his children's university and living in Paris, which was followed by the masculine voice-over guarantee that 'you can get there from here'. However, these 'greed merchants' did not mention the risks of buying complex financial products (Augar, 2005).

Materialism seems natural, and all animals and humans could become obsessive and defensive with protecting their possessions when they are in a survival situation. Because when food is scarce, animals and people need to fight for their survival (Achterhuis, 1988). Many variations to this argument float around in economic circles, even though this argument is illogical and not supported by evidence. Chapter 4 showed that animals will not only defend but also share food and shelter; thus, greed is neither 'natural' nor 'good' for the survival of the nation or the wealth of the nation. Much of human history is *not* peppered with materialism, and the concept of private property only emerged late in the Medieval period, as Chapter 4 showed. Research reveals that in non-collectivist cultures, people do not need to have their basic materialist needs fulfilled before they can focus on what is meaningful in life; only people in capitalist cultures seem to experience this materialist requirement for well-being (as will be elaborated in Chapter 12).

Thus, it seems to be the capitalist culture that has created the myth that materialism is normal and needed. Capitalism—and particularly the financial and neoliberal nature of modern economies—seems to depend on materialistic and self-oriented types of meaning summarised as 'greed'. The 2007/2008 meltdown not only revealed flaws in the design of the economic system but also in the existence of the greed culture (Mason, 2009). In response to this, countless books have appeared on post-materialistic economics: how to build an economy not on the foundations of materialism but on social and larger types of meaning. For this reason, a year after the collapse of Lehman Brothers, the time was ripe to give Elinor Ostrom the Nobel Prize for her economic work on the commons, which challenged the conventional wisdom that property can only be successfully managed by either private individuals or the state, as she focused on local commons without any regulation by central authorities or privatisation. Ultimately, Ostrom (1994, 1990) revealed the failure of the materialistic and self-oriented foundations of our economic system and proposed a structure based on social types of meanings and focusing on the larger good instead of private wealth and success (see Chapter 15).

Hedonistic Meanings

It is not only materialism that dominates capitalism. In the book *Brave New World* (Huxley, 1932/1998), individuals can take a pill, 'soma', to get 'the warm, the richly coloured, the infinitely friendly world of soma-holiday' and to 'raise a quite impenetrable wall between the actual universe and their minds'. Thus, people take pills to have joyful experiences, like Marx described that people in all times reach for 'opium' such as religion. Individuals can tap into many sources of hedonism, such as leisure and joyful activities, enjoying the beauty of music, art, eating, drinking, etc. Often, this is formulated in utilitarian terms of pain avoidance and pleasure seeking. Enjoyment is also often an embodied experience, such as tasting delicious food and hearing lyrical sounds from musicians, and can focus on the body by enjoying sports or joining a gym and fitness culture. Some individuals also connect with nature and animals.

Neil Postman (1985) argued that in our 'show business' era 'we amuse ourselves to death', like people taking *soma* in *Brave New World*. He describes how we have started to focus on the form, the aesthetics, and less on the content of our culture. For example, the form of television has made the news bulletins into shows that need to project drama and excitement. Social media such as Facebook and Twitter show merely a picture or a limited number of words. Politics have become entertainment, with the electorate voting actors and clowns into power (Kincheloe, 2002), such as President Trump governing the United States by sending angry tweets to his eagerly awaiting 62 million followers. Because of this focus on such superficial mediums, politics and economics are no longer about ideas and solutions but about the nice form and the nice experience, according to postmodern philosophers: 'the medium is the message' (McLuhan, 1994). Postman contends that television is altering the meaning of "being informed" by creating a species of information that might properly be called disinformation—misplaced, irrelevant, fragmented, or superficial information that creates the illusion of knowing something but which in fact leads one away from knowing'. Seeking immediate feelings of pleasure and avoiding pain has become one of the most important reasons for consumers to buy products or services and to vote for politicians. This has given rise to the 'happiness industry' of pharmaceutical companies, nudging governments, and creating happiness-boosting advertisements (Williams, 2016).

Self-Oriented Meanings

Capitalism is based on the pillars of materialism and hedonism, as the previous sections showed, but its determining aspect is possibly its focus on the self. The epitome of self-oriented meanings is Samuel Smiles, who wrote on the first page of the mid-Victorian Bible of liberalism with the much-telling title *Self-Help* in 1859:

Whatever is done for men or classes, to a certain extent this takes away the stimulus and necessity of doing for themselves; and where men are subjected to over-guidance and over-government, the inevitable tendency is to render them comparatively helpless. Even the best institutions can give a man no active aid. Perhaps the utmost they can do is, to leave him free to develop himself and improve his individual condition. But in all times men have been prone to believe that their happiness and well-being were to be secured by means of institutions rather than by their own conduct. (...)Englishmen feel that they are free, not merely because they live under those free institutions which they have so laboriously built up, but because each member of society has to a greater or less extent got the root of the matter within himself; and they continue to hold fast and enjoy their liberty, not by freedom of speech merely, but by their steadfast life and energetic action as free individual men. (...)It is this individual freedom and energy of action that really constitutes the prolific source of our national growth. For it is not to one rank or class alone that this spirit of free action is confined, but it pervades all ranks and classes; perhaps its most vigorous outgrowths being observable in the commonest orders of the people.

For Smiles, self-help means individual self-determination and continuous progress. He not only made the argument that a self-oriented spirit could facilitate success but also vice versa: if individuals fail economically, this is totally due to them not having 'the right spirit'. Naturally, this is a logical fallacy: when event 'A' predicts event 'B'—e.g., education can cause individuals to get a well-paid job— this does not imply that when 'B' does not occur this must be due to 'A'—e.g., not everyone who does not have a well-paid job is uneducated. Smiles' illogical reasoning excluded the possibility that the circumstances could be so bad that people failed in a socio-economic sense, regardless of their spirit. An individual's spirit can also be influenced by Keynesian 'animal spirits'—that is, by irrational thoughts and feelings and by influences from the market that people cannot control, such as mind manipulation.

However, it seems to have been Smiles' rigid self-help fallacy that formed the cornerstone of Thatcherism and Reaganism. Thatcher had a religious belief in the self-help citizen, possibly reflecting her own perseverance of climbing up the social ladder from grocer's daughter to first British female prime minister. She stimulated a meritocratic self-help culture of taking responsibility for one's own financial, educational, and social progress by thrift and rational decision making (Jones, 2012). Similar to Smiles, she seemed to fall into the fallacious guilt-trip trap: She sketched the image of good, rational self-help citizens who did not need to depend on others, as 'there is not such a thing as society', versus bad, benefit-seeking scoundrels dependent on the state because of their irresponsible habits: 'Go back, you flower people, back where you came from, wash your hair, get dressed properly, get to work on time and stop all this whining and moaning' (Thatcher, cited in Marquand, 1988, p. 165). She strongly believed in the self-oriented citizen who could succeed only if they would be rational enough, a conviction that was eagerly taken over by tabloids condemning benefit seekers and other 'scoundrels' (Vos, Roberts, & Davies, 2019).

Smiles and Thatcher offered a functionalist version of self-help. You only have yourself to blame for any mishaps, and you should not expect society to help you. Thatcher used the concept of self-help in a functionalist way, as self-care was not merely about the care of the self for the sake of the self but was redefined in purely economic terms as self-sustenance. The self became a means to an economic end, with 'identity economics' as its culmination point (see Chapter 7).

Philosopher Michel Foucault (1976/2012) elaborated the economic–political history of 'care for the self'. Historically, self-care is related to taking seriously what our passions (*pathos*) are and what is authentically meaningful to ourselves. Thus, it is not about being a strict functionalist judge deciding what is good and what is bad and feeling guilty when we do not live the lives we want and blaming others when they are not successful. For Foucault, self-care is not merely about rational control and ascesis, but about a critical–intuitive approach, living life to the fullest, with a mild though critical listening to the totality of our experiences, including our ambiguities, paradoxes, uncertainties, and our struggle with the reality of limiting socio-economic circumstances. Similarly, for Adam Smith self-interest included a social awareness, like the Ancient Greek concept of *prudence,* and not a solipsistic just-do-it-on-your-own mentality (as he wrote in his *Moral Sentiments*, as described in Chapter 5). Philosopher Martin Heidegger (1927/1996) made a sharp distinction between different ways of relating to ourselves; he preferred the term 'self-care' over 'self-help', as this is a more holistic concept that includes the social context. Self-care can also transcend our current socio-economic circumstances to include the opportunity of using our full potential, even parts we have not explored before; thus, self-care is not functionalist and instead reaches towards social, larger, and existential–philosophical types of meaning.

Thus, self-oriented meanings are more than self-help and selfishness, which are just narrow examples. Of course, the term 'self' is used in a loose way as there may not be such a thing as a true self or an essence (Vos, 2018). Self-oriented meanings include resilience, which is the ability to cope successfully with difficult life situations with attributes such as flexibility, perseverance, and hope. This also includes self-efficacy, such as setting specific activities or goals, planning, organizing, and exercising self-discipline. To be able to effectively master the situation, individuals also have to experience self-acceptance, autonomy, and self-expression. Finally, this includes self-care, which means looking after oneself and fulfilling one's own needs to recover and continue in difficult situations.

It is this story of self-development and success that became central in neoliberalism, in contrast with moral or rational liberalism, which still focused more on other individuals and material conditions. This led to the emergence of 'the century of the self', to use the title of Adam Curtis' 2002 documentary. The birth of the discipline of psychology seems to be both the result and the cause of this self-oriented culture, with people like Sigmund Freud explaining how we could become more resilient and in control of ourselves via developing self-insights in talking therapies. This self-orientation can nowadays be found in most capitalist cultures and in individuals with strong capitalist values (see previous chapter).

Margaret Thatcher was the Iron Lady of Self-Help. The socio-economic turn towards the self and the functionalisation of self-help is possibly one of Thatcher's largest cultural legacies. In her 'pseudo-Leninist' style, she expressed this idea in strong wording, as seen above, and supported this with a restrictive social welfare system, tax reduction for higher incomes, and tax increase for lower incomes (Jones, 2012). However, this British version of the American Dream seemed to become more like a socio-economic nightmare. Thatcher's policies not only increased negative freedom, predominantly for the well-to-dos, but she also decreased the real opportunities for self-help (Farrall & Hay, 2014; Seldon & Collings, 2014). For example, her policies meant a marginal and absolute reduction in the opportunities for those with lower incomes, increased unemployment (1.5 million in 1979, 3.3 million in 1984, and 1.9 million in 1990), a slowing-down of social mobility growth, and an almost doubling of the socio-economic inequality, with the top decile in the United Kingdom owning more than half of all the wealth (Buscha & Sturgis, 2018; Major & Machin, 2018). This created the largest absolute poverty rate in Europe (28% of all children lived below the poverty line at the end of her government period; Nelson, 2006). It has been argued that Thatcher's policies had no foundations in economic research or neoliberal philosophy but merely reflected the interests and power of a small political establishment (Giddens, 1993, p. 233). However, from a meaning-oriented perspective, it was not mere cronyism of the Establishment (Jones, 2016) that caused the socio-economic nightmare: It was a self-oriented, functionalist perspective on life.

Neoconservative Social and Larger Types of Meaning

The previous chapter showed that the more capitalist a country is, the more its citizens focus on materialist, hedonist, and self-oriented types of meaning. In addition, the previous sections elaborated each of these types of meaning. Whereas neoliberalism—such as displayed by the Mont Pelerin Society, Thatcher, and Reagan—seemed to pay little attention to social and larger types of meaning, other capitalist perspectives exist that do pay attention to social and larger types of meaning in addition to the other neoliberal ideas. Among these is neoconservatism, which is a neoliberal perspective with the addition of specific types of social and larger meaning in life that is particularly oriented around American nationalism and imperialism. Several authors have argued that neoconservatism is the American variant of European neoliberalism. In contrast with the open materialist, self-oriented, and functionalist approach of neoliberalism in European countries such as the United Kingdom, the United States seems to hide capitalism behind a thin veil of social and larger types of meanings, and, therefore, preserves the term neoconservative over neoliberal Drolet, 2013).

Neoconservatism started as a response to what neoconservatives regarded a decline of social and larger types of meaning in the 1960s and 1970s, or as sociologist Leo Strauss asserted: 'the crisis of the West consists in the West's having become uncertain of its purpose' (East, 1977). He described how social movements had hijacked the term 'liberation' for hedonism, materialism, and consumerism. For Strauss, liberalism itself was in crisis as its modern form is oriented towards universal freedom that bears the intrinsic risk of extreme relativism and nihilism, making any meaning go—resulting in complete moral *laissez-faire, laissez-passer*. Strauss saw this as value-free meaninglessness and a hedonist 'permissive egalitarianism', which was just another face of the brutal nihilism expressed, for example, in Nazi and Stalinist regimes. He opposed this modern liberalism and preferred the ancient liberalism that is oriented towards human excellence and includes moral ideas about absolute good and evil. Strauss believed that the only solution was to restore vital ideas and faith from the past, such as the Greek Classics and Judeo–Christian heritage. This included a complete overhaul of the liberal education system to teach restraint and sobriety. Strauss was joined in the new right movement by many others who felt that in modern times, the meaning of community, family, and virtues was replaced with superficial types of meaning. This included conservative Catholics, evangelicals, Lawrence Mead's neo-paternalism, and the communitarian movement in social welfare (Cooper, 2017).

What types of social and larger meanings do neoconservatives promote? Family values and raising children are important, as well as following what is socially expected, social virtues, tradition, and supporting the community and the nation (Drolet, 2013). Religion, particularly Judaeo–Christian values, play an important role in this movement. Irving Kristol called this 'American bourgeois populism' (in Reflections, p. xiiii): 'fitting the individual into the American communities in such a way that this explains to the American people why they are right, and why the intellectuals are wrong'. According to Kristol, some people are wise, and some are unwise, and this difference needs to be said aloud in society. Kristol's statement was picked up by American nationalists, who considered the ultimate purpose in neoconservatism to be the promotion of the American version of democracy within and outside the United States. This means creating peace in-house, as well as promoting American business interests in other countries through military and political strength. Many neoconservatives seem to have a relatively aggressive interventionalist stance towards other cultures, such as bringing democracy or Western values in general to countries such as Iraq or Afghanistan (Drolet, 2013; Kristol, 1998).

Thus, neoconservatives do not seem to leave individuals completely free to decide for themselves which specific social and larger meanings they want to fulfill. Values such as personal growth, authenticity. and justice are excluded from the neoconservative agenda; instead, individuals are stimulated to strive for human excellence and political virtue. According to neoconservatives, it is the task of intellectuals and politicians to lead people back from their meaninglessness into the light of true virtues. Because if there is one thing that social sciences have shown, according to neoconservatives, it is that individuals often do not reason or think rationally. They require a strong state: without a Leviathan-state, individuals will act towards each other like wolves, as Thomas Hobbes and, later, Karl Schmitt showed. Therefore, Strauss argued that 'perpetual deception of the citizens by those in power is critical because they need to be led, and they need strong rulers to tell them what's good for them' (Drury, 1999). A strong hand is sometimes needed to prevent enemies attempting to negate one's lifestyle, Strauss argued in a heated debate with Schmitt in Weimar Germany.

Thus, neoconservatives promote an authoritarian type of moral monism instead of meaning-oriented pluralism. This even includes condoning materialist and self-oriented types of meaning, as long as these are for the greater good of the United States. For example, many adherents influenced George W. Bush to invade Iraq in 2003 (Drolet, 2013). Many of them continued their support, even when it became clear that the invasion was based on a lack of evidence that Iraq had weapons of mass destruction and that economic gains for American corporations had also played a role in the decision making. Such political lies are condoned for the greater good because the average citizen is seen as passive; as long as some form of democracy is restored, invasions of foreign countries are justified (this has been called a polyarchic concept of democracy; Drolet, 2013).

It seems that materialist struggles were translated into neoconservative schemas of social and larger types of meaning. For example, in the 1970s neoconservatives attacked the idea of benefits for unemployed or sick people—in line with Margaret Thatcher and her right hand, Keith Joseph—as they argued that their problem was not socio-economic in nature but moral issue; the underclass is demoralised, and this is why a culture of dependency on benefits and drugs has emerged. For example, Kristol promoted the idea of a conservative welfare state that supports the youngest and eldest individuals in society but stimulates anyone else to take up their 'moral' self-help responsibility for themselves. There is no such thing as a purely materialistic problem: almost every material situation reflects one's own morality. Similarly, neoconservatives envisioned crime control as segregating high-risk groups from the rest of society, even by the death penalty. Thus, an authoritarian tone emerged in the debate, even though there is little empirical evidence confirming that benefit seeking is a moral problem and that hard, controlling measures can improve a sense of morality and lift individuals out of poverty (Abramowitz & Withorn, 2018).

Neoconservatism seems to uniquely combine functionalism with a narrow definition of social and larger types of meaning. The movement has received significant support from evangelicals—particularly those living in the American Bible Belt (Drolet, 2013). Although evangelicalism focuses more on the social community and larger religious values than other neoconservatives, they seem to have a similar functionalist outlook on life, albeit a combined servitude to the market with servitude towards God. A good example of this is Walmart, which grew on the soil of both economic and Christian principles (Moreton, 2019). The ethics of hard-work, strict upbringing and a serving attitude fit the neoconservative trends well; thus, evangelicals have migrated to the forefront of the modern Republican party. The popularity of evangelicalism may be explained by its strong functionalist model of community building and teaching via Bible groups and evangelical outreach.

However, one may argue that functionalism distorts the social and larger types of meaning. These social and larger types of meaning seem to be more the result of mind manipulation, social control, and conformism than a belief in the inherent meaningfulness of social relationships and larger meanings. As Drolet (2012, p. 9) writes: 'History cannot be the source of moral meanings for human societies since historical progress is not moral or metaphysical progress but simply the progress of man's control.' That is, the functionalist focus on life is maintained, for example in the form of authoritarianism, strict religious hierarchies (see Chapter 5) or meaning manipulation (Chapter 11). Individuals focus on the community or on specific ethical rules because they are forced into doing so. There may be little subjective freedom and critical intuition involved in choosing these social and larger types of meaning.

This contradicts what Church reformer Martin Luther (1520/2016) wrote in his pamphlet *The freedom of the Christian*—that individuals need to have a free will to be able to choose God for His own sake and not for the sake of their being forced to choose God. Meaning cannot be imposed. Love for 'liberal democracy' cannot be imposed on the Iraqi or Afghanistan people—modernising at gunpoint (Whyte, 2018; Simons & Chifu, 2017; Roberts, 2007). An authentic decision needs to be made in freedom. Similarly, empirical studies show that the more individuals feel that they are forced into believing something is meaningful, the less meaningful and the less authentic this feels (Vos, 2018). Social and larger types of meaning seem to lose their inherent meaningfulness with a functionalist approach, as they become an empty shell around the remaining self-oriented materialist goals and meaning-manipulative techniques of American politics (as will be explained in Chapter 12). Consequently, neoconservatism seems to preserve the Capitalist Life Syndrome:

> According to neoconservatives, it is this unconditional commitment to the notion of the common good that humanises and gives meaning to the life of the individual citizen. Without this commitment, life is mere animal existence, without context or history. And it is the absence of this existential

commitment that renders liberal societies to be vulnerable to their enemies today. As Kristol argues, the liberal state defines the common good as consisting mainly of personal security under the law, personal liberty under the law, and a steadily increasing material prosperity for those who apply themselves to that end. It is, by the standards of previous civilisations, a vulgar conception of the common good: there is no high nobility of purpose, no selfless devotion to transcendental needs, no awe-inspiring heroism. (Drolet, 2012, p. 201)

One popular propagandist for neoconservatism in the field of meaning in life is Canadian psychologist Jordan Peterson. He does not hide his functionalist approach to life and even called his best-selling book *12 Rules for Life, An Antidote to Chaos*, reducing individuals to either rule followers or chaos creators. His idea of meaning seems to be the opposite of a phenomenological/critical–intuitive approach and the off-modern (Chapter 16). He searches for Aristotelean goals like human excellence, and he argues that all human actions should be oriented efficiently towards these goals as self-control, as Strauss propagated. He describes how in the universe things fall apart and culture degenerates; therefore, people have to act correctly to prevent others from collapsing, which is a highly anthropocentric perspective (Chapter 14). Thus, he offers an optimistic vision of the human potential to achieve goals, a vision that individuals suffering from the Capitalist Life Syndrome may be longing for and which may explain his popularity.

Some authoritarian trends can also be found in Peterson's work (see Chapter 12). For example, he bases his perspective of meaning on a Darwinist survival of the fittest, urging his readers to 'stand up straight with your shoulders back, fight back' and 'be aggressive enough'. Other people do not seem inherently meaningful in Peterson's universe, and people are stimulated to 'make friends with people who want the best for you', ultimately a self-oriented reduction of social relationships. Subsequently, based on his neoconservative rules, he accuses women, transgenders, and left-leaning students of not being aggressive enough. Thus, Peterson seems to offer a narrow personal interpretation of meaning in life and to ignore the large body of research literature on the wider plurality of meanings and the evolutionary necessity of morality and mutual aid.

Conclusions

The previous chapter showed that the more capitalist a country is, the more individuals focus on materialist, hedonist, and self-oriented types of meaning. Naturally, there are exceptions to this generalisation, and many neoconservatives and religious individuals will, for instance, stand for social and larger types of meaning. As Chapter 6 showed, since the 2007/2008 financial crisis, there has been renewed interest in social and larger types of meanings in the form of moral and meaning-oriented economics. The focus of this new trend does not lie on nationalism, American hegemony or religiosity like in neoconservatism but in nature, real care for other people, authenticity. and self-realisation. Furthermore, this new trend adds a critical–intuitive approach to doing justice to individual differences, in contrast with neoconservatism. This trend indicates that Strauss' basic assumption was wrong, and that the only possible answer to the purposelessness of society is to impose a nationalistic hegemony on people via a strong state. It is possible to develop a society that has a strong focus on social and larger types of meaning but is not based on neoconservatism.

Key Points

1. Individuals often experience multiple types of meaning in daily life.
2. Individuals in capitalist countries often focus on materialist, hedonist, and self-oriented types of meaning.
3. The 2007/2008 financial meltdown may be understood as the result of a culture oriented towards materialist and self-oriented meanings, particularly greed.
4. American neoconservatism may be understood as the addition of a limited range of social and larger types of meaning to the capitalist focus on materialist/hedonist/self-oriented meanings.

Chapter 10

The Capitalist Approach to Meaning: Functionalism

Capitalist discourse is something that is madly astute. It works like clockwork, couldn't work better. It's so good at getting consumed that it is consuming itself. (Lacan, 1972, conference lecture, University of Milan)

Historical Context

The 'Great War' ended only a decade ago, Stalin killed the people's hopes for freedom during the Russian Revolution by reigning with steel power, brown shirts have started marching on German streets, and fascists have only just been defeated in the London battle of Cable Street. Meanwhile, people in America seem to have become complacent with their selfish materialistic and hedonistic lifestyle, taking liberty for granted and uncritically allowing new forms of tyranny to emerge, as Alexis de Tocqueville predicted a century ago (1835/2003). The world is in crisis, and this is primarily a crisis of our perspectives on liberty.

This seemed to be the common feeling among the 26 men in the conference room in Paris on 26 August 1938. This was also possibly one of the few things they could agree on, as they differed on many other topics such as the name of their new approach. Finally, the term 'neoliberalism' won, to show that they stood in the historic tradition of the liberal fight for freedom, albeit with their own new definition.

Another topic they agreed on was their fight against statist doctrines, which Lippmann (1938) described as:

Their [statist] doctrine is that disorder and misery can be overcome only by more and more compulsory organization. Their promise is that through the power of the state men can be made happy. Throughout the world, in the name of progress, men who call themselves communists, socialists, fascists, nationalists, progressives, and even liberals, are unanimous in holding that government with its instruments of coercion must, by commanding the people how they shall live, direct the course of civilization and fix the shape of things to come. They believe in the overhead planning and control of economic activity. (pp. 3–4)

The Lippmann Colloquium was named after the author of this citation from the book *The Good Society*, Walter Lippmann. In this book, he wrote that just like innovations in machine technics—such as the recent inventions of electricity, radio, and phone—new inventions had to be made in political technics. The old political technic involved governments imposing top-down control on people, as in the Russian plan economy or the Nazi war economy. The American government had responded similarly to the Big Depression: Roosevelt's New Deal included an increase in regulations, financial reforms, public work projects, subsidies, and benefits. Roosevelt used the term 'liberal' for this political programme, but Lippmann questioned this term as he felt that the freedom of the individual was impinged on by the increase in government control. This is the same old paradoxical political technics that he saw with Hitler, Stalin, and even his friend Keynes: attempts to create freedom by limiting freedom. He thought that these politicians had forgotten the freedom that had been gained by political changes since Medieval feudalism, such as 'liberation from the bondage of authority, monopoly, and special privilege'.

Thus, Lippmann feared the increase of authoritarian collectivism and an increase in state size due to people forgetting the real meaning of freedom. To reinstate the liberal philosophy, new political technics had to be developed. But these technics could not be based on the idea of a rational government and society as the rational liberals had believed. All rulers, administrators, and citizens are fallible and irrational beings: 'They are men, and so their powers are limited.' Society may also have become too massive to control because of the increase in scale created by radio, newspapers, cars, and trains. Like adherents of the Austrian School and the new discipline of psychology, Lippmann criticised the idea that economic behaviour could be predicted and rationally controlled since most of public life is irrational, habitual, customary, and unconscious. The free mind cannot and should never be controlled by others; we are all driven by a will to be free. The freedom of the state is a means to the freedom of the individual. All participants of the *Colloque Lippmann* seemed to agree with this Lippmannian analysis of the world crisis as a problem of statism and irrationalism.

What were the new neoliberal technics that they proposed during the Colloquium? Although they wanted a small state, they refuted the idea that the government should remain totally passive and silent because individual citizens cannot be totally trusted due to their irrationality. The state should not allow '*laissez-faire, laissez-passer*'—for example, by accepting any criminal or irrational behaviour. The first technic that a state must offer is setting the basic conditions that individuals need to be able to act freely in the market—for example, by making contracts enforceable by law, protecting private property, insuring financial risks, minimising monopolies, regulating bankruptcy, and organising and inspecting the market. Tax income should not be handed as a financial gift to poor people but should be used to improve the conditions of the market, such as offering public health, education, and public works. Thus, the state should guarantee the negative freedom of individuals—that is, freedom from oppression. This implied that the state should also not give positive interventions for individuals, such as offering basic income, housing, or jobs like in a planned economy—as this would imply an impingement on individual freedom by the state. Individuals should be free to decide their own housing, job, etc.

Most Colloquium members agreed with this first state technic, and many agreed with Lippmann's proposed second technic, although some were uncertain or opposed it (1938, p. 231):

> The economy requires not only that the quality of the human stock, the equipment of men for life, shall be maintained at some minimum of efficiency, but that the quality should be progressively improved. To live successfully in a world of the increasing interdependence of specialized work requires a continual increase of adaptability, intelligence, and of enlightened understanding of the reciprocal rights and duties, benefits and opportunities, of such a way of life.

Lippmann meant that for individuals to be able to progress in their use of their freedom, they need to completely adjust to the needs of the market—for example, via flexibility of the labour market and an education system focused on economic needs.

Thus, neoliberal state technics actively seek to re-form the social order so that individuals will fulfill the needs of the market (Lippmann, 1938). This meant that the individual becomes a variable in the function of the state. Ultimately, the philosophy of neoliberalism that started around the Lippmann Colloquium is a functionalist philosophy of life, alienating individuals from their own meaning and subjecting their personal meaning to the meaning of the market (cf. Mirowksi & Plehwe, 2009/2015). As with national socialism and Stalinism, individuals became a function of the neoliberal imagination. Lippmann's proposal of mind manipulation seems to infringe on the freedom of individuals and, therefore, appears inconsistent with his idea of the freedom of the individual. However, this little impingement on individual freedom is for the benefit of the greater good of the free market and the wealth of the nation—a small cost for a large benefit. As Colloquium participant Marjolin argued, neoliberals did not 'favour freedom in and of itself. If we are liberals, it is because we think that freedom must make it possible to realize certain values: achieve the maximum of social justice and defend [ourselves] against external aggressions.' Thus, for several Colloquium participants, the concept of freedom had lost its inherent meaningfulness and become a variable in a neoliberal function. Whereas rational liberalism would sacrifice everything to secure individual freedom, neoliberalism would sacrifice everything, including the individual, for the functioning market. The symbol of individual freedom became more important than real individual freedom. Or as Slavoj Zizek said cheekily about the doctrine of neoliberalism: 'You are free to do anything as long as it involves shopping' (Mirowksi & Plehwe, 2009/2015, p. 321).

Underlying the discourse of the Lippmann Colloquium is an implicit disdain for the ordinary citizen, worker, and consumer, who allegedly cannot cope with their individual freedom. It seemed that many participants agreed with De Tocqueville's criticism of traditional liberalism as inherently leading to complacency and mediocrity (1835/2003). One of the Colloquium participants, Michael Polanyi, argued that

> the mental derangement that threatens our civilization stems from a state of permanent perplexity, in which society's frame of mind becomes more and more prone to civil unrest. Individuals seek a purpose and are profoundly frustrated by the invisibility of the hand that guides them in a market-based system. The lack of clear directed purpose leaves individuals befuddled and perplexed, in contrast to the clear, purposeful actions demanded of individuals in centrally planned regimes. As a result, the individual in a market economy is plunged into perplexity with regard to the scope of his social duties. Deeply seeking a purpose, and finding it intangible in the liberal economic order, man embraces illiberal movements that promise clear directed actions.

Von Mises agreed that 'the masses have certain penchant for cruelty, revenge and even sadism', which Ortega y Gasset underlined by speaking about 'a revolt of the masses against liberalism' (Reinhoudt & Audier, 2018, p. 28). The new liberalism that the Colloquium was discussing should answer this moral decline, and Lippmann concluded that they had 'to play their role in a decisive struggle for the defence of civilisation, in re-establishing order in the minds of man so that they may formulate their individual wills clearly' (Reinhoudt & Audier, p. 110).

Thus, the Colloquium participants distrusted the concrete individual but trusted the abstract market forces. An elitist version of the Enlightenment Ideal can be read in their discussions, where it was proposed that the Colloquium participants knew better than the rest of the population how to 're-establish order in the minds of man'. Experts on the Invisible Hand, such as successful business leaders and economists, should guide ordinary people in the right direction of what is meaningful for them. Thus, the neoliberal state technics involve functionalisers, people who make others a more efficient variable in the societal function via neoliberal education and meaning manipulation, and the functionalized, people who are being manipulated.

As argued in Chapter 5, the belief in the goodness of the market and the natural better-ness of market leaders is a neoliberal imagination and symbol. As several speakers argued in the Colloquium, not enough ordinary people seem to believe in this, and therefore political technics should be used to 'educate' people—that is, to manipulate them. Ultimately, the neoliberal order in society can only survive by imposing the neoliberal imagination and symbols on people via 're-establishing order in the minds of man'. It remains unclear to which extent mind manipulation is allowed or even needed in the neoliberal state according to the Colloquium participants. The absolute minimum seemed clear, as they seemed to agree that explicit propaganda like under Stalin or Hitler should not be allowed. However, the absence of an explicit discussion regarding to what extent states can manipulate individual minds is telling, particularly as Lippmann had written about the role of journalism, and the books from Bernays about *Propaganda* were ranking high on the best-selling book lists. Possibly, the Colloquium participants were not aware of the extent to which people can be manipulated in subtle ways, as we are nowadays more aware of how, for example, Cambridge Analytica has used Facebook to subliminally nudge people to vote for Brexit and Trump. Possibly, the Colloquium participants believed in the strength of individuals to counter negative mind manipulation, although this is inconsistent with their general disdain for ordinary workers. Possibly, they did not see the negative effects as, for example, Lippmann (2018, 2017a) had a Romantic ideal about professional journalism being able to tell readers what is really going on in society. Whatever the reason is that the limitations of mind manipulation were ignored during this first discussion on neoliberalism, the emergence of neoliberal imaginations has caused the growth of a large and professional mind manipulation industry (Chapter 11).

The Lippmann Colloquium provides an insight into the changing lights in economics, although this group did not have an immediate impact because WWII broke out. However, the Colloquium's spirit can be read in the 1944 publication of Von Hayek's *Road to Serfdom*, which was written in the heat of the war against fascism. Like Lippmann, Hayek argued that modern societal crises are caused by state interventions. He also argued that state planning inevitably leads to totalitarianism because it requires 'that the will of a small minority be imposed upon the people'. The state should only exist to guarantee the functioning of the markets, with the meaning of both states and citizens reduced to market functions. Although less explicit than Lippmann, Hayek also suggested the need for political technics to educate the population and guide their meanings in the direction of the market. Hayek's book received much criticism, for example, by claiming that planning *must* lead to oppression, even though that may be merely one *possibility* among many (Wootton, 1946) since empirical research suggests that social-welfare states even outperform free-market economics (Sachs, 2006, 2006a). However, *Road to Serfdom* meant that neoliberalism was not going to leave the public debate and the political imagination.

Three years later, Von Hayek invited participants from the Lippmann Colloquium to join another meeting with colleagues to discuss the state of liberalism in Mont Pelerin near Montreux, Switzerland. Although there was a large diversity of opinions, a common vision of what came to be known as The Mont Pelerin Society confirmed the quartet of Lippmann's and Hayek's theories: anti-collectivism, small state, political technics, and condescension towards the average citizen (Mirowski & Plehwe, 2009/2015; Hartwell, 1995). Ultimately, they wanted to rescue 'the central values of civilisation'—that is, freedom of the individual and more particular, the freedom of individuals in the market. However, participants disagreed about the extent to which governments should be active and aggressive; particularly in Germany, Ordoliberals such as Rustow believed strongly that the state should actively order and regulate individuals to safeguard the market function (Dardot & Laval, 2009/2017). Many other institutions, research, and lobby groups emerged from the Mont Pelerin Society. Many members would become crucial advisors of politicians such as Ronald Reagan and Margaret Thatcher, whose policies were focused on decreasing the dependency of individuals on the state while increasing the use of meaning manipulation technics (see chapter 6).

Definitions

My first holiday job as a 14-year-old started at the conveyor belt. A big stumping machine dropped pancakes, and I had to collect six pancakes and put these in a plastic package while my colleague at the end of the belt put all pancake packages in a box. My manual actions adjusted quickly to the tempo of the conveyor belt. I became one with the automated process and reached a state of mindlessness and self-alienation due to the repetitive movement: the boundary between me and machine fell away in my experience, and I lost all sense of self and time. My flow became so efficient that I even had more than a second break after each package that I finished, and my floor manager complimented me.

However, at the end of the afternoon, a manager in a grey white-lined suit visited the factory hall. Without talking with employees or looking them in their eyes, he noted their manual actions. When he looked at my hands, he responded with a shock as he saw the missing fingers at my left hand; this was how I was born, even though it did not affect my functioning in daily life or in this factory. 'Hey, you,' he shouted at me over the banging and hissing noises of the machines, 'you cannot work here because of your hand. You're fired!' I looked desperately at my floor manager, who had just complimented me for my swift work, but he quickly turned his head away.

I had lost my job because the higher manager assumed that I could not function well, even without asking me or my floor manager about my actual functioning. My body had become a cog in the pancake machine, an anonymous function in his managerial eyes. I was quickly introduced to the Human Resources Manager, who explained her role as managing the human resources like floor managers overlook material resources. In her explanation, employees were just another type of capital, a potential to efficient making money that she could easily replace for a more perfect resource—with ten fingers. She added: 'You should be happy that you got fired because you can find a better job elsewhere; the work here is boring.' Thus, not only had my body become an extension of the machine, even my thoughts and feelings had become manipulatable and replaceable variables in their economic function.

Functionalism is the process that robs individuals of their inherent meaningfulness and renders them to a function of a larger social structure, economic system, or state. Individuals are not treated as aims in themselves, but as abstract and disposable variables in a larger function. This goes back to the etymology of capitalism, whose literal translation is: the science that regards objects and people as movable properties, such as 'caput', livestock (Chapter 2). I did not have meaning in myself; my frustration was a disruption for the HR manager. I derive my meaning from a larger goal. The complexity and pluralities of my meaning are reduced to this economic goal of packing as many pancakes as possible and making as much profit as possible for the company, regardless of what my job subjectively meant for me. I had been functionalized; my body had become a replaceable part of the pancake factory, and I was not treated as a person with inherent meaningfulness.

Functionalisation of Bodies
How is this separation between being a body for the system and subjective meaning possible? Both Jesus and philosophers such as Aristotle have used the metaphor of the body, where all parts are related in a hierarchy as, for example, the hand serves the head. In some traditional social societies, individuals were not seen as a goal in themselves but had to fulfill the position that they were allocated at the social–cosmic–divine ladder like a farmer was expected to farm and if farming was not be successful, he would be deemed meaningless (Vos, 2017). At the end of the Middle Ages, the social hierarchy disappeared as Enlightened philosophers and Reformist theologians started to question the higher cosmic–divine position of the clergy and political leaders. A new hierarchy emerged within people: the difference between body and mind. As philosopher Rene Descartes wrote, there is a separation between our bodily experiences and our thinking; I could doubt the existence of my body but not the existence of my thinking ('I think; therefore I am'). His contemporaries started to see the mind as a little man, homunculus, that controlled the body like the control panel of a machine. This body-machine should be trained as the slave of the homunculus. Thus, first the body and the mind were separated, and then the body was regarded the slave of the mind. This separated the embodied reality from our imaginations and symbols and created 'the fiction of the thinkable world' (Steinberg, 2005).

Functionalisation of People

Some people are better than others at controlling their body with their mind, and some people are guided by better values than others. This is what some self-acclaimed Enlightened thinkers believed. These Enlightened individuals, the functionalisers, should guide the unenlightened: they should teach them the right ideas and the right way to control and manipulate their bodies, for example, in workhouses for the poor. Thus, the bodies of ordinary people became slaves to the ideas of a so-called Enlightened Elite. This enslavement of bodies was ultimately for the benefit of the greater good that the Enlightened had determined, such as the wealth of nations. It was good for the overall wealth of everyone that factory workers had to almost kill their bodies in their work for a low wage. It was good for unenlightened individuals and for their civilisation in Africa that Western colonisers and slave tradesmen were so kind as to help them. *Thus, they explained.* The bodies of ordinary individuals became a function of the industry, just as along the conveyor belt the hands of the factory worker become a symbolic extension of the machine (see next sections for references).

Functionalisation of Slaves

The functionalisation of bodies and people seems to underlie the large-scale slave trade and colonialism that kings and tradesmen committed themselves to from the 16th century onwards. Whereas the lives of certain humans had been regarded as meaningless when they did not fit the medieval social–cosmic–divine order, they were still not deemed meaningful in the functionalist era. The social order was replaced by a functionalist order with self-acclaimed functionalisers at the top specifying what function individuals had to fulfill, based on a narcissistic version of Enlightenment ideals. Whereas slavery previously had been justified by speaking about slaves as part of the natural order of the universe, slavery started to be seen as crucial for the economy and good for slaves as they were given the opportunity of a well-disciplined life.

For example, in the 17th century, the Dutch West India Company started to use Cape Coast Castle in what is now Ghana to collect slaves bought from local tribes and to prepare them for transport to their colonies in America. The underground dungeon in this fortress was a human petri dish, sorting out the weak from the strong slaves by giving limited food and water and letting the weakest die before being shipped off across the Atlantic. This dark hole of terror and death stood in direct juxtaposition to the lavish European living quarters and commanding offices.

The arguments from some white abolitionists were still functionalist, as they merely described how the 'functioning' of the slaves had been misrepresented; they did not speak about the inherent meaningfulness of each human being and their right to freely determine their own functions. For example, Quaker Anthony Benezet wrote after years of teaching black people that 'the notion entertained by some, that the blacks are inferior *in their capacities*, is a vulgar prejudice'. Captain William

Wilberforce wondered in 1789 whether 'slave trade would help their civilization'. Slavery was regarded as not functioning well, but the underlying idea that human beings could be regarded as variables in an economic function remained unquestioned. A more radical abolition movement seemed impossible during the American Civil war because of the existing functionalist perspectives and the role of capitalists who depended on modern forms of slavery. Consequently, functionalism and slavery has continued in many forms, ranging from the Nazi final solution of extinguishing Jewish and other 'inferior' people, to today's wage slaves in factories of international fashion brands.

Criticism of Functionalism

In Europe, a more radical sentiment emerged, questioning the idea that humans can be functionalized—i.e. enslaved—in any form. As Schopenhauer wrote (1851/2000): 'Poverty and slavery are only two forms of the same thing, the essence of which is that a man's energies are expended for the most part not on his own behalf but that of others; the outcome being partly that he is overloaded with work, partly that his needs are very inadequately met.' During the 19th century, many philosophers felt that this functionalist world view did not do justice to the lived experiences and inherent meaningfulness of individuals. These so-called life philosophers, such as Schopenhauer, Nietzsche, and Dilthey, put the 'lived experience' of individuals central: that is, the irreducible subjective experience of the totality, complexity, and dynamics of life, where body and mind are not simple things that can be separated, and where individuals are done injustice when they become part of someone else's function. Life is not a mechanical process but evolves organically. Life philosophers, whose ideas were later taken over by phenomenologists and existential philosophers, tried to do justice to the irreducible lived experiences of meaning in life. Thus, these philosophers and sociologists started to question the functionalising spirit of capitalism. Their most popular explanations will now be described: 'rationalization', 'commodification', 'technology', and 'governmentality'.

Rationalization

Rationalisation is a sociological term that means the replacement of traditions, values, and emotions as motivation for behaviour with concepts based on rationality and reason. For example, a bureaucratic government is based on the rational idea of efficiency. Max Weber (2013) believed that the emergence of Calvinist religion meant that people shifted their focus in life towards a rational means of economic gain to deal with their 'salvation anxiety', even though later they abandoned their religion but remained rational. Comparative economic studies have rejected Weber's thesis, as religion only seemed to play a dominant role in the specific geographical region where he had done his research but not elsewhere (Tubadii, Moeller, & Nijkamp, 2014;

Stasavage, 2014; Blum & Dudley, 2001). However, many authors agree with Weber's explanation that people did not only become secular, but their full perspective on society became more rational. Both capitalist enterprises and bureaucratic state apparatus evolved according to rational models. Weber described this process as the institutionalization of purposive, rational economic and administrative action. This implied the transformation of a traditional approach to society, with pre-given social hierarchies, to nations organised according to rational laws. Similarly, Adorno and Horkheimer (1944/1997) have criticized the societal process of rationalisation, to which they attribute 'the sinking of mankind into a new kind of barbarism' instead of 'entering into a truly human condition'.

However, the concept of rationalisation seems to have fallen out of fashion in 21st century sociology, as the term 'ratio' seems ambiguous and unclear and has been criticized not only by neoliberals but also by the Frankfurt School (Habermas, 1985). In our daily life, most of our actions are not explicitly based on rational reasoning but on an intuitive and non-reflected understanding of our life-world and the meanings that we share with other people.

Commodification

Commodification means that goods, services, ideas, and people are not seen as meaningful and ends in themselves but as commodities or objects of trade. For Karl Marx, a commodity is always the product of human labour offered for sale on the market. Commodification involves a complex process that is not only influenced by economic and technical factors but also by political factors such as property rights and access to resources. Commodity fetishism means that social relationships do not have meaning in themselves anymore—for example, I love my co-worker not for being the person who she is but for her economic function, which can be exchanged in market trade; treat my co-worker not as an end in herself, but as an instrument in my job.

This concept of commodification solved the old economic debate over the difference between value and price and between meaning and money. The meaning household of an individual cannot be simply reduced to its use value—for example, using my colleague for my ends or exchange value, such as selling a slave or a football player. Price is then the *monetary expression* of exchange value, although exchange value is not always expressed in monetary terms. According to the labour theory of value, product values in an open market are regulated by the time that a worker needs to produce them; thus workers create the surplus value of the products and services that can be sold for money on the market. Commodification, therefore, is a functionalist transformation of goods, services, ideas, and people into real, imaginary, or symbolic material. An example of becoming real material is the football player whose body is used for the club owner. Imaginary material is an imagined exchange value, such as the banknote that gives an imaginary 'IOU'. A symbol is a powerful imagine that has started to become meaningful in itself and causes actions, such as the strong symbolic power of money.

Although commodification is always functionalist, functionalisation is not always commodified, as not all functionalist approaches focus on material or price. Money also played a relatively small role in feudal society, even though feudalism was not only traditional but also functionalist in nature, just as the meaning of individuals was only regarded as their function in the social–cosmic–divine order. For example, a peasant did his job on the land of the lord not necessarily as a deliberate exchange or with the expectation of something in return—money or protection by the lord—as many historians seem to assume; peasants simply fulfilled their role because this is simply what was expected. There was no surplus that workers added to the land on which they worked since their products and services were immediately taken and used by the lord or by themselves. Only when technological innovations increased the productivity of the land and the outcome of the labour, did workers add surplus value with the time and resources that they invested in the product, which they could exchange on the market for something else. Thus, the Marxist concept of commodification combines functionalism, materialism, and monetarism.

Technology
Technology is the term that Martin Heidegger used to describe the spirit of modern economics (Heidegger,1954/1977; Eldred, 2005). Our technological approach to life transforms objects, humans, and our full world from having meaning *among themselves* to having meaning in their *use for something else*. For example, whereas a landscape was an idyllic experience for the Romantic, it became a resource for making money for the industrial capitalist. The world has been transformed into objects functioning for something else. What happens with technological developments and seeing the world as Cartesian machines is that our ontology changes: that is, we start to understand phenomena from the perspective of their technological functioning ('present at hand') and not from our daily practice and interaction within our life-world ('at-handness'). Whereas, for example, Aristotle looked at phenomena from the totality of four different perspectives—*aitia*—this potentiality became reduced to the perspective of *actualitas*: We see all phenomena as material standing ready for use to achieve material–economic goals.

Thus, the essence of technology is the set-up (*ge-stell*): In our technological perspective, everything is set up for something; it is on standby with the possibility of being ordered for another goal (Eldred, 2005). This implies that the large potential that humans have is reduced to being on standby for something to happen, instead of humans being treated as meaningful and as meaning creators in themselves. Technology strips humans of their unique ability to ask themselves questions and change their perspectives towards their meaning; instead of freely experiencing their own wide potential of meaning in life, they are set up for something. Individuals are no longer aware of their own meaning household but have become part of the larger meaning household of their socio-economic–political set-up. Consequently, the totality of being human and the reality of our life-world are reduced to mere imaginary or symbolic functions. This process is relatively close to Marx's concept of commodification (Hemming, 2013; Marcuse, 2005; Eldred, 2005). This Heideggerian concept of technology would later become the core of Michel Foucault's concept of governmentality.

Self-Governmentality

Self-governmentality is the term that Foucault developed at the end of his life, and which others such as Nikolas Rose have elaborated. This neologism combines governing ('*gouverner*') and mentality ('*mentalité*'), and thus describes 'the "how" of governing, that is, the calculated means of directing how we behave and act' (Jeffrys & Sigley, 2009) or the 'government rationality' (Gordon, 1991, p.13). More general, governmentality includes all techniques and strategies by which a society is rendered governable. 'Government refers to more or less systematized, regulated and reflected modes of power (a "technology") that go beyond the spontaneous exercise of power over others, following a specific form of reasoning (a "rationality") which defines the telos of action or the adequate means to achieve it' (Lemke, 2014).

The term 'government' refers in modern language to actions of the state or administration, but Foucault traces its etymological roots to self-control, guidance for children, soul direction, etc. Thus, governmentality means actions by the state and actions by the self. Foucault is interested in how the modern state, in its neoliberal forms, has developed and how this development is intertwined with the development of the subject, and particularly by self-governmentality or technologies of the self. Just as state techniques control individuals to attain maximum wealth for the nation, individuals use techniques of the self to control their bodies, minds, and lifestyle to achieve well-being. Although state governmentality and self-governmentality have possibly always influenced each other, in the neoliberal state these approaches strongly intertwine. Von Mises wrote that it is not by nature that men know how to conduct—govern—themselves but only thanks to education and to the market offering Lippmannian 'political technics'.

Foucault describes how in the neoliberal imagination, the retreat of state government, in rhetoric such as the small, lean, fit, or flexible state, is paralleled by an increase in self-governmentality. This not only implies Smilean self-help but citizens looking after their own social risks such as illness, unemployment, and poverty—*help yourself economically, but the state also won't rescue you!* This also implies that the individual takes over the state role of controlling social behaviour by policing one's own thoughts and feelings. Self-care does not merely mean focusing on a materialistic type of meaning—e.g., getting enough money to buy food, clothes, and shelter; it also implies the totality of political technologies that individuals impose on themselves to adjust and control themselves to fit the socio-economic system. Thus, neoliberalism increases the functionalist approach to life, although the focus shifts away from the state to the individual as functionaliser; that is, whereas citizens were treated as a manipulatable variable in the larger state function, they start to manipulate themselves. Neo-liberalism implies both an increased functionalist approach to life as well as a shift from society to individual. Whereas totalitarian regimes impose top-down external power on their citizens—for example by using violence—in neoliberalism there is a bottom-up process by which citizens impose internal power on themselves. This is internalised fascism: Individuals develop oppressive attitudes of power against themselves and others, and thereby support the authoritarian power of the Establishment.

For example, many American states have seen a 'self-esteem movement' since the 1990s, which attributes social problems such as unemployment, alcoholism, and criminality to a lack of self-esteem. Naturally, this is reminiscent of Smilean–Thatcherite–Reaganite self-help citizens. Self-esteem is a technology in the sense that it is specialised knowledge of how to esteem ourselves to estimate, calculate, measure, evaluate, discipline, and judge ourselves (Cruikshank, 1999). However, what happened in reality is that although these social topics were previously the state's responsibility, individuals started to focus on their own role and to continuously assess themselves to check whether they are not causing social problems. Thus, socio-economic inequality, racism, and capitalism are not seen as the root of problems; rather, the management of the self is. The zenith of self-governmentality is the self-help culture with book titles such as 'Get Rich in Seven Steps' and 'Get Slim in Five Weeks', thus making the state obsolete in offering people financial security and food regulations about fat and sugar. This self-oriented functionalist variation of Lippmannian 'political technics', 'anthropotechnics,' makes us try to do better and better according to the adage 'you must change yourself' (Sloterdijk,2010). Thus, this self-esteem culture projects self-oriented and materialist success as the ultimate ethical goals; being jobless, obese, or poor becomes a moral problem caused by a lack of self-discipline. Ultimately, this implies that an individual's meaning in life is not independent on the functioning of the state, as liberals had imagined, but it becomes a variable in the function of the socio-economic system.

Functionalisation of Human Rights

"I was just following orders. An order is an order." Adolf Eichmann explained to his judges that he was just coordinating the train system and that he could not reject the orders from his commanders. He presented himself as a good man, a loving husband and father, who just followed orders. His plea of following superiors' orders was echoed by many other Nazis and collaborators during the post-WWII Nuremberg Trials. Seen from a phenomenological perspective, they argued that their individual meaning in life had been completely determined by the social structure, the functionalist spirit, and the mind manipulation. They were the victims of the spirit of their time, not the aggressor. Is this on a fundamental level what Hannah Arendt

(1964) wrote about the banality of evil: that any ordinary human is vulnerable to be swayed by the perspectives of their time? That their evil self-governmentality was the result of the evil government? That their immoral meaning in life was caused by their immoral culture? Did Foucault not suggest that individuals can never be free from biopolitics? That it isn't even in our sense of freedom to deviate from the socio-politically dominant perspectives determined by our social context? Can I only be free when I have first learned to be free?

Or is the alternative true, and is each individual free and able to determine his or her own perspectives and decisions at all times and in all places? This is what Eichmann's judges assumed when they did not accept his plea of superior orders, as Nuremberg Principle IV stated that: 'The fact that a person acted pursuant to order of his Government or of a superior does not relieve him from responsibility under international law, provided a moral choice was, in fact, possible to him.' Thus, they believed that each individual is responsible. Eichmann had had countless opportunities to resist, even without risking his own life. His responsibility even reached beyond his own life, as the value of millions of human beings could not be reduced to the function of him doing his job or trying to survive. Other people were inherently meaningful in and of themselves and should never have been functionalized by his superiors nor by him.

The post-WWII soul searching gave rise to the idea that functionalisation per se was the problem and that individuals should be legally protected against becoming functionalised. Therefore, the first sentence of the *preamble* of the Universal Declaration of Human Rights in 1948 states that 'recognition of the inherent dignity and of the equal and inalienable rights of all members of the human family is the foundation of freedom, justice and peace in the world.' All human beings are born free and equal in dignity and rights; have the right to life, liberty, and security of person; and cannot be held in slavery or servitude. Everyone has the right to freedom of thought, conscience, and religion.

Did the legalisation of human rights mean the end of functionalisation? No. The anti-functionalist human rights seem to have become functionalised themselves: They have become a bureaucratic tick-the-box exercise and not an active campaign for social justice, starting from the inherent meaningfulness of individuals (Moyn, 2018). As research indicates, human rights gave governments and companies the legal justification to continue their functionalist approach, although the functionalisation has gone underground, behind the sight of the public and inside our minds by Foucauldian self-governmentality. For example, on the surface, governments like that in the United Kingdom seem to tick all human-rights boxes, but they have become more concerned with doing the minimum instead of actively lifting individuals out of poverty and empowering people. That is, the damning 2018 report from the United Nations described how the post-2008 crash austerity measures have hit the poorest unequally hard, even though the government did not seem to have violated human rights on paper as they offered the bare minimum of benefits and housing.

Consequently, the United Kingdom has become the most unequal Western country with the largest group of socio-economically deprived individuals stuck in a poverty trap (Vos, Roberts, & Davies, 2019).

The subscription of countries to human rights has been questioned by politicians worldwide, ranging from the United Kingdom to the United States. Subsequent British PMs Theresa May and Boris Johnson have pleaded to step out of the Convention of Human Rights and to exit the European Union, as they argue that this will help British companies get rid of European regulations and bureaucracies (*The Independent*, 18/01/2019, 24/11/2019). May said that such laws and regulations should be given up to make the market more flexible and appealing for new companies. Ultimately this would improve the overall competitiveness and wealth of the British economy, and thus the post-individual-rights market that May imagined would ultimately be good for all, including workers because it would improve employment. Similarly, the Human Rights Watch Report 2019 described how under president Trump, the 'United States continued to move backward on human rights at home and abroad' by passing 'laws, implementing regulations, and carrying out policies that violate or undermine human rights', such as 'reducing over-incarceration in the United States, implementing an array of anti-immigration policies, and working to undermine a national insurance program that helps Americans obtain affordable health care'. Examples of policies and practices that seem to violate or limit human rights include harsh criminal sentencing, racial disparities and policing, poverty, increasing numbers of hate crimes, and violation of rights of immigrants, refugees, and women. Trump justifies these changes with economic figures: 'America is being respected again, and America is winning again, because we are finally putting America first' (White House Briefing, 27/07/2018). The wealth of America is more important than the rights of individual Americans? Individuals need to be sacrificed for the wider wealth?

Thus, it seems that political leaders on both sides of the Atlantic Ocean project a functionalist perspective in which individual rights need to be sacrificed to function for the greater good. May, Johnson, and Trump seem to justify their actions as following neoliberal orders: they obey the market. This seems to contradict the post-WWII spirit of the Human Rights Convention. The Devil's Advocate from the Nuremberg Trials may ask: Could Trump, May, and Johnson's pleas regarding their superior orders from the market pass Nuremberg II standards?

McDonaldisation

The society that May and Trump imagine is highly functionalist or, in simpler words: McDonaldised. The previous sections offered macro-economic explanations of functionalism. Functionalisation does not merely affect our professional life but all aspects of our being, including our family and home life, our psychological well-being, our understanding of knowledge and truth, and psychotherapy (Rose, 1989). How can functionalism be characterised in our daily life-world? How does functionalism rob individuals of their meaningfulness and render them to a larger function? What could I tell my 14-year old self in the pancake factory? To answer such questions, sociologist George Ritzer (1992) simplified his explanation of functionalism by calling this 'the McDonaldisation' of society. Although this simplification lacks some depth, it is useful for educational purposes. The following is an overview of Ritzer's examples, along with other examples based on the literature review from Chapter 7. Within capitalist systems, meaning is approached in the following functionalist ways:

Anonymous abstraction.
The individual becomes an anonymous abstract phenomenon within the larger structure. For example, McDonald's does not have waiters; customers need to queue at the counter or digitally order their food, and become a number that is called out when food is ready.

Predictability
The flipside of anonymous abstraction is predictability by standardised and uniform services. Wherever a client visits a McDonalds, they will receive approximately the same type of products and services. It is this predictability that has made the yellow "M" one of the world's best-recognised symbols.

Goal-orientation
Individuals have a function towards a larger goal that lies outside themselves or their current situation. McDonald's offers the option to get your hunger satisfied, and if you are not hungry, they will make you feel hungry by the idealised pictures of delicious food on the wall. The goal of the employee is to make money for the company's shareholders.

Maximisation
As the advertisement from Pepsi Max suggests, *Live life to the max!* Whatever you do, do it to the max: get the highest educational degree or their highest position in your field, and as long as you have not achieved these positions you are a failure and have something to strive for. Meaning becomes a structurally unfulfillable desire. Do not order a BigMac, but a triple burger!

Efficiency and Efficiency Improvement (Continuous Progress)
You should try to get to your highest goal as quickly as possible with the least number of resources. Efficiency at McDonald's means that every aspect of the organization is geared toward minimising time.

Social Control

A core characteristic of companies such as McDonald's is that all human aspects are standardised, put in uniform, and stripped of their human uniqueness and variability. For example, several court cases have been lost by employees wanting to look different by having piercings or wearing a burqa. Social control also implies the use of carrots and sticks, rewards and punishments, even though research shows that this simplistic idea of social control is ineffective (Kohn, 1999).

Physical Control

The body has become an object of control that we try to master in our gym and running exercises. Foucault connected technologies of the self with biopolitics— that is, with submission to a larger goal. McDonald's employees are expected to follow automated or even ISO-certified procedures.

Obsession with Self-Control

Not only the body but also our sense of self become objects of mastery. Emotions and virtues are expected to be malleable to the goals of the company, and if employees cannot fit into the company's system, they can follow training on 'self-management'. This obsession with the self is only possible because the subjective self is in the first place distinguished from the body and explained as an object that can be controlled like the body or any physical object. For example, in many jobs, individuals are expected to swallow their subjective feelings, put on a big smile, and use their emotions when communicating with customers (Hirschman, 1997). Mental health has particularly become subject to functionalisation. In our previous book (Vos, Roberts, & Davies, 2018), we describe how mental health and mental health care have become functionalised. That is, the subjective meaning and well-being of the individual are replaced with the standardised diagnostic manuals and treatment manuals.

Calculability

Meaning has become quantifiable in number of sales or money rather than being subjective like an individual's taste. McDonald's 'developed the notion that quantity equals quality, and that a large amount of product delivered to the customer in a short amount of time is the same as a high-quality product. They run their organization in such a way that a person can walk into any McDonald's and receive the same sandwiches prepared in precisely the same way. This results in a highly rational system that specifies every action and leaves nothing to chance' (Macionis & Gerber, 2010, p.112).

Monetarisation

Meaning is often calculable in financial terms. Thus, meaning can be bought. Advertisements continuously try to imprint the idea of the buy-a-bility of meaning:

buy this car and you will be happy, go on this adventurous holiday and you will have the time of your life, and buy this vacuum cleaner and you will have more time left for the things that really matter to you. Often, the more money you have, the larger the meaning is that you can get: a triple burger will make you smile more than having the classic BigMac, according to the commercials.

Randomness
The goals become interchangeable. For the company, it does not matter whether they sell a triple burger or a BigMac, although their income could be slightly bigger with the triple. The tastes of customers can change; therefore, they can choose a different product every time and, therefore, the menu offers many options to randomly replace your choice. Similarly, in life, meaning becomes random and replaceable, like randomly ordering any McMeaning from the menu of life (Vos, 2018).

Flexibility
Sociologist Richard Sennett (1998) describes the corrosion of character in neoliberalism. In the past, virtues such as perseverance and long-term commitment and loyalty were praised, but this has now been replaced with the neoliberal adage of flexibility. Many long-term contracts have been replaced by temporary job agencies, organisations have become flatter and thus the roles have become more replaceable. Individuals are expected to be flexible when they work and when they are with the family, and employers expect employees to continuously check their email on their mobile phone even at home; flex-time has become a duty instead of a right. Companies are continuously reorganising and adjusting to new demands of the market, and thus individual employees are expected to adjust to the latest insights from HR. This means that people are expected to tolerate uncertainty, risks, and lack of work routines. Relationships become more superficial than in the past because of the increased changeability. There is a loss of skill and craftmanship; although individuals may know how to do atomised activities, they do not know the full process of production like a craftsman did (Sennett, 2008). For example, McDonald's staff are often on flex-contracts and working continuously changing shift hours.

Individual Failure
A consequence of the functionalisation of control is the idea that individuals are responsible for their failures. This means feelings of guilt and shame when they have not been able to perfectly control their actions, body, or self. For example, companies such as Enron use rank-and-yank systems, where individual employees are literally organised in order of successfulness so that the least successful individuals get fired regardless of the reason for their failure (Verhaeghe, 2012).

Using Instruments/Technology
Whereas craftsmen worked directly with their material—like a baker directly kneads the bread—many modern workers focus mainly on a control panel and thus lack immediate material contact. There is a loss of embodied connection with our immediate world, and our connection with our professional world is mediated by machines that are owned by our employer. Like McDonald's employees click on a button to get Coke splashed into a plastic cup.

Conclusion
All these are examples of McDonaldisation, functionalisation, of society. Either one or multiple examples occur in capitalist societies, and they reduce the complexity, plurality, and inherent meaningfulness of individuals to socio-economic functions.

Pareto's Failure

Economic functions are aggregates and averages of many, sometimes millions of, individuals, and each of them has their own statistical error—that is, we cannot precisely predict how one specific individual behaves. Not everyone behaves precisely the same way; we only know generic trends (cf. Von Mises, 1948). As the participants in the Lippmann Colloquium concluded in 1938, humans often behave irrationally. It is easy to overlook the variation and dispersion of individual scores, and econometrists may already become excited if their model explains half of the variation between individuals, ignoring that half of the individual scores are not perfectly explained. We are inclined to look at what we expect to see, and not at what we do not see (Taleb, 2011, 2005). When the application of the statistical model on real data fails because the assumptions of the model are not met, this is counterintuitively called 'market failure,' whereas this is actually a model failure. We ask the wrong questions: 'Which shares will grow quickest' should be 'What is the structure of the market and where are the exceptions to the trends'. If we want to reduce the statistical error and would like to predict people's behaviour better, we need to look inside individual minds—how they make sense of their situation and what they find meaningful. We may need heterodox statistics to plot this (Lee, 2009). However, by definition, meaning cannot be perfectly functionalized; this is freedom of meaning.

The same functionalist failure applies to the Pareto-Optimal. Vilfredo Pareto studied economic equilibrium in terms of solutions to individual problems of objectives and constraints, and he was the first to argue that utility maximation does not need to be cardinal (i.e., the exact amount that someone wanted of something) just the ordinal amount (how much they wanted it more than something else—X versus Y; (Mazzucato, 2018). For example, would an individual prefer to stay unemployed when the amount of extra income from their job compared to their unemployment benefits is marginally low? To find the optimal solution in a national balance of supply and demand of work and welfare costs, several assumptions need to be met. All obstacles to equilibrium—such as monopolies, government interventions, and meaning manipulation—need to be obliterated. However, real markets rarely meet such conditions, and thus error enters the model. Still, governments often base their welfare policies on such functions with such unrealistic conditions: *If we raise unemployment benefits, how many more people would stay at home instead of starting to work?* The question to be or not to be unemployed has a complex meaning for individuals, depending on many other variables such as the importance of material wealth and success, a sense of fatalism or self-efficacy, and the culture such as Thatcherite shaming of the unemployed.

Statistical functions start failing even more in meaning-oriented economies, as individuals will more often make intuitive decisions on the basis of their subjective meaning household, and individuals will go off the main paths in our 'off-modern era' (Boym, 2006). This may become the end of econocracy—that is, being state-governed by economic functions (Earle, Moran, & Ward-Perkins, 2017). For example, current economic models predict that an individual will buy a product such as bread in a supermarket because of its functionality—having the right ingredients, being cheap, etc. However, in the meaning-oriented trend, individuals will buy a loaf of bread from their local baker who they know personally or will look at the ecological production of the bread, etc. Whereas functionality included a limited number of materialist and hedonist meanings, in the meaning economy an unlimited number of possible meanings are included.

Whereas governments with big budgets may get away with ignoring Pareto's margin of error, individual companies and investors often do not have this luxury. As a seller, you do not know what the best price is for the optimal sale; it is a matter of trial and error. If you see that you can sell your product well for £10, then you can try out a rise of £1. Our economy is fundamentally based on trial and error; we live in a risk society (Beck, 1992). However, for individuals risk means the potential of loss, and people are loss averse; thus, they will try to reduce their personal risk while hoping that the risks for others will increase. Risk can be reduced by understanding the minds of buyers; therefore, companies spend much on economic analyses and behavioural economics. Another option is creating a monopoly or cronyism; countless stories of entrepreneurial corruption have come to the surface, such as ENRON, or secret price deals like British construction company Carillion. For example, American 'pharma bro' Martin Shkreli acquired the drug Daraprim, used in the treatment of AIDS-related illnesses and raised the price of a single dose from $13.50 to $750; similarly, pharmaceutical giant Valeant silently reduced its R&D costs, bought companies that had monopolies in the market, and had a chain of pharmacies set up to sell their products (McLean, 2016). London's housing market is another example where alternatives have been killed to keep the demand of houses high and the supply of new buildings low, such as having expensive transport that forces people to live near their work in Central London, offering rental benefits to pay any income gap, etc. (Dorling, 2015).

Another risk-reducing alternative is creating demand by telling people what they need—by mind manipulation. For example, Pfizer's marketing targeted women and told them that pre-menstrual syndrome is not normal; therefore, they offered a miracle drug against this, which is really Prozac, their anti-depressant (Davies, 2013).

Conclusions

Many economic models are only valid when they are seen from a functionalist perspective as the Lippmann Colloquium proposed. When models do not fit the data of real people, these models may not get adjusted, but the people get adjusted. By a lack of strict government regulations and controls, as neoliberals argued, companies can get away with corruption and manipulation. The question may be asked whether it would be more effective and beneficial for society to revisit the functionalist assumptions on which this system is built since individuals are meaningful in themselves and functionalist reduction of their inherent meaningfulness seems to lead to economic failure, corruption, and mind manipulation.

Key Points

1. Functionalism means that individuals are not treated as aims in themselves but as abstract and disposable variables in a larger function.
2. Functionalism is related to the sociological and philosophical concepts of rationalisation, commodification, technologies of the self, and self-governmentality.
3. Characteristics of a functionalist approach to life are an anonymous abstraction, predictability, goal-orientation, maximisation, efficiency and efficiency improvement, company control, physical control, self-control, calculability, monetarization, randomness, flexibility, failure attributed to the self, use of instruments/technology and hierarchy of functionalisers and functionalised.
4. Neoliberalism is based on a functionalist philosophy of life.
5. The functionalist assumptions make the ideal of Pareto optimality unrealistic, but companies may try to make it work via corruption and mind manipulation.

Chapter 11

Capitalist Relationship Between Individual and Society: Mind Manipulation

Economics is the method. The object is to change the soul. (Thatcher, *Sunday Times*, 7/5/1988)

Propaganda works best when those who are being manipulated are confident they are acting on their own free will. (Quote attributed to Joseph Goebbels)

A Brief History of Neoliberal Propaganda

The 1910s were a decade of revolution or, better said, attempts thereof. The workers' hopes in Russia were smashed by the Bolshevik oligarchy, and the Great War was raging on the Continent. In this hot era, the suffragette movement was growing quickly. *Smash the patriarchy! Claim your rights, sisters!* And then there was this emancipated man, Bernard Bernays, who offered to help with a big parade, and a big media team. Yes, why not? He offered the marching women 'torches of freedom', cigarettes to break the taboo that only men could smoke. The pictures of these smoking women in the newspapers brought a shockwave to society, quickly followed by a spike in tobacco sales. Smoking became a favorite symbol of rebellion. The cigarette smoke hid the harsh reality that Bernays was paid by the tobacco industry to get half of the population smoking as women had rarely been seen smoking before due to the taboo of smoking women (Bernays,1923/2015).

Neoliberalism would not have succeeded without people like Bernays, who instigated the discipline of *propaganda* or *public Relations*, PR, and neither would Hitler have been able to raise the amount of support that Bernays did. Bernays applied the insights from his uncle 'Sigi', Sigmund Freud, to help companies sell their products and governments control the population. Bernays' autobiography (1965/2015a) reads like a *Who's Who* for government and corporate mind manipulators, and -reading behind the over-positive image that he tried to sketch of himself—his role in, for example, the coup in Guatemala to protect the interests of United Fruit Corporation, which held an almost complete monopoly on the American market. Nowadays, any serious enterprise has a PR officer, and governments hire consultants to 'nudge' citizens (Thaler & Sunstein, 2008).

It seems that Bernays delineates two types of propaganda. Superficial propaganda sells specific products or services that do not require a change of perspective. Deep propaganda not merely sells a product immediately, as advertising has done for centuries, but also transforms the buyer's 'philosophy of life' (Pitkin, 1932) and their perspectives on what appears as meaningful and less meaningful, so that the product appears as the logical next-desired step in the fulfillment of their new world. Deep PR works by changing the circumstances, not merely the willingness to buy a product, such as the social taboo of smoking women had to be broken. For example, deep PR for piano sales would focus on showing how cool having a music room is: Create the space before you sell the product that can fill this space. PR varies by levels of depth. The deepest level of propaganda is teaching a materialist and functionalist perspective—ultimately the Capitalist Life Syndrome. Products and services can only be sold, and neoliberalism can only survive, because of the 'engineering of consent' by changing the social circumstances (Lippmann, 2017).

Of course, PR is not a totally new invention. Even the Romans offered *panem et circenses* (bread and circuses) to appease the population and get away with atrocities. Religious institutions may also have been used as 'opium for the people' to keep them too high on the drugs of religion to see the structural inequalities and atrocities of the system. However, Bernays has put PR on the agenda as the central technology for enterprises and states, leading to the self-governmentality of citizens and customers who tell themselves that they are free even though they are not. Propaganda is a modern technic of the self; it includes psychological action and warfare, re-education and brainwashing, public and human relations (Ellul, 1973).

In this book, mind manipulators are also referred to as 'mind mafia'. This is not merely a rhetoric trick, as there are similarities between the mafia and the organisation of mind manipulation. Both are organised groups that started as private firms protecting powerful individuals or families to win the competition with rivals and win over the hearts and minds of the population. Mind manipulation is often not transparent and open for examination by researchers or journalists, and it often happens behind the screens (Streatfield, 2008; Taylor, 2006; Winn, 2000; Bowart 1977). Mind manipulation includes getting support for legal and illegal activities, extending the norms and habits in a country such as creating public support for wars— renamed as 'humanitarian interventions'— and paying out banks after the 2007/2008 crash. The methods may include intimidation, albeit that mind mafia seem to use more subtle psychological 'political technics' than direct physical threats (Streatfield, 2008; Taylor, 2006; Winn, 2000; Bowart 1977). Similar ideas are conveyed by Roberto Saviano, researcher and expert on the Italian mafia, who compared how neoliberal governments and the mafia function. He has, for instance, argued that the United Kingdom is 'the most corrupt country in the world' and that Brexit makes 'the UK even more exposed to the organised crime' (*The Independent*, 29/05/2016). Mind mafia may include corruption and other white-collar crimes, but more often it acts in the grey zone of the law, by manufacturing public consent for activities that have not been regulated yet, or which may be included as an exception to common laws. An example is the Trickle-Down Myth, which has been used to justify low taxes and tax havens for the rich, even though there is no empirical evidence that the money from rich individuals will trickle down to the wider population (Akinci, 2017; Herzog, 2016; Bertrand & Morse, 2016; Sewell, 2013). The most explicit example is possibly the company Cambridge Analytica, which used Facebook information to target potential voters for President Trump and for Brexit (Wylie, 2019; Kirk, 2017).

The Moral Necessity of Mind Manipulation

Bernays, Lippmann, and others envisaged mind manipulation as morally good and even socially crucial. Bernays believed that public relations will create 'a smoothly functioning society where everyone is guided imperceptibly throughout our lives by a benign group of rational manipulators' (1928/1955, p.16). Bernays' vision elaborates Walter Lippmann's argument in *Public Opinion* (1922, pp. 195, 251) that 'the democratic El Dorado' is impossible in modern mass society as individuals are irrational and disoriented by external stimuli: the common good eludes the public opinion entirely. Consequently, we need to break the dogma that the voice of the people is the voice of God and that elected politicians should, therefore, serve the people; leaders are not servants, but people should serve the larger perspective that politicians have to *lead* them. People should vote for the best manipulator, the person who can create the right circumstances in which citizens will behave according to neoliberal values. Lippmann (2010) stated that freedom is not the aim but the method because people are 'too feeble' and 'indifferent' to manage freedom:

> The goal is never liberty, but liberty for something or other. For liberty is a condition under which activity takes place, and men's interests attach themselves primarily to their activities and what is necessary to fulfil them, not to the abstract requirements of any activity that might be concerned. If we substitute the word indifference for liberty, we shall come much closer to the real intention that lies behind the classical argument. It is that the traditional core of liberty, namely, the notion of indifference, is too feeble and unreal a doctrine to protect the purpose of liberty, which is the furnishing of a healthy environment in which human judgment and inquiry can most successfully organise human life. Too feeble, because in time of stress nothing is easier to insist, and by insistence to convince, that tolerated indifference is no longer tolerable because it has ceased to be indifferent. (p. 8)

Lippmann concluded elsewhere (2017) that

Therefore, democracy requires a supra-government body of detached professionals to sift the data, think things through, and keep the national enterprise from blowing up or crashing to a halt. The major issues must be framed, the crucial choices made, by the "responsible administrator". It is on the men inside, working under conditions that are sound, that the daily administration of society must rest.

As Bernays (1922) wrote later: "those [committees of wise men] who manipulate this unseen mechanism of society constitute an invisible government which is the true ruling power of our country" (p. 37).

In these texts, we recognise the disdain for the general public and the neoliberal narcissism that permeated the 1938 Lippmann Colloquium, a tendency that was also pervasive in American neo-conservatism (Drolet, 2013). The complexity of modern society and choice overload *require* manipulators, and as long as the manipulators have good intentions, as did the neoliberals and neoconservatives, they have an important role to play. This is particularly the case in times of crises—for example, against fascism or communism: 'Propaganda is good or bad depending upon the merit of the cause urged, and the correctness of the information published' (Bernays, 1922). So, neoliberalism says that the average free human being should be fundamentally mistrusted, whereas a superman-neoliberal should lead them (which is fundamentally a similar argument as Hitler made about Arian superiority).

The ideology of neoliberal propaganda to guide the population was quickly applied in a large scale by politicians. For example, Joseph Goebbels, Hitler's propaganda man, had read, and most likely applied, Bernays' work in practice, and Stalin employed experts on brainwashing (Tye, 2002). During WWII, Bernays advised the US Information Agency, Army and Navy, in creating public support and willingness to subscribe to the war. In the 1950s, Bernays advised politicians solving the Watergate Scandal. Meanwhile, the CIA developed its handbooks on brainwashing and torture, which are still used today with prisoners in Guantanamo Bay and in invaded countries such as Iraq and Afghanistan (Taylor, 2006). Propaganda has become the main tool for creating popular consent for government policies.

In the United Kingdom, nobody knew better how to apply propaganda in politics than Keith Joseph, Margaret Thatcher's right hand, who promoted 'determined, tireless government action' because individuals cannot be trusted to lead the free market on their own (Denham & Garnett, 2001, p. 182). Joseph was directly influenced by the ideas of the Mont Pelerin Society, particularly via lectures at the Institute of Economic Affairs, where he had introduced Thatcher to ideas like Hayek's and Friedman's. Like Hayek, he believed in market and morals. Joseph said that the main problem of their era was a lack of purpose and responsibility in the people: 'Drugs, drunkenness, teenage pregnancies, vandalism, an increase in drifting—now called by new names, but basically vagrancy are the very opposite of freedom, which begins with self-discipline. We must fight the battle of ideas in every school, university, publication, committee, TV studio even if we have to struggle our toe-hold there; we have the truth in the remoralisation of public life.'

Joseph believed politics should focus on 'a battle of ideas', even if this literally included work camps for brainwashing. During his career as advisor to Thatcher—initially, he tried to become PM with Thatcher as his right hand—he almost directly applied Bernays' ideas. He initiated many public debates, even about controversial topics such as birth control of uneducated people and 'underserving benefit claimants', even though prestigious economic bodies told him that his presentation of facts was clearly inaccurate (Denham & Garnett, 2001, p. 258). He promoted censorship of television and education and told his colleagues not to worry about accusations of McCarthyism and being "red under the bed": 'the facts will support us later' (Denham & Garnett, 2001, p. 288). His white and green papers, which were made public in 2014, show how much of a mastermind of mind manipulation he was. For example, he advised breaking the community spirit and thus prevent uprisings against the system by a deliberate divide-and-conquer strategy in council housing, and by defunding community centres and sports clubs. Break neighbourhood communities and trade unions, and lower their benefits and government support, to break the collectivism that had led to fascism and communism and transform individuals into Smilesian self-help citizens. Even decades later, former deputy Prime Minister Nick Clegg admitted that the Conservative Party had refused to build more council houses in order to break class awareness in neighbourhoods (*The Independent*, 3/9/2016).

Together with politicians such as Calvin Coolidge, Joseph saw a crucial role for education to 'produce' the right circumstances in which people would feel that they freely choose neoliberal values, such as dedicating their work lives to commercial companies and voting Tory. As education minister, Joseph deliberately reshaped the education programme to focus mainly on a business-relevant core such as mathematics and language, and he checked individual syllabi to get rid of critical thinking skills and political sciences in the curriculum (Vos, Roberts, & Davies, 2019). The creation of the Ofsted Office for Standards in Education as well as SAT tests ensured that both teachers and students would focus only on this core programme. By merging polytechnic and universities, he lowered the standard of critical thinking and refocused on business-oriented vocational skills. This way of policing the mind via education seems more efficient than using regular political technics and police forces on the streets (Aronowitz, 1984).

Like his preceding minister of education, Thatcher, Joseph started to defund universities and stimulate university–business partnerships so that universities would lose their status as sanctuaries of independent thinking (Sanderson, 2018). He transformed the education system as a teacher of obedience and commercial information instead of critical skills and facts (Vos, Roberts, & Davies, 2019). The independence of scientific research has been undermined by corporate influences and research grants (Sanderson, 2018). In the late 1980s, independent academic committees started to be expelled from government ministries in European countries and replaced by outsourcing of scientific reports that 'empirically confirm' what the minister wanted to hear. Consequently, civil servants could select the researchers that fit the government policies (deductive governmentality). The mechanisms of feedback and evaluation of governmental policies have become ineffective and non-transparent (Institute for Government, 2019). Thus, it seems that knowledge has lost the relatively independent status it had in the past and has become to some extent buyable in the international 'War on Science' (Otto, 2016).

The consequence of the neoliberal propaganda machine seems to be that in capitalist countries we may not completely own our emotions and thoughts, as we are manipulated by companies and governments. The wars of our era, and those of the future, seem to be primarily fought in the mind, not on the streets and the battlefields (Roberts, 2007). The economy does not function in a value-neutral way, as has been argued by classical economists, but by the meanings that powerful players in the market impose on others (see Chapter 4).

This chapter sketches the intricate ways that governments, corporations, culture, mental health care providers, and socio-economic circumstances manipulate the thoughts and feelings of citizens and customers, not only to create specific meanings in them but to make them imagine that they are free in deciding for these meanings— i.e., the mind hijack and fatalism behind the Capitalist Life Syndrome. In recent years, the ways that mind manipulation works have increasingly come into the daylight, with obvious social media manipulation during election campaigns, and presidents shedding their critics by shouting 'fake news' in their tweets. Organisations such as Full Fact show how rhetoric in the public domain is often based on selective, tweaked, or fully made-up facts. Despite the increasing visibility of the manipulation mechanism, the influence of mind manipulation on people's lives seems to go relatively unchallenged, and many people may even not be aware how they have been manipulated.

Governmental Mind Manipulation

Every great world-changing movement driven by an idea must first spread this idea using propaganda. After propaganda has converted the entire population over to an idea, only a handful of men are needed to finish the job. The art of propaganda consists in putting a matter so clearly and forcibly before the minds of the people as to create a general conviction regarding the reality of a certain fact, the necessity of certain things and the just character of something that is essential. The art of propaganda consists precisely in being able to awaken the imagination of the public through an appeal to their feelings, in finding the appropriate psychological form that will arrest the attention and appeal to the hearts of the national masses. (Hitler, 1925/2007, pp. 23,155)

These words come from Adolf Hitler, but they may equally have come from other influential politicians in the 20th or 21st century. As neo-Marxist Gramsci (1994) wrote, whereas rulers would previously mainly dominate the material means of production, in modern societies they focus on the Lippmannian 'political technics' and Bernaysian 'propaganda' of large-scale mind manipulation. Gramsci described how the ruling-class in modern societies tries to establish a cultural hegemony by dominating the beliefs, explanations, perceptions, values, and mores of the majority, so that their worldview becomes the accepted norm. They aim to inculcate people with the idea that socio-economic inequality and the dominance of the rich is common sense, that it is inevitable and beneficial for everyone, instead of viewing this as a social construct that only benefits the small ruling class. Subsequently, the working class starts to identify their own good with the good of the bourgeoisie, and they help to maintain the status quo instead of revolting, which Foucault (2001/2008, 1988) would later call self-governmentality. It is easier to control people via cultural hegemony than via military or political coercion, according to Gramsci and Foucault.

The strongest rejection of government mind manipulation can possibly be found from proto-anarchist Proudhon (2004), who argued that all governments inherently imply mind manipulation: 'To be governed is to be watched, inspected, spied upon, directed, law-driven, numbered, regulated, enrolled, indoctrinated, preached at, controlled, checked, estimated, valued, censured, commanded, by creatures who have neither the right nor the wisdom nor the virtue to do so.'

However, together with Proudhon, Gramsci (1994) describes that ordinary citizens can become aware that they are manipulated by the state, which creates a 'crisis of hegemony'. When people become conscious, they can either turn against the mind manipulation by directly trying to dethrone press barons or companies like Cambridge Analytica ('war of maneuver'), or they can establish a counter-hegemony of alternative perspectives on meaning in life ('war of position') by re-valuing alternative cultures, mass media, and ideologies. Part III will exemplify such alternatives to mind manipulation that embrace a plurality of perspectives of meanings instead of the monocultures of mind mafia.

It has been argued that the state can determine all societal areas, including religion, education, family, law, political systems, trade unions, communications such as press, and cultures such as literature, arts, and sports (Althusser, 1971/2014). Translated into the meaning framework, it may be argued that the propaganda of the state can serve each of the six types of meaning.

First, manipulation may help politicians to get elected and have success in creating better *material* circumstances for the population. An example is the targeting on Facebook of individuals who may be interested in switching their vote, for instance in the election of President Trump. The Brexit campaign included fake news, such as saying that the European Union does not allow curved bananas or that the EU costs £350 million per week. Another example is the leader of the opposition in British Parliament in 2019 who is the most smeared politician in history, according to an independent research report entitled 'From Watchdog to Attack Dog' (Cammaerts et al., 2019).

Second, some individuals, particularly those with more antisocial traits—and who are statistically overrepresented in leadership roles in governments and corporations—may enjoy the process of manipulation and having power over people. It has been said that politicians may have more authoritarian and controlling traits than the general population (Weinberg 2011).

Third, manipulation can be ego-saving for politicians by shifting the population's focus, and possibly also their own self-perception, away from their faults and mistakes. A clear example is the propaganda of the American Department of Defence about the Operation Iraqi Freedom that tried to control the public image of the war as just and downplayed atrocities such as Abu Ghraib (Guo & Chen, 2015; Ahmad, 2014).

Fourth, manipulative rhetoric can help to build, or undermine, a sense of community and belonging and stimulate social values and altruism or its opposite—egoism and self-help. For example, after 9/11, George Bush Jr tried to create a sense of national community by focusing on external enemies: 'You are either with us or you are against us!' (Mackay, 2005)

Fifth, some manipulators believe that their perspective is best for humanity and that they serve a larger purpose, as the condescending statements of some members of the Lippmann Colloquium show.

Sixth, manipulation can also give a sense of certainty to the manipulated and the manipulators instead of living with the anxieties, complexities, ambiguities, paradoxes and risks of complex modern life, as Lippmann and Bernays argued.

Governments can use manipulation technics from the smallest to the largest level. For example, tax officers use psychological techniques to 'nudge' the behaviour of individual citizens by the way letters have been formulated and repressive regimes of benefit assessments have been structured. Positive reinforcement and indirect suggestions have been used to 'nudge' customers and citizens into behaviour such as paying taxes (Thaler & Sunstein, 2009). Nudging techniques focus on our use of judgmental heuristics in economic decisions by altering the environment so that when a heuristic or 'System 1 decision-making' is used, the resulting choice will be the most positive or desired outcome. An example is placing junk food next to the cash registers in a store to trigger last-minute sales. A less refined system of nudging can be found in many modern workplaces that have a culture of carrots and sticks, punishments and rewards to manipulate workers into the right direction: 'Do this and you will get that!' But in many cases punishments and rewards fail and lead to human suffering, as hundreds of research studies have shown (Kohn, 1999). All these models do not take the customers or employees as ends in themselves and do not focus on the meanings of the products, services, and work for them.

Naomi Klein (2007) hypothesized that politicians often use crises as an argument to push through their opinion: 'To solve this crisis, we have no other option...' TINA: There Is No Alternative! For example, whipping up public fear and anger over the risk of terrorist attacks by radical Islamists created a parliamentary majority for a new Terrorism Act in the United Kingdom in 2018, which has given unprecedented powers to the police, intelligence services, and even private policing; subsequently many corporations with connections to 10 Downing Street have profited from this act. Furthermore, elections can be rigged by presenting politicians with similar political ideas as different, creating the illusion of a choice where there are no actual differences—such as the way New Labour copied many ideas of the Conservative Party and vice versa. Similarly, dictatorial regimes such as China and Iran have elections where citizens choose between individuals with similar political programmes; research shows that this sense of freedom of voting while trusting the government competence helps citizens feel more satisfied with their government, even though they have no real freedom (Guriev & Treisman, 2015). Another way to manipulate politics is by manipulating the opposition—for instance, via polarising police infiltrates in left movements (Lubbers, 2012). Some governments also give the idea that national debt is to some extent unavoidable— for example, in times of war; however, politicians seldom explain how corporate interests determine the loans to pay for these wars as, for instance, the American Fed is an independent corporation, and the European Central Bank is strongly influenced by corporate powers (Hudson, 2015a).

As described, Keith Joseph was one of the first UK politicians, even before Thatcher, who used aggressive language towards unemployed and poor people needing benefits for their survival, and he claimed that 'undeserving benefit claimants' should not be allowed to have children or have the right to vote. Joseph created the public image of benefit seekers as scoundrels and social parasites, an image that was quickly taken over by British newspapers. Receiving benefits became synonymous with the idea that you are not good enough or that you have a moral problem. Joseph also used generic terms, which saved him from providing evidence and being confronted by individual benefit-seekers who were not scoundrels; he called such individuals 'exceptions to the rule'. Newspapers eagerly confirmed the myth of benefit fraud, with headings such as '£20k benefit cheat who said he was unable to walk filmed' (*The Sun*, 28/09/2018), 'Anger, as government pays out £2.3Billion to benefits cheats' (*The Sun*, 09/05/2019), and 'A judge has let off a £73k benefits cheat' (*The Sun*, 19/01/2019). However, these newspapers do not seem to report as frequently that £13 billion in benefits have remained unclaimed by people who have the right to this, five times the amount of 'frauds' (*The Independent*, 13/4/2017). It is also rarely mentioned that there is a large disparity between the number of 4,000 civil servants tracking down benefit fraud and the 500 civil servants going after tax evasion by large companies and taxpayers with assets over £1 million, even though benefit fraud annually accounts for approximately £2 billion and tax evasion for £73 billion (FullFact, 9/7/2018). In such a climate of structural representativity bias, it is unsurprising that most of the British population believes that benefit fraud is endemic and that there is little public outrage over tax evasion by big companies.

These examples of government manipulation may come with large costs for democracy, as this means that the few impose their will on the many. *Democracy is dead, long live democracy!* The institutions of parliament and courts fulfill an important symbolic role in modern societies, but their actual democratic nature has been questioned. For example, representatives in the British House of Commons and the American Congress represent only 30% of the full population, when compared with socio-demographic characteristics. Sixty per cent of the members of the British Parliament own at least one other house that they rent out, in contrast with 2% of the general population; however, they are also the so-called 'representatives' who need to make decisions about the housing market that directly influences their own wealth (Smith, 2017). It has been argued that many political systems, such as those in the United Kingdom and the United States consist of many revolving doors for politicians, large corporations, and journalists (Jones, 2016). Furthermore, powerful manipulators may try to rewrite the rules and the definitions of where the mark lies in court and in parliament. For example, American president Donald Trump has selected the judges who need to examine allegations over the manipulation of voters that helped him to power. The British Prime Minister Boris Johnson has been accused of telling lies about the European Union to achieve the Brexit vote—for example, by writing on the side of a bus that the EU costs the British taxpayer £35 million per year. However, the court ruled that it is not up to the court to determine the extent to which politicians can misrepresent facts as this is a political decision, thus leaving lying politicians with a majority in parliament unchallenged (Kirk, 2017). Furthermore, the political powers of independent bodies such as the Ombudsman are limited, and several countries ignore the judgment from courts such as the European High Court and the International Court in The Hague. Additionally, several countries, including the United Kingdom and the United States publicly considered unsubscribing from the European or the Universal Declaration of Human Rights.

The free press has the potential to vilify any political transgressions. Therefore, Lippmann appealed to the professionalisation of the press to fulfill, an important social role. However, the history of the press, and its alleged freedom, is tainted by media barons distorting truth seeking and imposing their values (Curran, 2012), and revolving doors between journalists and politicians (Jones, 2014). In the United States, restrictions were lifted in 1987 that previously required broadcasters to present political topics in a way that was honest, equitable, and balanced; this removal has enabled news channels to broadcast fake news on a large-scale. The neoliberal model transformed the press, broadcasting, and other media into extensions of the capitalist system. Because newspapers and other media sources mainly depend on advertising income, they need to present news in such a way that it appeals to the largest possible audience and thus becomes attractive to advertisers. However, this may imply sensationalising news and confirming the perspectives of advertisers (Jones, 2014).

Consequently, the media rarely criticise the fundamental materialist and functionalist perspectives that underlie the political and economic system as their advertisers would disapprove of this. The marketisation of the press has even transformed traditionally left-leaning newspapers such as *The Guardian* into uncritical publishers of positive news about psychiatric drugs because their main advertisers appear to be psychopharmaceutical companies (Roberts in Vos, Roberts, & Davies, 2019). The media can make or break politicians and, therefore, it is understandable that politicians try to appease media barons; for example, when Murdoch decided that his press emporium would support New Labour Blair instead of the Tory party, this meant a significant shift in tone of their news as well as in the voting behaviour among their readers. Consequently, British prime ministers hold on average 10 meetings per year with Murdoch, which is more than with academic researchers (*The Guardian*, 2/2/2017). Media Barons make the news by framing, ignoring events, agenda-setting, creating pseudo-events, etc.

Herman and Chomsky (1988) write that media have become dependent on profit making, advertisers, information from press officers from the large companies and bureaucracies, flak and enforcements to media statements, and the ideological war on terror (or, in the past, anti-communism). They conclude that in many countries, mass communication media 'are effective and powerful ideological institutions that carry out a system-supportive propaganda function, by reliance on market forces, internalized assumptions, and self-censorship, and without overt coercion' (1988, p. 13).

Thus, checks and balances—and in general *Trias Politica*—do not work when large-scale government mind manipulation is allowed. This can lead to a vicious circle of the always-increasing manipulative power of the manipulators and the emergence of an undefeatable oligarchy. This violates the idea of an open society, based on the falsifiability of government rhetoric and actions (Popper, 2012). However, the public imagination is one of democracy and freedom. It seems that 'on the ruins of neoliberalism', antidemocratic politics has risen (Brown, 2019). This has led to a structural crisis in neoliberal propaganda democracies, leading to riots of disillusioned and angry citizens such as the yellow vest movement in France. '*I know that I am free, but why do I not feel free?*' asks the self-conscious citizen (Zizek, 2010).

Corporate Mind Manipulation

Success belongs to marketers who have a thorough understanding of individuals' and masses' mental processes and social-connection patterns and how their publics know what they think they know and what their motives are, and, as a consequence, are able to create and provide them with robust Meaning to conquer awareness and channel intent toward a desired outcome. (Ferzini, 2012, p. 3)

How can companies sell? Whereas until recently, the material functionality of the product or service mainly determined sales, this is nowadays increasingly achieved by the ability to give consumers a positive hedonistic experience, a sense of self-transformation, and, preferably, a connection with their social and larger values (Chapter 7). Thus, companies need to create the psychological connection between their product/service and its potential meaningfulness for the individual as well as suggest that their product/service is the only real meaning—for example, via meaning-manipulating slogans: 'Panasonic: Ideas for life', 'Pepsi: Live life to the max', 'Coca Cola: The real thing' (Chapter 2). Clients may not have wanted 'a real thing', 'maximising life,' or 'ideas for life', but advertisements suggest that they have been missing these, and nobody wants to think of themselves as lacking ideas for life, living life to a minimum, or being satisfied with fakeness. Thus, companies do not need to fulfill an existing nee, as the starting point can be anything as long as the desire for this can be manipulated. This commercial mind manipulation can go on under the radar as corporations focus on targeted micro-campaigns, particularly via social media such as Facebook, Twitter, and Instagram. Messages can be micro-targeted and can even be subliminal—brief exposure to a message with an impact on consumer behaviour but unconscious to the consumer. Our era of social media targeting would have been Bernays' PR Valhalla.

As Bernays recommended, companies and governments often set the right circumstances to sell products. For example, if estate agents want to sell houses and banks want to sell mortgages, housing should be both scarce and desired so that people are willing to spend the most money possible on buying houses. This requires, for example, a structural housing shortage, a volatile rental market that tenants want to escape by buying their own place, TV programs about the fun of buying and renovating houses and gardening, etc. Many of these TV programs are directly sponsored by construction companies and banks. In contrast, there are few TV programs on foreclosures, failed house renovations, happy tenants, etc. There is a housing-obsessive culture that seems to be further fostered by parliamentary votes (Dorling, 2015). It has been said that it is not coincidental that most members of the British House of Commons are London landlords themselves, and that they have consistently voted against proposals to increase the number of houses—e.g., building council housing, cheap public transport to villages and towns outside Greater London—to benefit housing and help keep rents and mortgages high (Walker & Jeraj, 2016; Dorling, 2015).

The most fundamental circumstance that any sales require is public trust in the market, such as reassuring words from the chair of the Federal Bank or the European Central Bank. Consumers also need to trust that the product or service they buy is what is promised—for example, via a good legal system, consumer organisations, and the National Ombudsman. Such circumstances set implicit trust for large productivity and sales.

However, it is not important for sales that an economic sector is efficiently regulated; what matters is the *imagination* and the *symbol* politics of regulatory bodies. Since the 1970s, increasing numbers of regulation policies have been privatised, which means they are written and maintained by the sectors themselves. This privatisation of regulation creates structural volatility of the market. An example is British railway services. Public and political acceptance of privatisation of British railway services since 1994 has depended on safeguarding the reliability and costs of the services. To guarantee this, the Office for Rail and Road set the quality and safety benchmarks for the tenders. Systematic research shows that privatisation led to an exponential increase in fares while the quality and reliability of services have decreased, most likely because there were doubts about the independence and the lax rules of the government regulator—e.g., requirements for structurally low ticket prices, sufficient space, and good working conditions (Jupe & Funnell, 2015; Preston & Robins, 2013; Bowman, 2013; Alexandersson, & Hultén, 2006; Parker, 2004). It has been suggested that Virgin received its tender of the long-distance train lines by bullying and cronyism. Thus, the regulatory body had a symbolic function and sketched the image of the highest quality and fair-priced railway services, whereas in reality private companies could get away with anything. It seems that privatisation of former government activities has been socially justified by giving powers to regulatory bodies, but when the bodies are partial and lax, the social foundations for privatisation fall away. It seems that either very strict rules should be developed for regulatory bodies, or privatisation is not socially justified. However, as long as (semi-)private companies can hold up the façade of fair regulation, they can keep both citizen support and political support (Jupe & Funnell, 2015; Preston & Robins, 2013; Bowman, 2013; Alexandersson, & Hultén, 2006; Parker, 2004).

Corporations and governments seem to hide how they manipulate minds. One strategy is offering an overwhelming quantity of information, including conflicting information, which conceals fundamental flaws as it is difficult to find a needle in a haystack. An example is multinational giants such as the Unilever Group, whose advertisements compete with themselves—e.g., their products Biotex, Sun, Robijn, and Sunil are all washing powders and liquids available on the Dutch market. The public believes that there is a structural difference between products and that they have a free choice, whereas in reality Unilever has a monopoly in this market. Furthermore, the complexity of the impenetrable web of incestuous relationships between members of the Bildenberg Group often makes it difficult for journalists to discover and publish structural faults such as corruption and cronyism, and thus this group lacks clear checks and balances.

An example of how these corporate manipulation strategies intertwine resulted in the largest student rent strike in history, in London in 2016. To an increasing extent, universities depend on accommodation rents and building sales for their income, and some London colleges have even replaced their core function of conducting academic research with construction works (Hale & Vina, *Financial Times,* 23/6/2016). Student accommodation companies often have a monopoly to offer housing for students. For example, the University Partnerships Programme (UPP) is one of the largest companies whose student accommodations at the University of the City of London was only regarded 'affordable' to 0.8 per cent of the students. Long-term lease agreements mean that UPP has an effective monopoly on the provision of student accommodations, barring universities from entering into similar agreements with other companies. This gave UPP freedom to set their own rent charges from students, which income goes, via Jersey-based subsidiaries, to the People's Bank of China, the Communist Party-controlled Chinese central bank, and the Dutch pension provider PGGM. It is interesting that individuals with main decision-making powers in the national regulatory body overseeing the student accommodations had financial interests in the construction industry and former university boards (Anonymous Report, Student Union UCL, 2016). Thus, behind the façade of organisational complexity and revolving doors, and in contrast with reality, corporations sold the idea of affordable quality accommodation.

Cultural Mind Manipulation

Culture just provides fun, doesn't it? Or not? Is culture a tool to shift the audience's perspective? Countless philosophers of art and culture have asked these questions. These doubts came to the forefront in the postmodernist and post-structuralist debates. Postmodernism brought the idea that there is no one truth or reality but only an unlimited number of perspectives. Authors such as Foucault concluded that everything is ideology and mind manipulation and that there is no a space free from government and corporate influences.

Thus, is all resistance against manipulation futile, and should we accept any mind meddling? Anything goes? Can we merely select the manipulations we prefer and, thus, allow subjective taste, hedonism, and aesthetics to replace guidance by moral norms? For example, individuals can select which social media channels they want to be influenced by, but even that choice is itself influenced by their social context. Individuals do not follow one big story in their lives, such as the ultimate truth or meaning of life—except possibly the big narrative of postmodernism or neoliberalism itself—but create a bricolage of small stories, which could be stories or mini-stories that governments or corporations have provided. Postmodernism seems to create a fatalistic and relativistic ideology and thus support the mind manipulation. Fredric Jameson evolves this idea in his book *Postmodernism, or the Cultural Logic of Late Capitalism* (1991). He shows how relativist postmodernism serves capitalism and how this is another systematic commodification of capitalism itself. That is, the functionalist approach to meaning is supported by postmodern and poststructuralist philosophers such as Lyotard and Derrida. Postmodernists are skeptical about the ability to experience absolute meaning or truth. Any meaning can be explained by the socialisation and social context of individuals and, more important, by the socio-economic system in which they live. Personal meaning is like living in the movie *The Matrix*, in which individuals are continuously manipulated. However, in contrast with the movie, postmodernists seem to believe that we cannot step out of the matrix of manipulation, and we cannot know what is true and what is false. To extrapolate their perspective: if there are no truths or falsehoods, anything goes (*laissez-faire*). We can randomly exchange one meaning for another. There is nothing absolute in how we live our lives, and our sense of meaning is merely one of the functions within the wider social system (Baudrillard, 1998). Postmodernism has laid the foundations for the meaning manipulation machinery by which the capitalist system survives, and which leads individuals to the Capitalist Life Syndrome. Thus, postmodernism seems to be a functionalist philosophy on which modern capitalism is built, and vice versa; functionalist capitalism has possibly also influenced the emergence of postmodernist philosophy (Jameson, 1992; Nealon, 2012). Consequently, many individuals seem to search desperately for guidance in life (Frankl, 1948). They feel lost because all the cultural and social signs in the capitalist system send them in different directions, while they are simultaneously told they should not trust any inner/psychological signs of direction.

The entertainment industry, such as Hollywood and game developers, use explicit and implicit ways to sell products, such as offering customers to play a game for free but where they will need to pay to access the highest levels (Graber & Dunaway, 2017; Street, Inthorn, & Scott 2015; Coleman & Freelon, 2015). For example, in several countries, the army facilitates and pays the development of war films and first-person shooter games to make war look cool and attract recruits. The weapons industry and the gun lobby point at the threats in society to make people buy their products for self-protection (Wasson & Grieveson, 2018). The American weapons lobby, the National Rifle Association, seems only able to sell guns by evoking emotions of threat and fear, even though independent research has shown time and again that the largest threat in the United States is the wide availability of guns themselves (Kleck, 2017). These examples indicate that corporations use the collective imagination of the population to sell their products and use cultural products as a symbol to justify and bridge reality with this imagined world.

Conclusions

This chapter has sketched several domains of public life in which governments and companies deliberately manipulate people's minds. It may be argued that the capitalist lifestyle can only be sustained through this mind manipulation, as the manipulation hides the real money and power interests and creates the circumstances under which customers and citizens will align with the aims imposed by the industry and the state. Of course, individuals are told that they are free, but this is the essence—as Adolf Hitler wrote in *Mein Kampf*—as people do not want to feel coerced into believing or behaving.

> All that was required of them (i.e., the brain-washed masses) was a primitive patriotism which could be appealed to whenever it was necessary to make them accept longer working hours or shorter rations. Even when they became discontented, as they sometimes did, their discontent led nowhere, because, being without general ideas, they could only focus it on pretty specific grievances. The larger evils invariably escaped their notice. (Orwell,1949/1983)

Key Points

1. Mind manipulators or 'mind mafia' regard the group of corporations, governments, and other privileged people who use psychological, social, and political means to manipulate and stimulate public support for their idea, product, or service.
2. Mind manipulation works by creating the right circumstances under which individuals think that they are making a free decision, although they have been pushed in a specific direction.
3. Rulers in many different empires have used mind manipulation technics, but in the 20th century a larger, more systematic, and professional focus lies in creating public consent and selling products and services via propaganda and public relations.
4. Mind manipulation has been justified and stimulated by the belief that certain people are better than others in pushing people in the right moral direction.
5. Mind manipulation can be found in politics, private companies, culture, and many other places.
6. Mind manipulation creates public consent for capitalism and sustains the Capitalist Life Syndrome. Without mind manipulation, consent is small and people would openly resist the capitalist lifestyle. Politicians such as Keith Joseph have deliberately created socio-economic conditions that stimulate the Capitalist Life Syndrome via education, housing, and benefits policies.

Chapter 12

The Capitalist Individual:
Individual, Fatalistic, and in Existential and Psychological Crises

Keeping people hopeless and pessimist—see, I think there are two ways in which people are controlled—first of all, frighten people and secondly demoralize them. (Benn, 2013)

Individual Causes of the Capitalist Life Syndrome

Interviewer: Are you a predator?
Scott Tucker: Am I a predator? No. I mean, it's just a business. There was a demand, consumer, and you know, the business was built around that.
Interviewer: Do you think you're a moral person?
Scott Tucker: I'm a businessperson.

These are the final words of Scott Tucker in the documentary series *Dirty Money*. Tucker was known to the broad public as an amateur racing driver in his Ferrari. However, in 2016 he was arrested and sent to jail for almost 17 years for his role in various payday lending operations. His online company AMG Services offered payday loans even in states where such high-interest loans were restricted or illegal. He hid behind complex legal structures, such as deals with Native American tribes to claim ownership of his business and invoke sovereign immunity from prosecution. He made over $400 million from false claims, mail fraud, racketeering, fraud, and money laundering, leaving over 5 million individuals struggling to pay off their debts.

What has made Tucker into this competitive machine—either in his Ferrari or on the phone with innocent lenders? What made him disconnect— 'just doing a business'—from 'morality'? What made him treat consumers as a function of his business? Little is known about Tucker's personal background, except for his going to a strict Jesuit boys' high school. However, even the exploitative behaviour in his early professional life gives us little to guess about his childhood: Was is competitive and authoritarian?

The previous chapters have described how capitalism is characterised by a materialist, hedonist, self-oriented and functionalist culture, and how this culture is promoted by mind manipulation. However, some individuals seem almost immune to this manipulation, whereas others seem to uncritically take over the capitalist culture or even become its ultimate advocate, like Scott Tucker. What explains these individual differences? The following paragraphs will discuss the complex interaction between social and intra-psychological factors, according to psychological research.

Social Situation
WWII gave rise to countless psychological experiments to understand how seemingly normal people like Eichmann could succumb to atrocities. For example, in the infamous Milgram experiment, a research leader asked research participants to assist in an experiment in which they had to administer shocks to a learner, even though in reality these shocks were not administered. Approximately two-thirds of all participants would give shocks, which would have led to the death of the learner if this would have been real (Blass, 1999). Similar findings were found in Zimbardo's prison experiments in which volunteers were allocated to the role of prisoner or prison guard, but guards would become too sadistic towards the prisoners and thus the experiment had to be terminated prematurely. These findings have been explained as the process of dehumanisation, where others are no longer seen as fellow humans with their own meaningfulness. Under the right circumstances almost anyone could disconnect from their evolutionary built-in empathy and desire for mutual aid to survival of the fittest.

One of the circumstances that trigger this functionalist shift is an ambiguous and uncertain situation in which people feel that they are not able or lack the expertise to decide, particularly in a crisis of conflict of conscience. They shift their individual responsibility to an expert, such as looking at the experiment leader who nodded when they continued giving shocks or doing sadistic interrogations of 'prisoners'. To extrapolate these findings, one may argue that ordinary citizens trust and follow economists and politicians as experts, in times of economic or existential uncertainty or crisis. Whereas the country's 'experts' follow materialist, hedonist, and self-oriented functions—particularly in times of economic or political crisis—it is likely that individuals will merge themselves into their culture, even if this implies dehumanisation of others and themselves.

The situation in which individuals are reminded of death and their own finitude makes them focus more on conservative values (Greenberg, Koole, & Pysczinski, 2014). For example, when research participants in New York subliminally saw pictures of 9/11, they became more nationalistic and focused more on family values. This has been explained as an evolutionary neurological response: In times of crisis, individuals focus on conserving what they have. This has been particularly evident in times of economic or political crisis when individuals become more nationalistic and authoritarian in their voting behaviour. It seems that in response to crises such as 9/11 or the 2007/2008 crash, individuals focus in functionalist ways on materialist and self-oriented types of meaning. Klein (2007) has argued that politicians have deliberately been using, or creating, public shocks to push through their capitalist agenda. For example, there was little public support for an American invasion of Afghanistan and Iraq, but 9/11 gave the sense of crisis and neoconservative support. Capitalism thrives in crises.

Socialisation

Children often take over the perspectives of their parents. It has been argued that this socialisation process is important for our survival as in our early years we depend on care from others and, therefore, try to behave in such ways that we get their protection and support, including following their expectations (Jost et al., 2003). Not only parents but also peers have an important role in internalising the perspectives from our subcultures because we depend on others for social approval and self-respect. During our sturm-und-drang adolescence years, we develop our own perspectives on life, individuation–separation, but modern research doubts that individuals fundamentally change the perspectives that they have developed earlier in life. For example, when an individual grows up with strong materialistic goals, it is unlikely that they will totally reject all materialism. Individuals do have some degrees of freedom to decide and design their own perspectives, but—like radio broadband— the width of the degree of variation seems to have been set earlier in life, just as Scott Tucker's psychopathic actions could be regarded as the result of his upbringing with capitalist and authoritarian values.

For example, private boarding schools are infamous for their authoritarian atmosphere; 'the Boarding School Syndrome' teaches children a functionalist, self-oriented, and materialist perspective on life (Schaveren, 2015). It has been suggested that British private schools are 'engines of privilege', as children in such schools are likely to have higher socio-economic positions later in life (Kynaston & Green 2019). In their later top positions, such as management or conservative politics, they can act out on their authoritarian upbringing and impose their narrow life perspective on others. Thus, private and boarding schools can be one cog in the machine creating a capitalist culture among managers and politicians.

However, not all children growing up in harsh environments become psychopaths. Lawrence Kohlberg (1984) did research on the development of moral reasoning. He found that there is an evolution in children's morality as they grow up. For example, at the youngest age, children focus on pre-conventional morality—such as obedience, individualism, punishment and reward;   conventional morality, focusing on maintaining relationships and status quo, and post-conventional morality follow larger universal principles. Thus, generally speaking, individuals shift from a materialist and self-oriented functionalist perspective to a more social and larger critical–intuitive perspective in their moral reasoning. This shift seems to follow the improvement of neurological and cognitive functions. However, not all children develop post-conventional moral reasoning. Many hypotheses have been developed to explain these differences. Culture and education do not have significant effects, but a positive parenting style and secure attachment style seem to predict individuals developing post-conventional morality.

Authoritarian Upbringing
One's moral development seems to be strongly determined by an authoritarian upbringing. This was the main thesis from Theodor Adorno and colleagues (Adorno, Frenkel-Brunswik, Levinson, & Sanford, 1950/2019). He studied individuals with authoritarian personality, which is a combination of conventionalism, authoritarian submission, authoritarian aggression, anti-intellectualism, anti-intraception, superstition and stereotyping, power and toughness, destructiveness, cynicism, projectivity, and exaggerated concerns over sex. Adorno argued that extremely harsh and punitive parenting makes children feel angry at their parents, but fear of parental disapproval or punishment leads them to not directly confront their parents but instead to identify with and idolize authority figures. In a similar psychoanalytic way of reasoning, Wilhelm Reich argued in his book *The Mass Psychology of Fascism* that when children learn from their parents to suppress their sexual desires, they expend the repressed energy in authoritarian idealism. They learn to control their rebellious and sexual impulses and the anxiety associated with such feelings. Nazi political ideology and practice exploited these psychological mechanisms of repressive families and further exacerbated this with a baneful religion, a sadistic educational system, terrorism of the party, fear of economic manipulation, fear of other races, and public tolerance of violence against minorities.

Although the psychodynamic language of Adorno's and Reich's explanations has been rejected, countless studies have proven that an authoritarian upbringing leads to an authoritarian adult life. Michael Milburn and Sheree Conrad (2016) argued that frequent childhood punishment, abuse, neglect, and, in general, authoritarian parenting leads to seeing the world as a hostile place in which individuals need to fight for their own survival. These individuals often show displaced aggression by their anger towards and rejection of others in society, even though the original cause of their anger is their parents. There is a strong relationship between authoritarian upbringing and support for neoliberal economic policies and government violence against enemies. For example, support for George W. Bush and the war on terror went hand in hand with approval of various forms of physical punishment for children (Hetherington & Weiler, 2009). Thus, a significant number of individuals supportive of the self-help ideology and aggressive neoliberal interventions have been confronted with intolerable pains as a child; in response, they have created an imaginative and symbolic perspective—and identified with the aggressor by becoming the aggressor themselves to cope with this harsh reality. Having learned to tolerate their own pains, they expect others to similarly tolerate their pains.

An authoritarian upbringing teaches people from a young age onwards that individuals are variables in someone else's function and that they are not meaningful in themselves. This functionalist approach can be reinforced and triggered by later life circumstances, such as a sense of political and economic crisis and survival of the fittest. Corporate cultures can also exacerbate these authoritarian trends. An extreme example of authoritarian individuals are psychopaths. Since the 2007/2008 crash, an increasing number of books and studies have been published to understand why so many investors, managers, and CEOs on Wall Street, and in banks and multinational entities show anti-social traits. Whereas only 1 per cent of the population show psychopathic tendencies, in senior positions in business this is 3–11% (Dutton, 2012; Hare, 1994). These 'snakes in suits' (Baibak & Hare, 2007) are common at higher levels of corporations, and they thrive under bosses who are abusive themselves and further exacerbate the authoritarian work culture by bullying, conflict, stress, staff turnover, and absenteeism (Boddy, 2011). This seems to create a vicious cycle, where authoritarian managers create a culture that stimulates authoritarian behaviour of materialist–hedonist selfishness and functionalism.

Capitalist Perpetuum Mobile
Bernays wrote that to sell something the right circumstances need to be created so individuals feel that they are freely choosing to buy a product. The examples in this section have shown how social and economic circumstances influence individual meaning in life. Capitalism seems to function as a perpetuum mobile, pulling individuals into its movement. Individuals are more likely to experience the Capitalist Life Syndrome when they have had an authoritarian upbringing and were spoon-fed neoconservative ideas by their parents, teachers, and religious leaders. More oil is thrown onto this functionalist–materialist fire by psychopathic work cultures and politicians declaring a continuous state of crisis. Individuals may feel that they are existentially trapped, as they experience a gaping ravine between the imagination of the American Dream—and its variations in other Western countries—that they were taught and the harsh reality of daily life with its quickly increasing socio-economic inequality and decreasing social mobility. In such situations, individuals can fall back on authoritarian coping mechanisms learned early in life. This makes it more likely that they will support a neoliberal ideology and raise their children in similar capitalist and authoritarian ways.

Some politicians seem to have deliberately created socio-economic conditions that increase the likelihood of this neoliberal perpetuum mobile. For example, Keith Joseph and Margaret Thatcher reshaped education around neoliberal and neoconservative work skills, reduced employee rights and unions, reduced sickness and unemployment benefits, and thus gave way to a sense of continuous survival of the fittest; Reagan and Bush used similar interventions (Chapter 5). Such politicians sustained the culture of denial by creating external enemies—such as communists, the war on terror, immigrants, or the European Union—which shifted the anger over their own harsh upbringing and socio-economic circumstances towards others. All these government interventions stimulate the capitalist perpetuum mobile.

In sum, authoritarian upbringing and socio-economic situations of continuous crisis and survival of the fittest can lead individuals to develop the Capitalist Life Syndrome. On a macro-economic scale, this also implies that socio-economic inequality and low social mobility in capitalist countries foster the Capitalist Life Syndrome, as the more individuals struggle for their survival the more likely it is that they develop materialist, self-oriented, and functionalist approaches to life. They deny that the capitalist system is the cause of their struggles and instead take over capitalist perspectives and may support neoliberal and neoconservative values. This denial and displacement of emotions is called in psychoanalysis 'reaction formation', which is a defence mechanism in which emotions and impulses that are anger or anxiety producing or are perceived unacceptable are mastered by exaggeration of the directly opposing tendency.

The research in Chapter 7 confirms this idea. The more unequal a country is and the lower the social mobility, the more individuals focus on materialist, hedonist, and self-oriented values and the more individuals approach life in functionalist ways (Worldwide Survey of Meaning in Chapter 7; Figure 8.1.). This relationship is even stronger when time is included: The more unequal and less socially mobile a country has become during the last decade, the more likely it is that citizens show characteristics of the Capitalist Life Syndrome. Thus, individual and socio-economic circumstances seem to exacerbate each other with a capitalist perpetuum mobile, continuously creating Scott Tuckers who create new Scott Tuckers.

> "What do you want to be when you grow up," the goat asked her ambitious lamb.
> " A wolf," answered the lamb." (Ljupka Cvetanova, *The New Land*)

Sense of Freedom

These studies on the societal trends and the capitalist perpetuum mobile may sound deterministic. However, there are always individual differences, with some freedom to develop self-insight and make one's own decisions (Chapter 7). This begs the question: How free are we to determine our own life? We may possibly never be able to answer this ontological question as we do not have a God's eye point of view. However, there is much research on the sense of freedom that individuals experience. This sense of freedom often depends on the culture in which people live and the dominant societal narratives. However, even when individuals are taught, they are the function of the socio-economic structure; for example, in the USSR there are individuals who feel that they have some degree of freedom within the given limitations of their situation.

Figure 12.1. Worldwide Survey of Meaning in Life: Relationship Between the Average Effect of GINI Inequality Coefficient and Social Mobility (Hedges' g; x-axis) and Types of Meaning and Approaches to Meaning (Hedges' g; y-axis)

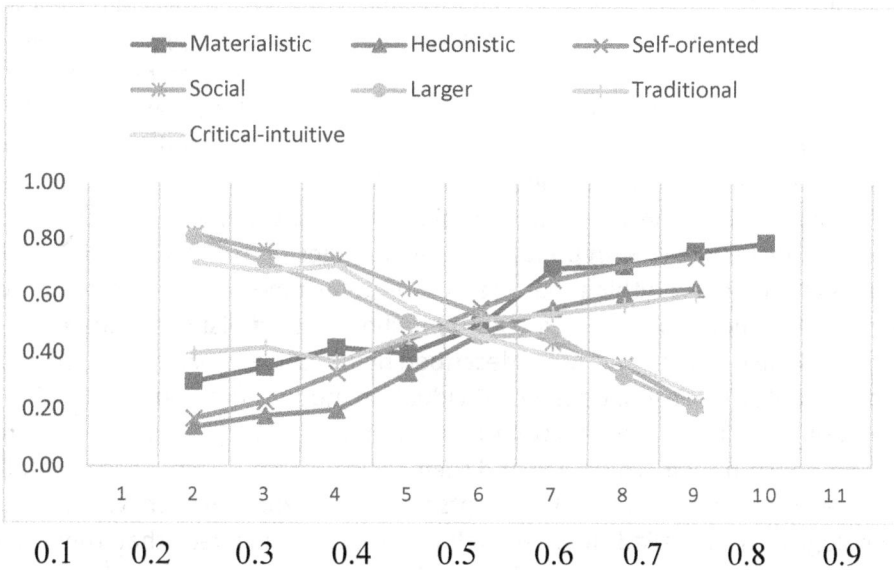

Moral and rational liberals focus on individual freedom, and capitalism is still promoted as *the* symbol of freedom. However, the question is: *Whose* freedom is this? Ordinary citizens seem impotent against corporate and government mind manipulation, while socio-economic inequality and social mobility have been rising in capitalist countries since the end of the 20th century (Chapter 10). Although the socio-economic circumstances of many have improved since 1900, this trend of improvement has hit a ceiling and has reversed. A small establishment has gained more power and wealth than the rest; the average CEOs at major American corporations get paid more than 100 times as much as their average workers (Pikkety, 2016). The pilgrim fathers' dream of the land of the free may be the nightmare of others, not only ordinary workers but, in the first place, displaced indigenous people and ethnic minorities (Freeman, 2016).

Neoliberals have argued that governments should guarantee the negative freedom of people, such as freedom from oppression. Many laws and regulations have been established to safeguard personal property, risk insurance, functioning of the market, basic health and safety protection, etc. However, these negative laws and regulation also mean positive freedom for a small few; for example, many laws have benefited large corporations, and whereas large companies have large lobbying power, such as the American Chamber of Commerce, individuals have little power (Reich,2016). The top five oil companies receive a combined $4 billion in annual tax breaks, Google receives $632 million in government subsidies for data centres, the United States Department of Agriculture spends $20 billion every year on subsidies for the largest producers, and the bailout of the AIG group has put $314 billion of taxpayer money at risk. Research over a 20-year period shows that large corporations and wealthy individuals have a 60% chance that a law will be passed if they want it to be, whereas 'the preferences of the average American appear to have only a minuscule—near zero—statistically non-significant impact upon public policy' (Gilens & Page, 2014). Consequently, whereas roughly 77% of Americans said they trusted government to do the right thing in the 1980s, this has decreased to 20% today (Reich, 2016). Thus, neoliberal regulations seem to stimulate inequality.

It is not remarkable that many studies show that many individuals in capitalist countries feel fatalistic, with population percentages up to 70% (Chapter 8). Fatalism is the idea that everything has been pre-determined by one's socio-economic situation. The more capitalistic a country is the more fatalistic individuals are (WSM: Pearson's R=.67, p<.01). Karl Marx described how capitalism alienates individuals, and Friedrich Nietzsche described how individuals in modern times are determined by the perpetuum mobile of a societal will to power. Individuals feel trapped in a situation of powerlessness in their workplace and their social position. This sense of fatalism may be the result of countless failed attempts to improve the situation, which behavioural psychologists have called 'learned helplessness'. People feel that their wish for a better work situation for themselves and others is unachievable (Bourdieu, 1998). Camus (1942/2013) compared this feeling with the mythical figure of Sisyphus, who was doomed to roll a stone up a hill until it rolled down again and then to roll it up again—for eternity. Are ordinary citizens doomed to this eternal inferno?!

This sense of fatalism is fostered by an expert culture of economists and politicians claiming, 'capitalist realism: the widespread sense that not only is capitalism the only viable political and economic system but also that it is now impossible to even *imagine* a coherent alternative to it' (Fisher, 2009, p.2). Thatcher hammered the idea that There Is No Alternative (TINA), and this argument also dominated post-2008-crash politics. *We have no alternative than to rescue the banks, letting CEOs and investors get away with their psychopathic behaviour while imposing austerity measures on the average citizen.* Paradoxically, individuals are told that people are still

> lucky that we don't live in a condition of Evil. Our democracy is not perfect. But it's better than the bloody dictatorships. Capitalism is unjust. But it's not criminal like Stalinism. We let millions of Africans die of AIDS, but we don't make racist nationalist declarations like Milosevic. We kill Iraqis with our aeroplanes, but we don't cut their throats with machetes as they do in Rwanda, etc. (Badiou, 2001)

Thus, in the collective imagination, the symbol of TINA tells us what we should see as real, but this seems far from real (Zizek, 2013). Our system is based on cognitive dissonance between what we are told about how neoliberalism benefits everyone, and what is really happening (Mirowski, 2013). This neoliberalist paradox tells says freedom is for the few, not for the many.

Existential Crisis

Life is complex and inherently paradoxical and ambiguous, and human beings continuously face unsolvable paradoxes and ambiguities, not only in the economy but everywhere in life. This is our *conditio humana*. Individuals may never be able to grasp the total complexity of the socio-economic system in which they live. The processes of globalisation and digitalisation seem to have made our life-world even more complex and overwhelm us by an unlimited number of choices and unstoppable growth of information available on the internet. This can trigger intense feelings of existential anxiety and loneliness in this quickly expanding universe of options. This means that people do not merely fear specific situations, such as losing their current job or becoming ill. They are afraid of the system and the human condition as such. Their gaze gets trapped into the abyss of life. Research indicates that many individuals in capitalist countries feel stuck in such an existential crisis (Chapter 8; also Vos, 2018).

Although it seems realistic to assume that we will never be able to completely understand and control our complex social reality, we are not doomed to existential despair. Existential philosophers believe that individuals are never completely determined by their socio-economic circumstances. In each situation, individuals have two options to cope with this situation: Either they embrace the complexities and paradoxes of life (authentic choice), or they try to deny and avoid them by rendering reality into simplistic categories or holding onto fundamentalist and traditionalist ideas (inauthentic choice). In existential terms, we always have the ontological freedom to change our attitude towards the situation, even though we may not be free as perceived from the ontic perspective on our socio-economic life-world (Irwin, 2015). For example, individuals may not be able to overcome their unemployment due to macro-economic conjunctures or financial crisis, but they can change how to deal with this situation. An individual could become fatalistic, depressed, and anxious due to the impossibility of keeping or getting a job, or the individual could decide to take an active stance and continue applying for jobs. Ultimately, individuals have the choice to change their perspective on their situation. *It is annoying that I lost my job, but employment is NOT the only and most important meaning in my life; I still am a son, a father, and a friend (social meaning), and I have a social and larger responsibility to remain ethical and help to make the world a better place (larger meaning). I realise that I am not merely a function of the economy but that I have the freedom to determine my own meaning.* In a Meaning-Oriented Economy, these authentic and hopeful perspectives are promoted, while we remain realistic about our situation.

Mental Health in Crisis

Imagine you go to a doctor with a bleeding toe, and in response, the doctor removes your tonsils. You would call this a medical error. Similarly, health professionals can make errors in their psychological diagnoses and the etiological models they create about the causes of mental health problems. 'You need to develop more beneficial ways of thinking and feeling!', a stereotypic cognitive behavioural therapist could say; or a psychodynamic psychotherapist could recommend, 'let us dig in your childhood to see what went wrong then.' Such psychological interventions could be very appropriate for certain clients, but not when patients suffer because of their socio-economic situation—like stress from work, unemployment, benefits, a political crisis, discrimination, financial uncertainty, a climate crisis, etc. We cannot and should not individualise such problems as their cause and solution primarily lie in society and not merely in the individual. Chapter 7 showed that on the most fundamental level capitalism can cause mental health problems because of its focus on materialist, hedonist, self-oriented and functionalist approaches to life. Traditional psychotherapeutic and psychiatric approaches try to teach clients some coping mechanisms to deal better with the difficult life situations, but they may not structurally remove the socio-economic and meaning-oriented causes, just as a band-aid does not cure gangrene. (Vos, Roberts, & Davies, 2019)

The reality of our socio-economic struggles needs to be acknowledged when professionals examine problems in mental and physical health. The personalisation of such problems and the creation of a self-help culture. 'You are crazy, not society; change yourself, not the system' seems political. There are few psychological issues that have completely developed in isolation from society, as the expression and amelioration of most problems are embedded in the reality of social, economic, and political interactions (Vos, Roberts, & Davies, 2019). We may argue that all mental health problems that individuals experience may to some extent be an indicator of social problems, with individual mental health symptoms, like fever, indicating an underlying societal disease.

All psychotherapy and psychiatry are essentially community therapy and social work, and the disconnection of these disciplines from their socio-economic context may be regarded as a political and economic activity (Vos, Roberts, & Davies, 2019). For example, until the beginning of the 20th century, individuals with mental health problems were cast away from society and put in asylums so they could not harm society and could become a human zoo—as, for example, the psychiatric centre of Bethlem in London whose 100,000-plus visitors a year watched the crazy people locked in cages. Crazy individuals had no place in society and the economy. With the birth of psychology and psychotherapy at the end of the 19th century, mental health was no longer seen as an issue of outsiders but as an experience that could apply to all of us. In his early work, Sigmund Freud paid attention to the social situation of his patients, such as paying attention to their stories of incest and sexual abuse; but later in his career Freud decided that all these horrific stories could not have really happened and—possibly to be able to cope psychologically with the overwhelming reality of the cruelty and suffering in the stories of his clients. Freud concluded that these stories were mere fantasies and the result of frustrated drives. Freud's decision to attribute problems to the individual and not to the social reality has had large political consequences. Because psychology started as a discipline that individualised problems and ensured that individuals were set aside as outsiders, like the crazy people in Bethlem, many of the main psychotherapeutic approaches primarily focus on the individual and not on their social context, their socio-economic situation (Vos, Roberts, & Davies, 2019).

In the '60s and '70s, the idea of individualised psychology and psychiatry came under attack by critical psychiatrists and pedagogues like Ronnie Laing and Paulo Freire. They showed how psychiatry and psychotherapy can function to oppress individuals, either literally by drugging down critics of the system or by stimulating people to blame themselves instead of expressing their anger at the system and demanding socio-political change. As described before in this book, Michel Foucault has shown how neoliberal governments have conveniently used the self-help culture of modern psychiatry and psychotherapy. Instead of governments governing individuals, it is more efficient to let people govern themselves, as previous chapters showed. A clear example is that since 2014 unemployed individuals in the United Kingdom can be forced to receive psychotherapy, even though they may not have any mental health problems; this gives them a clear message that it is their own fault they are unemployed rather than due to the system (Vos, Roberts, & Davies, 2019).

Elsewhere, we describe on the basis of many studies that mental health is in crisis (Vos, Roberts, & Davies, 2019). Not only is the large prevalence of mental health problems in Western countries the result of our crises like the Capitalist Life Syndrome, but also the mental health system itself is in crisis. There are clear capitalist interests involved in modern mental health services such as the Improved Access to Psychological Therapies (IAPT) in the United Kingdom. For example, all initiators of IAPT and 83% of the members in its guideline committees have direct financial interests such as receiving financial support from the pharmaceutical industry or wearing double hats by both managing and evaluating the IAPT system they have created themselves. Consequently, whereas the official figures from these self-evaluations report that over 50% of individuals recover from this mental health care, independent reports suggest this may be less than 10%. This new mental health care system entails partial or complete privatisation and services being paid by governments or health insurances for the number of people they can cure within a minimum number of sessions; this has created a system that focuses on quick and dirty solutions and not necessarily on structural psychological solutions, which may require more sessions and greater expertise from mental health professionals. It is not surprising that there is a relapse crisis in many of these Western mental health services since clients often do not structurally improve in pharmaceutical or psychological therapies and may need additional mental health support. This inefficient and corrupt mental health system is internationally promoted by neoliberal economists and has been enforced on countries during periods of financial crisis, such as Greece experienced.

Why does the mental health care system seem to fail in some capitalist countries? In our previous book (Vos, Roberts, & Davies, 2019), I describe four hypotheses. First, politicians may have been inadvertently manipulated by mental health lobbyists—for instance, because they did not have sufficient expertise in mental health. Second, politicians and economists may see mental health care as 'just' another sector that should be privatised, like almost all sectors. Third, it could also be the case that the trend of individualisation in mental health care stimulates the self-help culture espoused, for example, by Margaret Thatcher so individuals will attempt to search for problems and solutions inside themselves instead of asking for help. A failing mental health service can be very beneficial for neoliberal governments, as it steers attention away from the government to the individual. This spirit can be clearly read in the papers from Sir Keith Joseph, who deliberately wanted to use socio-economic, educational and mental health structures to manipulate voters: Individuals with socio-economic and mental health problems should be supported enough to be productive workers but not feel empowered enough to start a revolution. Finally, the modern mental health care system could stimulate people to avoid reality, even literally, with online and virtual reality mental health tools. The pills and brief talking therapies create a symbolic narrative about individuals taking responsibility for their own well-being while the economy allegedly offers them full freedom for self-development. Thus, mental health can become a key domain for mind manipulation, sustaining the capitalist perpetuum mobile.

Conclusions

This chapter discussed four characteristics of the Capitalist Life Syndrome: individualism, fatalism, existential and psychological crises. This shows, on the one hand, how all individuals are influenced by their upbringing and socio-economic situation and, on the other hand, how they keep some opportunities for individual freedom.

Individuals can develop self-insight and change their attitude towards their situation. This was the key message of psychiatrist Viktor Frankl, who wrote in his book *Man's Search for Meaning* (1948/1985) that even in the direst situations, such as being a prisoner in a concentration camp, individuals may not be able to completely change their circumstances—escape was not an option for most prisoners—but everyone has the ability to transcend the situation in their mind. For example, in the concentration camp, individuals kept their sense of freedom, meaning, and hope by small actions such as sharing an empathic gaze with a fellow inmate or appreciating small moments such as seeing the sunset in the mountains around Auschwitz. Those who kept a sense of meaning were more likely to survive the horrors of the camp, while those who lost any sense of social, larger, and existential meaning withered away. Similarly, research shows that the ability to keep a sense of social and larger meaningfulness can help individuals cope with their daily-life struggles under capitalism (Chapter 8). This ultimate sense of freedom and hope forms the foundation of the Meaning-Oriented Economy, which will be elaborated in Part III.

Key Points

1. Individuals can internalise capitalist values due to the interaction of their authoritarian upbringing, neoconservative education, and psychopathic work culture.
2. Many individuals experience a sense of fatalism and helplessness about their ability to improve their life, possibly as the result of failing socio-economic mobility and political narratives.
3. There is a crisis in mental health, as well as in mental health care. Never have so many individuals experienced mental health problems as in modern capitalism, and never has mental health care so greatly financially profited from people's suffering. Mental health also seems to be a key domain for mind manipulation, sustaining the capitalist perpetuum mobile.

Chapter 13

Functionalist–Materialist Theories of Change

The lunacy continues and has every chance of becoming a way of life unless we stop it soon. Men are getting so used to wars that psychiatric wings (…) are planning how to break the news to the men when the war is over. (Spike Milligan, 2019)

Delivering Capitalism by Joystick

'Officially the British army was not there, but I was there. We were told that we are bringing freedom to Yemen. We are fighting Al Qaida and ISIS. I am a joystick expert, knowing how to conduct drone strikes.' My client stopped briefly to swallow, and I saw a tear welling in his eye. 'Until some months ago. I could not stay, as my conscience grew on me. I was asked to bomb a school where terrorists would be hiding, but the drone image showed children. One push on the button and they would have been dead. I could not do that. The war is senseless. Even if I would have killed terrorists, would we have changed the spirit of the people? We would have given them more reason to hate us. We cannot bring democracy by joystick.'

During the last century, the United States and the United Kingdom have been involved in most major wars in the world. According to the Watson Institute of International and Public Affairs, more than $5.9 trillion has been spent in post-9/11 wars.

One of the most frequently heard justifications for so-called 'humanitarian interventions' is to bring 'freedom'. However, the previous chapters have shown that freedom is an ambiguous concept. On a superficial level, these interventions mean regime change, rebuilding state control, bringing a working democracy, and opening the market to capitalist endeavours. This is an outmoded vision that views states as independent unified states that control markets and rely on authoritarianism when needed. The economic and political realities are often much more complex (Ghani & Lockhart, 2009). On a deeper level, the aim of humanitarian interventions seems to create a change of spirit and perspective, such as promoting economic and political freedom à la the West. However, although bombs and boots may put a different person in power, this may not really change the spirit of the people (Whyte, 2018; Simons & Chifu, 2017; Roberts, 2007). For example, Bush and Blair told us that they expected a brief and clean war, but even after more than a decade fighting, there are still military missions ongoing in Iraq and Afghanistan. Research shows that less than half of all so-called humanitarian interventions since the 1990s have been effective, and often at a large cost of human lives (Seybolt, 2007). Therefore, we need to seriously ask ourselves: What is the underlying theory of capitalist change, and why is this theory failing in practice?

The underlying model seems to be of functionalist–materialist change. The failing states that the international community intervenes in are often characterised by a combination of a lack of state control over people—leading to internal riots or civil war and a chaotic or closed economic market—and a traditional approach to life (Ghani & Lockhart, 2009). On the most simplistic level, military interventions assume that bringing a functionalist change in material circumstances will subsequently change the people's spirit. Military interventions are inherently functionalist, as they treat individual citizens, and even a whole country, not as aims in themselves but as an abstract and disposable variable in the large function of international law, order, and markets. A complex plan of targets and goals is rolled over the country, and individual citizens are expected to respond flexibly to bombs and boots.

However, countless psychological studies show that, for instance, seeing foreign soldiers with guns patrolling the streets does not evoke a sense of wanting to adjust but instead a sense of vulnerability, authoritarianism, and anger (Whyte, 2018; Simons & Chifu, 2017; Roberts, 2007). Authoritarian interventions often provoke an authoritarian spirit in the people, which may aggravate the conflict (Peksen, 2011). The change from traditionalism to functionalism is one that cannot be enforced quickly by bombs and boots, particularly in the case of strongly religious countries (Seybolt,2007).

A totally different ballgame is the aim to transform a country towards an open economy oriented around materialist, hedonist, and self-oriented goals. These are values that may be opposite to the social and larger types of meaning in the life of the people. A market economy assumes a unique capitalist perspective on life, but such a perspective cannot be simply imposed on people. For example, research on the transition of former East-bloc countries indicates that the formal opening of the market did not quickly lead to significant changes in the spirit of the people (Chapter 8). Similarly, the history of economics in Part I shows that the complex evolution of economic ideas takes centuries and does not merely include the development of new materialist infrastructure, such as building industry or creating government institutions, but also a change in perspectives. The idea that cultural and economic evolution follows the same linear pattern and mechanisms everywhere has been strongly rejected by anthropological studies; instead, multilinearity and plasticity are required to understand cultural and economic transitions (Caldararo, 2014).

Idealistic and Materialist Models of Transition

Humanitarian interventions that aim to change the people's spirit, such as my client bombing Yemen, often provoke the opposite: resistance and polarisation of opinions (Whyte, 2018; Simons & Chifu, 2017; Peksen, 2011; Syebolt, 2007). The common response from the people doing the military intervention is to fight this opposition or to integrate it into a new system, such as giving high positions to local tyrants in the formal government.

This seems to be what Georg Wilhelm Friedrich Hegel (1807/1976) might have advised on the basis of his dialectical explanation of the spirit. He explained how an oppressive ideology (thesis) can lead to a counter response (antithesis), which could finally be integrated in a new stable situation (synthesis). He saw social change always as a response to a paradoxical situation. Simplistically said, this could mean that the spirit does not change for the sake of the inherent meaningfulness of the new situation—'this is inherently a truly good situation'— but for the functionalist sake of the thesis—'this is better than how the situation was' (but it is irrelevant how much better this synthesis is, and at what cost this has come).

However, the traditional interpretation is that Karl Marx found this German Ideology of Hegel too abstract. Instead, Marx believed that social changes are always embedded in concrete material praxis:

> Along with the constantly diminishing number of the magnates of capital, who usurp and monopolize all advantages of this process of transformation, grows the mass of misery, oppression, slavery, degradation, exploitation; but with this too grows the revolt of the working class, a class always increasing in numbers, and disciplined, united, organized by the very mechanism of the process of capitalist production itself. The monopoly of capital becomes a fetter upon the mode of production, which has sprung up and flourished along with, and under it. Centralization of the means of production and socialization of labour at last reach a point where they become incompatible with their capitalist integument. This integument is burst asunder. The knell of capitalist private property sounds. The expropriators are expropriated. (Marx & Engels, 1867/1990,p.78)

Thus, according to Marx, the way that the materialist means of material production is distributed in the population leads to a significant inequality between a class of owners and a class of workers. Belonging to a class determines what you will see as your meaning in life. For example, growing up as the son of bakers makes it more likely that you will become a baker than a banker. Your personal meaning determines how your work interacts with the material world—for example, by getting alienated from the bread that you are selling when you are no longer kneading the dough but operating the buttons of a bread-baking machine. Similarly, social transition happens via an increasing awareness of our materialist (dys)functioning in society. Capitalism leads to wealth accumulation, centralisation, monopolizing, and overproduction/underconsumption, which leads to large differences in socio-economic circumstances in capitalist societies. The most direct way to class consciousness is materialist suffering in daily life: the relatively low income, the unemployment, the de-skilling of unemployment, the monotony of simple work, and the hunger. These dire circumstances make the class difference felt and embodied rather than a mere abstract Hegelian theory. Revolutions start in dire materialist conditions and our sense of being a functionalist member of a class, and we feel that this functionalist materialism does not do justice to our meaning potential.

It is understandable, that many revolutionaries have applied Marx in functionalist and materialist ways. For example, Mao Tse-Tung (1939) wrote about the materialist conditions of the Chinese Revolution:

> The ruthless economic exploitation and political oppression of the peasants by the landlord class forced them into numerous uprisings against its rule(…). It was the class struggles of the peasants, the peasant uprisings and peasant wars that constituted the real motive force of historical development.

Seen from a functionalist and materialist perspective, individual citizens may even need to lose their inherent meaningfulness for the sake of revolution, according to Che Guevara (2003):

> Revolution is impersonal; it will take their lives, even utilizing their memory as an example or as an instrument for domesticating the youth who follow them. (…) We executed many people by firing squad without knowing if they were fully guilty. At times, the Revolution cannot stop to conduct much investigation; it has the obligation to triumph.

However, despite the writing and actions of these revolutionaries, it is too simplistic to reduce Marx to mere materialist functionalism, as Chapter 6 has shown, and as neo-Marxist Gramsci (1994a) argued, saying that such an interpretation is 'primitive infantilism' in contrast with 'the authentic testimony of Marx'. That is, the principle of causal primacy of the forces of production, like Tse-Tung and Guevara write about, could be seen as a flaw in Marxist interpretations. Instead, he envisaged a critical–relativist perspective on historical change. Both economic and cultural changes reflect the same underlying historical processes, and it is difficult to say which sphere has primacy over the other. Thus, from a phenomenological perspective, someone's perspective on life cannot be distinguished from their actions.

To explain Gramsci's point, let us zoom in on the Marxist concept of alienation as an example. This could be read not only from a materialist perspective but also from a meta-perspective about materialism—that is, alienation does not merely imply that my product is not 'mine' anymore; a difference has grown between me and my product. The problem is that I look at myself and the world around me in terms of materialism. Alienation also implies a similar meta-perspective on functionalism. The problem is not merely that I am regarded a 'human instrument' or 'human resource' that can be paid for and randomly replaced. The problem is also that I think of myself as a function of something else and not as a means in myself, and similarly that I do not think of other people and objects as being meaningful in themselves. Marx shows how our perspective on the plurality and complexity of meaning has become narrow-minded, and how this narrow mindset reproduces itself via its own products—that is, we think in functionalist–materialist ways and this stimulates us to see and treat ourselves in functionalist–materialist ways.

Whereas Marx's communist utopia was post-materialist and post-functionalist, he described the revolution towards this utopia in functionalist and materialist terms, like Mao and Che elaborated. For example, Marx calls on workers of the world to unite, to demand the ownership and power over the production processes. The richness and power should be taken out of the hands of the few to be shared among the many. During the revolutionary stage, Marx does not ask fundamental questions about why we need materialism and functionalism at all. He fights the functionalist inequality in material conditions, but he does not fight the idea of materialism and functionalism.

However, a revolution from this perspective may further propagate material functionalism and feed the capitalist perpetuum mobile (see previous chapter). People continue their dependency on 'the means of materialist mass-production', albeit owned by the people instead of by the establishment, which makes these means even more valuable; it also will make individual owners fight even harder to keep their property, which Marx himself at one point described as 'capitalism without capitalists'. The fight against powerholders in society puts them on an even larger pedestal, and the attempt of workers to take over the ownership of the means of production can make them more focused on material goals. The goal of fully automated luxury communism is still a materialist, functionalist imagination, albeit that material wealth has changed hands. Marx's focus on materialism and functionalism in the first stage of the revolution may be compared to fighting with guns to convince our enemy to lay down their guns. The reality is that the enemy will most likely not put down their guns but instead start an endless arms race. Meanwhile, the use of guns becomes habitual to the fighters—the alienation that war creates—which makes the post-war dream even less likely. Having a gun in your hands transforms everyone you see into a potential target—i.e., a functionalist, materialist object.

This failure of functionalist–materialist revolution may be seen in the failure of the Russian Revolution (Faulkner, 2017). Certain types of material changed hands;

factories and land were taken away from the few by the State, but materialism and functionalism continued to exist. One type of functionalism was replaced by another: Instead of being wage slaves oppressed by a factory owner, citizens became slaves of the State, with the Stasi now controlling every domain of their life. The materialism–functionalism of the old governing oligarchy was replaced by the materialism–functionalism of the new government. The Stalinist allergy against post-materialist meanings was reflected in many of Stalin's speeches, and in the prohibition of religion. Stalin had used Marx's functionalist–materialist revolution to create a functionalist–materialist society in which the Capitalist Life Syndrome was replaced by the Communist Life Syndrome. The Kremlin did not create Marx's dream of a critical–intuitive society predominantly oriented towards social and larger types of meaning.

Another example of materialist functionalism is the reliance of traditional left activists on labour unions as the main mechanism of change and building of social movements (Sverke, 2019; Kelly, 2015). However, in capitalist countries, many people do not see themselves as a member of a class or as a labourer anymore (Chapter 8). They lack a sense of belonging to a community. They are self-help individuals, focused on developing their personal identity in the experience economy. This is, for example, reflected in the large decline in union membership. Thus, whereas in Marx's time, unions and political leaders could appeal to a sense of social community, ordinary citizens seem to have a less social perspective on life. A traditional appeal to their labour mindset may therefore not suffice to create political change in contemporary Western societies. Gramsci (1994a) offered an even more radical critique of trade unions, which he described as vulgar economism and liberalism, as he believed that many unionists often fight for their own materialist interests and do not look beyond their own immediate economic gains as congruous with the universal progress of society.

Therefore, if the Marxists want to have an effective revolution, they must be non-materialist and non-functionalist to be able to get away from the self-fulfilling prophecy of our functionalist–materialist situation. The capitalist perpetuum mobile needs to be broken. The full spirit needs to be changed, not only the material circumstances. Post-materialist/post-functionalist activists could break this cycle of dependency by shifting their functionalist focus from materialist and hedonist goals to freeing human beings for their wider range of meanings in life (Bookchin, 1982). Greedy individuals should not be fought, but materialism and self-orientations as such should be undermined. Powerholders should not be fought, but the idea of power should be negated. Not only should economic inequality be fought, but we should give importance to how to create a meaningful society, here and now. Why wait to live a meaningful life until the end of the struggle, when we do not know whether we will win the struggle at all, and if we win we do not know when that will be.

Post-materialist/post-functionalist revolutions mean that political actions should be driven by factors such as the ethical call from our conscience because we are undeniably struck by the pain of another human being: 'humanitarian intervention is justified when it is a response to acts that shock the moral conscience of mankind' (Walzer, 1977). The meaningfulness and irreducible otherness of the other are causes in themselves that demand to be done justice, like doing justice for the sake of justice or loving for the sake of love. Our conscience calls for change when we feel that our freedom or the freedom of others is too much impinged on, in whatever form of oppression. Societies change when the needs and meanings of people remain structurally unfulfilled (Caldarado, 2014). We come into action to listen to them and help others fulfill their unique potential. This seems to be a recursive argument: A lack of freedom for people to fulfill their meaning potential asks for more freedom. The inherent meaningfulness of the freedom of individuals to fulfill their meaning potential is the core of non-functionalist revolution.

This post-materialist revolution will not bring us to a permanent state of bliss like a Communist Valhalla, but it requires a continuous revolution, a continuous sensitivity to examine where our potential of meanings gets reduced and where to fight for justice (Trotsky, 1923). When there is no criticism and no call for revolution anymore, then we need to worry. Being human implies continuously brushing up our social sensitivity (social meaning) and fighting for justice (larger meaning).

Maslowian Basic Needs Models of Transition

We have seen how both capitalist and Marxist models are based on materialist ideas of social change (although there are many exceptions to these stereotypes of capitalism and Marxism). Many of these ideas seem to be based on a variation of the Hierarchy of Needs theory from psychologist Abraham Maslow. This theory states that the basic material needs of individuals must be fulfilled before individuals can realise their potential of social and larger meanings. First, give people food and shelter before they can find meaning in life and fight for social change.

However, few systematic studies have been conducted to test Maslow's hypothesis, and the existing research shows that Maslow's model only works in capitalist countries. In non-capitalist countries, material conditions are neither sufficient nor necessary for self-realisation and social change (Bouzenita, 2016; Wachter, 2003; Gambrell & Cianci, 2003; Wahba & Bridwell, 1976). For example, giving money and building homes and industries does not immediately change the spirit of people in a non-capitalist country, as exemplified by the large-scale failure of so-called 'humanitarian interventions'. The reason for this is that in less-capitalist countries, many individuals do not have a strong functionalist focus on materialist, hedonist, or self-oriented types of meaning, but they (also) focus on social and larger meanings.

Formulated more formally, this research refutes the Marxist idea that the societal superstructure follows from the materialist base. Socio-economic circumstances do not completely determine the meanings of a population. There is no pyramidal hierarchy of needs in which individuals first need to fulfill lower materialist needs before they can experience life as meaningful. For example, individuals in communist countries were guaranteed work, housing, and transport, but the picture of their daily life was gloomy; the USSR seemed bound to fail due to its functionalist focus on materialist meanings and its lack of freedom for social and larger meanings. Thus, citizens are not mere functions of their socio-economic conditions—although individuals are, of course, to some extent influenced by their circumstances—and money and power may increase the practical opportunities to fulfill their meaning potential.

The failure of the Maslowian model of the Hierarchy of Needs also seems to explain the failure of micro-credits, which were hyped by developmental economists in the 1990s and 2000s (Duvendack & Palmer-Jones, 2011; Westover, 2008). Individuals who were unable to receive a loan from a regular bank were offered small financial loans to start their own company and to receive training, to become ultimately a profitable company. However, these micro-credit programmes have been shown to have only small or even negative effects in the long term, and created debt and dependency of already poor individuals (Duvendack & Palmer-Jones, 2011; Westover, 2008). Furthermore, business failure and financial dependency seemed to undermine the self-esteem of small business owners.

> For example, when I spoke with a local tailor in Dar Es Salaam, Tanzania, he told me that he had received a loan to buy a new Singer sewing machine and to improve his shop. To be able to repay the loan, he needed a larger income than before. He found it difficult to increase his profits, because there had not been a change in the demand for tailored clothes, and he experienced more competition from other tailors who had also increased their productivity thanks to micro-credits. Meanwhile, Uganda had made trade deals with China so that cheap clothes were dumped on the Ugandan market. He struggled to repay the loan and was forced to work more hours. One could say that the banker had not conducted a good market analysis, or that the tailor should have been offered marketing skills training. However, there was a more fundamental problem. Most of his customers were friends and family, and he did not want to charge them more money than he had done, even though due to that he struggled financially. He told me that it is more important to help others than to make a profit: Social meaning trumps material profit. The situation made him feel trapped, and he did not know how to get out of this poverty trap. Thus, his social and larger meanings clashed with the materialist and self-oriented meanings from his bankers. Any developmental aid model should start bottom up, from the perspective of ordinary people like this tailor.

Another example of the failure of Maslowian reasoning can be found approximately 1,000 kilometres west of the Tanzanian tailor, in Uganda.

We sat in the refreshing shadow of a baobab at the end of a hot Ugandan afternoon. We were about to have a conversation that would turn my Western world-view upside down. I looked at the nine meager children around me; they must have been around ten years old. The yellow patchy hair suggested that some of them were in a late stage of Aids. Many of them had lived from 'a bob for a job' on the streets as long as they could remember, as their parents had died. Their life must be hard, I thought. But instead of speaking about the negative -and reinforcing feelings of desperation that I expected them to have, I asked for the positive: 'What are the most important things in your life?' Their eyes started to shine, and eager answers rolled over one another. 'Friends,' 'Helping others', 'Learning', 'Being a good person'. I asked them what made them get up from their bed or their sleeping place in the morning and start searching for job and food. 'I do it for my two younger sisters: I feed them.' 'I want to make this country better.' 'My love for the people and the animals on the streets.' I asked about their dreams for the future. Like all children, some had unrealistic dreams like becoming a top footballer. 'I want to become the first female president.' Are you never worried about the future of your country? I asked. 'Yes, of course. But worrying does not help. When problems come, we will deal with them then.' 'We can only do what is good, here and now.'

Their answers surprised me, and I started to realise that I had projected my Western idea of needing to fulfill our basic materialist needs before we can live a meaningful life. Instead, they showed me that meaning can be found everywhere, anytime. Meaning even seems to be the driver of their survival activities; without meaning, they would possibly not feel motivated to get up in the morning. This conversation debunked the (neo)colonial myth that in these so-called 'survival economies', people only struggle and do not experience their lives as meaningful. Many research studies have confirmed this: struggle for survival and social/larger meaning are not opposites but can co-exist; -all living creatures are endowed with survival and mutual-aid instincts, although people in less-capitalist countries focus less on materialist self-oriented values and more on social and larger meanings. In capitalist countries, we have been spoon-fed the idea that our personal materialist needs must be fulfilled, albeit just some basic needs. Consequently, when we lose our income, house, or health, we feel that life has become meaningless. Furthermore, our (neo)colonial mindset sees other people as variables of their materialist functions: when they lack economic success, their life must be meaningless. However, the meaningfulness of life is unconditional. When you do not indoctrinate people from a young age onwards that meaning in life depends on materialist and self-oriented success, then life does not feel meaningless when they are not successful. Their social and larger meanings make them more resilient to cope with dire circumstances, and their life remains meaningful, possibly more meaningful than how rich capitalist individuals see themselves.

These nine children had deconstructed my Western concepts of meaning. One of the boys saw how touched I was by their stories, and without speaking he took my wrist and put a small bracelet around it, made from long grass and a piece of iron chain he must have found somewhere. He could not have made his point better—following his intuition, symbolically connecting and showing larger meaning in life. I knew that he had just given me the revolutionary answer to the quest for meaning that I had been on since I had met the elderly man as a young student (see Introduction).

Conclusions

This chapter showed that materialist conditions are neither sufficient nor necessary to live a meaningful life. Social and larger meanings are unconditional. Consequently, the functionalist–materialist ideals of social change, which stereotypically underlie both capitalism and Marxism, seem to fail. The spirit of people cannot be changed by powerholders sitting behind the joystick of a drone or by throwing cash at them. Change comes from within a people when they feel that their meaning potential is structurally unfulfilled, particularly when this involves a lack of political freedom (social and larger meanings), which seems a more important motivator for change than a lack of economic freedom (materialist, self-oriented meanings). Thus, socio-political change is not merely created by analysing what is wrong with materialist conditions and by demanding functionalist–material change, but by transcending these conditions and focusing on social connections and larger visions and beliefs. This is where a meaning-oriented perspective on economics can stop the perpetuum mobile from sustaining the ten characteristics of the Capitalist Life Syndrome that were discussed in this second part of the book. The next part will examine how sustainable change is emerging in the Meaning-Oriented Economy.

Key Points

1. Both capitalist and Marxist models of socio-economic transition and humanitarian political–military interventions often have a functionalist focus on materialist types of meaning.
2. The idea that individuals require the fulfillment of basic needs before they can live a meaningful life is based on a capitalist ideology and does not apply to less-capitalist countries. Fulfillment of material needs is neither necessary nor sufficient for change in less capitalist countries.

3. Functionalist–materialist interventions cannot change the spirit of people when they do not already have a functionalist and materialist perspective.
4. Research indicates that a functionalist–materialist focus is not effective in non-capitalist countries and has limited slow effects on transitioning towards capitalism.
5. Both neo-Marxist and existential philosophers describe how models of socio-economic change should do justice to the complexity and plurality of meaning in life.
6. Socio-economic change does not only happen for functionalist, materialist, or self-oriented reasons, but also for the inherent meaningfulness of people. Individuals can experience a call for change when a limited perspective is imposed on them and they lack the freedom to fulfill their meaning potential.

Part III

The Meaning-Oriented Economy

Chapter 14

Meaning-Oriented Perspectives
on Economics & Transition

Radical transformation of society requires personal and social change first or at least simultaneously. (Quote attributed to Thai politician Sulak Sivaraksa)

Ten Perspectives

Have all economic ideals failed or become impossible in our 21st century? Do we live in a post-economists' society? We have seen how rational and moral liberalism was based on the ideal of rational citizen-consumers, but psychologists have shown that humans are highly irrational. The neoliberal model proposes a mind-manipulating government to protect the market, but its sacrifices of democracy and individual freedom are inconsistent with its own philosophy and are regarded as morally unjustifiable by increasing numbers of people. We may never be able to complete liberate ourselves from this Nietzschean will to power, according to Foucault, as our minds are always manipulated, and we cannot live in an abstract vacuum outside the societal mind games (Coolsaet, 2015). The alternative of returning to classical Marxist–collectivist values of unifying workers all over the world seems out of date in our individualist era (Chapter 13). We have seen how both capitalist and Marxist economic models seem to fail as they are to some extent based on assumptions of materialist functionalism. Thus, people who want societal change may need a radically different perspective on society, not merely a shift of authors writing the same story with different words.

The Meaning-Oriented Economy offers a possible answer. Chapter 6 has shown how a meaning-oriented perspective has already started to emerge from post-materialist economics. A Meaning-Oriented Economy has a predominantly non-functionalist approach towards social or larger meanings, seen from a complex interaction between individual and society, with a plurality of meanings. Research in Chapter 7 also showed that individuals with a meaning-oriented perspective on the economy have better existential, social, psychological, and physical well-being. This chapter will elaborate on the emergence of the Meaning-Oriented Economy. This will start by explaining how capitalism is based on a dualist view of mind versus body, whereas the Meaning-Oriented Economy is non-dualistic. This will be followed by a non-dualistic description of the recent meaning-oriented turn.

Cosmocentrism

Some of the world's oldest petroglyphs (carvings in rocks) can be found in Bella Coola, a hidden valley in British Columbia, Canada. Some 10,000 years ago, the first-nation people created an elaborated area full of symbols in the rocks. A returning pattern in these carvings in this area is a circle in a circle in a circle. A first nation elder explained the meaning of this petroglyphic symbol to me: 'The inner circle symbolises the physical self and all our material possessions, the second circle the community of people, animals and nature, and the outer circle the spiritual world of the universe, Spirit, death and life. All circles are connected with each other: the outer requires the inner, and vice versa.'

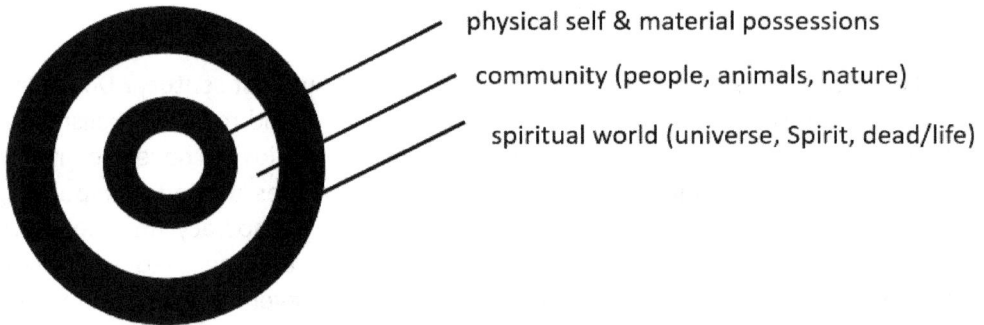

physical self & material possessions

community (people, animals, nature)

spiritual world (universe, Spirit, dead/life)

For the first-nation people on the west coast of what is nowadays called Canada, economic behaviour, the inner circle, is always embedded in the social and spiritual worlds. *Homo economicus*, if there is someone like that, is always part of a community and a universe and can only be understood from within these larger perspectives. This also implies that all economic behaviour has inherently a social and spiritual meaning: 'When we share with others, we share with ourselves' (Navajo saying); 'By caring for others we care for the spirits.' (Mohawk saying). We are part of nature and the universe, not a transcendent species without any impact and responsibility for creating balance and harmony (Deloria, 2012, 2003). The first-nation people have many examples of a free-gift economy, such as *pow-wows* and giveaways that are social events, spiritual events, and economic happenings at the same time. At the end of such spiritual ceremonies, there is space for individuals to give away belongings (Cashdan, 2019; Deloria, 2012, 2003; Moore, 1993). The gift has economic, social, and spiritual meanings at the same time. Thus, the economy of the first-nation people balanced all these different types of meaning simultaneously: materialist/self-oriented, social, larger and existential–philosophical (Deloria, 2012, 2003). This is called cosmocentrism, the idea that the universe is harmoniously ordered and integrated and that humans have the responsibility to maintain this stability and harmony.

First-nation philosopher Vine Deloria (2012, 2003) wrote that possibly the largest difference between the first nation and capitalist economic philosophies is the Cartesian dualism of the latter. That is, for most nations in history all dimensions are at least to some extent intertwined (descriptive), and these should be balanced in actions (normative). Capitalism seems only possible because of a split between the materialist world and other worlds, whereas many collectivist economies seem to assume a non-split of physical–communal–universal being. Consequently, the colonisation of Northern America by European settlers did not only have a materialist meaning, the stealing of first-nation land and freedom, but also meant a loss of community and spirit. Cosmocentrism was replaced by anthropocentrism. The physical land was robbed of its social and spiritual meaning and became a product in the hands of financial interests. Even today American courts have decided that an interstate oil pipeline could go through holy land; the courts seem to ignore the meaning that the land has for the multiple circles of first-nation people. The capitalist system that was enforced on these people did not do justice to the complex balancing that they had been maintaining for millennia. Capitalism splits the economic process off from the community and the larger perspectives. The economic activity was no longer balanced with social and spiritual interests in the economic domain. It may be hypothesized that this split explains why a large number of first-nation individuals experience bad mental health such as depression or substance misuse (Fleming & Ledogar, 2008).

Almost all non-Western social-economic philosophies show similar non-reductionist ideas that focus on balancing physical, social, and spiritual domains. No religion could ever think of cutting or even loosening the bond between nature, community, and individual, and accordingly do not focus on the Cartesian ratio but on intuitive experiences and symbols that transcend divisive concepts in space and time (Cassirer,1944/1992). For example, the Upanishads describe the intertwining of *damah* (self-restraint), *daya* (compassion/love for all life), and *dāna* (charity). Ancient Aztecs had a complex system of communal land and property possession, and their system intertwined community and spirituality. The Ancient Egyptian Book of the Dead suggested how the economy should be part of the current community and spirituality. The Japanese concept of Ikigai implies a subtle balance between what you love, what you are good at, what the world needs, and what you can be paid for. The Dark and Middle Ages were dominated by guilds and craftsmen who would put community and the quality of the product or service first over any profit. These are all examples of social economies that were introduced in Chapter 4.

How does this collectivist cosmocentrism work on an individual level, seen from a phenomenological perspective? In our daily lives, Western individuals do usually not reflect on meaning in life, and we do not split the material world from our social and spiritual world, as we 'simply' live a meaningful life—no ratio involved. We feel that we are inside the hot flow of experiencing of what is meaningful to us, such as the meanings that we have been taught or we have chosen in our life. We usually only start to reflect on our meanings and explicitly ask questions about meaning when something unexpectedly disrupts our flow of experiencing, such as unexpected life events, accidents, a serious physical disease, unemployment, economic crisis, or a life-changing collective trauma such as 9/11 (Vos, 2018). Thus, like the native Americans say, in our daily life experiences, we intuitively balance the unseparated material, social, and spiritual worlds. However, capitalism brings with it the counter-intuitive idea of the rational *Homo calculus* with its dominant functionalist focus on the physical world, artificially separated from its self-oriented, social, larger and existential types of meaning.

The Meaning-Oriented Economy builds on the indigenous cosmocentrist models whereby our critical intuition balances all six types of meaning. Therefore, to exemplify the Meaning-Oriented Economy, the next chapters will give many examples of indigenous people.

Meaning as Driver of Socio-Economic Change

As determine in the previous chapter, seen from a meaning-oriented perspective, socio-political change does not start from a functionalist–materialist focus but from the critical intuition that one's meaning potential is done injustice. The Capitalist Life Syndrome inherently creates existential and psychological tensions that lead to its own demise. As Marx said in 1850: capitalism 'will carry within it the seeds of its own destruction'. That is, the increasing functionalisation and growing focus on materialist, hedonist, and self-oriented types of meaning can lead to an existential and psychological crisis. The capitalist dream is revealed as mere imagination and symbols in the harsh reality of daily life. It is this sense of existential urgency and psychological pressure that forces individuals to consider personal change and demand social change. People realise that they suffer due to the oppression in the capitalist system (Guba-McCallister, 2019). Thus, the Capitalist Life Syndrome leads to a sense of being trapped and existential and mental health crisis. This can reach a point that an individual concludes: *If nothing changes, I will die physically, psychologically or existentially; therefore, something MUST change.*

This is not merely a socio-economic revolution, but an existential revolution. That is, it is not merely one 'thing' or 'aspect' that is not done justice in our life: The pressure comes from the totality of our being, which feels it is done injustice (Dilthey, 2010). Tension builds up in all types of meaning: We feel that we are struggling to find materialist, self-oriented, social, larger, and existential meaning in life. Karl Jaspers calls this a boundary situation in life. We are not confronted with one specific problem, boundary, or limitation in our life, but we start to feel that our totality, and the totality of our fellow humans, is done injustice in the current functionalist system. We have become replicable cogs in a complex functionalist machine blindly running towards materialist, hedonist, and self-obsessed goals. It is our sense of inherent meaningfulness that calls for change: *We are worth it, to spread our wings wider than what our situation allows us*. We are more than a cog in the machine, we are more than just an employee, and our life is more than living from kick to kick. Our sense of community, connecting, and belonging to humankind and wanting a better world for all call for change.

Research on national crises or political–economic transition show how citizens are not only struggling with their socio-economic situation, but their complete sense of meaning is shattered (Chapter 8). For example, after the fall of communism, individuals felt disoriented and had not only to develop a new economy but also a new perspective on life. However, to some extent there was some overlap between the functionalism and the materialism of both communism and capitalism, which led to some continuation of fundamental perspectives on life. After the 2007/2008 crash, individuals started to question the functionalist, materialist and self-oriented perspectives more, and as such they seemed to experience an existential crisis in which they had to redesign a new perspective on life. The loss of work or the foreclosure of one's house meant that people started to ask themselves what they have been working for all these years. In capitalist countries, there are many vulnerable groups of individuals struggling to survive.

Thus, there seems to be a mutual interactive relationship between material circumstances and meaning. On the one hand, the previous chapter has debunked the Maslowian myth that people need basic material needs fulfilled to live a meaningful life, and that poor material conditions automatically lead to people going on the streets to demand social change. For example, poorer countries have a higher average general life satisfaction than rich countries. On the other hand, socio-economic inequality, bad housing situations, negative neighbourhoods, a lack of green space, and social isolation can lower one's happiness and life satisfaction, particularly for individuals for whom material success and status are important (Chapter 8). However, people do not necessarily need much economic wealth to experience life as meaningful and to feel satisfied with life. As long as they have some sense of political freedom, belonging to a community, and social fairness (i.e., social and larger types of meaning), they have the resilience to cope with the materialist struggles. Thus, as long as individuals feel that they have social and political opportunities and fairness, they do not feel an existential urgency to demand social change. However, when the social and political opportunities to realise their meaning are structurally undermined or individuals experience a deep sense of socio-economic unfairness, their existential and psychological pressures can reach a boiling point: *revolución!*

This theoretical explanation of social change will become much clearer in the next section and chapters. The next section will give an overview of the evidence for the transition from capitalism to a Meaning-Oriented Economy. The next four chapters will describe four different ways of what a meaning-oriented society could look like. This loosely follows the political activism model from Olin Wright (2010). Chapter 14 will describe how individuals may find meaning within capitalism, Chapter 15 explores meaning outside capitalism, Chapter 16 describes the fight against capitalism, and Chapter 17 sketches meaning beyond capitalism.

Evidence for the Meaning-Oriented Turn

Sociological Evidence

Chapter 6 previously introduced the turn towards meaning in the economy. Not only psychologists have reported these trends, but also economists. For example, in 2016, PricewaterhouseCoopers (PwC) published a report about the World Economic Forum showing that many of the major CEOs believe that the Meaning-Oriented Economy will reach a tipping point around 2020. In their 2017 book, Drewell and Larsson cite a study from Quattroporte, which used data from more than 100 million internet users and 1 billion tweets; it showed that since approximately 2012 the attention has more than doubled for topics on the sharing economy, entertainment, living debt-free, impact of investments, and circular economy. Furthermore, Hurst (2017) cite research on an increase in employment in meaning-oriented sectors of the economy between 2010 and 2020, such as social work (24%), education (15%), health (29%), and care and services (27%). Drewell, Larsson and Hurst refer to the Millennial and Xennial generations who are particularly interested in meaning-oriented topics such as material minimalism, social connections, ethics, and political activism. However, many of these trends could also indicate the emergence of the experience economy, instead of a meaning-oriented transition. These do not clearly distinguish the experience economy from the Meaning-Oriented Economy (Chapter 8).

Some support for the meaning-oriented turn was provided by the World Values Survey, which is the largest longitudinal study available on cross-cultural values. Inglehardt (2019,1997) concludes on the basis of 40 years of data analyses that there is a worldwide 'post-materialist' trend. He gives examples of how people value social relationships, community, and ecological protection more than in the past. However, the survey only focuses on the question of *what* is changing, not *how* people are changing, as it does not include questions about functionalism or post-functionalism. It seems that Inglehardt has a relatively monistic and functionalist perspective himself, which seems to imply a historical fallacy as his perspective is the result of his cultural-historical perspective. In his questionnaire, he gives people the Manichean option of comparing the values of survival (which he equates with materialism) with the values of self-expression (post-materialism). However, this does not seem to give the pluralistic option that people can have multiple simultaneous meanings; for example, neoliberalism is characterised by a combination of materialism and self-orientation, whereas the post-materialist economies in this chapter focus on social and larger meanings.

Thus, although these generic studies indicate a meaning-oriented turn, there are many questions about their methodology. Therefore, it is important to zoom in and examine what researchers say about the meaning-oriented changes for specific groups: consumers, employees, investors, and creators and owners of businesses. The following overview is based on the literature review in Chapter 6, and many of these examples are based on Dik, Byrne, and Steger (2013/2017).

Meaning-Oriented Consumers
Consumers start to buy products not merely for their functionality or nice experience, but with a focus on the overall meaning—e.g., the overall behaviour of the company, such as tax evasion, environmental track record, and employment practices such as paying a living wage to all employees and no/low bonuses for management. There is a trend towards consumers buying products more locally to prevent environmental costs of transport and to support individual businesses. Furthermore, there is a large increase in companies that focus on sharing resources, such as Uber, Couchsurfing, Airbnb, eBay, Zipcar, and WeWork (although these companies have been criticised for their materialist aims, and the unfair treatment of employees by not offering them the rights of a contract worker). Increasing numbers of companies tailor their products and services around the customer, not merely to offer them a nice experience, but to fulfill their meaning. For example, the start-up company One Medical Group in San Francisco offers a GP service without waiting lists, where appointments are made online, and where there is no time pressure during consultations (Hurst, 2017).

Meaning-Oriented Employees
The stereotypic functionalist manager views employees merely as a commodity to be purchased at the lowest price possible, a tool for achieving the goals set by the company owner. For example, Graeber (2018) described how in neoliberal economies there are many 'bullshit jobs' that are without a clear meaning and may be boring, repetitive, dangerous, dehumanizing, and often filled by less-educated workers. However, companies are starting to give more importance to employees. Work can no longer be thought of without considering social and larger types of meaning.

As early as the 1970s, Studs Terkel (2011) observed in his ground-breaking study that employees do not merely work for financial sustenance; they search for meaning in their employment, which they want to see as worthwhile and providing a sense of purpose. In the 1970s there may have been fewer job opportunities for individuals to realise their meanings, but this has exponentially increased since then: In 1975 17% of the S&P 500 was composed of intangible assets, whereas in 2015 this has risen to 84% (Drewell & Larsson, 2017). For example, Daniel Pink shows in his book *Drive*

(2011) how professionals do not merely want to work for a salary or a nice experience, but search for self-management and self-direction. A career is a self-chosen path of what individuals find personally meaningful. This also implies a good person–environment fit is important so an individual's meaning fits in the organisation. This also includes organisations designing jobs for the individual employees, as well as job crafting by the employee, for instance by changing tasks, job relations, and job perceptions. People seem to engage more with their work when the work offers an attractive identity, is challenging but not too-challenging, has clear roles, offers meaningful rewards, gives employees and opportunity to be heard, and offers important relationships and competent supervision (Kahn & Fellows in Dik, Byrne, & Steger, 2013/2017). Another trend is that employees are seen more as independent, as in companies such as Uber and Airbnb. Similarly, the number of start-ups is growing exponentially, which may reflect a desire for freedom and the possibility for entrepreneurs to follow what is meaningful for small (Drewell & Larsson, 2017).

Thus, work has become an important source of meaning for individuals. Anna Tavis (2015) has developed a measure to examine the meaningfulness of work: the Workforce Purpose Index, which consists of multiple components. Tavis discovered that less than 28% of the American population regards their work as meaningful. Employees describe the following as the most meaningful: education, non-commercial organisations, agriculture and forestry, entertainment, health, the aerospace and car industry, research. The least meaningful are wholesale, retail, public facilities, construction, estate agents, advertising and public relations, catering, technology, transport, finances, accounting, banks, and insurances. Furthermore, Tavis found that employees who experience work as more meaningful receive better evaluations from managers, have more leadership roles, stay longer in their positions, and experience more job satisfaction by contributing to staff/colleagues and society as a whole.

Meaning-Oriented Organisation Structure
Company structures are also transforming. Companies are formulating a clearer purpose that does not merely include profit but also social and ecological meanings. For example, companies can aim for social justice and equal opportunities in society, offer opportunities for individuals to realise their human potential, share empowering knowledge or resources for free or at small prices, or connect people with one another. Ulrich and Ulrich (2010) describe a meaningful ('abundant') organisation as one that strengthens others, sustains both social and fiscal responsibility, aligns organisation purposes and individual motivation, makes high-performing teams high-relating teams, creates positive work that affirms and connects people, develops employees' competence and commitment, and shapes their sense of contribution. Thus, companies are being reorganised in such a way that they overcome static organisational paradigms and foster collaboration via self-management and evolution of the organisation's purpose via inclusion of all relevant voices. Examples are

American apparel brand Patagonia, Dutch health care organisation Buurtzorg, international steel manufacturer Nucor, and energy giant AES. These organisations are designed more often to foster the creation of human value, such as the bottom-up organization structure Semler (2002) has created in Semco International, with self-management teams that manage their own work and are supported in community building, peer support, and self-development.

Meaning-Oriented Leadership

The meaning-oriented organisation also requires a different type of leadership (e.g. Dik, Byrne, & Steger, 2013/2017). Meaning-oriented leaders are described more often as authentic, visionary, and empowering. They do not see their personnel as functionalist mechanics helping them to fulfill the goals of the company owners but as ends in themselves. Consequently, they use rewards and punishments as little as possible and instead create a work culture that stimulates the intrinsic motivation and self-determination of employees. Meaning-oriented leaders also stimulate team cohesion and social support, possibly not only because social meaning is inherently valuable for them but also because it is good for the company, as many studies show that positive work relationships lead to greater job satisfaction and productivity and lower sickness leave

Meaning-Oriented Human Resources Management

The search for meaning for employees goes beyond the traditional functionalist paradigms in HRM, which helped the company owners to make optimal use of their personnel. The Meaning-Oriented Economy implies a shift towards facilitating employees in finding a sense of meaning in work and including personnel in the formulation of the company's purpose and the organisation design. A crucial transition is that meaningful work becomes an end in itself. Meaning-oriented HRM helps all staff to find meaning in everyday tasks, stimulate relationships, personal growth, balance work and private life, regards colleagues as friends and family, views work as a craft, stimulates the idea of winning through collaboration, stimulates learning through experimenting and risk taking, and focuses on a good fit between the individual and the work tasks (Hurst, 2017).

Meaning-Oriented Finance

Institutional investors are starting to focus not merely on financial profit but on post-materialist meanings beyond this, such as considerations about the environment, social, and governance. Increasing numbers of investors have started to have social and green investment wallets. Examples are the Finance Initiative of the United Nations Environment Programme and the Principles for Responsible Investment, which has grown since 2006 into a network of over 1600 responsible institutional investors worth almost $70 trillion. There is also an increase in peer-to-peer lending platforms and crowdfunding, which has increased from €1.1 billion in 2013 to €5.4 billion in 2015 (Drewell & Larsson, 2017).

Meaning-Oriented Education

Education is inherently about meaning (Vos, Roberts, & Davies, 2019). There is no such a thing as a value-neutral fact. Therefore, governments often attempt to impose reforms to shape the curriculum and offer a 'hidden curriculum' of values and shaping of behaviour (Forrester & Garrett, 2016; Vallence, 1973; Freire, 1970/2018). Some of the most radical reforms happened under the Thatcher and Reagan administrations, which explicitly attempted to reduce the teaching of critical thinking skills and refocus education around a core curriculum of knowledge and skills for future white-collar jobs. Not only did the new programs focus predominantly on materialist and self-oriented values, while reducing social and larger meanings, education underwent a functionalist turn as well, turning schools into vocational, goal-directed learning factories where pupils learn for school tests instead of a love for learning (Forrester & Garrett, 2016; Vallence, 1973; Freire, 1970/2018). Internal motivation for learning was undermined by test-oriented teaching. Aronowitz & Giroux (1986/2003, p. 24) provide a gloomy summary of the resulting educational 'Bleak House': 'Instead of helping students to think about who they are and what they should do … teachers have been trained to use techniques, control student discipline, teach a given subject effectively and organise a day's activities as efficiently as possible.' Education prepares students to live in a functionalist, materialist–hedonist and self-oriented economy. What is at stake is not just the ability to be creative but the capacity for conceptual thought itself, which weakens the foundations of democracy, as awareness, self-reflection .and critical thinking are necessary for active citizenship. However, many authors report a slow but remarkable trend in capitalist countries: the role of meaning in education is becoming more acknowledged. A good example is the Finnish education model, which gives much autonomy to individual schools, teachers, and pupils and enables pupils to choose from a wide range of subjects that feel meaningful to them, including life-skills modules. This Finnish meaning-oriented education model ranks among the best in teaching professional and social skills (Vos, Roberts, & Davies, 2019).

Conclusions

The research literature is crystal clear: The economy in Western countries is changing. Whereas capitalist meanings have determined most economic stakeholders in the past, there seems to be a conscious trend to be open to a wide range of meanings, including non-functionalist approaches towards social and larger types of meaning. We saw examples from a meaning-oriented turn in consumption, employment, organisation structures, leadership, HRM, finances, and education.

This meaning-oriented transition is not a functionalist–materialist revolution as Marx described; this change started with the inherent meaningfulness of nature and people calling for justice to be done. Natural and social resources are no longer seen as mere cogs in the profit-making machine but as inherently meaningful. The planet deserves to be taken seriously in our production and consumption process. The workplace should help employees to find meaning and offer authentically meaningful products and services to customers. Whereas the Meaning-Oriented Economy offers a silent revolution in the West, it seems in line with the perspectives that indigenous people have had for thousands of years. To further exemplify the Meaning-Oriented Economy, the following chapters will elaborate four ways that individuals can experience meaning within, outside, against, and beyond capitalism.

Key Points

1. A Meaning-Oriented Economy has a predominantly non-functionalist approach towards social or larger meanings, seen from a complex interaction between individual and society, with a plurality of meanings. Research shows that individuals with a meaning-oriented perspective on the economy have better existential, social, psychological, and physical well-being.
2. A meaning-oriented perspective is based on a non-Cartesian dualistic model that transcends oppositions such as self–other and body–mind. From a non-dualistic perspective, all types of meaning are connected, and all are needed to live a full, meaningful life.
3. Research on societal transitions indicates a complex model in which individual and social processes interact; not merely materialist situations change but people's fundamental perspective on life changes.
4. The growth of the spirit of capitalism can lead to its own demise because the growing functionalisation and the increased focus on materialist, hedonist, and self-oriented types of meaning can build up existential and psychological pressures that can reach a tipping point and demand fundamental change. This is phenomenologically experienced as a call of conscience, as people feel that the totality of individuals is no longer done justice by capitalist perspectives.
5. The last chapters of this book describe how individuals can experience meaning within, outside, against, and beyond capitalism.

Chapter 15

Islands of Anarchy:
Meanings within Capitalism

'Our job is to create a sense of purpose!'(Mark Zuckerberg, 2017, in Zizek, 2019)

Islands of Meaning

Living a meaningful life within capitalism is like creating islands of meaning in the ocean of capitalism. Individuals can create their own meaningful spaces without changing the system. Capitalism remains functionalistally oriented towards materialism, hedonism, and the self, but individuals create personally meaningful moments and places.

Creating islands of meaning often starts small, like the fully suited-up businessman who rebels within the system by wearing the Donald Duck socks that his children gave him on Father's Day. My daily life may, in general, feel boring or mechanical, but I live for these moments that I can go wild and feel free; I look forward to my modern *panem et circences*, such as adventure holidays, ecstatic concerts, booze and drug trips, etc. These are all decisions that focus on experiences that feel more meaningful than my grey daily life, although these examples remain superficial. I can also decide to start small-scale projects that focus on social and larger meanings, like guerrilla gardening (gardening in public spaces) or volunteering at my community centre. Islands of meaning can also be reflected in deciding to work fewer hours and spend more time with family, volunteering, or in leisure activities. Islands of meaning can also be reflected in shopping behaviour: I decide not to buy meat in bulk anymore but go to the butcher, or I buy my bread from the local baker instead of at the supermarket chain. Thus, islands of meaning range from small to large.

These islands can also seep into the enterprise organisation. For example, company aims can transform into 'Meaning Inc.', as Bains et al. (2007) describe. Making money and attaining material success are no longer the sole purpose of the company; creating positive production processes and working relationships between the employees are similarly important goals. For employees, pride and recognition for their unique contributions are important motivations in addition to salary. Sales do not come at disproportional costs to workers and nature. Employees feel that they do not merely work to make a living but are making a positive contribution to society via their work. Customers are not viewed merely from a materialist perspective as money spenders but as fellow humans who need social connection and a moral approach as much as a materialistically functional product. New values of companies include fairness, equality, empathy, community spirit, and human concern. These values reflect a wide plurality of different types of meaning but with the main focus on social and larger meanings. Such values are experienced as authentic, and short-term material gains may be sacrificed for following long-term values. This implies that leaders become compassionate visionaries to guide in building and sharing values throughout the organisation and beyond. This almost becomes a form of lean manufacturing, where all resources and processes are focused on shared meanings. This can be reflected in flat, democratic, and employee-centred organisational structures that offer individuals a sense of belonging and ownership in both processes and outcomes (Laloux, 2014).

A good example of a meaning-oriented company is Semco, run by the Brazilian entrepreneur Ricardo Semler (2003), who gave workers the responsibility for their work process and organisation without targets set by higher management: 'too much structure can strangle the soul'. Semco's profits increased 40-fold over 20 years with little staff turnover, which Semler attributes to the ethos of the right work/life balance, with hammocks for employees during the day, Retire-a-Little plans, and abolition of the control and boarding-school mentality giving way to real trust in his employees. Workers can flexibly create their own agenda according to their biorhythms and personal meanings and situation: for example, someone could enjoy a sunny Monday on the beach and work on a chilly Sunday. The workplace also offers individuals opportunities to use their talents and realise their calling in life. Also, for those for whom the job is just a way to make a living the workplace, or some aspects of it, opens up many opportunities to realise meanings and talents that they may have not considered before.

Another example is the social market economy, or Rhine Capitalism, which dominates West-European countries such as Germany. The Rhine model is more than a slightly adjusted form of Anglo-Saxon capitalism, as it offers a completely different perspective on life (Peters & Weggeman, 2019). It acknowledges the importance of social and larger meanings both in organisations and in the economy. Key concepts include solidarity, team play, and personal autonomy, and continuous learning; it is principle-led, both task and process oriented, and tailored to unique contexts. Profit is not based on increasing the financial margins but by limiting costs for management and inefficient procedures, by having experts show the way forward, and by putting the customer central. Instead of managers or shareholders who know little about the content of the companies and who have no direct skin in the game, experts lead organisations from the bottom up, with freedom for intelligent disobedience and with the help of a large back-office. Thus, responsibilities are decentralised and tailored to the unique meanings of employees; for example, work councils play an important role in deciding the organisation structure, tasks, and aims of organisations. This means that shareholders are replaced by all stakeholders as the orientation of the company aligns with the motto *Liberté, égalité et fraternité!* (Peters & Weggeman, 2019). In this spirit, on a macro-economic level, the Dutch polder model displays a pragmatic recognition of pluriformity and cooperation despite differences, and, the government, trade unions, and employer's unions negotiate to find common ground, a cultural attitude that has been attributed to the Dutch history of having to collaborate in their fight against water and foreign invasions (Hendriks, 2017).

Research on quality of life and happiness indicates that individuals living in countries with some type of these welfare economics have the highest scores (Delson, 2000). It seems that a large civil society as the Dutch poldermodel espouses is associated with a thriving economy (Van Zanden & Prak, 2013). For example, whereas the Netherlands had been haunted by high unemployment and rising public deficits in the 1970s and 1980s, it turned overnight into a flourishing economy in the 1990s. However, more research is needed, particularly because the concept of the polder model is often used as an ambiguous umbrella term, and because its praxis is crumbling (Keune, 2016).

Thus, from a meaning-oriented perspective, these types of welfare and negotiation economies seem to be some of the most meaningful. It may be argued that both the freedom of the capitalist system and the financial safety net of the welfare state facilitates individuals to optimise what is meaningful for them: this freedom allows creative exploration of new opportunities, and the welfare state allows the possibility of a safety net in case of failure.

Most of these examples are possible without changing the capitalist system. Mackey and Sisodia (2013) write that they see opportunities to marry purpose and capitalism into 'conscious capitalism'. They argue that purpose should be authentic, and the organisation structure should be non-functionalist. Thus, they believe in the opposite of what Friedman wrote about when he mentioned that taking care of customers, employees, and business philanthropy are means to an end in his frequently cited 1970 treatise *'The social responsibility of business is to increase its profits'*. Mackay and Sisodia argue that centring a company around meaning does not undermine the fundamentals of a free market, competition, and private property. The opposite is true as free-enterprise capitalism enables a company to do good: 'Business is good because it creates value, it is ethical as it is based on voluntary exchange and it is noble because it can elevate our existence and it is heroic because it lifts people out of poverty and creates prosperity.' (Mackey & Sisodia, 2013, p.21) They argue that the problem is not capitalism but *crony capitalism*—the materialist, functionalist and selfish reduction of the large potential that capitalism has to offer in their imagination. Conscious capitalism consists for them of individual enterprises who 'do right because it is right': they centre around higher purpose and core values, which are revealed in conscious leadership, culture and management and stakeholder integration. For them, corporate social responsibility is a neologism, as each corporation has the potential to be social and adding an ethical dimension is not a burden or sacrifice but an inherent part of the business. Subsequently, they write that conscious capitalism leads to larger profits precisely because it does not directly focus on profits; they cite research showing that in conscious companies, investments and stock market returns are larger, and they have larger sales, lower marketing and administrative costs, and lower employee turnover. Later in this chapter we will see some limitations to these arguments. However, it may be argued that what Mackay and Sisodia plea for is no longer capitalism, as all perspectives they offer on meaning are different from the spirit of capitalism as described in Part II.

The Third Way

Around the turn of the last millennium, there was a political trend to create spaces for meaning without changing the global capitalist system. Tony Blair led New Labour, Bill Clinton New Democrats, and Gerhard Schroder Das Neue Mitte. Although they all developed their own version, they shared the philosophy called 'The Third Way', a metaphor to describe their alternative to both capitalism and socialism, focused around the ideal of the reflexive, self-responsible individual who has the 'moral thread of self-actualisation [which means] authenticity and being true to oneself' (Giddens, 1991, p.97).

The Third Way has been described as a response to 'the death of communism and socialism' with the fall of the Wall. What the Third Way ideologists particularly rejected was what Walter Lippmann called 'statism': a large welfare state, bureaucracy, planned economy, and nationalisation of economic functions such as public transport and electricity. They embraced the ideal of global capitalism, which meant the emergence of a free, privatised global market, unhindered by borders and regulations: 'the left could become comfortable with markets, with the role of business in the creation of wealth, and the fact that private capital is essential for social investment' (Giddens, 1991, p.34).

The economic ideology of socialism may be dead, but in the Third Way's interpretation its social values survive: fairness, social justice, liberty and equality of opportunities, cosmopolitanism, solidarity, and responsibility for others. This includes the neoconservative idea that a stable sense of self needs to be established in a stable community, such as a family or a nation. These Third Way adherents believed that these values are inherently meaningful but that the market does not offer them as these values are under attack by gangster capitalism, Thatcherite selfishness, social atomism, and greed.

In the political arena these social values were quickly blended with some form of authoritarianism. For example, New Labour's mantra 'duty and responsibilities' was based on Keith Joseph's idea that the public debate and symbol politics can influence citizen behaviour, and Blair explicitly invited behavioural economists to 'bend public behaviour to more beneficial outcomes' (Halpern, 2010,p.241). Blair continued the Thatcherite red herring of labeling individuals on benefits as 'citizen-consumers' and 'scoundrels'. Reforms of the welfare state were framed as not only cost-reducing but also giving incentive to work; for example, the American Welfare to Work and the British Job centres used benefits as incentives and coercion to unemployed and sick people, by creating a culture of fear of losing benefits and not having enough to live on. Thus, New Labour translated the imagination of social society and symbol politics into a functionalist reality.

Third Way politicians were enthusiastic promotors of enterprises and believed that everyone would benefit from this via the miracle of an Invisible Hand. They introduced a new type of 'knowledge entrepreneur' and 'network entrepreneur'. They believed that in the global free market, creative individuals and decentralised groups would flourish and develop new creative products and services, for example in IT. These individuals would be self-realising and creatively follow their own meaning. A specific role could be fulfilled by the renewed idea of civil society, such as third sector and local communities.

However, it seems that the Third Way has failed. Many politicians have become disillusioned in the Third Way, and voters punished politicians in many countries by voting against them (Halpern, 2010). This failure has been attributed to several causes. First, many politicians believed that as long as workers are flexible and have the right skills and values, the free global market will make them flourish: 'we are what we make of ourselves' (Giddens, 1991, p. 75). To help people get equal opportunity, Third Way ideologists hammered on 'education, education, education'. However, this focus on the supply side of the market seemed to ignore that there was insufficient demand and that not each individual had enough personal resources to realise their potential (Jynaston & Green, 2019). There are structural thresholds in the market for small-scale entrepreneurs, such as requiring starting capital and competing with monopolists. Furthermore, the idea failed because not everyone has the financial, cognitive, social, and emotional capability to use the opportunities of education and training; for example, graduates from private schools have much better chances of success than those from public schools (Jynaston & Green, 2019). Consequently, the only thing that the Third Way did was to realise the Smilesian–Thatcherite self-help citizen.

Second, there seems to be a large gap between the political imaginations/symbols of the Third Way and economic reality. Faucher-King and Gales (2010) show in their analyses that, for example, under New Labour social inequality increased, absolute poverty grew, and social mobility decreased. Many government duties were privatised or covered in private–state partnerships, but the motivations of sub-contractors were often more focused on making a profit than delivering good quality. The quality-check was deregulated to independent regulators or to economic sectors themselves, which often meant nepotism and revolving doors between the regulator and the regulated.

Under Clinton, many protections for consumers and regulations for corporations were rewritten, while rights and lobby groups for companies increased (Reich, 2016). This meant that in their daily life, many citizens did not see any of the values that politicians had been speaking about. It has been argued that the privatisation of public contracts can lead to a lowering of the quality standards and transforming public works into a tick-the-box exercise that would only minimally fulfill the criteria of regulatory and government bodies (LeGrand & Robinson, 2018; Kishimoto, Petitjean, & Steinfort, 2017).

> One example was given by a project manager on road works in London, who wants to remain anonymous (personal communication, 2019). He gave the example of citizens complaining about a pothole in the road. This complaint would lie on the pile of complaints that the council had received, and they would prioritise solving the cases that were the most dangerous and had the largest number of complaints. The council has a procurement contract with his private company to fill an X number of potholes. Under pressure of making maximum profit, the company uses the cheapest material to fill the pothole, which would satisfy the council, but which would quickly become a new pothole that would require new repairs and new income for the company. Thus, privatisation led to the inefficiency of road works, and the company did not experience a responsibility towards the community to deliver reliable roads.
>
> A similar example was reported by an anonymous regulator in British waterworks, who described how the standards for water providers were set low and directly reflected the impact of corruption and nepotism (personal communication, 2019). Thus, the privatisation and opening of the market led to lower quality of services for the general population and increased the social inequality in political and economic power.

Third, the trust in the market has led to increased deregulation and self-regulation by the banking sector, leading to unlimited growth of complex financial products. The ultimate consequence of this was the 2007/2008 crash and historically low trust in the free market (Tooze, 2018; Whitham, 2018; Sornette, 2017).

Fourth, politicians said that their focus on humanitarian values led them to international 'humanitarian interventions' and 'fixing failed states' such as Yugoslavia and Iraq. However, it was later discovered that the decisions for these wars were based on lies, and that financial gains were, to some extent, more direct reasons (see Chapter 6).

In sum, the Third Way created imaginations that contrasted starkly with the reality of people's daily life. Although in word the focus lay on social and larger values, the reality seemed more oriented towards materialist, hedonist, and self-oriented types of meaning. Individuals did not always seem to be regarded as meaningful in themselves but had to play their role in the larger societal function and were manipulated by the authoritarian public debate and coercive job coaches (Jynaston & Green, 2019; Faucher-King and Gales (2010). Ultimately, this led to an increased sense of fatalism and helplessness on the left, as the plan of the Big Society that had been called the last option for left ideology failed. These characteristics are similar to neoliberalism, albeit with a different name (Jordan, 2010). Perry Anderson concluded in the New Left Review (2000,p.7) that 'The third way is the best ideological shell of neoliberalism today'.

Meaning-Oriented Public Space

Socio-economic changes often go hand in hand with a change in the use of public space—i.e., the physical places where people can meet and meaning can happen (Sennett, 1976). Whereas work and private life were barely separated until the late Middle Ages, the urbanization and the emergence of the concept of 'private property' led people to develop sharper distinctions between private and public. A small elite had already been distinguishing itself from peasants and servants via walled castles and mansions, but in the 16th century larger parts of the population started to create separate islands of personal meaning—for example, via door locks and fences. Additionally, individuals started to distinguish themselves from one another by personalized design, as Pierre Bourdieu (2013) writes. For example, the living room was not a place anymore where people had to make a living but became a place where the interior design and paintings reflected their personality.

Thus, a difference emerged between neutral public spaces and meaningful personal spaces, whereas before public spaces were entwined with opportunities for personal connections and meaning. Sociologist Richard Sennett (1976) compared the design of Covent Garden with that of Trafalgar Square in London. Covent Garden was built in 1630 to stimulate the connection between people. Anyone who visits Covent Garden can experience this: The old market halls are buzzing with energy, buskers, live performances, and a relaxed atmosphere where friends can meet one another. In contrast, Trafalgar Square was built in the 19th century as a large open space, similar to the rebuilding of Paris by Hausmann. The cosiness of the small shops and sense of containment created by the arches of the market hall have been replaced by straight lines, grandiose fountains, and column with a statue of Lord Nelson on the top. Trafalgar Square feels impersonal, a place for showing off but not really connecting with others. Trafalgar Square has now become a place for tired tourists to sit down next to the fountains, countless pigeons, and mass protests. It is not a place to have a nice chat and a drink in a cosy environment with a friend. Trafalgar Square offers a functionalist design with the pre-given goal of evoking a sense of grandeur and nationalism, while Covent Garden offers the large potentiality of social meetings, artistic performances, shopping for specialty items, etc. Thus, the architect directed the form, material, and construction of Trafalgar Square towards pre-set goals, whereas the architect of Covent Garden used the form, material, and construction to offer many opportunities for people to meet and enjoy one another.

Functionalist designs help to optimise the functioning of buildings and public spaces. For example, the neoliberal functionalism of the Aylesbury Council Estate in London offered many homes to many people during a period in which there was a large shortage of housing. The homes provide all basic functions, such as a bedroom, living room, bathroom, and a kitchen. However, relatively little attention was given to what it is like to live there. This culminated in the hyper-functionalism of design and architecture of public spaces in the latter half of the 20th century. Additionally, under Margaret Thatcher, community centres and parks were closed, and communities started to centre around shopping complexes (Johnson, 2011). The central meeting place in modern neighbourhoods in the United Kingdom became shopping paradises, such as the Elephant and Castle centre that offered the first megastores in Europe. There are few gardens, few other colours than grey, all doors have the same colour and shape, and tenants are not allowed to change the looks. Thus, functionalist designs try to use the smallest number of materials and building efforts to create the maximum impact with the simplest forms. Formulated philosophically, the complex interaction of the four Aristotelean *aitia* of form, material, construction process, and goals was streamlined efficiently to merely achieve the basic goals.

The emergence of the Meaning-Oriented Economy also brings a transformation of public spaces (Vos, 2017b). The anonymous brutalist architecture from the '70s and '80s gets replaced with places where people feel at home and that they can make their own. The cattle-block structures of traditional offices in which individuals had been working between three low walls are being replaced by light, open office structures or artistic espresso bars where people bring their laptop. Open restaurant kitchens have become a trend so that customers can enjoy the cook's theatre performance.

On a superficial level, one may argue that this is a mere inauthentic experience economy, focused on profit making. For example, you do not walk into a store where they sell M&M's; you walk into a full experience where all your senses are affected— smell, taste, vision. Fashion stores do not sell clothes anymore but a lifestyle, with books and hipster gadgets lying next to socks and suits. Undoubtedly, there is a functionalist trend where public spaces reduce customers or visitors into a profitable experience machine. We are being nudged.

On another level, some third spaces, such as libraries and station waiting rooms, are also changing into experiential places where a variety of meanings start to cross over from material functions (lending books), hedonism (enjoying coffee, games), self-oriented (self-development via books), social (meeting, connecting and belonging) to larger (contributing to an ethical and better world), and existential–philosophical (fundamental sense of connectedness and freedom) meanings. Urban planners, architects, and designers use a diversity of physical cues and nudges to enable these meanings, such as how chairs are positioned towards each other, use of colours, natural materials and plants, round forms and variation. The meaning-oriented public spaces are often developed together with the local public and all stakeholders. 'Make it better than home. Make it better than retail. Even better than Starbucks. Make it honest, informal, inspiring, different and personal,' so writes Aat Vos in his book *How to Create a Relevant Public Space* (2017b).

Meaningful Global Networks

Public space does not exist merely in reality but also online. In *Second Life* individuals build their own avatar and in *Sim City* people build their own space. Virtual reality offers a variety of tailorable space, where the avatars of players can meet and interact, often in ways that feel more authentic than meeting a real person in a real physical space, as all avatar outfits and spaces are chosen by the individual to reflect what they find meaningful. The gaming industry is booming, possibly because it offers new ways to experience and express personal meanings, which is more than Postman's (2006) fatalistic interpretation that modern entertainment makes us 'amuse ourselves to death'. Research shows that gamers often describe their experiences as meaningful, connecting. and important in life (Kolo & Baur, 2004). It is clear that the internet has transcended its initial function of information-sharing and hedonism and has become a platform where many meanings can emerge.

Social media giants such as Facebook are some of the main sources of meaning manipulation, intentionally or unintentionally. For example, Facebook experienced a storm of public outrage when it was discovered that it had sold profile information to mind manipulation firms such as Cambridge Analytica. Each profile of an individual has around 5000 data points, which can be used in algorithms for targeted advertising campaigns. For example, possible voters against the EU were shown advertisements by the Leave Campaign such as 'The EU want to kill our cuppa tea', 'Islamist terrorism is a real threat to our way of life. Act now before we see an Orlando style of attack here'. Researchers have argued that these targeted campaigns led to the majority vote for Brexit (Goodwin & Heath, 2016). Consequently, in 2018, Facebook guru Mark Zuckerberg was called to the public pillory of parliamentary investigations in the United Kingdom and United States, facing much criticism. Social media users also expressed concern about how Facebook prioritises certain news items to certain individuals, including fake news. This led to large user campaigns to leave Facebook. Essentially, users were saying that they felt Facebook was too functionalist and materialist and did not care about them and their inherent meaningfulness but only about money and the wider capitalist system.

Facebook responded to the outrage by recruiting more staff to weed out fake news: 'fake news is not our friend'. Furthermore, Zuckerberg announced in June 2019 several changes in order to focus more on 'meaningful content' rather than functionalism, materialism, and self-obsession (theadminzone.com). The changes mean that Facebook will focus less on self-enhancement via posts on your personal profile ('see how cool my breakfast was') and more on interaction in groups. Zuckerberg has decided that meaningful content can be defined as the number of comments, shares, and positive responses to group posts, such as love or shocked-face emojis. A neutral emoji reflecting sadness or anger is not 'meaningful', even though this could feel meaningful for an individual—e.g., a sad face could implicate meaningful support in response to a post about the loss of a loved one. However, it is not the individual user who decides what is meaningful. The 'meaningfulness' of our engagement with Facebook is ultimately directed by Facebook algorithms, and we will not be able to argue or tailor their functionalist approach. Thus, meaningful content equals active user engagement, not a self-defined pluralistic sense of meaningfulness. Although this is an example of meaning under capitalism, this seems to be a very narrow perspective,

Neo-Fascism and Brexit

The failure of Third Way politics was followed by a trend towards neoconservative, populist, nationalist, and even neofascist politicians in many Western countries at the start of the 21st century (Bastow & Martin, 2003). Nationalism and neo-fascism may offer people a sense of meaning. The romantic ideal of The Nation and The Ideal Race can give a sense of belonging and community, something that people may feel they lack in the materialist era of global capitalism, although this is a narrow example of a social meaning. They simultaneously claim their personal rights and feel entitled; their self-oriented narcissism may be understood as a response to the functionalisation of the economy, where individuals are not seen for who they are but in which governments, for example, benefit seekers are punished and coerced into work. *I matter! I want to be seen for who I am! I want to set my own meanings!* Individuals' obsession with imaginations and symbols such as the confederate flag or the swastika may help them flee from the fatalism and struggles in daily life into the dream of a struggle-free Utopia. These dreams are often a combination of anti-capitalism, anti-communism, anti-Semitism, and anti-immigrant (Bastow & Martin, 2003).

A similarly narrow post-materialist imagination of nationalism can be found in the vote of British people to leave the European Union. Research shows that a combination of motivations led to this vote, including a rejection of immigration and a sense of taking back control as a nation, which have been described as thinly veiled forms of nationalism or even racism (Faulkner & Dhati, 2017; Kirk, 2017; Calhoun, 2017; Ashcroft, 2016). People did not want to be functionalised by the European Union; they wanted to determine their own meaning as a country. The Leave Campaign often used words such as 'British values', appealing to their idea of an existential crisis. The Brexit vote gave people a sense of control over the complex globalised world: They could steer away from the fatalism of the failed Third Way and the neoliberal financial crisis of 2007/2008 (Fetzer, 2019). The Brexit campaigns appealed strongly to the emotions of people, as did the experience economy. Mind manipulation groups such as the Cambridge Analytica, which targeted undecided right-wing voters via Facebook set the circumstances in such a way that individuals felt that they made an independent decision to leave the EU, even though they had been nudged by a media flood of rants about foreigners, costs of the EU, etc. (Fuchs, 2018). Ultimately, for many, Brexit may have been a reaction formation, whereby they projected their frustration about the capitalist system and their own life onto European institutions. Thus, Brexit may be regarded as the result of the Capitalist Life Syndrome, which has been decades in the making since Keith Joseph and Margaret Thatcher.

Conclusions

This chapter showed many examples of businesses and politicians offering islands of meaning within the capitalist system. People can rest and, get energised and hopeful by having brief moments and small spaces that feel meaningful in a meaningless world. Just as Karl Marx criticized religion for giving false meaning because it does not address underlying socio-economic problems, the examples in this chapter may pose a similar danger of being an opium for the people. These small, meaningful moments may help individuals to just bear their circumstances and survive but can also prevent them from taking political action against structural injustices. People flee to these islands of meaning and depend on them for their emotional survival, but their attention is shifted away from the underlying problems.

Islands of meaning can also get occupied by neoliberal values, and authentic meaning can transform into mere hedonist experiences, particularly when emotional labour is involved (Hochschild, 1983). Starbucks' employees are required to manipulate their emotions to sell the product with passion and a big smile, regardless of whether this is authentic or not. The danger of the 'Meaning Inc. Economy' is that meaning can be used merely to increase productivity, lower costs, and increase the profits; the real costs of this could be a sense of authenticity.

Do we always have the opportunity to be authentic? Is real authenticity possible at all? Does the drive towards authenticity add an extra psychological burden that is exploited by capitalists? Adorno asked these questions in his book *Jargon of Authenticity* (1973). He shows how the concept of authenticity can be used in a functionalist manner to make quick money, in a similar way that Pine and Gilmore argued in their book on the experience economy. For example, travel companies do not merely sell a flight with accommodations and a tour guide; they sell 'authentic tours' and 'get off the beaten path, away from the tourist crowds and delve deeper into the authentic local way of life'. This example shows how the jargon of authenticity and meaning can be used in functionalist ways for mere materialist and hedonist purposes. Seen from a pragmatic–phenomenological perspective, we may never know whether or not we are truly authentic or meaningful. We can only critically analyse ourselves and our situation to intuit how authentic we are. We need to remain reflexive and be aware of how we may become exploited. Because *meaning sells!*

Key Points

1. Individuals, governments and corporations can create small spaces and moments that feel meaningful without structurally changing the capitalist system.
2. Politicians who followed the philosophy of The Third Way intended to combine social and larger types of meaning with a capitalist system, but in practice, they mainly promoted neoliberal practices.
3. Public space is undergoing a transformation from impersonal, brutalist constructions to personal spaces in which a plurality of meanings can happen.
4. Social media offer a space and an escape that can feel meaningful for people, but which can also be misused to promote selfish materialist goals.
5. Although individuals may be able to experience meaning without changing the capitalist system, this bears an inherent risk of sliding into superficial and functionalist approaches to life.

Chapter 16

Going Off-Road:
Meanings Outside Capitalism

Off-modern paths

In the 21st century, modernity is our antiquity. We live in its ruins, which we incorporate into our present. Unlike the thinkers of the last fin de siècle, we neither mourn nor celebrate the end of history. We have to chart a new road between unending development and nostalgia, find an alternative logic for the contradictions of contemporary culture. Instead of fast-changing [prefixes] post, anti, neo, trans and sub—that suggest an implacable movement forward, against or beyond, I propose to go off: off as in off the path, or way off, off-roadway, off-brand, off the wall and occasionally off-colour. Off-modern is a detour into the unexplored potentials of the modern project. It recovers unforeseen pasts and ventures into the side alleys of modern history, at the margins of error or major philosophies, economic, and technological narratives of modernization and progress. It opens into the modernity of what-if, and not only post-industrial modernization as it was. (Boym, 2017, p. 3)

If modernism is the path that former big ideologies such as liberalism and communism have been walking, postmodernism is the path on which neoliberalism walks (cf. Jameson, 2007). However, there is an alternative to both paths of (neo)liberalism and (neo)Marxism. Based on her experiences of growing up in Communist Russia and later emigrating to the United States, Svetlana Boym (2017) describes an alternative to both modernism and postmodernism: the off-modern. She calls on individuals to be critical of the usual paths and not to accept the unchosen paths that they were forced to go into. Instead, she asks individuals to go off-road, off the big narratives, explore the unexplored, and let our critical-intuition tell us what is meaningful.

The hiker who feels free enough to wander off the usual road experiences some freedom in the habitual world. Boym calls this 'estrangement,' using the term of the artist Viktor Shklovsky (2015). This is not merely estrangement *from* the world, such as stoicism, Christian ascesis, or capitalistic alienation wandered away from our connections with the life-world. Shklovsky describes estrangement *for* the world—that is the freedom of meaning, reframing, a new beginning, new perspectives.

> What Shklovsky is getting at here is a radical dislocation from one's usual point of view, a reframing and recontextualization of reality; one moreover that affords an entirely different set of possibilities—for perception, understanding and action—which enhance one's (and other's) life. From initially being an artistic technique, estrangement morphed into an existential art and practice of freedom. This is what Boym has in mind when she speaks of estrangement for the world—it breathes new life into the possibilities of being and resurrects the ordinary marvelous under the all-encompassing challenges of life.' (Roberts, 2017, p. 62)

The ability to overtake neoliberalism when we go off-modern does not imply a quantitative increase in success or linear progress, but a qualitative leap. Helfrich and Bollier (2019) call this an ontological change ('Ontowandel'): our full understanding of Being and Truth change. People develop totally new perspectives and revisit pre-existing perspectives that have been left unexplored by capitalism, communism, or colonialism.

Thus, the off-modern does not merely estrange us from our habitual perspectives—for example, by critically reflecting on the limitations of capitalist perspectives, as critical theorists and Foucault did. The off-modern estranges us *for* the world as it 'recovers modern perspectivism, the logic of making strange and polymorphous versatility, and the play of perspectives' (Boym, 2017, p.35) Boym describes here how going off-modern leads to the co-existence of a plurality of individual meanings, each based on personal critical–intuitive journeys. She calls this *prospective nostalgia*, which is not about what has not been in the past or what is not yet but a longing for unexplored pluralities, searching 'with a spyglass what is hidden in plain view in our ever-fleeting here and now' (Boym, 2017, p.40) Thus, we have to listen critically to what our intuition tells us is truly meaningful instead of letting ourselves be determined by the linear history and by mind manipulation. This implies creativity, art, intuition, self-compassion, experimentation, and connectedness with our surrounding world.

This chapter explores several examples of off-modern, outside capitalism. These examples are not merely a reaction to the Capitalist Life Syndrome, like linear progress or Hegelian Dialectics, but come from inner drives and pre-existing traditions. In contrast with the big imaginations and symbolic language of (post)modernist philosophies, many of these off-modern examples start modestly from the bottom up. Many examples also reveal how people try to intuitively balance different types of meaning, such as the interests of the family, society, and nature (critical–intuitive cosmocentrism). Functionalism seems absent—no mind mafia—but, instead, critical–intuitive individuals who are not mere variables in statistical functions but seen for who they are. These stories will not be told by the conquerors but by the individuals in their social embedding.

Indigenous Economies

Indigeneity refers to people who originally lived in a place before colonialists or immigrants invaded it. Indigenous perspectives on the economy have never disappeared but may have been muted or transformed during (post)colonialism. Unfortunately, decolonisation does not necessarily mean that indigenous perspectives have resurfaced; instead, many have argued that the perspectives of the colonisers continue to dominate former colonies (Bales, 2012; Fischer, 2009; Bargh, 2007; Hochschild, 1998). For example, the post-colonial elite and government follow neoliberal ideologies, even when this contradicts indigenous views. This post-colonial neoliberal elite is often supported by money and political and military power from former colonisers, albeit under the cover of developmental aid (Bales, 2012; Fischer, 2009; Bargh, 2007; Hochschild, 1998). For example, for decades, the IMF has offered financial support under strict one-size-fits-all conditions of economic reconstruction; 'Structural Adjustment Policies' such as privatisation and opening of the market for foreign investors were accepted by the new elite in former colonies accepted, who promoted these economic packages to their own population as inevitable—'TINA'. These new elites also seem to have no alternative themselves because by giving up capitalist ideologies and following alternative indigenous they risk losing international support or may even be labeled pariahs and toppled in a coup. Consequently, indigenous perspectives continue being suppressed, and former colonies remain enslaved by capitalism. Although people have regained legal and political rights, their minds remain colonized, and they see meaning from post-colonialist functionalist–materialist perspectives (Bales, 2012; Fischer, 2009; Bargh, 2007; Hochschild, 1998).

Many indigenous cultures imagine or symbolise how we can live a meaningful life outside capitalism, off-modern. For example, the South-African term *ubuntu* is an abbreviation of the Xhosa proverb *Umuntu ngumuntu ngabantu*, which translates as 'a human being is a human being only through its relationship to other human beings (Marx, 2002, p.52). This includes ideals such as solidarity, hospitality, community, unity, and harmony. The ideal and praxis of *ubuntu* played a major role in the post-Apartheid reconciliation process to give a sense of common postcolonial identity, memory, belonging, and sovereignty (Fox, 2011). Similarly, the concept of *ujamaa*, which means family or brotherhood and asserts that a person becomes a person *through the people* or community, played an important role when Tanzania became independent. After the genocides in Rwanda, the concept of *agaciro*, roughly translated as "dignity" or "value", helped to give a communal sense of self-worth, self-determination, and dignity (Rutazibwa, 2014). The Kenyan coat of arms includes the word *harambee*, which means 'all pull together', such as in community self-help events. The Maori concept of *utu* means balance and harmony within a civilisation, which includes rituals and ceremonies around authentic gift-giving as well as revenge. Whereas such 'off-modern' indigenous concepts were ignored until the recent past, there is growing awareness and legal protection for indigeneity—for example, in the 2007 Declaration on the Rights of Indigenous Peoples.

The power of indigenous economic perspectives can be seen in the silent revolution that started in the 1990s in South America. Until then, many governments had followed the Washington Consensus and had often received financial, economic, and military support from American governments and multinational corporations (Klein, 2007). This seems to have caused large socio-economic inequality, with natural resources such as coal and oil in the hands of the few and with *haciendas* as modern versions of former slave plantations. The extraction of raw materials, mainly oil, has been wreaking havoc on the natural environment and destroying irreplaceable biological and cultural diversity. In response, in the late 1980s and 1990s, new social movements formed that were based on identity rather than class, possibly in line with the international trend of the experience economy. This indigenous identity was often strongly rooted in material poverty and exploitation (Fischer, 2009). This led to the 1991 multicultural constitution in Colombia, the movement toward socialism and the presidency of Evo Morales in Bolivia, and the emergence of the Confederation of Indigenous Nationalities in Ecuador. These indigenous movements became even more popular after the 2008 global economic crisis.

The South American indigenous movements often centre around the concept of living well, *vivier bien* in Spanish, *sumac kawsay* in the language of Quechua people in the Andes, or *suma qamana* for the Aymara (Ranta, 2018). This describes a way of doing things that is community-centric, ecologically balanced, and culturally sensitive. *Buen vivir* focuses on the attainment of the good life, which can be found within a community, and in harmony with other people and nature. This is built on the indigenous idea of cosmocentrism: the material world and the self, the social world, nature, the universe, and the spiritual domain are all inter-related. The new constitution of Ecuador outlines *buen vivir* as a set of rights for humans and for nature; this embraces a bio-pluralistic view, eliminating the separation between nature and society. Although *buen vivir* is mainly supported by left-wing political parties, it radically transcends traditional left ideas such as traditional Marxism, refuted by indigenous politicians for its functionalist–materialist focus that they see as the opposite of *buen vivir*.

Indigenous religions are complexes of attitudes, beliefs, and practices fine-tuned to harmonize with the lands on which the people live, such as the rain dance of the Hopi tribe in Arizona, a religious ritual that transcends space and time by connecting with the land and the ancestors (Deloria, 2003). Similarly, the harmony and balance of *buen vivir* can only be attained when people do not only live on the land, produce, and consume but also *own* the land. 'Land is paramount; humans must serve the land both directly by cultivating it and through workshop of the telluric spirits' (Ranta,

2018, p. 67). Their cosmocentrist perspective does not separate private properties like capitalism. Only by working with the land and in relationship with other people can a balance be achieved among individuals, people, and nature, and large-scale land ownerships and monopolies disrupt this harmony. Thus, the concept of living well includes landownership, ecological sustainability, and territorial sovereignty for local communities. In Bolivia and several other countries, this concept led in the 1990s to devolution of government tasks and an increase in communal landownership. Consequently, a system emerged in which the state and a plurality of local communities co-exist ('plurinationalism'). In Brazil, this meant the emergence of the landless rural workers' movement (Movimento dos Trabalhadores Rurais Sem Terra), which fought for landownership as a self-sustainable way of life for the rural poor and which won large land reform in 1988.

In the same period that *buen vivir* became more politically accepted in South America, the ideological movement of Zapatista gained popularity in the Chiapas in Mexico. Their ideology, *neozapatismo*, centres around the concept of mutual aid: 'For everyone, everything. For us, nothing.' (*Para todos todo, para nosotros nada*). Zapatista started its armed struggle on 1 January 1994, when the North American Trade Agreement (NAFTA) came into power, which they saw as detrimental for ordinary Mexican people. The Zapatistas oppose neoliberal globalisation and call for democratisation and bottom-up political participation. Despite many political and military setbacks, many indigenous communities have gained more control over local resources and they to practice horizontal autonomy, build schools, hospitals, and sustainable agro-ecological systems, experience equitable gender relations, and promote international solidarity.

These examples show how many indigenous people across the globe follow non-functionalist, social and larger types of meaning, often embedded in millennia of experience—many with longer histories than capitalism. Their indigenous off-modern perspectives offer alternatives to capitalism, appealing to many oppressed and young people across the globe.

Commons & Cooperatives

Communism and neoliberalism seem to have in common that both mistrust common people to manage common resources such as land, fisheries, and other natural resources, feeling that either governments or corporations should own and manage these. For example, Garret Hardin (1968) used the term 'the tragedy of the commons' to describe the situation that when multiple farmers need to share a piece of land, they will follow their self-interest without looking after the common land as they will let their animals over-graze and destroy the land. This phenomenon has been replicated in many economic experiments on so-called prisoner dilemma games, in which research participants had to make economic decisions in situations where they shared resources with others. The traditional response of economists to this tragedy is the call for a Leviathan-state or corporations led by experts who allegedly know better than commoners how to manage commons—a living social structure in which people manage common problems in self-organised ways (Helfrich & Bollier, 2019; Ostrom, 1990, 2015).

Governments or corporations are not the only two solutions to managing common resources, according to Nobel-prize winner Elinor Ostrom. Neither state nor privatisation is needed. Individuals can self-organise, manage resources together, and solve such common pooled-resource problems as long as the right conditions are there. Ostrom describes how individuals decide their economic strategy on the basis of norms and a cost-benefit analysis of cooperation. Decentralised community-based approaches do not always work, though (Ostrom, 2012) as certain conditions need to be present, including clear boundaries to facilitate exclusion (where can our sheep not graze?), internal rules within the community to prevent using too much of the resources, adjusting rules to the unique local situation, monitoring and enforcing rules and agreements, and having clear procedures for dispute resolution. For example, the Zapatista movement or the Rojeve community in Syria are based on systems with such conditions.

However, Ostrom's model is based on many implicit existential assumptions. She assumes that individuals interact with one another in rational ways, that individuals want to collaborate because this is in their best self-interest, and that the main shared goal is materialist prosperity for all. However, earlier cited research shows that people do not calculate rational functions and often make decisions on the basis of their intuition, social and larger values. For example, rules of morality and justice play a role in the distribution of common resources—e.g., 'You have lived here longer than I, so you deserve a larger piece of land'. For many people, sharing and managing resources together is based on a deep sense of social meaning: belonging, altruism, and giving. It can even be a world-view or ontological position (Helfrich & Bollier, 2019), as individuals realise that they are always in relationships with others and that every action directly or indirectly impacts others (freedom in relationship), such as *ubuntu* and *vivir bien*. Striving for harmony is an ontological and spiritual aim for many. All commons seem to combine the triad of people acting with careful self-determination, self-organisation via equality, and social bonds (Helfrich & Bollier, 2019).

More radically formulated than Ostrom, commons have a large potential of providing a sense of meaningfulness for its stakeholders, as it can be based on non-functionalist cooperation whereby each individual is seen as meaningful in themselves and not as an economic function. The direct involvement of individuals in the commons can also imply that they can experience a sense of control, social connection, and a larger perspective, which can all be important sources of meaning. When a common is based on a sense of social meaning, and not merely viewed as materialist competition, collaboration with others is not experienced as a limitation of one's own freedom (negative freedom) but as the exercise of one's freedom and synergetic enhancement of one's meaning in life (positive freedom). Or as George Barrett writes in *Objections to Anarchism* (1921, p. 348–49): 'To get the full meaning out of life we must co-operate, and to co-operate we must make agreements with our fellow-men. But to suppose that such agreements mean a limitation of freedom is surely an absurdity; on the contrary, they are the exercise of our freedom'.

Commons lead to a polycentric system of governance, which means that multiple individuals or institutions have a role in the governing process, such as plurinationalism in Bolivia. This can take many forms. The most common of commons are consumer cooperatives, worker cooperatives, multi-stakeholder cooperatives, and digital platform cooperatives. According to the Worldwatch Institute, in 2012 approximately one billion people in 96 countries had become members of at least one cooperative. Research shows that coops are typically more economically resilient than other enterprise types; for example, 80% of coops survive the first five years compared to 41% of other types (www.uk.coop.uk, 2015). Next to economic reasons, one may argue that this resilience is caused by the focus on social and larger types of meaning and not merely on materialist self-enrichment, as research shows that social and larger meanings increase psychological resilience, perseverance, and hardiness. Many coops reinvest a part of their profit in local community projects and have a clear vision and mission statement, aiming to serve larger ethical goals.

The first successful coop was the Rochdale Society of Equitable Pioneers, which was started in 1844 by 28 weavers and other artisans in Rochdale, England, who set up their own store to sell food they could not otherwise afford. Their coop was based on the Rochdale principles, which most coops still follow: voluntary and open membership; democratic member control; economic participation by members; autonomy and independence; education, training, and information; cooperation among cooperatives; concern for the community. Since then, countless coops have formed in many economic sectors such as supermarkets, banks, housing coops, and energy coops. During the Spanish Civil War, many factories and companies were owned by the workers. In countries such as Argentina, there are large industrial and services coops. Furthermore, in recent years, the number of cooperative digital platforms, such as Wikipedia, have quickly emerged.

However, many variations and pseudo-coops have also emerged, such as Uber and Airbnb that allow individuals rent out their car and taxi-service or their houses to others via online platforms. However, these platform-companies are run for profit, and individual sellers have little democratic voice in them except for deciding when and where to offer their product or service (Stone, 2017; Quattrone, 2016). Thus, the idea of cooperatives seems in danger of materialism, functionalism, and capitalist exploitation.

Islamic Economies

Islam is one of the world's largest religions, with 1.8 billion followers. Like any large religion or ideology, there is a heterogeneity of perspectives and movements within Islam. For example, Islamic socialists such as Shariati claim that the prophet Mohammed envisioned a classless society, based on equality and justice. Others claim that the Qur'an and Hadith reveal the vision of laissez-faire capitalism as it has been argued that sovereignty only belongs to God and thus no person, class, or group can create laws and regulations for others (Toor, 2011; Tripp, 2006).

Whatever perspective one has on Islam, the religion seems to promote social and larger types of meaning. Examples are Islamic banks, which often have social purposes, and the *zakat*, the giving of donations to the less fortunate. Many Western Muslims develop plural selves, integrating both 'western'-neoliberal and Islamic values. (Nasr Abu Zayd, 2006) The Arab Spring Revolution in 2010 also offered some opportunities for pluralism to emerge within Mediterranean Islamic countries, which attempted to reveal and undermine the so-called 'non-Islamic' authoritarianism of the regimes and demand democracy and 'western' concepts of individual freedom (Ramadan, 2012).

Freedom seems to be a contested concept in Islam, as it is in many religions and ideologies. On the one hand, some critics have argued that Islam is a functionalist religion that brings non-freedom and fatalism for the individual because it demands the submission of the believer who needs to obey the Sharia laws; thus, individuals are not seen as meaningful in themselves but merely as servants of Allah. On the other hand, it has been argued that 'Western countries' could learn much from the concept of freedom in Islam as the freedom in neoliberalism seems restricted to achieving materialist self-interest, whereas freedom in Islam is oriented towards social and larger purposes (Khuri, 1998). While the neoliberal obsession with individual freedom (e.g., freedom from state interventions) is negative in nature, freedom in Islam can be positive as it says what it wants— a sense of belonging, altruism, ethics, justice, and a better world for all—and not only what it does not want. Particularly in mystic movements such as Sufism, believers use a critical–intuitive approach and not merely a reductionist–functionalist approach as in neoliberalism. However, naturally, given the heterogeneity of Islamic interpretations, it is difficult to give a conclusive answer, as in certain countries a more authoritarianist reading of Islam is followed, which limits, for instance, the freedom of women and LGBTQI+ people.

It has been argued that 'many' Muslims have radicalised in the 20th century, in response to the aggressive propaganda of neoliberalism and military interventions by Western countries (Gray, 2005). More generally formulated, the Capitalist Life Syndrome seems to have led Muslim believers into the hands of fanatics who promised more meaningful alternatives to capitalism. The anti-rationalist rhetoric of Bin Laden and Al Zawahiri—calling for a *jihad*, a battle of the heart—rejects the cold, rationalist functionalism of neoliberalism. Extremist Muslims such as Al Qaida and ISIS seem to have radicalised their vision and methods in response what, in their eyes, is the materialism and hedonism that capitalism preaches. They condemn the exploitation of man by man and attack the plundering by capitalists and imperialists. Furthermore, the emergence of the Religious Radical Life Syndrome can be fed by individual life experiences, such as suffering socio-economic hardships, an authoritarian upbringing, economic sanctions, and invasions by Russia and United States (Durward, 2016; Eland, 1998). Radicalisation may not only be a response to Western materialism and hedonism but also to the demise of Muslim states themselves, as it has been argued that many Muslim states lack a spiritual daily life, leading to a 'quest for meaning and peace of heart. Viewed in this light, Muslim-majority societies are profoundly bereft of serenity, coherence and peace. The time has come for spiritual and religious emancipation' (Ramadan, 2012, p.141) Often, Muslim extremism is a response to both trends inside and outside Muslim-majority countries, with a variety of social and larger goals. For example, the 1979 Iranian Revolution started as a protest to establish the rule of the oppressed—Khomeini said that Islam stands for justice and class balance—although the revolution was quickly taken over, with help of neoliberal Western powers, by conservative orthodoxy (Behdad & Nomani, 2006). The West-versus-East and Islamophobic stereotypes do not do justice to common existential crises. From a meaning-oriented perspective, Muslim extremism has much in common with neoliberal and neoconservative extremism, with their functionalist and authoritarian perspective on life, the idea of linear progress in history, and the belief in a Romantic ideal that even justifies the use of violence.

Conclusions

Walking where many have walked before can give a sense of stability and security. However, this path may be too small to fit all people due to its popularity, and much of the landscape may remain unexplored by staying on the path. Therefore, people may want to go off the beaten track, with indigenous, cooperative, or Islamic initiatives, and inspire people ranging from Podemos in Spain, and Syriza in Greece to the 'umbrella protests' in Hong Kong. The examples in this chapter show how people search for a wide range of meanings, in freedom and non-functionalist harmony with other people and nature. Naturally, there is often no clear boundary between being, inside or outside capitalism, as capitalism is not a physical object or space with clear borders; many of these initiatives, such as coops, happen within capitalist systems and may not fundamentally fight the wider system but merely give a partial temporary escape from it. These examples also do not offer a panacea and can be vulnerable to aggressive attacks and take-overs by capitalists (Ostrom, 2012).

Key Points

1. This chapter described examples of meaning outside capitalism, characterized as 'off-modern', like going off the beaten path, as anarchist punks did.
2. Examples included indigenous economies, commons, and cooperatives.
3. Communism was criticised for having similar perspectives on life as capitalism, which risks individuals getting stuck in the Communist Life Syndrome.
4. Islamic economic perspectives were described, like all religions, as being two-faced, supporting both the Meaning-Oriented Economy as well as the Religious Radical Life Syndrome.

Chapter 17

Fighting the System: Meanings Against Capitalism

The crisis consists precisely in the fact that the old is dying and the new cannot be born; in this interregnum a great variety of morbid symptoms appear. (Gramsci, 1994)

Reaching the Tipping Point

The capitalist lifestyle seems to bring suffering in the daily life of many people, not only material but also psychological (see chapters 8 and 12). However, as previous chapters have shown, many people seem to respond to the suffering by copping out via denial and avoidance or even via defending the hand that hits them (Chapter 12). Psychologists have argued that when suffering and frustration last long enough, such defence mechanisms may start to break, and individuals can develop a crisis in mental health, identity, morality, and meaning in life (Vos, 2017, 2016, 2016a). According to Karl Marx, the Capitalist Life Syndrome will inevitably lead to political action and possibly even to revolution: the seeds of its destruction seem to be sown in its own cloth due to the long-term suffering of the masses (Chapter 13). Thus, the Capitalist Life Syndrome may give rise to a critical mass demanding change. This process of how the Capitalist Life Syndrome can transform into activism is well described by activist Saul Alinsky in *Rules for radicals* (1971/1989):

> Today's generation is desperately trying to make sense out of their lives and out of the world. They have rejected their materialist backgrounds, the goal of a well-paid job, suburban home, automobile, country club membership, first-class travel, status, and everything that meant success to their parents. They have had it. They watched it lead their parents to tranquilisers, alcohol, long-term endurance marriages or divorces, high blood pressure, frustration and the disillusionment of the good life. They have seen the almost unbelievable idiocy of our political leadership. The young are inundated with a barrage of information and facts so overwhelming that the world has come to seem an utter bedlam, which has them spinning in a frenzy, looking for

what man has always looked for from the beginning of time, a way of life that has some meaning or sense. A way of life means a certain degree of order where things have some relationship and can be pieced together in a system that at least provides some clues what life is about. There is a feeling of death hanging over the nation. Today's generation faces all this and says 'I don't want to spend my life the way my family and their friends have. I want to do something, to create, to be me, to do my own thing to live. The older generation doesn't understand and worse doesn't want to. I don't want to be just a piece of data to be fed into a computer or a statistic in a public opinion poll, just a voter carrying a credit card. (...) The young react to their chaotic world in different ways. Some panic and run, rationalizing that the system is going to collapse anyway of its own rot and corruption, so they are copping out, going hippie or yippie, taking drugs, trying communes. Others went for pointless sure-loser confrontations and say: 'well we tried and did our part' and then they copped out too. Others stick with guilt, not knowing where to go to and go berserk. (p. xiv–xv)

According to Alinsky, political activism seems to start with the feeling that our personal meanings are under attack, that the dominant meanings of the majority in society are too narrow-minded, or that social core values are undermined. This is often first felt on a personal and embodied level, in the form of psychological frustration, relational conflicts, a sense of alienation, or a general lack of life fulfillment. Individuals face ethical conflicts, such as being required to commit themselves to mind-killing, anti-social, or unecological jobs inconsistent with their values of self-fulfillment, altruism, and natural protection. There is a discrepancy between how the world is and how it should be, between self-interest and self-sacrifice, between power and love, between stability and unity, between change and diversity, and between imagination and hope (Chambers, 2003/2018). People can try to deny or avoid such paradoxes for a long time and fool themselves with justifications such as 'TINA' or hiding behind others—'I do what others do'—and the mind manipulation works hard to keep the capitalist perpetuum mobile going (chapters 11–12). A sense of fatalism and existential stress is inherent in capitalist life, and instead of changing society, people change themselves, until they cannot change any more (chapter 8).

Thus, societal change does not necessarily start with negative materialistic conditions, as Marx described the conditions of revolution. Instead, it seems to start with a crisis in meaning in life, and the success of the social movement depends on the meaning that they are able to reclaim in society. This chapter will discuss some of the most frequently cited research on social movements and political activism, along with findings from new meta-analytical research. This will show how political activism rises from long-term frustrated meaning in life, and how activist events are most effective when they address a meaningful topic with meaningful methods that appeal to the broader population and to those in power. This is what I call the Meaning-Oriented Activism Model (MOAM). Section 2 will give a broad overview of the field of research on social movements and where MOAM fits in this. Section 3 will show the role of meaning in movements, and section 4 will apply the ten meaning-oriented perspectives to political activism.

Research on Social Movements

Karl Marx was one of the first philosophers to explicitly theorise how social movement could be built and could become successful. Marx seemed to mainly base his model of revolution on theoretical analysis, generally in line with Hegel's dialectics (Draper, 1977). However, modern empirical research has shown that effective social movements are more complex and that, for example, class is regarded as only one of the multiple possible unifying aims of social movements (Laclau & Mouffe, 2014). The following is an historic overview of research on social movements, with a specific focus on the role of meaning (based on: Berberoglu, & Al-Sayed, 2019; Lawson, 2019; Roggeband & Klandermans, 2017; Staggenborg, 2015; Della Porta & Diani, 2015; Johnston, 2014; Pinard, 2011; Day, 2005).

The first stage of research mainly consisted of historians who were often critical of revolutions. They described social movement as exceptions to the normal equilibrium in society, when people acted irrationally as if having a physical disease, following the stages of symptoms, cramping, fever, delirium, and convalescence. Their interpretations of historical cases have been disproven by later empirical researchers.

The second stage focused mainly on uprising in 'The Third World'. The researchers described how relative materialistic deprivation could lead to social instability as people feel frustrated when they cannot realise their aspirations and when their expectations fail. The J-curve theory described, for example, that social movements emerge when people are frustrated about the lack of socio-economic improvement and equality, particularly after a period in which their expectations or false hopes were rising due to a temporary improvement in the general socio-economic circumstances that was followed by an economic downturn. Although this research could explain more social movements than the first research stage, their model still seemed too simplistic to explain when and where all social movements start. Later research showed that it was not the objective deprivation per se that mattered, but the subjective meaning that this had for people. Furthermore, materialistic circumstances per se do not explain why social change happens, but the perception is that there is a social or larger injustice behind this deprivation—for example ,because only one specific racial group is maltreated more than others.

The third stage looked at macro-level structures that could lead to the emergence and success of social movements. For example, revolutions have started because of farmers rising up in response to the commercialisation of agriculture, or because of international inequality, military conflict, and migration. Although these models mainly focused on objective resources, they started to include factors such as ideologies, agency, and political culture, showing that religious and ideological conflicts could also explain social movements. For example, in 'The Third World,' uprisings happen due to dependent state development, which exacerbates social tensions; repressive, exclusionary, personalistic regimes, which polarised opposition; an economic turndown, which acted as a final straw in radicalising the opposition; and a world-systemic opening, which acted as to loosen external constraints (Foran, 2005, in: Lawson, 2019). Later research has shown that these objective structural circumstances alone do not explain why revolutions happen, but it is the impingement of social and larger types of meaning on the perception of people that makes them rise up against the state.

The fourth stage predominantly uses an integrative approach to social movements, combining multiple factors on international, national, and group levels. This research does not attempt to identify a complete overview of all factors leading to revolution, which is impossible because there are too many, but focuses on 'the precariousness of instability'. Fourth-stage research focuses, for example, on how states become unstable due to dependent trade relations, elite disunity, insecure standards of living, and unjust leadership; consequently, the legitimacy of the state becomes questioned by people, and social movements could emerge (Goldstone, 2001).

The factors are not important in themselves; they only matter when they are widely perceived as meaningful within a coherent narrative framework. That is, the general framing of the societal situation is crucial, as the social and cultural context determines people's actions. Thus, the mind manipulation of the people by state and enterprises plays an important role in explaining injustices. This explains, for example, post-materialist revolutions where the focus does not lie on specific materialistic deprivation but on socio-economic inequality, post-2008 austerity measures, and capitalism in general, which are seen in general as unjust by movements such as Occupy Wall Street, Podemos, Syriza, DiEm25, and like-minded groups (Pinard, 2005; Melucci, 1989; Offe, 1987). The Black Lives Matter movement explicitly puts the meaningfulness of a disenfranchised group on the political agenda, particularly fighting against racism and discrimination by law enforcement and states.

This fourth stage of research could be summarised by asking the question 'Why do social movements emerge?', in contrast with the 'when' and 'how' questions from the other stages (Pinard, 2011). Researchers in this fourth stage give explicit attention to the motivations of individual activists, which seem to cover all different types of meanings (Pinard, 2011; Taylor, 2010; Klandermans, 2004). This research will be integrated in the Meaning-Oriented Activism Model, which will be explained in the next two sections. This model will give a comprehensive answer to the question 'why'.

Meaning-Oriented Activism Model

What makes individuals turn the corner and conclude 'I cannot accept this any longer; I need to act! I demand societal change'? The degree of support for and participation in social movements seems to depend on multiple factors, as the four stages of research on social movements have shown.

Deprivation of Social and Larger Types of Meaning

Macro-economic factors such as economic deprivation do not predict on their own whether people will rise up or not (materialist meaning; Ostby, 2013; Lichbach, 1989; Parvin, 1973). Social-economic inequality does not directly predict uprisings and civil wars, but it is predictive when combined with a sense of belonging to an ethnic group or class that is discriminated against. Thus, inequality per se does not lead to unrest, but when this inequality is regarded as structural discrimination of a social group (social meanings), then it can be a catalyst (Weinberg & Bakker, 2015; Bate & Mumme, 2013). For example, people are more likely to rise up in response to low social mobility, which means that individuals cannot develop themselves (self-oriented meaning) (Houle, 2017). High food prices can lead to uprisings when citizens see this as unfair to their group (Bush, 2009). Social welfare policies can limit the unfair socio-economic distribution of wealth in a country and can, therefore, reduce the likelihood of uprising (Burgoon 2006), whereas in contrast austerity measures and benefit cuts are perceived as unjust and can lead to riots (Ponticelli & Voth, 2018).

Thus, the sense of social justice and ethics seem to be ultimate motivators behind uprisings (social and larger types of meaning), or as Che Guevarra (2003) said: "Allow me to say, at the risk of appearing ridiculous, that the true revolutionary is motivated by great feelings of love.' When citizens are not only dissatisfied about their material conditions but also experience democratic dissatisfaction, the use of violence during uprisings is also more likely (Shaheen, 2015). Furthermore, the meaning of social change cannot be imposed by others but needs to come from inside, as, for instance, research shows that international sanctions and military interventions only contribute 15% to the likelihood of success of political campaigns (Chenoweth & Murphy, 2011).

These examples show that what matters is not the materialist life situation per se, but the self-oriented, social, and larger meaning it has for individuals (Shaheen, 2015). The more personal, social, and larger types of meanings remain unfulfilled, the more likely it is that people will rise up. This also means that frustration of economic freedom (which focuses predominantly on materialist, hedonist, and self-oriented meanings) is less likely to lead to riots than unfulfilled political freedom (which focuses more on self-oriented, social and larger meanings). Similarly, we have already seen in the Worldwide Survey of Meaning in Life (Chapter 8) that economic freedom does not predict one's sense of fulfillment of meaning in life, but that political freedom does. When individuals feel that they cannot live a meaningful life due to structural political oppression, such as in the former USSR, they are more likely to rise up. The WSM also showed that the more an individual's meanings are unfulfilled, and the more the political system contradicts their own economic values, the more they support protesting, civil disobedience, or revolution (WSM:R=.33,p<.01;R=.28,p<.05). This is understandable. Imagine that if living a rich person's lifestyle is one's ultimate dream but the political situation makes this impossible, one naturally person will be more likely to take to the streets. Imagine that if someone is an ethnic minority, such as an indigenous American, and they experience structural, personal, and social discrimination, they are more likely to rise up. Understandably, the more individuals feel that their meanings remain unfulfilled, the lower are their mental health and life satisfaction (WSM: resp.R=.34,p<.01, R=.37,p<.01). And, vice versa, the more people suffer from mental health problems and the lower the average life satisfaction is, the more likely it is that individuals will support an uprising (WSM:R=.28, p<.05, R=.36, p<.01). Thus, the more social and larger meanings remain unfulfilled in a country, the more likely it is that individuals experience internal psychological pressures that could make them go onto the streets and demand change.

Social and Larger Meanings as Campaign Aims
To find further evidence for the role of meaning in political activism, I conducted secondary meta-analyses on all political campaigns between 1900 and 2006 that Chenoweth and Murphy (2006) had collected and combined this with the WSM data. I also added information about the aims of each campaign (Carter, Clark, & Randle, 2015) and categorised each campaign for the extent to which it aimed at each of the six types of meaning (1=not at all, 5=completely). The result was clear: most campaigns aimed at a mixture of meanings, but those that mainly focused on materialist and self-oriented meanings were significantly smaller in size and less successful at achieving their aims than those that focused strongly on social and larger types of meaning (N=201;Hedges'g=.43,p<.01;g=.47,p<.01). There is more population support for campaigns that address social and larger types of meaning, such as opposition to authoritarian regimes like Milosevic in Serbia. Furthermore, the amount of economic unfreedom did not predict the likelihood of uprisings (p=.09), but the amount of political unfreedom did (g=.53,p<.01). This undermines the ideas from neoliberals such as Friedman (1980) that economic freedom is the condition for political freedom and that economic unfreedom may lead to social unrest.

Social and Larger Meanings as Campaign Methods
The ends do not always justify the means. When individuals use violence, the likelihood of public support is twice as small compared to non-violent action (Chenoweth & Murphy, 2006). The reason for this is that violent methods are only supported by a small part of the population. Violence may conflict with their larger sense of justice and ethics; thus, the movement needs to be in line with the social and larger types of meaning that individuals have. Violent campaigns may also require

more skills training, and thus may fail to recruit a robust, diverse, and broad-based enough membership that can erode the power base of the adversary. Loyalty shifts for the police and army are more likely when activists do not violently oppose them but appeal to a shared meaning (Chenoweth & Murphy, 2006). Alternatively formulated, the more individuals focus on materialist aims, the more likely it is that they will use violence, whereas the more they focus on social and larger aims the more likely it is that they will use non-violent means ($g=.31, p=.06$). Furthermore, economic boycotts and strikes are less likely to be successful when individuals feel that their material meanings are fulfilled ($g=-.29, p<.01$) and that their country is economically equal ($g=-.26, p<.01$). Consequently, it may be argued that social welfare policies and progressive taxes may work—like Roman bread and circuses—to appease the public and prevent civil uprising (Burgoon, 2006).

Propaganda Framing

As described previously, materialistic deprivation per se does not lead to uprising; however, people need to feel aggrieved about this because of the meaning that it has for them. Thus, this depends on how the deprivation is framed by the individuals themselves, by the social movement, and by the wider media in the country (McAdam, 2010; Johnston & Noakes, 2005). The framing of the situation is important to identify the problem (diagnostic framing), explain solutions (prognostic framing), and engage people in action (motivational framing) (Benford & Snow, 2000). Particularly important is the framing of the situation as unjust for specific social groups or for mankind at large, which leads to a moral indignation against those responsible (Gamson, 1992; Gamson, Fireman & Rytina, 1982). A clear example of framing is how the British government framed the widely felt socio-economic injustice in the country; the United Kingdom is the most unequal country in the world, not as the consequence of their failed national policies but as the result of immigration and the European Union. This framing led to the Brexit revolution.

Movement Resources

Successful framing also includes framing of individual and collective agency, the likelihood of success of the social movement, and identity, the sense of being part of a community versus 'the enemy'. Thus, injustice (social and larger type of meaning), agency, and identity (self-oriented and social types of meaning) are crucial ingredients to the successful framing of a social movement. Successful social movements are resilient in the long-term. They are not only short-lived momentums of action but require disruption, sacrifice, and escalation (Engler & Engler, 2016). This resilience and commitment require that the movement has clear meanings that energise people and give them direction and hope when they inevitably experience setbacks. Research indicates that individuals who have a strong sense of social or larger meaning are more resilient at coping with stressful life situations (Vos, 2016). People need to feel strengthened and self-determined (Sharp, 2005, 2008). Thus, it can be expected that campaigns will be more resilient, and activists will be more committed when they have a strong sense of social and larger meaning.

Conclusion

Empirical research shows that individuals are more likely to support and participate in social movements (S) when there is a combination of factors: Deprivation of social and larger types of meaning (D), social and larger meanings as campaign aims (A), social and larger meanings as campaign methods (M), counter-propaganda framing (F) and movement resources (R):(S=D+A+M+F+R).

Implications

We could derive from this model that the size of public support for a social movement, and its likelihood of success, can be improved by changing any of these factors. The more people feel structurally deprived for unjust reasons, the more likely is it that they will rise up. This implies, that individuals should, for instance, not merely attribute their deprivation to their individual decisions or bad fate but should see the problem as discrimination of their total socio-economic group. Education and framing could help people become aware of the social and larger injustice behind their individual struggles, and to connect struggles of different individuals together: 'the personal is political'. It could take a long time, or an aggravation or crisis in their life situation, before some individuals may accept the fact that they are struggling. They could deny their feelings about their struggles, saying to themselves and others that they are doing fine even though they are not. The social movement should not aim to change the material situation of a small group of individuals—such as teachers in one school demanding a higher salary; rather, it should focus on the structural, social, and larger injustice behind the material problem—such as stopping the structural oppression and abuse of teachers by the state. The methods should be in line with larger ethics and social justice, such as public-friendly strikes, positive engagement with the general public, and having an open community atmosphere. There needs to be a clear promotion of the unjust cause of the problem, clear political aims and logical strategy, and a wide variety of reasons why individuals should support and participate. Finally, effective new movements seem to have professionalised their use of resources (Soborski, 2019; Day, 2005). This includes education of the general public, training in activist skills, efficient communication methods, efficient and just decision-making and accountability procedures, psychological support and debriefing, and transparency of this to new participants.

Counter-revolutionary activities are all actions by the state or groups with commercial interests to stop the social movement. They could target the same variables to counter the revolution, and the revolutionaries should be aware of this and, in turn, counter this counter-revolution. The state will ensure that individuals are not suffering too much to feel 'Okay' enough not to rebel against the state. Any socio-economic inequalities will be attributed to the individual and will be framed in the Smilesian narrative of the self-help citizen. Individuals could also be distracted from their personal suffering—for example. because the government focuses on an external enemy or literally starts a military war. The state can try to frame the social movement as merely focusing on their selfish aims and show how the social movement is doing injustice to the wider population, for example, because their occupations or protests disrupt the daily life of ordinary, innocent citizens. The police could undermine the peaceful strategies of the movement by deliberately escalating protests by provoking aggression from protestors, or they could infiltrate movements to create internal competition and struggles within the social movement. Negative framing of the social movement will be one of the main strategies of the counter-revolution, particularly to cast the social movement as a group of radicals whom the rest of the population do not want to associate themselves with; this will include using media friendly to the state, spreading fake news, using bots, etc. The state could also undermine the resources of social movements. The most important resources are possibly time and energy; by making sure that people need to spend all their time on working hard to survive, they have no time and energy left to organise themselves and protest. This also includes making it more difficult for people to rise up—for example, by increasing criminal punishment for activists, undermining the rights of trade unions, forbidding strikes, etc. The recent years seem to have seen many examples of these counter-revolutionary strategies used by the American and British governments.

Ten Perspectives on Meaning-Oriented Activism

Political Imagination, Symbols, and Reality

Philosopher Paul Ricoeur (1957) identified an ontological difference between two forms of politics. *Le politique*, which I call Politics with a capital 'P', is the formal reflection and theory after the fact, such as the imaginations and symbols that politicians use in their rhetoric and mind manipulation (Apter, 2018). In contrast, *la politique*, politics with a small 'p', is about the concrete, empirical, and diverse manifestations of politics in daily life. Whereas Politicians may focus on convincing the population of one absolute true meaning for everyone, this is often in contrast with the diversity of daily life experiences of ordinary citizens. Mind manipulation often plays a crucial role in simplifying the collective narrative—attempting to conflate political reality with Political rhetoric—like the conqueror writing the history books and leaving out other versions.

Activists have the advantage of appealing to the political immediacy of daily life experiences, whereas politicians can be stuck in Political reflection and symbolic rhetoric (Engler & Engler, 2016). The appeal to the lived experiences of raw reality gives activists an advantage. Therefore, successful campaigns will show the tragic stories of individuals. A television camera zooming in on a person crying can create more public support than a minister's brilliant theoretical speech, particularly in our experience economy. Theories are not the only motor of societal change; many psychologists show that individuals do not change by merely having a class-consciousness, vision, or intention (e.g., Prochaska, Festinger, Ajzen, Kuhn). A utopian vision needs to be shared by a significant number of individuals in society who have a raw lived experience of discontent about the current societal system, and who feel able to use their skills to change society in the direction of the envisaged future. Thus, societal change seems to require three components, like fire requires fuel, oxygen, and heat. This Revolution Triangle consists of the fuel of the vision, the heat of the existential frustration, and the oxygen of a sense of self-efficacy. Individuals need to be frustrated about the perceived difference between how society is and how they would like society to be, and particularly their own role; this is also what the WSM-plus meta-analysis showed: the larger the gap between wished meaning and realised meaning—like Marxist alienation or cognitive dissonance—the larger the likelihood of support for and action of civil uprising (see previous section). However, this needs to be supported by self-efficacy, the sense of freedom, and opportunities for change: *yes, we can!* (Vos, 2016)

This does not mean that activists should not appeal to people's imagination. Strong visionaries such as Martin Luther King, Mahatma Gandhi, and Nelson Mandela did not only tell people what was wrong with current Politics but offered an alternative vision of a society based on social and larger meanings such as equity and justice. A positive vision can undermine the sense of fatalism and powerlessness and can persuade people that change is both desirable and possible (Poppovic, 2016). Clear political aims and a coherent ideology seem to be crucial aspects of successful social movements (Soborski, 2018; Day, 2005).

Like imaginations, symbols often play an important role in political movements, such as the demonstrations in Hong Kong in 2014 used the umbrella as a symbol— 'the umbrella revolution'. The opposition that ultimately ousted Milosevic from his presidency used the symbol of a raised fist, reminiscent of the black fist of the American Black Power Movement. A symbol can also be a place, such as Tiananmen Square in Beijing or the Wall Street Stock Exchange (Alinksy, 1971).

Types of Meaning
Activist organiser Bill Moyer (2001) wrote about the different meanings that activism has in different stages of political campaigns. Normal times in which a critical social problem is not widely recognised are followed by a period in which activists show the failure of the official institutes. This is followed by the ripening of the conditions for social change, such as an increasing public recognition of the problems. A trigger event can help the movement take off on large-scale; this trigger can be any event revealing to the public how widely held values are violated by powerholders. This starts to create a public perception of failure, and the majority public opinion shifts, leading to

change. Subsequently, any societal change needs to be maintained by continued critiques and checks and balances (Moyer, 2001).

Different stages of social movement require different actions (Moyer, 2001). For example, activists can fulfill the role of a citizen, rebel, change agent, or reformer. Whereas the citizen and reformer will use the democratically available means available to inform the public and lobby powerholders, the rebel and change agent will use direct action to enforce change. This is the famous debate among protestors: Do we need new institutions and lobbying, or should we organise mass protests? Most likely, we need both, but at different stages of the movement (Engler & Engler, 2016). Therefore, successful movements are often broad and include people coming from different angles, such as Martin Luther King and Malcolm X, who both contributed to the success of the Civil Rights Movement, even though the former used non-violent means and the latter advocated violence.

Thus, it seems that a one-size-fits-all activist does not exist: Political struggle has different meanings for different individuals in different stages of the social movement. This multiplicity of meanings seems crucial for the success of a movement. A movement also needs to be more than merely an action-oriented campaign with one specific goal; it needs to appeal to a wide audience. Thus, a broad ecology of change with multiple meanings is needed: 'When mass mobilizations, established organizations, and alternative communities see themselves as complementary, they can create a movement ecosystem that allows diverse approaches to promote change to flourish' (Engler & Engler, 2016, p.103).

How can previously politically unengaged individuals start to see meaning in activism? Slavoj Popovic was involved in the OTPOR campaign against Milosevic. He writes in his book *Blueprint for Revolution* (2016) that a long-term campaign often starts with politicising citizens, for example by getting them involved in micro-activism of small political problems in daily life, such as demonstrating against uncollected dog poop on the street. Everything becomes achievable when it is broken down into small, playful steps. By achieving small steps, individuals feel empowered and start to believe that they can achieve change; their experiences contradict the fatalistic narrative that 'the powerholders are few but strong, and we are weak but many'. Self-esteem building and achieving small materialist and hedonist goals can help citizens become open to fighting for social and larger topics. One of Gandhi's first political protests was the salt march, where he addressed the daily life reality that poor people could not afford to buy salt; this helped raise awareness for the position of the poor and empowered people in such a way that this led in the long term to the decolonisation of India. Thus, it is important that campaigns address all types of meaning, from small to large, so that the actions become appealing to a broad public and not only to a handful of hardcore activists. More abstract meanings can be addressed later in the campaign (Poppovic, 2016).

As mentioned above, the most effective campaigns address all types of meanings but focus mainly on social and larger types of meaning. The following are some possible examples from the practice of activism (based on Klandermans, 2004, 1997; Taylor, 2010, 1989).

Materialist activism. Citizens often become involved in politics through fighting for materialist goals such as the reduction of the salt price, according to Popovic. The advantage of materialist goals is that they are visible, well-defined, and achievable. *We want a salary raise!*

Hedonist activism. Activism needs to be fun, light-hearted, and creative to appeal to a broad audience, instead of merely imagining serious images such as Tiananmen Square bloodshed. For example, comedian-activist Mark Thomas has written *100 Acts of Minor Dissent* (2014), which are small ,hilarious actions he has done to show the failures of the system, such as holding a tea party in a public space with 'no loitering' signs or placing '*Daily Mail* free zone stickers' in neighbourhoods. Activism can be fun and playful. *We demand fun!*

Self-oriented activism. Self-expression and self-development can be important motivations for people to get engaged in campaigns. They can be creative by making banners or brainstorming about creative strategies. They can learn new skills, such as organising and public speaking, which can offer a sense of self-efficacy and pride. *Let's be creative!*

Social activism. This seems to be an important aspect of effective movements. Political campaigns can give a sense of belonging and feeling respected for who you are, which are experiences that individuals often miss in daily society. Activists can get a sense of fulfillment by helping others and building community. However, big mass demonstrations can give a sense of alienation and functionalism—'I am just a cog in a big machine'—and could demotivate individuals to remain politically involved. *We are cool; you are cool. Join us and let's help one another!*

Larger activism. The more generic the formulated campaign aims are—such as 'prevent climate change' or 'create ethical employment laws'—the more people are able to feel some personal connection; Who wouldn't be for climate change and for unethical employment laws? An appeal to ethics and justice often gives a campaign a more emotional loading. Furthermore, activists who can connect the campaign with their own religion often feel more committed to the campaign. *Can your conscience accept that you let Mother Earth and Father Society die? No? Then, join us!*

Approach to Meaning

Historically, many campaigns were organised by trade unions. People were directly involved in local branches, and they personally knew their union rep (Sverke, 2019; Kelly, 2015). Modern unions are often large and impersonal, and membership participation may be reduced to annual payment of membership fees. Often, hierarchical organisational structures and bureaucratic procedures have emerged. Negotiations with employers and governments are often rational, and reasonable comprises are made. Bureaucracy can be an efficient way to disempower social movements (Stewart, 2001). Thus, the union movement in countries such as the United Kingdom has become a functionalist one. This functionalisation seems to make members feel unengaged, apathetic, and unmotivated to get involved in political activism. In contrast, a critical–intuitive approach to activism starts with the daily life experiences of people, like early days of the union movement. Individual meanings and individual relationships within the movement matter, regardless of its size. People are stimulated to critically listen to their intuitive sense of what is just and unjust, instead of coming up with rational explanations.

Individual and Social Structure
Political campaigns usually start by revealing how some group of powerful individuals are oppressing other people—for instance, by showcasing the role of mind manipulation (Chambers, 2003/2018). For example, Democratic candidate for the presidential election in 2020, Bernie Sanders, started his campaign by revealing the lies of President Trump. Similarly, pro-EU campaigners in the United Kingdom showed how newspapers have been lying about the EU and how Cambridge Analytica collided with Facebook to use manipulative techniques on social media.

How can political powerholders see the meaningfulness of a political campaign, and change? Some activists seem to create strawmen by sketching powerholders stereotypically as merely driven by greed and selfishness, a strategy that can cause polarisation and failure of the movement. Naturally, rich and powerful individuals can also experience a wide range of meanings in life, and they can also feel a lack of life fulfillment when they merely focus on materialist and hedonist goals. Their defence mechanisms are often meant to protect what they know and what they think is the only option for a meaningful life for themselves and for their friends. Therefore, political activists could start with a 'power mapping' of these 'pillars of power'—who they are, what keeps them in power, and, ultimately, what power means to them, and how these meanings could be used to change their behaviour in favour of the political campaigners (Chambers, 2003/2018). Thus, the aim of political activism is to connect the campaign with the pre-existing meanings of the powerholders—how they benefit or how they can fulfill their personal meaning in life by supporting this campaign, achieve similar goals in different ways to reach their personal goals and garner public admiration? Campaigns should focus on win–win strategies. It seems easier to reframe the campaign aims in terms of the powerholders' meanings than to change the meanings of the powerholders, as it seems difficult to completely counter their functionalist–materialist perspectives, which are often the result of life-long experiences of authoritarian upbringing and self-reinforced life scripts.

An exception is dilemma action (Engler & Engler, 2016; Chenoweth & Murphy, 2006; Chambers, 2003/2018). This is a type of non-violent civil disobedience designed to create a response dilemma or lose–lose situation for powerholders. They are forced to either concede some public space to protesters or make themselves look absurd or heavy handed by acting against the protest. This has also been associated with political jiu-jitsu techniques, where the force of the powerholders is used against themselves. For example, the climate campaign Extinction Rebellion (XR) has been blocking streets and public buildings in London, such as putting a boat in concrete in the middle of Oxford Circus and gluing and chaining themselves onto this boat (Shah, 2019; Extinction Rebellion, 2019). To remove the protestors, the police would need to use force to get rid of the glue, chains, and boat. However, allowing the protestors to hold their demonstration congested the traffic and gave the movement more media attention. After almost a week, the police had to intervene, and the videos of police officers using violence went viral on social media. Simultaneously, the protestors remained non-violent and were kind to police officers; in addition, they accepted their court proceedings. So the public image was created of good activists bullied by bad officials. This created large public support and led to the British government formally stating that there is a climate crisis, a statement that was one of the goals of XR.

History
History is rewritten by the conquerors, and thus activists may need to show how the history books leave out information. Historical analyses can help to understand power structures, and sketching historical parallels can help to understand the dangers and options that people have. For example, Faulkner and Dhati (2017) used the definition of fascism and looked at examples such as national socialism during WWII; they compared this with the current situation of the election of Trump, other populists, and the Brexit vote.

Existential Urgency
Chambers (2003/2018) argued that effective campaigns appeal to our human condition—such as all of us are born, will die, and have differences (natality, mortality, and plurality). Not only practical issues are at stake—uncollected dog poop on the street—but our full human condition: the demise of norms and virtues that can lead to chaos and violence. People need to feel an existential urgency in the campaign, such as reflected in the name of Extinction Rebellion: rebel now or become extinct forever due to climate change (Shah, 2019; Extinction Rebellion, 2019).

Insights from existential philosophers and psychotherapists could be used to make people aware of the existential urgency of the political campaign. For example, the explicit use of existential theory and exercises has worked in public workshops to recruit new activists for the climate movement Extinction Rebellion (personal experience). They explained Blaise Pascal's wager. This involved asking people to compare a situation in which they risk eternal hell by not acting or do not risk this by acting; even though they may not be sure whether hell or paradise will be waiting, it is better to be safe than sorry. Irvin Yalom's deathbed imaginative experiment asked individuals to imagine that they are dying and to compare three ways they could have lived their lives that made them most satisfied: they did not try to change the world, they tried to change the world but failed, and they tried to change the world and succeeded. The life story of Viktor Frankl was used as an example of how individuals are able to find some freedom to act and create meaningful change in people, even though Frankl was imprisoned in the concentration camp of Auschwitz. People were asked to phenomenologically bracket the assumptions that they had about activism and instead have an open mind about opportunities to get involved in the movement as they explored different types of meaning that activism could have for them.

Mental Health and Individuation
Change starts when people feel that the meanings on which their life depends are at stake (see chapters 13–14). This can create inner tensions such as fatalism, anxiety, and depression. People fight with themselves and with one another over the question of whether they should accept the situation, ignore or deny reality, or take to the streets and demand change. For people to decide to take action, they need to feel psychologically strong enough to do so, and they need psychological support if they feel frustrated or traumatised during activism. Therefore, mental health problems are a driver of activism as well as a point of attention for a movement. Voluntary mental health care and peer support groups can help to empower people and build psychological resilience (Vos, Roberts, & Davies, 2019).

Successes and Failures of Contemporary Progressive Movements

Several authors have argued that social movements since the turn of the millennium seem to have different aims and strategies than those of any previous movements (Soborski, 2019; Day, 2011). This goes hand in hand with the observation that worldwide the number and size of social movements have increased during the last decades. They have grown larger than in the period 1968–1975, which has officially gone into the history books as a rebellious era (Engler and Engler, 2016). Examples of recent movement are Occupy Wall Street, anti-Trump rallies, Black Lives Matter, Podemos, Syriza, #metoo, Extinction Rebellion, the Hong Kong umbrella uprising, Chilean and Brazilian resistance movements. It can be hard to discern commonalities among them, but the Meaning-Oriented Activism Model could explain some of their common successes and failures.

Deprivation
Popular revolts happen against the background of a period of low, unstable growth in the advanced economies, accompanied by increasing inequality and poverty due to long-term privatisation and welfare and public services cuts in the name of austerity in the wake of the financial crisis. The rest of the world has also experienced a halt in economic growth after the boom of the 1990s which had in some places led to

experiments in redistribution and in other places to corruption and inequality. In countries such as Chile, Lebanon, Iran, and Hong Kong, people rise up against their authoritarian leaders. Meanwhile, countries in the Middle East are still in the aftermath of the War on Terror, and the authoritarian response to the Arab Spring by their rulers. Furthermore, the massive displacement of people from Iraq, Syria, and Africa has triggered nationalistic and xenophobic responses in Europe. Although these societies have very different histories and political systems, they have in common that people rise up due to forms of deprivation that they have framed as unjust, unequal, or undemocratic to their specific social or economic group. In contrast with previous periods, many of these modern social movements see class as only one of the many struggles, not as the main struggle (Laclau & Mouffe, 2014).

Movement Aims

Expression of anger and frustration over the deprivation is only the first step. A social movement also will need to formulate clear political aims and a coherent ideological framework. Several authors have argued that many contemporary movements are more focused on frustration expression and less on the clear formulation of aims (Soborski, 2019; Day, 2011; Pinard, 2005; Melucci, 1989). They have, for instance, summarised the Occupy movement with the question: 'We are the 99%, but what do we want?' Similarly, the climate movement Extinction Rebellion has been criticised for having political aims that are too generic and unlikely to achieve structural change: The government must declare a climate and ecological emergency, halt biodiversity loss, reduce greenhouse gas emissions to net-zero by 2025, and create a citizen's assembly on climate and ecological justice. This does not include a clear strategy of how governments could be convinced to not only give verbal support but enact real policy change. There is also little elaborated vision on intersectionality, such as the specific impact that climate change has on the poorest people, and on how the wider political and socio-economic system has created and reinforced climate change, such as the materialistic focus of the Capitalist Life Syndrome and how this could be changed.

Thus, the social movements seem to aim at expressing frustration over what they do not want (negative identity) without giving clear guidance about the alternative that they do want (positive identity). On the one hand, the openness of these aims enables movements to grow fast since it does not exclude individuals for having different personal aims. On the other hand, the social movements could become so broad or uncritical that it becomes unclear what the movements stand for and that people with conflicting interests could join. It is also difficult to identify when the movement has achieved its goals; to celebrate success when the goals are unclear could lead to frustration and fatigue in the participants in the long term. To achieve actual change, this neutral or negative identity of the movement should be transformed into a positive identity, stating clear political aims and an ideological position on each of the ten meaning-oriented perspectives in the previous section.

Movement Methods

It has been argued that in modern progressive movements, an historical inversion of form and content has happened. Whereas movements in the past had a strong ideology but sometimes inconsistent methods, the current movements have a strong methodology but a weak ideology (Boggs, 1977). This inversion seems to be the response to previous authoritarian movements with hierarchical leadership and bureaucratic structures. There was an inconsistency between the aims that some movements were striving for and the methods they used: 'How could one get an egalitarian and free society to issue from authoritarian organisation?' (Guillaime in Soborski, 2019). Consequently, many modern movements do not have a formal central power structure, and their decision-making process is decentralised and egalitarian (Laclau & Mouffe, 2014). Key principles are horizontality, direct democracy, autonomy, creativity, flexibility, and spontaneity. Clear examples of this 'fetishization of form over content' are globalist movements at World Social Forums, Indigados, Occupy, and Extinction Rebellion. Thus, for these movements, not only the destination is meaningful, but also the journey towards the destination. The methodology itself has social and larger meanings.

On the one hand, participation in the movement can feel meaningful from the first moment onwards, whereas new activists in previous traditional movements could feel not listened to and could feel stuck in meaningless bureaucracies. On the other hand, the focus seems to have moved to organising protests instead of building a strong and coherent resistance movement (Simon, 2020). That is, a protest is a march, a demonstration, slogans, and placards. These protests can give meaning to the activists and can pull new activists in because they can contribute to personal meanings such as playfulness, feeling confident, a sense of community, and solidarity. However, these tactics can only get us so far, as, for example, when a successful demonstration is followed by police enforcement.

Extinction Rebellion has possibly been one of the most effective movements in recent history to put climate change in the news by blocking the central streets of London; however, the police quickly developed tactics to minimise disruption and close down encampments; as London Mayor Sadiq Khan put it, the key thing was to ensure 'business as usual'. Thus, marches and protests on their own do not lead to structural change. For that, a long-term strategy with clear aims and ideology are needed. Resistance means that one symbolic disruption is followed by other large-scale actions such as strikes, occupations, and other forms of direct action to stop the full societal machine from running. For example, during the U.S. Civil Rights Movement in the 1950s and 1960s, racist laws were openly violated— most famously by Rosa Parks, who refused to move out of a whites-only bus seat. This was followed by thousands of black activists, who defied violent police and racist mobs in mass direct-action protests. In contrast, the Stop the War Coalition was the biggest social movement the United Kingdom has ever seen, with huge protest marches and lobbies, but there was little civil disobedience to disrupt the economy, the military machine, or the government. The anti-capitalist movement from 1999–2002 was more radical, as world summits from Seattle to Genoa were sieged by global activists in an attempt to shut them down, but they lacked a strategy to lobby and enforce long-term systemic change.

Furthermore, some of the new social movements have developed a new type of bureaucracy. This is not the bureaucracy of formal procedures that are imposed from the top down by the movement leadership; rather, it is the tyranny of extreme democracy. For example, in new groups many meetings can be spent on finetuning the decision-making and accountability procedures, and achieving consensus on decision-making can be time-consuming due to the difficulty of getting everyone to agree on everything.

At the other extreme are movements such as Extinction Rebellion, which consist of autonomous individuals or small sub-groups that decide their own actions; this strategy has been called 'swarming', like birds in a swarm moving in the same direction even though there is no central leadership or pre-determined plan. The disadvantage of swarming is that not each activist may have the skills and resources to act autonomously, and it may be difficult to coordinate the common long-term strategy.

In general, this trend of methodological puritanism and quarrelling seems to have contributed to the fragmenting of the progressive movement in general. If social movements want to be efficient, they will need to be pragmatic as well as doing justice to the social and larger meanings of their methodology. They will particularly need clear unifying aims from which the methodologies should logically follow.

Propaganda Framing
The largest battle between revolutionaries and counter-revolutionaries regards propaganda and framing. Chapter 11 has already elaborated how mind mafia is a key component to keep the existing powers and prevent change. It seems that the ruling class often has the upper hand due to their connections within the media (Jones, 2014).

For example, British Labour leader Jeremy Corbyn has possibly introduced one of the most anti-capitalist election manifestos in the recent history of his political party, and he was supported by a large young progressive grass-roots movement. However, he quickly became the most smeared politician in history (Cammaerts et al., 2019). During election times, his opponents spent millions on negative advertising, created fake websites, and accused Corbyn of racism even though his voting record factually shows that he is possibly one of the most anti-racist parliament members (*The Guardian*, 20/2/2019; BBC, 21/2/2019; *Jewish News*, 28/11/2018). An estimated 7% of the social media advertising of Labour was biased, compared with 88% of Conservative advertising (FullFact, 17/12/2019). These campaigns included the implicit message that Corbyn could not be trusted with economics, even though there is no evidence that conservative governments are better for the economy than Labour (Barclay, 10/12/2019; Alston, 22/05/2019). The effect of the smear campaign was that a majority of the population disliked Corbyn, which was the main reason they voted against him even though they were unable to explain why: 'I just don't like him' (Ashcroft Polls, 17/12/2019). Psychologists call this 'conditioning'—like Pavlov's dog—whereby people started to associate Corbyn unconsciously with negative feelings. Ironically, population surveys also indicated that a majority of the British population supported the content of Corbyn's manifesto (*The Independent*, 22/11/2019; YouGov, 12/11/2019). When people are confronted with the cognitive dissonance between their dislike of Corbyn and their liking his policies, they seem to respond fatalistically: 'everyone lies', 'Corbyn lies too', and 'all politicians are bad'. Similarly, over 80% of the regular readers of *The Sun* do not believe that their newspaper tells the truth (Populus poll, 12/12/2012). Thus, truth does not seem to matter in these propaganda campaigns, and framing can break or make a politician and a social movement.

If progressive movements want to be effective, they will need to control the framing. A pro-active counter-propaganda programme is needed to show the problems with the neoliberal propaganda. This includes campaigning to forbid lies in political advertising, which is already supported by 87% of the general British population (The Coalition for Reform in Political Advertising/YouGov, 17/12/2019). People should be more critically educating in schools, the media, and workshops within the social movement. Furthermore, the smear campaigns should be used against the smearers; for example, Labour could have put the smearing of Corbyn and the untrustworthiness of Tory fake news more generally, at the heart of their own campaign. False prophets on economics should be attacked in the media with clear evidence. Furthermore, modern marketing campaigns should be used to take into account the dominant ways that people digest information and get socially involved, such as via social media, movies, and games. This also implies surpassing and restructuring meaningless bureaucracies in political organisations and movements, such as relatively flat leadership structures and pragmatic decision-making procedures. However, most of all, a clear vision is needed that offers a distinct meaning-oriented alternative to the suffering in current society.

Conclusions

Meaning is at the core of the cause, aims, and methods of successful political campaigns. These research findings also seem to indicate that the Capitalist Life Syndrome may trigger a successful global uprising because of capitalism's functionalist focus on materialist meanings instead of social and larger types of meaning, a lack of political freedom, and mental health problems. The Capitalist Life Syndrome seems to create internal and social pressures that cannot be suppressed in the long term. Indeed, research seems to suggest that since the 2008 financial crisis the number of uprisings in capitalist countries is increasing, such as the Occupy movement, Yellow Vest Movement in France, London Riots in 2011, nationwide demonstrations against the Trump administration, Extinction Rebellion, etc. (Burgum, 2018; Winlow, Hall, Briggs & Treadwell, 2015; Anyon, 2014). Some of these campaigns were short lived, but together they seem to be part of a wider ecology of change that is gradually but structurally eroding capitalist perspectives on life (Engler & Engler, 2016). They provide hope since any social movement only becomes truly effective when it enables people to experience personal meaning in their political actions and to hope for a fulfilling life.

Key Points

1. The Meaning-Oriented Activism Model states that individuals are more likely to support and participate in social movements (S) when there is a combination of factors: deprivation of social and larger types of meaning (D), social and larger meanings as campaign aims (A), social and larger meanings as campaign, Methods (M), counter-propaganda framing (F) and movement resources (R)—(S=D+A+M+F+R).

2. Research indicates that political campaigns are more effective when they address a wide range of meanings, particularly social and larger meanings, when they are not too functionalist, underline existential urgency, psychologically empower activists, and connect the meanings of the campaign with the meanings of powerholders.

3. If anti-capitalist social movements want to be effective, they need to focus on the deprivation of social and larger types of meaning, social and larger meanings as campaign aims, social and larger meanings as campaign methods, having meaningful propaganda and framing, being prepared to counter the fake news from the counter-revolution movements, and having sufficient resources. The movement needs to have a positive identity, stating clear political aims and ideological position about each of the ten meaning-oriented perspectives.

Chapter 18

Meaning-Oriented Economy:
Meanings Beyond Capitalism
(A Personal Perspective)

A map of the world that does not include Utopia is not even worth glancing at, for it leaves out the one country at which humanity is always landing. (Wilde, 1891)

Be realistic, demand the impossible! (Guevara,2003)

Meaning-Oriented Real Utopias

Imagine an island where everyone lives a meaningful life, people are happy, and there are no differences and conflicts between people. This is because materialist greed and selfishness are abolished, along with money and private property. This is *Utopia*, as Thomas More described it in 1516.

The Greek word 'utopia' may be translated as 'a good non-existing place' (Achterhuis, 1988). In the narrow sense, utopia is a pure figment of imagination which does not need to be realised. However, capitalist utopia is more than mere imagination, as it relies on symbols such as the free market and the self-help citizen. Whereas imagination may be put aside as innocent fantasies, symbols can have the power of Platonic ideas or templates prescribing our meaning in life (see Chapter 4). In a capitalist utopia, mind mafia use Lippmannian 'political technics' and Bernaysian 'propaganda' to promote neoliberal meanings; thus, this symbolic utopia stimulates a 'perverse desire that you are not only allowed but even solicited to realize' (Zizek, Lecture at University of Buenos Aires, 8 May 2014).

Thus, utopias seem to be either figments of imagination or enforced symbols. It is not surprising that utopias have developed a bad reputation in our postmodern era (Achterhuis,1988). However, another type of utopia is possible, which is not mere imaginary and symbolic Politics, but involves the complex political reality of the concrete life-world (Ricoeur, 1957). This Real Utopia is the result of the inner pressures that individuals experience in response to the real raw experiences of their

Capitalist Life Syndrome. It forces its own birth, like contractions of our mental womb, according to Zizek (2014): 'The true utopia happens when the situation is so without issue, without the way to resolve it within the coordinates of the possible that out of the pure urge of survival you have to invent a new space. Utopia is not kind of free imagination. Utopia is a matter of innermost urgency, you are forced to imagine it, it is the only way out, and this is what we need today.'

How are meaning-oriented utopias possible in this context of neoliberal postmodernism and mind mafia? According to several authors on real utopias, this is possible by returning to the life-world of individuals, to the real experiences of pressure and suffering that the Capitalist Life Syndrome brings. Additionally, teach citizens to listen critically to their own intuition and to do justice to the plurality of voices in our socio-economic transactions (see Chapter 6). Thus, these authors argue, do not just copy–paste the mind mafia but think and critically intuit the underlying meanings that our suffering reveals. *Intuitio Aude! Critico Aude!* Our critical intuition can help us to differentiate between manipulated utopic symbols and imaginations, and real utopias that offer off-modern opportunities for a meaning-oriented society, as Olin Wright describes (2010):

> 'Real Utopia' seems like a contradiction in terms. Utopias are fantasies, morally inspired designs for social life unconstrained by realistic considerations of human psychology and social feasibility. Realists eschew such fantasies. What is needed are hard-nosed proposals for pragmatically improving our institutions. Instead of indulging in utopian dreams we must accommodate to practical realities. The Real Utopia Project embraces this tension between dreams and practice. It is founded on the belief that what is pragmatically possible is not fixed independently of our imaginations but is itself shaped by our visions. Self-fulfilling prophecies are powerful forces in history, and while it may be Pollyannaish to say 'where there is a will there is a way', it is certainly true that without 'will' many 'ways' become impossible. (p. 20)

We have already seen in chapters 7 and 14 that increasing numbers of people are leaving the idea of a capitalist utopia for a meaning-oriented society. How does a meaning-oriented real utopia look like? Seen from the ten meaning-oriented perspectives (Chapter 3) this may include the following. A meaning-oriented utopia offers individuals the freedom to develop their own types of meaning, whatever these are. Individuals and society are in a complex dynamic interaction of pluralistic meanings. Where individual meanings conflict, as different perspectives inevitably conflict, social and larger types of meanings prevail, such as the sense of belonging, community, altruism, justice, ethics, larger perspectives, and protecting the vulnerable, the voiceless, future generations, and nature. Functionalism is replaced by a critical–intuitive perspective that does justice to the inherent meaningfulness of each individual and that does not reduce individuals to numbers but offers a new bottom-line guaranteeing the well-being of each individual. Individuals are not merely passively determined by the limitations and the negative freedom of society, but societal structures actively offer positive freedom to open individuals for their individual critical intuition and for their meaning potential. This offers a realistic sense of freedom, as people recognise real limitations such as the finitude of our planet and the vulnerability and pains of our fellow humans. We can learn about the limitations of our utopic ideals and become realistic by critical historiographic lessons on human failures and successes. Ultimately, this utopia will offer existential and psychological well-being. These are ten possible perspectives on meaning-oriented real utopias.

The following sections will offer some specific suggestions of how we could create a meaning-oriented real utopia. These suggestions are directly derived from the research mentioned in Part II (deductive methodology), but obviously their effectiveness in real life still needs to be proven. Whereas the rest of the book is descriptive in nature, this chapter is more prescriptive and based on the fundamental value that each individual deserves to live a meaningful life (see last section for self-reflection).

The Human Right to a Meaningful Life

The Universal Declaration of Human Rights starts with describing human nature, from which the other articles are derived (i.e., 'Natural Law'). Article 1 states that 'all human beings are born free and equal in dignity and rights. They are endowed with reason and conscience and should act towards one another in a spirit of brotherhood.' In line with modern understanding of biology (Chapter 4), the uniqueness of human nature is our reflexive capacity to make a free, rational, and conscious decision to either follow our survival-of-the-fittest instincts or our drive towards mutual aid. Our uniqueness is to choose what we find meaningful. However, in this formulation the vague word 'dignity' has been interpreted, and misused, in many ways (section 9.4). This article could, therefore, benefit from specification: 'Each individual is meaningful in themselves, and is endowed with the ability to discover, express and act upon what they personally experience as meaningful in life, in a spirit of brotherhood.' In other words, the first article could explicitly state the human right of a meaningful life.

The spirit of brotherhood means that social and larger meanings ultimately guide the interaction between people. Furthermore, the declaration already states that humans not only have a reason, which can be manipulated by mind mafia, but their conscience can make a critical–intuitive distinction between more meaningful and less meaningful. Therefore, Article 3 is logically derived from the human nature described in Article 1: 'Everyone has the right to life, liberty and security of person'. In other words, people have the right to be themselves, human, including experiencing, deciding, and expressing their own meaning. Thus, the change of the first article could be paralleled with an addition to the third: 'Everyone has the right to a self-chosen meaningful life.'

The human right to a meaningful life is the cornerstone of a meaning-oriented society. It seems that without these additions, the Universal Declaration remains a disguise and tick-the-box exercise for functionalist materialism (section 9.4). Individuals should not be forced by any states, corporations, or economic systems to incorporate any specific perspective on meaning. Therefore, articles 18 and 19 on the freedom of thought, conscience, and religion could be strengthened. These articles currently state that people have freedom of opinion and expression but does not explicitly prohibit mind manipulation. Article 19 could, therefore, include 'the right not to be compelled to take over the thoughts, conscience, religion, or opinions from other individuals, groups, or governments'. The collective, or its parliamentary representatives, should not decide what is meaningful for the individual, but the individual could decide whether to join the collective or not. The only limitation is the situation where individuals violate human rights, such as Hitler should not have the right to realise his Final Solution, as this violates other people's rights to a meaningful life.

The consequence of the human right to a meaningful life is that states have a duty to actively protect individual meanings and to pro-actively enable citizens to develop and realise their own meanings—for example, via offering critical education, forbidding meaningless jobs, and providing basic material conditions. The human right to a meaningful life becomes the anvil on which all societal, economic, and legal systems could be shaped. This human right is not a fixed Valhalla that solves all problems; instead, the human right to a meaningful life assumes a 'permanent revolution'—that is, a continuous checking and balancing of the freedom of individuals to determine their own meaning.

Minimum National Meaning

The traditional focus of neoliberalism seems to lie in achieving the largest Gross National Product (GNP) possible. GNP is a monetary measure of the market value of all the produced goods and services. However, GNP has not only been criticised for being an ineffective indicator of economic health but also for its materialist focus. Therefore, Bhutan introduced the concept of Gross National Happiness (GNH) in 1972. Similarly, in 2011, the United Nations Assembly passed the resolution 'Happiness: towards a holistic approach to development', which urged member nations to follow Bhutan's example and start measuring happiness. They called happiness a 'fundamental human goal', although they did not go so far as to call this a human right. Although happiness appears to be a narrow hedonist term (see Chapter 7), economists have operationalised this in broader terms of social and larger types of meaning; therefore, a better term and aim could be 'Gross National Meaning'. The four formal pillars of GNH are creating sustainable and equitable socio-economic development, environmental conservation, preservation, and promotion of culture, and good governance. In Bhutan, GNH is measured with objective measures, subjective surveys, and interviews on the nine domains of psychological well-being, health, time use, education, cultural diversity and resilience, good governance, community vitality, ecological diversity and resilience, and living standards. Over time, other indicators have evolved such as the OECD Better Life Index and the World Happiness Report.

These indicators include a broad range of post-materialist meanings in life. However, moving the political goals away from selfish materialism may not be enough to guarantee a meaningful life for each individual as GNH is still measured and applied *functionalistally*. For example, according to Human Rights Watch reports, before the democratic turn in 2008, the Bhutan government used the argument of GNH cultural preservation to justify the ethnic cleansing of the non-Buddhist population of ethnic Nepalese of Hindu faith. Bhutan focused on the statistical average happiness or meaning and artificially manipulated these figures by literally removing the statistical outliers. This genocide did not do justice to the inherent meaningfulness of each individual. Thus, focusing on the average meaning of a country is a functionalist approach that could in its worst version even justify genocides. Therefore, a non-functionalist approach to National Meaning is needed.

To protect individual meaning, Michael Lerner (1997) calls for a new bottom-line, the individual rights for conditions that lead to a meaningful life. Like a National Minimum Wage, the National Minimum Meaning (NMM) is the lowest level of meaningfulness that states can guarantee their citizens. It will be difficult to guarantee that every day and every situation is completely meaningful to each individual, but what matters is the minimum level of fulfillment of meaning in their daily life. For example, people may need to work at a job that they do not always find meaningful, but the job may enable them to afford other meaningful activities in their life; however, the job could not be a completely meaningless 'bullshit job' (Graeber, 2018).

It may be argued, that all citizens should be able to experience that a minimum 40% of all their meanings in life get fulfilled at least 'somewhat' or 'much' (percentages lower than this are strongly correlated with large fatalism and helplessness, psychological stress, and psychopathology; Pearson's $R=.65, p<.01$; $R=0.55, p<.01$ in WSM). However, the meaning of the NMM is subjective, as certain individuals may tolerate a lower level of meaning than others; therefore, national debates should continuously update the NMM level that a country strives for.

What physical conditions are needed to achieve the NMM level? Nobel Prize Winner Amartya Sen reflected on this question. He emphasized that we should not merely look at how individuals function but at their *capability* to function at a minimum level, and to experience a minimum amount of freedom of choice and desire fulfillment, 'to achieve outcomes that they value and have reason to value' (2009, p. 291). Sen conceptualises capability as a reflection of the freedom to achieve meaningful 'functionings', which he describes as 'beings and doings' such as being healthy, having a good job, having financial safety, being happy, having self-respect, and being calm—thus, freedom to determine one's own wide range of meanings (Sen,1992). Capabilities are the functionings—i.e., meanings—that an individual can realistically fulfill. Such formulations of capability have two parts: functionings/meanings and the freedom of opportunity to fulfill these functionings/meanings. This includes factors inside the person, such as their unique perspectives on life, as well as outside factors such as economic conjunctures and political climate. This implies that conditions for the NMM level include both external as well as internal factors and both subjective utilities as well as objective resources. For example, an individual may have the money to start their own company, but without self-esteem, knowledge, and skills the company would either fail or not start at all.

Although Sen refuses to give a list of minimum capabilities because he believes that the minimum could be formulated by the unique stakeholders in the unique situation, Martha Nussbaum (2000) provides a comprehensive formulation of 10 capabilities that any decent state could guarantee as a minimum. The most fundamental seems to be the citizens' capability to plan their own life and develop their conscience. Individuals should be able to freely determine and experience their emotions—including love, grief, and anger—without being afraid of interference from others, and thus without mind mafia. This not only implies that governments should protect individual meanings from impingement but that they should also actively help citizens become aware of their meaning potential and their opportunities in life as well as teach critical thinking—for example, via education. The other capabilities that Nussbaum identifies cover almost all types of meaning: individuals should be able to live a human life of normal length and in good health and with bodily integrity; they should also have some control over their situation, such as the right to participate politically and have their properties protected (materialist meaning). Individuals should be able to play and have fun (hedonist meaning). Individuals should be able to optimally use their senses, imagination, and thought through, for example, literacy, education, arts, freedom of expression, and religion (self-oriented meaning). Individuals should be free to engage in social types of meanings—that is, to live with and toward other humans as well as animals, plants, and nature—belonging to a community and being altruistic, as well as receiving self-respect within this community (social and larger meanings).

Thus, we could argue that following from the universal human right to a meaningful life, states could guarantee a National Minimum Meaning that consists of the realistic capability of its citizens to fulfill all types of meaning in their lives, or at least in 40%.

Meaning-Oriented Checks and Balances

In More's Utopia, individuals always seem to focus on social and larger meanings –and thus be considerate of others—even when they are passionate about their own meaningful projects. However, reality tells that when something is very meaningful for individuals, they can commit themselves passionately to it and defend their perspectives whenever they can. They will let the world know what and why it is meaningful, and they will recommend it to others. This can be constructive as meaning can enthuse and empower others, help people develop larger perspectives via public debates, and stimulate research, development, and productivity. However, individuals can also be so passionate that they try anything to make their meaning happen, even at the cost of others: 'You MUST accept my meaning in life, regardless of what you think and feel'. The meaningfulness of one person can become the meaninglessness of the other person.

Therefore, societal mechanisms may be needed to mediate conflicting meanings in order to remain focused on NMM and on the human right to a meaningful life. In other words, we need checks and balances. Traditionally, elected parliamentary representatives debate differences in public meanings until agreement, or a meaningful amount of support, is achieved and laid out in the law. The government introduces and executes laws in ways it deems meaningful, but its executive meanings are continuously checked by parliament, the legislative power. The judiciary ensures that both parliament and government fulfill their role and will mediate when meanings of citizens conflict. This model of the separation of legislative, executive, and judiciary powers was developed by the philosopher Montesquieu to check and balance differences in meaning.

However, the emergence of the large-scale mind mafia in the 20th century seems to undermine the fairness of checks and balances (see Chapter 11). For example, it has become questionable as to what extent elections in a digital era can lead to a fair representation of the voters' voice; there is a direct correlation between the amount of money that candidates can spend on their campaigns and the likelihood that they get elected (Austin & Tjernstrom, 2003). Money usually does not directly buy votes, but it buys mind manipulation, such as paying Cambridge Analytica to use targeted social media campaigns to influence the Brexit vote and the presidential election of Donald Trump (Wylie, 2019; Kirk, 2017; Goodwin & Heath, 2016). More general, the media in many Western countries are concentrated in the hands of a small group of moguls such as Rupert Murdoch, who owns the most influential newspapers and TV stations in the United Kingdom (Jones, 2014; Curran, 2012). In this situation, journalists cannot completely fulfill their independent role of criticising the meanings of the government, parliament and courts, as Lippmann envisioned. Furthermore, parliaments struggle to hold government accountable and check their work when ministers and civil servants deliberately mislead parliament, such as when American

President George W. Bush and British PM Tony Blair lied about the existence of weapons of mass destruction which led to the American–British invasion of Iraq (Guo & Chen, 2015; Ahmad, 2014). Furthermore, the demographics of parliament members are merely representative of a minority of the population in the United Kingdom and the United States (Smith, 2013). For example, more than half of British MPs rent out a second house, which most likely will influence their voting behaviour on housing bills (Darling, 2015). Finally, judges in American supreme courts are often selected by governments, and thus the judiciary power is limited by government manipulation.

In sum, these examples show how a new power has emerged that unchecks and disbalances—the meaning manipulation by mind mafia. Therefore, a fourth meta-power is needed in addition to Montesquieu's Trias Politica to safeguard the checks and balances, to minimise the influence of mind manipulation on the system, and to guarantee the human right to a meaningful life. Pierre Rosanvallon (2018, p. 263) argues that this new meta-power needs to be based on three poles: 'a council on democratic performance, charged with formalising the legal basis for principles underlying a permanent democracy (integrity of elected officials and transparency of government institutions foremost among them); public commissions, responsible for evaluating the democratic character of public policy deliberation and the steps taken by administrative agencies to put policies into effect, in addition to sponsoring public debate on all relevant issues; and civic organizations, watchdog groups devoted to specifically monitoring government performance (especially with regard to responsiveness, responsibility, and the clarity of political speech) and working to promote citizen involvement, training, and education. In addition, we would also need an independent commission on media checks and balances, such as the current Independent Press Standards Organisation, Press Complaints Commission, and press regulators like Ofcom. Finally, we would also need a similar independent commission on checks and balances in the commercial domain. Examples of such existing institutions with similar aims but less power are the national Ombudsman and consumer protection organisations such as Which? Magazine. This also includes independent regulatory bodies instead of regulators set up by economic sectors themselves. In contrast with existing bodies, these committees and organisations should be unified and truly independent and get more legal powers as the fourth authority of the mind manipulation regulator.

Meaning-Oriented Education

The British mind manipulation mastermind Keith Joseph saw education as the core place to win 'the battle of ideas' in favour of neoliberalism (Sanderson, 2018; Denham & Garnett, 2001; Wright & Bottery, 2002; Wilkin, 1996). Western education has been strongly narrowed-down to a core curriculum that teaches knowledge, skills, and obedience from which the main economic sectors benefit (Forrester & Garrett, 2016; Vallence, 1973; Freire, 1970/2018).

However, the capacity for critical reflection is key for developing democracy (Arendt, 1970). An alternative is possible, such as the WHO Life Skills Education Programme. The Finnish school system, 'the miracle of education' (Niemi et al., 2016), is a good example; it includes a broad curriculum and schools having independence in the selection of the goals and methods of teaching (Vos, Roberts, & Davies, 2019). Instead of government bodies such as the Office for Standards of Education (Ofsted) deciding the content and methods of pupil tests, there could be bodies to guarantee the freedom of teaching, both the overall curriculum as well as the independence of the content of the specific syllabi, books, and teaching methods. The independence of education could be regarded as a fundamental right that directly derives from the human right to a meaningful life. We have two options, according to Freire (1970/2018): education as a practice of freedom or as an instrument to facilitate integration into the status quo.

Any school curriculum could include not only professional knowledge and skills but also life skills, teaching children and young people how to live a meaningful life. For example, in Finland school subjects include personal growth, cultural identity internationalism, media skills, communication, participatory citizenship and entrepreneurship, responsibility for the environment, well-being and a sustainable future, safety and traffic, and technology (Määttä, & Uusiautti, 2012). This also includes training in critical thinking skills, such as critical use of social media. Arts and humanities also play an important role to stimulate critical thinking, creativity, and intuitive skills, all crucial skills to living a meaningful life. Furthermore, several schools follow democratic principles advocated by John Dewey (1923) by lifting discipline and instead focusing on what is meaningful for children, such as having weekly meetings where children discuss mutually agreed-on codes and how to cope with breaches (Forrester & Garratt, 2016).

Children could also be able to develop their meaning in life free from oppressive powers and childhood abuse, neglect, and poverty, which could later lead to authoritarian attitudes (Milburn & Conrad, 2016). Governments could enforce explicit anti-authoritarian laws to break the intergenerational vicious cycle of authoritarianism. This not only implies anti-spanking laws and support for advanced child protection services; it also assumes forbidding authoritarian private/boarding schools for the privileged and instead supporting community activities where children can learn to listen to their own critical intuition via play, creativity, and fun, ranging from after-school activities to state-supported community centres, sports associations, or vouchers for music and art lessons.

Meaning-Oriented Communities

Communities can play an important role in meaning-oriented societies. They may provide a sense of belonging and offer opportunities to help others and receive help

(Vos, 2017). Communities can also stimulate democratic decision making and meaningful commitment to our direct material surroundings, such as neighbourhoods looking after their green space and other commons (Ostrom, 2006). This does not mean that communities are the only possible source of support and democracy. To stimulate these social and larger meanings, governments may want to decentralise powers that can be more meaningfully led by citizens than by bureaucrats—such as maintenance of green space. Community centres and neighbourhood councils could receive funding to give ample opportunities to individuals to find meaning in their social contexts, such as sports associations, hobby clubs, and neighbourhood councils. The long-term financial costs of this devolution of money, power, and meaning may be less than the actual costs, as these communities will improve the sense of meaningfulness, self-efficacy, and citizenship in individuals, which will pay off indirectly via increased productivity and fewer costs for mental and physical health care.

Meaning-Oriented Work and Income

In a meaning-oriented society, individuals have the right to meaningful work. More precisely, work enables individuals either within the workplace or via the income that it provides to live a life that feels for at least 40% meaningful.

Employees could be stimulated to experience a plurality of meanings via work. They could find meaning in the materialist process and surroundings, such as the activities themselves, and the physical public space in which they work (materialist meaning). They could find meaning in the control that they have over their own work and in the self-development and resilience that they experience in striving towards high but achievable goals (self-oriented meaning). Employees could also find meaning in the social aspect that the workplace can have for them, such as the relationships with colleagues (social meaning). Jobs can also help employees to focus on larger meanings, such as civil servants can explicitly aim to help to improve society or offer a service that is deeply meaningful to customers (larger meaning). The flipside of the right to meaningful work is the duty of employers and governments to prevent 'bullshit jobs' (Graeber, 2018). For example, automation could replace human beings in monotonous and hyper-specialised jobs such as packing pancakes at conveyor belts.

In meaning-oriented organisations, decisions are made by people who have 'skin in the game'. For example, Chang (2012) describes how the 2007/2008 crash was caused by investors and bankers who were only interested in making a quick profit. Profit was artificially created by increasing the margins instead of improving the quality of products and services. They took large risks and experimented on a large scale as they did not carry personal financial risks. Ordinary employees and small enterprises had to pay the price for bankers and investors playing roulette. Thus, the direction of companies was predominantly guided by materialist, hedonist, and self-oriented reasons, despite the plurality of meanings that the workplace, products, and services can have for employees, customers, and the wider economy. In meaning-oriented organisations, all investors and managers need to have skin in the game, such as employees owning company shares. Employees and experts could be directly involved in deciding the aims and methods of the company via representative work councils, such as the Rhine Model and the Dutch Poldermodel (Peters & Weggeman, 2019; Van Zanden & Prak, 2013). In addition, large companies could have stakeholder councils, where the voice from all formal *and informal* stakeholders and their representatives can be heard, including the neighbourhood, schools, and nature. This will most likely not only make companies more meaningful to all stakeholders, but also make them more innovative and cost efficient, as well as more resilient to socio-economic shocks.

Individual entrepreneurs could be supported to start their own companies and would not need to compete with giants with unreasonably large power. For example, large companies can afford more expensive mind manipulation than small companies, and thus they are more likely to succeed than small companies. Therefore, monopolies, cronyism, and unreasonable powers of corporations that limit the freedom of small and medium-sized enterprises to realise their meanings may be prohibited.

States could support individuals to realise their meanings by providing personal investment grants. This is not like microcredits that need to be repaid; rather, it is a one-time lump sum that can be used to start a company, follow education or training, or invest in automation. Fees for higher education can also come from this money bag, but individuals who do not attend higher education can use this money for other purposes to similarly improve their status in the market. A personal investment grant is one of the clear initiatives that could directly help individuals develop and realise their own plan in life. It has been suggested that each citizen could receive a stake of $80,000 at the age of 21, and those who have done well must pay back their stake, with interest, upon their death via inheritance tax (Ackermann & Alstott, 1999).

Furthermore, one of the largest stimulations of the freedom to choose our own meaning in life is the introduction of a universal basic income. This gives the individual more freedom to find jobs and activities that they find meaningful, instead of being forced to accept meaningless jobs or experience low self-esteem because of the guilt culture surrounding benefit seeking. Such income is universal, meaning that each individual receives a uniform amount (De Wispelaere & Stirton, 2004). Public support for universal basic income is quickly increasing, from 12% of the American population in 2008 to 48% in 2018; 46% of supporters would pay higher personal taxes to support it and 80% of supporters say companies could pay higher taxes to fund the program (Gallup, 26 February 2018). In the United Kingdom, 49% supports the idea and only 29% opposes it (IPSOS, 8 September 2017). Whereas politicians in many countries have been theoretically debating the universal basic income, countries such as the Netherlands, Belgium, and Finland are successfully implementing large-scale experiments or have introduced a universal basic income unofficially 'via the back door' of tax deductions (Van Parijs & Vanderborght, 2017; Vanderborght, 2014; Bregman, 2014). The introduction of universal basic income is not stopped by its economic feasibility or its public support, which are positively supported by a robust body of empirical evidence, but by its political feasibility (De Wispelaere & Noguera, 2012).

Universal basic income has also been supported by some neoliberal authors as it offers a cost-efficient welfare system, instead of the cost inefficiency of benefit systems (Torry, 2016; Van Parijs et al., 2006). However, most neoliberals seem to reject the idea of universal basic income because it seems to contradict the Smilean–Thatcherite–Josephian ideal of the self-help citizen. Some neoliberals regard benefit seekers as having a moral problem and deem them too lazy to work; they believe that generous benefits or basic income would reinforce their idleness. However, this assumption is not supported by any empirical evidence. Research indicates the opposite: a universal basic income stimulates the sense of self-efficacy and helps unemployed individuals to find work quicker than in a benefit-based system (De Wispelaere & Stirton, 2012a). Ultimately, it seems that the question is not whether a universal basic income works but whether politicians want to give up the self-governmentality that they try to impose via the restrictive and punitive benefit system.

Furthermore, Nick Srnicek and Alex Williams (2015) write that the ideal of a universal basic income could only be implemented together with the demands of full automation, a short work week, and regarding care as work. Without using the term 'meaning', what they suggest is that a universal basic income without guaranteeing NMM is not desirable. Meaningless jobs could be replaced by automation, and the profits from increased automation could be used to partially pay for the universal basic income (such as taxation or public ownership of automatization). People could work two or three days to have enough time to engage in meaningful activities other than their job, such as relationships, participating in community activities, or taking care of commons such as the public green. Finally, Srnicek and Williams argue that care activities such as parenting or supporting parents could also be regarded as work for which people could receive an income. This combination of demands could help to create more freedom to live a meaningful life.

Meaning-Oriented Knowledge and Research

Whereas agrarian and industrial economies flourished thanks to increased productivity, the flourishing of modern economies seem to depend on innovation, research, and education. Increasing proportions of the GNP depend on sectors such as IT, finances, higher education, etc. However, neoliberal economies seem to limit the learning capability of countries, as market forces logically lead to the stagnation of learning, research, and development (Stiglitz & Greenwald, 2014). Ideas are for sale, for example, via R&D investments, research grants, or companies starting their own university, such as Google University and Facebook University (Stiglitz & Greenwald, 2014). Academic creativity seems to be killed by the profit obsession and the military–hierarchical bureaucracies of universities (Roberts, 2018). The biopolitical organisation of universities seems to lead to destructive self-governmentality and to the corrosion of academic freedom.

As if this were not enough, postmodernism seems to have killed the ideal of truth, and neoliberalism seems to have used this for its own benefits (Jameson, 1991). For example, American President Trump has received much public support for his unsupported claim that research on climate change and the human cause of it is a hoax, even though 98% of all climate researchers say that the human impact on climate changes is real (Jordan, 2019). Many governmental departments in Western countries have also disbanded their independent research advisory boards since the late 1980s; since then, civil servants have been expected to buy reports from external consultants to support the government position (Chapter 11). Thus, knowledge, truth, and academia seem to have lost their independence, and, consequently, their important role of providing independent checks and balances (Otto, 2016).

As many authors have argued, critical thinking should become dangerous and sexy again. Knowledge and research should be independent from the meaning of the oligarchy of corporate powers and government officials. Education and knowledge creation should be free from external impositions and serve the wide meaning potential of the full population: Knowledge should be treated as a common (Otto, 2016; Frischmann, Madison & Strandburg, 2014). Only with such a refreshed status can real innovation happen. New critical universities need to be established that share knowledge as commons, which are meaningful in themselves and which are not owned by any particular individual. These places bring people together and invite them to reach beyond biopolitics and the polarization of opinions to create new visions and communities that can lead to action and lasting change. These are 'festivals of ideas where all contributions are equally valued'. Ultimately, these critical universities could raise a NEW VOICE: learning New ideas, sharing both Expertise and experiences, exploring What to do now instead of merely saying what is wrong, creating new Vision, building Open communities, being Intersectional and interdisciplinary, being Critical and creative, and Empowering individuals. 'Because together we can raise a NEW VOICE!' (London Critical University, Mission statement, September 2019).

Meaning-Oriented Consumption

Chapter 6 described how consumption is becoming increasingly meaning oriented instead of being obsessed with the functionality of the product or service. People buy at their local baker's because they know him/her/them and know that the products are healthier and more ecological than supermarket bread. By buying or not buying, consumers have an almost unlimited, but often unused, power to determine which companies fail and which succeed.

However, consumers are often unaware of the multiplicity of meanings that are involved in products or services. Some laws already exist to make consumers aware of some possible meanings, such as the legal obligation to write the ingredients on a label or to give an information sheet with financial products. Similarly, logos are printed on the packaging of products to show their ecological or social stewardship, as a stamp from the Forest Stewardship Council (FSC) guarantees the ecological sustainability of a wood product, the Marine Stewardship Council (MSC)stamp guarantees sustainable fishing, and a Fair Trade logo guarantees that all partners along the trade chain have a fair income. However, most of these information sheets and logos are placed irregularly on products and mainly focus on materialist and ecological meanings.

Just as customers have a right to know the ingredients or material of the product they buy, they could have the right to know the social and ecological meanings of a product. This could reflect the grey reality and not merely the black-or-white situation of placing or not placing a logo on a product, such as offering a range from 1, meaning bad, to 5, meaning good. Furthermore, there could be a consistent assessment of all the meaning of a product or service, and not merely a meaning that is convenient for an economic sector; for example, salmon may be harvested ecologically but the fishermen get paid little (e.g., a package of salmon could be marked MSC5 and Fair Trade1).

The inconsistency of information sheets and logos are caused by the fact that these are provided either by the economic sector itself or by relatively small NGOs. Furthermore, in the current system, it is unclear how fair the advertising of a product or service is; therefore, a new mind-manipulation logo could be introduced that would assess to what extent the meaning of a product or service has been manipulated. It could be the task of the government or a new mind manipulation regulator to provide such independent assessments of products and services.

Meaning-Oriented Mental Health Care

Elsewhere, we have described how mental health care has become a key domain of government and corporate mind manipulation, popularised by politicians such as Keith Joseph (Vos, Roberts, & Davies, 2019). For example, Joseph suggested in his white papers that mental health care should be just good enough to enable people to perform well enough in their jobs, but it should not empower people to rise up (Conservative Party Archive, 2016). Consequently, it seems unsurprising, that there is a structural lack of funding for public mental health care and prevention programmes, and that the diagnostic, therapeutic, and mental health care systems seem mainly governed by individuals with direct personal financial interests (Vos, Roberts, & Davies, 2019).

Instead of being shaped to fit standardised mental health care, individuals could receive individual mental health vouchers that they could use with any mental health care provider they want (Vos, Roberts, & Davies, 2019). Mental health advocates could have a stronger role in informing clients about the options they could choose from and identify the type of therapy that may be most relevant for their current situation. This could include the opportunity of humanistic, existential, relational, and critical psychotherapies that focus on empowering individuals within the reality of their socio-economic context. Instead of immediately searching for problems in the individuals, mental health care providers could start with a systematic assessment of how the social context gives rise to distress (Vos, Roberts, & Davies, 2019). Such an ecological system of diagnosing and treating is already emerging. For example, the British Psychological Society has been promoting the Power Threat Meaning Framework. This replaces the question that therapists traditionally start with—'What is wrong with you?'—with four others: 'What has happened to you?' (How has power operated in your life?); 'How did it affect you?' (What kind of threats does this pose?); 'What sense did you make of it?' (What is the meaning of these situations and experiences to you?); 'What did you have to do to survive?' (What kinds of threat response are you using?) (Johnstone et al., 2018). Developments like this can empower individuals to explore, express, and act upon what is truly meaningful for them in life instead of blaming them for their mental health problems.

Philosophical–Existential Types of Meaning

The profound conflict in this century is(…) between history and nature. (Camus, 1951/2012)

Chapter 1 introduced the idea of existential–philosophical types of meaning, but this book is bereft of examples of these types of meaning. The reason for this is the abstract nature of these meanings and because few people have written about this, except for existential philosophers. However, in a meaning-oriented society, these relatively silent meanings could get a voice. The examples of future generations and nature are merely a small number of countless instances.

Future generations cannot directly plea for their rights in the present moment, as they have not been born yet. However, we may have a direct responsibility for them. For example, our invisible bond with future generations could exert an ethical appeal on us not to leave our countries with an enormous debt, a dictatorship, or destroyed nature. Protecting future generations can be seen as inherently meaningful, but often in daily life we do not think of them since we literally cannot envisage them. Short-term perspectives often receive more reinforcement in our current economic system, such as cutting a forest gives a forest owner direct income; therefore, instead, positive longitudinal projects could be rewarded and longitudinal destruction punished. We may ask ourselves critical questions from a pluralistic meaning-oriented perspective. Who are we to prioritise our right to a meaningful life over the rights of our children to have a meaningful life? Are their rights not equally important? Should violations or destruction of their future potential meanings be equally legally punishable as a direct crime against a person currently alive?

Some philosophers have argued that all nature is meaningful in itself (Stone, 1972). We should approach nature not as a thing ('it') but with full respect as a fellow being ('thou'); like with other human beings, we should be in a dialogue with nature and not impose our monologue: 'All real living is meeting' (Buber, 2002). This implies that animals, plants, and nature, in general, have a universal right to a meaningful life, albeit obviously that their meaning is not defined by their self-conscious decisions. Natural destruction could to some extent be treated as a crime against humans. Indeed, an increasing number of philosophers and courts have stated that the meaningfulness of nature could not be violated. Philosopher Christopher Stone (1972) argued that trees have legal standing, and a US court argued that inanimate objects have the standing to sue in court (Sierra Club vs. Morton, 405US727, 1972). Nature has a legal status as a ship can have legal status. For example, in 2012, New Zealand's Whanganui River was legally declared a person with standing, albeit with human guardians, so that legal actions could protect its interests.

This means that acting against nature and future generations could not merely depend on gentlemen's agreements such as the Paris Climate Agreement, or on civil courts, but also on criminal courts (NGO Stop Ecocide, 2019).

Final Reflections

This chapter described what a real utopia of a meaning-oriented society could look like. Examples were provided on how the inherent meaningfulness of individual citizens, consumers, future generations, and nature could be protected. These are not mere imaginations; Chapter 6 has shown an international development towards a Meaning-Oriented Economy. Although we may not have actively chosen this system, governments and civil services are already acting more and more on the basis of protecting the plurality and self-realisation of meanings (Rubin, 2016). However, other chapters have shown the threats that the current economic powers pose towards the inherent meaningfulness of individuals, future generations, and nature, and it seems important that we create and support institutions to check and balance these powers if we want to guarantee a meaningful life to each citizen.

The normative tone of this chapter was different from other chapters, in which I tried to be more scientifically descriptive. My use of words such as 'should' and 'must' is based on what I perceive as meaningful: protecting and stimulating a meaning-oriented society. Striving towards this meaning-oriented utopia is only one of the options, as previous chapters showed how individuals could also find meanings within, outside, or against capitalism. The examples in this chapter may be utopic, but, as Gramsci wrote, my intellect may be pessimistic, my will is optimistic. I believe in the inherent meaningfulness of helping others to live a self-chosen, meaningful life. What matters is doing justice to the meaningfulness of individuals and their personal meanings.

I started this book with the conversation that I had as a psychology-student with an elderly man. I have carried his riddle with me for decades, sometimes explicitly but usually implicitly I tried to answer his question about how we can do justice to individual meanings within our current economic constellation. Although it took me much studying and many life experiences, this book is its result. I have discovered that economics is not the neutral science that it claims to be. Instead, all economic models are based on subjective perspectives on meaning in life. Consequently, the fundamental question is not which economic or political label we want to put on ourselves, but which types of meaning and which approach we want in life. This is a personal question that nobody can answer except for yourself, even though some economists and politicians have passionately tried to manipulate our individual answers, with the emergence of the intricate system of mind mafia as its culmination point. I think that we need to learn to listen critically to what our own intuition tells us about meaning.

On my journey, I have discovered that I get less inspired by the limited perspectives of economic gurus than by the concept of mutual aid in the animal realm, social economies, indigenous tribes, African street children, and even work at the conveyer belt in a pancake factory. Often without the intellectual and cultural luggage on which neoliberalism is built, the phenomenology of these experiences reveals how a more meaningful society is possible. They offer inspiration, vision and hope. That is what we desperately need in our era of economic, social and ecological crises.

Because everyone deserves to live a meaningful life.

Key Points

1. Utopias traditionally focus either on free imagination or imposed symbols. The alternatives are Real Utopias, which start in the lived-experiences of the life-world.
2. A meaning-oriented society is based on the universal human right to a meaningful life and offers a Minimum National Meaning to each citizen.
3. The National Minimum Meaning consists of the realistic capability of all citizens in a state to fulfill all types of meaning in their lives, or at least in 40% of it, without manipulation by the mind mafia.

4. Mind manipulation seems to endanger the checks and balances in the political system. Therefore, a fourth power could be established in addition to the Trias Politica of legislative–executive–judicial powers to guarantee the fairness and independence of the other powers, minimise the impact of mind manipulation, and safeguard the human right to a meaningful life.

5. A meaning-oriented society offers meaning-oriented education, communities, knowledge, research, and mental health care, and does justice to the meaningfulness of future generations, nature and other unheard voices.

Afterword

'Infectious diseases are no respecters of wealth, power or personal merit. Pandemic infectious disease is one situation where we cannot accept Margaret Thatcher's view that "there is no such thing as society". With a fast-spreading respiratory virus, for example, everyone is ultimately in the same boat'.
(Doherty, 2013)

'We may be on the same boat, but when the Titanic goes down, the only question that matters is who will go first on the lifeboats. This is an issue of economics and meaning in life, not of virology'.
(author's comment to Doherty)

The COVID-19 and the Capitalist Life Syndrome

When I wrote the final words of the last chapter, it felt as if I were closing the door behind me, coming home from a long journey. I have taken the reader as a companion on my journey from the animal realm and early humans in the first chapters, via capitalism and Marxism, to the post-capitalist utopias in the last chapters. We have reconnected with old acquaintances in our home countries and have explored cultures far away. We have completed our journey: We can put our backpack in the corner of the room, hang up our coat, take off our shoes, and plump down in our comfy chair to rest and recover! Alas, world history has decided that there is no time to rest. Sitting in my comfy chair was just a brief respite to catch my breath.

On the day that I sent the publisher my manuscript, there was a newsflash about an unknown virus raging through Wuhan and Hubei regions in China, triggering the local government to order a full lockdown. In the following weeks, the 2019 novel coronavirus (SARS-CoV-2) travelled quickly across the world, affecting millions of people and killing hundreds of thousands. The size of this pandemic leaves the pandemics of other coronaviruses like SARS-Cov and MERS, and possibly even the fatal Ebola epidemic, behind. People fear that we may be running towards a pandemic the size of the 1918 Spanish Flu and the Black Death in 1346, which wiped out almost half of the world population. *World-wide panic! Save the elderly and vulnerable individuals with underlying diseases! Get your personal protective equipment now! Lock yourself up in your house with all the toilet paper that you can find in the stores!*

Or is there something else going on at the same time as the biomedical threat? Could it be that, although we need to take this pandemic very seriously from an epidemiological perspective, we have also been taken hostage by the narratives from our politicians and the explanations from our pharmaceutical companies? Is the COVID-19 pandemic the ultimate example of the Capitalist Life Syndrome? Are the biomedical pandemic, our socio-economic system, and our understanding of meaning in life intertwined? Of course, people can easily see that the pandemic has a devastating impact on the economy, but this pandemic is more than biomedical and socio-economic. It is also a pandemic of a specific perspective on life—the Capitalist Life Syndrome that I have described in this book. We may even argue that this pandemic could be a culminating point of the Capitalist Life Syndrome. Therefore, in this Afterword, I will explore how *The Economics of Meaning in Life* can help us understand the political framing and socio-economic impact of the COVID-19 pandemic.

The Pandemics of the Capitalist Life Syndrome

The world history of health and illness has often been categorized into three ages of transition (Hardt, 2015). For example, according to Abdel Omran (1971), the earliest is the Neolithic age of pestilence and famine, which was characterized by high mortality and low life expectancy, with many infectious diseases, malnutrition, and famine. The age of receding pandemics that followed centuries later started with modern medicine and the public hygiene movement, leading to a progressive decline of mortality rates and fast population growth. Finally, our current age has seen a fading away of pandemics and an increase in life expectancy, although new diseases such as cardiovascular diseases, cancer, violence, accidents, and substance abuse have emerged because of our lifestyles. An example of this is the staggering increase of so-called 'deaths of despair' from suicide, drug overdose, and alcoholism, which are associated with people's low socio-economic status and low social mobility (Case & Deaton, 2020; Deaton, 2013).

However, Omran's expectation that pandemics would become less frequent and have a smaller impact on society has been proven wrong. 'Despite continuing progress in many areas, including enhanced human and animal surveillance and large-scale viral genomic screening, we are probably no better able today to anticipate and prevent the emergence of pandemic influenza than five centuries ago' (Morens, Taubenberger, Folkers & Fauci, 2010). We may have entered a new age of pandemics (Quick & Fryer, 2018). Microbes have adjusted to our lifestyle, and our lifestyle has opened new opportunities for their fast transmission (Hardt, 2015). Thus, pandemics continue to have a significant impact on the world population. This is not due to a lack of medicinal expertise, like in the first age, but because of our socio-economic situation, as Omran identified in the third age, which leads some experts to speak of an 'outbreak culture' that is associated with our socio-economic lifestyle (Sabeti & Salahi, 2018). Therefore, I propose a fourth age in the world history of health and illness: The era of pandemics caused by the Capitalist Life Syndrome. In the next paragraphs, I will give examples of how capitalism has (partially) caused, facilitated, divided, exacerbated, and extended the modern outbreak culture.

Causal factors

Epidemiologists have described how our capitalist lifestyle may have contributed to the causation and spread of viruses such as COVID-19. Many pandemics start with the infection of some wildlife or domestic animal species. Although the pathogen crossover from one species to another seems unpredictable, the likelihood of such crossovers increases because of our lifestyles. For example, rapid deforestation has increased human contact with unknown animal species, and SARS-Cov and SARS-CoV-2 seem to have come from bats and civets. Human water storage, such as wells and pools, also become infection beds for malaria-bearing mosquitoes. In addition, climate change has caused global coverage by Aedes species, with Zika and dengue mosquitoes creating pandemics in northern countries such as the United States.

The increase in food demand, combined with the industrial scale of animal farming, has transformed farms into mass factories of animals near human civilization, where infections such as foot and mouth disease can quickly spread and cross over to humans. The increased demand for livestock and the decreased margins of profit have motivated many animal farmers to give antibiotics to their animals, which may lower the effectiveness of antibiotics and may impact the human immune system.

Furthermore, it seems that SARS-CoV-2 was spread via wet markets of live animals in Wuhan. Until the 1990s, there was little trade in live animals in such wet markets, but the increase in wealth in China has also increased the demand for rare animals in culinary dishes that were in the past only imaginable for the ultra-rich.

Facilitating factors

Epidemics and pandemics cannot happen without dense and mobile populations that foster the spread of infection beyond a specific location. It seems that global capitalism has fostered the concentration and connection of people. For example, the age of the great explorers like Columbus was also the age of pandemics for indigenous people, such as native Americans, who were killed not only by rifles but also by new viruses such as smallpox brought by Europeans. Later, the Black Death was brought to Europe via boats from places like Egypt. The 1918 flu virus was brought home by soldiers returning from the front and was transmitted to Asia by traders on the Trans-Siberia Express. Similarly, the COVID-19 pandemic would most likely have remained in Wuhan if people had not travelled on a large scale, including internationally, for the Chinese New Year. The worldwide interconnectedness of our economies makes it easy for viruses to spread like wildfire.

Dividing Factors

'We are in this together' seems to be the mantra of politicians during the COVID-19 pandemic. However, research clearly shows that 'we' are not in this together. People are rarely together in health and illness: There are considerable health disparities, with the poorest having the most substantial risk of infection and illness (Marmot, 2020; Case & Deaton, 2020; Deaton, 2013; Singer, 2009; Adler & Newman, 2002). Many pandemics, such as tuberculosis, become a disease of the poor, and COVID-19 also seems to have the largest impact on ethnic minorities and individuals with the lowest socio-economic status. The current pandemic offers poignant examples of how existing health inequalities predict more severe symptoms and an increased likelihood of death (Health Foundation UK, 2020). For example, people face the virus from uneven starting points, with individuals in the most socio-economically deprived areas more likely to have chronic life conditions that put them at a greater risk of developing a severe form of COVID-19 (Intensive Care National Audit and Research Centre Report, 2020; Croxford, BBC, 12 April 2020).

However, governments have been refusing to publish recommendations from experts on health inequalities during the COVID-19 pandemic (Woodcock, 2020). The only available data comes from the UK Office for National Statistics (7 May 2020) who described the unequally large impact of COVID-19 on ethnic minority groups:

> COVID-19-related death for males and females of Black ethnicity is 1.9 times more likely than those of White ethnicity (...) males in the Bangladeshi and Pakistani ethnic group were 1.8 times more likely to have a COVID-19-related death than White males when age and other socio-demographic characteristics and measures of self-reported health and disability were taken into account; for females, the figure was 1.6 times more likely.

This reminds us of the words of civil rights activist Audre Lorde who said, 'Institutionalized rejection of difference is an absolute necessity in a profit economy which needs outsiders as surplus people'.

Exacerbating factors. Many mechanisms have exacerbated the infection risks for vulnerable groups (Nuffield Trust, Georghiou & Appleby, 27 April 2020). For example, although countries went into a full lockdown, many individuals with low socio-economic status (e.g., waste collectors, supermarket staff, postal delivery services, police officers, nurses and other health care workers) had to continue working outdoors, which involved an increased risk of infection. Politicians have labelled these frontline workers as 'key workers' and 'supermen' during the pandemic, but these symbolic words seem to disguise the harsh reality of the daily exposure to infections, with, for example, 45 bus drivers and approximately 200 health care workers dying from COVID-19 in the United Kingdom (Siddique & Marsh 2020). The use of the Superman symbol creates the impression that these key workers work from the goodness of their heart. However, although some may work for altruistic reasons, many individuals did not have another option than to work; otherwise they would lose their job and be left with no or little benefits.

Furthermore, research indicates that quarantine is ineffective, or even detrimental, during coronavirus pandemics when people live in small housing conditions and overcrowded neighbourhoods, which increases the risk of the virus spreading. Research also indicates that other socio-economic factors such as having less money to buy vitamin-rich food and greater psychological stress create an impaired immune system that could result in more severe cases of COVID-19, (Berkman, Kawachi & Glymour, 2014; O'Campo & Dunn, 2011; Singer, 2009; Marmot & Wilkinson, 2005).

Governments have also been criticized for exacerbating the pandemic by prioritizing the economy over people. For example, American president Donald Trump and British Prime Minister Boris Johnson have been criticized for starting large-scale testing and quarantine measures much too late and for advocating a return to work and schools much too early (The British House of Commons, Parliamentary Debate, 19 May 2020).

Years before the outbreak of COVID-19, scientists warned Western governments about the risk of such a pandemic and urged them to prepare by increasing staffing and equipment. However, the required pandemic strategies were never implemented because of a structural lack of resources allocated by politicians (Carrington, 2020). For example, privatization and underfunding during the last decade meant that the British National Health Services were already struggling to offer adequate care to all patients due to privatization and underfunding during the last decade (El-Gingihy, 2018). The COVID-19 pandemic flooded this already overstretched health care system. The lack of preparedness required that all available health care resources be allocated to the care of COVID-19 patients; consequently, less urgent and routine care, such as cancer screening, had to be postponed, even though this also has increased mortality rates.

A select committee of the British parliament is at this moment of writing investigating what the government could have done differently. This includes delving into the reasons why Prime Minister Boris Johnson had rejected multiple offers to buy much-needed personal protective equipment for health care workers and ventilators for patients. As a consequence of Johnson's rejection of these offers, health care staff had to cover themselves with makeshift protection such as bin bags with holes cut in them, while they had to decide which patients should live and who should die because they did not have enough ventilators for all patients.

The so-called free market also seems to have influenced the lack of equipment. COVID-19 tests were delivered worldwide very slowly because few companies were allowed to produce test kits due to a monopoly, although it has been widely acknowledged that the early availability of testing helps stop the spread of the virus. Researchers have also been criticized for withholding research findings for their advantage in selling treatments or vaccines (Stiglitz, 2020).

In sum, although the overstretched health services may already have been struggling to cope with the increased demand for care, COVID-19 has grown to proportions of a collective crisis due to poor political decisions and planning.

Extending Factors

COVID-19 will most likely go into the history books as one of the greatest crises of recent generations, and possibly of human history in general (Faulkner, 2020). We can see the crisis unfolding before our eyes: The COVID-19 pandemic is causing an unprecedented economic depression. In the first months of the pandemic, the GDP shrank by more than one-third (UK Office for Budget Responsibility, 14 April 2020) and 40 million Americans and one million Britons have lost their jobs, with numbers rising (Aratani, 2020). The socio-economic impact of the pandemic does not seem to be borne equally by different echelons of society. Although many parliaments have quickly passed emergency bills to allocate large sums of money to support those hit hardest by COVID-19, they have been criticized for offering too little too late. Some of these bills, such as the emergency COVID-19 Legislation in the United Kingdom, include clauses that strengthen the powers of employers, for example, to lay off staff, which politicians argue is crucial for the economy. Money comes before people. In some cases, businesses have acted faster than governments to reduce the health risks to employees and customers; in other situations, there has been a public outcry at what has appeared to be putting business interests ahead of social good, despite the government support available. For example, Amazon, Sports Direct, and pub chain Wetherspoon used the crisis to make all staff redundant or forced them to work in unsafe circumstances (Health Foundation UK, 2020). It reminds us of the former mayor of Chicago speaking about the 2007–2008 financial crash: 'You never want a serious crisis to go to waste. And what I mean by that is an opportunity to do things that you think you could not do before.'

This list of causal, facilitating, dividing, and extending factors shows how the current pandemic is not merely biomedical but is intertwined with the economic pandemic of capitalism (Berkman, Kawachi & Glymour, 2014; O'Campo & Dunn, 2011; Singer, 2009; Marmot & Wilkinson, 2005). We live in the fourth stage of the world history of pandemics, where capitalism and pandemics are connected. Why does this role of capitalism receive so little attention in the media? Why do even the most critical people on social media defend government policies? Could this be the Capitalist Life Syndrome? The next sections will explore these questions, using the phenomenological methods of the ten perspectives (see Chapter 4).

Corona-Capitalism

The Capitalist Life Syndrome and the coronavirus pandemic are so intertwined that we could identify a new phenomenon: Corona-Capitalism. We could define this as follows, with the help of the ten phenomenological perspectives:

> Corona-Capitalism is the economic, social, and political system in which a country's health care policies and the population's perception of the coronavirus pandemic are controlled by a small group of powerful individuals and private enterprises to increase their own powers and profits. Corona-Capitalism is characterized by attempts to control the public symbols and imaginations about the pandemic more than the actual spread of the virus. Corona-capitalists frame the pandemic in materialistic and self-oriented terms of functionalistic survival of the fittest and use mass panic to create public consent for large-scale authoritarian interventions and for pumping public money into private companies. Corona-Capitalism is associated with a large impact on the physical, psychological, and existential well-being and daily lives of many citizens.

Table 1.1. Ten perspectives on Corona-Capitalism

Question	Perspective	Corona Capitalism
Name?	Name of system	Corona Capitalism
Status?	Ontological status	Symbol & imagination
What?	Type of meaning	Materialistic Self-oriented
How?	Approach to meaning	Functionalistic
Where?	Relationship between individual and society	Authoritarian enforcement
When?	Development over time	Influences from government, science, and media
Who?	Emergence of individual meaning	Manipulation of risk perception, panic, and meaning
Whose?	Sense of freedom	Negative freedom, inequality, helplessness
Why?	Existential ground	Existential angst and anger
Which?	Impact on daily life	Mental health problems, low quality of life, low life satisfaction

Ontological Status: From the Illusion of a Biomedical Reality to Symbols and Imagination

This is far from the first time that humans have confronted a large-scale pandemic. However, people seem shocked, like Albert Camus wrote in his book *The Plague* (1956/2012): we knew in theory that pestilences happen and will always happen in human history, but when it strikes ourselves it takes us by surprise. Whereas before the pandemic we may have ignorantly lived our daily lives, based on the invisible pillars of our belief in health and control over our own lives and the grandeur of unlimited human progress that capitalism has fed us, COVID-19 openly points the finger at our hubris. We find ourselves in one of these situations where life throws up events beyond our control, and it is in these moments that we undergo our ultimate test of character, as Camus described in *The Plague*. Will we hold onto the capitalistic dreams of functionalistic control, materialism, and selfishness? Will we uncritically swallow authoritarian measures of government? Will we fight tooth and nail in the supermarket against our neighbours over the limited stock of toilet rolls and bottles of hand sanitizer? Or will we rise above ourselves, like the Phoenix rising from its ashes, to create something new with social and larger meaning?

Anyone who has followed social media, popular magazines, and newspapers during the pandemic is aware that everything can be doubted, except for one thing: the reality of the pandemic and the necessity for large-scale lockdowns. The daily briefings by politicians and scientists seem to be accepted as God's Holy Words. The saddest example is the couple who died from drinking chlorine after Donald Trump suggested that chlorine may prevent or kill the virus. This couple was not an exception, as one would hope; after Trump's briefing, health services received thousands of phone calls with questions about drinking or injecting chlorine. It seems that during the first months of the pandemic our imaginations went into overdrive, while our reality-testing capability declined. It was almost as if we framed our personal experiences with the templates that were handed down by Hollywood movies about extinction, zombies, and the end of the world, -from movies such as *Outbreak, 93 Days* and *Contagion* to *World War Z* (Lynteris, 2019). Thus, what we are looking at here is not Reality but the mere symbols and imaginations of politicians and pharmaceutical companies that are presented to us as reality. As we have seen in this book, capitalism dominates via symbols and imagination, and this pandemic does not seem any different. It is the control over these symbols and imaginations that Corona-Capitalists are fighting for.

Types of Meaning: Materialistic and Self-Oriented

Materialistic Meaning

What is the COVID-19 pandemic? The standard medical answer tells that COVID-19 is a respiratory illness caused by a virus that can lead to symptoms such as fever, coughing, sore throat, shortness of breath, and sometimes a lack of taste and smell. Some patients progress to severe pneumonia and respiratory or multiple organ failure (Jiang, Deng, Zhang, Cai, Cheung & Xia, 2020; Singhai, 2020). COVID-19 is caused by the 2019-novel coronavirus (SARS-CoV-2), which is the third large Coronavirus outbreak in less than 20 years, after Severe Acute Respiratory Syndrome (SARS) in 2002-2003 and the Middle East Acute Respiratory Syndrome (MERS) in 2012. Although compared to some other pandemics and even seasonal flu, SARS-CoV-19 seems to have a lower mortality rate, it seems to affect more individuals, due to larger transmission risks and quicker mutations (Sohrabi, et al., 2020; World Health Organization, 2020).

The virus causes mild symptoms in 80 percent of patients, severe in 13 percent and critical in 6 percent, with larger mortality in elderly individuals and those with underlying medical conditions (Emami, Javanmardi, Pirbonyeh, & Akbari, 2020; Sun, Lu, Xu, Sun, & Pan, 2020). To date, there is no vaccine available, and treatment includes symptom management, supportive care, and isolation. As the virus spreads from human to human via respiratory droplets and other bodily secretions, recommended prevention includes frequent hand washing, social distancing, covering coughs and sneezes with a tissue, and keeping unwashed hands away from the face. Consequently, to stop the exponential spread of the virus via human contact, more than one-third of all countries worldwide have executed nationwide lockdowns (Mahase, 2020; World Health Organization, 2020).

Non-Hedonistic and Self-Oriented Meaning

Does the previous medical-text-book-like paragraph tell the full story? No: it feels as if we have taken the soul out of the body. If we regard our own body and our health risks only in such biomedical terms, we seem to treat our body as an objective machine that has nothing to do with ourselves. As Jean-Paul Sartre (1956/2001) stated, we could say that we look with a medical gaze at our body, but this is not our full lived experience. As countless empirical studies have shown, individuals perceive health risks differently than what medical doctors have told them: Their body has a subjective meaning that reaches beyond the biomedical gaze (Vos, 2011).

Whereas before the pandemic our body was possibly a source of hedonistic pleasure—such as enjoying good food, drinks, sports, or sex—those infected with COVID-19 may lose their taste, smell, and joy. Even individuals who remain healthy may experience their bodies as viral time bombs for themselves or others.

Thus, we often do not only look at our body with a biomedical perspective: We are simply submerged in our subjectively lived experience of our body as part of our full life. Martin Heidegger (1927) differentiates this internal experience of life from the external approach of the biomedical aspects of the body—*körper* in German. Heidegger calls this internal experiential approach to the body 'leib', which is etymologically derived from the German word for life, *leben*. This immediately brings mortality and finitude into our body experience: Our body is about life and the absence of life—death. Our body is not merely a machine that can be eternally repaired and replaced; it is a limited being. Our internal experience of our own finitude cannot be done justice in biomedical terms. We cannot objectively look, as a medical doctor does, at the expiry date of our body because we have our own subjective experience of it as an embodied being that is fragile and that will die one day. The biomedical approach lacks a perspective on this subjective experience of being limited in time, stretching between birth and death.

Consequently, governments that impose a lockdown on their citizens also seem to impose existential anxiety. People become afraid of going outside, not merely because they do not want to break the rules but because they are afraid of getting or spreading COVID-19 and ultimately of suffering and death. This is what Heidegger (1927) calls angst, being confronted with the fact that our body can fail and die, which can provoke a feeling of threat and anxiety. Stay home and save lives, that is what our governments tell us, and we do so because of the angst their message provokes.

We seem obsessed with the material world. Our subjective experience of our body as part of the totality of our life, including all its subjective meanings, seems less relevant than the control over our body as a biomedical machine. This materialistic perspective seems to extend to the unequal impact that the pandemic has on different socio-economic groups, as discussed above. Whereas on the one end of the socio-economic spectrum, one quarter of the full Western population may file for unemployment (Armstrong, 2020; Duncan, 2020), at the other end are those individuals who have benefited from the pandemic. As one manager of a hedge fund said, 'When there is fear and increased uncertainty in the market, which is what shorter-term investors focus on, we find there is a great opportunity' (ProActive Investors UK, 5 March 2020). The blatant profiteers are investors benefiting from short-selling; these include Novacyt PLC, which has the monopoly on the Primedesign diagnostic test; companies like Reckitt that produce disinfectants and personal protective equipment; take-away food companies, postal delivery services such as Amazon, and home entertainment such as Netflix. Politicians have justified big payouts for companies, such as financing the flight sector while cutting salaries of health care workers by calling them essential for the economy. Pharmaceutical companies have received historically unequalled public funding for research and development of vaccinations and treatment. The clearest example of how the economy comes before people was given by the lieutenant governor of Texas, Dan Patrick, who told Fox News on 24 March 2020 that he would rather die than see public health measures damage the US economy. He said that he believed that 'lots of grandparents' across the country would agree with him: 'My message is: let's get back to work, let's get back to living, let's be smart about it, and those of us who are 70-plus, we'll take care of ourselves.'

Social Meaning

The biomedical approach is not only limited because it is oriented to the materialist world but also because it primarily focuses on our self and seems to leave out the wider social world in which we are thrown and towards which our bodies are oriented (Heidegger, 1927, pp. 90–108; Heidegger 1921/1995, GA21, pp. 52–59). Physical being is intrinsically interwoven with one's social world. My being means something to others, and the being of others means something to me. My existential loyalties to others could even be more meaningful than my own survival: I would be willing to give up my own life to prevent the unnecessary suffering of others. This is also why we stay home during the pandemic: to prevent others from getting sick.

Thus, this pandemic makes us more aware than ever of how we are all inter-related and inter-dependent. This has also motivated many healthy individuals to help their neighbours, as more than 1,000,000 individuals in the United Kingdom are doing by volunteering in the National Health Services. However, social meanings are also affected in a negative way. In contrast with the political mantra of 'we are in this together', the numbers of people living on the streets and depending on food banks are soaring (Shelter UK, 2020; Trussel Trust, 2020). The cold numbers of deaths that politicians read out on TV each day do not seem to do justice to, for example, the pain that I feel for my friend who died from COVID-19. Boris

Johnson called health care workers supermen in March 2020, but only three months before this he won the general election with a political program premised on cutting wages of health care workers. Social symbols and social reality seem far away from each other.

> But, you know, I feel more fellowship with the defeated than with saints. Heroism and sanctity do not really appeal to me, I imagine. What interests me is being a man. (Camus, 1956/2012)

Larger & Existential–Philosophical Meaning

In our daily life, we do not reflect on our body, and we do not need to use biomedical terms, as we simply live our embodied daily life: Our material body and our subjective experiences are intertwined (Heidegger, 1919/1920, GA58, p. 160). It is only when our body fails or gets threatened that we start reflecting and using medical terminology (Vos, 2018, 2016, 2014). During and after this pandemic, we need to reconstruct our perception of our body. Whereas our body had previously been an unquestioned part of our lived experience—body, life, and world—we suddenly feel alienated from our bodies as potential biomedical time bombs (Vos, 2011). Pandemics disrupt the immediacy of our daily life experience by making us aware of our health risks, the fragility of our body, and ultimately of the human condition.

As argued previously, the idea that epidemiologists and virologists show us the full reality is an illusion; this pandemic inherently has symbolic and imaginary meanings. We see that the biomedical approach leaves out the subjective meanings of our body, life, and world, an approach that seems interwoven with capitalist perspectives that appear to ignore subjective meanings of the body and stick to the materialistic–functionalistic narrative that the medical doctors and pharmaceutical industries offer.

However, individuals have the freedom *not* to deal with themselves and others merely from this reductionist biomedical–capitalist approach and instead try to do justice to the complexities and subjectivities of their experiences. This is the difference between inauthenticity and authenticity, or between anthropocentric and cosmocentric approaches to the pandemic. As the First-Nation Canadians in Bella Coola explained to me, whereas biomedical science focuses predominantly on the inner circle of the embodied self and may even try to increase its reach, the cosmocentric approach aims to balance the embodied self with the broader circles of the social world and the universe in which our body is already embedded. The petroglyphs in the Bella Coola Valley visualized self, world, and universe as intertwined circles within circles.

Similarly, Western philosophers and theologians have used words such as 'soul' to describe the unity of existential paradoxes such as body–biology, life–death, world–self (Heidegger, 1921/1995,, pp. 233–239; Visser, 2009). That is, in our soul, we may phenomenologically experience the freedom of time and space—'time–play–space'(Heidegger, 1927)—to decide to either do justice to the complexities and subjectivities of body, life, and world or opt for biology, death, and self. Simply put, they claim that our soul has to decide to be authentic or inauthentic. In a similar sense, religious people have been describing COVID-19 as a spiritual crisis. They are correct in that this pandemic seems to bring us to the boundaries of our existence (Jaspers, 1921) and confront us with the existential decision of whether we want to do justice to our embodied self, others, and our wider universe.

> Each of us has the plague within him; no one, no one on earth is free from it. And I know, too, that we must keep endless watch on ourselves lest in a careless moment we breathe in someone's face and fasten the infection on him. What is natural is the microbe. All the rest—health, integrity, purity (if you like)—is a product of the human will, of a vigilance that must never falter....What does it mean, the plague? It's life, that's all (Camus, 1956/2012).

Approach to Meaning:
Functionalistic Control and Survival of the Fittest

Ultimately, the fate of what has traditionally been called our 'soul' may be at stake, as COVID-19 seems to threaten our most fundamental approach to life, self, and being. We may realize that life as such may not continue after the COVID-19 pandemic since it is not merely a virus that affects a few individuals or one country but impacts the entire globe. COVID-19 may rip us out of our daily life and place us in a battle royale deathmatch—fighting against one another for our lives, like real-life *Hunger Games* (Collins, 2008) and thus reducing the potential of our human spirit to a mere animalistic survival of the fittest. Has the COVID-19 pandemic become the battleground between the Capitalist Life Syndrome and the Meaning-Oriented Society?

The functionalist survival-of-the-fittest approach seems to be the sign of an underlying struggle about what is truly meaningful in life, a struggle that was already there before the pandemic and which will most likely continue afterwards. As the philosopher Giorgo Agamben (2020, epub, suggests:

> Our society no longer believes in anything but bare life. It is obvious that Italians are disposed to sacrifice everything—the normal conditions of life, social relationships, work, even friendships, affections and religious and political convictions—to the danger of getting sick. Bare life—and the danger of losing it—is not something that unites people, but blinds and separates them.

Politicians argue that it is crucial to get the pandemic under control, and to achieve this they try to control citizens. Just as Margaret Thatcher justified her most controversial policies by claiming 'there is no alternative' (TINA), prime ministers and presidents use the same argument for their draconian measures such as a nationwide lockdown. Zizek (2020, p. 86) wrote, 'I fear barbarism with a human face—ruthless survivalist measures enforced with regret and even sympathy, but legitimized by expert opinions'. It seems that politicians may sacrifice individual citizens to achieve this illusion of control—for example, by arguing for 'herd immunity' instead of prevention and self-isolation. Thus, dehumanization seems to have become ordinary political language, reminding us of the cold jargon of functionalist capitalism (and also of functionalist communism, as the pandemic policies from the Chinese state seem to suggest).

Although politicians seem to create the illusion that they are in control, reality seems far away. Despite consecutive governments having been warned about the potential threat of a pandemic, research indicates that most countries were unprepared for the size of the pandemic, with insufficient equipment and staffing. For example, the defunding and privatization of the national health services of more than a decade left the United Kingdom unprepared to cope with this crisis (El-Gingihy, 2019). The large numbers of Americans without health insurance made it more likely that infected individuals would not receive adequate prevention and treatment and could subsequently risk infecting others. Furthermore, the size of the post-pandemic economic crisis shows the fragility of the economic system. Thus, the pandemic does not reveal governments in control, but seems to show the structural lack of control and the socio-economic fragility of our system.

The pandemic shows how our society is stuck in 'the death spiral of a rich society', as Haque (2019) writes. Economic wealth, social opportunities and health care are not distributed equitably. This brings the average person into a struggle for self-preservation—literally when there is no safety net of social welfare and national health care. Consequently, these individuals have little energy left to focus on political activism, community building and enriching society with culture and art.

Our elites have succeeded in one vital task—what an Emile Durkheim might have called "social reproduction." They have managed to reproduce society in their image. What does the average Anglo-American aspire to be, do, have? To be rich, powerful, careless, selfish, and dumb, now, mostly. We do not, as societies or cultures, value learning or knowledge or magnanimity or great and noble things, anymore. We shower millions on reality TV stars and billions on "investment bankers." The average person has become a tiny microcosm of the aspirations and norms of elites — they're not curious, empathetic, decent, humane, noble, kind, in pursuit of wisdom, truth, beauty, meaning, purpose. We have become cruel, indecent, obscene, comically shallow, and astonishingly foolish people. That's not some kind of jeremiad.

Literally nobody on planet earth wants worse lives excepts us. We are the only people on earth who thwart our own social progress, over and over again—and cheer about it. How did we become these people? How did we become tiny microcosms of our arrogant, ignorant, breathtakingly stupid elites? Because we are perpetually battling for self-preservation. Life has become a kind of brutal combat to the death. For jobs, for healthcare, for money, for the tiniest shreds of resources necessary to live. We wake up and fight one another for these things, over and over again. That is what our lives amount to now—gladiatorial combat. People who are battling for self-preservation can't take care of anyone else. If I ask the average Brit or American to consider paying for their society's healthcare, education, elderly care, childcare, increasingly, the answer is: LOL. In America, it always has been. Why is that? The reason couldn't be simpler. People cannot even take care of themselves and their own. How can they take care of anyone else— let alone everyone else? A more technical, formal way to say that is: our societies have now become too poor to afford public goods and social systems. But public goods and social systems are what make a modern, rich society. What is a society without decent healthcare, schools, universities, libraries, education, parks, transport, media—

available to all, without life-crippling "debt"? It is not a modern society at all. (Haque, 2019)

Relationship Between Individual and Society: The Power of Science, Media, and the Deep State

The COVID-19 pandemic seems to have revealed the roles that science, media and a so-called deep state may play in our daily lives.

Science

Scientific research and academia were already in crisis before the COVID-19 pandemic; the public had become increasingly skeptical about the neutrality of researchers since the turn of the millennium. The idea of absolute truth had tumbled from its pedestal and seemed to have been replaced by the belief in Twitter and YouTube heroes (Vos, Roberts, & Davies, 2019). At the end of the 1990s, many countries kicked scientists out of governmental committees, and instead civil servants invited external researchers to write scientific reports (scientific conclusions for sale?). The COVID-19 pandemic seems to have brought scientists back to the political arena, and the idea of truth has had an unexpected return, possibly under the auspices of existential angst. Politicians have put scientists on a pedestal to justify their decisions during the pandemic, and the public seems to crave certainty and clear guidance in this unsettled time. However, it seems impossible for scientists to live up to these extreme expectations because of the uncertain nature of pandemics. Consequently, scientists have become the focus of criticasters and countless conspiracy theories.

Science during pandemics is not the same as science in ordinary times; it may be called extra-paradigmatic science (Giordano, 2020; Bjorkdahl & Carlsen, 2019). From all the countless viruses going around the world, researchers have to identify those that could spiral into a severe pandemic, and they need to do this as soon as possible so they can give recommendations on how to stop the spread at an early stage. However, they can only classify the virus when multiple people have been infected, which takes time because of the incubation period; meanwhile, the virus continues spreading. The available data is far from absolute in the early stage of pandemics, as symptoms may vary and not every infected individual will infect each person they meet. This involves uncertainty and risk calculations, not black-or-white conclusions. Because of the uncertain nature of viruses, researchers will always be criticized—either for having warned people too early about a potential pandemic on the basis of too little information or for having acted too late because they wanted to wait for enough information to advise on the basis of solid evidence. However, several scientists argue that the best of both options—doing too little too late, or doing too much too early—is the latter: 'the main problem is that no one will ever get in trouble for measures that are too draconian. They will only get in trouble if they do too little. So, our politicians and those working with public health do much more than they should do.' (Goetzsche, 2020)

Another problem is how to communicate these uncertain scientific findings, and how to ensure that people take the right preventive actions. Communication of public health risks involves a fragile balance, between making sure that people act quickly when needed without overestimating the actual risks and creating a panic. Effective risk communication involves knowledge about how laypeople subjectively interpret risks and how to nudge people (Vos, 2011). This knowledge is becoming increasingly critical, as we seem to live in a global risk society where many aspects of our daily lives are not determined by black-or-white information but by statistical calculations of the likelihood that scenarios could happen (Beck, 2009). However, non-specialists often find it difficult to accurately interpret statistical risks, apply these to their own lives, and take reasonable actions. Consequently, the ways the public interprets risks often tells more about their pre-existing subjective meanings in life, need for certainty, and media influence than about scientific risks (Vos, 2011). It is this uncertainty and subjectivity of health risk interpretations that can easily be manipulated by influential individuals for their profit.

Scientists seem to be forced to make decisions that are not always in the interests of the general public; most of their research is now funded by commercial companies and not by neutral bodies or states. Sabeti and Salahi (2018) describe how this has corrupted researchers and made government responses fail during the Ebola pandemic in 2014 (p. 56):

> Pressure mounts among researchers to be the first to discover a pathogen or an outbreak. Public health agencies strive for publicity in their effort to maintain legitimacy. For-profit companies aim to create and license technologies essential to outbreak response. It might appear that aggressive, highly motivated people and rushed work are exactly what is needed to combat a fast-spreading virus. But aggression and urgency can lead to deception, secrecy, and attempts to put obstacles in the way of competitors. "Human nature

is that we are invested in our own gains and our own philosophy and our own organizations," said Sheila Davies of Partners in Health. Although these impulses are critical to pushing forward research development, the incentives are not set up to benefit those who are in greatest need.

In this context of pandemics, Judy Mikovits and Kent Heckenlively even titled their book *Plague of Corruption* (2020). Similar commercial corruption of science seems to have happened during the COVID-19 pandemic (Gomez, 2020). As the German specialist in pulmonology and former chairman of the Assembly of the Council of Europe, Dr. Wolfgang Wodarg, describes the current pandemic:

> Politicians are being courted by scientists...scientists who want to be important to get money for their institutions. Scientists who just swim along in the mainstream and want their part of it. And what is missing right now is a rational way of looking at things. We should be asking questions like "How did you find out this virus was dangerous?", "How was it before?", "Did not we have the same thing last year?", "Is it even something new?" That is missing. (Wodarg in *OffGuardian*, 24 March 2020)

While scientists and politicians already had to struggle to make the best decisions for the population in the uncertain context of the pandemic, commercial interests tried to influence their research and decisions. For example, critical journalists have shown that during the COVID-19 pandemic, several leading scientists on government advisory committees, such as SAGE in the UK, had direct ties to the pharmaceutical industry. SAGE presented their recommendations as 'scientific', but analyses of the minutes of their meetings indicate that their advice was often directly influenced or vetoed by politicians (Busby, 2020; Medical Professionals and Scientists for Health, Freedom and Democracy, statement, 28 May 2020; Morales & Ring, 2020; Lintern, 2020; Young, 2020). Journalists have also questioned the quality of the data used by these government advisory committees and argued that several public health policies follow from suspect data from companies with commercial interests (Davey, Kirchgaessner & Boseley, 2020; Fitzgerald & Crider, 2020). Several pathologists and funeral directors have also told the press how guidance on autopsies was changed early during the pandemic, which made concluding that individuals had 'died from' COVID-19 more unreliable (e.g.,

Dr. John Lee in *The Spectator*, 30 May/2020; Dr. Hugo de Jonge in *Tubantia*, 23 May 2020; Dr. Malcolm Kendrick in *RTV*, 28 Nay 2020; Davis, 2020). Consequently, critical journalists and scientistshave casted doubts about the accuracy of the number of COVID-19 deaths announced in daily press briefings in the White House and 10 Downing Street, and about the health policies that followed from these figures (Corbett, 2020; German Network for Evidence-Based Medicine, 20 March 2020; Ioannidis, 2020, 2020a; Levitt, 2020; Roussell in *Off Guardian*, 24 March 2020; Tailano, 2020).

The best example of ambiguous science involves mathematician Niall Ferguson. His statistical model of the spread of the virus was pivotal in convincing the British government to enforce a nationwide lockdown that shuttered businesses and forced millions into furlough or unemployment (Conn, Lawrence, Lewis, Carrell, Pegg, Davies, & Evans, 2020). Ferguson's research has also been cited by American top-epidemiologist Anthony Fauci to argue for far-reaching control of the population. However, Ferguson's models were based on empirical evidence at that time indicating relatively little scientific evidence that nationwide lockdowns were more efficient than group-specific lockdowns (Briggs, 17 May 2020). Ferguson's theoretical model has been criticized for its lack of social realism (Epstein, 19 March 2020; Gorbatenko, 2020). For example, Ferguson assumed a limitless exponential model for how individuals infect one another: person one could infect persons two and three, who both could infect persons four to seven, etc. However, individuals mainly meet the same people in their limited social network of friends, colleagues, and relatives, and thus there is a limit to the number of people that one person may infect. It may have been sufficient for the most vulnerable individuals to self-isolate (Tegnell, 2020). Furthermore, lockdowns have substantial psychological and socio-economic side effects, including creating psychological stress that decreases immune system functioning and increases infection risk (Brookes, 2020). However, the mathematical and economics-focused models of the advisors seemed to lack this social and psychological complexity, which may be attributed to a lack of psychologists on the medical advisory boards of British and American governments (Constello, 27 April 2020).

Consequently, researchers at the universities of Oxford and Edinburgh have not been able to recreate Ferguson's computer model (O'Toole, 2020; Parliamentary Select Committee Minutes, 4 June 2020). Within three months after his initial advice, Ferguson had to admit that his model was wrong, and that countries without a lockdown have not seen a worse pandemic trajectory (Johns, 2 June 2020). Subsequently, governmental advisors have admitted that they may have exaggerated their response and that COVID-19 did not do as much harm as they had initially communicated (coronavirus press briefing Downing Street, 6 May 2020). A significant number of excess deaths could have been prevented, as they may have been caused by the lockdown instead of by the virus according to 600 American physicians in *Forbes*, 23 May 2020 (see also Knightly, 2020; Brooke, 2020). 'Is our fight against Coronavirus worse than the disease?' (Katz, 2020) Thus, scientists seem to have played an important but controversial role in the decision making during the pandemic, potentially mixing science with power and money.

Media

Most people heard about COVID-19 for the first time via the news, newspapers, or social media, and not, for example, from their direct contact with epidemiologists (Kwok, Li & Chan, 2020). Thus, for many individuals, this pandemic started first as a social construct that only later became a daily life reality to them. This also includes the possibility that individuals took over the explicit and implicit misinterpretations from the sources that informed them about the pandemic. We often base our (mis)interpretations of health risks on the (mis)interpretations of others who may base their ideas on the (mis)interpretations of yet others (Vos, Gomez-Garcia, Oosterwijk et al., 2012): COVID-19 seemed to spiral down into a similar whisper-game.

Media and politicians may have unintentionally shared their misinterpretations of COVID-19, as many people are biased in their communication of health risks to others (Vos, Gomez-Garcia, Oosterwijk et al., 2012). For example, several organisations, such as the Swiss Policy Research Institute, criticise mainstream media for their inaccurate and disproportionately fear-inducing reports about COVID-19. It may also be that some individuals have intentionally exaggerated risks and created panic, in line with Bernard Bernays' propaganda and Keith Joseph's policies. This is not unlikely. A meta-analysis of studies on COVID-19 indicates that media cause almost half of the panic during pandemics (Vos, 2020). Stockpiling and other panic behaviour during pandemics seem to be a direct result of media sensationalism. Fear increases media income and creates a vicious cycle: Frightened individuals will follow the media to get more information about the pandemic, which will make them more frightened, which will make them follow more media, etc.

Deep State
To what extent have governments, companies, or what some have dubbed
'the deep state' (Hellinger, 2018; Lofgren, 2016) created or used COVID-19
to manipulate people? During any collective trauma, countless memes go
round on social media as people desperately search for a straightforward
explanation of the crisis and try to reduce complexity and uncertainty in
order to create a sense of uniqueness in an era of collective trauma
(Douglas, Sutton & Cichocka, 2017; Imhoff & Lamberty, 2017; Jolley &
Douglas, 2017; Friesen, Campbell & Kay, 2014).

During the 1832 cholera outbreak, people attacked medical doctors for
'deliberately poisoning the poor to harvest their bodies for medical school
anatomy lessons' (McMillen, 2016). Similarly, some self-acclaimed
defenders of the truth go further on social media by arguing that
pharmaceutical companies may have had a hand in causing the pandemic
to increase their profits, or even control people by secretly implanting them
with a chip when they get vaccinated, with the Bill and Melinda Gates
Foundation at the forefront as primary funders of vaccination research and
the World Health Organisation (Wakefield, 2020). At the time of writing
this, although some hypotheses seem theoretically feasible, there seems to
be a lack of conclusive evidence, which is used by conspiracy theorists to
argue that companies and governments do not want the truth to come out.

A weaker version of conspiracy theories is that people in power may not have
deliberately created COVID-19 but may use this situation for their benefit. For
example, neoliberal economist Milton Friedman (1980) seemed to suggest that
neoliberal policies could easily be pushed through in times of crisis. In normal
times, citizens scrutinize governmental policies, but in times of crisis, they accept
that extraordinary measures are needed to cope with extraordinary threats. Thus,
it may be in the interests of powerholders to exaggerate the sense of threat in the
population if they want to push through a radical agenda. As we will see later,
when people are reminded of mortality and fragility, they seem to (partially) shut
down critical thinking and accept more extreme government policies than they
would do during ordinary times—just as Bernays helped to create a political crisis
in Guatemala so that the United Fruit Company could keep their plantations
(L'Etang, 1999). Thus, it does not seem surprising that in this historical context of
mind manipulation by media some people have described COVID-19 as the
ultimate 'PsyOp'—even though they have only indirect evidence for the current
pandemic as a PsyOp (Ryan, 2020)?

It is difficult to conclude who may be using the collective existential threat of
COVID-19 to push through their radical policies. However, some journalists have
argued that the British Prime Minister has already used the pandemic to delay
Brexit negotiations with the European Union indefinitely so that he could enforce
a Hard Brexit (Cowburn, 2020). Other journalists have argued that the self-

isolation of individuals may lead to further atomization of society and the fragmentation of political opposition. Furthermore, the government's response to COVID-19 may foster authoritarianism; police have received the authority to arrest anyone suspected of having COVID-19 in several countries. COVID-19 could also be used for nationalist and anti-globalist political purposes: For example, the British Prime Minister could 'blame immigrants, journalists, people of colour, liberals and other enemies' (Gawthorpe, 2020). Furthermore, a repeated claim on left social media is that the shortage of staff and resources in national health services aims to create public consent to buy medical services from commercial companies and to further privatize national health services. They cite Chomsky (2011): 'That is the standard technique of privatization: defund, make sure things do not work, people get angry, you hand it over to private capital. If they can succeed in defunding it—they have been trying for decades.'

> At the beginning of a pestilence and when it ends, there is always a propensity for rhetoric. In the first case, habits have not yet been lost; in the second, they are returning. It is in the thick of a calamity that one gets hardened to the Truth—in other words, to silence. (Camus, 1956/2012)

Development Over Time: The Conquerors Write the History Books

In the previous sections, we have seen how the materialist, self-oriented, and functionalist perspectives of capitalism have framed and possibly aggravated the COVID-19 pandemic, with a potentially controversial role for scientists, media, and a deep state. There seems to be less public attention on the human dimension of the pandemic, such as the intertwined inequalities in wealth and health. How has the public mood been able to shift so quickly towards this materialist functionalism? Why have even the usually most critical people on social media defended government policies?

We can find a possible answer in the chapter on mind manipulation. In line with Michel Foucault, we might argue that there are two ways for a government to make a population do what it wants—in this case, stopping citizens from spreading the virus. First, a government could explicitly tell their people what to do and threaten them with fines or imprisonment if they disobey. *Thou shalt do what I say, not because my demands are inherently meaningful but because I punish violators!* This authoritarian strategy seemed to have been used to a greater or lesser extent by governments across the globe. A refined version was implemented by the Chinese government, which put a technological track-and-trace system in place, connecting phones, social media, bank accounts, and CCTV to follow citizens and send them into self-isolation if they had been in touch with any sick person or if they showed any symptoms. Softened versions of this digital track-and-trace system have been developed in Western countries, by companies such as Google and implemented by several states such as the United Kingdom.

An authoritarian strategy requires the image of a strong leader, harsh language, and indisputable science, which seemed to transform the daily press conferences from the White House and 10 Downing Street almost into a theatre act. This strategy implies that the government needs to hold up its strong façade for a long time and mute dissenting voices. For example, any scientific doubts need to be brushed away, even though uncertainties are inherent in science during pandemics. Several scientists critical of national strategies have been arrested or sent to psychiatric wards, including professors Li Wenliang and Chen Zhaozhi in China, Anastasia Vasilieva in Russia, and Thomas Binder in Switzerland. Meanwhile, there have been occasional reports of social media such as Facebook and YouTube deleting posts and profiles from criticasters and conspiracy theorists, including David Icke. Facebook has started to inform users which posts it regards as including 'fake news'. Freedom of speech and science is the price of this authoritarian strategy, whose emotional impact is that people may not internalize the meaning of the governmental message but instead may feel frustrated and angry about the governmental measures. This bears the risk that citizens could turn their anger against the government and that politicians could consequently lose at the next elections. Therefore, this strategy seems too risky for politicians in the long term.

Therefore, the second strategy of self-governmentality seems more efficient. This strategy aims to use minimum government threats, enlarge the perceived threat, and appeal to citizens' consciences. Key to this is the idea is that citizens should act in freedom rather than feel forced. This strategy has created conflicting messages such as 'You can go outdoors to do your grocery shopping or do physical exercise, but you should still feel guilty when you do'; 'You could open your business, but you must feel irresponsible' (because if we tell you as government that you need to close your company, we may need to financially compensate you;, but if you decide to close it yourself, we do not need to pay you). Social psychological research indicates that paradoxes and uncertainties and any forms of intermittent reinforcement of behaviour are efficient ways to make people obey, 'just to be on the safe side'.

Self-governmentality shifts the responsibility of public health from the government to the self-help citizen. This motivates citizens to look after themselves and one another, which excuses government from the expectation of providing health care and benefits. Self-governmentality also means that any failures could be attributed to citizens instead of governmental policies. The tabloids and social media seem to be keen supporters of this blame-game by continuously showing pictures of individuals not being in lockdown.

Self-governmentality transforms feelings of anger towards the government over their lack of preparedness for the pandemic and the unnecessary and unequal human suffering into feelings of guilt over one's failures (cf., Milburn & Conrad, 2016). We should not blame the system, but individuals. Furthermore, populist politicians could not only turn the anger towards citizens themselves, but they could also use the anger, or even incite hatred, towards ethnic minority groups, as reflected in anti-China rhetoric and xenophobic incidents in the United States and United Kingdom.

As described in an earlier chapter of the book, research on Terror Management Theory shows how a reminder of one's mortality can trigger a conservative response. Hundreds of psychological experiments have shown that individuals facing an existential threat often become more conservative, supporting strong leaders and focusing on traditional conformist values (Burke, Kosloff & Landau, 2013; Burke, Martens & Faucher, 2010). This Terror Management Theory has been used to explain how the 1918 flu pandemic contributed to the popularity of national socialism in Germany and other affected countries. Seen from this perspective of the denial of our mortality, it is, unfortunately, not surprising that racist incidents have happened and that countries have closed their physical borders and refused to share vaccines and treatments with other countries (Serhan & McLaughlin, 2020). The support for conservative governments has also been increasing despite rising death figures (Butchireddygari, 2020). All these reactions are responses to existential terror.

Seen from a rational perspective, we have always been at risk to become ill and die from complications from, for example, seasonal influenza. Of course, COVID-19 seems to affect slightly more people, and its mortality rates seem greater than that of the annual seasonal flu—at least this is what scientists and governments tell us (healthline.com, 12 March 2020). It may be this existential uncertainty that people seem to find difficult to live with. As one person said, 'I would prefer to have the certainty that I will get sick and die than that I have to live with uncertainty' (Vos, 2011). People want certainty, even if this means drastic measures.

People could also have become psychologically numb—like a 'psychological herd immunity'—to hearing numbers in daily press briefings and countless social media posts. The initial fear associated with these numbers wears off, say psychologists, because of the effects of gradual exposure, habituation, and desensitization—like a sliding scale. Consequently, people may accept horrific situations and authoritarian governments that they would not accept at the start. This explains how non-democratic decisions and authoritarian policies from governments receive broad public support during COVID-19. Paradoxically speaking, the more citizens hear about failing politicians, the less they will insist on full accountability 'because all politicians are corrupt, and we will never see any accountability'. In the end, individuals start to feel helpless and apathetic after seeing their loved ones die, their economy collapse, and their freedom taken away.

> But what are a hundred million deaths? When one has served in a war, one hardly knows what a dead man is, after a while. And since a dead man has no substance unless one has actually seen him dead, a hundred million corpses broadcast through history are no more than a puff of smoke in the imagination. (Camus, 1956/2012)

Individual Meaning: The Psychological Impact

Previous sections have already described how pandemics can affect people's mental health, with feelings such as existential angst, guilt, anger, and helplessness. During a systematic literature review and meta-analysis examining the psychological impact of pandemics, (Vos, 2020) discovered 26 studies that described the psychological impact of COVID-19 in 104,361 participants. Almost 60% of all health care workers experienced acute traumatic stress, and almost one-third experienced moderate to severe symptoms of depression, general distress, insomnia, or anxiety. One-third of all COVID-19 patients and the general population also reported these psychological symptoms. I compared research on COVID-19 with 44 studies encompassing 28,499 participants during the SARS and MERS pandemics. The impact of COVID-19 is almost twice as significant in some participants. One-third of all health care workers and 15% of the general population experienced psychological symptoms. In the most extreme cases, coronavirus patients may suffer from acute respiratory distress syndrome, sepsis, or may need ventilation. One in two of these extreme cases report severe post-traumatic stress, insomnia, and unemployment even years after hospital treatment (Chlan & Savik, 2011; Davydow, Desai, Needham, & Bienvenu, 2008; Davydow, Hough, Langa, & Iwashyna, 2013). Patients treated for severe COVID-19 disease may experience similar long-term psychological effects.

Several factors explain the mental health impact of COVID-19, SARS, and MERS. Health care workers suffer from more mental health problems when they feel dissatisfied with the organization, training, and support at work, as well as the lack of personal protective equipment and funds allocated by the government. They also report more stress due to a lack of social support from colleagues, friends, and family, and when they are in direct contact with infected patients. In the general population, individuals experienced more psychological problems when they belonged to a physically or mentally vulnerable population, such as having an underlying physical disease or being older. Furthermore, individuals with poor socio-economic status experienced more psychological problems. The lockdown also increased mental health problems, with half of the isolated individuals having acute post-traumatic stress disorder or depression. Thus, a large part of the psychological impact of pandemics is caused by political decisions that involve a lack of adequate equipment, inefficient health care organization, long-term nationwide lockdown, and socio-economic inequality.

How worried should we be about these figures? On the one hand, we could argue that this psychological impact is a normal response to the abnormal situation of pandemics. The anxiety helps people take actions to prevent spreading the virus. On the other hand, the figures are very large: In normal times, between 2% and 15% of the population report such symptoms, whereas 20% of health care workers still report moderate to severe mental health problems several years after the SARS/MERS pandemic. Several studies have also reported waves of suicides at the end of pandemics. Therefore, it is important to organize large-scale screening for mental health problems and offer tailored mental health care, particularly to health care workers and patients (Duan & Zhu, 2020; Liu, Yang, Zhang, Wu, Xiang, Liu, Hu, & Zhang, 2020; Zhang, Wu, Zhao, & Zhang, 2020). But even more important, governments should prevent the causes of psychological stress by offering the right equipment, organizing health care efficiently, keeping nationwide lockdown as brief as possible, and minimizing the socio-economic impact, particularly by protecting the most socio-economically vulnerable groups.

Freedom: Symbolic and Negative

The meta-analysis also showed that quarantine, either nationwide lockdown and/or self-isolation, is associated with symptoms of post-traumatic stress, depression, and insomnia. Interview studies on the impact of quarantine reveal similar conclusions (Brooke, 2020). The meta-analysis indicates why quarantine could have a large psychological impact.

First, individuals in quarantine are less physically active; research suggests that physical inactivity can worsen mental well-being (Bauman, 2004; Hoare, Milton, Foster, & Allender, 2016; Penedo & Dahn, 2005). Second, individuals report that they engage less in leisure activities and feel bored (Marafa & Tung, 2004), which may prevent them from releasing psychological and physical stress (Aldana, Sutton, Jacobson, & Quirk, 1996; Weng & Chiang, 2014). Third, people report less social contact, particularly individuals without a partner or those feeling stigmatized (Best, Manktelow, & Taylor, 2014; Jeong et al., 2016). Research shows a strong relationship between lack of social contact and poor mental health (Hawkley & Cacioppo, 2010; Heinrich & Gullone, 2006; Holt-Lunstad, Smith, Baker, Harris, & Stephenson, 2015; Mushtaq, Shoib, Shah, & Mushtaq, 2014). Fourth, individuals may worry over their financial future, job loss, or housing situation (Atkeson, 2020; Jeong et al., 2016; Stephany et al., 2020; Yilmazkuday, 2020). Fifth, large families seem to experience more psychological distress, possibly from the emotional impact of quarantine on children and family interactions (Brooke, 2020; Grechyna, 2020; Liu, Bao, Huang, Shi, & Lu, 2020). Sixth, inadequate supplies may deteriorate people's dietary and health behaviour, which could subsequently impact their emotional state (Jeong et al., 2016). Seventh, it may be argued that the psychological impact of quarantine could lead to reduced immune system functioning and greater infection risk (Biondi & Zannino, 1997; Garfin, Thompson, & Holman, 2018; Segerstrom & Miller, 2004).

Finally, self-isolation can also lead to suicides. Figures from previous pandemics suggest that suicide rates will increase by more than one-third, possibly creating approximately 200,000 deaths worldwide during the COVID-19 pandemic. This is not far from the total number of deaths due to COVID-19 itself. The cure may be worse than the disease.

In sum, these studies seem to have in common that people struggle with living a meaningful and satisfying daily life within the constraints of quarantine (Pereira, Silva, & Dias, 2020; Tabri, Hollingshead, & Wohl, 2020; Vos, 2020). Lack of freedom is physically and psychologically unhealthy.

They considered themselves free and no one will ever be free as long as there is plague, pestilence and famine. (…) The evil that is in this world always comes of ignorance, and good intentions may do as much harm as malevolence, if they lack understanding. On the whole, men are more good than bad; that however isn't the real point. But they are more or less ignorant, and it is this that we call vice or virtue. (Camus, 1956/2012)

Existential Perspective: Coping with Existential Threat

The COVID-19 pandemic is also a pandemic of its existential interpretation. That is, politicians have called the coronavirus an 'existential threat to the nation' (Diamond & Cook, 2020) and an 'existential threat to the economy' (Gawthorpe, 2020). A search in Google combining the words 'existential' and 'Corona' gives 1.5 million results. Many media channels seem to underline how extraordinary the COVID-19 situation is. Some researchers have argued that all media need to exaggerate and make news look extreme and thrilling to attract readers (Curran, 2012). Therefore, it seems that media respond to a collective crisis by suggesting that we are experiencing a unique existential break in our timeline. This reminds us of the headlines in newspapers in the days after the attack on the Twin Towers in New York: 'The world will never be the same anymore' (Vos, 2003). For example, people still remember where they were when they heard about that attack. There seems to be a life before 9/11 and a life after 9/11, like Before Christ and After Christ. Will there also be life before COVID-19 and life after COVID-19?

Psychiatrist–philosopher Karl Jaspers (1919) wrote that situations like this pandemic could be a boundary situation in life. That is, COVID-19 could shatter people's assumptions about life in such a way that they start to question the current situation and possibly fundamental assumptions about life in general (Janoff-Bulman, 2010). What is shaken by the pandemic is not merely their biomedical risks but all their assumptions about life. The confrontation with life's inevitable finitude and suffering can open people's eyes to our existential reality.

On the one hand, people could run away for the complexity and uncertainties of the situation. For example, some people ask existential questions such as why people get sick and why people have to die. They try to find an ultimate meaning that could explain their suffering, such as a bigger plan that God has with COVID-19, or try to explain the pandemic as a conspiracy by a deep state. These interpretations have in common the idea that the pandemic can ultimately be explained, which seems to make the pandemic a little be less threatening. People seem to be trying to control the uncontrollable and to find meaning in the meaningless because they find it difficult to hold the paradox of experiencing personal meaning in the here and now while accepting the absence of an absolute ultimate true meaning in life (Vos, 2015).

On the other hand, individuals could learn existential lessons during pandemics. For example, they could learn that they cannot be totally in control of every situation in life and that they cannot understand and predict all life events. They could also start to prioritize social and larger types of meaning in life over materialistic, self-oriented, and hedonistic meanings, as the journalist Gabriel Tupinamba wrote (in Zizek, 2020, p.135):

> I really can feel something heroic about this new ethics—everybody works day and night from their home office, participating in video conferences and taking care of children or schooling them at the same time, but nobody asks why he or she is doing it, because it's not any more a question of so 'I get money and can go to vacation etc.', since nobody knows if there will be vacations again and if there will be money. It's the idea of a world where you have an apartment, basics like food and water, the love of others and a task that really matters, now more than ever. The idea that one needs 'more' seems unreal now.

Impact on Daily Life

The final perspective on the pandemic involves the impact of the threat of COVID-19 on people's daily lives. COVID-19 seems to have a significant impact, from self-isolation, hospitalization, and losing loved ones to needing to work from home, financial uncertainties, and unemployment.

Individuals also seem to relate in new ways to other people. On the one hand, they may see and treat others no longer as fellow human beings but as mere potential virus-spreaders who should be feared. Because of their existential anxiety, some individuals may overlook their commonalities in suffering and feel thrown back onto themselves. On the other hand, they could develop a sense of unity and belonging as humanity: 'We are in this together'. Relationships could feel more valuable and intense, and people could reach out more to others. However, it seems crucial that individuals have the willpower, social skills, and technological means to reach out towards each other from their homes. For example, homeless and older people may have fewer means to stay in contact with others.

Possibly the most significant practical challenge involves the effects of self-isolation or working from home, which can decrease social contact and increase loneliness (Hawkley & Cacioppo, 2003). Similarly, children seem to struggle with the social constraints of home confinement (Wang, Zhang, Zhao, Zhang & Jiang 2020). However, working from home could also enable parents to better combine work/family life, which could improve mental health (Shephard-Banigan et al., 2016), although having the entire family working from home may be more complex to practically arrange, lead to more distractions, and may negatively impact mental health.

Empirical Evidence for the Detrimental Impact of Corona-Capitalism

This is Corona-Capitalism: materialist, self-oriented, functionalist, authoritarian, self-governed, and having a significant and unequal impact on the lives of people. What empirical evidence does Corona-Capitalism have? I have conducted a new meta-analysis in which I combined the country characteristics of Chapter 8 with the number of infected individuals and the number of deaths attributed to COVID-19 according to the figures from the World Health Organisation on 16 May 2020 (although I am aware of the criticism regarding the reliability of these figures). This study indicated that the more capitalistic a country is, the more people are infected, and the more people have died from COVID-19[1]. Thus, these

---

[1] To be precise: the infection and mortality rates correlate with larger overall capitalism scores for countries (R=.31, .39), more privatisation (R=.49, .45), more competitiveness (R=.44, .42), larger socio-economic inequality (R=.34, .47), smaller social mobility (R=-.48, -.41), an average lower better life (R=-.51, -.44), and more mental health problems (R=.42, .35). A combination of the average scores in the World Wide Survey of Meaning in Life also showed that the more people are infected and die from COVID-19, the more people on average focus on materialistic meaning in life (R=.28, .21); the more they focus on self-oriented meanings (R=.22, .24); the more their economic values are oriented towards capitalism (R=.19, .17); and the more they are functionalistic (R=.24, .27). Understandably, larger numbers of infections and deaths were correlated with larger scientific and fatalistic determinism (R=.26, .28) and less controllability and safety (R=.29, .27). Although these correlations are relatively small, they were all significant (p<.05). Furthermore, preliminary analyses of 562 participants in our Psychological COVID-19 Survey (corona-research.com) suggest that individuals experienced a larger mental health impact and supported authoritarian government strategies more when they had a more functionalistic, materialistic, and self-oriented attitude (R=.44, .33, .35), when they reported socio-economic struggles in daily life (R=.47), or when they worked in health care (R=.49).

studies seem to confirm the intertwining of the COVID-19 pandemic and the Capitalist Life Syndrome.

The Post-Corona Society

The old world is dying, and the world struggles to be born; now is the time of monsters. (Gramsci, 2000)

This Afterword has shown how the Capitalist Life Syndrome and the COVID-19 pandemic are intertwined. Their connection is so strong that I have recommended identifying a fourth stage in the world history of health and illness: the pandemic of Corona-Capitalism. As long as there is capitalism, there will be pandemics like COVID-19. But how long will capitalism exist?!

On the one hand, politicians could use the situation to normalize dehumanized policies and create a new normal: 'There is no alternative: You have to use bin bags as personal protective equipment as we have nothing else; bin bags are better than nothing'. The focus may shift away from offering quality care and human rights to a tick-box exercise: 'Look, we are giving personal protective equipment, albeit bad PPE'. Furthermore, authors such as Naomi Klein (2007) have warned that this pandemic is precisely what neoliberal governments want, a shock doctrine to push through authoritarian policies, austerity measures, mass redundancies, etc. It is a remarkable coincidence that the pandemic seems to offer the 'The Great Reset' of the world economy that the World Economic Forum has decided that our main focus should be for the next years (weforum.org, 29 June 2020). There may be a tendency for governments to create or use a state of exception like this as a normal governing paradigm, according to Giorgi Agamben (in Zizek, 2020, p.74): 'We might say that once terrorism was exhausted as a paradigm for exceptional measures, the invention of an epidemic could offer the ideal pretext for broadening such measures beyond any limitation.' In recent years, 'the state of fear [has] diffused into individual consciousnesses and translates into a real need for states of collective panic, for which the epidemic offers the ideal pretext' (ibidem). Thus, is this pandemic just the dress rehearsal for more upcoming crises (Latour, 2020)?

On the other hand, COVID-19 has also already changed the economic policies in many countries. Several governments, including neoliberal politicians in the United Kingdom and the United States, have offered monetary policies and quantitative easing to prevent an economic depression and support the most vulnerable in society. COVID-19 also seems to put frontline workers in a different light: In several European countries, people started clapping for frontline workers outside their houses on a specific evening each week. COVID-19 seems to create a larger valuation of frontline workers and knowledge workers over other workers, which also seems to change public opinion about wages of frontline and knowledge workers and the public accessibility of national health care and benefits. COVID-19 seems to present us with a new socio-economic reality based on new economic values. This is in line with the trend towards a meaning-oriented economy that we have seen throughout this book.

People also seem to have become more critical of politicians and the socio-economic status quo. For example, angry parents at over 100 schools across the United Kingdom have kept their children at home because they disagree with the education system. Progressive politicians and activists have also used the pandemic to demand an equal economy, universal basic income, universal basic services, and full accountability and transparency of the government. Simultaneously, a global uprising emerged to demand an end to racism and socio-economic inequality after the death of American George Floyd, who died due to disproportionate police violence because of his black skin colour. The Black Life Matters movement seemed to be triggered by the angst and anger regarding the unequal impact of the pandemic, which laid bare the underlying structural socio-economic inequalities. Like other recent horizontal activist movements such as the Extinction Rebellion, these demonstrations are mainly organized bottom-up by young people, who seem to feel an existential urgency in the current political climate; they have nothing to lose by demonstrating and risking arrest. *Rebel or die!*

Many citations in this chapter come from *The Plague*, written by the existential philosopher Albert Camus (1956/2012), possibly the most famous novel on people's responses to a pandemic. It is not surprising that this book suddenly is selling well during the COVID-19 pandemic (Flood, 2020). Camus described the fictional story of the French-Algerian city of Oran, which was quarantined because of the plague. In the initial stage of the lockdown, some citizens responded with hysteria, whereas others rejected all warnings. Later, some individuals took advantage of the situation by looting or bribing health officials and guards, while others tried to help their fellow citizens and felt a strong sense of connectedness and social belonging. Camus seemed to suggest that people fundamentally have the option to either respond authentically to the pandemic—accepting the situation and taking responsibility for themselves and others—or inauthentically by denying or exaggerating the situation or using it to their advantage. According to Camus, we have some amount of individual freedom to determine our approach to the pandemic. Do we choose to obey the Capitalist Life Syndrome, or do we try to create a meaning-oriented economy, albeit for ourselves and the people directly around us? The answer to this question could determine our future: The socio-economic system can only change when we decide not to identify ourselves any longer with our economic and political hostage takers.

> What is true of all the evils in the world is true of [this pandemic] as well. It can also make individuals rise above themselves. (…) The only way to deal with an unfree world is to become so absolutely free that your very existence is an act of rebellion. (Camus, 1956/2012)

When you finish reading a book, you end the journey that the author took you on. However, a good book never reaches its destination, as it inspires you to start your own meaningful journey. May the journey you began with this book never end.

London, United Kingdom, 29 June 2020.

Appendices:

Resources for Researchers

Appendix 1. Overview of Publications on Moral Economics

Name, Year	Title	Topic
Aronson, 2017	We: Reviving social hope	Critical analysis of inequality in the USA, and a call for social hope.
Bowles, 2016	The moral economy: Why good incentives are no substitute for good citizens	Using well-designed incentives and policies to stimulate good citizenship.
Brown, 2017	Buddhist economics: An enlightened approach to the dismal science	Economics based on Buddhist values.
D'Alisa, Demaria & Kallis, 2015	Degrowth: A vocabulary for a new era	Critical analyses of the need for growth and consumption; proposing a post-consumption economy.
Etzioni, 1988	The moral dimension: Toward a new economics	Showing moral dimensions in economics, and analysing the human motivations of utility/hedonism and morals.
Green, 2009	Good value: Reflections on money, morality and an uncertain world	Capitalism fulfills deep human drives towards exploration and exchange. However, there may be duties, morals, and human needs which are not fulfilled by the current capitalism.
Jackson, 2017	Prosperity without growth: Foundations for the economy of tomorrow	Economics beyond the growth paradigm.
Leadbeater, 2011	What's mine is yours: How collaborative consumption is changing the way we live.	The emergence of businesses and initiatives, particularly online, where people share resources and services with one another.
Lerner, 2006	The left hand of God: Healing America's political and spiritual crisis.	Analysis of the paradox of citizens voting for neoliberal politics from which they do not benefit. A call for a new bottom line in economics, based on meaning, personal responsibility, connections, and caring.
Mackey & Sisodia, 2013	Conscious capitalism: Liberating the heroic spirit of business	Describing business grounded in ethical consciousness: free enterprise capitalism to lift people out of poverty, foster cooperation and human progress. Examples from American businesses focusing on purpose, stakeholder integration, conscious leadership, and conscious culture and management.
Mason, 2015	Post-Capitalism: A guide to our future	A critical analysis of capitalism, and showing hope in cooperative and self-managed online spaces, leading to new forms of ownership and more social equality and sustainability.
Nelson, 2018	Economics for humans	Showing how social responsibility is part of business. Debunking the myth of economy as a machine and calling for qualities that also make businesses thrive—e.g., ethics, social and environmental values.

Nolan, 2009	Crossroads: The end of wild capitalism & the future of humanity	Diagnosis of economic threats to humanity and ways to develop a more collaborative economy.
Nussbaum, 2011	Creating capabilities: The human development approach	Describing the capability approach that Nussbaum and Sen have developed. Taking human capabilities as starting point of economic progress, including needs for dignity and self-respect.
Palmarozza & Rees, 2006	From principles to profit: The art of moral management	Describing the benefits and possibilities of moral management, including topics such as morality, virtue, truth, love, service, creativity, and multiple roles of the leader.
Payutto, 1994	Buddhist economics: A middle way for the market place	Economy based on Buddhist principles.
Pollard, 1996	The soul of the firm	Management committed to the development of its employees.
Porritt, 2006	Capitalism as if the world mattered	Showing environmental and humane crises related to capitalism; suggestions for a sustainable capitalism that will work for the people and the planet.
Ropke, 1960	Humane economy: The social framework of the free market	Critical analyses of the free market, and showing the humane and moral implications.
Rubin, 2015	Soul, self & society: The new morality and the modern state	The current system of the state is showing a new ethics, with human self-fulfillment at its heart. Our modern era is characterised by a morality of higher purposes and the rise of a new morality of self-fulfillment, which encourages people to a meaningful and rewarding life-path. It demands people respect one another's choices, mutuality of interactions, public positions allocated according to merit, and fulfillment of everyone's basic needs.
Sachs, 2008	Common wealth for a crowded planet	Suggestions for a plan to solve severe cries of population growth, climate change, severe poverty, by focusing on cooperation and technology.
Scharmer, 2009	Theory U: Leading from the future as it emerges: The social technology of presencing	Methodology to use our attention more fully, uncover our blind spots ,and connect with our authentic self, in the process of presence and sensing.
Schoene, 2015	Fair economics: Nature, money and people beyond neoclassical thinking	Analysis of fairness in economic thinking from Aristotle to Adam Smith and beyond. Describes the impact on nature and people, and how social and environmental values could be included in economics.
Schumacher, 1963	Small is beautiful	Showing how modern economics is oriented towards material wealth and ignores social and environmental topics.
Semler, 1994	Maverick! The success story behind the world's most unusual workplace	Egalitarian organisational structure.

Sundararajan, 2016	The sharing economy: The end of employment and the rise of crowd-based capitalism	Diagnosis of the rise of sharing economy and crowd-based capitalism, such as Uber and AirBnB.
Thurow, 1996	The future of capitalism: How today's economic forces shape tomorrow's world	Describing the emergence of a new type of capitalism that focuses on skills ('man-made brainpower'), social investments in infrastructure, education, and knowledge.
Tirole, 2017	Economics for the common good	Description of changes in the field of economics, including topics such as the common good; a call for focusing more directly on the common good in economics.
Tronto, 2013	Caring democracy: Markets, equality and justice	Caring as foundations of economy and economics.
Walzer, 1983	Spheres of justice: A defence of pluralism and equality	Describing the importance of pluralism and equality in economy, and including topics such as free time, kinship, recognition, and political power.
Wilson, 1993	The moral sense	Describing the importance of morality within economics, and how morality has always been part of the economic debates.
Yelle, 2019	Sovereignty and the sacred: Secularism and the political economy of religion	Critical analysis of the role of religion in politics and economics, and a call to include religious concepts and values in economic and political thinking.
Yunus, 2010	Building social business: The new kind of capitalism that serves humanity's most pressing needs	Social businesses use the energy of capitalism to fulfill human needs rather than reward shareholders. Examples ranging from multinationals to microcredits.
Zingales, 2012	A capitalism for the people: Recapturing lost genius of American prosperity	Capitalism without cronyism and inequality, based on morality.

Appendix 2. Overview of Publications on Meaning-Oriented Economics

Name, year	Title	Topic
Bains et al., 2007	Meaning Inc: The blueprint for business success in the 21st century	Helping corporations become more meaning-oriented: positive change in society, flourishing of others, inspiring mission, engagement, pride, trust, and a feeling special in employees.
Csikszentmihalyi, 2003	Good business: leadership, flow and the making of meaning	Finding flow in business—e.g., via leadership and organisational structure, and subsequently leading to flourishing of the company.
Deci, 1975	Intrinsic motivation	Describing the psychological and economic benefits of intrinsic motivation, for instance in work.
Dik, Byrne & Steger, 2013/2017	Purpose and meaning in the workplace	Psychological research on the role of meaning in the workplace.
Diller, Shedroff, & Rhea, 2008	Making meaning: How successful businesses deliver meaningful customer experiences	Giving meaningful experiences to customers.
Drewell & Larsson, 2017	The meaningful economy: A megatrend where meaning is a new currency	Describing the role of meaning in many aspects of the modern economy.
Drucker, 1984	Sinnvoll Wirtschaften: Notwendigkeit und Kunst, die Zukunft zu meistern (Meaningful economics: Necessity and art to master the future)	Economics beyond profit maximation.
Gilbert, 2005	The workplace revolution: Restoring trust in business and bringing meaning to our work	Personal strategies and corporate methodologies for improving the overall health of jobs.
Graeber, 2018	Bullshit jobs	Describing the psychological and social impact of meaninglessness in jobs and the economy.
Hurst, 2017	De betekeniseconomie (The meaning economy)	Why meaning matters in work, and how work could become more meaningful for employees and customers.
Joyce, 1987	The historical meanings of work	Describing the different meanings that work had for people in different eras.
Laloux, 2014	Reinventing organizations: A guide to creating organizations inspired by the next stage of human consciousness	How to focus workplaces on authenticity, communication, passion, and purpose.
Lerner, 1997	The politics of meaning: Restoring hope and possibility in an age of cynicism	Showing how social and larger values have left modern politics, and how religious and spiritual values could enrich politics.
Naylor, Willimon & Osterberg, 1996	The search for meaning in the workplace	Wide-ranging discussion of possible meanings in work.
Pink, 2009	Drive: The surprising truth about what motivates us	Work focusing on self-direction, learning, and creating, connecting, and contributing to the world.
Sisodia, Wolfe & Sheth, 2015	Firms of endearment: How world-class companies profit from passion and purpose.	Meaning-oriented companies are more profitable than non-meaning-oriented companies
Spence, 2009	It's not what you sell, it's what you stand for. Why every extraordinary business is driven by purpose	Examples of companies with a clear purpose—that is, a clear statement about the difference they try to make in the world beyond money.
Ter Borg, 2003	De zineconomie (The meaning economy)	Meaning is no longer a by-effect of the economy, but people search for meaning in the economy.

| Ulrich & Ulrich, 2010 | The why of work | How to create meaning in one's work—e.g., via understanding needs of customers and employees, personalising work, and using checklists and many other tools. |

Appendix 3. Systematic Review of Literature
on Capitalism and Meaning

Table A3.1. Methodology of the Systematic Review of Literature on Capitalism and Meaning

Aims Study 1 aimed to conduct a systematic literature review of all empirical and conceptual studies on the relationship between capitalism and meaning in life. The review was conducted in multiple rounds (see Figure 1), in line with PRISMA and MOOSE-guidelines (Liberati, Altman, Tezlav, et al., 2009; Stroup, Berlin, Morton, Williamson, Rennie et al., 2000).
Literature search It was decided not to specify the specific criteria for capitalism and meaning in life, except for authors using these terms. Thus, this study gives an overview of studies that included both the terms capitalism and meaning. The following search terms operationalised meaning: 'meaning in life, meaningful life, living meaningful*, search for meaning, life meaning, meaning-oriented, meaning-centred, meaning-focused, noetic, purpose in life, purpose of life, life purpose, purposes in life, purposes of life, life's purpose, purposeful, goal in life, goal of life, goals of life, goals in life, life's goal*, value* in life, life's value*, significance of life, life destiny, destiny in life, destiny of life, life* essence, essence of life, sense of life, life satisfaction, aims in life, aims of life, life* aims, meaning-making, existential*'. The following search terms operationalised 'capitalism' or 'meaning-oriented economies': 'capital*, market economy, neoliberal*, liberal, econom*, privatization, self-interest, competition, competitive market, wage labour, free market, supply and demand, meaning economy, Meaning-Oriented Economy, meaning-focused economy, purpose economy, purposeful economy'. The following search engines were used: Pubmed, Web-of-Knowledge, PsycInfo, PsycTest, Medline, Embase, scholar.google.com, Scopus. * Asterisks indicate phrases that may include additional words when they appear in the literature.
Selection of literature All titles and abstracts were initially screened for eligibility. Studies were excluded though thorough reading of the abstracts and on the basis of full-text manuscripts. Studies were included when they described any type of meaning with the following characteristics: 1. Any type of qualitative, quantitative, or conceptual method, including reviews, 2. The relationship between meaning in life and capitalism, 3. Explicitly used the term 'meaning' and 'capitalism' or their pre-defined synonyms. The findings from the included studies were analysed via an adjusted version of thematic analyses (Braun & Clarke, 2006): 1. In each article, each unique relationship between 'meaning' and 'capitalism' was identified and recorded in an EXCEL spreadsheet; 2. Similar relationships across articles were preliminarily categorised on the basis of their general content and were given a preliminary name; each category contained types of meaning from at least three articles; 3. The preliminary categories were combined with one another until multiple levels of categorisation were created, with each having between three and six sub-categories. To improve the reliability of the findings, two researchers independently categorised the meanings, which had a high inter-rater reliability for the selection of studies (Kappa=.80) and for the categorisation (Kappa=.82).

Table A3.2. Results of the Systematic Literature Review of Capitalism and Meaning

Theme	References
Critical philosophy	
Ancient Greek theories	Critchley, 1995; McCarthy, 1992; Pike, 2019; Prasch, 2013; Van Staveren, 2013
Marxist theories	Dudnik, 2018; Goux, 1990; Mészáros, 2006; Ollman & Bertell, 1976; Schumpeter, 2010
Foucauldian theories	Foucault, 2012; P. Kelly, 2016; Lemke, 2010; McDonald & O'callaghan, 2008; Vatter, 2009
Existential & phenomenological theories	Brockelman, 2008; Dion, 2014 ; Duppe, 2011; Flynn, 1986; Heidegger, 1977; Irwin, 2015; Sartre, 1974, 2007
Bourdieu's theories	McAlexander, Dufault, Martin, & Schouten, 2014; Peters, 2012
Tocqueville's theories	McLendon, 2006
Maslowian theories	Bouzenita & Boulanouar, 2016; Stum, 2001
Capability theories	Muffels & Headey, 2013
Critical theory	Althusser, 2014; Fremstad, 1977; Gane, 1990; Horkheimer & Adorno, 1982; H. Marcuse, 2005, 2013
Other theories	Da Rosa, 2019; Dardot & Laval, 2014; Guattari & Deleuze, 2000; Jameson, 1993; Knight, 2008; Lewis, 2004; Löwy, 2009; Metz, 2003; Sennett, 1998, 2007, 2008, 2012; Žižek, 1989
Relationship between meaning and macro-economic phenomena	
Relationship between positive psychology and capitalism in general	Meyers & van Woerkom, 2017; Millán, 2016; Riaz, Riaz, & Batool, 2014
Relationship between happiness and capitalism in general	Carabelli & Cedrini, 2011; van de Vliert, Janssen, & Giebels, 2002
Relationship between life satisfaction and capitalism in general	
Relationship between social capital, meaning, and capitalism in general	Abdallah, Thompson, & Marks, 2008; Ambrey, Ulichny, & Fleming, 2017; Ardahan, 2014; Ateca-Amestoy, Aguilar, & Moro-Egido, 2014; W. E. Baker, 2003; Bartolini & Sarracino, 2015; Bjornskov, 2003; Calvo, Zheng, Kumar, Olgiati, & Berkman, 2012; Colombo & Stanca, 2014; Dowd et al., 2014; Elgar et al., 2011; Freitag, 2003; Han, Kim, & Lee, 2013; Helliwell & Barrington-Leigh, 2010, 2012; John F. Helliwell & Putnam, 2013; Hommerich & Tiefenbach, 2018; Hooghe & Vanhoutte, 2011; Inaba, Wada, Ichida, & Nishikawa, 2015; Jagodzinski, 2010; Jorm & Ryan, 2014; Joubert, Wan, Bhatt, & Chan, 2015; Jovanović, 2016; Kirkbesoglu & Sargut, 2016; Kroll, 2011; Kuo, 2015; Kwok, Cheng, & Wong, 2015; Leerattanakorn & Wiboonpongse, 2017; Lucchini, Della Bella, & Crivelli, 2015; Menon, Pendakur, & Perali, 2015; Millán, 2016; Morris, Messal, & Meriac, 2013; Nicholas, 2012; Ning, 2017; Okulicz-Kozaryn, 2010; Orlowski & Wicker, 2015; Pei, 2008; Ponce, Rosas, & Lorca, 2014; Portela, Neira, & Salinas-Jimenez, 2013; Richards, 2016; Suhail & Chaudhry, 2004; K. Takahashi et al., 2011; Theurer & Wister, 2010; Tjosvold, XueHuang, Johnson, & Johnson, 2008; Richards, 2016; Van Tongeren, Green, Davis, Hook, & Hulsey, 2016; Vemuri & Costanza, 2006; Vemuri, Grove, Wilson, & Burch, 2011; Suhail, 2004; Verduyn, Ybarra, Resibois, Jonides, & Kross, 2017; Weckroth, Kemppainen, & Sorensen, 2015; Woo & Kim, 2018; Wulff, 2009; Yamaoka, 2008; Yetim & Yetim, 2014; Yip et al., 2007; Zou, Su, & Wang, 2018

Relationship between *psychological capital,* meaning, and capitalism in general	Bockorny & Youssef-Morgan, 2019; Bradley, 2015; Choi, Cho, Jung, & Sohn, 2018; Culbertson, Fullagar, & Mills, 2010; Howatt, 2013; Karatepe & Karadas, 2015; Kwok et al., 2015; Li, 2018; Li, Wu, & Zhang, 2011; Millán, 2016; Murgic, Rijavec, & Miljkovic, 2019; Singhal & Rastogi, 2018; Yuan, 2017; Zhang, Ewalds-Kvist, Li, & Jiang, 2019
Relationship between *natural capital,* meaning, and capitalism in general	Abdallah et al., 2008; Ambrey & Fleming, 2014; Cooper, 2011; Gu, Huang, Zhang, & Wang, 2015; Howell, Passmore, & Buro, 2013; Ojala, 2013; Takahashi, Tandoc, Duan, & Van Witsen, 2017; Thorpe & Jacobson, 2013; Vemuri & Costanza, 2006; Vemuri et al., 2011; Yeatts, Cready, Pei, Shen, & Luo, 2014; S. Zhang, Liu, Zhu, & Cheng, 2018; Zorondo-Rodríguez et al., 2016
Relationship between *income/ income paradox* and meaning	Degutis & Urbonavicius, 2013; Easterlin, Laura Angelescu McVey, Malgorzata Switek, Onnicha Sawangfa, & Jacqueline Smith Zweig, 2010; Easterlin, McVey, Switek, Sawangfa, & Smith Zweig, 2010; Easterlin, McVey, Switek, Sawangfa, & Zweig, 2013; Ferrer-i-Carbonell & Gerxhani, 2016; Fischer & Torgler, 2013; Gleibs, Morton, Rabinovich, Haslam, & Helliwell, 2013; Groot, Van den Brink, & van Praag, 2007; Guiso, Sapienza, & Zingales, 2003; Hitaj, 2011; Keuschnigg & Wolbring, 2012; Knies, 2012; Lin, 2001; Menon et al., 2015; Montgomerie & Tepe-Belfrage, 2019; Navarro & Sanchez, 2018; Ning, 2017; Oishi & Diener, 2014; Renneboog & Spaenjers, 2012; Schnell, 2009; Suhail & Chaudhry, 2004; Tang, 2014; Van Hoorn & Sent, 2016; Ward & King, 2016; Zatzick, Deery, & Iverson, 2015
Relationship between *socio-economic inequality/welfare state,* and meaning	Bilajac, Marchesi, Tesic, & Rukavina, 2014; Bjornskov, Dreher, & Fischer, 2007, 2008; Buttrick, Heintzelman, & Oishi, 2017; Choi, Kim, & Park, 2016; Clench-Aas & Holte, 2018; Dabla-Norris, Kochhar, Suphaphiphat, Ricka, & Tsounta, 2015; Davidson, Pacek, & Radcliff, 2013; Easterlin, 2012; Fujishiro, Xu, & Gong, 2010; Gilens & Page, 2014; Graafland & Lous, 2018; Greider, 1998; Grouden & Jose, 2014; Jetten, Haslam, & Barlow, 2013; Peck, 2002; Piston, 2014; Radcliff, 2001; Rousseau, 1999; Ryff, 2017; Ryff, Keyes, & Hughes, 2003; Shin, 2018; Stiglitz, 2012; Tcherneva, 2015; Ward & King, 2016; Zhang et al., 2018
Relationship between *housing/ neighbourhood/public space*, and meaning	Aminzadeh et al., 2013; Chuluun & Graham, 2016; Clark & Lisowski, 2018; Eibich, Krekel, Demuth, & Wagner, 2016; Hoogerbrugge & Burger, 2018; Iqani & Baro, 2017; Lewicka, 2011a, 2011b; Lewicka, 2013; McKnight & Block, 2011; Millán, 2016; O'Brien, 2002; Plaut, Markus, Treadway, & Fu, 2012; Rodgers, 2012; Sennett, 2017; Teck-Hong, 2012; Vos, 2017
Relationship between meaning and *evolutionary economics*	Alexander, 2017; Bekoff, 2000; Bowles & Gintis, 2013; De Waal, 2010; DeVore & Lee, 1968; England, 1994; Frank, 2012; Holland, 2009; Provine, 1988; Katz, 2000; Keltner, 2009; Kropotkin, 1922; Provine, 1988; Vanberg, 2014; Wilson, 1993; Wright, 1995
Relationship between *economic freedom,* meaning, and economics	Gehring, 2013; Graafland & Compen, 2015; Graafland & Lous, 2018; Spruk & Kešeljević, 2016; Tsai, 2009; Wolcott, 2019; Xin & Smyth, 2010
Relationship between *political freedom and unfreedom/ authoritarianism,* meaning, and economics	Beck & Germann, 2019; Jorm & Ryan, 2014; Korsunskiy, 2018; Mattioli, 2017; Radcliff, 2001; Rode, 2013; Tandoc & Takahashi, 2013
Meaning in transition towards capitalism	
General economic development	Abadía-Barrero, 2015; Algan, 2014; Bartolini, Mikucka, & Sarracino, 2017; Bergheim, 2007; Breen, 2004; Buscha & Sturgis, 2018; Cohen & Ackland, 2012; De Soto, 2000; Easterlin, 2009,

	2012, 2014; Fedyukin, 2018; Goh, 2009; Guriev & Melnikov, 2018; Guriev & Zhuravskaya, 2009; Heyat, 2004; Piontek, 2010; Ram, 2008; Reyes-García, 2012; Stetsenko & Arievitch, 2010; Thurnwald, 2018
Post-communism/welfare state	Andren & Martinsson, 2006; Bjornskov et al., 2008; Brockmann, Delhey, Welzel, & Yuan, 2009; Ci, 1994; Danziger, Carlson, & Henly, 2001; Dragone & Ziebarth, 2017; R. A. Easterlin, 2009; Easterlin, 2014; Inglehart, Foa, Ponarin, & Welzel, 2013; Morgan & Wang, 2018; S. H. Schwartz & Bardi, 1997; Stojanovic, 2010; Tsai, 2009; Zeng & Eisenman, 2018
Post-Arab Spring	Silver, Caudill, & Mixon, 2017
Post-colonialism & post-statism	Hirt, Slaev, & Anderson, 2012
Post-financial crisis	Bjerg, 2014; Bowman & Rugg, 2013; Frank, Davis, & Elgar, 2014; Gonzalez, Oosterlynck, Ribera-Fumaz, & Rossi, 2018; Habibov & Afandi, 2015; Murphy & Scott, 2014; Panas, 2013; Pezirkianidis, Stalikas, Efstathiou, & Karakasidou, 2016
Post-natural disaster/trauma	Lowe, Manove, & Rhodes, 2013; Park, 2005, 2010; Park & Ai, 2006; Schulenberg, Drescher, & Baczwaski, 2014; Scott & Weems, 2013; Scott, Martin, & Schouten, 2014; Tosone et al., 2003; Toussaint et al., 2017; Triplett, Tedeschi, Cann, Calhoun, & Reeve, 2012; Updegraff, Silver, & Holman, 2008; Wlodarczyk et al., 2016; Palgi et al., 2012; Ren, 2009; Aten, O'Grady, Milstein, Boan, & Schruba, 2014; Aten et al., 2019; Bakic & Ajdukovic, 2019; Blix, Hansen, Birkeland, Nissen, & Heir, 2013; Bradfield, Wylie, & Echterling, 1989; Chan, Sha, Leung, & Gilbert, 2011; R. L. Collins, Taylor, & Skokan, 1990; Dolan, 2007; Drescher et al., 2012; Drescher, Schulenberg, & Smith, 2014; Dursun, Steger, Bentele, & Schulenberg, 2016; Feder et al., 2013; Garrison & Sasser, 2009; H. A. Giroux, 2006; Gowan, Kirk, & Sloan, 2014; Guo, Gan, & Tong, 2013; Hackbarth, Pavkov, Wetchler, & Flannery, 2012; Haynes et al., 2017; Hussain & Bhushan, 2013; Ishida, 2011; Kalayjian, 1999; Kalayjian & Diakonova-Curtis, 2018; Kalayjian & Eugene, 2009; Karanci & Acarturk, 2005; Li Fan & Chen, 2009; McElroy-Heltzel et al., 2018; Miles & Crandall, 1983; Noviana, Miyazaki, & Ishimaru, 2016; Palgi et al., 2012; Ren, 2009
Micro-economic projects in non-capitalist countries	García, Cova, Rincón, & Vázquez, 2015; Huhn, 2014; Masferrer-Dodas, Rico-Garcia, Huanca, Reyes-Garcia, & Team, 2012; Raffaelli, Tran, Wiley, Galarza-Heras, & Lazarevic, 2012; Ranganathan, 2014
Meaning in vulnerable groups in capitalist countries	—
Meaning in homeless, unemployed & low-waged	Abeyta, Routledge, Kersten, & Cox, 2017; Bearsley & Cummins, 1999; Bender, Thompson, McManus, Lantry, & Flynn, 2007; G. Blau, Petrucci, & McClendon, 2013; Carboni, 1990; Caron, 2012; Danaher, 2017; Garapich, 2014; Ilan, 2013; Kunze & Suppa, 2017; Lai, 1998; Miller, 2011; Myck & Oczkowska, 2018; Norton, Nizalova, & Murtazashvili, 2018; Polakow, 2007; Rew, Slesnick, Johnson, Aguilar, & Cengiz, 2019; Ehrenreich, 2010; Ghidina, 1992; Hultman & Hemlin, 2008; Hultman, Hemlin, & Olof Hörnquist, 2006; Machell, Disabato, & Kashdan, 2016; Mills & Codd, 2008; Skevington, 2009
Meaningless jobs	Bales, 1999; Graeber & Cerutti, 2018; Isaksen, 2000; Kreiner, Ashforth, & Sluss, 2006; Lucas & Buzzanell, 2004; Malott, Hill, & Banfield, 2013; Steger, Littman-Ovadia, Miller, Menger, & Rothmann, 2013; Tyler, 2011; Tyner, 2016

Meaning in ethnic minority groups	Baessler, Oerter, Fernández, & Romero, 2003; Boggs, 1970; Chigbo, 2011; Eksner, 2015; Jagire, 2011; Jervis, Spicer, & Manson, 2003; Keyes, 2009; Kiang & Fuligni, 2010; Kiang, Peterson, & Thompson, 2011; Kiang & Witkow, 2015; Kim, Son, & Nam, 2005; Lin, 2008; Lu, Marks, & Apavaloiae, 2012; Mattis, 2002; Nuñez & Sansone, 2016; Pan, 2011; Pan, Fu Keung Wong, Joubert, & Chan, 2007; Pan, Wong, Joubert, & Chan, 2008; Pang, 1994, 1996; Saito, 2014; Vellem, 2015; Yuen, 2013
Meaning in immigrants & refugees	Ager & Ager, 2010; Alvarez de Davila, 2015; Basoglu, 2006; Bek-Pedersen & Montgomery, 2006; Chen, 2008; Chu, Shen, & Yang, 2017; Comaroff & Comaroff, 2002; Dunn & O'Brien, 2009; Ekblad, 1993; Erman, 2001; Gladden, 2013; Gregory & Prana, 2013; Hart & Singh, 2009; Hutzell & Peterson, 1986; Idemudia, Williams, Madu, & Wyatt, 2013; Lam & Chan, 2004; Lim, 2018; Madison, 2006; Magat, 1999; Major & Machin, 2018; Massey & Akresh, 2006; A. R. Morgan, Rivera, Moreno, & Haglund, 2012; Okazaki & Abelmann, 2014; Peterson & Plamondon, 2009; Purser, 2009; Puvimanasinghe, Denson, Augoustinos, & Somasundaram, 2014; Russell & Stage, 1996; Schweitzer, Melville, Steel, & Lacherez, 2006; Spencer & Le, 2006; Suárez-Orozco & Suárez-Orozco, 2009; Sutker, Davis, Uddo, & Ditta, 1995; Taloyan, Johansson, Saleh-Stattin, & Al-Windi, 2011; Tempany, 2009; Wilchek-Aviad, 2015; Wong & Tsang, 2004; Xie, Xia, & Zhou, 2004; Yost & Lucas, 2002
Meaning in young people	Abdullah, 2019; Brassai, Piko, & Steger, 2012; Chatterjee & Basu, 2010; Duke, Skay, Pettingell, & Borowsky, 2009; Erikson, 1963; Heilman, 1998; Hewitt, 2014; Hewlett, Sherbin, & Sumberg, 2009; Hou, Kim, & Benner, 2018; How & Strauss, 2000; Kelly, Zimmer-Gembeck, & Boislard-P, 2012; Kline, 2011; Langer, 2002; Leung & Shek, 2018; Negru-Subtirica, Pop, Luyckx, Dezutter, & Steger, 2016; Ojala, 2013; Schulenberg, Smith, Drescher, & Buchanan, 2016; Schulze, 1992; Selivanova, 2017; Shek, 2005; Yunus, 2014
Meaning in elderly	Baum, 1988; Bickerstaff, Grasser, & McCabe, 2003; Chang & Patricia, 2000; Choi, Kim, Shin, Lee, & Jung, 2003; Depaola & Ebersole, 1995; Ebersole & Depaola, 1987, 1989; Erichsen & Büssing, 2013; Fry, 2000; Hofer et al., 2014; Ju, Shin, Kim, Hyun, & Park, 2013; Klaas, 1998; Krause, 2003, 2004, 2005, 2007; Luborsky, 1993; MacKinlay, 2002; Nyqvist, Forsman, Giuntoli, & Cattan, 2013; Oakes, 2008; Plaud & Guillemot, 2015; Reker, 1997, 2005; Reker, Peacock, & Wong, 1987; Sarvimäki & Stenbock-Hult, 2000; Steptoe, Deaton, & Stone, 2015; Takkinen & Ruoppila, 2001; Theurer & Wister, 2010; Trice, 1990; Wagnild & Young, 1990; Wijk & Grimby, 2008; Van Ranst, 1997; Troutman, Nies, & Bentley, 2010
Meaning in parents	
Meaning in individuals with severe mental or physical disease	Argentzell, Håkansson, & Eklund, 2012; Léonard & Arnsperger, 2009 See for a review of the other articles duplicate of the systematic literature review on meaning in chronic and life-threatening physical illness: Vos, 2016, 2016a
Meaning in women	Barchiesi, 2014; Boncompte & Paredes, 2019; Butler, 2011; Dzbankova & Sirucek, 2013; Shaw, 2014; Williams, 2014; Beutel & Marini, 1995; Broadhead, 2018; Carr, 1997; Chamberlain & Zika, 1988; Collischon, 2019; Edwards & Holden, 2001; Emslie & Hunt, 2009; Evangelista, Kagawa-Singer, & Dracup, 2001; Fletcher, 1998
Meaning in LGBTQI+	Allan, Tebbe, Duffy, & Autin, 2015; Cox, Dewaele, Van Houtte, & Vincke, 2010; Erez & Shenkman, 2016; K. A. Foster, Bowland, & Vosler, 2015; Halkitis et al., 2009; King & Noelle, 2005; King & Smith, 2004; Langdridge, 2014; Patterson & Riskind, 2010; Riggle,

	Rostosky, & Danner, 2009; Riggle, Rostosky, & Horne, 2010; Riggle, Whitman, Olson, Rostosky, & Strong, 2008; Szymanski & Mikorski, 2016; Taber & Briddick, 2011
Meaning in addiction alcohol, drugs, internet	Bozoglan, Demirer, & Sahin, 2013; Carroll, 1993; Cheng & Li, 2014; Coleman, Kaplan, & Downing, 1986; Cook, 2004; Didelot, Hollingsworth, & Buckenmeyer, 2012; Galanter, 2006; Jacobson, Ritter, & Mueller, 1977; Ko et al., 2008; Konkolÿ Thege, Stauder, & Kopp, 2010; Lyons, Deane, & Kelly, 2010; Marsh, Smith, Piek, & Saunders, 2003; R. A. Martin, MacKinnon, Johnson, & Rohsenow, 2011; Miller, 1990; Miller & Bogenschutz, 2007; Nicholson et al., 1994; O'Connell, Tondora, Croog, Evans, & Davidson, 2005; Oakes, 2008; Okasaka, Morita, Nakatani, & Fujisawa, 2008; Roos, Kirouac, Pearson, Fink, & Witkiewitz, 2015; Röpke, 2014; Ross, 2008; Schnetzer, Schulenberg, & Buchanan, 2013; Sellman, 2010; Sherman & Fischer, 2002; Steger, Mann, Michels, & Cooper, 2009; Thege, Bachner, Kushnir, & Kopp, 2009; Thurang, Rydström, & Bengtsson Tops, 2011; Waisberg & Porter, 1994; Wiklund, 2008; Wolf, Katz, & Nachson, 1995; Young-Hall, 2001; Zhang et al., 2015
Meaning in terrorism & radical extremism	Agathangelou, 2010; Chudinov & Sgem, 2014; Clymer, 2004; Halperin, Canetti, Hobfoll, & Johnson, 2009; Krieger & Meierrieks, 2010; Kruglanski, Gelfand, Bélanger, Hetiarachchi, & Gunaratna, 2015; Marcuse, 2006; Salzman, 2008; Steger, Frazier, & Zacchanini, 2008; Walters, 2002; Zygmuntowski, 2016
Characteristics of individual lifestyles in capitalist countries later in this article renamed as 'Capitalist Life Syndrome'	
Materialism & identification with products/brands, consumerism, hedonism	Atkinson & Elliott, 2008; Avery, 2007; Barber, 2008; Baudrillard, 2016, 2018; Bauer, Wilkie, Kim, & Bodenhausen, 2012; Belk & Pollay, 1985; Campbell, 1987; Carù, Caru, & Cova, 2007; Chang & Arkin, 2002; Chen, Peng, & Saparito, 2002; Ci, 1999; Csikszentmihalyi, 2004b; De Graaf, Wann, & Naylor, 2014; Dittmar, Bond, Hurst, & Kasser, 2014; Dittmar & Kapur, 2011; Easterlin & Crimmins, 2018; Elliott, 1997; Frank, 2001; Friedman, 2005; Graham & Oswald, 2010; Guitart, 2011; S. Hall, 2012; Henderson-King & Mitchell, 2011; Hirschman & Holbrook, 1982; Holbrook & Hirschman, 1982; Huta, 2007; Izberk-Bilgin, 2013; James, 2007, 2008; Kale, 2006; Kashdan & Breen, 2007; Kasser, 2002, 2016; Kasser, Ryan, Couchman, & Sheldon, 2004; T. E. Kasser & Kanner, 2004; Kielburger & Kielburger, 2009; La Barbera & Gürhan, 1997; Marcuse, 2013; McGrath, 2016; Merish, 2000; Migone, 2007; Miles, 1998; Rindfleisch, Burroughs, & Wong, 2008; Roscoe, 2014; Rosenberg, 2013; Sarracino & Mikucka, 2019; Sayre & Horne, 1996; Skidelsky & Skidelsky, 2012; Stecker, 1981; Stolle, Hooghe, & Micheletti, 2005; Swinyard, Kau, & Phua, 2001; Tsang, Carpenter, Roberts, Frisch, & Carlisle, 2014; Twenge & Campbell, 2009; Twenge & Foster, 2008; Twitchell, 1999; Wuthnow, 1995; Zhao & Belk, 2008
Meaning manipulation via advertising and biased journalism, social media, and entertainment	Ewen, 2008; Freberg, Graham, McGaughey, & Freberg, 2011; Herman & Chomsky, 2010; Jhally, 2014; Jiaxun, 2006; Kohn, 1999, 2000; Steger & Dik, 2009; Scott et al., 2014; Stavrakakis, 2000; Steger & Dik, 2009; Sternberg, 1999; Thaler & Sunstein, 2009; Wu, 2017; Yani-de-Soriano & Slater, 2009; Zuboff, 2019
Self-promotion, narcissism, 'identity economics', 'psychopaths', greed	Lord & Brown, 2003; Pacifico & Gomes, 2019; Pacquing, 2017; Sullivan, 2011; Vaknin, 2009; Verhaeghe, 2012; Adams, 2016; G. Akerlof & Kranton, 2010; Boyd, 1996; Di Fabio, 2015; A. Di Fabio &

	Kenny, 2018; Di Fabio, Palazzeschi, & Bucci, 2017; Hearn, 2008; Jakovljevic & Tomic, 2016; Akerlof & Kranton, 2000; Catlin & Epstein, 1992; Adams, 2016; Akerlof & Kranton, 2011; Baumeister, 1999; Campbell et al., 1996; Campbell, Hoffman, Campbell, & Marchisio, 2011; Davis, 2010; Davis, 2003; Eckhardt & Houston, 1998; Emmons, 1987; Fine, 1986; Folbre, 2009; Foster, Campbell, & Twenge, 2003; Giddens, 1991; Gini, 2013; Gruba-McCallister, 2007; Herrmann-Pillath, 2017; Hogg & Terry, 2001; Horkheimer, 1982; Ibarra, 1999; Jacoby, 1980; Kelly, 2016; Krekels & Pandelaere, 2015; Kunneman & Brinkman, 2009; Lasch, 1980, 2018; Layton, 2014; Levin, 1987; Mäkinen, 2012; Lunbeck, 2014; Mazlish, 1982; Meglino & Korsgaard, 2004; Moran, 2014; Rand, 1964; Saltman, 2013; Schlegel, Hicks, Arndt, & King, 2009; Sen, 2007; Sengupta & Sibley, 2018; Seuntjens, Zeelenberg, van de Ven, & Breugelmans, 2015
Quick-fix life satisfaction	Hyland, 2015a, 2015b; Noys, 2014; Schneider & du Plock, 2012
Flexibility, uncertainty, gig economy	Arthur & Rousseau, 1996; Bauman, 2013; Beck, Lash, & Wynne, 1992; Bowe, Bowe, & Streeter, 2009; Kidder, 2006; Kuhn, 2016; Prassl, 2018
Choice overload & decision-making difficulties	Chernev, Böckenholt, & Goodman, 2015; Corsani, 2015; Iyengar & Kamenica, 2006; Kasser, Cohn, Kanner, & Ryan, 2007; O'Toole & Lawler, 2008; Reed, Reed, Chok, & Brozyna, 2011; Scheibehenne, Greifeneder, & Todd, 2010; Schwartz, 2004, 2010; Swenson, 2014; Wolcott, 2019
Meritocracy	Carlone et al., 2016; Machonin, 1994; Stavrositu, 2014; Young, 2017
Rationalisation & utilitarianism	Bartels & Pizarro, 2011; Corlett, 1988; Angelo Corlett, 1988; Goh, 2009; Metz, 2003; Scarre, 2002
Fatalism, TINA, helplessness, hopelessness, nihilism	Abeyta et al., 2017; Acevedo, 2005; Amsler, 2016; Aronson, 2017; Binkley, 2011; Casey, 2011; De Genova, 1995; Diken, 2008; J. Dixon & Frolova, 2011; Fassin, 2010; Fisher, 2009; Foucault, 2012; Foucault, Davidson, & Burchell, 2008; Hamzaoglu, Ozkan, Ulusoy, & Gokdogan, 2010; Hoedemaekers, 2016; Jost et al., 2017; Kristol, 1973; Kroker, 2004; Lemke, 2010; Liodakis, 2016; Martinko & Gardner, 1982; McMurtry, 1973; Merrifield, 1993; Munck, 2003; Pereboom, 2011; Polanyi, 1947; Rucker & Galinsky, 2008; Rustin, 1992; Sobol-Kwapinska, 2013; Weller, 2010; Žižek, 2017
Existential moods (see also existential and theoretical publications	Bahmad, 2019; Irwin, 2015; Neilson, 2015; Sharp, 2018; Tran, 2013; Vida, 2016
Meaning-oriented economy later in this article renamed as 'meaning-orientation towards the economy'	
Meaning-oriented macro-economy in general	Baumol, Litan, & Schramm, 2007; Berman, 1970; Brown, 2017; Drewell & Larsson, 2017; Drucker, 1997; Graen & Grace, 2015; Honoré, 2005; Hurst, 2016; Jackson, 2016; Jensen, 1996; Nelson, 2018; Oteman & van Lienden, 2014; Palmarozza, 2006; Payutto & Evans, 1994; Ranta, 2018; Reed et al., 2011; Rubin, 2015; Schumacher, 2011; Sedlacek, 2011; Seligman, Ernst, Gillham, Reivich, & Linkins, 2009; Tian, 2010; Tirole, 2017; Tronto, 2013; M. Yunus, 2010
Meaning in business in general	Bains, 2011; Banerjee & Wahl, 2014; Gilbert, 2005; Semler, 2001; Sisodia, Wolfe, & Sheth, 2003; Spence, 2009; Van Gelderen, 2006; Viviers & Eccles, 2012
Ecologically sustainable economy & connection with nature	Isaakgun, 2016; Kasser, 2017; Knight & Rosa, 2011; Krueger, Schulz, & Gibbs, 2018; Lawn, 2011; Mitrut, Balaceanu, Gruiescu, & Serban, 2015; Patrizi, Capineri, Rugani, & Niccolucci, 2010; Pretty,

	2013; Tkachenko & Hromovyk, 2018; Wood, Logsdon, Lewellyn, & Davenport, 2015; Banyte, Brazioniene, & Gadeikiene, 2010; D'Alisa, Demaria, & Kallis, 2014; Engelbrecht, 2009; Foster, 2002; Harrison, 2013; Hawken, Lovins, & Lovins, 2013; Iranzo, 2015; Isaak, 2016; Jacobs & Mazzucato, 2016; Leary, Tipsord, & Tate, 2008; Poon, Teng, Chow, & Chen, 2015; Sachs, 2008; Schoene, 2015; Vermeir & Verbeke, 2008
Post-materialistic consumerism	Alexander, 2011; Botsman & Rogers, 2011; Cherrier, 2007; Featherstone, 1982; Hall, 2012; T. C. Johnston & Burton, 2003; Kielburger & Kielburger, 2009; Lamla, 2009; Ozcaglar-Toulouse, 2007; Price, Feick, & Guskey, 1995; Rucker & Galinsky, 2008; Shaw, Grehan, Shiu, Hassan, & Thomson, 2005; Tosh, Ralph, & Campbell, 2000
Altruism, corporate social responsibility, neocommunitarianism, & moral and compassionate economy	Aguinis & Glavas, 2019; Barman, 2016; Benioff, 2009; Bowles, 2016; Brittan, 1996; Driscoll, 2015; Ellis, 2004; Etzioni, 2010; Fyfe, 2005; Goldsworthy, 2010; Grant, 2009; Grayson & Jane, 2017; Green, 2009; Gutierrez-Zamano, 2005; Hirschberger, 2013, 2015; Hoffman & McNulty, 2012; Lane, 1991; Lewis & Mackenzie, 2000; Lotufo, Neto, & Gouvêa, 2015; Lu, Jiang, Zhao, & Fang, 2019; Lugo, 2017; J Mackey & R Sisodia, 2013; John Mackey & Raj Sisodia, 2013; McCrea, Walker, & Weber, 2013; Ostrom, 1990; Porritt, 2012; Röpke, 2014; Scerri & Lam, 2015; Schwartz, Keyl, Marcum, & Bode, 2009; Sundararajan, 2016; Theurer & Wister, 2010; Young, 2003
Experience economy	Birch, 2008; Boswijk, Peelen, Olthof, & Beddow, 2012; Boswijk, Thijssen, & Peelen, 2005; Csikszentmihalyi & Csikszentmihalyi, 1975; Garcia, 2016; Grandey, Fisk, Mattila, Jansen, & Sideman, 2005; Hjorth, 2007; Krueger, 1991; Lonsway, 2013; Piët, 2003; Pine & Gilmore, 1998, 2013; Pine, Pine, & Gilmore, 1999; Schulze, 1992; Snel, 2011; Snir & Harpaz, 2002; Sundbo & Darmer, 2008; Sundbo & Sorensen, 2013
Meaning-oriented finance & investment	Dixon & Monk, 2014; Harrington & Harrington, 1992; Mackenzie & Lewis, 1999; Rubaltelli, Lotto, Ritov, & Rumiati, 2015; Schwartz, 2003
Meaning-oriented business leadership & visionaries	Van Dierendonck, Haynes, Borrill, & Stride, 2004; Springett, 2004; Walumbwa, Avolio, Gardner, Wernsing, & Peterson, 2008; Walumbwa, Avolio, & Zhu, 2008; Walumbwa et al., 2011; Arnold, Turner, Barling, Kelloway, & McKee, 2007; Avolio & Gardner, 2005; Avolio, Reichard, Hannah, Walumbwa, & Chan, 2009; Avolio, Walumbwa, & Weber, 2009; Bass, 1988; Bass & Bass, 2009; Boddy, Miles, Sanyal, & Hartog, 2015; Bouchikhi & Kimberly, 2008g58; M. E. Brown, Treviño, & Harrison, 2005; Burpitt & Bigoness, 1997; Collins, Collins, & Porras, 2005; Csikszentmihalyi, 2004a; Gardner, 2010; Gardner, Avolio, Luthans, May, & Walumbwa, 2005; George, 2003; George, Sims, McLean, & Mayer, 2007; Gerstner & Day, 1997; Gray & Jones, 2018; Gupta, 1996; Hackman & Hackman, 2002; Hall, 2004b; Hochschild, 2012; Hoover & Gorrell, 2009; Ilies, Morgeson, & Nahrgang, 2005; Judge & Piccolo, 2004; Kark & Shamir, 2013; Kark, Shamir, & Chen, 2003; Lee, McNulty, & Shaffer, 2013; Lennick & Kiel, 2007; Luthans & Avolio, 2003; Martin, 2013; May, Chan, Hodges, & Avolio, 2003; Palmarozza, 2019; Podolny, Khurana, & Hill-Popper, 2004; Rubin, 2015; Sanders, Hopkins, & Geroy, 2003; Schaubroeck, Lam, & Cha, 2007; Smircich & Morgan, 1982; Snel, 2011; Springett, 2004; Voelpel, Leibold, & Tekie, 2006; Walumbwa, Avolio, Gardner, Wernsing, & Peterson, 2008; Walumbwa, Avolio, & Zhu, 2008; Walumbwa et al., 2011

Meaning-oriented work, intrinsic work motivation & vocation and career	Aguinis & Glavas, 2019; Baker, Jacobs, & Tickle-Degnen, 2003; Berg, Grant, & Johnson, 2010; Berkelaar & Buzzanell, 2015; Blustein, 2006; Bunderson & Thompson, 2009; Byrne, Palmer, Smith, & Weidert, 2011; Chen, 2001; Claes & Quintanilla, 1993; Deci, Koestner, & Ryan, 1999; Deci & Ryan, 2010; Dik, Byrne, & Steger, 2013; Dik & Duffy, 2009; Dik et al., 2015; Dik, Steger, Fitch-Martin, & Onder, 2013; Duffy, Dik, & Steger, 2011; Fouad & Kantamneni, 2008; Freedman, 2008; Gagné & Deci, 2005; Gibson, 2004; Grant, 2008a, 2008b; Guion & Landy, 1972; Hall & Chandler, 2005; Hansen, 1994; Harpaz & Fu, 2002; B. Harrington & Hall, 2007; Herzberg, 2017; Holland, 1959, 1997; Ibarra, 2004; Joo & Lee, 2017; Kosine, Steger, & Duncan, 2008; Lane, 1991; Leider, 2015; Levy, 2005; Malka & Chatman, 2003; Markow & Klenke, 2005; Murtaza, 2011; Naylor, Willimon, & Österberg, 1996; Parsons, 1909; Pattakos, 2010; Patterson & Riskind, 2010; Pink, 2011; Riza & Heller, 2015; Rosso, Dekas, & Wrzesniewski, 2010; Steger & Dik, 2009, 2010; Steger, Pickering, Shin, & Dik, 2010; Super, 1957; Super, Savickas, & Super, 1996; Terkel, 2011; Ulrich & Ulrich, 2010; Wrzesniewski, Berg, & Dutton, 2010; Wrzesniewski, McCauley, Rozin, & Schwartz, 1997
Meaning-oriented work-person fit & job crafting	Arthur, Bell, Villado, & Doverspike, 2006; Bakker, 2010; Berg, Wrzesniewski, & Dutton, 2010; Blau, 1987; Bono & Judge, 2003; Briscoe & Hall, 2003; Briscoe, Hall, & DeMuth, 2006; Bujold, 2004; Chatman, 1989; Clegg & Spencer, 2007; Cools, Van den Broeck, & Bouckenooghe, 2009; Dawis, 2005; Dawis & Lofquist, 1984; Dik & Hansen, 2011; Don Gottfredson & Duffy, 2008; Durr & Tracey, 2009; Edwards, Cable, Williamson, Lambert, & Shipp, 2006; Edwards, Caplan, & Van Harrison, 1998; Guan, Deng, Bond, Chen, & Chan, 2010; Hall, 1996, 2004a; Harms, Roberts, & Winter, 2006; Heller, Watson, & Ilies, 2004; Jansen & Kristof-Brown, 2006; Johnson, 2005; Kohn & Schooler, 1982; Kreiner, 2006; Kristof-Brown, Zimmerman, & Johnson, 2005; Livingstone, Nelson, & Barr, 1997; Lofquist & Dawis, 1991; Lyons & O'brien, 2006; Lyons, 2008; MacDonald-Dennis, 2015; Nur Iplik, Can Kilic, & Yalcin, 2011; Oh et al., 2014; Salzinger, 1991; Savickas, 1997, 2002, 2005, 2013; Savickas et al., 2009; Scroggins, 2008; Steijn, 2008; Taber & Briddick, 2011; Tziner & Meir, 1997; Van Vianen, Nijstad, & Voskuijl, 2008; Vogel & Feldman, 2009; Wrzesniewski & Dutton, 2001
Meaning-oriented workplaces & HR	Argandoña, 2003; Avolio & Walumbwa, 2006; Aycan, Kanungo, & Sinha, 1999; Branson, 2008; Capabilities Group, 2011; Cardador & Rupp, 2011; Chiaburu & Harrison, 2008; Cohen-Meitar, Carmeli, & Waldman, 2009; Dirks, 2000; Fairlie, 2011; Fenwick & Lange, 1998; Grant, 2007; Hackman, 1980; Kahn, 1992; Kahn & Fellows, 2013; Kantartzis & Molineux, 2011; Karakas, 2010; Laloux, 2014; Macey & Schneider, 2008; Moorman & Byrne, 2013; Morrison, Burke, & Greene, 2007; Nuñez & Sansone, 2016; Parker, 2014; Pontefract, 2016; Pratt & Ashforth, 2003; Vuori, San, & Kira, 2012; Wagner-Marsh & Conley, 1999; Wrzesniewski, Dutton, & Debebe, 2003
Meaning-oriented volunteering & NGOs	Anderson et al., 2016; Dempsey & Sanders, 2010; Jaunmuktane, 2012; Jenkinson et al., 2013; Koschmann, 2012; Onyx & Warburton, 2003; Rodell, 2013; Wilensky, 1996; Wilson, 2000; Schnell, 2012; Schnell & Hoof, 2012; Sherman, Michel, Rybak, Randall, & Davidson, 2011; Thoits, 2012
Meaning-oriented products, fair trade, services, advertising & pricing	Abolhasani, Oakes, & Oakes, 2017; Adams & Boscarino, 2015; Buhl, 1992; Diller, Shedroff, & Rhea, 2005; Doran, 2009, 2010; Leigh, Peters, & Shelton, 2006; Liozu, Boland, Hinterbuber, &

	Perelli, 2015; Stephan Liozu, Hinterhuber, Perelli, & Boland, 2012; Pharr, 2011
Meaning-oriented education & child raising	Agger, 2015; Akbaş, 2012; Aronowitz & Giroux, 2003; Cavazos Vela, Castro, Cavazos, Cavazos, & Gonzalez, 2015; MacDonald-Dennis, 2015; Heller-Sahlgren, 2018; Hong, 2014; Kirillova, Kirillova, Abramova, Gavrilova, & Vaibert, 2017; Lengyel et al., 2019; Lin, 2013; P. M. Miller, 2012; Patton, Parker, & Pratt, 2013; Samuel, Bergman, & Hupka-Brunner, 2013; Schneider & du Plock, 2012; Seligman et al., 2009; Teschers, 2018; Wright, 2011; Yu & Ren, 2014; Giroux, 2014; MacDonald-Dennis, 2015
Meaning-oriented work/life balance, leisure time	Bailey & Fernando, 2012; Bonebright, Clay, & Ankenmann, 2000; Boniwell & Zimbardo, 2004; Burke, Jones, & Westman, 2013; Emslie & Hunt, 2009; Gao & Jin, 2015; Haar, Russo, Suñe, & Ollier-Malaterre, 2014; Hobson, 2013; Ilies, Liu, Liu, & Zheng, 2017; Iwasaki, 2007; Jones, Burke, & Westman, 2006; Judge & Watanabe, 1993; Kuo, 2015; Melamed, Meir, & Samson, 1995; Neulinger, 1982; Noonan, 2009; Rain, Lane, & Steiner, 1991; Snir & Harpaz, 2002
Meaning-oriented media & meaning-oriented use of social media	Dmitrovsky, 2019; D. Edwards & Cromwell, 2018; Giroux & Pollock, 2010; Goodwin, 2012; Green & Jenkins, 2011; Hofer, 2013; Holmes, 2008; Johnston, Tanner, Lalla, & Kawalski, 2013; Langlois, 2009; Munzel, Galan, & Meyer-Waarden, 2018; Rockwell, 2019; Holmes, 2008; Marmor-Lavie, Stout, & Lee, 2009
Meaning-oriented art, culture, & subculture	Jeon, 2018; Kwon & Park, 2018; Lewin & Williams, 2009; Seppala & Hellman, 2014; Vos, 2016
Meaning-oriented spaces & design	Kindyis, 2014; Levinthal & Warglien, 1999; Morgeson, Dierdorff, & Hmurovic, 2010; Schwanen & Wang, 2014; Spielmann, Babin, & Manthiou, 2018; Vosyliute & Kaunas, 2008; Williams, 2002; Williams & McIntyre, 2001
Meaning-oriented sports	Brady & Grenville-Cleave, 2017; Brymer, 2013; Diamant, 1991; Ronkainen, Kavoura, & Ryba, 2016; Ronkainen & Nesti, 2017
Meaning-oriented tourism	Blomfield, 2009; Caton, 2012; Cavagnaro, Staffieri, & Postma, 2018; Collins-Kreiner, 2018; Fennell, 2006; Filep, 2012; Heintzman, 2013; Jamal & Stronza, 2008; Kirillova, Lehto, & Cai, 2017, 2017a, 2017b; Kujawa, 2017; Li & Chan, 2017; Margry, 2008; Matteucci & Filep, 2017; Mattis, 2002; McCabe & Johnson, 2013; Robledo, 2015; Ross, 2013; Sirgy & Uysal, 2016; Xue, Manuel-Navarrete, & Buzinde, 2014; Zahra & McIntosh, 2007

Appendix 4. Meta-Analysis of Capitalism and Types of Meaning in Life

Table A4.1. Methodology of Meta-Analysis of Capitalism and Types of Meaning in Life

Operationalisation of meaning Individuals seem to give a uniquely subjective answer when they are asked about meaning in life. However, many individuals share similar answers. We previously conducted a systematic literature review of all research on what individuals describe as valuable, meaningful, important or motivational in life. This yielded 45,710 individuals in 107 studies. Thematic analysis identified five overarching types and 29 sub-types of meaning. The data from this review were used for secondary analyses to calculate correlations between the type and sub-types of meaning, on the one hand, and the extent to which the country in which the study was conducted can be characterised as capitalist, on the other hand. Therefore, the data in this study consist of the 107 studies on meaning in life, which have been published elsewhere (Vos, 2020). In this study, we identified five overarching types and 29 sub-types of meaning. For each study, we scored these types and sub-types in two different ways. We created a score on a scale from 1–type/subtype of meaning is totally unimportant to 5–type/subtype of meaning is totally important. If the study already included a score on a scale, this was recalculated to this 5-point scale with the same proportion (e.g. a score of 6 on a scale from 1–unimportant to 7–important was recalculated as 6/7 x 5 = 4.3). Studies that did not report a score were not included. As an alternative method, we also created a dichotomous scale from 0–type of meaning is not mentioned to 1–type of meaning is mentioned; however, this did not have enough variation between countries to show any statistical significance (e.g., 'materialist types of meanings' were reported in all countries that showed no differences between countries on a dichotomous scale, whereas countries do differ in the extent to which they focus on materialism on a 1-5 scale).
Operationalisation of capitalism Capitalism is a broad concept with many associations and many variations (e.g., Hall & Soskice, 2001; Peck & Theodore, 2005). However, many definitions describe capitalism as an economic system based on the private ownership of the means of production and their operation for profit. Characteristics of capitalism include private property, self-interest, competition, capital accumulation, wage labour, prices set by the market's supply and demand, freedom to choose consumption production and investment, and a small government. Of course, there are many variations, such as the decentralised liberal market economy of the United Kingdom and the United States, and the more coordinated market economy of Germany and Japan (Hall and Soskice, 2001). Given this pluriformity, in order to examine the relationship between the different types of meaning in life and capitalist values, a multiplicity of characteristics of capitalism should be analysed. Therefore, for each study, we identified the country in which the data was recorded, and calculated multiple capitalism scores for each country on the basis of publicly available economic data. We used six aggregate scores to operationalise capitalism. Additionally, we used five aggregate scores for phenomena that are often associated with capitalism.
Operationalisation of health We tested mental health both on the individual level as well as the country-level.
Analyses We calculated correlations between the 5 types and 29 sub-types of meaning on the one hand and the 9 characteristics of capitalism with Pearson's Correlation. We used Spearman's Rank correlations and partial correlations to examine whether the relationship between capitalism and meaning could be explained by study-related factors and cultural factors. *Mediation analyses-* We inserted the data from the 107 studies into Comprehensive Meta-Analysis software. We tested mediation via meta-regression analyses, similarly to Baron and Kenny (1986) and

Preacher and Hayes (2008), while taking the standard deviation for each study into account by data pooling and using random models. This is a relatively robust technique against violations of normality, with a priori power of .80 with medium effects at sample sizes larger than 70 (Fritz & MacKinnon, 2007). With regression analyses, mediation is assumed to be present when the types and sub-types of meaning (M) mediate the relationship between the characteristics of capitalism (C) and the mental health outcomes (H). Four mediation steps have to be fulfilled. 1. Capitalism and meaning need to correlate (C&M), which is aim 1 of this study. 2. Capitalism needs to predict mental health (C→H). 3. Meaning needs to predict mental health (M→H). 4. When meaning is included in the analyses, capitalism explains mental health less as compared with Step 2 (C→M→H). Either the beta decreases but remains significant (i.e., 'partial mediation') or the beta becomes non-significant (i.e., 'complete mediation').

We use the expression 'direct effect' to indicate that the capitalism directly predicts mental health, and that the Beta is not influenced by the inclusion of meaning in analyses (i.e., mediation in Step 4 is not significant). We use the expression 'indirect effect' to indicate that capitalism indirectly predicts the outcomes via the partial or complete mediation of meaning (i.e., mediation in Step 4 is significant). The word 'effect' without adjective indicates analyses between variables I–P, I–O or P–O in steps 1, 2, and 3. Steps 2–4 were calculated with linear regression analysis and standardized betas (cf. Vos, 2011). Effect sizes were described with Pearson's correlation coefficients (.10 is small, .30 moderate, .50 large), and f^2 in case of multiple regression (.02 is small, .15 medium, .35 large). Alpha was set at .05 and was not corrected for number of statistical estimations because of this study's explorative aim.

Table A4.2. Methodology of Meta-Analysis on Capitalism and Types of Meaning in Life: National Measures Included in the Study

Construct	Name	Description	Authors
Direct measures of capitalism	Overall capitalism score (OC)	Overall score based on privatisation, competitiveness, and economic freedom (see below)	Pryor, 2010
	Privatisation (PR)	Overall score based on: substantial and legally protected private ownership of the means of production, which includes: Private investment as a share of total investment; Rule of law; Judicial independence; Impartial courts; Protection of intellectual property; Law and order; Legal enforcement of contracts; Judicial indicators combined (Pryor, 2010)	Gwartney et al., 2007; Heritage Foundation 2008; Beach and Kane, 2008
	Competitiveness (CO)	Overall score for competitive markets, based on Business freedom; Price controls; Competition in domestic banking; Collective bargaining at central level (Pryor, 2010)	Gwartney et al., 2007; Heritage Foundation 2008; Beach and Kane, 2008
	Economic freedom (EF)	Overall score based on: lack of interest rate regulation; Trade freedom; Investment freedom; Financial freedom; Labour freedom (Pryor, 2010)	Gwartney et al., 2007; Heritage Foundation 2008; Beach and Kane, 2008
	Market competitiveness (MC)	The extent to which the market is coordinated either by the market or by strategy	Hall and Gingerich, 2004
Indirect measures of capitalism	Political freedom (PC)	The extent of political freedom was measured, as several neoliberal economists such as Friedman (1980) have argued that economic freedom is a necessary and sufficient condition for political freedom.	Pryor, 2010
	Social mobility (SM)	The movement of individuals and groups within or between socio-economic strata in a society	World Bank, 2018
	GINI coefficient (GINI)	Socio-economic inequality	World Bank, 2018
	Gross Domestic Product (GDP)	To compensate for irrelevant exchange rate variations, we used GDP based on purchasing-power parity.	Credit Suisse, 2017
Mental health	Individual mental health (IMH)	Pooled scores on a wide range of psychometric instruments	Vos, 2019

		measuring mental health in the studies included in the meta-analyses	
	Average mental health in a country (MHC)	Average mental health in a country	OECD (www.oecd.com, 21 June 2019)
	Average life satisfaction in a country (LSC)	Average life satisfaction in a country	OECD (www.oecd.com, 21 June 2019)
	Average Better Life Index in a country (BLI)	The Average Better Life Index in a country includes a variety of benchmarks reflecting the overall quality of life in a country (housing, income, jobs, community, education, environment, governance, health, life satisfaction, safety and work-life balance).	OECD (www.oecd.com, 21 June 2019)
Covariables	Cultural dimensions	Individualism-collectivism, uncertainty avoidance, power distance, masculinity–femininity, long-term orientation, indulgence–self-restraint	Hofstede: www.hofstedeinsight.com, 19 June 2019
	Study-related factors	year of publication, sample size, male/female proportion, education level, income	

Table A4.3. Findings of Meta-Analysis on Capitalism and Types of Meaning in Life: Overview of Types of Meaning in Life

Types and sub-types of meaning in life	Characteristics of Capitalism							
	Direct characteristics					Indirect characteristics		
	Overall Capital-ism Score	Private owner-ship	Compet-itive markets	Economic freedom	Compet-itive market coordin-ation	Political freedom	Social mobility	GDP
I. MATERIALISTIC-HEDONISTIC TYPES OF MEANING								
Overall score	.40 (.01)	.32 (.05)	.44 (.01)	.36 (.05)	.42 (.01)	NS	NS	NS
Material conditions	.46 (.01)	.44 (.01)	.48 (.01)	.40 (.01)	.46 (.01)	NS	.28 (.05)	.31 (.05)
Professional–educational success	.39 (.01)	.38 (.05)	.40 (.01)	.37 (.05)	.38 (.01)	NS	.32 (.05)	.22 (.05)
Hedonist–experiential experiences	.38 (.01)	.30 (.05)	.40 (.01)	.24 (.05)	.43 (.01)	NS	NS	NS
Health	.10 (.05)	NS	.18 (.05)	.11 (.05)	.20 (.05)	.24 (.01)	.24 (.01)	.12 (.05)
Nature	-.27 (.05)	-.22 (.05)	-.34 (.01)	-.28 (.05)	-.28 (.05)	NS	NS	-.28 (.05)
II. SELF-ORIENTED TYPES OF MEANING								
Overall score	.30 (.01)	.31 (.01)	.38 (.01)	.36 (.01)	.38 (.01)	NS	NS	NS
Resilience	.23 (.05)	.21 (.05)	.26 (.01)	.20 (.05)	.28 (.01)	NS	NS	NS
Self-efficacy	.36 (.01)	.29 (.01)	.38 (.01)	.40 (.01)	.37 (.01)	.10 (.05)	NS	NS
Self-acceptance	.29 (.05)	.28 (.05)	.30 (.05)	.32 (.01)	.32 (.05)	.11 (.05)	NS	NS
Autonomy	.42 (.01)	.42 (.01)	.46 (.01)	.39 (.01)	.42 (.01)	.22 (.05)	NS	NS
Creative self-expression	.31 (.05)	.38 (.05)	.32 (.05)	.28 (.05)	.32 (.05)	.24 (.01)	.22 (.05)	NS
Self-care	.30 (.05)	.28 (.05)	.28 (.05)	.33 (.01)	.31 (.05)	NS	.25 (.05)	NS
Authenticity	-.23 (.05)	-.18 (.05)	-.26 (.01)	-.21 (.05)	-.25 (.01)	NS	NS	NS
III. SOCIAL TYPES OF MEANING								
Overall score	-.39 (.01)	-.32 (.01)	-.46 (.01)	-.35 (.01)	-.44 (.01)	NS	NS	NS
Feeling socially connected	-.30 (.05)	-.22 (.05)	-.40 (.01)	-.29 (.01)	-.43 (.01)	.20 (.05)	-.14 (.05)	-.24 (.05)
Belonging to a community	-.48 (.01)	-.42 (.01)	-.54 (.01)	-.49 (.01)	-.49 (.01)	.18 (.05)	-.25 (.05)	-.25 (.05)
Following social expectations	-.22 (.05)	-.18 (.01)	-.26 (.05)	-.23 (.05)	-.24 (.05)	.12 (.05)	-.27 (.05)	-.22 (.05)
Altruism	-.51 (.01)	-.48 (.01)	-.55 (.01)	-.46 (.01)	-.53 (.01)	NS	NS	NS
Giving birth and taking care of children	-.33 (.05)	-.29 (.01)	-.32 (.05)	-.35 (.01)	-.29 (.05)	NS	-.10 (.05)	-.16 (.05)
IV. LARGER TYPES OF MEANING								
Overall score	-.32 (.01)	-.20 (.05)	-.37 (.01)	-.32 (.05)	-.35 (.01)	NS	NS	NS
Specific purpose in life	-.33 (.05)	-.22 (.01)	-.36 (.05)	-.31 (.05)	-.33 (.05)	NS	NS	NS
Personal growth	NS	NS	NS	NS	NS	NS	NS	NS
Sense of temporality	-.30 (.05)	-.24 (.05)	-.36 (.05)	-.28 (.05)	-.38 (.05)	NS	NS	NS
Justice & ethics	-.34 (.05)	-.32 (.05)	-.38 (.01)	-.35 (.05)	-.36 (.01)	.20 (.05)	NS	-.25 (.05)
Spirituality & religion	-.28 (.05)	NS	-.30 (.05)	-.25 (.05)	-.31 (.05)	-.14 (.05)	NS	NS
V. EXISTENTIAL-PHILOSOPHICAL MEANINGS								
Overall score	NS	NS	NS	NS	NS	NS	NS	NS
Being-alive	NS	NS	NS	NS	NS	NS	NS	NS
Uniqueness	.10 (.05)	NS	.18 (.05)	.20 (.05)	.20 (.05)	NS	NS	NS
Connectedness with the world	NS	NS	NS	NS	NS	NS	NS	NS
Individual freedom	.09 (.01)	.06 (.05)	.14 (.05)	10 (.05)	.14 (.05)	.26 (.01)	.22 (.05)	NS

Individual responsibility	-.10 (.05)	-.11 (.05)	-.18 (.05)	-.12 (.05)	-.14 (.05)	NS	NS	NS
Gratitude to life as a gift	-.24 (.05)	-.18 (.05)	-.25 (.05)	-.01 (.01)	-.22 (.05)	NS	NS	NS

Note: *Each cell represents: Pearson's Correlation between a score on the (sub)type of meaning and a score on a characteristic of capitalism (p-value). NS Not Significant.*

Table A4.4. Findings of Meta-Analysis on Capitalism in Life: Results from the Mediation Regression Analyses

Predicted mental health (H)	Characteristics of capitalism (C)								Type of meaning (M)					Total model statistic *f²*
	Privatisation	Compe-titiveness	Economic freedom	Competitive market coordination	Political freedom	Social mobility	Gini	GDP	Materialistic & hedonistic	Self-oriented	Social	Larger	Existential-philosophical	
Individual mental health	-.15/ns	-.39/ns	-.20/ns	-.33/ns	.46/.20	.39/.15	-.38/ns	Ns	-.54	-.39	.51	.39	.28	.65
Average country mental health	-.23/ns	-.31/ns	-.19/ns	-.32/ns	.42/.28	.32/.11	-.42/ns	Ns	-.48	-.36	.49	.37	Ns	.54
Average country life satisfaction	-.15/ns	-.28/ns	-.21/ns	-.29/ns	.29/.17	.26/.09	-.32/ns	Ns	-.46	-.34	.41	.33	Ns	.44
Average country Better Life Index	.12/ns	.19/ns	.13/ns	.12/ns	.19/.11	.18/.06	-.16/ns	ns	-.28	-.27	.29	.28	ns	.39

Note: *Table shows standardized betas for mental health-variables (H) predicted directly by capitalism variables (C) or by the types of meaning in life (M), or by mediation (C→M→H). The overall capitalism score was not included, as its* *sub-components were already included in the regression model. Subtypes of meaning in life showed similar findings as types of meaning, but these are not presented to keep this table simple. Only significant predictors, mediators, and total models are presented. P-values <.05. R^2 is an explained variance of total model, f^2 the corresponding effect size. Constant and error terms are not presented to keep table simple. The mediation rows show two betas for capitalism: prediction without/with inclusion of the meaning-mediators in the regression equation; a reduction of the ß implies partial mediation (e.g., .81/.40); when ß become non-significant (ns), this implies complete mediation (e.g., .81/ns).*

Appendix 5. Interview study

Table A5.1. Methodology of Interview Study

Interview questions
The interview consisted of the following questions: 'What do you experience as your meaning in life?' 'How do you know what is meaningful in your life, and what is not meaningful?' 'How do you feel that capitalism helps you to experience meaning in life?' 'How do you feel that capitalism hinders you to experience meaning in life?' 'How does capitalism influence your moods and mental health?' 'Do you feel that you will be able to overcome the limitations of capitalism on your life, and if so: how?' Prompts and follow-up questions were aimed at stimulating the participants to elaborate their answer, clarify, give examples, and summarise.
Recruitment
Individuals were recruited online via social media, and interviews were conducted via Zoom.us Inclusion criteria included: self-identified pro-capitalist or anti-capitalist attitudes, speaking English, and not suffering from psychosis or any other cognitive impairment that could impact the interview. As there were more eligible participants than needed for this study, capitalist and non-capitalist participants were selected one by one on the basis of matching age, education, and income. This study was conducted between November 2017 and April 2018 by British company Meaning Online Ltd and followed the ethical guidelines of the British Psychological Society.
Analysis
The data were analysed with Interpretative Phenomenological Analysis (Smith, 2012).

Table A5.2. Findings of Interview Study: Socio-Demographic Characteristics of Participants

Socio-demographic variable	Capitalist participants	Non-capitalist participants
Age	M= 41.4 years, SD= 7.1 years	M= 39.9 years, SD=9.2 years
Years of education	M=15.6 years, SD=3.2 years	M=17.3 years, SD=2.8 years
Gender	4 men, 4 women	4 men, 4 women
Average annual income in USD	M=45.259 USD, SD=27.235	M=38.241, SD=23.450
Country	UK=4, USA=2, Ireland=1, Netherlands=1	UK=4, USA=2, Germany=1, Netherlands=1

M=mean, SD= Standard Deviation

Table A5.3. Findings of Interview Study: Overarching Themes and Themes Derived from the Interviews of 8 Self-Proclaimed Capitalists and 8 Self-Proclaimed Anti-Capitalists

Interview question	Capitalists (total N=8)	Anti-capitalists (total N=8)
'What do you experience as your meaning in life?'	**Materialistic meanings (8)** -Being successful in job (8) -Buying stuff (6) -Living in a good house and good physical circumstances (5) **Hedonistic meanings (6)** -Joyful experiences (holiday, food, leisure) (6) **Self-oriented meanings (6)** -Perseverance (5) -Autonomy (5) **Social meanings (7)** -Connections with family (6) -Connections with friends (6) -Giving birth and raising children (4) **Larger meanings (3)** -Spirituality or religion (3) -Personal growth (2) **Existential-philosophical meanings (3)** -Individual freedom (2) -Uniqueness (1)	**Hedonistic meanings (5)** -Connection with animals and nature (5) **Self-oriented meanings (5)** -Authenticity (4) -Resilience (3) **Social meanings (8)** -Helping others (8) -Connections with family (7) -Connections with friends (7) -Belonging to a community (7) -Giving birth and raising children (5) **Larger meanings (8)** -Ethics and justice (8) -Specific purpose in life (4) -Personal growth (3) -Spirituality or religion (3) -Temporality (2) **Existential–philosophical meanings (5)** -Individual responsibility (5) -Connectedness with the world (3) -Individual freedom (1) -Gratitude to life (1)
'How do you know what is meaningful in your life, and what is not meaningful?'	**Randomness of meaning (6)** -There is no absolute true meaning (5) -Any type of meaning can be replaced by any other random type of meaning (4) -'I just do what I do' (2) **Demanding approaches (4)** -Feeling in control of realising one's meaning (4) -Setting goals and expecting life will fulfill these (3) **Traditional approaches (3)**	**Intuition (6)** -Meditation or mindfulness (3) -Personal journey and self-insight (2) -Intuition (2) -Perceiving meaning (2) **Critical analyses of what we are told is meaningful by others, and particularly by advertisements and social media (6)** **Absoluteness of meaning (4)** -Meaning is beyond doubt (4) -Universal truth of meaning (2)

	-Doing what others do (2) -Following religion (2) -Following expectations from others (1)	**Traditional approaches (2)** -Guidance from spirituality (2)
'How do you feel capitalism helps you to experience meaning in life?'	**Capitalism gives money and opportunity for meaning (8)** -Money helps to buy meaningful experiences (6) -Capitalism gives many meaningful opportunities due to competition (3) -Being able to do a job that feels meaningful to me (3)	**Stimulates materialistic and self-oriented types of meaning (6)** -Helping individuals to realise self-oriented meanings in life (4) -Helping individuals to realise material dreams (3)
'How do you feel that capitalism hinders you to experience meaning in life?'	**Social limitations (8)** -Poor work/life balance, e.g., little time for family (7) -Uncertainty (2) **Climate crisis (1)**	**Individual limitations (6)** -Difficult or impossible to live outside of capitalist values (6) -Being powerless (6) -Having to work for an employer (4) **Social limitations (8)** -Stimulation of materialism (7) -Stimulation of selfishness (6) -Disrupting communities & loneliness (4) **Ecological and climate crisis (4)**
'How does capitalism influence your moods and mental health?'	**Positive mood (8)** -Happiness (5) -Flow and passion (2) **Negative mood (5)** -Lack of life fulfillment and emptiness of life (4) -Irritability and burnout (4) -Uncertainty and anxiety about future (4) -Decision-making problems (3) -Depression (1)	**Negative mood (8)** -Uncertainty and anxiety (8) -Helplessness and fatalism (7) -Depression (3) -Emptiness of life (3) -Loneliness (3)
'Do you feel that you will be able to overcome the limitations of capitalism in your life, and, if so, how?'	**Limitations cannot be completely overcome (5)** **Sources of overcoming limitations (4)** -Self-development (2) -Skills development (2)	**Limitations cannot be completely overcome (7)** **Sources of overcoming limitations (8)** -Anti-capitalist struggle as a community, e.g., via unions or protests (4)

		-Self-development and meditation/mindfulness (2) -Perseverance (2) -Skills development (2)

Note: *Numbers reflect the number of participants who reported this theme or subtheme. Texts in **bold font** are overall themes; texts in* regular *font are sub-themes.*

Appendix 6. Worldwide Survey of Meaning in Life

Table A6.1. Hypotheses of Worldwide Survey of Meaning in Life

(1)	The following experiences have strong relationships with one another (either in the form of The Capitalist Life Syndrome or The Economic Meaning-Orientation): (a) Capitalist values (b) Prioritising meaning in daily life decisions (c) Types of meaning (d) A functionalistic versus an intuitive–critical approach to meaning (e) Fatalism, determinism, and lack of controllability (f) Existential moods (g) Mental health and quality of life, mediated by types of meaning
(2)	Unfulfilled meaning in life: (a) There is a significance difference between imagined types/sub-types of meaning and realised types/sub-types of meaning (b) The realisation of meaning depends on individual income, national GDP, social mobility, political freedom. and socio-economic equality (c) The fulfillment of meaning (i.e., the difference between imagined and realised meaning) correlates positively with mental health (d)
(3)	Covariables: Cultural and socio-demographic variables do not correlate with: (a) Types of meaning, economic values, and mental health; (b) The tested relationships in hypotheses 1–3.

Table A6.2. Methodology of Worldwide Survey of Meaning in Life

---

Overall

In contrast to studies 1–3, Study 4 included both characteristics of the economy and health of the country in which the participant lives and individual variables. The next table will show the questionnaires that operationalised the constructs in this study.

Method for hypothesis 1

Hypothesis 1 was tested by calculating Pearson's correlations between the variables. As further validation and to test the mediation effects, a Structural Equation Model (SEM) was developed on the basis of the hypotheses and the multiple operationalisations of each variable. Initially, multilevel SEM was developed to test the degree and effects of dependency between individuals within a country. Missing data was imputed with multiple regression imputation (Schafer, 1997; Little & Rubin, 2002). *Mplus* was used, which allows multiple likelihood estimation of multilevel SEM with robust standard errors and χ^2 test of model of fit (Muthen & Muthen, 2004). Fit indices included chi-square values, Comparative Fit Index (CFI), Standardised Root Mean Residuals (SRMR), and Root-Mean-Square Error of Approximation (RMSEA), with a 90% confidence interval, and the p for test of close fit. A good model fit would mean that chi-square is non-significant—preferably with a p-value of about .50—CFI is larger than .90, TLFI larger than .95, and RMSEA is smaller than .08.

Method for hypothesis 2

Hypothesis 2 was tested by using Student T-tests and standardised Cohen's D for the difference between imagined and realised types and sub-types of meaning. Pearson's correlations were calculated between realised types and sub-types of meaning and individual income, national GDP, social mobility, political freedom, and socio-economic equality. Pearson's correlations also described the relationship between the fulfillment of meaning (i.e., the difference between imagined and realised meaning) and mental health. These hypotheses were further tested by inclusion of these variables in SEM.

Method for hypothesis 3

Hypothesis 3 was tested by using Pearson's correlations and partial correlations between cultural and socio-demographic variables, and all the other variables included in this study. This was further tested by inclusion in SEM.

Recruitment

This study was advertised via social media and free and paid survey websites between April and July 2019 at the Metanoia Institute in London and received approval from the Metanoia ethical committee.

Table A6.3. Psychometric Instruments Included in Worldwide Survey of Meaning in Life

Hypothesis		Questionnaire	Scales	Authors
1	Capitalist values	Materialist Values Scale (MVS)	Materialism (overall score)	Richins & Dawson, 1992
		Economic Values Inventory (EVI)	Economic Unfairness (EVI-EU), Economic Efficacy (EVI-EF), Anti-Price Controls (EVI-PC), Anti-business (EVI-AB), Anti-social Welfare EVI-AS)	O'Brien & Ingels, 1987
		World's Smallest Political Quiz (WSPQ)	Liberal–conservative (WSPQ-LC), Left-right (WSPQ-LR)	McGee, 2016
		Country-specific characteristics of capitalism	See Table A4.2.	See Table A4.2.
	Basing decisions in daily life on meaning	Prioritising Meaning Questionnaire (PMQ)	Prioritising Meaning (overall score)	Russo-Netzer, 2018
	Imagined types of meaning	Meaning Quintet Questionnaire Imagined meanings version (MQQ-I)	Imagined materialistic–hedonistic type of meaning (MQQ-I-M), Imagined self-oriented type of meaning (MQQ-I-S), Imagined social type of meaning (MQQ-I-So), Imagined larger type of meaning (MQQ-I-L), Imagined existential–philosophical type of meaning (MQQ-I-E)	Vos, 2019, 2018, 2016
	Functionalistic versus intuitive-critical approach to meaning	Meaning Attitude Scale (MAS)	Traditional approach (MAS-T), Functionalistic approach (MAS-F), Critical–intuitive approach to meaning (MAS-CI)	Vos, 2019b
	Fatalism, determinism, and lack of controllability	Free Will and Determinism Scale (FWDS)	Free will (FWDS-W) Scientific determinism (FWDS-S), Fatalistic determinism (FWDS-F), Randomness (FWDS-R)	Vohs & Schooler, 2008
	Existential moods	World Assumptions Questionnaire (WAQ)	Controllability of events (WAQ-E), Comprehensibility (WAQ-C), Predictability of people (WAQ-P), Trustworthiness (WAQ-T), Goodness of people (WAQ-G), Safety and vulnerability (WAQ-S)	Kaler, 2009
		Psychological Well-Being Scale (PWBS)	Self-acceptance (PWBS-S), Mastery (PWBS-M), Autonomy (PWBS-A),	Ryff, 1989

			Relationships (PWBS-R), Personal growth (PWBS-G), Purpose in life (PWBS-P)	
		Meaning in Life Questionnaire (MLQ)	Presence of meaning (MLQ-P), Search for meaning (MLQ-S)	Steger, 2012
	Mental health and quality of life	Satisfaction with Life Scale (SWLW)	Life satisfaction (overall score)	Diener, Emmons, Larsen, Griffin, 1985
		PANAS Positive Affect / Negative Affect Scale (PANAS)	Positive affects (PANAS-P), Negative affects (PANAS-N)	Thompson, 2007
		SF-6D	Quality of life (overall score)	Whitehurst, Bryan & Lewis, 2011
2	Imagined types of meaning	See above	See above	See above
	Realised types of meaning	Meaning Quintet Questionnaire (MQQ) – realised meanings version	Realised materialistic–hedonistic type of meaning, Realised self-oriented type of meaning, Realised social type of meaning, Realised larger type of meaning, Realised existential–philosophical type of meaning	Vos, 2019, 2018
	Unfulfilled types of meaning	Calculation of scores: Imagined MQQ – Realised MQQ	Unfulfilled Meaning	Vos, 2019
	Individual income, national GDP, social mobility, political freedom, and socio-economic equality	Individual income	Financial Well-Being Scale – Short	CFPB, 2019
		National GDP	See Table A4.2.	See Table A4.2.
		Social mobility	See Table A4.2.	See Table A4.2.
		Political freedom	See Table A4.2.	See Table A4.2.
		Socio-economic equality	See Table A4.2.	See Table A4.2.
3	Cultural dimensions	Hofstede's cultural dimensions	See Table A4.2.	See Table A4.2.
	Socio-demographic variables	Vos' Socio-demographics & Living Situation Questionnaire (VSLQ)	World region Country Region type Housing Age Gender Sexual orientation Years of education Work type Sense of ethnic belonging Religion Active in religion Relationship status Children number Large life changes in last year Income in USD	Vos, 2011, 2019

Acronyms are shown between (brackets).

Table A6.4. Socio-Demographic Characteristics of the Sample in the Worldwide Survey of Meaning in Life

Sociodemographic characteristic	Results	Results
Total N		1281
Country**	**Europe**	
	United Kingdom	113
	Netherlands	57
	Austria	32
	Germany	25
	France	23
	Italy	16
	Hungary	13
	Poland	9
	Spain	8
	Iceland	8
	Portugal	6
	Romania	6
	Belgium	6
	Luxemburg	3
	Switzerland	3
	Greece	2
	Croatia	1
	Serbia	1
	North America	
	United States	87
	Canada	64
	Latin & South America	
	Brazil	47
	Colombia	21
	Chile	19
	British Guiana	11
	Surinam	9
	Trinidad	7
	Paraguay	1
	Africa	
	Ghana	21
	South Africa	19
	Uganda	17
	Tunisia	16
	Mozambique	13
	Morocco	12
	Russia	97
	Middle East	
	Israel	47

	United Arabic Emirates	36
	Palestine	23
	Egypt	21
	Pakistan	9
	Lebanon	5
	Syria	2
	Southeast Asia	
	India	98
	Japan	67
	Philippines	32
	Indonesia	21
	Malaysia	19
	Singapore	13
	Australasia	
	Australia	53
	New Zealand	42
Region type	Large city	691
	Small city	237
	Village	256
	Countryside	97
Housing situation	Living with partner	362
	Living with partner and child(ren)	321
	Living alone	259
	Living with extended family	183
	Living with others (non-relatives)	156
Age (mean, st. dev.)		31.4 (11.2)
Gender	Female	730
	Male	540
	Non-binary	11
Sexual orientation	Heterosexual	1061
	Homosexual or bisexual	217
Years of education (mean, st. dev.)		9.7 (6.7)
Work situation	Employed	431
	Self-employed	329
	Student	267
	Unemployed	131
	Retired or sick	123
Work type	Vocationally trained craftsperson, technician, IT specialist, nurse, artist or similar	551
	Generally trained office worker or secretary	231
	Academically trained professional or similar	141
	Unskilled or semi-skilled manual worker	216
	Manager	139
Sense of ethnic belonging	To a majority group	1037
	To a minority group	123
	To a very small minority group	121
Religion	Roman Catholic	398

378

(multiple possible)	Protestant	207
	Muslim	321
	None	298
	Hindu	176
	Spiritual or Something-ist	165
	Buddhist	115
	Jewish	57
	Daoism, Confucianism, Shinto, or Jainism	32
	Sikh	13
	Other	39
Relationship status	Married	451
	Single	327
	Relationship	324
	Widowed	121
	Other	58
Children	None	499
	Pregnant	127
	Number of children (mean, standard deviation)	2.1 (1.7)
Large life change in last year	None	671
	Yes	610
Salary in US Dollars (mean, standard deviation)		$31,671 ($23,319)

Note: *Figures present numbers and (percentages of total sample between brackets). *Calculated score on the basis of answers; **Only described if mentioned by more than 10% of participants; N=number; M=mean; SD=Standard Deviation*

Table A6.5. Findings of Worldwide Survey of Meaning in Life: Pooled Between-Individuals and Between-Countries Correlation Matrices of the Latent Variables

	Capitalist characteristics of country (non-capitalist to capitalist)	Individual capitalistic values (non-capitalist to capitalist)	Individual types of meaning (material–hedonistic–self-oriented to social-larger types)	Individual approach to meaning (critical–intuition to functionalism)	Individual sense of freedom (no freedom to full freedom)	Individual existential concerns (no concerns for many concerns)	Individual well-being (bad well-being to good well-being)
Capitalist characteristics of country	-	.52**	.46**	.42*	.37*	.44*	.35*
Individual capitalistic values	.88**	-	.52**	.46**	.42*	.46**	.34*
Individual types of meaning	.80**	.93**	-	.49**	.39**	.43*	.36*
Individual approach to meaning	.71**	.89**	.86**	-	.37**	.47*	.37*
Individual sense of freedom	.63**	.79*	.76**	.56*	-	.39*	.33*
Individual existential concerns	.66*	.69*	.70*	.71*		-	.36*
Individual well-being	.59*	.59*	.66**	.64**			-

Note: *Explanation of the range of the scores on each latent variable is described between (brackets). The lower and upper matrices are the pooled between-individuals and between-countries correlation matrices, respectively, *p<.05. **p<.01.*

Table A6.6. Findings of Worldwide Survey of Meaning in Life: A Multilevel Structural Equation Model on The Capitalist Life Syndrome and the Economic Meaning-Orientation

The meaning of the acronyms of the observed variables (in boxes) can be found in the tables above. The circles represent the latent variables. For simplicity, the measurement errors, disturbances, and covariances among exogenous latent variables are not presented. Be aware that four perspectives of the Capitalist Life Syndrome are not operationalised in this model, as these perspectives are more abstract in nature and/or are already measured by other variables included in this model due to conceptual overlap.

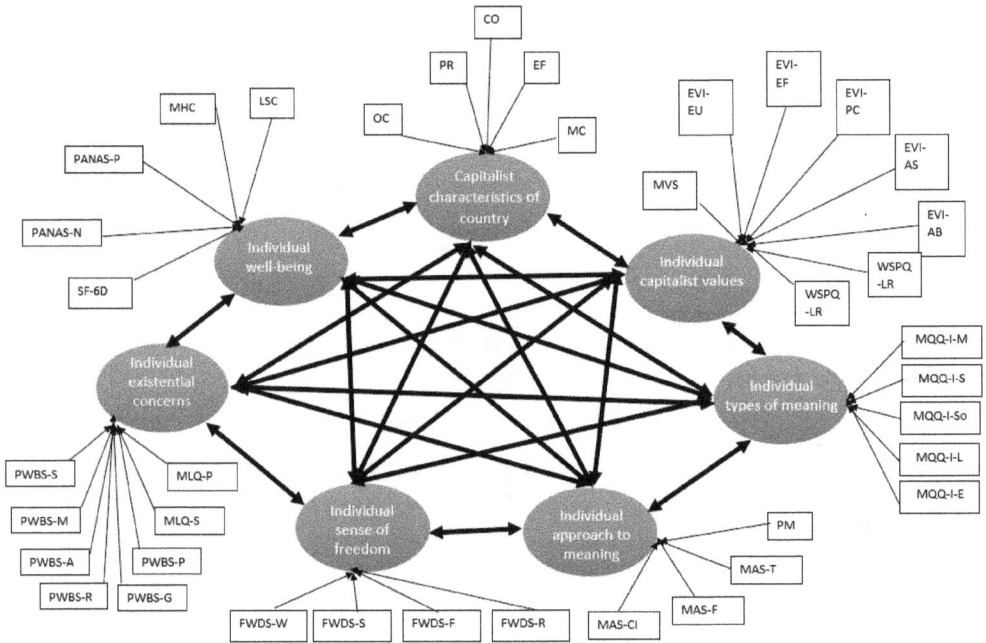

References

Abramovitz, M., & Withorn, A. (2018). Playing by the rules: Welfare reform and the new authoritarian state. In *Without justice for all*:151–172. Routledge: New York.

Achterhuis, H. (2010). *De utopie van de vrije markt.* Lemniscaat: Utrecht.

Achterhuis, H. (1988). *Het rijk van de schaarste: van Thomas Hobbes tot Michel Foucault.* Ambo: Baarn.

Abdullah, T., & Brown, T. L. (2011). Mental illness stigma and ethnocultural beliefs, values, and norms: An integrative review. *Clinical Psychology Review*, 31(6): 934–948.

Ackerman, B., & Alstott, A. (1999). *The stakeholder society.* Yale University Press: London.

Adler, N. E., & Newman, K. (2002). Socio-economic disparities in health: pathways and policies. *Health Affairs*, 21(2), 60–76.

Adorno, T. W., & Horkheimer, M. (1944/1997). *Dialectic of enlightenment.* Verso: London.

Adorno, T. (1964/2002). *The jargon of authenticity.* Routledge: London.

Adorno, T., Frenkel-Brenswik, E., Levinson, D. J., & Sanford, R. N. (1950/2019). *The authoritarian personality.* Verso Books: London.

Agamben, G. (2020). The Invention of a Pandemic. *European Journal of Psychoanalysis.* [Advanced online version]

Aghion, P., & Griffith, R. (2008). *Competition and growth: reconciling theory and evidence.* MIT press: Cambridge MA.

Aghion, P., Akcigit, U., & Howitt, P. (2014). What do we learn from Schumpeterian growth theory?. In *Handbook of economic growth*: 515–563). Elsevier: Cambridge MA.

Akerlof, G. A., & Shiller, R. J. (2010). *Animal spirits: How human psychology drives the economy, and why it matters for global capitalism.* Princeton University Press: New Jersey.

Akerlof, G. A., & Kranton, R. (2010). Identity economics. *The Economists' Voice*, 7(2): 30–45.

Akerlof, G. A., & Kranton, R. E. (2000). Economics and identity. *The Quarterly Journal of Economics*, 115(3): 715–753.

Aldana, S. G., Sutton, L. D., Jacobson, B. H., & Quirk, M. G. (1996). Relationships between leisure time physical activity and perceived stress. *Perceptual and Motor skills, 82*(1), 315-321.

Alexander, R. (2017). *The biology of moral systems.* Routledge: London.

Alexandersson, G., & Hultén, S. (2006). *Competitive tenders in passenger railway services: Looking into the theory and practice of different approaches in Europe.* University of Trieste: Trieste.

Alinsky, S. D. (1971/1989). *Rules for radicals: A practical primer for realistic radicals.* Vintage: New York.

Althusser, L. (1971/2014). *On the reproduction of capitalism: Ideology and ideological state apparatuses.* Verso: London.

Anderson, P. (2000). Renewals. *New Left Review*, 2(1): 11.

Apter, E. (2018). *Unexceptional politics: On obstruction, impasse, and the impolitic.* Verso: London.

Arendt, H. (1964). *Eichmann in Jerusalem.* Viking: New York.

Aristotle, A. (unknown/2019). *Aristotle's politics.* Clarendon: Oxford.

Aristotle, A. (unknown/2019a). *Aristotle's ethics.* Clarendon: Oxford.

Armstrong, G. (2020). The billionaires behind the crisis. *Eyes on the ties.* https://news.littlesis.org/2020/04/01/the-billionaires-behind-the-crisis-how-the-rich-powerful-put-their-wealth-above-public-health/?fbclid=IwAR0eGgfCI8agnJjMmCLfutSsXHt6vxlVAskZ1PqIfjeIQtrjynviLJZpM-g

Armstrong, J. (2002). *Conditions of love: The philosophy of intimacy.* Norton: London.

Armstrong, K. (2006). *The great transformation: The beginning of our religious traditions.* Anchor: Harlow.

Arnold, A. (2017). Why YouTube stars influence millennials more than traditional celebrities. *Forbes*, 20 June 2017.

Aronowitz, S., & Giroux, H. A. (2003*). Education under siege: The conservative, liberal and radical debate over schooling.* Routledge: London.

Atkinson, D., & Elliott, L. (2008). *The gods that failed: How blind faith in markets has cost us our future.* Random House: New York.

Augar, P. (2005). *The greed merchants: How the investment banks played the free.* Penguin: London.

Austin, R., & Tjernstrom, M. (2003). *Funding of political parties and election campaigns.* Cambridge University Press: Cambridge

Badiou, A. (2001). On evil: An interview with Alain Badiou, by Cox, C. & Whallen, M. *Cabinet*, 5: 1–5.

Babiak, P., & Hare, R. D. (2007). *Snakes in suits.* HarperCollins: New York.

Bains, G. (2011). *Meaning Inc: The blueprint for business success in the 21st century.* Profile Books: London.

Bales, K. (2012). *Disposable people: New slavery in the global economy, updated with a new preface.* University of California: California.

Bargh, M. (Ed.). (2007). *Resistance: An indigenous response to neoliberalism.* Huia Publishers: New Zealand.

Barrett, G. (1921). *Objections to anarchism.* Freedom Press: London.

Barro, R. J., & McCleary, R. (2003). *Religion and economic growth.* Harvard University: Cambridge MA.

Bassiry, G. R., & Jones, M. (1993). Adam Smith and the ethics of contemporary capitalism. *Journal of Business Ethics*, 12(8), 621–627.

Bastow, S., & Martin, J. (2003). *Third way discourse: European ideologies in the twentieth century.* Edinburgh University Press: Edinburgh.

Baten, J., & Mumme, C. (2013). Does inequality lead to civil wars? A global long-term study using anthropometric indicators (1816–1999). *European Journal of Political Economy*, 32: 56–79.

Baudrillard, J. (1998). *The Consumer Society*, (trans. Chris Turner).

Bauman, A. E. (2004). Updating the evidence that physical activity is good for health: an epidemiological review 2000–2003. *Journal of science and medicine in sport*, 7(1), 6-19.

Bauman, Z. (2013). *Liquid modernity*. John Wiley & Sons: London.

Baumol, W.J., Litan, R. E., & Schramm, C.J. (2007). *Good capitalism, bad capitalism, and the economics of growth and prosperity*. Yale University Press: London.

Beck, U. (2009). *World at risk*. Polity: London.

Beck, U., Lash, S., & Wynne, B. (1992). *Risk society: Towards a new modernity*. SAGE: London.

Becker, G. S. (1976). Altruism, egoism, and genetic fitness: Economics and sociobiology. *Journal of Economic Literature*, 14(3): 817–826.

Becker, G. (1996). *Preferences and values. Accounting for taste*. Harvard University Press: Cambridge MA.

Bekoff, M. (2000). Animal emotions: Exploring passionate. *BioScience*, 50(10): 861–870.

Benford, R. D., & Snow, D. A. (2000). Framing processes and social movements: An overview and assessment. *Annual review of sociology*, 26(1), 611–639.

Benjamin, W. (1996). Capitalism as religion. *Selected writings*, 1: 1913–1926. Harvard University Press: Cambridge MA

Benn, T. (2013). *The Benn Diaries: 1940–1990*. Random House: London.

Bentham, J. (1789/1970). *An introduction to the principles of morals*. Athlone: London.

Berberoglu, & Al-Sayed. (2019). *The Palgrave handbook of social movements, revolution, and social transformation*. B. Berberoglu (Ed.). Palgrave Macmillan.

Berkman, L. F., Kawachi, I., & Glymour, M. M. (Eds.). (2014). *Social epidemiology*. Oxford University Press: Oxford.

Berlin, I. (2017). Two concepts of liberty. In *Liberty reader* (pp. 33–57). Routledge.

Berman, M. (2009). *The politics of authenticity: Radical individualism and the emergence of modern society*. Verso: London.

Bernays, E. L. (1965/2015a). *Biography of an idea: The founding principles of public relations*. Open Road: London.

Bernays, E. L. (1923/2015). *Crystallizing public opinion*. Open Road: London.

Best, P., Manktelow, R., & Taylor, B. (2014). Online communication, social media and adolescent wellbeing: A systematic narrative review. *Children and Youth Services Review*, 41, 27-36. Biondi, M., & Zannino, L. (1997). Psychological stress, neuroimmunomodulation, and susceptibility to infectious diseases in animals and man: a review. *Psychotherapy & Psychosomatics*, 66(1), 23.

Billing, E. (1951). *Our calling*. Augustana Book Concern: Rock Island.

Bintliff, J. (2002). *Going to market in antiquity*. Franz Steiner: Stuttgart.

Bjørkdahl, K., & Carlsen, B. (2019). Introduction: Pandemics, publics, and politics—Staging responses to public health crises. In *Pandemics, Publics, and Politics*. Palgrave: Singapore.

Blum, U., & Dudley, L. (2001). Religion and economic growth: Was Weber right? *Journal of Evolutionary Economics*, 11(2): 207–30.

Boddy, C. R. (2011). The corporate psychopaths theory of the global financial crisis. *Journal of Business Ethics*, 102(2): 255–259.

Bok, D. (2010). *The politics of happiness: What government can learn from the new research on well-being*. Princeton University Press: New Jersey.

Bollier, D., & Helfrich, S. (Eds.). (2014). *The wealth of the commons: A world beyond market and state*. Levellers Press: Amherst MA.

Bookchin, M. (1982). *The ecology of freedom*. New Dimensions Foundation: London.

Boswijk, A., Thijssen, T., & Peelen, E. (2007). *The experience economy: A new perspective*. Pearson Education: Harlow.

Boudreaux, D. (1994). Schumpeter and Kirzner on competition and equilibrium. *The Market Process: Essays in Contemporary Austrian Economics*. Elgar: Aldershot.

Bourdieu, P. (1998). *Practical reason: On the theory of action*. Stanford University Press: Redwood.

Bourdieu, P. (2013). *Distinction: A social critique of the judgement of taste*. Routledge: London.

Bouzenita, A. I., & Boulanouar, A. W. (2016). Maslow's hierarchy of needs: An Islamic critique. *Intellectual Discourse*, 24(1): 62–81.

Bowles, S., & Gintis, H. (2013). *A cooperative species: Human reciprocity and its evolution*. Princeton University Press: New Jersey.

Bowman, K., & Rugg, A. (2010). *TARP, the auto bailout, and the stimulus: Attitudes about the economic crisis*. American Enterprise Institute for Public Policy Research: Washington DC.

Bowman, K., & Rugg, A. (2010). *Polls on the environment and global warming*. American Enterprise Institute for Public Policy Research: Washington DC.

Bowman, A., Folkman, P., Froud, J., Johal, S., Law, J., Leaver, A., ... & Williams, K. (2013). *The Great Train Robbery: rail privatisation and after*. Centre for Research on Socio-Cultural Change: Manchester.

Brown, W. (2019). *In the ruins of neoliberalism: The rise of antidemocratic politics in the West*. Columbia University Press: New York.

Boym, S. (2006). *The off-modern*. Bloomsbury: New York.

Braun, V., & Clarke, V. (2006). Using thematic analysis in psychology. *Qualitative Research in Psychology*, 3(2), 77-101.

Bregman, R. (2017). *Utopia for realists: And how we can get there*. Bloomsbury: New York.

Bronk, R., & Bronk, V. F. R. (2009). *The romantic economist: Imagination in economics*. Cambridge University Press: Cambridge.

Brooks (2020) The psychological impact of quarantine and how to reduce it: Rapid review of the evidence. *The Lancet* 395(10227): 912-920.

Bruckner, P. (2012). *The paradox of love*. Princeton University Press: New Jersey.

Buber, M. (1996). *Paths in utopia*. Syracuse University Press: New York.

Buber, M. (2002). *The Martin Buber reader: Essential writings*.

Burgoon, B. (2006). On welfare and terror: Social welfare policies and political–Economic roots of terrorism. *Journal of Conflict Resolution*, 50(2): 176–203.

Burke, B. L., Kosloff, S., & Landau, M. J. (2013). Death goes to the polls: A meta-analysis of mortality salience effects on political attitudes. *Political Psychology*, 34(2), 183–200.

Burke, B. L., Martens, A., & Faucher, E. H. (2010). Two decades of terror management theory: A meta-analysis of mortality salience research. *Personality and Social Psychology Review*, 14(2), 155–195.

Buscha, F., & Sturgis, P. (2018). Declining social mobility? Evidence from five linked censuses in England and Wales 1971–2011. *The British Journal of Sociology*, 69(1): 154–182.

Bush, R. (2010). Food riots: Poverty, power and protest. *Journal of Agrarian Change*, 10(1): 119–129.

Busby, M. (2020, 9 May). UK scientists hit back at attempts to discredit scientific basis for lockdown. *The Guardian*.

Butchireddygari L. (2020, March 19). Is one generation taking the coronavirus less seriously than others? Not really. *FiveThirtyEight*. https://fivethirtyeight.com/features/is-one-generation-taking-the-coronavirus-less-seriously-than-others-not-really/

Butler, J. (2002). *Gender trouble*. Routledge: London.

Cammaerts, B., Brooks, D., Magalhaes, J.C., Jimenez-Martinez, C. (2019). *From watchdog to attack dog. Journalistic representations of Jeremy Corbyn in the British Press*. London School of Economics Report.

Caldararo, N. L. (2013). *The Anthropology of Complex Economic Systems: Inequality, Stability, and Cycles of Crisis*. Lexington Books: Washington DC.

Campbell, T. (2014). *Adam Smith's science of morals*. Routledge: London.

Camus, A. (2012). *The rebel: An essay on man in revolt*. Vintage: New York. (Original work published in 1951)

Camus, A. (2012). *The plague*. Vintage: London.(Original work published in 1956)

Camus, A. (2013). *The myth of Sisyphus*. Penguin UK. (Original work published in 1942)

Carrington, D. (2020, 29 March). UK strategy to address pandemic threat not properly implemented. *The Guardian*.

Carter, A., Clark, H., Randle, M. (2016). *A guide to civil resistance: A bibliography of social movements and nonviolent action*. Merlin Press: London.

Cartwright, N. (2007). *Hunting causes and using them: Approaches in philosophy and economics*. Cambridge University Press: Cambridge.

Case, A., & Deaton, A. (2020). *Deaths of despair and the future of capitalism*. Princeton University Press: Princeton.

Cashdan, E. (2019). *Risk and uncertainty in tribal and peasant economies*. Routledge: London.

Cassirer, E. (1944/1992). *An essay on man: An introduction to a philosophy of human culture*. Yale University Press: London.

Cassirer, E., Kristeller, P. O., & Randall, J. H. (Eds.). (2011). *The Renaissance philosophy of man: Petrarca, Valla, Ficino, Pico, Pomponazzi, Vives*. University of Chicago Press.

Chambers, E.T. (2003/2018). *Roots for radicals: Organizing for power, action, and justice*. Bloomsbury: New York.

Chang, H. J. (2012). *23 things they don't tell you about capitalism*. Bloomsbury: New York.

Chen, C. C., Peng, M. W., & Saparito, P. A. (2002). Individualism, collectivism, and opportunism: A cultural perspective on transaction cost economics. *Journal of Management*, 28(4): 567–583.

Chenoweth, E., & Stephan, M. J. (2011). *Why civil resistance works: The strategic logic of nonviolent conflict*. Columbia University Press: New York.

Chlan, L., & Savik, K. (2011). Patterns of anxiety in critically ill patients receiving mechanical ventilatory support. *Nursing research*, 60(3 Suppl), S50.

Chomsky, N. (2011, 7 April). *The state-corporate complex: a threat to to freedom and survival*. Lecture, University of Toronto.

Chow, G.C. (2015). *China's economic transformation*. John Wiley: London.

Collins, R. (2009). *Violence: A micro-sociological theory*. Princeton University Press.

Cooper, M. (2017). *Family values: Between neoliberalism and the new social conservatism*. MIT Press: Cambridge MA.

Cronin, B. (Ed.). (2016). *Handbook of research methods and applications in heterodox economics*. Edward Elgar: Cheltenham MA.

Cruikshank, B. (1999). *The will to empower: Democratic citizens and other subjects*. Cornell University: Ithaca.

Cruver, B. (2002). *Anatomy of greed: The unshredded truth from an Enron insider*. Carroll & Graf: New York.

Curran, J. (2012). *Media and power*. Routledge: London.

Csikszentmihalyi, M. (2004). *Good business: Leadership, flow, and the making of meaning*. Penguin: London.

Csikszentmihalyi, M. (1997). *Finding flow: The psychology of engagement with everyday life*. Basic Books: London.

Cohen, N. (2018). *The know-it-alls: The rise of Silicon Valley as a political powerhouse and social wrecking ball*. Oneworld: London.

Conn, D., Lawrence, F., Lewis, P,m Carrell, S., Pegg, D., Davies, H. & Evans, R. (2020, 29 April). Revealed: the inside story of the UK's Covid-19 crisis. *The Guardian*.

Cook, P. (2002). Competition and its regulation: Key Issues. *Annals of Public and Cooperative Economics, 73*(4): 541–558.

Coolsaet, W. (2015) *Nietzsche over de wil tot macht. Foucault in zijn spoor.* Pelckmans: Turnhout.

Corbett (2020, 17 April). Episode 376 – Lies, damned lies and the coronavirus statistics. *The Corbett Report.*

Costello, A. (2020, 27 April). The government's secret science group has a shocking lack of expertise. *The Guardian.*

Cowburn, A. (2020, 5 March). Boris Johnson spokesman insists coronavirus will not delay Brexit transition. *The Independent.*

Curran, J. (2012). *Media and power.* Routledge: London.

Dabla-Norris, E (2015). *Causes and consequences of income inequality: A global perspective.* International Monetary Fund.

Dardot, P., & Laval, C. (2014). *The new way of the world: On neoliberal society.* Verso: London.

Davey, M., Kirchgaessner, S & Bosely, S. (2020, 3 June). Surgisphere: governments and WHO changed COVID-19 policy based on suspect data from tiny US company. *The Guardian.*

Davies, G. (2010). *History of money.* University of Wales Press: Cardiff.

Davies, J. (2013) *Cracked: Why psychiatry is doing more harm than good.* Icon: London.

Davies, W. (2015). *The happiness industry: How the government and big business sold us well-being.* Verso: London.

Davis, I. (2020, 8 May) COVID 19 is a statistical nonsense. *The OffGuardian.*

Davydow, D. S., Desai, S. V., Needham, D. M., & Bienvenu, O. J. (2008). Psychiatric morbidity in survivors of the acute respiratory distress syndrome: a systematic review. *Psychosomatic medicine, 70*(4), 512-519.

Day, R. J. (2005). *Gramsci is dead: Anarchist currents in the newest social movements.* Pluto Press.

Deaton, A. (2013). *The great escape: Health, wealth, and the origins of inequality.* Princeton University Press: Princeton.

Della Porta, D., & Diani, M. (Eds.). (2015). *The Oxford handbook of social movements.* Oxford University Press.

Delsen, L. (2000). *Exit poldermodel? Sociaal–economische ontwikkelingen in Nederland.* Van Gorcum: Utrecht.

Deleuze, G., & Guattari, F. (1988). *A thousand plateaus: Capitalism and schizophrenia.* Bloomsbury: New York.

Deloria, V. (2012). *Metaphysics of modern existence.* Fulcrum: Ann Arbor.

Deloria, V. (2003). *God is red: A native view of religion.* Fulcrum: Ann Arbor.

Denham, A., & Garnett, M. (2001). From guru togGodfather: Keith Joseph, New Labour and the British conservative tradition. *The Political Quarterly, 72*(1): 97–106.

Descartes, R. (1629/2003). *The treatise of man.* Prometheus: London

De Tocqueville, A. (1835/2003). *Democracy in America.* Regnery: Washington DC.

De Waal, F. (2010). *The age of empathy: Nature's lessons for a kinder society.* Broadway: London.

De Waal, F. (1996). *Good natured: The origins of right and wrong in humans and other animals.* Cambridge, MA: Harvard University Press.

Dewey, J. (1903). *Democracy in education. The elementary school teacher.* University of Chicago: Chicago

De Wispelaere, J., & Stirton, L. (2004). The many faces of universal basic income. *The Political Quarterly, 75*(3): 266–274.

De Wispelaere, J., & Noguera, J. A. (2012). On the political feasibility of universal basic income: An analytic framework. In *Basic Income Guarantee and Politics*: 17–38). Palgrave Macmillan: New York.

Diamond D., & Cook, N. (2020, 24 February). Trump faces 'black swan' threat to the economy and reelection. *Politico.*

Dik, B. J., Byrne, Z. S., & Steger, M. F. (2013). *Purpose and meaning in the workplace.* American Psychological Association: Washington DC.

Dilthey, W. (2010). *Selected works, Volume III: The formation of the historical world in the human sciences.* Princeton University Press: New Jersey.

Doherty, P. C. (2013). *Pandemics: What everyone needs to know.* Oxford University Press: Oxford.

Douglas, K. M., Sutton, R. M., & Cichocka, A. (2017). The psychology of conspiracy theories. *Current Directions in Psychological Science,* 26(6), 538–542.

Draper, H. (1977). *Karl Marx's theory of revolution* (Vol. 1–V). NYU Press.

Drewell, M. & Larsson, B. (2017). *The rise of the meaningful economy: A megatrend where meaning is a new currency.* CreateSpace Independent Publishing Platform: Europe.

Dreyfus, H., & Taylor, C. (2015). *Retrieving realism.* Harvard University Press.

Drolet, J. F. (2011). *American neoconservatism: The politics and culture of a reactionary idealism.* Hurst: London

Drosos, D. G. (1996). Adam Smith and Karl Marx: Alienation in market society. *History of Economic Ideas,* 325–351.

Drury, S. B. (1997). *Leo Strauss and the American right.* St. Martin's Press: New York.

D'Souza, D. (1997). Justice to Ronald Reagan. *Washington Times*: 23 November.

Duan, L., & Zhu, G. (2020). Psychological interventions for people affected by the COVID-19 epidemic. [epub ahead of print] *The Lancet Psychiatry.*

Duncan, C. (2020, 19 April). Coronavirus: more than 6.5 million jobs to be lost in UK lockdown, study predicts. *The Independent.*

Düppe, T. (2011). *The making of the economy: A phenomenology of economic science.* Lexington: Washington DC.

Durward, R. (2016). *Religion, conflict and military intervention.* Routledge: London.

Dutton, K. (2012). *The wisdom of psychopaths.* Random House: New York.

Duvendack M., Palmer-Jones R., Copestake J.G., Hooper L., Loke Y., & Rao N. (2011). *What is the evidence of the impact of microfinance on the well-being of poor people?* EPPI-Centre, Social Science Research Unit, Institute of Education, University of London.

Earle, J., & Moran, C. Ward-Perkins, Z. (2017). *The econocracy–The perils of leaving economics to the experts.* Manchester University Press: Manchester.

East, J. P. (1977). Leo Strauss and American conservatism. *Modern Age*, 21(1): 2–15.

Eckhardt, G. M., & Houston, M. J. (1998). Consumption as self-presentation in a collectivist society. *ACR Asia-Pacific Advances*, 3: 52–58.

Eldred, M. (2005). *Capital and technology: Marx and Heidegger*. Artefact: London.

Eland, I. (1998). Does US intervention overseas breed terrorism? *Cato Institute Foreign Policy Briefing*, *50*: 1–24.

El-Gingihy, Y. (2018). *How to dismantle the NHS in 10 easy steps: The blueprint that the government does not want you to see*. John Hunt Publishing: Abingdon.

Ellul, J. (1973). *Propaganda: The formation of men's attitudes*. Vintage: New York.

Emami, A., Javanmardi, F., Pirbonyeh, N., & Akbari, A. (2020). Prevalence of underlying diseases in hospitalized patients with COVID-19: a systematic review and meta-analysis. *Archives of academic emergency medicine*, 8(1): 26-32.

Engler, M., & Engler, P. (2016). *This is an uprising: How nonviolent revolt is shaping the twenty-first century*. Bold Type: New York.

European Commission (2015). *25 years after the fall of the Iron Curtain: The state of integration of East and West in the European Union*. Publications Office of the European Union.

Farrall, S., & Hay, C. (2014). *The legacy of Thatcherism: Assessing and exploring Thatcherite social and economic policies*. Oxford University: Oxford.

Faucher-King, F., & Le Galès, P. (2010). *The new labour experiment: Change and reform under Blair and Brown*. Stanford University Press: Cambridge MA.

Faulkner, N. (2017). *A People's History of the Russian Revolution*. Pluto: London.

Faulkner, N. (2020, 26 June). *History's greatest crisis has begun*. Mutiny. timetomutiny.org

Faulkner, N., & Dathi, S. (2017). *Creeping fascism: Brexit, Trump and the rise of the far right*. Public Reading Rooms: London.

Ferguson, N. (2008). *The ascent of money: A financial history of the world*. Penguin: London.

Ferzini, F. (2012). *Marketing propaganda: From attention to the meaning economy*. CreateSpace Independent Publishing Platform: Europe.

Finer, H. (1946). *Road to reaction*. Dobson: London.

Fischer, E. F. (Ed.). (2009). *Indigenous peoples, civil society, and the neo-liberal state in Latin America*. Berghahn: Oxford.

Fisher, M. (2009). *Capitalist realism: Is there no alternative?* Hunt: London.

Fitzgerald, M., & Crider, C. (2020). Under pressure, UK government releases NHS COVID data deals with big tech. *Open Democracy*.

Fleming, J., & Ledogar, R. J. (2008). Resilience and indigenous spirituality: A literature review. *Pimatisiwin*, 6(2): 47–65.

Flood, M. (2020, 5 March). Publishers report sales boom in novels about fictional epidemics. *The Guardian*.

Foley, D. K. (2009). *Adam's fallacy: A guide to economic theology*. Harvard University: Cambridge MA.

Force, Pierre. *Self-interest before Adam Smith: A genealogy of economic science* (Vol. 68). Cambridge University Press, 2003.

Forman-Barzilai, F. (2010). *Adam Smith and the circles of sympathy: Cosmopolitanism and moral theory* (Vol. 96). Cambridge University Press.

Fotaki, M. (2009). Maintaining the illusion of a free health care in post-socialism: A Lacanian analysis of transition from planned to market economy. *Journal of Organizational Change Management*, 22(2): 141–158.

Foer, F. (2017). *When Silicon Valley took over journalism*. The Atlantic: London.

Fox, G. (2011). Remembering ubuntu: Memory, sovereignty and reconciliation in post-apartheid South Africa. *PlatForum*, 12: 79–93.

Foucault, M. (1988). *Technologies of the self: A seminar with Michel Foucault*. University of Massachusetts: Cambridge MA.

Foucault, M. (1965/2013). *Archaeology of knowledge*. Routledge: London.

Foucault, M. (1976/2012). *The history of sexuality* (Vol. 3)*: The care of the self*. Vintage: New York.

Foucault, M. (2001/2008). *The birth of biopolitics: Lectures at the Collège de France, 1978–1979*. Springer.

Foucault, M., Dreyfus, H. L., & Rabinow, P. (1982). M*ichel Foucault: Beyond structuralism and hermeneutics. The subject and power*. University of Chicago: Chicago.

Frank, T. (2001). *One market under God: Extreme capitalism, market populism, and the end of economic democracy*. Anchor: Canada.

Frankl, V.E. (1978). *The unheard cry for meaning: Psychotherapy and humanism*. Simon & Schuster: New York.

Frankl, V. E. (1949/1985). *Man's search for meaning*. Simon and Schuster: New York.

Freire, P. (1996). *Pedagogy of the oppressed* (revised). Continuum: New York.

Frey, B. S. (2008). *Happiness: A revolution in economics*. MIT: Cambridge MA.

Friedman, M. (1953). The methodology of positive economics. *Essays in positive economics*, 3(3): 145–178.

Friedman, M. (1980). *Free to choose*. Harcourt: New York.

Friedman, M. (1977). *From Galbraith to economic freedom*. Transatlantic: London.

Friedman, M. (1972). Have monetary policies failed? *The American Economic Review*, 62(1–2): 11–18.

Friedman, M. (2007). The social responsibility of business is to increase its profits. In *Corporate ethics and corporate governance* (pp. 173–178). Springer: Berlin.

Friesen, J., Campbell, T., & Kay, A. (2014). The psychological advantage of unfalsifiability: The appeal of untestable religious and political ideologies. *Journal of Personality and Social Psychology,* 108(3): 515–525.

Frischmann, B. M., Madison, M. J., & Strandburg, K. J. (Eds.). (2014). *Governing knowledge commons*. Oxford University: Oxford.

Fromm, E. (1976/2013). *To have or to be?* A&C Black: London.

Fukuyama, F. (2006). *The end of history and the last man*. Simon & Schuster: New York.

Fullbrook, E. (Ed.). (2003). *The Crisis in Economics: the post-autistic economics movement: the first 600 days*. Routledge: London.

Fullbrook, E. (Ed.). (2004). *A guide to what's wrong with economics*. Anthem Press: London.

Furnham, A., Bond, M., Heaven, P., Hilton, D., Lobel, T., Masters, J., ... & Van Daalen, H. (1993). A comparison of Protestant work ethic beliefs in thirteen nations. *The Journal of Social Psychology*, 133(2): 185–197.

Galbraith, J. K. (1987). *A history of economics: The past as the present*. Hamish Hamilton.

Gambrel, P. A., & Cianci, R. (2003). Maslow's hierarchy of needs: Does it apply in a collectivist culture. *Journal of Applied Management and Entrepreneurship*, 8(2): 143–167.

Gamson, W. A. (1992). *Talking politics*. Cambridge university press.

Gamson, W. A., Fireman, B., & Rytina, S. (1982). *Encounters with unjust authority*. Dorsey Press.

Garcia, T. (2016). *La vie intense. Une obsession moderne*. Autrement: Paris.

Garfin, D. R., Silver, R. C., & Holman, E. A. (2020). The novel coronavirus (COVID-2019) outbreak: Amplification of public health consequences by media exposure. *Health Psychology*. [online publication: March 2020].

Gawthorpe, A. (2020, 14 March). Be careful. Trump may exploit the coronavirus crisis for authoritarian ends. *The Guardian*.

Gazzaniga, M. S. (Ed.). (2012). *Handbook of psychobiology*. Elsevier: London.

German Network for Evidence-Based Medicine (2020). *Covid19: where is the evidence? Report*. https://www.ebm-netzwerk.de/de/ueber-uns/wer-wir-sind

Ghani, A., & Lockhart, C. (2009). *Fixing failed states: A framework for rebuilding a fractured world*. Oxford University Press: Oxford.

Giddens, A. (1971). *Capitalism and modern social theory: An analysis of the writings of Marx, Durkheim and Max Weber*. Cambridge University Press: Cambridge.

Giddens, A. (1993). Modernity, history, democracy. *Theory and Society*, 22(2): 289–292.

Giddens, A. (2013). The third way: The renewal of social democracy. John Wiley: New York.

Gilens, M., & Page, B. I. (2014). Testing theories of American politics: Elites, interest groups, and average citizens. *Perspectives on politics*, 12(3): 564–581.

Giordano, P. (2020). *How contagion works. Science, awareness and community in times of global crises*. Weidenfeld & Nicolson: Great Britain.

Giroux, H. A., & Pollock, G. (2010). *The mouse that roared: Disney and the end of innocence*. Rowman & Littlefield: Maryland.

Goetzsche, P. (2020, 21 March). Corona: an epidemic of mass panic. *Deadly Medicines*.

Goldstone, J. A. (2001). Toward a fourth generation of revolutionary theory. *Annual Review of Political Science*, 4(1), 139–187.

Gomez, L. D. T. (2020). *COVID-19:* Analysis of corruption in public procurement. Epub on Academia.edu

Goodwin, M. J., & Heath, O. (2016). The 2016 referendum, Brexit and the left behind: An aggregate-level analysis of the result. *The Political Quarterly*, 87(3): 323–332.

Gorbatenko, D. (2020). Lockdowns May Be Worse Than Doing Almost Nothing. *SSRN 3566853*. [Epub ahead of print]

Gordon, C., Burchell, G., & Miller, P. (1991). *Governmental rationality: An introduction. The Foucault effect studies in governmentality*. Harvester Wheatsheaf: Hemel Hempstead.

Graeber, D., & Cerutti, A. (2018). *Bullshit jobs*. Simon & Schuster: New York.

Gramsci, A. (1994). *Letters from prison*. Columbia University Press: Cambridge MA.

Gramsci, A. (1994a). *Gramsci: Pre-prison writings*. Cambridge University Press: Cambridge MA.

Gramsci, A. (2000). *The Gramsci reader: selected writings, 1916-1935*. NYU press.

Gray, J. (2015). *Al Qaeda and what it means to be modern*. Faber & Faber: London.

Grechyna, D. (2020). Health Threats Associated with Children Lockdown in Spain during COVID-19. [online publication: March 2020]. *SSRN: 3567670*.

Green, J., & Jenkins, H. (2011). How audiences create value and meaning in a networked economy. In *The handbook of media audiences*: 109–132.

Greenberg, J., Koole, S. L., & Pyszczynski, T. A. (Eds.). (2004). *Handbook of experimental existential psychology*. Guilford Press: London.

Guba-McCallister, F. (2019). *Embracing disillusionment: Achieving liberation through the demystification of suffering*. University Professors Press.

Guevara, E. C. (2003). *Che Guevara reader: Writings on politics and revolution*. Ocean Press: Lancing.

Guiso, L., Sapienza, P., & Zingales, L. (2003). People's opium? Religion and economic attitudes. *Journal of monetary economics*, 50(1): 225–282.

Guriev, S., & Treisman, D. (2015). *How modern dictators survive: An informational theory of the new authoritarianism*. National Bureau of Economic Research.

Guthrie, D. (2001). *Dragon in a three-piece suit: The emergence of capitalism in China*. Princeton University: New Jersey.

Habermas, J. (1985). *The theory of communicative action* (Vol. 2): *Lifeworld and system: A critique of functionalist reason*. Beacon: Boston.

Halpern, D. (2010). *The hidden wealth of nations*. Polity: London.

Hancké, B. (Ed.). (2009). *Debating varieties of capitalism: A reader*. Oxford University: Oxford.

Hankinson, R. J. (2001). *Cause and explanation in ancient Greek thought*. Oxford University: Oxford.

Hannah, S. (2020). *From protest to resistance*. www.timetomutiny.org

Haque, U. (2019, 9 December). This is how a society dies. *Eudaimonia*. https://eand.co/this-is-how-a-society-dies-35bdc3c0b854

Hardt, M. D. (2015). *History of infectious disease pandemics in urban societies*. Lexington Books: Lanham.

Hare, R.D. (1994). Predators: The disturbing world of the psychopaths among us, *Psychology Today*, 27 (1): 54–61.

Hausman, D., McPherson, M., & Satz, D. (2016). *Economic analysis, moral philosophy, and public policy*. Cambridge University Press: Cambridge.

Hawkley, L. C., & Cacioppo, J. T. (2003). Loneliness and pathways to disease. *Brain, Behavior, and Immunity*, 17(1), 98–105.

Hayek, F. A. (1976). *The mirage of social justice* (Vol. 2): *Law, legislation, and liberty*. University of Chicago: Chicago.

Hayek, F. A. (1960/2013). *The constitution of liberty*. Routledge: New York.

Hayek, F. A. (1948). The meaning of competition. *Individualism and Economic Order*, 92: 98–121.

Hayek, F. A. (1945). The use of knowledge in society. *The American Economic Review*, 35(4): 519–530.

Hayek, F. A. (1944/2014). *The road to serfdom*. Routledge: New York.

Hayek, F. V. (1941). The counter-revolution of science. *Economica*, 8(31), 281–320.

Health Foundation UK. (2020). *Will COVID-19 be a watershed moment for health inequalities?* Report. https://www.health.org.uk/publications/long-reads/will-covid-19-be-a-watershed-moment-for-health-inequalities

Heath, E. (2013). *Adam Smith and self-interest*.

Hegel, G. W. F. (1807/1976). *Phenomenology of spirit*. Galaxy: London.

Heidegger, M. (1919/1920, 2012). *Basic problems of phenomenology*. Continuum: New York.

Heidegger, M. (1921/1995). *Aristotle's Metaphysics*. Indiana University Press: Bloomington.

Heidegger, M. (1954/1977). *The question concerning technology*. Harper & Row: New York.

Heidegger, M. (1954). *Wissenschaft und Besinnung*. Klostermann.

Heidegger, M. (1927/1996). *Being and time*. SUNY: London.

Heidegger, M. (1921/1995). *Aristotle's metaphysics*. Indiana University Press: Indiana.

Heidegger, M. (1914). *Die lehre vom urteil im psychologismus: Ein kritisch-positiver beitrag zur logik*. Klostermann.

Heilbroner, R. L., & Milberg, W. (2012). *The making of economic society*. Pearson Education Company.

Heinzelman, K. (1980). *The economics of the imagination*. University of Massachusetts: Cambridge MA.

Hellinger, D. C. (2018). *Conspiracies and conspiracy theories in the age of trump*. Springer.

Helm, J., Lee, R., & DeVore, I. (1968). *Man the hunter*. Aldine: Chicago.

Hemming, L. P. (2013). *Heidegger and Marx: A productive dialogue over the language of humanism*. Northwestern University Press: Hennessy

Hendriks, F. (2017). *Polder politics: The re-invention of consensus democracy in the Netherlands*. Routledge: New York.

Herman, E. S., & Chomsky, N. (2010). *Manufacturing consent: The political economy of the mass media*. Random House: New York.

Hetherington, M. J., & Weiler, J. D. (2009). *Authoritarianism and polarization in American politics*. Cambridge University: Cambridge.

Herzog, L. (2016). The normative stakes of economic growth; Or, why Adam Smith does not rely on "trickle down". *The Journal of Politics*, 78(1): 50–62.

Hirschberger, G. (2015). Terror management and prosocial behaviour: A theory of self-protective. In *The Oxford handbook of prosocial behaviour*: 166–206.

Hirschman, A. O. (1997). *The passions and the interests: Political arguments for capitalism before its triumph*. Greenwood: Westport.

Hirschman, E. C., & Holbrook, M. B. (1982). Hedonistic consumption: emerging concepts, methods and propositions. *Journal of marketing*, 46(3): 92–101.

Hitler, A. (1925/2007). *My Struggle*. Jaico: Mumbai.

Hoare, E., Milton, K., Foster, C., & Allender, S. (2016). The associations between sedentary behaviour and mental health among adolescents: a systematic review. *International journal of behavioral nutrition and physical activity, 13*(1), 108.

Hobbes, T. (1651/2016). *Leviathan*. Penguin: London.

Hochschild, A. (1999). *King Leopold's ghost: A story of greed, terror, and heroism in colonial Africa*. Harcourt: New York.

Hochschild, A. R. (1983). *The managed heart*. Berkeley University: San Francisco.

Hoffman, W. M., & McNulty, R. E. (2012). Transforming faith in corporate capitalism through business ethics. *Journal of Management, Spirituality & Religion*, 9(3): 217–236.

Holt-Lunstad, J., Smith, T. B., Baker, M., Harris, T., & Stephenson, D. (2015). Loneliness and social isolation as risk factors for mortality: a meta-analytic review. *Perspectives on psychological science, 10*(2), 227-237.

Honoré, C. (2014). *In praise of slowness*. Orion: London.

Horkheimer, M. (1972). *Critical theory: Selected essays*. A&C Black: London.

Horkheimer, M. (2013). *Critique of instrumental reason*. Verso: London.

Houle, C. (2019). Social mobility and political instability. *Journal of Conflict Resolution*, 63(1): 85–111.

Howe, N. & Strauss, B. (2017). *Millennials rising: The next generation*. Vintage: London.

Hsieh, T. (2010). *Delivering happiness: A path to profits, passion, and purpose*. Hachette: London.

Hudis, P. (2012). *Marx's concept of the alternative to capitalism*. Brill: Leiden.

Hudson, M. (2015). *Killing the host: How financial parasites and debt bondage destroy the global economy*. ISLET: Washington DC.

Hudson, Michael (2017). *J is for junk economics: A guide to reality in an age of deception*. ISLET: Washington DC.

Hurst, A. (2016). *The purpose economy expanded and updated: How your desire for impact, personal growth and community is changing the world*. Elevate: London.

Husserl, E. (1999). *The essential Husserl: Basic writings in transcendental phenomenology*. Indiana University: Bloomington.

Husserl, E. (1934/1970). *The crisis of European sciences and transcendental phenomenology: An introduction to phenomenological philosophy*. Northwestern University Press.

Huxley, A. (1932/1998). *Brave New World*. Vintage: London.

Iacoboni, M. (2009). Imitation, empathy, and mirror neurons. *Annual Review of Psychology*, 60: 653–670.

Imhoff, R., & Lamberty, P. K. (2017). Too special to be duped: Need for uniqueness motivates conspiracy beliefs. *European Journal of Social Psychology*, 47(6), 724–734.

Inglehart, R. (1997). *Modernization and postmodernization: Cultural, economic, and political change in 43 societies*. Princeton University: New Jersey.

Inglehart, R. (2018). *Culture shift in advanced industrial society*. Princeton University: New Jersey.

Intensive Care National Audit and Research Centre (2020). *Report on 2249 patients critically ill with Covid-19*. https://www.icnarc.org/About/Latest-News/2020/04/04/Report-On-2249-Patients-Critically-Ill-With-Covid-19

Ioannidis, J. P. (2020). A fiasco in the making? As the coronavirus pandemic takes hold, we are making decisions without reliable data. *Stat*, 17.

Ioannidis, J. P. (2020a). Coronavirus disease 2019: The harms of exaggerated information and non-evidence-based measures. *European Journal of Clinical Investigation*, 50(4), e13222.

Irwin, D. A. (2015). *Free trade under fire*. Princeton University: New Jersey.

Isaak, R. (2016). The making of the ecopreneur. In *Making Ecopreneurs: 63–78*. Routledge: New York.

James, O. (2007). *Affluenza: How to be successful and stay sane*. Random House: New York.

James, O. (2008). *The selfish capitalist: Origins of affluenza*. Random House: New York.

Jameson, F. (1991). *Postmodernism, or, the cultural logic of late capitalism*. Duke University: Durham.

Janoff-Bulman, R. (2010). *Shattered assumptions*. New York: Simon and Schuster.

Jaspers, K. (1921/2013). *Psychologie der weltanschauungen*. Springer. London.

Jaspers, K., & Salamun, K. (1949). *Vom ursprung und ziel der geschichte*. Artemis: Zurich.

Jeffreys, E., & Sigley, G. (2009). Governmentality, governance and China. In *China's governmentalities: 13–35*. Routledge: New York.

Jensen, R. (2001). *The dream society: How the coming shift from information to imagination will transform your business*. McGraw Hill: New York.

Jeong, H., Yim, H. W., Song, Y.-J., Ki, M., Min, J.-A., Cho, J., & Chae, J.-H. (2016). Mental health status of people isolated due to Middle East Respiratory Syndrome. *Epidemiology and health, 38*.

Jhally, S. (2014). *The codes of advertising: Fetishism and the political economy of meaning in the consumer society*. Routledge: New York.

Jiang, F., Deng, L., Zhang, L., Cai, Y., Cheung, C. W., & Xia, Z. (2020). Review of the clinical characteristics of coronavirus disease 2019 (COVID-19). *Journal of general internal medicine*, 1-5.

Jo, T. H., Chester, L., & D'Ippoliti, C. (Eds.). (2017). *The Routledge handbook of heterodox economics*. Routledge: London.

Johns, S. (2020, 2 June). Neil Ferguson says UK must keep transmission reducted by 65% to control pandemic. *Imperial College London*.

Johnston, H. (2014). *What is a social movement?* John Wiley & Sons: New York.

Johnston, H., & Noakes, J. A. (Eds.). (2005). *Frames of protest: Social movements and the framing perspective*. Rowman & Littlefield Publishers.

Johnstone, L., Boyle, M., Cromby, J., Dillon, J., Harper, D., Kinderman, P., & Read, J. (2018). *The power threat meaning framework*. British Psychological Society: Leicester.

Jolley, D., & Douglas, K. M. (2017). Prevention is better than cure: Addressing anti-vaccine conspiracy theories. *Journal of Applied Social Psychology*, 47(8), 459–469.

Jones, O. (2015). *The establishment: And how they get away with it*. Melville House: London.

Jordan, B. (2010). *Why the third way failed: Economics, morality and the origins of the 'big society'*. Policy: London.

Jost, J. T., Glaser, J., Kruglanski, A. W., & Sulloway, F. J. (2003). Political conservatism as motivated social cognition. *Psychological bulletin*, 129(3): 339-351.

Jupe, R., & Funnell, W. (2015). Neoliberalism, consultants and the privatisation of public policy formulation: The case of Britain's rail industry. *Critical Perspectives on Accounting*, 29: 65–85.

Kagarlitsky, B. (2002). *Russia under Yeltsin and Putin: neo-liberal autocracy*. Pluto: London.

Kahneman, D., & Tversky, A. (2013). Prospect theory: An analysis of decision under risk. In *Handbook of the fundamentals of financial decision making: 99-127*. University of British Colombia: Canada.

Kahneman, D. (2011). *Thinking, fast and slow*. Macmillan: London.

Kasser, T., Cohn, S., Kanner, A. D., & Ryan, R. M. (2007). Some costs of American corporate capitalism: A psychological exploration of value and goal conflicts. *Psychological Inquiry*, 18(1): 1–22.

Kasser, T. E., & Kanner, A. D. (2004). *Psychology and consumer culture: The struggle for a good life in a materialist world*. American Psychological Association: Washington DC.

Katz, D. (2020, 20 March). Is Our Fight Against Coronavirus Worse Than the Disease? *New York Times*.

Keen, S. (2011). *Debunking economics: The naked emperor dethroned?* Zed: London.

Keppler, J. H. (2010). *Adam Smith and the economy of the passions*. Routledge: New York.

Keune, M. (Ed.). (2016). *Nog steeds een mirakel? De legitimiteit van het poldermodel in de eenentwintigste eeuw*. Amsterdam University Press: Amsterdam.

Keynes, J. M. (1937). The general theory of employment. *The Quarterly Journal of Economics*, 51(2): 209–223.

Kiefer, T.M. (2002). *Anthropology*. Harvard University: Cambridge MA.

Kiel, L. D., & Elliott, E. W. (1996). *Chaos theory in the social sciences: Foundations and applications*. University of Michigan: Ann Arbor.

Klandermans, B. (2004). The demand and supply of participation: Social–psychological correlates of participation in social movements. In *The Blackwell companion to social movements*: 360–379.

Klandermans, P. G. (1997). *The social psychology of protest*. Oxford: Blackwell.

Klein, N. (2007). *The shock doctrine: The rise of disaster capitalism*. Macmillan: London.

Kline, G. L. (1988). The myth of Marx' materialism. In *Philosophical Sovietology*: 158–203. Springer: Dordrecht.

Knightly, K. (2020, 6 May) COVID19: are ventilators killing people? *The OffGuardian*.

Knowlton, B., & Grynbaum, M. M. (2008). Greenspan shocked that free markets are flawed. *New York Times*, 23 November.

Kohn, A. (1999). *Punished by rewards: The trouble with gold stars, incentive plans, A's, praise, and other bribes*. Harcourt: London.

Kohlberg, L. (1981). *Essays on moral development*. Harper & Row: San Francisco.

Kołakowski, L. (2005). *Main currents of Marxism: The founders, the golden age, the breakdown*. Norton: London.

Kolo, C., & Baur, T. (2004). Living a virtual life: Social dynamics of online gaming. *Game studies*, 4(1): 1-31.

Khuri, R. K. (1998). *Freedom, modernity, and Islam: Toward a creative synthesis*. Syracuse University: New York.

Kleck, G. (2017). *Point blank: Guns and violence in America*. Routledge: London.

Kristol, I. (1995). *Neoconservatism: The autobiography of an idea*. Simon and Schuster: New York.

Kocieniewski, D. (2012). Since 1980s, the kindest of tax cuts for the rich. *The New York Times*. 12 February

Kropotkin, P. (1902/2012). *Mutual aid: A factor of evolution*. Courier: Evansville.

Krugman, P. (2009). *Reagan did it*. New York Times, 31 August.

Kuhn, T. S. (2012). *The structure of scientific revolutions*. University of Chicago: Chicago.

Kwok, K. O., Li, K. K., Chan, H. H., Yi, Y. Y., Tang, A., Wei, W. I., & Wong, Y. S. (2020). Community responses during the early phase of the COVID-19 epidemic in Hong Kong: Risk perception, information exposure and preventive measures. [epub ahead of print]. *medRxiv*.

Kynaston, D., & Green, F. (2019). *Engines of privilege: Britain's private school problem*. Bloomsbury: New York.

Lacan, J. (2001). *Ecrits: A selection*. Routledge: New York.

Laclau, E., & Mouffe, C. (2014). *Hegemony and socialist strategy: Towards a radical democratic politics*. Verso Trade.

Laing, R. (2010). *The divided self: An existential study in sanity and madness*. Penguin: London.

Laloux, F. (2014). *Reinventing organizations: A guide to creating organizations inspired by the next stage in human consciousness*. Nelson Parker: Millis.

Lane, R. E. (2000). *The loss of happiness in market democracies*. Yale University: London.

Laslett, P. (2015). *The world we have lost: Further explored*. Routledge: Abingdon.

Latour, B. (2020, 29 March). Imaginer les gestes-barrières contre le retour à la production d'avant-crise. *AOC Analyse Opinion Critique*. https://aoc.media/opinion/2020/03/29/imaginerles-gestes-barrieres-contre-le-retour-a-la-production-davant-crise/.

Lawson, G. (2019). *Anatomies of revolution*. Cambridge University Press.

Lawson, N. (2011). *Memoirs of a Tory radical*. Biteback: London.

Lee, F. (2009). *A history of heterodox economics: Challenging the mainstream in the twentieth century*. Routledge: London.

Lehmann, H., & Roth, G. (Eds.). (1995). *Weber's Protestant ethic: Origins, evidence, contexts*. Cambridge University Press.

Lemke, T. (2014). The risks of security: Liberalism, biopolitics, and fear. The government of life. In *Foucault, biopolitics, and neoliberalism* (pp. 59–74). Fordam: New York.

Lerner, M. (1997). *The politics of meaning*. Addison-Wesley: Boston.

Levinas, E. (1979). *Totality and infinity: An essay on exteriority*. Springer: New York.

Levitt, M. (2020, 22 March). Why this Nobel Laureate predicts a quicker coronavirus recovery: we are going to be fine. *Los Angeles Times*.

Levy, N. (2005). Downshifting and meaning in life. *Ratio*, 18(2): 176–189.

Lewis, M. (2010). *Liar's poker*. Norton: London.

Liberati, A., Tetzlaff, J., & Altman, D. G. (2009). Preferred reporting items for systematic reviews and meta-analyses: The PRISMA statement. *Annals of Internal Medicine*, 151(4), 264–269.

Lichbach, M. I. (1989). An evaluation of "does economic inequality breed political conflict?" studies. World Politics, 41(4): 431–470.

Lintern, S. (2020, 13 June). Chief nurse dropped from Downing Streets coronavirus briefing after refusing to back Dominic Cummings. The Independent.

Lippmann, W. (2018). Liberty and the news. Routledge: New York.

Lippmann, W. (2017). Public opinion. Routledge: New York.

Lippmann, W. (2017a). The good society. Routledge: New York.

Liu, J. J., Bao, Y., Huang, X., Shi, J., & Lu, L. (2020). Mental health considerations for children quarantined because of COVID-19. The Lancet Child & Adolescent Health. [Epub ahead of print]

Liu, S., Yang, L., Zhang, C., Xiang, Y. T., Liu, Z., Hu, S., & Zhang, B. (2020). Online mental health services in China during the COVID-19 outbreak. [epub ahead of print]. The Lancet Psychiatry.

Locke, J. (1689/1988). Two treatises of government. Cambridge University: Cambridge.

Lofgren, M. (2016). The deep state: The fall of the constitution and the rise of a shadow government. Penguin: London.

Lovejoy, A. (2017). The great chain of being: A study of the history of an idea. Routledge: New York.

Löwy, M. (2009). Capitalism as religion: Walter Benjamin and Max Weber. Historical Materialism, 17(1): 60–73.

Lubbers, E. (2012). Secret manoeuvres in the dark. Pluto: London.

Luther, M. (2016). The freedom of a Christian, 1520: The annotated Luther study edition. Fortress Press: London.

Lynteris, C. (2019). Human extinction and the pandemic imaginary. Routledge.

Määttä, K., & Uusiautti, S. (2012). How do the Finnish family policy and early education system support the well-being, happiness, and success of families and children? Early Child Development and Care, 182(3): 291–298.

MacIntyre, A. (1981). After virtue: A study in moral theology. University of Notre Dame: Paris.

Mackey, J., & Sisodia, R. (2013). Conscious capitalism, with a new preface by the authors: Liberating the heroic spirit of business. Harvard Business Review: Boston.

Macionis, J., & Gerber, L. (2010). Sociology. Pearson: Canada.

Mahase, E. (2020). Coronavirus: covid-19 has killed more people than SARS and MERS combined, despite lower case fatality rate. British Medical Journal. [Epub ahead of print]

Makortoff, K. (2020, 28 May). Covid-19 crisis pushes US jobless claims above 40m – as it happened. The Guardian.

Major, L. E., & Machin, S. (2018). Social mobility and its enemies. Penguin: London.

Määttä, K., & Uusiautti, S. (2012). How do the Finnish family policy and early education system support the well-being, happiness, and success of families and children?

Mandeville, B. (1705). The fable of the bees. Liberty: London

Marafa, L. M., & Tung, F. (2004). Changes in participation in leisure and outdoor recreation activities among Hong Kong people during the SARS outbreak. World Leisure Journal, 46(2), 38-47.

Marcuse, H. (2013). One-dimensional man: Studies in the ideology of advanced industrial society. Routledge: New York.

Marcuse, H. (2005). Heideggerian Marxism. University of Nebraska: Lincoln.

Marmot, M., & Wilkinson, R. (Eds.). (2005). Social determinants of health. Oxford University Press: Oxford.

Marmot, M. (2020). Health equity in England: The Marmot review 10 years on. British Medical Journal, 368.

Marx, K. (1974). Surveys from exile. Vintage Books.

Marx, K. (1939/2005). Grundrisse: Foundations of the critique of political economy. Penguin: London.

Marx, K. (1867/1990). Capital. Penguin: London.

Marx, K., & Engels, F. (1846/2011). The German ideology. Martino Fine: London.

Marx, K. (1844/2014a). On the Jewish question. Routledge: London.

Marx, K. (1844/2014b). Economic and philosophical manuscripts. Routledge: London.

Marx, K. (1844/1975) Comments on James Mill. Routledge: London.

Marx, W. (1975). Hegel's phenomenology of spirit: A commentary on the preface and introduction. Routledge: London.

Marshall, A. (2009). Principles of economics. Cosimo: New York.

Marquand, D. (1988). The unprincipled society: New demands and old politics. Cape: London.

Mason, P. (2009). Meltdown: The end of the age of greed. Verso: London.

Mauss, M. (2002). The gift: The form and reason for exchange in archaic societies. Routledge: New York.

Mazzucato, M. (2018). The value of everything: Making and taking in the global economy. Hachette: London.

McAdam, D. (2010). Political process and the development of black insurgency, 1930–1970. University of Chicago Press.

McCabe, I. B. (2008). Orientalism in early modern France: Eurasian trade, exoticism and the ancient regime. Berg: Oxford.

McCloskey, D. N. (1998). The rhetoric of economics. University of Wisconsin: Madison.

McCloskey, D. (2006). The bourgeois virtues: Ethics for a capitalist age.

McLuhan, M. (1994). Understanding media: The extensions of man. MIT: Cambridge MA.

McMillen, C. W. (2016). Pandemics: A very short introduction (Vol. 492). Oxford University Press: Oxford.

McNulty, P. J. (1968). Economic theory and the meaning of competition. The Quarterly Journal of Economics, 1: 639–656.

Megill, A. (2001). Karl Marx: The burden of reason. Routledge: London.

Melucci, A. (1989). Nomads of the present: Social movements and individual needs in contemporary society. Vintage: London.

Mészáros, I. (2006). Marx's theory of alienation. Aakar: New Delhi.

Mikovits, J., & Heckenlively, K. (2014). Plague. Skyhorse: New York.

Milburn, M. A., & Conrad, S. D. (2016). *Raised to rage: The politics of anger and the roots of authoritarianism*. MIT Press.

Mill, J. S. (1859/1966). *On liberty*. Palgrave: London.

Mirowski, P., & Plehwe, D. (Eds.). (2015). *The road from Mont Pelerin*. Harvard University: Cambridge MA.

Mirowski, P. (2013). *Never let a serious crisis go to waste: How neoliberalism survived the financial meltdown*. Verso: London.

Mitchell, D. (2019). *Making foreign policy: Presidential management of the decision-making process*. Routledge: New York.

Mitsuhashi, Y. (2018). *Ikigai: Giving every day meaning and joy*. Hachette: London.

Moore, J. H. (1993). *The political economy of North American Indians*. University of Oklahoma: Norman.

Morales, A. & Ring, S. (2020, 29 April). Johnson's top aide pushed scientists to back UK lockdown. *Bloomberg*.

Morens, D. M., Taubenberger, J. K., Folkers, G. K., & Fauci, A. S. (2010). Pandemic influenza's 500th anniversary. *Clinical Infectious Diseases*, 51(12), 1442–1444.

Moreton, B. (2009). *To serve God and Wal-Mart*. Harvard University: Cambridge MA.

Mount, F. (2012). *The new few: Or a very British oligarchy*. Simon & Schuster: New York.

Moyer, B., MacAllister, J., & Soifer, M. L. F. S. (2001). *Doing democracy: The MAP model for organizing social movements*. New Society: Gabriola.

Moyn, S. (2018). *Not enough: Human rights in an unequal world*. Harvard University: Cambridge MA.

Mushtaq, R., Shoib, S., Shah, T., & Mushtaq, S. (2014). Relationship between loneliness, psychiatric disorders and physical health? A review on the psychological aspects of loneliness. *Journal of Clinical and Diagnostic Research*, 8(9), WE01.

Nealon, J. (2012). *Post-postmodernism: Or, the cultural logic of just-in-time capitalism*. Stanford University: Redwood.

Nelson, R. H. (2014). *Economics as religion: From Samuelson to Chicago and beyond*. Pennsylvania State University: Pennsylvania.

Newell, B. R., Lagnado, D. A., & Shanks, D. R. (2015). *Straight choices: The psychology of decision making*. Psychology Press: Hove.

Nisbet, R. (2017). *History of the idea of progress*. Routledge.

Nomani, F., & Behdad, S. (2006). *Qass and labor in Iran: Did the revolution matter?* Syracuse University Press: New York.

Nussbaum, M. C. (2011). *Creating capabilities*. Harvard University: Cambridge MA.

O'Campo, P., & Dunn, J. R. (Eds.). (2011). *Rethinking social epidemiology: Towards a science of change*. Springer Science & Business Media: London.

Offe, C. (1987). Challenging the boundaries of institutional politics: Social movements since the 1960s. In Maier, C.S. (Ed.), *Changing boundaries of the political* (pp. 63–105.

Offer, J. (Ed.). (2000). *Herbert Spencer: Critical Assessments*. Taylor & Francis: New York.

Ollman, B., & Bertell, O. (1976). *Alienation: Marx's conception of man in a capitalist society*. Cambridge University: Cambridge.

Omran, A. R. (1971/2005) The epidemiological transition: A theory of the epidemiology of population change. *The Milbank Quarterly*, 83(4): 731–757.

Orwell, G. (1949/1983). *Nineteen Eighty-Four*. Penguin: London.

Østby, G. (2013). Inequality and political violence: A review of the literature. *International Area Studies Review*, 16(2): 206–231.

Ostrom, E. (1990). *Governing the commons: The evolution of institutions for collective action*. Cambridge University: Cambridge.

Ostrom, E., Gardner, R. ^ Walker, J. (1994). *Rules, games, and common-pool resources*. University of Michigan: Ann Arbor.

Ostry, J. D., Loungani, P., & Furcery, D. (2016). Neoliberalism: Oversold? *Finance & Development*, 53(2).

O'Toole, J. (2020, 3 June). Professor Lockdown Ferguson admits crippling restrictions made no difference – where's the outrage? *Russian TV*.

Oyserman, D., Coon, H. M., & Kemmelmeier, M. (2002). Rethinking individualism and collectivism: Evaluation of theoretical assumptions and meta-analyses. *Psychological Bulletin*, 128(1): 3–10.

Parker, D. (2004). *The UK's privatisation experiment: The passage of time permits a sober assessment*. Centre for Economic Studies, University of Munich.

Parvin, M. (1973). Economic determinants of political unrest: An econometric approach. *Journal of Conflict Resolution*, 17(2): 271–296.

Peksen, D. (2012). Does foreign military intervention help human rights? *Political Research Quarterly*, 65(3): 558–571.

Penedo, F. J., & Dahn, J. R. (2005). Exercise and well-being: a review of mental and physical health benefits associated with physical activity. *Current opinion in psychiatry*, 18(2), 189-193.

Pereira, E. R., Silva, R. M. C. R. A., & Dias, F. A. (2020). Psychological phases and meaning of life in times of social isolation due the COVID-19 pandemic a reflection in the light of Viktor Frankl. *Research, Society and Development*, 9(5), 122953331.

Peterson, J. B. (2018). *12 rules for life: An antidote to chaos*. Random House: New York.

Peterson, J. B. (2002). *Maps of meaning: The architecture of belief*. Routledge: New York.

Pigou, A. C. (1941). *Equilibrium and employment*. McMillan: London.

Pikketty, A.G. (2014). *Capital in the twenty-first century*. Belknap: Cambridge MA.

Pinard, M. (2011). *Motivational dimensions in social movements and contentious collective action*. McGill-Queen's Press MQUP.

Pine, B. J., Pine, J., & Gilmore, J. H. (1999). *The experience economy: Work is theatre & every business a stage*. Harvard Business: Cambridge MA.

Pitkin, W. B. (1932). *Consumer, his nature and his changing habits*. McGraw Hill: New York.

Polanyi, K., & MacIver, R. M. (1944). *The great transformation*. Beacon: Boston.

Ponticelli, J., & Voth, H. J. (2019). Austerity and anarchy: Budget cuts and social unrest in Europe, 1919–2008. *Journal of Comparative Economics*. [Epub ahead of print]

Popovic, S., & Miller, M. (2015). *Blueprint for revolution: How to use rice pudding, lego men, and other nonviolent techniques to galvanize communities, overthrow dictators, or simply change the world*. Spiegel & Grau: New York.

Popper, K. (2012). *The open society and its enemies*. Routledge: New York.

Porter, M. E. (2000). Location, competition, and economic development: Local clusters in a global economy. *Economic Development Quarterly*, 14(1): 15–34.

Postan, M. M. (1973). *The medieval economy and society: An economic history of Britain, 1100–1500* (Vol. 1). University of California: Berkeley.

Postman, N. (2006). *Amusing ourselves to death: Public discourse in the age of show business*. Penguin: London.

Poteete, A. R., Janssen, M. A., & Ostrom, E. (2010). *Working together: Collective action, the commons, and multiple methods in practice*. Princeton University: New Jersey.

Pounds, N. J. G. (2014). *An economic history of medieval Europe*. Routledge: New York.

Preston, J., & Robins, D. (2013). Evaluating the long term impacts of transport policy: The case of passenger rail privatisation. *Research in Transportation Economics*, 39(1): 14–20.

Pribram, K. H. (1958). *Comparative neurology and the evolution of behavior*. University of Wisconsin: Madison.

Price, L. L., Feick, L. F., & Guskey, A. (1995). Everyday market helping behavior. *Journal of Public Policy & Marketing*, 14(2): 255–266.

Proudhon, P. J., & Robinson, J. B. (2004). *General idea of the revolution in the nineteenth century*. Courier: London.

Proudhon, P. J. (1876). *What is property?: An inquiry into the principle of right and of government*. Tucker: Lisle.

Quick, J. D., & Fryer, B. (2018). *The end of epidemics: The looming threat to humanity and how to stop it*. St. Martin's Press: New York.

Ranta, E. (2018). *Vivir bien as an alternative to neoliberal globalization: Can indigenous terminologies decolonize the state?* Routledge: New York.

Rayack, E. (1987). *Not so free to choose: The political economy of Milton Friedman and Ronald Reagan*. Praeger: New York.

Reich, R. B. (2016). *Saving capitalism: For the many, not the few*. Vintage: New York.

Reich, W. (1970). *The mass psychology of fascism*. Macmillan: London.

Reinhoudt, J., & Audier, S. (2018). *The Walter Lippmann colloquium. The birth of neo-liberalism*. Palgrave Macmillan: London.

Renneboog, L., & Spaenjers, C. (2012). Religion, economic attitudes, and household finance. *Oxford Economic Papers*, 64(1): 103–127.

Ricoeur, P. (1957). Le paradoxe politique. *Esprit*, 250(5): 721-745.

Ritzer, G. (1992). *The McDonaldization of society*. Pine Forge: Newbury.

Roberts, R. (2017). *The off-modern: Psychology estranged*. Hunt: London.

Roberts, R. (2015). *Psychology and capitalism: The manipulation of mind*. Hunt: London.

Roggeband, C., & Klandermans, B. (Eds.). (2017). *Handbook of social movements across disciplines*. Springer.

Rose, N. (1990). *Governing the soul: The shaping of the private self*. Routledge: New York.

Rothbard, M. N. (1995). *Economic thought before Adam Smith*. Elgar: Camberley.

Rothschild-Whitt, J. (1979). The collectivist organization: An alternative to rational–bureaucratic models. *American Sociological Review*: 509–527.

Rubin, E. L. (2015). *Soul, self, and society: The new morality and the modern state*. Oxford University: Oxford.

Rutazibwa, O. U. (2014). In the name of human rights: The problematics of EU ethical foreign policy in Africa and elsewhere. *Afrika Focus*, 27(1): 96–101.

Ryan, K. (2020, 6 June). Is the Coronavirus scare a psychological operation? *Off-Guardian*.

Ryman, J. A., & Turner, C. A. (2007). The modern Weberian thesis: A short review of the literature. *Journal of Enterprising Communities: People and Places in the Global Economy*, 1(2): 175–187.

Sabeti, P., & Salahi, L. (2018). *Outbreak culture: The Ebola crisis and the next epidemic*. Harvard University Press: London.

Sachs, J. D. (2006). *The end of poverty: Economic possibilities for our time*. Penguin: London.

Sackett, R. D. F. (1997). *Time, energy, and indolent savage: A quantitative cross-cultural test of the primitive affluence hypothesis*. University of California: Berkeley.

Salecl, R. (1994). *The crisis of identity and the struggle for new hegemony in the former Yugoslavia*. Verso: London.

Samuelson, P. A. (1948). Foundations of economic analysis. *Science and Society*: 13 (1):93–95.

Sartre, J. P. (1956/2001). *Being and nothingness*. Citadel Press.

Sartre, J. P. (1967). *Essays in existentialism*. Citadel: New York.

Scarre, G. (1996). *Utilitarianism*. Routledge: London.

Schaverien, J. (2015). *Boarding school syndrome: The psychological trauma of the privileged child*. Routledge: New York.

Schrank, Z., & Running, K. (2018). Individualist and collectivist consumer motivations in local organic food markets. *Journal of Consumer Culture*, *18*(1): 184–201.

Schulze, G. (1992). Die erlebnisgesellschaft: kultursoziologie der gegenwart. Campus-Verlag: Frankfurt.

Schumacher, E. F. (2011). *Small is beautiful: A study of economics as if people mattered*. Random House: New York.

Schwartz, S. H. (2012). An overview of the Schwartz theory of basic values. *Online readings in Psychology and Culture*, *2*(1): 11–31.

Schwartz, S. H. (2007). Cultural and individual value correlates of capitalism: A comparative analysis. *Psychological Inquiry*, *18*(1): 52–57.

Schwartz, T. (2013). Companies that practice 'conscious capitalism' perform 10x better. *Harvard Business Review*, *2*:4–20.

Shaheen, S. (2015). *Social uprisings: Conceptualization, measurement, causes and implications*. University of Marburg: Marburg.

Sharp, G. (2012). *From dictatorship to democracy: A conceptual framework for liberation*. The New Press: New York.

Sharp, G. & Finkelstein, M. (1973). *The politics of nonviolent action*. Sargent: Boston.

Shklovsky, V. (2015). Art, as device. *Poetics Today*, *36*(3): 151–174.

Sedlacek, T. (2011). *Economics of good and evil: The quest for economic meaning from Gilgamesh to Wall Street*. Oxford University Press: Oxford.

Segerstrom, S. C., & Miller, G. E. (2004). Psychological stress and the human immune system: a meta-analytic study of 30 years of inquiry. *Psychological bulletin*, *130*(4), 601.

Seldon, A., & Collings, D. (2014). *Britain Under Thatcher*. Routledge: London.

Semler, R. (2003). *The seven-day weekend: Finding the work/life balance*. Century: London.

Semler, R. (2001). *Maverick!: The success story behind the world's most unusual workplace*. Random House: New York.

Sen, A. K. (2009). *The idea of justice*. Harvard University Press: Cambridge MA.

Sen, A. (2007). *Identity and violence: The illusion of destiny*. Penguin Books: India.

Sen, A. K. (1992). *Inequality re-examined*. Oxford University Press: Oxford.

Sennett, R. (2017). *The fall of public man*. Norton: London.

Sennett, R. (2008). *The craftsman*. Yale University: New Jersey.

Sennett, R. (1998). *The corrosion of character: The personal consequences of work in the new capitalism*. Norton: London.

Serhan, Y.S. & McLaughlin, T. (2020, 13 March). The other problematic outbreak: As the coronavirus spreads across the globe, so too does racism. *The Atlantic*.

Seybolt, T. B. (2007). *Humanitarian military intervention: The conditions for success and failure*. Stockholm International Peace Research Institute: Stockholm.

Schopenhauer, A. (1851/2000). *Parerga and Paralipomena*. Oxford University Press: Oxford.

Shelter UK (2020). *Annual report 2019*. England.shelter.org.uk

Shepherd-Banigan, M., Bell, J. F., Basu, A., Booth-LaForce, C., & Harris, J. R. (2016). Workplace stress and working from home influence depressive symptoms among employed women with young children. *International Journal of Behavioral Medicine*, 23(1): 102–111.

Siddique & Marsh, S. (2020, 22 May). NHS staff feel like 'cannon fodder' over lack of coronavirus protection. *The Guardian*. https://www.theguardian.com/society/2020/mar/22/nhs-staff-cannon-fodder-lack-of-coronavirus-protection

Silverman, E. J. (2009). *The prudence of love: How possessing the virtue of love benefits the lover*. Rowman & Littlefield: Lanham.

Singh, A. (2004). *Multilateral competition policy and economic development: A developing country perspective on the European Community proposals*. United Nations Conference on Trade and Development.

Singer, M. (2009). *Introduction to syndemics: A critical systems approach to public and community health*. John Wiley & Sons: New Jersey.

Singhal, T. (2020). A review of coronavirus disease-2019 (COVID-19). *The Indian Journal of Pediatrics*, 1-6.

Sisodia, R., Wolfe, D., & Sheth, J. N. (2003). *Firms of endearment: How world-class companies profit from passion and purpose*. Pearson Prentice Hall: New Jersey.

Skidelsky, E., & Skidelsky, R. (2012). *How much is enough? Money and the good life*. Penguin: London.

Skidelsky, R. (1996). *Keynes*. Oxford University Press: Oxford.

Sloterdijk, P. (2014). *You must change your life*. John Wiley: New York.

Smiles, S. (1890). *Self-help*. Donohue: Henneberry.

Smith, S. W. (2003). *Labour economics*. Routledge: New York.

Smith, A. (1776/2010). *The wealth of nations: An inquiry into the nature and causes of the wealth of nations*. Harriman House: Petersfield.

Smith, A. (1759/2010). *The theory of moral sentiments*. Penguin: London.

Soborski, R. (2018). *Ideology and the future of progressive social movements*. Rowman & Littlefield International Limited, an affiliate of Rowman & Littlefield, Lanham, Maryland.

Sohrabi, C., Alsafi, Z., O'Neill, N., Khan, M., Kerwan, A., Al-Jabir, A., ... & Agha, R. (2020). World Health Organization declares global emergency: A review of the 2019 novel coronavirus (COVID-19). International Journal of Surgery.

Sowell, T. (2013). *"Trickle down theory" and tax cuts for the rich* (No. 635). Hoover: Berkeley.

Spadafora, D., & Spada, J. (1990). *The idea of progress in eighteenth-century Britain*. Yale University: New Jersey.

Srnicek, N., & Williams, A. (2015). *Inventing the future: Post capitalism and a world without work*. Verso: London.

Staveren, I. van (2013). *The values of economics: An Aristotelian perspective*. Routledge: London.

Staggenborg, S. (2015). *Social movements*. Oxford University Press: USA.

Stasavage, D. (2014). Was Weber right? The role of urban autonomy in Europe's rise. *American Political Science Review*, *108*(2): 337–354.

Stavrakakis, Y. (2007). *Lacanian left*. Edinburgh University: Edinburgh.

Steinberg, M. (2005). *The fiction of a thinkable world: Body, meaning, and the culture of capitalism*. New York University: New York.

Stephany, F., Stoehr, N., Darius, P., Neuhauser, L., Teutloff, O., & Braesemann, F. (2020). Which industries are most severely affected by the COVID-19 pandemic? A data-mining approach to identify industry-specific risks in real-time. *MyIDEAS: April 2020*.

Stewart, A. (2000). *Theories of power and domination: The politics of empowerment in late modernity*. Sage.

Stiglitz, J. E., & Greenwald, B. C. (2014). *Creating a learning society: A new approach to growth, development, and social progress*. Columbia University: New York.

Stockinger, P. (2016). *Digital archives, cultural identity and diversity, meaning economy*. Council of Europe Conference.

Stone, C. D. (1972). Should trees have standing—Toward legal rights for natural objects. *Southern California Law Review 45*: 450–492.

Stroup, D. F., Berlin, J. A., Morton, S. C., Olkin, I., Williamson, G. D., Rennie, D., ... & Thacker, S. B. (2000). Meta-analysis of observational studies in epidemiology: A proposal for reporting. *Jama*, *283*(15), 2008–2012.

Sun, P., Lu, X., Xu, C., Sun, W., & Pan, B. (2020). Understanding of COVID-19 based on current evidence. *Journal of medical virology*, *92*(6), 548-551.

Sundbo, J., & Sorensen, F. (Eds.). (2013). *Handbook on the experience economy*. Elgar: Aldershot.

Swatos Jr, W. H., & Kaelber, L. (2016). *The Protestant ethic turns 100: Essays on the centenary of the Weber thesis*. Routledge: London.

Tabri, N., Hollingshead, S., & Wohl, M. (2020). Framing COVID-19 as an Existential Threat Predicts Anxious Arousal and Prejudice towards Chinese People. [online publication: March 2020]. *medRxiv*.

Taleb, N. (2005). *The black swan: Why don't we learn that we don't learn*. Random House: New York.

Taliano, M. (2020). SARS-CoV-2: fear versus data/International Journal of Antimicrobial Agents Available online 19 March 2020, 105947. *International Journal of Antimicrobial Agents*, *105947*.

Taylor, B. C. (2003). Postmodernism, ethnography, and communication studies. In *Expressions of ethnography: Novel approaches to qualitative studies* (pp. 65–76). SUNY: London.

Taylor, C. (1989). *Sources of the self: The making of the modern identity*. Harvard University: Cambridge MA.

Taylor, K. (2006). *Brainwashing: The science of thought control*. Oxford University: Oxford.

Taylor, V. (1989). Social movement continuity: The women's movement in abeyance. *American Sociological Review*, 761–775.

Taylor, V. (2010). Culture, identity, and emotions: Studying social movements as if people really matter. *Mobilization*, *15*(2), 113–134.

Tegnell, A. (2020, 24 March). The world stands still... except for Sweden. *Die Zeit*.

TenHouten, W. D. (2016). *Alienation and affect*. Taylor & Francis.

Tkachenko, T., & Mileikovskyi, V. (2018). Geometric basis of the use of green constructions for sun protection of glazing. In *International Conference on Geometry and Graphics* (pp. 1096–1107). Springer: New York.

Thurnwald, R. (2018). *Economics in primitive communities*. Routledge: New York.

Tcherneva, P. R. (2015). Trends in US income inequality. *Real-World Economics Review*, 64: 20–35.

Terkel, S. (2011). *Working: People talk about what they do all day and how they feel about what they do*. The New Press: New York.

Tett, G. (2009). *Fool's gold: How unrestrained greed corrupted a dream, shattered global markets and unleashed a catastrophe*. Hachette: London.

Thaler, R., & Sunstein, C. (2008). *Nudge: The gentle power of choice architecture*. Yale University: New Haven.

Thomas, M. (2015). *100 acts of minor dissent*. September: London.

Torry, M. (2016). *The feasibility of citizen's income*. Palgrave Macmillan: New York.

Toffler, A. (1984). *Future shock*. Bantam: London.

Trilling, L. (2009). *Sincerity and authenticity*. Harvard University: Cambridge MA.

Tronto, J. C. (2013). *Caring democracy: Markets, equality, and justice*. New York University: New York.

Trussel Trust (2020). *UK food banks report busiest month ever, as coalition urgently calls for funding to get money into people's pockets quickly during pandemic*. Report. https://www.trusselltrust.org/2020/06/03/food-banks-busiest-month/

Tse-Tung, M. (1939). The Chinese Revolution and the Chinese Communist Party. In *Selected works of Mao Tse-Tung*. Foreign Languages Press: Beijing.

Tubadji, A., Moeller, J., & Nijkamp, P. (2014). Was Weber right? The cultural capital root of socio-economic growth examined in five European countries. *International Journal of Manpower*, *35*: 56–88.

Tye, L. (2002). *The father of spin: Edward L. Bernays and the birth of public relations*. Macmillan: London.

Ulrich, D. (2011). Leaders who make meaning meaningful. *Human Resource Management International Digest*, *19*(2): 36–52.
United Kingdom Office for National Statistics. (2020, 7 May 2020). *Coronavirus-related deaths by ethnic group, England and Wales*.
  https://www.ons.gov.uk/peoplepopulationandcommunity/birthsdeathsandmarriages/deaths/methodologies/coronavir usrelateddeathsbyethnicgroupenglandandwalesmethodology
United Nations (2019). *UN Human Rights report on Venezuela*. United Nations: Washington DC.
Valente, J. (2003). Lacan's Marxism, Marxism's Lacan. In *The Cambridge Companion to Lacan*, 153–72. Cambridge University: Cambridge.
Valéry, P. (2016). *La crise de l'esprit*. FV Éditions: Paris.
Vanderborght, Y. (2002). Basic income in Belgium and the Netherlands. Implementation through the back door? In *IXth Congress of the Basic Income European Network,* Geneva.
Van Parijs, P. (1992). *Arguing for basic income*. Verso: London.
Van Parijs, P., & Vanderborght, Y. (2017). *Basic income: A radical proposal for a free society and a sane economy*. Harvard University: Cambridge MA.
Van Zanden, J & Prak, M. (2013). *Nederland en het poldermodel*. Bert Bakker: Utrecht.
Vattimo, G., & Zabala, S. (2014). *Hermeneutic communism: From Heidegger to Marx*. Columbia University: New York.
Verhaeghe, P. (2012). *What about me? The struggle for identity in a market*. Scribe: London.
Visser, G. (2008). *Gelatenheid: Gemoed en hart bij Meister Eckhart: Beschouwd in het licht van Aristoteles' leer van het affectieve*. SUN.
Visser, G. (1999). *De druk van de beleving*. SUN: Utrecht.
Visser, G. (2009). *Niets cadeau: een filosofisch essay over de ziel*. Valkhof Pers.
Vivenza, G. (2001). *Adam Smith and the classics: The classical heritage in Adams Smith's thought*. Oxford University Press.
Voegelin, E. (1986). *Political religions*. Mellen: New York.
Von Mises, L. (2002). *Epistemological problems of economics*. Ludwig von Mises Institute: Auburn.
Von Mises, L. (1998). *Human action: A treatise on economics*. Ludwig von Mises Institute: Auburn.
Von Mises, L. (1977). *Critique of Interventionism*. Ludwig von Mises Institute: Auburn.
Von Mises, L. (1912). *The theory of money and credit*. Ludwig von Mises Institute: Auburn.
Vos, A. (2017). *How to create a relevant public space*. Nai010 uitgevers/publishers: Rotterdam.
Vos, J. (2003, March). De wereld zal nooit meer zijn zoals het was. *De Sofa*.
Vos, J. (2011). *Opening the psychological black box in genetic counselling*. PhD Thesis. Department of Clinical Genetics, Faculty of Medicine, Leiden University Medical Center (LUMC), Leiden University.
Vos, J. (2014). Meaning and existential givens in the lives of cancer patients: A philosophical perspective on psycho-oncology. *Palliative & supportive care*, *13*(4), 885-900.
Vos, J. (2015). Meaning and existential givens in the lives of cancer patients: A philosophical perspective on psycho-oncology. *Palliative & Supportive Care*, *13*(4): 885–900.
Vos, J. (2016). Working with meaning in life in chronic or life-threatening disease: A review of its relevance and the effectiveness of meaning-centred therapies. In Schulenberg & Russo-Netzer (Eds.), *Clinical perspectives on meaning* (pp. 171–200). Springer, Cham.
Vos, J. (2016). Working with meaning in life in mental health care: A systematic literature review of the practices and effectiveness of meaning-centred therapies. In *Clinical Perspectives on Meaning*: 59–87. Springer: Cham.
Vos, J. (2018a). *Meaning in life: An evidence-based handbook for practitioners*. Palgrave Macmillan: London.
Vos, J. (2018b). Death in existential psychotherapies: A critical review. In Menzies, R.E., Menzies, R.G., & Iverach, L. (Eds.) *Curing the dread of death: Theory, research and practice* (pp. 145–160).
Vos, J., Roberts, R., & Davies, J. (2019). *Mental health in crisis*. SAGE: London.
Vos, J. (2020). Prevalence and predictors of the psychological impact of the COVID-19 pandemic compared with SARS and MERS: a meta-analysis. *Under review*.
Vos, J., Gómez-García, E., Oosterwijk, J. C., Menko, F. H., Stoel, R. D., van Asperen, C. J., ... & Tibben, A. (2012). Opening the psychological black box in genetic counseling. The psychological impact of DNA testing is predicted by the counselees' perception, the medical impact by the pathogenic or uninformative BRCA1/2-result. *Psycho-Oncology*, *21*(1), 29–42.
Vos, J., Menko, F. H., Oosterwijk, J. C., van Asperen, C. J., Stiggelbout, A. M., & Tibben, A. (2013). Genetic counseling does not fulfill the counselees' need for certainty in hereditary breast/ovarian cancer families: an explorative assessment. *Psycho-Oncology*, *22*(5), 1167-1176.
Wachter, K. (2003). Rethinking Maslow's needs. *Journal of Family and Consumer Sciences*, *95*(2), 68–88.
Wahba, M. A., & Bridwell, L. G. (1976). Maslow reconsidered: A review of research on the need hierarchy theory. *Organizational Behavior and Human Performance*, *15*(2): 212–240.
Wakefield, J. (2020, 6 June). How Bill Gates became the voodoo doll of Covid conspiracies. *BBC News*.
Walker, R. & Jeraj, S. (2016) *The rent trap: How we fell into it and how we get out of it*. The Left Book Club: London.
Walzer, M. (1977). *Just and unjust wars*. Basic Books: New York.
Wang, G., Zhang, Y., Zhao, J., Zhang, J., & Jiang, F. (2020). Mitigate the effects of home confinement on children during the COVID-19 outbreak. [epub ahead of print]. *The Lancet*.

Waszek, N. (1984). Two concepts of morality: A distinction of Adam Smith's ethics and its stoic origin. *Journal of the History of Ideas, 45*(4), 591–606.

Weber, M. (2013). *The Protestant ethic and the spirit of capitalism*. Routledge: New York.

Webley, P., Burgoyne, C., Lea, S., & Young, B. (2002). *The economic psychology of everyday life*. Psychology Press: Hove.

Weinberg, A. (Ed.). (2011). *The psychology of politicians*. Cambridge University: Cambridge.

Weinberg, J., & Bakker, R. (2015). Let them eat cake: Food prices, domestic policy and social unrest. *Conflict Management and Peace Science, 32*(3): 309–326.

Weng, P.-Y., & Chiang, Y.-C. (2014). Psychological restoration through indoor and outdoor leisure activities. *Journal of Leisure Research, 46*(2), 203-217. World Health Organization. (2020). *Mental health and psychosocial considerations during the COVID-19 outbreak, 18 March 2020* (No. WHO/2019-nCoV/MentalHealth/2020.1). World Health Organization.

West, E. G. (1969). The political economy of alienation: Karl Marx and Adam Smith. *Oxford Economic Papers, 21*(1), 1–23.

Westover, J. (2008). The record of microfinance: The effectiveness/ineffectiveness of microfinance programs as a means of alleviating poverty. *Electronic Journal of Sociology, 12*(1): 1–8.

White, G. (Ed.). (1988). *Developmental States in East Asia*. Springer: New York.

Wingren, G. (1957). *Luther on Vocation*. Muhlenberg: Philadelphia.

Wood, E. M. (2002). *The origin of capitalism: A longer view*. Verso.

Woodcock, A. (2020, 12 June). Coronavirus: Boris Johnson under pressure to publish report recommending measures to protect ethnic minorities. *The Independent*.

Wolf, M. J. (1999). *The entertainment economy. The mega-media forces that are re-shaping our lives*. Penguin: New York.

Wright, E. O. (2010). *Envisioning real utopias*. Verso: London.

Yilmazkuday, H. (2020). Coronavirus effects on the US unemployment: Evidence from Google Trends. *SSRN: 3559860*.

Young, T. (2020, 12 June). The science was right – it was the Government that was wrong. *The Telegraph*.

Zayd, N. Ḥ. A. (2006). *Reformation of Islamic thought: A critical historical analysis*. Amsterdam University: Amsterdam.

Zhang, J., Wu, W., Zhao, X., & Zhang, W. (2020). Recommended psychological crisis intervention response to the 2019 novel coronavirus pneumonia outbreak in China: A model of West China Hospital. [epub ahead of print]. *Precision Clinical Medicine*.

Žižek, S. (2006). *How to read Lacan*. Granta: Cambridge.

Zizek, S. (2011). *Living in the end times*. Verso: London.

Žižek, S. (2013). *Welcome to the desert of the real: Five essays on September 11 and related dates*. Verso: London.

Žižek, S. (2015). *Trouble in paradise: From the end of history to the end of capitalism*. Melville House: New York.

Žižek, S. (2019). *The relevance of the communist manifesto*. Polity: Cambridge.

Zizek, S. (2020). *PANDEMIC!: Covid-19 Shakes the World*. John Wiley & Sons.

References from the Systematic Literature Review on Meaning and Capitalism[2]

Abadía-Barrero, C. E. (2015). The transformation of the value of life: Dispossession as torture. *Medical Anthropology, 34*(5), 389–406.

Abdallah, S., Thompson, S., & Marks, N. (2008). Estimating worldwide life satisfaction. *Ecological Economics, 65*(1), 35–47.

Abdullah, M. (2019). Five childhood experiences that lead to a more purposeful life. *Greater Good Magazine Berkeley*.

Abeyta, A. A., Routledge, C., Kersten, M., & Cox, C. R. (2017). The existential cost of economic insecurity: Threatened financial security undercuts meaning. *The Journal of Social Psychology, 157*(6), 692–702.

Acevedo, G. A. (2005). Turning anomie on its head: Fatalism as Durkheim's concealed and multidimensional alienation theory. *Sociological Theory, 23*(1), 75–85.

Adams, R. E., & Boscarino, J. A. (2015). Volunteerism and well-being in the context of the World Trade Center terrorist attacks. *International Journal of Emergency Mental Health, 17*(1), 274.

Adams, T. V. (2016). *The psychopath factory: How capitalism organises empathy*. London: Duncan Baird Publishers.

Agathangelou, A. M. (2010). Bodies of Desire, terror and the war in Eurasia: Impolite disruptions of (neo) liberal internationalism, neoconservatism and the 'new' imperium. *Millennium–Journal of International Studies, 38*(3), 693–722.

Ager, W., & Ager, A. (2010). The psychology of enforced mobility. In S. C. Carr (Ed.), *The psychology of global mobilit*. (pp. 151–170). New York, NY: Springer Science + Business Media.

Agger, B. (2015). *Speeding up fast capitalism: Cultures, jobs, families, schools, bodies*. New York: Routledge.

Aguinis, H., & Glavas, A. (2019). On corporate social responsibility, sensemaking, and the search for meaningfulness through work. *Journal of Management, 45*(3), 1057–1086.

Akbaş, O. (2012). Reasons for high school students to mistrust most people: A study in the context of values education. *Educational Sciences: Theory & Practice, 12*(2), *12*(2), 603–608.

Akerlof, G., & Kranton, R. (2010). *Identity economics*. Princeton: Princeton University Press.

Akerlof, G. A., & Kranton, R. E. (2000). Economics and identity. *The Quarterly Journal of Economics, 115*(3), 715–753.

Akerlof, G. A., & Kranton, R. E. (2011). *Identity economics: How our identities shape our work, wages, and well-being*. Princeton: Princeton University Press.

Alexander, R. (2017). *The biology of moral systems*. New York: Routledge.

Algan, Y. (2014). Discussion. In A. E. Clark & C. Senik (Eds.), *Happiness and economic growth: Lessons from developing countries.* (pp. 23–27). New York, NY: Oxford University Press.

Allan, B. A., Tebbe, E. A., Duffy, R. D., & Autin, K. L. (2015). Living a calling, life satisfaction, and workplace climate among a lesbian, gay, and bisexual population. *The Career Development Quarterly, 63*(4), 306–319.

Althusser, L. (2014). *On the reproduction of capitalism: Ideology and ideological state apparatuses.* London: Verso Trade.

Alvarez de Davila, S. (2015). *The lived-experiences of Latino meatpacking workers in a small Midwest town: An existential and emotional conflict of migration.* (76). ProQuest Information & Learning.

Ambrey, C., & Fleming, C. (2014). Public greenspace and life satisfaction in urban Australia. *Urban Studies, 51*(6), 1290–1321.

Ambrey, C., Ulichny, J., & Fleming, C. (2017). The social connectedness and life satisfaction nexus. *Feminist Economics, 23*(2), 1–32.

Aminzadeh, K., Denny, S., Utter, J., Milfont, T. L., Ameratunga, S., Teevale, T., & Clark, T. (2013). Neighbourhood social capital and adolescent self-reported wellbeing in New Zealand: A multilevel analysis. *Social Science & Medicine, 84*, 13–21.

Amsler, S. (2016). Learning Hope. An epistemology of possibility for advanced capitalist society. In *social sciences for an other politics* (pp. 19–32): Springer.

Anderson, D., Prioleau, P., Taku, K., Naruse, Y., Sekine, H., Maeda, M., ... Yanagisawa, R. (2016). Post-traumatic stress and growth among medical student volunteers after the March 2011 disaster in Fukushima, Japan: implications for student involvement with future disasters. *Psychiatric Quarterly, 87*(2), 241–251.

Andren, D., & Martinsson, P. (2006). What contributes to life satisfaction in transitional Romania? *Review of Development Economics, 10*(1), 59–70.

Ardahan, F. (2014). The Impacts of social capital and some demographic variables on life satisfaction: Antalya case. *Anthropologist, 18*(3), 76–-776.

Argandoña, A. (2003). Fostering values in organizations. *Journal of Business Ethics, 45*(1–2), 1–28.

Argentzell, E., Håkansson, C., & Eklund, M. (2012). Experience of meaning in everyday occupations among unemployed people with severe mental illness. *Scandinavian Journal of Occupational Therapy, 19*(1), 49–58.

Arnold, K. A., Turner, N., Barling, J., Kelloway, E. K., & McKee, M. C. (2007). Transformational leadership and psychological well-being: The mediating role of meaningful work. *Journal of occupational health psychology, 12*(3), 193.

Aronowitz, S., & Giroux, H. A. (2003). *Education under siege: The conservative, liberal and radical debate over schooling*. New York: Routledge.

Aronson, R. (2017). *We: Reviving social hope*. Chicago: University of Chicago Press.

Arthur Jr, W., Bell, S. T., Villado, A. J., & Doverspike, D. (2006). The use of person–organization fit in employment decision making: an assessment of its criterion-related validity. *Journal of Applied Psychology, 91*(4), 786.

Arthur, M. B., & Rousseau, D. M. (1996). Introduction: The boundaryless career as a new employment principle. In *The boundaryless career: A new employment principle for a new organizational era* (pp. 3–20).

Ateca-Amestoy, V., Aguilar, A. C., & Moro-Egido, A. I. (2014). Social interactions and life satisfaction: Evidence from Latin America. *Journal of Happiness Studies, 15*(3), 527–554.

Aten, J. D., O'Grady, K. A., Milstein, G., Boan, D., & Schruba, A. (2014). Spiritually oriented disaster psychology. *Spirituality in Clinical Practice, 1*(1), 20.

Aten, J. D., Smith, W. R., Davis, E. B., Van Tongeren, D. R., Hook, J. N., Davis, D. E., ... O'Grady, K. (2019). The psychological study of religion and spirituality in a disaster context: A systematic review. *Psychological Trauma: Theory, Research, Practice, and Policy*, 27–53.

Atkinson, D., & Elliott, L. (2008). *The gods that failed: How blind faith in markets has cost us our future*. London: Random House.

Avery, J. (2007). *Saving face by making meaning: The negative effects of consumers' self-serving response to brand extension.* (68). ProQuest Information & Learning.

Avolio, B. J., & Gardner, W. L. (2005). Authentic leadership development: Getting to the root of positive forms of leadership. *The Leadership Quarterly, 16*(3), 315–338.

Avolio, B. J., Reichard, R. J., Hannah, S. T., Walumbwa, F. O., & Chan, A. (2009). A meta-analytic review of leadership impact research: Experimental and quasi-experimental studies. *The Leadership Quarterly, 20*(5), 764–784.

Avolio, B. J., & Walumbwa, F. O. (2006). Authentic leadership: Moving HR leaders to a higher level. In *Research in personnel and human resources management* (pp. 273–304). London: Emerald Group Publishing.

Avolio, B. J., Walumbwa, F. O., & Weber, T. J. (2009). Leadership: Current theories, research, and future directions. *Annual Review of Psychology, 60*, 421–449.

Aycan, Z., Kanungo, R. N., & Sinha, J. B. (1999). Organizational culture and human resource management practices: The model of culture fit. *Journal of Cross-Cultural Psychology, 30*(4), 501–526.

Baessler, J., Oerter, R., Fernández, B. M., & Romero, E. M. (2003). Aspects of meaning of life in different subcultures in Peru. *Psychological Reports, 92*(3, Pt.2), 1119–1130.

Bahmad, J. (2019). Transnational hauntings: Globalization, social inequality, and the specters of radical Islam in Laila Marrakchi's Marock (2005). *Expressions Maghrebines, 18*(1), 99–106.

Bailey, A. W., & Fernando, I. K. (2012). Routine and project-based leisure, happiness, and meaning in life. *Journal of Leisure Research, 44*(2), 139–154.

Bains, G. (2011). *Meaning Inc: The blueprint for business success in the 21st century.* New York: Profile Books.

Baker, N. A., Jacobs, K., & Tickle-Degnen, L. (2003). A methodology for developing evidence about meaning in occupation: Exploring the meaning of working. *OTJR: Occupation, Participation and Health, 23*(2), 57–66.

Baker, W. E. (2003). *Achieving success through social capital.* Zagreb: Mate, škola ekonomije i managementa.

Bakic, H., & Ajdukovic, D. (2019). Stability and change post-disaster: Dynamic relations between individual, interpersonal and community resources and psychosocial functioning. *European Journal of Psychotraumatology, 10*(1), 13.

Bakker, A. B. (2010). Engagement and" job crafting": Engaged employees create their own great place to work.

Bales, K. (1999). *Disposable people. New slavery in the global economy.* Berkeley: University of Los Angeles Press.

Banerjee, S., & Wahl, M. F. (2014). Values and corporate governance systems. *Values in shock: The role of contrasting management, economic and religious paradigms in the work place,* 381–387.

Banyte, J., Brazioniene, L., & Gadeikiene, A. (2010). Expression of green marketing developing the conception of corporate social responsibility. *Inzinerine Ekonomika-Engineering Economics, 21*(5), 550–560.

Barber, B. R. (2008). *Consumed: How markets corrupt children, infantilize adults, and swallow citizens whole.* WW Norton & Company.

Barchiesi, F. (2014). Review of The problem with work: Feminism, marxism, antiwork politics, and postwork imaginaries. *Work, Employment and Society, 28*(2), 335–337.

Barman, E. (2016). *Caring Capitalism.* Cambridge: Cambridge University Press.

Bartels, D. M., & Pizarro, D. A. (2011). The mismeasure of morals: Antisocial personality traits predict utilitarian responses to moral dilemmas. *Cognition, 121*(1), 154–161.

Bartolini, S., Mikucka, M., & Sarracino, F. (2017). Money, trust and happiness in transition countries: Evidence from time series. *Social Indicators Research, 130*(1), 87–106.

Bartolini, S., & Sarracino, F. (2015). The dark side of Chinese growth: Declining social capital and well-being in times of economic boom. *World Development, 74,* 333–351.

Basoglu, M. (2006). Rehabilitation of traumatised refugees and survivors of torture. *British Medical Journal, 45*(5): 132–145.

Bass, B. M. (1988). Evolving perspectives on charismatic leadership.

Bass, B. M., & Bass, R. (2009). *The Bass handbook of leadership: Theory, research, and managerial applications.* New York: Simon and Schuster.

Baudrillard, J. (2016). *The consumer society: Myths and structures.* London: Sage.

Baudrillard, J. (2018). On consumer society. In *Rethinking the subject* (pp. 193–203). New York: Routledge.

Bauer, M. A., Wilkie, J. E., Kim, J. K., & Bodenhausen, G. V. (2012). Cuing consumerism: Situational materialism undermines personal and social well-being. *Psychological Science, 23*(5), 517–523.

Baum, S. K. (1988). Meaningful life experiences for elderly persons. *Psychological Reports, 63*(2), 427–433.

Bauman, Z. (2013). *Liquid modernity.* New York: John Wiley & Sons.

Baumeister, R. F. (1999). *Self-concept, self-esteem, and identity.*

Baumol, W. J., Litan, R. E., & Schramm, C. J. (2007). *Good capitalism, bad capitalism, and the economics of growth and prosperity.* New Jersey: Yale University Press.

Bearsley, C., & Cummins, R. A. (1999). No place called home: Life quality and purpose of homeless youths. *Journal of Social Distress and the Homeless, 8*(4), 207–226.

Beck, M., & Germann, J. (2019). Managerial power in the German model: The case of Bertelsmann and the antecedents of neoliberalism. *Globalizations, 16*(3), 260–273.

Beck, U., Lash, S., & Wynne, B. (1992). *Risk society: Towards a new modernity.* London: Sage.

Bek-Pedersen, K., & Montgomery, E. (2006). Narratives of the past and present: Young refugees' construction of a family identity in exile. *Journal of Refugee Studies, 19*(1), 94–112.

Bekoff, M. (2000). Animal emotions: Exploring passionate natures—Current interdisciplinary research provides compelling evidence that many animals experience such emotions as joy, fear, love, despair, and grief—We are not alone. *BioScience, 50*(10), 861–870.

Belk, R. W., & Pollay, R. W. (1985). Materialism and magazine advertising during the twentieth century. *ACR North American Advances.*

Bender, K., Thompson, S. J., McManus, H., Lantry, J., & Flynn, P. M. (2007). *Capacity for survival: Exploring strengths of homeless street youth.* Paper presented at the Child and Youth Care Forum, July.

Benioff, M. (2009). *Compassionate capitalism: How corporations can make doing good an integral part of doing well:* ReadHowYouWant. com.

Berg, J. M., Grant, A. M., & Johnson, V. (2010). When callings are calling: Crafting work and leisure in pursuit of unanswered occupational callings. *Organization Science, 21*(5), 973–994.

Berg, J. M., Wrzesniewski, A., & Dutton, J. E. (2010). Perceiving and responding to challenges in job crafting at different ranks: When proactivity requires adaptivity. *Journal of Organizational Behavior, 31*(2–3), 158–186.

Bergheim, S. (2007). *The happy variety of capitalism: Characterised by an array of commonalities.*

Berkelaar, B. L., & Buzzanell, P. M. (2015). Bait and switch or double-edged sword? The (sometimes) failed promises of calling. *Human Relations, 68*(1), 157–178.

Berman, M. (1970). *The politics of authenticity: Radical individualism and the emergence of modern society.* New York: Atheneum.

Beutel, A. M., & Marini, M. M. (1995). Gender and values. *American Sociological Review,* 436–448.

Bickerstaff, K. A., Grasser, C. M., & McCabe, B. (2003). How elderly nursing home residents transcend losses of later life. *Holistic Nursing Practice, 17*(3), 159–165.

Bilajac, L., Marchesi, V. V., Tesic, V., & Rukavina, T. (2014). Life satisfaction, optimism and social capital. *Psychiatria Danubina, 26*, 435–441.

Binkley, S. (2011). Happiness, positive psychology and the program of neoliberal governmentality. *Subjectivity, 4*(4), 371–394.

Birch, S. (2008). *The political promotion of the experience economy and creative industries*. Samfundslitteratur.

Bjerg, O. (2014). *Making money: The philosophy of crisis capitalism*. London: Verso.

Bjornskov, C. (2003). The happy few: Cross-country evidence on social capital and life satisfaction. *Kyklos, 56*(1), 3–16.

Bjornskov, C., Dreher, A., & Fischer, J. A. V. (2007). The bigger the better? Evidence of the effect of government size on life satisfaction around the world. *Public Choice, 130*(3–4), 267–292. doi:10.1007/s11127-006-9081-5

Bjornskov, C., Dreher, A., & Fischer, J. A. V. (2008). Cross-country determinants of life satisfaction: Exploring different determinants across groups in society. *Social Choice and Welfare, 30*(1), 119–173. doi:10.1007/s00355-007-0225-4

Blau, G., Petrucci, T., & McClendon, J. (2013). Correlates of life satisfaction and unemployment stigma and the impact of length of unemployment on a unique unemployed sample. *Career Development International, 18*(3), 257–280. doi:10.1108/cdi-10-2012-0095

Blau, G. J. (1987). Using a person–environment fit model to predict job involvement and organizational commitment. *Journal of Vocational Behavior, 30*(3), 240–257.

Blix, I., Hansen, M. B., Birkeland, M. S., Nissen, A., & Heir, T. (2013). Posttraumatic growth, posttraumatic stress and psychological adjustment in the aftermath of the 2011 Oslo bombing attack. *Health and Quality of Life Outcomes, 11*(1), 160.

Blomfield, B. (2009). Markers of the heart: Finding spirituality in a bus marked "Tourist". *Journal of Management, Spirituality and Religion, 6*(2), 91–105.

Blustein, D. (2006). The psychology of working: A new perspective for career development, counseling, and public policy. Mahwah, NJ,: Lawrence Erlbaum Associates Publishers. http://dx.doi. org/10.1037 ….

Bockorny, K., & Youssef-Morgan, C. M. (2019). Entrepreneurs' courage, psychological capital, and life satisfaction. *Frontiers in Psychology, 10*, 6. doi:10.3389/fpsyg.2019.00789

Boddy, C., Miles, D., Sanyal, C., & Hartog, M. (2015). Extreme managers, extreme workplaces: Capitalism, organizations and corporate psychopaths. *Organization, 22*(4), 530–551.

Boggs, J. (1970). The myth and irrationality of Black capitalism. *The Review of Black Political Economy, 1*(1), 27–35.

Boncompte, J. G., & Paredes, R. D. (2019). Human capital endowments and gender differences in subjective well-being in chile. *Journal of Happiness Studies: An Interdisciplinary Forum on Subjective Well-Being*. doi:10.1007/s10902-019-00085-y

Bonebright, C. A., Clay, D. L., & Ankenmann, R. D. (2000). The relationship of workaholism with work–life conflict, life satisfaction, and purpose in life. *Journal of Counseling Psychology, 47*(4), 469.

Boniwell, I., & Zimbardo, P. G. (2004). Balancing time perspective in pursuit of optimal functioning. *Positive Psychology in Practice, 12*, 141–155.

Bono, J. E., & Judge, T. A. (2003). Self-concordance at work: Toward understanding the motivational effects of transformational leaders. *Academy of Management Journal, 46*(5), 554–571.

Boswijk, A., Peelen, E., Olthof, S., & Beddow, C. (2012). *Economy of experiences*: European Centre for the Experience and Transformation Economy Amsterdam.

Boswijk, A., Thijssen, T., & Peelen, E. (2005). *Een nieuwe kijk op experience economy: Betekenisvolle belevenissen*: Pearson Education.

Botsman, R., & Rogers, R. (2011). *What's mine is yours: How collaborative consumption is changing the way we live* (Vol. 5): Collins London.

Bouchikhi, H., & Kimberly, J. R. (2008). *The soul of the corporation: How to manage the identity of your company*: Pearson Prentice Hall.

Bouzenita, A. I., & Boulanouar, A. W. (2016). Maslow's hierarchy of needs: An Islamic critique. *Intellectual Discourse, 24*(1).

Bowe, J., Bowe, M., & Streeter, S. (2009). *Gig: Americans talk about their jobs*: Broadway Books.

Bowles, S. (2016). *The moral economy: Why good incentives are no substitute for good citizens*: Yale University Press.

Bowles, S., & Gintis, H. (2013). *A cooperative species: Human reciprocity and its evolution*: Princeton University Press.

Bowman, K., & Rugg, A. (2013). Five years after the crash: What Americans think about Wall Street, banks, business, and free enterprise. *AEI Paper & Studies*.

Bozoglan, B., Demirer, V., & Sahin, I. (2013). Loneliness, self-esteem, and life satisfaction as predictors of Internet addiction: A cross-sectional study among Turkish university students. *Scandinavian Journal of Psychology, 54*(4), 313–319.

Bradfield, C., Wylie, M. L., & Echterling, L. G. (1989). After the flood: The response of ministers to a natural disaster. *Sociological Analysis, 49*(4), 397–407.

Bradley, K. (2015). *Educators' positive stress responses: Eustress and psychological capital*. (75). ProQuest Information & Learning, Retrieved from http://search.ebscohost.com/login.aspx?direct= true&AuthType= sso&db=psyh&AN=2015-99051-028&site=ehost-live&authtype=sso&custid=s5409946 Available from EBSCOhost psych database.

Brady, A., & Grenville-Cleave, B. (2017). Introducing positive psychology and its value for sport and physical activity. In *Positive psychology in sport and physical activity* (pp. 7–19): Routledge.

Branson, C. M. (2008). Achieving organisational change through values alignment. *Journal of Educational Administration, 46*(3), 376–395.

Brassai, L., Piko, B. F., & Steger, M. F. (2012). Existential attitudes and Eastern European adolescents' problem and health behaviors: Highlighting the role of the search for meaning in life. *The Psychological Record, 62*(4), 719–734.

Braun, V., & Clarke, V. (2006). Using thematic analysis in psychology. *Qualitative Research in Psychology, 3*(24), 77.

Breen, R. (2004). R., Luijkx (2004a), Social mobility in Europe between 1970 and 2000. *R. Breen, Social Mobility in Europe*, 37–75.

Briscoe, J., & Hall, D. (2003). Being and becoming protean: Individual and experiential factors in adapting to the new career. Unpublished technical report. DeKalb, IL: Department of Management, Northern Illinois University, DeKalb.

Briscoe, J. P., Hall, D. T., & DeMuth, R. L. F. (2006). Protean and boundaryless careers: An empirical exploration. *Journal of Vocational Behavior, 69*(1), 30–47.

Brittan, S. (1996). *Capitalism with a human face*: Harvard University Press.

Broadhead, S. (2018). Pedagogical possibilities for unruly bodies. *Gender and Education, 30*(5), 683–684. doi:10.1080/09540253.2018.1451627

Brockelman, T. (2008). *Zizek and Heidegger: The question concerning techno-capitalism*: A&C Black.

Brockmann, H., Delhey, J., Welzel, C., & Yuan, H. (2009). The China puzzle: Falling happiness in a rising economy. *Journal of Happiness Studies, 10*(4), 387–405. doi:10.1007/s10902-008-9095-4

Brown, C. (2017). *Buddhist economics: An enlightened approach to the dismal science*: Bloomsbury Publishing USA.

Brown, M. E., Treviño, L. K., & Harrison, D. A. (2005). Ethical leadership: A social learning perspective for construct development and testing. *Organizational Behavior and Human Decision Processes, 97*(2), 117–134.

Brymer, E. (2013). Extreme sports as transformational tourism. *Transformational Tourism: Tourist Perspectives, 111*.

Buhl, K. (1992). A meaning-based model of advertising. *Journal of Consumer Research, 19*, 317–338.

Bujold, C. (2004). Constructing career through narrative. *Journal of Vocational Behavior, 64*(3), 470-484.

Bunderson, J. S., & Thompson, J. A. (2009). The call of the wild: Zookeepers, callings, and the double-edged sword of deeply meaningful work. *Administrative Science Quarterly, 54*(1), 32–57.

Burke, R. J., Jones, F., & Westman, M. (2013). *Work-life balance: A psychological perspective*: Psychology Press.

Burpitt, W. J., & Bigoness, W. J. (1997). Leadership and innovation among teams: The impact of empowerment. *Small group research, 28*(3), 414–423.

Buscha, F., & Sturgis, P. (2018). Declining social mobility? Evidence from five linked censuses in England and Wales 1971–2011. *The British Journal of Sociology, 69*(1), 154–182.

Butler, J. (2011). *Gender trouble: Feminism and the subversion of identity*: Routledge.

Buttrick, N. R., Heintzelman, S. J., & Oishi, S. (2017). Inequality and well-being. *Current Opinion in Psychology, 18*, 15–20. doi:10.1016/j.copsyc.2017.07.016

Byrne, Z., Palmer, C., Smith, C., & Weidert, J. (2011). The engaged employee face of organizations. *The new faces of organizations in the 21st century, 1*, 93–135.

Calvo, R., Zheng, Y. H., Kumar, S., Olgiati, A., & Berkman, L. (2012). Well-being and social capital on planet Earth: Cross-national evidence from 142 countries. *Plos One, 7*(8), 10. doi:10.1371/journal.pone.0042793

Campbell, C. (1987). *The romantic ethic and the spirit of modern consumerism*: Springer.

Campbell, J. D., Trapnell, P. D., Heine, S. J., Katz, I. M., Lavallee, L. F., & Lehman, D. R. (1996). Self-concept clarity: Measurement, personality correlates, and cultural boundaries. *Journal of Personality and Social Psychology, 70*(1), 141.

Campbell, W. K., Hoffman, B. J., Campbell, S. M., & Marchisio, G. (2011). Narcissism in organizational contexts. *Human Resource Management Review, 21*(4), 268–284.

Capabilities, C. (2011). The human development approach. In: Cambridge, MA: Harvard University Press.

Carabelli, A., & Cedrini, M. (2011). *The economic problem of happiness: Keynes on happiness and economics.* Paper presented at the Forum for Social Economics.

Carboni, J. T. (1990). Homelessness among the institutionalized elderly. *Journal of Gerontological Nursing, 16*(7), 32–37.

Cardador, M. T., & Rupp, D. E. (2011). Organizational culture, multiple needs, and the meaningfulness of work. In *The handbook of organizational culture and climate* (pp. 158–175).

Carlone, H. B., Benavides, A., Huffling, L. D., Matthews, C. E., Journell, W., & Tomasek, T. (2016). Field Ecology: A modest, but imaginable, contestation of neoliberal science education. *Mind Culture and Activity, 23*(3), 199–211. doi:10.1080/10749039.2016.1194433

Caron, J. (2012). Predictors of quality of life in economically disadvantaged populations in Montreal. *Social Indicators Research, 107*(3), 411–427.

Carr, D. (1997). The fulfillment of career dreams at midlife: Does it matter for women's mental health? *Journal of Health and Social Behavior, 38*(4), 331–344. doi:10.2307/2955429

Carroll, S. (1993). Spirituality and purpose in life in alcoholism recovery. *Journal of Studies on Alcohol, 54*(3), 297–301.

Carù, A., Caru, A., & Cova, B. (2007). *Consuming experience*: Routledge.

Casey, T. (2011). Capitalism, crisis, and a zombie named TINA. In *The Legacy of the Crash* (pp. 38–59): Springer.

Catlin, G., & Epstein, S. (1992). Unforgettable experiences: The relation of life events to basic beliefs about self and world. *Social Cognition, 10*(2), 189–209.

Caton, K. (2012). Taking the moral turn in tourism studies. *Annals of Tourism Research, 39*(4), 1906–1928.

Cavagnaro, E., Staffieri, S., & Postma, A. (2018). Understanding millennials' tourism experience: Values and meaning to travel as a key for identifying target clusters for youth (sustainable) tourism. *Journal of Tourism Futures, 4*(1), 31–42.

Cavazos Vela, J., Castro, V., Cavazos, L., Cavazos, M., & Gonzalez, S. L. (2015). Understanding Latina/o students' meaning in life, spirituality, and subjective happiness. *Journal of Hispanic Higher Education, 14*(2), 171–184.

Chamberlain, K., & Zika, S. (1988). Religiosity, life meaning and wellbeing: Some relationships in a sample of women. *Journal for the Scientific Study of Religion*, 411–420.

Chan, C. L., Sha, W., Leung, P. P., & Gilbert, K. R. (2011). Inspiring hope and transforming grief: Community capacity building for victims of the Sichuan earthquake in China. *Grief Matters: The Australian Journal of Grief and Bereavement, 14*(2), 52.

Chang, L., & Arkin, R. M. (2002). Materialism as an attempt to cope with uncertainty. *Psychology & Marketing, 19*(5), 389–406.

Chang, S. O., & Patricia, M. B. (2000). Meaning in life among the elderly. *Journal of Korean Academy of Nursing, 30*(2), 259–271.

Chatman, J. A. (1989). *Matching people and organizations: Selection and socialization in public accounting firms.* Paper presented at the Academy of Management proceedings.

Chatterjee, I., & Basu, J. (2010). Perceived causes of suicide, reasons for living and suicidal ideation among students. *Journal of the Indian Academy of Applied Psychology, 36*(2), 311–316.

Chen, C. C., Peng, M. W., & Saparito, P. A. (2002). Individualism, collectivism, and opportunism: A cultural perspective on transaction cost economics. *Journal of Management, 28*(4), 567–583.

Chen, C. P. (2001). On exploring meanings: Combining humanistic and career psychology theories in counselling. *Counselling Psychology Quarterly, 14*(4), 317–330.

Chen, C. P. (2008). Career guidance with immigrants. In *International handbook of career guidance* (pp. 419–442). Springer.

Cheng, C., & Li, A. Y.-l. (2014). Internet addiction prevalence and quality of (real) life: A meta-analysis of 31 nations across seven world regions. *Cyberpsychology, Behavior, and Social Networking, 17*(12), 755–760.

Chernev, A., Böckenholt, U., & Goodman, J. (2015). Choice overload: A conceptual review and meta-analysis. *Journal of Consumer Psychology, 25*(2), 333–358.

Cherrier, H. (2007). Ethical consumption practices: Co-production of self-expression and social recognition. *Journal of Consumer Behaviour: An International Research Review, 6*(5), 321–335.

Chiaburu, D. S., & Harrison, D. A. (2008). Do peers make the place? Conceptual synthesis and meta-analysis of coworker effects on perceptions, attitudes, OCBs, and performance. *Journal of Applied Psychology, 93*(5), 1082.

Chigbo, K. (2011). *The unheard cry of the Igbo people: A study of meaning in life in the meta-psychology of Abraham Joshua Heschel*: Xlibris Corporation.

Choi, Y. E., Cho, E., Jung, H. J., & Sohn, Y. W. (2018). Calling as a predictor of life satisfaction: The roles of psychological capital, work–family enrichment, and boundary management strategy. *Journal of Career Assessment, 26*(4), 567-582. doi:10.1177/1069072717723092

Choi, Y., Kim, J.-H., & Park, E.-C. (2016). The impact of differences between subjective and objective social class on life satisfaction among the Korean population in early old age: Analysis of Korean longitudinal study on aging. *Archives of Gerontology and Geriatrics, 67*, 98–105. doi:10.1016/j.archger.2016.07.006

Choi, S. O., Kim, S. N., Shin, K. I., Lee, J. J., & Jung, Y. J. (2003). Development of elderly meaning in life (EMIL) scale. *Journal of Korean Academy of Nursing, 33*(3), 414–424.

Chu, Y., Shen, C., & Yang, J. (2017). Country-level bonding, bridging, and linking social capital and immigrants' life satisfaction. *Applied Research in Quality of Life.* doi:10.1007/s11482-017-9556-1

Chudinov, S. I., & Sgem. (2014). Extremist rationality in suicide terrorism. In *Anthropology, Archaeology, History and Philosophy* (pp. 735–742). Sofia: Stef92 Technology Ltd.

Chuluun, T., & Graham, C. (2016). Local happiness and firm behavior: Do firms in happy places invest more? *Journal of Economic Behavior & Organization, 125*, 41–56. doi:10.1016/j.jebo.2016.01.014

Ci, J. (1999). Disenchantment, desublimation, and demoralization: Some cultural conjunctions of capitalism. *New Literary History, 30*(2), 295–324.

Ci, J. (1994). *Dialectic of the Chinese revolution: From utopianism to hedonism*: Stanford University Press.

Claes, R., & Quintanilla, S. A. R. (1993). Work meaning patterns in early career. *The European Work and Organizational Psychologist, 3*(4), 311–323.

Clark, W. A. V., & Lisowski, W. (2018). Wellbeing across individuals and places: How much does social capital matter? *Journal of Population Research, 35*(3), 217–236. doi:10.1007/s12546-018-9207-x

Clegg, C., & Spencer, C. (2007). A circular and dynamic model of the process of job design. *Journal of Occupational and Organizational Psychology, 80*(2), 321–339.

Clench-Aas, J., & Holte, A. (2018). Measures that increase social equality are effective in improving life satisfaction in times of economic crisis. *Bmc Public Health, 18*, 11. doi:10.1186/s12889-018-6076-3

Clymer, J. A. (2004). *America's culture of terrorism: Violence, capitalism, and the written word*: UNC Press Books.

Cohen-Meitar, R., Carmeli, A., & Waldman, D. A. (2009). Linking meaningfulness in the workplace to employee creativity: The intervening role of organizational identification and positive psychological experiences. *Creativity Research Journal, 21*(4), 361–375.

Cohen, M. H., & Ackland, G. J. (2012). Boundaries between ancient cultures: Origins and persistence. *Advances in Complex Systems, 15*(1–2), 30. doi:10.1142/s0219525911003220

Coleman, S. B., Kaplan, J. D., & Downing, R. W. (1986). Life cycle and loss—The spiritual vacuum of heroin addiction. *Family Process, 25*(1), 5–23.

Collins-Kreiner, N. (2018). Pilgrimage-tourism: Common themes in different religions. *International Journal of Religious Tourism and Pilgrimage, 6*(1), 3.

Collins, J. C., Collins, J., & Porras, J. I. (2005). *Built to last: Successful habits of visionary companies*: Random House.

Collins, R. L., Taylor, S. E., & Skokan, L. A. (1990). A better world or a shattered vision? Changes in life perspectives following victimization. *Social Cognition, 8*(3), 263–285.

Collischon, M. (2019). Relative pay, rank and happiness: A comparison between genders and part- and full-time employees. *Journal of Happiness Studies, 20*(1), 67-80. doi:10.1007/s10902-017-9937-z

Colombo, E., & Stanca, L. (2014). Measuring the monetary value of social relations: A hedonistic approach. *Journal of Behavioral and Experimental Economics, 50*, 77–87. doi:10.1016/j.socec.2014.03.001

Comaroff, J., & Comaroff, J. L. (2002). Alien-nation: Zombies, immigrants, and millennial capitalism. *The South Atlantic Quarterly, 101*(4), 779–805.

Cook, C. C. (2004). Addiction and spirituality. *Addiction, 99*(5), 539–551.

Cools, E., Van den Broeck, H., & Bouckenooghe, D. (2009). Cognitive styles and person–environment fit: Investigating the consequences of cognitive (mis)fit. *European Journal of Work and Organizational Psychology, 18*(2), 167–198.

Cooper, M. E. (2011). *Life as surplus: Biotechnology and capitalism in the neoliberal era*: University of Washington Press.

CCorlett, J. A. (1988). Perloff, utilitarianism, and existentialism: Problems with self-interest and personal responsibility. *American Psychologist, 43*(6), 481-483. doi:10.1037/0003-066X.43.6.481.b

Corsani, A. (2015). Transformation of labor and its temporalities: Chronological disorientation and the colonization of non-working time. *Logos*(3), 5–71. Retrieved from <Go to ISI>://WOS:000378493600004

Cox, N., Dewaele, A., Van Houtte, M., & Vincke, J. (2010). Stress-related growth, coming out, and internalized homonegativity in lesbian, gay, and bisexual youth. An examination of stress-related growth within the minority stress model. *Journal of Homosexuality, 58*(1), 117–137.

Critchley, P. (1995). Aristotle and the public good. *San Francisco, CA: Acadmia. edu.*

Csikszentmihalyi, M. (2004a). *Good business: Leadership, flow, and the making of meaning*: Penguin.

Csikszentmihalyi, M. (2004b). Materialism and the evolution of consciousness.

Csikszentmihalyi, M., & Csikszentmihalyi, I. (1975). *Beyond boredom and anxiety* (Vol. 721). Jossey-Bass: San Francisco.

Culbertson, S. S., Fullagar, C. J., & Mills, M. J. (2010). Feeling good and doing great: The relationship between psychological capital and well-being. *Journal of Occupational Health Psychology, 15*(4), 421–433. doi:10.1037/a0020720

D'Alisa, G., Demaria, F., & Kallis, G. (2014). *Degrowth: A vocabulary for a new era*: Routledge.

da Rosa, R. R. (2019). Neoliberalism, de-democratization, subjectivity. *Argumentos-Revista de Filosofia*(21), 154–165. Retrieved from <Go to ISI>://WOS:000465313600013

Dabla-Norris, M. E., Kochhar, M. K., Suphaphiphat, M. N., Ricka, M. F., & Tsounta, E. (2015). *Causes and consequences of income inequality: A global perspective*: International Monetary Fund.

Danaher, J. (2017). Will life be worth living in a world without work? Technological unemployment and the meaning of life. *Science and Engineering Ethics, 23*(1), 41–64.

Danziger, S. K., Carlson, M. J., & Henly, J. R. (2001). Post-welfare employment and psychological well-being. *Women & Health, 32*(1–2), 47–78. doi:10.1300/J013v32n01_03

Dardot, P., & Laval, C. (2014). *The new way of the world: On neoliberal society*: Verso Trade.

Davidson, R., Pacek, A. C., & Radcliff, B. (2013). Public policy and human happiness: The welfare state and the market as agents of well-being. In H. Brockmann & J. Delhey (Eds.), *Human happiness and the pursuit of maximization: Is more always better?* (Vol. 8, pp. 163–175). New York, NY: Springer Science + Business Media.

Davis, J. B. (2010). *Individuals and identity in economics*: Cambridge University Press.

Davis, J. E. (2003). The commodification of self. *The Hedgehog Review, 5*(2), 41–50.

Dawis, R. V. (2005). The Minnesota Theory of Work Adjustment.

Dawis, R. V., & Lofquist, L. H. (1984). *A psychological theory of work adjustment: An individual-differences model and its applications*: University of Minnesota Press.

De Genova, N. (1995). Gangster rap and nihilism in black America: Some questions of life and death. *Social Text*(43), 89–132.

De Graaf, J., Wann, D., & Naylor, T. H. (2014). *Affluenza: How overconsumption is killing us--and how to fight back*: Berrett-Koehler Publishers.

Deleuze, G., & Guattari, F. (2000). *A thousand plateaus: Capitalism and schizophrenia*. London: Athlone Press.

De Soto, H. (2000). *The mystery of capital: Why capitalism triumphs in the West and fails everywhere else*: Basic Civitas Books.

de Waal, F. Primates and philosophers: How morality evolved.

De Waal, F. (2010). *The age of empathy: Nature's lessons for a kinder society*: Broadway Books.

Deci, E. L., Koestner, R., & Ryan, R. M. (1999). A meta-analytic review of experiments examining the effects of extrinsic rewards on intrinsic motivation. *Psychological Bulletin, 125*(6), 627.

Deci, E. L., & Ryan, R. M. (2010). Intrinsic motivation. *The Corsini encyclopedia of psychology*, 1–2.

Degutis, M., & Urbonavicius, S. (2013). Determinants of subjective wellbeing in Lithuania. *Inzinerine Ekonomika-Engineering Economics, 24*(2), 111–18. doi:10.5755/j01.ee.2.24.2.2024

Dempsey, S. E., & Sanders, M. L. (2010). Meaningful work? Nonprofit marketization and work/life imbalance in popular autobiographies of social entrepreneurship. *Organization, 17*(4), 437–459.

Depaola, S. J., & Ebersole, P. (1995). Meaning in life categories of elderly nursing home residents. *The International Journal of Aging and Human Development, 40*(3), 227–236.

DeVore, I., & Lee, R. B. (1968). *Man the hunter*: Aldine-Atherton.

Di Fabio, A. (2015). The new purposeful identitarian awareness for the twenty-first century: Valorize themselves in life construction from youth to adult to late adulthood. In A. Di Fabio & J.-L. Bernaud (Eds.), *The construction of the identity in 21st century: A festschrift for Jean Guichard* (pp. 157–168). Hauppauge, NY: Nova Science Publishers.

Di Fabio, A. (2018). Intrapreneurial self-capital: A key resource for promoting well-being in a shifting work landscape. *Sustainability, 10*(9), 11. doi:10.3390/su10093035

Di Fabio, A., Palazzeschi, L., & Bucci, O. (2017). In an unpredictable and changing environment: Intrapreneurial self-capital as a key resource for life satisfaction and flourishing. *Frontiers in Psychology, 8*, 5. doi:10.3389/fpsyg.2017.01819

Diamant, L. (1991). *Mind-body maturity: Psychological approaches to sports, exercise, and fitness*: Taylor & Francis.

Didelot, M. J., Hollingsworth, L., & Buckenmeyer, J. A. (2012). Internet addiction: A logotherapeutic approach. *Journal of Addictions & Offender Counseling, 33*(1), 18–33.

Dik, B. J., Byrne, Z. S., & Steger, M. F. (2013). *Purpose and meaning in the workplace*: American Psychological Association.

Dik, B. J., & Duffy, R. D. (2009). Calling and vocation at work: Definitions and prospects for research and practice. *The Counseling Psychologist, 37*(3), 424–450.

Dik, B. J., Duffy, R. D., Allan, B. A., O'Donnell, M. B., Shim, Y., & Steger, M. F. (2015). Purpose and meaning in career development applications. *The Counseling Psychologist, 43*(4), 558–585.

Dik, B. J., & Hansen, J.-I. C. (2011). Moderation of PE fit-job satisfaction relations. *Journal of Career Assessment, 19*(1), 35–50.

Dik, B. J., Steger, M. F., Fitch-Martin, A. R., & Onder, C. C. (2013). Cultivating meaningfulness at work. In *The experience of meaning in life* (pp. 363–377): Springer.

Diken, B. (2008). *Nihilism*: Routledge.

Diller, S., Shedroff, N., & Rhea, D. (2005). *Making meaning: How successful businesses deliver meaningful customer experiences*: New Riders.

Dion, M. (2014). *Financial crimes and existential philosophy*. Dordrecht: Springer.

Dirks, J. M. (2000). *Spirituality of work: The new opiate or a postmodern search for meaning in life?* Paper presented at the PUB DATE 2000-12-00 NOTE 567p.; Conference organized by Research into Adult and Vocational Learning (RAVL) at the University of Technology, Sydney (UTS). Gleebooks," Studies in Continuing Education," and the Faculty of Education at UTS provided some financial assistance.

Dittmar, H., Bond, R., Hurst, M., & Kasser, T. (2014). The relationship between materialism and personal well-being: A meta-analysis. *Journal of Personality and Social Psychology, 107*(5), 879.

Dittmar, H., & Kapur, P. (2011). Consumerism and well-being in India and the UK: Identity projection and emotion regulation as underlying psychological processes. *Psychological Studies, 56*(1), 71–85.

Dixon, A. D., & Monk, A. H. B. (2014). Frontier finance. *Annals of the Association of American Geographers, 104*(4), 852–868. doi:10.1080/00045608.2014.912543

Dixon, J., & Frolova, Y. (2011). Existential poverty: Welfare dependency, learned helplessness and psychological capital. *Poverty & Public Policy, 3*(2), 1–20.

Dmitrovsky, A. L. (2019). Journalism theories: Why they do not work? (The problem of a synergistic approach to journalistic phenomena). *Theoretical and Practical Issues of Journalism, 8*(1), 36–56. doi:10.17150/2308-6203.2019.8(1).36-56

Dolan, M. J. (2007). Government-sponsored chaplains and crisis: Walking the fine line in disaster response and daily life. *Hastings Const. LQ, 35*, 505.

Don Gottfredson, G., & Duffy, R. D. (2008). Using a theory of vocational personalities and work environments to explore subjective well-being. *Journal of Career Assessment, 16*(1), 44–59.

Doran, C. J. (2010). Fair trade consumption: In support of the out-group. *Journal of Business Ethics, 95*(4), 527–541.

Doran, C. J. (2009). The role of personal values in fair trade consumption. *Journal of Business Ethics, 84*(4), 549–563.

Dowd, A. M., Marshall, N., Fleming, A., Jakku, E., Gaillard, E., & Howden, M. (2014). The role of networks in transforming Australian agriculture. *Nature Climate Change, 4*(7), 558-563. doi:10.1038/nclimate2275

Dragone, D., & Ziebarth, N. R. (2017). Non-separable time preferences, novelty consumption and body weight: Theory and evidence from the East German transition to capitalism. *Journal of Health Economics, 51*, 41–65. doi:10.1016/j.jhealeco.2016.11.002

Drescher, C. F., Baczwaski, B. J., Walters, A. B., Aiena, B. J., Schulenberg, S. E., & Johnson, L. R. (2012). Coping with an ecological disaster: The role of perceived meaning in life and self-efficacy following the Gulf oil spill. *Ecopsychology, 4*(1), 56–63.

Drescher, C. F., Schulenberg, S. E., & Smith, C. V. (2014). The Deepwater Horizon oil spill and the Mississippi Gulf Coast: Mental health in the context of a technological disaster. *American Journal of Orthopsychiatry, 84*(2), 142.

Drewell, M., & Larsson, B. (2017). *The meaningful economy*. Poland: The Foresight Group.

Driscoll, M. (2015). Hyperneoliberalism: Youth, labor, and militant mice in Japan. *Positions-Asia Critique, 23*(3), 545–564. doi:10.1215/10679847-3125887

Drucker, P. F. (1997). *Sinnvoll wirtschaften: Notwendigkeit und kunst, die zukunft zu meistern*: Econ-Verlag.

Dudnik, S. I. (2018). Karl Marx and problem of humanism. *Vestnik Sankt-Peterburgskogo Universiteta-Filosofiya I Konfliktologiya, 34*(4), 462–473. doi:10.21638/spbu17.2018.401

Duffy, R. D., Dik, B. J., & Steger, M. F. (2011). Calling and work-related outcomes: Career commitment as a mediator. *Journal of Vocational Behavior, 78*(2), 210–218.

Duke, N. N., Skay, C. L., Pettingell, S. L., & Borowsky, I. W. (2009). From adolescent connections to social capital: Predictors of civic engagement in young adulthood. *Journal of Adolescent Health, 44*(2), 161–168.

Dunn, M. G., & O'Brien, K. M. (2009). Psychological health and meaning in life: Stress, social support, and religious coping in Latina/Latino immigrants. *Hispanic Journal of Behavioral Sciences, 31*(2), 204–227.

Duppe, T. (2011). *The making of the economy. A phenomenology of economic science.* Lanham: Lexington Press.

Durr II, M. R., & Tracey, T. J. (2009). Relation of person–environment fit to career certainty. *Journal of Vocational Behavior, 75*(2), 129–138.

Dursun, P., Steger, M. F., Bentele, C., & Schulenberg, S. E. (2016). Meaning and posttraumatic growth among survivors of the September 2013 Colorado floods. *Journal of Clinical Psychology, 72*(12), 1247–1263.

Dzbankova, Z., & Sirucek, P. (2013). *Rationality in economics—Male and female perspectivES.* Slany: Melandrium.

Easterlin, R. A. (2009). Lost in transition: Life satisfaction on the road to capitalism. *Journal of Economic Behavior & Organization, 71*(2), 130–145. doi:10.1016/j.jebo.2009.04.003

Easterlin, R. A. (2012). Life satisfaction of rich and poor under socialism and capitalism. *International Journal of Happiness and Development, 1*(1), 112–126.

Easterlin, R. A. (2014). Life satisfaction in the transition from socialism to capitalism: Europe and China. In A. E. Clark & C. Senik (Eds.), *Happiness and economic growth: Lessons from developing countries.* (pp. 6–31). New York, NY: Oxford University Press.

Easterlin, R. A., & Crimmins, E. M. (2018). American youth are becoming more materialistic. In *Citizen Politics in Post-Industrial Societies* (pp. 67–83): Routledge.

Easterlin, R. A., McVey, L. A., Switek, M., Sawangfa, O., & Zweig, J. S. (2010). The happiness–income paradox revisited. *Proceedings of the National Academy of Sciences, 107*(52), 22463-22468.

Easterlin, R. A., McVey, L. A., Switek, M., Sawangfa, O., & Zweig, J. S. (2010). The happiness–income paradox revisited. *PNAS Proceedings of the National Academy of Sciences of the United States of America, 107*(52), 22463–22468. doi:10.1073/pnas.1015962107

Easterlin, R. A., McVey, L. A., Switek, M., Sawangfa, O., & Zweig, J. S. (2013). The happiness-income paradox revisited. In B. S. Frey & A. Stutzer (Eds.), *Recent developments in the economics of happiness.* (pp. 220-225). Northampton, MA: Edward Elgar Publishing.

Ebersole, P., & DePaola, S. (1989). Meaning in life depth in the active married elderly. *The Journal of Psychology, 123*(2),171–178.

Ebersole, P., & Depaola, S. (1987). Meaning in life categories of later life couples. *The Journal of Psychology, 121*(2), 185–191.

Eckhardt, G. M., & Houston, M. J. (1998). Consumption as self-presentation in a collectivist society. *ACR Asia-Pacific Advances.*

Edwards, D., & Cromwell, D. (2018). Propaganda blitz: How the corporate media distort reality. London: Pluto Press.

Edwards, J. R., Cable, D. M., Williamson, I. O., Lambert, L. S., & Shipp, A. J. (2006). The phenomenology of fit: Linking the person and environment to the subjective experience of person–environment fit. *Journal of Applied Psychology, 91*(4), 802.

Edwards, J. R., Caplan, R. D., & Van Harrison, R. (1998). Person–environment fit theory. *Theories of Organizational Stress, 28,* 67.

Edwards, M. J., & Holden, R. R. (2001). Coping, meaning in life, and suicidal manifestations: Examining gender differences. *Journal of Clinical Psychology, 57*(12), 1517–1534.

Ehrenreich, B. (2010). *Nickel and dimed: On (not) getting by in America*: Metropolitan Books.

Eibich, P., Krekel, C., Demuth, I., & Wagner, G. G. (2016). Associations between neighborhood characteristics, well-being and health vary over the life course. *Gerontology, 62*(3), 362–370. doi:10.1159/000438700

Ekblad, S. (1993). Psychosocial adaptation of children while housed in a Swedish refugee camp: Aftermath of the collapse of Yugoslavia. *Stress Medicine, 9*(3), 159–166.

Eksner, H. J. (2015). Meaning-making and motivation in urban zones of marginalization: Mapping the ecocultural context of educational goals. *British Journal of Sociology of Education, 36*(4), 595–613. doi:10.1080/01425692.2013.835712

Elgar, F. J., Davis, C. G., Wohl, M. J., Trites, S. J., Zelenski, J. M., & Martin, M. S. (2011). Social capital, health and life satisfaction in 50 countries. *Health & Place, 17*(5), 1044–1053. doi:10.1016/j.healthplace.2011.06.010

Elliott, R. (1997). Existential consumption and irrational desire. *European Journal of Marketing, 31*(3/4), 285–296.

Ellis, T. (2004). The era of compassionate capitalism. Executive MBA dissertation, Henley Management College, Henley-on-Thames.

Emmons, R. A. (1987). Narcissism: Theory and measurement. *Journal of Personality and Social Psychology, 52*(1), 11.

Emslie, C., & Hunt, K. (2009). 'Live to work' or 'work to live'? A qualitative study of gender and work–life balance among men and women in mid-life. *Gender, Work & Organization, 16*(1), 151–172.

Engelbrecht, H. J. (2009). Natural capital, subjective well-being, and the new welfare economics of sustainability: Some evidence from cross-country regressions. *Ecological Economics, 69*(2), 380–388. doi:10.1016/j.ecolecon.2009.08.011

England, R. W. (1994). *Evolutionary concepts in contemporary economics*: University of Michigan Press.

Erez, C., & Shenkman, G. (2016). Gay dads are happier: Subjective well-being among gay and heterosexual fathers. *Journal of GLBT Family Studies, 12*(5), 451–467.

Erichsen, N.-B., & Büssing, A. (2013). Spiritual needs of elderly living in residential/nursing homes. *Evidence-Based Complementary and Alternative Medicine, 2013*.

Erikson, E. H. (1963). *Childhood and society* (2nd ed.). Erikson-New York: Norton.

Erman, T. (2001). Rural migrants and patriarchy in Turkish cities. *International Journal of Urban and Regional Research, 25*(1), 118–133.

Etzioni, A. (2010). *Moral dimension: Toward a new economics*: Simon and Schuster.

Evangelista, L. S., Kagawa-Singer, M., & Dracup, K. (2001). Gender differences in health perceptions and meaning in persons living with heart failure. *Heart & Lung, 30*(3), 167–176.

Ewen, S. (2008). *Captains of consciousness advertising and the social roots of the consumer culture*: Basic Books.

Fairlie, P. (2011). Meaningful work, employee engagement, and other key employee outcomes: Implications for human resource development. *Advances in Developing Human Resources, 13*(4), 508–525.

Fassin, D. (2010). Coming back to life: An anthropological reassessment of biopolitics and governmentality. In *Governmentality* (pp. 193–208): Routledge.

Featherstone, M. (1982). The body in consumer culture. *Theory, Culture & Society, 1*(2), 18–33.

Feder, A., Ahmad, S., Lee, E. J., Morgan, J. E., Singh, R., Smith, B. W., ... Charney, D. S. (2013). Coping and PTSD symptoms in Pakistani earthquake survivors: Purpose in life, religious coping and social support. *Journal of Affective Disorders, 147*(1-3), 156–163.

Fedyukin, I. (2018). "Westernizations" from Peter I to Meiji: War, political competition, and institutional change. *Theory and Society, 47*(2), 207–231. doi:10.1007/s11186-018-9313-y

Fennell, D. A. (2006). *Tourism ethics* (Vol. 30): Channel View Publications.

Fenwick, T., & Lange, E. (1998). Spirituality in the workplace: The new frontier of HRD. *Canadian Journal for the Study of Adult Education, 12*(1), 63–87.

Ferrer-i-Carbonell, A., & Gerxhani, K. (2016). Tax evasion and well-being: A study of the social and institutional context in Central and Eastern Europe. *European Journal of Political Economy, 45*, 149–159. doi:10.1016/j.ejpoleco.2016.09.004

Filep, S. (2012). Positive psychology and tourism. In *Handbook of tourism and quality-of-life research* (pp. 31–50). New York: Springer.

Fine, R. (1986). *Narcissism, the self, and society*. New York: Columbia University Press.

Fischer, J. A. V., & Torgler, B. (2013). Do positional concerns destroy social capital: Evidence from 26 countries. *Economic Inquiry, 51*(2), 1542–1565. doi:10.1111/j.1465-7295.2011.00441.x

Fisher, M. (2009). *Capitalist realism: Is there no alternative?* New York: John Hunt Publishing.

Fletcher, J. K. (1998). Relational practice: A feminist reconstruction of work. *Journal of Management Inquiry, 7*(2), 163–186.

Flynn, T. R. (1986). *Sartre and Marxist existentialism: The test case of collective responsibility*. Chicago: University of Chicago Press.

Folbre, N. (2009). *Greed, lust and gender: A history of economic ideas*. Oxford: Oxford University Press.

Foster, J. B. (2002). *Ecology against capitalism*: NYU Press.

Foster, J. D., Campbell, W. K., & Twenge, J. M. (2003). Individual differences in narcissism: Inflated self-views across the lifespan and around the world. *Journal of Research in Personality, 37*(6), 469–486.

Foster, K. A., Bowland, S. E., & Vosler, A. N. (2015). All the pain along with all the joy: Spiritual resilience in lesbian and gay Christians. *American Journal of Community Psychology, 55*(1–2), 191–201.

Fouad, N. A., & Kantamneni, N. (2008). Contextual factors in vocational psychology: Intersections of individual, group, and societal dimensions. *Handbook of counseling psychology, 4*, 40–425.

Foucault, M. (2012). *The history of sexuality* (Vol. 3): *The care of the self*. New York: Vintage.

Foucault, M., Davidson, A. I., & Burchell, G. (2008). *The birth of biopolitics: Lectures at the Collège de France, 1978–1979*. Amsterdam: Springer.

Frank, C., Davis, C. G., & Elgar, F. J. (2014). Financial strain, social capital, and perceived health during economic recession: A longitudinal survey in rural Canada. *Anxiety Stress and Coping, 27*(4), 422–438. doi:10.1080/10615806.2013.864389

Frank, R. H. (2012). *The Darwin economy: Liberty, competition, and the common good*. New Jersey: Princeton University Press.

Frank, T. (2001). *One market under God: Extreme capitalism, market populism, and the end of economic democracy*. Toronto: Anchor Canada.

Freberg, K., Graham, K., McGaughey, K., & Freberg, L. A. (2011). Who are the social media influencers? A study of public perceptions of personality. *Public Relations Review, 37*(1), 90–92.

Freedman, M. (2008). *Encore: Finding work that matters in the second half of life*: PublicAffairs.

Freitag, M. (2003). Social capital in (dis)similar democracies - The development of generalized trust in Japan and Switzerland. *Comparative Political Studies, 36*(8), 936–966. doi:10.1177/0010414003256116

Fremstad, J. (1977). Marcuse: The Dialectics of hopelessness. *Western Political Quarterly, 30*(1), 80–92.

Friedman, J. (2005). *Consumption and identity*. New York: Routledge.

Fry, P. S. (2000). Religious involvement, spirituality and personal meaning for life: Existential predictors of psychological wellbeing in community-residing and institutional care elders. *Aging & Mental Health, 4*(4), 375–387.

Fujishiro, K., Xu, J., & Gong, F. (2010). What does "occupation" represent as an indicator of socioeconomic status?: Exploring occupational prestige and health. *Social Science & Medicine, 71*(12), 2100–2107.

Fyfe, N. R. (2005). Making space for "neo-communitarianism"? The third sector, state and civil society in the UK. *Antipode, 37*(3), 536–557.

Gagné, M., & Deci, E. L. (2005). Self-determination theory and work motivation. *Journal of Organizational Behavior, 26*(4), 331–362.

Galanter, M. (2006). Spirituality and addiction: A research and clinical perspective. *American Journal on Addictions, 15*(4), 286–292.

Gane, M. (1990). Ironies of postmodernism: fate of Baudrillard's fatalism. *Economy and Society, 19*(3), 314–333.

Gao, L., & Jin, W. T. (2015). Work–family conflict mediates the association between job demands and life and job satisfaction in Chinese middle-level managers. *Current Psychology, 34*(2), 311–320. doi:10.1007/s12144-014-9259-9

Garapich, M. P. (2014). Homo Sovieticus revisited—Anti-institutionalism, alcohol and resistance among polish homeless men in london. *International Migration, 52*(1), 100–117. doi:10.1111/imig.12041

García, F. E., Cova, F., Rincón, P., & Vázquez, C. (2015). Trauma or growth after a natural disaster? The mediating role of rumination processes. *European Journal of Psychotraumatology, 6*(1), 26557.

Garcia, T. (2016). *La vie intense. Une obsession moderne*. Paris: Autrement.

Gardner, H. (2010). *Responsibility at work: How leading professionals act (or don't act) responsibly*: John Wiley & Sons.

Gardner, W. L., Avolio, B. J., Luthans, F., May, D. R., & Walumbwa, F. (2005). "Can you see the real me?" A self-based model of authentic leader and follower development. *The Leadership Quarterly, 16*(3), 343–372.

Garrison, M. B., & Sasser, D. D. (2009). Families and disasters: Making meaning out of adversity. In *Lifespan perspectives on natural disasters* (pp. 113–130): Springer.

Gehring, K. (2013). Who Benefits from economic freedom? Unraveling the effect of economic freedom on subjective well-being. *World Development, 50*, 74–90. doi:10.1016/j.worlddev.2013.05.003

George, B. (2003). *Authentic leadership: Rediscovering the secrets to creating lasting value*. New York: John Wiley & Sons.

George, B., Sims, P., McLean, A. N., & Mayer, D. (2007). Discovering your authentic leadership. *Harvard Business Review, 85*(2), 129.

Gerstner, C. R., & Day, D. V. (1997). Meta-analytic review of leader–member exchange theory: Correlates and construct issues. *Journal of Applied Psychology, 82*(6), 827.

Ghidina, M. J. (1992). Social relations and the definition of work: Identity management in a low-status occupation. *Qualitative Sociology, 15*(1), 73–85.

Gibson, D. E. (2004). Role models in career development: New directions for theory and research. *Journal of Vocational Behavior, 65*(1), 134–156.

Giddens, A. (1991). *Modernity and self-identity: Self and society in the late modern age*. New York: Stanford University Press.

Gilbert, M. (2005). *The workplace revolution: Restoring trust in business and bringing meaning to our work*. London Conari Press.

Gilens, M., & Page, B. I. (2014). Testing theories of American politics: Elites, interest groups, and average citizens. *Perspectives on Politics, 12*(3), 564–581.

Gini, A. (2013). *My job, my self: Work and the creation of the modern individual*. New York: Routledge.

Giroux, H. A. (2014). *Neoliberalism's war on higher education*. London: Haymarket Books.

Giroux, H. A. (2006). Reading Hurricane Katrina: Race, class, and the biopolitics of disposability. *College Literature, 33*(3), 171–196. doi:10.1353/lit.2006.0037

Giroux, H. A., & Pollock, G. (2010). *The mouse that roared: Disney and the end of innocence*: Rowman & Littlefield Publishers.

Gladden, J. (2013). Coping strategies of Sudanese refugee women in Kakuma Refugee Camp, Kenya. *Refugee Survey Quarterly, 32*(4), 66–89.

Gleibs, I. H., Morton, T. A., Rabinovich, A., Haslam, S. A., & Helliwell, J. F. (2013). Unpacking the hedonistic paradox: A dynamic analysis of the relationships between financial capital, social capital and life satisfaction. *British Journal of Social Psychology, 52*(1), 25–43. doi:10.1111/j.2044-8309.2011.02035.x

Goh, D. P. S. (2009). Chinese religion and the challenge of modernity in Malaysia and Singapore: Syncretism, hybridisation and transfiguration. *Asian Journal of Social Science, 37*(1), 107–137. doi:10.1163/156853109x385411

Goldsworthy, H. D. (2010). *Compassionate capitalism: Institutionalization and legitimacy in microfinance*: University of California, Irvine.

Gonzalez, S., Oosterlynck, S., Ribera-Fumaz, R., & Rossi, U. (2018). Locating the global financial crisis: –ariegated neoliberalization in four European cities. *Territory Politics Governance, 6*(4), 468–488. doi:10.1080/21622671.2017.1318713

Goodwin, T. (2012). Why we should reject 'nudge'. *Politics, 32*(2), 85–92.

Goux, J.-J. (1990). *Symbolic economies: after Marx and Freud*. New York: Cornell University Press.

Gowan, M. E., Kirk, R. C., & Sloan, J. A. (2014). Building resiliency: A cross-sectional study examining relationships among health-related quality of life, well-being, and disaster preparedness. *Health and Quality of Life Outcomes, 12*, 17. doi:10.1186/1477-7525-12-85

Graafland, J., & Compen, B. (2015). Economic freedom and life satisfaction: Mediation by income per capita and generalized trust. *Journal of Happiness Studies: An Interdisciplinary Forum on Subjective Well-Being, 16*(3), 789–810. doi:10.1007/s10902-014-9534-3

Graafland, J., & Lous, B. (2018). Economic freedom, income inequality and life satisfaction in OECD countries. *Journal of Happiness Studies, 19*(7), 2071–2093. doi:10.1007/s10902-017-9905-7

Graeber, D., & Cerutti, A. (2018). *Bullshit jobs.* New York, NY: Simon & Schuster.

Graen, G., & Grace, M. (2015). Positive industrial and organizational psychology: Designing for tech-savvy, optimistic, and purposeful millennial professionals' company cultures. *Industrial and Organizational Psychology: Perspectives on Science and Practice, 8*(3), 395–408. doi:10.1017/iop.2015.57

Graham, L., & Oswald, A. J. (2010). Hedonistic capital, adaptation and resilience. *Journal of Economic Behavior & Organization, 76*(2), 372–384. doi:10.1016/j.jebo.2010.07.003

Grandey, A. A., Fisk, G. M., Mattila, A. S., Jansen, K. J., & Sideman, L. A. (2005). Is "service with a smile" enough? Authenticity of positive displays during service encounters. *Organizational Behavior and Human Decision Processes, 96*(1), 38–55.

Grant, A. M. (2007). Relational job design and the motivation to make a prosocial difference. *Academy of Management Review, 32*(2), 393–417.

Grant, A. M. (2008a). Does intrinsic motivation fuel the prosocial fire? Motivational synergy in predicting persistence, performance, and productivity. *Journal of Applied Psychology, 93*(1), 48.

Grant, A. M. (2008b). The significance of task significance: Job performance effects, relational mechanisms, and boundary conditions. *Journal of Applied Psychology, 93*(1), 108.

Grant, A. M. (2009). Putting self-interest out of business? Contributions and unanswered questions from use-inspired research on prosocial motivation. *Industrial and Organizational Psychology, 2*(1), 94–98.

Gray, D., & Jones, K. (2018). The resilience and wellbeing of public sector leaders. *International Journal of Public Leadership, 14*(3), 138–154. doi:10.1108/ijpl-09-2017-0033

Grayson, D., & Jane, N. (2017). *Corporate responsibility coalitions: The past, present, and future of alliances for sustainable capitalism*: Routledge.

Green, J., & Jenkins, H. (2011). How audiences create value and meaning in a networked economy. In *The handbook of media audiences,*(pp. 109–127).Wiley Online Books.

Green, S. (2009). *Good value: Reflections on money, morality and an uncertain world.* London: Penguin UK.

Gregory, J. L., & Prana, H. (2013). Posttraumatic growth in Côte d'Ivoire refugees using the companion recovery model. *Traumatology, 19*(3), 223–232.

Greider, W. (1998). *One world, ready or not: The manic logic of global capitalism.* New York: Simon and Schuster.

Groot, W., van den Brink, H. M., & van Praag, B. (2007). The compensating income variation of social capital. *Social Indicators Research, 82*(2), 189–207. doi:10.1007/s11205-006-9035-9

Grouden, M. E., & Jose, P. E. (2014). How do sources of meaning in life vary according to demographic factors? *New Zealand Journal of Psychology, 43*(3).

Gruba-McCallister, F. (2007). Narcissism and the empty self: To have or to be. *Journal of Individual Psychology, 63*(2).

Gu, D., Huang, N. W., Zhang, M. X., & Wang, F. (2015). Under the dome: Air pollution, wellbeing, and pro-environmental behaviour among Beijing residents. *Journal of Pacific Rim Psychology, 9*(2), 65–77. doi:10.1017/prp.2015.10

Guan, Y., Deng, H., Bond, M. H., Chen, S. X., & Chan, C. C.-h. (2010). Person–job fit and work-related attitudes among Chinese employees: Need for cognitive closure as moderator. *Basic and Applied Social Psychology, 32*(3), 250–260.

Guion, R. M., & Landy, F. J. (1972). The meaning of work and the motivation to work. *Organizational Behavior and Human Performance, 7*(2), 308–339.

Guiso, L., Sapienza, P., & Zingales, L. (2003). People's opium? Religion and economic attitudes. *Journal of Monetary Economics, 50*(1), 225–282.

Guitart, M. E. (2011). The consumer capitalist society and its effects on identity: A macro cultural approach. *Revista Psicologia Política, 11*(21).

Guo, M., Gan, Y., & Tong, J. (2013). The role of meaning-focused coping in significant loss. *Anxiety, Stress & Coping, 26*(1), 87–102.

Gupta, R. K. (1996). Is there a place for the sacred in organizations and their development. *Journal of Human Values, 2*(2), 149–158.

Guriev, S., & Melnikov, N. (2018). Happiness convergence in transition countries. *Journal of Comparative Economics, 46*(3), 683–707. doi:10.1016/j.jce.2018.07.003

Guriev, S., & Zhuravskaya, E. (2009). (Un)Happiness in transition. *Journal of Economic Perspectives, 23*(2), 143–168. doi:10.1257/jep.23.2.143

Gutierrez-Zamano, E. G. (2005). *Looking into the 'hard mirror': Life history exploration of altruistic motivation and socialization.* (65). ProQuest Information & Learning.

Haar, J. M., Russo, M., Suñe, A., & Ollier-Malaterre, A. (2014). Outcomes of work–life balance on job satisfaction, life satisfaction and mental health: A study across seven cultures. *Journal of Vocational Behavior, 85*(3), 361–373.

Habibov, N., & Afandi, E. (2015). Pre- and post-crisis life-satisfaction and social trust in transitional countries: An initial assessment. *Social Indicators Research, 121*(2), 503–524. doi:10.1007/s11205-014-0640-8

Hackbarth, M., Pavkov, T., Wetchler, J., & Flannery, M. (2012). Natural disasters: An assessment of family resiliency following Hurricane Katrina. *Journal of Marital and Family Therapy, 38*(2), 340–351.

Hackman, J. R. (1980). Work redesign and motivation. *Professional Psychology, 11*(3), 445.

Hackman, J. R., & Hackman, R. J. (2002). *Leading teams: Setting the stage for great performances.* Cambridge: Harvard Business Press.

Halkitis, P. N., Mattis, J. S., Sahadath, J. K., Massie, D., Ladyzhenskaya, L., Pitrelli, K., ... Lowie, S.-A. E. (2009). The meanings and manifestations of religion and spirituality among lesbian, gay, bisexual, and transgender adults. *Journal of Adult Development, 16*(4), 250–262.

Hall, D. T. (1996). Protean careers of the 21st century. *Academy of Management Perspectives, 10*(4), 8–16.

Hall, D. T. (2004a). The protean career: A quarter-century journey. *Journal of Vocational Behavior, 65*(1), 1–13.

Hall, D. T. (2004b). Self-awareness, identity, and leader development. In *Leader development for transforming organizations* (pp. 173–196): Psychology Press.

Hall, D. T., & Chandler, D. E. (2005). Psychological success: When the career is a calling. *Journal of Organizational Behavior 26*(2), 155–176.

Hall, S. (2012). The solicitation of the trap: On transcendence and transcendental materialism in advanced consumer-capitalism. *Human Studies, 35*(3), 365–381.

Halperin, E., Canetti, D., Hobfoll, S. E., & Johnson, R. J. (2009). Terror, resource gains and exclusionist political attitudes among new immigrants and veteran Israelis. *Journal of Ethnic And Migration Studies, 35*(6), 997–1014.

Hamzaoglu, O., Ozkan, O., Ulusoy, M., & Gokdogan, F. (2010). The prevalence of hopelessness among adults: Disability and other related factors. *The International Journal of Psychiatry in Medicine, 40*(1), 77–91.

Han, S., Kim, H., & Lee, H. S. (2013). A multilevel analysis of the compositional and contextual association of social capital and subjective well-being in Seoul, South Korea. *Social Indicators Research, 111*(1), 185–202. doi:10.1007/s11205-011-9990-7

Hansen, J. (1994). The measurement of vocational interests. *Personnel selection and classification*, 293–316.

Harms, P. D., Roberts, B. W., & Winter, D. (2006). Becoming the Harvard man: Person-environment fit, personality development, and academic success. *Personality and Social Psychology Bulletin, 32*(7), 851–865.

Harpaz, I., & Fu, X. (2002). The structure of the meaning of work: A relative stability amidst change. *Human Relations, 55*(6), 639–667.

Harrington, B., & Hall, D. T. (2007). *Career management & work-life integration: Using self-assessment to navigate contemporary careers*. London: Sage.

Harrington, J. C., & Harrington. (1992). *Investing with your conscience: How to achieve high returns using socially responsible investing*: Wiley New York, NY.

Harrison, N. E. (2013). *Sustainable capitalism and the pursuit of well-being*. New York: Routledge.

Hart, K. E., & Singh, T. (2009). An existential model of flourishing subsequent to treatment for addiction: The importance of living a meaningful and spiritual life. *Illness, Crisis & Loss, 17*(2), 125–147.

Hawken, P., Lovins, A. B., & Lovins, L. H. (2013). *Natural capitalism: The next industrial revolution*. New York: Routledge.

Haynes, W. C., Van Tongeren, D. R., Aten, J., Davis, E. B., Davis, D. E., Hook, J. N., ... Johnson, T. (2017). The meaning as a buffer hypothesis: Spiritual meaning attenuates the effect of disaster-related resource loss on posttraumatic stress. *Psychology of Religion and Spirituality, 9*(4), 446.

Hearn, A. (2008). 'Meat, Mask, Burden': Probing the contours of the branded 'self'. *Journal of Consumer Culture, 8*(2), 197–217. doi:10.1177/1469540508090086

Heidegger, M. (1977). *The question concerning technology, and other essays*.

Heilman, E. E. (1998). The struggle for self: Power and identity in adolescent girls. *Youth & Society, 30*(2), 182–208.

Heintzman, P. (2013). Retreat tourism as transformational tourism. In *Transformational Tourism: Tourist Perspectives*: CAB International.

Heller-Sahlgren, G. (2018). Smart but unhappy: Independent-school competition and the wellbeing-efficiency trade-off in education. *Economics of Education Review, 62*, 66–81. doi:10.1016/j.econedurev.2017.10.005

Heller, D., Watson, D., & Ilies, R. (2004). The role of person versus situation in life satisfaction: A critical examination. *Psychological Bulletin, 130*(4), 574.

Helliwell, J. F., & Barrington-Leigh, C. P. (2012). How much is social capital worth? In J. Jetten, C. Haslam, & S. A. Haslam (Eds.), *The social cure: Identity, health and well-being*. (pp. 55–71). New York, NY: Psychology Press.

Helliwell, J. F., & Huang, H. F. (2010). How's the job? *Industrial & Labor Relations Review, 63*(2), 205–227. doi:10.1177/001979391006300202

Helliwell, J. F., & Putnam, R. D. (2013). The social context of well-being. In B. S. Frey & A. Stutzer (Eds.), *Recent developments in the economics of happiness*. (pp. 309–320). Northampton, MA: Edward Elgar Publishing.

Henderson-King, D., & Mitchell, A. M. (2011). Do materialism, intrinsic aspirations, and meaning in life predict students' meanings of education? *Social Psychology of Education, 14*(1), 119–134.

Herman, E. S., & Chomsky, N. (2010). *Manufacturing consent: The political economy of the mass media*. New York: Random House.

Herrmann-Pillath, C. (2017). *The economics of identity and creativity: A cultural science approach*. New York: Routledge.

Herzberg, F. (2017). *Motivation to work*. New York: Routledge.

Hewitt, S. A. (2014). *Young urban Bulgarians: Transition and disempowerment*. (74). ProQuest Information & Learning.

Hewlett, S. A., Sherbin, L., & Sumberg, K. (2009). How Gen Y and Boomers will reshape your agenda. *Harvard Business Review, 87*(7-8), 71–76, 153.

Heyat, F. (2004). Re-Islamisation in Kyrgyzstan: Gender, new poverty and the moral dimension. *Central Asian Survey, 23*(3-4), 275–287.

Hirschberger, G. (2013). Self-protective altruism. *Social and Personality Psychology Compass, 7*(2), 128-140. doi:10.1111/spc3.12013

Hirschberger, G. (2015). Terror management and prosocial behavior: A theory of self-protective altruism. In D. A. Schroeder & W. G. Graziano (Eds.), *The Oxford handbook of prosocial behavior.* (pp. 166–187). Oxford: Oxford University Press.

Hirschman, E. C., & Holbrook, M. B. (1982). Hedonistic consumption: Emerging concepts, methods and propositions. *Journal of Marketing, 46*(3), 92–101.

Hirt, S., Slaev, A., & Anderson, J. (2012). Planning after statism. *Journal of Architectural and Planning Research, 29*(4), 271–277. Retrieved from <Go to ISI>://WOS:000319849700001

Hitaj, E. (2011). *The relationship between income, wealth, and life satisfaction.* (72). ProQuest Information & Learning.

Hjorth, D. (2007). *Entrepreneurship and the experience economy.* Copenhagen: Copenhagen Business School Press DK.

Hobson, B. (2013). *Worklife balance: The agency and capabilities gap.* Oxford: Oxford University Press.

Hochschild, A. R. (2012). *The managed heart: Commercialization of human feeling.* Berkeley: University of California Press.

Hoedemaekers, C. (2016). 'Work hard, play hard': Fantasies of nihilism and hedonism between work and consumption. *Ephemera: Theory and Politics in Organization, 16*(3), 61–94.

Hofer, J., Busch, H., Au, A., Poláčková Šolcová, I., Tavel, P., & Tsien Wong, T. (2014). For the benefit of others: Generativity and meaning in life in the elderly in four cultures. *Psychology and Aging, 29*(4), 764.

Hofer, M. (2013). Appreciation and enjoyment of meaningful entertainment. *Journal of Media Psychology.*

Hoffman, W. M., & McNulty, R. E. (2012). Transforming faith in corporate capitalism through business ethics. *Journal of Management, Spirituality & Religion, 9*(3), 217–236. doi:10.1080/14766086.2012.729720

Hogg, M. A., & Terry, D. J. (2001). Social identity theory and organizational processes (pp. 1–12). In *Social identity processes in organizational contexts*: Psychology Press.

Holbrook, M. B., & Hirschman, E. C. (1982). The experiential aspects of consumption: Consumer fantasies, feelings, and fun. *Journal of Consumer Research, 9*(2), 132–140.

Holland, A. (2009). Darwin and the meaning in life. *Environmental Values, 18*(4), 503–516.

Holland, J. L. (1997). *Making vocational choices: A theory of vocational personalities and work environments*: Psychological Assessment Resources.

Holland, J. L. (1959). A theory of vocational choice. *Journal of Counseling Psychology, 6*(1), 35.

Holmes, S. (2008). Free marketeering: Review of The Shock Doctrine. *London Review of Books*, 3(2): 25–27.

Hommerich, C., & Tiefenbach, T. (2018). Analyzing the relationship between social capital and subjective well-being: The mediating role of social affiliation. *Journal of Happiness Studies, 19*(4), 1091–1114. doi:10.1007/s10902-017-9859-9

Hong, E. (2014). Liberal education reconsidered: Cultivating humanity in the knowledge society. *Asia Pacific Education Review, 15*(1), 5–12. doi:10.1007/s12564-013-9291-8

Honoré, C. (2005). *In praise of slowness: Challenging the cult of speed.* New York: HarperOne.

Hoogerbrugge, M. M., & Burger, M. J. (2018). Neighborhood-based social capital and life satisfaction: The case of Rotterdam, The Netherlands. *Urban Geography, 39*(10), 1484–1509. doi:10.1080/02723638.2018.1474609

Hooghe, M., & Vanhoutte, B. (2011). Subjective well-being and social capital in Belgian communities. The impact of community characteristics on subjective well-being indicators in Belgium. *Social Indicators Research, 100*(1), 17-36. doi:10.1007/s11205-010-9600-0

Hoover, J., & Gorrell, P. (2009). *The coaching connection: A manager's guide to developing individual potential in the context of the organization*: AMACOM Div., American Management Association.

Horkheimer, M. (1982). Egoism and the freedom movement: On the anthropology of the bourgeois era. *Telos, 1982*(54), 10–60.

Horkheimer, M., & Adorno, T. W. (1982). Dialectic of enlightenment. 1972, Trans. John Cumming. *New York: Seabury.*

Hou, Y., Kim, S. Y., & Benner, A. D. (2018). Parent–adolescent discrepancies in reports of parenting and adolescent outcomes in Mexican immigrant families. *Journal of Youth and Adolescence, 47*(2), 430–444.

How, N., & Strauss, W. (2000). *Millennials rising: The next great generation.*

Howatt, W. A. (2013). *Roles of internal locus of control and self-efficacy on managing job stressors and Ryff's six scales of psychological well-being.* (73). ProQuest Information & Learning.

Howell, A. J., Passmore, H.-A., & Buro, K. (2013). Meaning in nature: Meaning in life as a mediator of the relationship between nature connectedness and well-being. *Journal of Happiness Studies, 14*(6), 1681–1696.

Huhn, A. (2014). *Sustenance and sociability: Foodways in a Mozambican town.* (74). ProQuest Information & Learning.

Hultman, B., & Hemlin, S. (2008). Self-rated quality of life among the young unemployed and the young in work in northern Sweden. *Work, 30*(4), 461–472.

Hultman, B., Hemlin, S., & Olof Hörnquist, J. (2006). Quality of life among unemployed and employed people in northern Sweden. Are there any differences? *Work, 26*(1), 47–56.

Hurst, A. (2016). *The purpose economy, expanded and updated: How your desire for impact, personal growth and community is changing the world*: Elevate Publishing.

Hussain, D., & Bhushan, B. (2013). Posttraumatic growth experiences among Tibetan refugees: A qualitative investigation. *Qualitative Research in Psychology, 10*(2), 204–216.

Huta, V. (2007). *Pursuing pleasure versus growth and excellence: Links with different aspects of well-being.* (68). ProQuest Information & Learning.

Hutzell, R., & Peterson, T. (1986). Use of the Life Purpose Questionnaire with an alcoholic population. *International Journal of the Addictions, 21*(1), 51–57.

Hyland, T. (2015a). The commodification of spirituality: Education, mindfulness and the marketisation of the present moment. *Prospero (13586785), 21*(2).

Hyland, T. (2015b). McMindfulness in the workplace: Vocational learning and the commodification of the present moment. *Journal of Vocational Education & Training, 67*(2), 219–234.

Ibarra, H. (2004). *Working identity: Unconventional strategies for reinventing your career*: Harvard Business Press.

Ibarra, H. (1999). Provisional selves: Experimenting with image and identity in professional adaptation. *Administrative Science Quarterly, 44*(4), 764–791.

Idemudia, E. S., Williams, J. K., Madu, S. N., & Wyatt, G. E. (2013). Trauma exposures and posttraumatic stress among Zimbabwean refugees in South Africa. *Life Science Journal, 10*(3).

Ilan, J. (2013). Street social capital in the liquid city. *Ethnography, 14*(1), 3–24. doi:10.1177/1466138112440983

Ilies, R., Liu, X.-Y., Liu, Y., & Zheng, X. (2017). Why do employees have better family lives when they are highly engaged at work? *Journal of Applied Psychology, 102*(6), 956–970. doi:10.1037/apl0000211

Ilies, R., Morgeson, F. P., & Nahrgang, J. D. (2005). Authentic leadership and eudaemonic well-being: Understanding leader–follower outcomes. *The Leadership Quarterly, 16*(3), 373–394.

Inaba, Y., Wada, Y., Ichida, Y., & Nishikawa, M. (2015). Which part of community social capital is related to life satisfaction and self-rated health? A multilevel analysis based on a nationwide mail survey in Japan. *Social Science & Medicine, 142*, 169–182. doi:10.1016/j.socscimed.2015.08.007

Inglehart, R. F., Foa, R., Ponarin, E., & Welzel, C. (2013). Understanding the Russian malaise: The collapse and recovery of subjective well-being in post-communist Russia. National Research University Higher School of Economics Research Paper No. WP BRP, 32.

Iqani, M., & Baro, G. (2017). The branded skyline? A socio-semiotic critique of Johannesburg's architectural adverts. *African Studies, 76*(1), 102–120. doi:10.1080/00020184.2017.1285670

Iranzo, J. M. (2015). Economic crisis, degrowth and interaction rituals: A path towards sustainability. Papeles Del Ceic. *International Journal on Collective Identity Research*(1), 31. doi:10.1387/pceic.13010

Irwin, W. (2015). *The free market existentialist: Capitalism without consumerism*. New York: John Wiley & Sons.

Isaak, R. (2016). Ecopreneurship, rent-seeking, and free-riding in global context: Job-creation without ecocide. *Small Enterprise Research, 23*(1), 85–93. doi:10.1080/13215906.2016.1189090

Isaksen, J. (2000). Constructing meaning despite the drudgery of repetitive work. *Journal of Humanistic psychology, 40*(3), 84–107.

Ishida, R. (2011). Enormous earthquake in Japan: Coping with stress using purpose-in-life/ikigai. *Psychology, 2*(08), 773.

Iwasaki, Y. (2007). Leisure and quality of life in an international and multicultural context: What are major pathways linking leisure to quality of life? *Social Indicators Research, 82*(2), 233–264.

Iyengar, S. S., & Kamenica, E. (2006). Choice overload and simplicity seeking. University of Chicago Graduate School of Business Working Paper, 87, 1–27.

Izberk-Bilgin, E. (2013). Theology meets the marketplace. In *Consumption and spirituality*, 16, 41.

Jackson, T. (2016). *Prosperity without growth: Foundations for the economy of tomorrow*. New York: Routledge.

Jacobs, M., & Mazzucato, M. (2016). *Rethinking capitalism: Economics and policy for sustainable and inclusive growth*. New York: John Wiley & Sons.

Jacobson, G. R., Ritter, D. P., & Mueller, L. (1977). Purpose in life and personal values among adult alcoholics. *Journal of Clinical Psychology, 33*(S1), 314–316.

Jacoby, R. (1980). Narcissism and the crisis of capitalism. *Telos, 44*, 58–65.

Jagire, J. M. (2011). Spirit injury: The Impact of colonialism on African spirituality. In *Spirituality, education & society* (pp. 183–192): Brill Sense.

Jagodzinski, W. (2010). Economic social, and cultural determinants of life satisfaction: Are there differences between Asia and Europe? *Social Indicators Research, 97*(1), 85–104. doi:10.1007/s11205-009-9555-1

Jakovljevic, M., & Tomic, Z. (2016). Global and public mental health promotion. *Psychiatria Danubina, 28*(4), 323–333. Retrieved from <Go to ISI>://WOS:000388943300004

Jamal, T., & Stronza, A. (2008). 'Dwelling' with ecotourism in the Peruvian Amazon: Cultural relationships in local–global spaces. *Tourist Studies, 8*(3), 313-335. doi:10.1177/1468797608100593

James, O. (2007). *Affluenza: How to be successful and stay sane*. New York: Random House.

James, O. (2008). *The selfish capitalist: Origins of affluenza*. New York: Random House.

Jameson, F. (1993). Postmodernism, or the cultural logic of late capitalism. In *Postmodernism: A reader*, 62.

Jansen, K. J., & Kristof-Brown, A. (2006). Toward a multidimensional theory of person-environment fit. *Journal of Managerial Issues*, 193–212.

Jaunmuktane, A. (2012). Policies related to volunteer work. In S. Treija & I. Skuja (Eds.), *Research for rural development* (Vol. 2, pp. 230–235). Jelgava: Latvia University of Agriculture.

Jenkinson, C. E., Dickens, A. P., Jones, K., Thompson-Coon, J., Taylor, R. S., Rogers, M., ... Richards, S. H. (2013). Is volunteering a public health intervention? A systematic review and meta-analysis of the health and survival of volunteers. *BMC Public Health, 13*, 10. doi:10.1186/1471-2458-13-773

Jensen, R. (1996). The dream society. *Futurist, 30*(3), 9–13.

Jeon, H. (2018). *Exploring factors for sustainable success of festivals: Authenticity, customer satisfaction, and customer citizenship behavior.* (79). ProQuest Information & Learning.

Jervis, L. L., Spicer, P., & Manson, S. M. (2003). Boredom," trouble," and the realities of postcolonial reservation life. *Ethos, 31*(1), 38–58.

Jetten, J., Haslam, S. A., & Barlow, F. K. (2013). Bringing back the system: One reason why conservatives are happier than liberals is that higher socioeconomic status gives them access to more group memberships. *Social Psychological and Personality Science, 4*(1), 6–13. doi:10.1177/1948550612439721

Jhally, S. (2014). *The codes of advertising: Fetishism and the political economy of meaning in the consumer society.* New York: Routledge.

Jiaxun, H. (2006). Consumer research: The methodology of existential–phenomenology and its application. *Advances in Psychological Science, 5.*

Johnson, K.-B. A. Z. R. (2005). EC Consequences of individuals' fit at work: A meta-analysis of person–job, person–organization, person–group, and person–supervisor fit. *Personnel Psychology, 58*, 281–342.

Johnston, K., Tanner, M., Lalla, N., & Kawalski, D. (2013). Social capital: The benefit of Facebook 'friends'. *Behaviour & Information Technology, 32*(1), 24–36. doi:10.1080/0144929x.2010.550063

Johnston, T. C., & Burton, J. B. (2003). Voluntary simplicity: Definitions and dimensions. *Academy of Marketing Studies Journal, 7*(1), 19–36.

Jones, F., Burke, R. J., & Westman, M. (2006). Work–life balance: Key issues. *Work-life–balance: A psychological perspective,* 1–9.

Joo, B. K., & Lee, I. (2017). Workplace happiness: Work engagement, career satisfaction, and subjective well-being. *Evidence-based HRM–A global forum for empirical scholarship, 5*(2), 206–221. doi:10.1108/ebhrm-04-2015-0011

Jorm, A. F., & Ryan, S. M. (2014). Cross-national and historical differences in subjective well-being. *International Journal of Epidemiology, 43*(2), 330–340. doi:10.1093/ije/dyt188

Jost, J. T., Langer, M., Badaan, V., Azevedo, F., Etchezahar, E., Ungaretti, J., & Hennes, E. P. (2017). Ideology and the limits of self-interest: System justification motivation and conservative advantages in mass politics. *Translational Issues in Psychological Science, 3*(3), e1-e26. doi:10.1037/tps0000127

Joubert, L. B., Wan, A. H. Y., Bhatt, S., & Chan, C. L. W. (2015). An exploratory study of social capital and cancer survivorship: Meaning and interpersonal relationships among Chinese with cancer. *Illness, Crisis, & Loss, 23*(1), 33–44.

Jovanović, V. (2016). Trust and subjective well-being: The case of Serbia. *Personality and Individual Differences, 98*, 284–288. doi:10.1016/j.paid.2016.04.061

Ju, H., Shin, J. W., Kim, C.-W., Hyun, M.-H., & Park, J.-W. (2013). Mediational effect of meaning in life on the relationship between optimism and well-being in community elderly. *Archives of Gerontology and Geriatrics, 56*(2), 309 Ju, H., Shin, J. W., Kim, C.-w., Hyun, M.-h., & Park, J.-w.313.

Judge, T. A., & Piccolo, R. F. (2004). Transformational and transactional leadership: A meta-analytic test of their relative validity. *Journal of Applied Psychology, 89*(5), 755.

Judge, T. A., & Watanabe, S. (1993). Another look at the job satisfaction–life satisfaction relationship. *Journal of Applied Psychology, 78*(6), 939.

Kahn, W. A. (1992). To be fully there: Psychological presence at work. *Human relations, 45*(4), 321–349.

Kahn, W. A., & Fellows, S. (2013). *Employee engagement and meaningful work.*

Kalayjian, A. (1999). Coping through meaning: The community response to the earthquake in Armenia. In *When a community weeps: Case studies in group survivorship* (pp. 87–101).

Kalayjian, A., & Diakonova-Curtis, D. (2018). Meaningful world trauma outreach and prevention across cultures: Utilizing the 7-step integrative healing model for resilience and meaning-making. In G. J. Rich & S. Sirikantraporn (Eds.), *Human strengths and resilience: Developmental, cross-cultural, and international perspectives.* (pp. 131–150). Lanham, MD: Lexington Books/Rowman & Littlefield.

Kalayjian, A., & Eugene, D. (2009). *Mass trauma and emotional healing around the world: Rituals and practices for resilience and meaning-making* (2 volumes): ABC-CLIO.

Kale, S. (2006). Consumer spirituality and marketing. *ACR Asia-Pacific Advances, 3*(1): 72-85.

Kantartzis, S., & Molineux, M. (2011). The influence of Western society's construction of a healthy daily life on the conceptualisation of occupation. *Journal of Occupational Science, 18*(1), 62–80.

Karakas, F. (2010). Spirituality and performance in organizations: A literature review. *Journal of Business Ethics, 94*(1), 89–106.

Karanci, N. A., & Acarturk. (2005). Post-traumatic growth among Marmara earthquake survivors involved in disaster preparedness as volunteers. *Traumatology, 11*(4), 307–323.

Karatepe, O. M., & Karadas, G. (2015). Do psychological capital and work engagement foster frontline employees' satisfaction? A study in the hotel industry. *International Journal of Contemporary Hospitality Management, 27*(6), 1254–1278. doi:10.1108/ijchm-01-2014-0028

Kark, R., & Shamir, B. (2013). The dual effect of transformational leadership: Priming relational and collective selves and further effects on followers. In *transformational and charismatic leadership: The road ahead* (10th Anniversary Ed.; pp. 77–101): Emerald Group Publishing Limited.

Kark, R., Shamir, B., & Chen, G. (2003). The two faces of transformational leadership: Empowerment and dependency. *Journal of Applied Psychology, 88*(2), 246.

Kashdan, T. B., & Breen, W. E. (2007). Materialism and diminished well-being: Experiential avoidance as a mediating mechanism. *Journal of Social and Clinical Psychology, 26*(5), 521–539.

Kasser, T. (2002). *The high price of materialism*: MIT press.

Kasser, T. (2016). Materialistic values and goals. *Annual Review of Psychology, 67*, 489–514.

Kasser, T. (2017). Living both well and sustainably: A review of the literature, with some reflections on future research, interventions and policy. *Philosophical Transactions of the Royal Society a-Mathematical Physical and Engineering Sciences, 375*(2095), 13. doi:10.1098/rsta.2016.0369

Kasser, T., Cohn, S., Kanner, A. D., & Ryan, R. M. (2007). Some costs of American corporate capitalism: A psychological exploration of value and goal conflicts. *Psychological Inquiry, 18*(1), 1–22.

Kasser, T., Ryan, R. M., Couchman, C. E., & Sheldon, K. M. (2004). Materialistic values: Their causes and consequences. In T. Kasser & A.D. Conner (Eds.), *Psychology and Consumer culture: The struggle for a good life in a materialistic world,* (pp. 11–28). Washington, DC: American Psychological Association.

Kasser, T. E., & Kanner, A. D. (Eds.) (2004). *Psychology and consumer culture: The struggle for a good life in a materialistic world*: American Psychological Association.

Katz, L. D. (2000). *Evolutionary origins of morality: Cross-disciplinary perspectives*. Charlottesville, VA: Imprint Academic.

Kelly, M. S., Zimmer-Gembeck, M. J., & Boislard-P, M.-A. (2012). Goals, behavior and satisfaction: The associations of sexual orientation and gender with identity, intimacy, status and sex. In C. Bassani (Ed.), *Adolescent behaviour.* (pp. 71–94). Hauppauge, NY: Nova Science Publishers.

Kelly, P. (2016). *The self as enterprise: Foucault and the spirit of 21st century capitalism*. New York: Routledge.

Keltner, D. (2009). *Born to be good: The science of a meaningful life*. New York, NY: W W Norton & Co.

Keuschnigg, M., & Wolbring, T. (2012). Rich and satisfied? Theoretical considerations and empirical results on the association between wealth and life satisfaction. *Berliner Journal fur Soziologie, 22*(2), 189–216. doi:10.1007/s11609-012-0183-2

Keyes, C. L. (2009). The black–white paradox in health: Flourishing in the face of social inequality and discrimination. *Journal of Personality, 77*(6), 1677–1706.

Kiang, L., & Fuligni, A. J. (2010). Meaning in life as a mediator of ethnic identity and adjustment among adolescents from Latin, Asian, and European American backgrounds. *Journal of Youth and Adolescence, 39*(11), 1253–1264.

Kiang, L., Peterson, J. L., & Thompson, T. L. (2011). Ethnic peer preferences among Asian American adolescents in emerging immigrant communities. *Journal of Research on Adolescence, 21*(4), 754–761.

Kiang, L., & Witkow, M. R. (2015). Normative changes in meaning in life and links to adjustment in adolescents from Asian American backgrounds. *Asian American Journal of Psychology, 6*(2), 164.

Kidder, J. L. (2006). *"It's the job that I love": Bike messengers and Edgework.* Paper presented at the Sociological Forum, July.

Kielburger, C., & Kielburger, M. (2009). *Me to we: Finding meaning in a material world*. London: John Wiley & Sons.

Kim, S. S., Son, H., & Nam, K. A. (2005). Personal factors influencing Korean American men's smoking behavior: Addiction, health, and age. *Archives of Psychiatric Nursing, 19*(1), 35–41.

Kindyis, T. (2014). Review of Explore everything: Place-hacking the city. *Crime, Media, Culture, 10*(3), 275–278. doi:10.1177/1741659014528415

King, L. A., & Noelle, S. S. (2005). Happy, mature, and gay: Intimacy, power, and difficult times in coming out stories. *Journal of Research in Personality, 39*(2), 278–298.

King, L. A., & Smith, N. G. (2004). Gay and straight possible selves: Goals, identity, subjective well-being, and personality development. *Journal of Personality, 72*(5), 967–994.

Kirillova, K., Lehto, X., & Cai, L. (2017a). Tourism and existential transformation: An empirical investigation. *Journal of Travel Research, 56*(5), 638–650.

Kirillova, K., Lehto, X., & Cai, L. (2017b). What triggers transformative tourism experiences? *Tourism recreation research, 42*(4), 498–511.

Kirillova, K., Lehto, X. Y., & Cai, L. (2017). Existential authenticity and anxiety as outcomes: The tourist in the experience economy. *International Journal of Tourism Research, 19*(1), 13–26.

Kirillova, O. V., Kirillova, T. V., Abramova, L. A., Gavrilova, I. V., & Vaibert, M. I. (2017). Psychological and pedagogical support of the formation of professional world outlook of the university students. *European Journal of Contemporary Education, 6*(2), 280–288. doi:10.13187/ejced.2017.2.280

Kirkbesoglu, E., & Sargut, A. S. (2016). Transformation of Islamic work ethic and social networks: The role of religious social embeddedness in organizational networks. *Journal of Business Ethics, 139*(2), 313–331. doi:10.1007/s10551-015-2637-x

Klaas, D. (1998). Testing two elements of spirituality in depressed and non-depressed elders. *The International Journal Of Psychiatric Nursing Research, 4*(2), 452–462.

Kline, K. (2011). Radical hermeneutics, adolescence, and twenty-first century critical pedagogy. In C. S. Malott & B. Porfilio (Eds.), *Critical pedagogy in the twenty-first century: A new generation of scholars* (pp. 53–67). Charlotte, NC: IAP Information Age Publishing.

Knies, G. (2012). Income comparisons among neighbours and satisfaction in East and West Germany. *Social Indicators Research, 106*(3), 471-489. doi:10.1007/s11205-011-9818-5

Knight, K. (2008). After Tradition?: Heidegger or MacIntyre, Aristotle and Marx. *Analyse & Kritik, 30*(1), 33–52.

Knight, K. W., & Rosa, E. A. (2011). The environmental efficiency of well-being: A cross-national analysis. *Social Science Research, 40*(3), 931–949. doi:10.1016/j.ssresearch.2010.11.002

Ko, C. H., Yen, J.-Y., Yen, C. F., Chen, C. S., Weng, C. C., & Chen, C. C. (2008). The association between Internet addiction and problematic alcohol use in adolescents: The problem behavior model. *CyberPsychology & Behavior, 11*(5), 571–576.

Kohn, A. (1999). *Punished by rewards:: The trouble with gold stars, incentive plans, A's, praise, and other bribes*: Houghton Mifflin Harcourt.

Kohn, M. L., & Schooler, C. (1982). Job conditions and personality: A longitudinal assessment of their reciprocal effects. *American Journal of Sociology, 87*(6), 1257–1286.

Konkolÿ Thege, B., Stauder, A., & Kopp, M. S. (2010). Relationship between meaning in life and intensity of smoking: Do gender differences exist? *Psychology and Health, 25*(5), 589–599.

Korsunskiy, A. G. (2018). Freedom as a philosopphical concept and political practice. *Vestnik Tomskogo Gosudarstvennogo Universiteta-Filosofiya-Sotsiologiya-Politologiya-Tomsk State University Journal of Philosophy Sociology and Political Science, 41*, 57–63. doi:10.17223/1998863x/41/7

Koschmann, M. A. (2012). Developing a communicative theory of the nonprofit. *Management Communication Quarterly, 26*(1), 139–146. doi:10.1177/0893318911423640

Kosine, N. R., Steger, M. F., & Duncan, S. (2008). Purpose-centered career development: A strengths-based approach to finding meaning and purpose in careers. *Professional School Counseling, 12*(2), 2156759X0801200209.

Krause, N. (2003). Religious meaning and subjective well-being in late life. *The Journals of Gerontology Series B: Psychological Sciences and Social Sciences, 58*(3), S160–S170.

Krause, N. (2004). Stressors arising in highly valued roles, meaning in life, and the physical health status of older adults. *The Journals of Gerontology Series B: Psychological Sciences and Social Sciences, 59*(5), S287–S297.

Krause, N. (2005). Traumatic events and meaning in life: Exploring variations in three age cohorts. *Ageing & Society, 25*(4), 501–524.

Krause, N. (2007). Evaluating the stress-buffering function of meaning in life among older people. *Journal of Aging and Health, 19*(5), 792–812.

Kreiner, G. E. (2006). Consequences of work–home segmentation or integration: A person–environment fit perspective. *Journal of Organizational Behavior: The International Journal of Industrial, Occupational and Organizational Psychology and Behavior, 27*(4), 485–507.

Kreiner, G. E., Ashforth, B. E., & Sluss, D. M. (2006). Identity dynamics in occupational dirty work: Integrating social identity and system justification perspectives. *Organization science, 17*(5), 619–636.

Krekels, G., & Pandelaere, M. (2015). Dispositional greed. *Personality and Individual Differences, 74*, 225–230.

Krieger, T., & Meierrieks, D. (2010). Terrorism in the worlds of welfare capitalism. *Journal of Conflict Resolution, 54*(6), 902–939.

Kristof-Brown, A. L., Zimmerman, R. D., & Johnson, E. C. (2005). Consequences of individuals' fit at work. *Personnel Psychology, 58*(2), 281–342.

Kristol, I. (1973). Capitalism, socialism, and nihilism. *The Public Interest, 31*(3), 3–16.

Kroker, A. (2004). *The will to technology and the culture of nihilism: Heidegger, Nietzsche and Marx*. Toronto: University of Toronto Press.

Kroll, C. (2011). Different things make different people happy: Examining social capital and subjective well-being by gender and parental status. *Social Indicators Research, 104*(1), 157–177. doi:10.1007/s11205-010-9733-1

Kropotkin, P. A. (1922). *Mutual aid: A factor of evolution*. Berlin: Knopf.

Krueger, D. W. (1991). *Emotional business: The meanings and mastery of work, money, and success*. New York: Avant Books.

Krueger, R., Schulz, C., & Gibbs, D. C. (2018). Institutionalizing alternative economic spaces? An interpretivist perspective on diverse economies. *Progress in Human Geography, 42*(4), 569–589. doi:10.1177/0309132517694530

Kruglanski, A. W., Gelfand, M. J., Bélanger, J. J., Hetiarachchi, M., & Gunaratna, R. (2015). Significance quest theory as the driver of radicalization towards terrorism. In *Resilience and resolve: Communities against terrorism* (pp. 17–30). London: World Scientific.

Kuhn, K. M. (2016). The rise of the "gig economy" and implications for understanding work and workers. *Industrial and Organizational Psychology, 9*(1), 157–162.

Kujawa, J. (2017). Spiritual tourism as a quest. *Tourism Management Perspectives, 24*, 193–200.

Kunneman, H., & Brinkman, F. (2009). *Voorbij het dikke-ik*. Utrecht: SWP.

Kunze, L., & Suppa, N. (2017). Bowling alone or bowling at all? The effect of unemployment on social participation. *Journal of Economic Behavior & Organization, 133*, 213–235. doi:10.1016/j.jebo.2016.11.012

Kuo, S. I. C. (2015). *Work and relationship balance in adulthood: An exploration of concurrent correlates, predictive validity, and developmental pathways*. (76). ProQuest Information & Learning.

Kwok, S., Cheng, L., & Wong, D. F. K. (2015). Family emotional support, positive psychological capital and job satisfaction among chinese white-collar workers. *Journal of Happiness Studies, 16*(3), 561–582. doi:10.1007/s10902-014-9522-7

Kwon, H. J., & Park, H. O. H. (2018). Cultural capital factors associated with life satisfaction in Korean baby boomers. *Journal of Public Health, 40*(1), E16–E24. doi:10.1093/pubmed/fdx128

La Barbera, P. A., & Gürhan, Z. (1997). The role of materialism, religiosity, and demographics in subjective well-being. *Psychology & Marketing, 14*(1), 71–97.

Laloux, F. (2014). *Reinventing organizations: A guide to creating organizations inspired by the next stage in human consciousness*. New York: Nelson Parker.

Lam, M., & Chan, T. (2004). Life themes in the narratives of young Chinese immigrants who have successfully adjusted to life in Hong Kong. *Journal of Youth Studies, 7*(4), 433–449.

Lamla, J. (2009). *Consuming Authenticity: A paradoxical dynamic in contemporary capitalism.*

Lane, R. E. (1991). *The market experience.* New York, NY: Cambridge University Press.

Langdridge, D. (2014). Are you angry or are you heterosexual? A queer critique of lesbian and gay models of identity development. In *Feeling queer or queer feelings?* (pp. 35–47). New York: Routledge.

Langer, B. (2002). Commodified enchantment: Children and consumer capitalism. *Thesis Eleven, 69*(1), 67–81.

Langlois, G. (2009). *The technocultural dimensions of meaning: Towards a mixed semiotics of the world wide web.* (70). ProQuest Information & Learning,

Lasch, C. (1980). The culture of narcissism. *Bulletin of the Menninger Clinic, 44*(5), 426.

Lasch, C. (2018). *The culture of narcissism: American life in an age of diminishing expectations.* New York: WW Norton & Company.

Lawn, P. (2011). Is steady-state capitalism viable? A review of the issues and an answer in the affirmative. In R. Costanza, K. Limburg, & I. Kubiszewski (Eds.), *Ecological Economics Reviews* (Vol. 1219, pp. 1–25). Malden: Wiley-Blackwell.

Layton, L. (2014). Some psychic effects of neoliberalism: Narcissism, disavowal, perversion. *Psychoanalysis, Culture & Society, 19*(2), 161–178.

Leary, M. R., Tipsord, J. M., & Tate, E. B. (2008). Allo-inclusive identity: Incorporating the social and natural worlds into one's sense of self. In H. A. Wayment & J. J. Bauer (Eds.), *Transcending self-interest: Psychological explorations of the quiet ego* (pp. 137–147). Washington, DC: American Psychological Association.

Lee, C. W., McNulty, K., & Shaffer, S. (2013). 'Hard Times, Hard Choices': Marketing retrenchment as civic empowerment in an era of neoliberal crisis. *Socio-Economic Review, 11*(1), 81–106. doi:10.1093/ser/mws015

Leerattanakorn, N., & Wiboonpongse, A. (2017). Happiness and community-specific factors. *Applied Economics Journal, 24*(2), 34–51. Retrieved from <Go to ISI>://WOS:000468230400003

Leider, R. J. (2015). *The power of purpose: Creating meaning in your life and work.* New York: Berrett-Koehler Publishers.

Leigh, T. W., Peters, C., & Shelton, J. (2006). The consumer quest for authenticity: The multiplicity of meanings within the MG subculture of consumption. *Journal of the Academy of Marketing Science, 34*(4), 481–493. doi:10.1177/0092070306288403

Lemke, T. (2010). Beyond Foucault: From biopolitics to the government of life. In *Governmentality* (pp. 173–192). New York: Routledge.

Lengyel, A., Szoke, S., Kovacs, S., David, L. D., Baba, E. B., & Muller, A. (2019). Assessing the essential pre-conditions of an authentic sustainability curriculum. *International Journal of Sustainability in Higher Education, 20*(2), 309–340. doi:10.1108/ijshe-09-2018-0150

Lennick, D., & Kiel, F. (2007). *Moral intelligence: Enhancing business performance and leadership success.* New York: Pearson Prentice Hall.

Léonard, C., & Arnsperger, C. (2009). You'd better suffer for a good reason: Existential economics and individual responsibility in health care. *Revue de Philosophie Économique, 10*(1), 125–148.

Leung, J. T. Y., & Shek, D. T. L. (2018). Parental sacrifice, filial piety and adolescent life satisfaction in Chinese families experiencing economic disadvantage. *Applied Research in Quality of Life.* doi:10.1007/s11482-018-9678-0

Levin, D. M. E. (1987). *Pathologies of the modern self: Postmodern studies on narcissism, schizophrenia, and depression.* New York: New York University Press.

Levinthal, D. A., & Warglien, M. (1999). Landscape design: Designing for local action in complex worlds. *Organization science, 10*(3), 342–357.

Levy, N. (2005). Downshifting and meaning in life. *Ratio, 18*(2), 176–189.

Lewicka, M. (2011a). On the varieties of people's relationships with places: Hummon's typology revisited. *Environment and Behavior, 43*(5), 676–709. doi:10.1177/0013916510364917

Lewicka, M. (2011b). Place attachment: How far have we come in the last 40 years? *Journal of Environmental Psychology, 31*(3), 207–230. doi:10.1016/j.jenvp.2010.10.001

Lewicka, M. (2013). Localism and activity as two dimensions of people–place bonding: The role of cultural capital. *Journal of Environmental Psychology, 36*, 43–53. doi:10.1016/j.jenvp.2013.07.002

Lewin, P., & Williams, J. P. (2009). The ideology and practice of authenticity in punk subculture. In P. Vannini and J.P. Williams (Eds.), *Authenticity in culture, self, and society* (pp. 65–83): Ashgate.

Lewis, A., & Mackenzie, C. (2000). Morals, money, ethical investing and economic psychology. *Human relations, 53*(2), 179–191.

Lewis, P. (2004). *Transforming economics: Perspectives on the critical realist project.* New York: Routledge.

Li, H., Fan, F.-M., & Chen, L.-Y. (2009). Disasters endow people with a positive meaning . *Journal of Capital Normal University* (Social Sciences Edition), *4*.

Li, T. E., & Chan, E. T. H. (2017). Diaspora tourism and well-being: A eudaimonic view. *Annals of Tourism Research, 63*, 205–206.

Li, Y. Z. (2018). Building well-being among university teachers: the roles of psychological capital and meaning in life. *European Journal of Work and Organizational Psychology, 27*(5), 594–602. doi:10.1080/1359432x.2018.1496909

Li, Z.-y., Wu, M.-z., & Zhang, A.-q. (2011). The relationship between psychological capital and job satisfaction, life satisfaction: Mediator role of work–family facilitation. *Chinese Journal of Clinical Psychology, 19*(6), 818–820.

Liberati, A., Altman, D. G., Tetzlaff, J., Mulrow, C., Gøtzsche, P. C., Ioannidis, J. P. A., ... Moher, D. (2009). The PRISMA statement for reporting systematic reviews and meta-analyses of studies that evaluate health care interventions: explanation and elaboration. *Journal of Clincal Epidemiology, 62*(10), 34.

Lim, S. S. (2018). Aspirations of migrants and returns to human capital investment. *Social Indicators Research, 138*(1), 317–334. doi:10.1007/s11205-017-1649-6

Lin, A. (2001). *Exploring sources of life meaning among Chinese.* Thesis, Trinity Western University, Langley, Canada.

Lin, H.-R. (2008). Searching for meaning: Narratives and analysis of US-resident Chinese immigrants with metastatic cancer. *Cancer Nursing, 31*(3), 250–258.

Lin, J. (2013). Education for transformation and an expanded self: Paradigm shift for wisdom education. In J. Lin, R. L. Oxford, & E. J. Brantmeier (Eds.), *Re-envisioning higher education: Embodied pathways to wisdom and social transformation* (pp. 23–32). Charlotte, NC: IAP Information Age Publishing.

Liodakis, G. (2016). *Totalitarian capitalism and beyond.* New York: Routledge.

Liozu, S., Boland, D., Hinterbuber, A., & Perelli, S. (2015). Mindful pricing. In L. Robinson (Ed.), *Marketing dynamism & sustainability-Things change, things stay the same.* (pp. 412–421). Coral Gables: Academic Marketing Science.

Liozu, S., Hinterhuber, A., Perelli, S., & Boland, R. (2012). Mindful pricing: Transforming organizations through value-based pricing. *Journal of Strategic Marketing, 20*(3), 197–209. doi:10.1080/0965254X.2011.643916

Livingstone, L. P., Nelson, D. L., & Barr, S. H. (1997). Person-environment fit and creativity: An examination of supply-value and demand-ability versions of fit. *Journal of Management, 23*(2), 119–146.

Lofquist, L. H., & Dawis, R. V. (1991). *Essentials of person–-environment-correspondence counseling.* Minnesota: University of Minnesota Press.

Lonsway, B. (2013). *Making leisure work: Architecture and the experience economy.* New York: Routledge.

Lord, R. G., & Brown, D. J. (2003). *Leadership processes and follower self-identity.* New York: Psychology Press.

Lotufo, Z., Jr., Neto, F. L., & Gouvêa, R. Q. (2015). Compassion in a competitive culture. In T. G. Plante (Ed.), *The psychology of compassion and cruelty: Understanding the emotional, spiritual, and religious influences.* (pp. 59–72). Santa Barbara, CA: Praeger/ABC-CLIO.

Lowe, S. R., Manove, E. E., & Rhodes, J. E. (2013). Posttraumatic stress and posttraumatic growth among low-income mothers who survived Hurricane Katrina. *Journal of Consulting and Clinical Psychology, 81*(5), 877.

Löwy, M. (2009). Capitalism as religion: Walter Benjamin and Max Weber. *Historical materialism, 17*(1), 60–73.

Lu, C., Jiang, Y., Zhao, X., & Fang, P. (2019). Will helping others also benefit you? Chinese adolescents' altruistic personality traits and life satisfaction. *Journal of Happiness Studies: An Interdisciplinary Forum on Subjective Well-Being.* doi:10.1007/s10902-019-00134-6

Lu, Y., Marks, L., & Apavaloaie, L. (2012). Chinese immigrant families and Christian faith community: A qualitative study. *Family and Consumer Sciences Research Journal, 41*(2), 118–130.

Luborsky, M. R. (1993). The romance with personal meaning in gerontology: Cultural aspects of life themes. *The Gerontologist, 33*(4), 445–452.

Lucas, K., & Buzzanell, P. M. (2004). Blue-collar work, career, and success: Occupational narratives of Sisu. *Journal of Applied Communication Research, 32*(4), 273–292.

Lucchini, M., Della Bella, S., & Crivelli, L. (2015). Social capital and life satisfaction in Switzerland. *International Journal of Happiness and Development, 2*(3), 250–268. doi:10.1504/ijhd.2015.072186

Lugo, C. R. (2017). The constitution of the common. *Direito E Praxis, 8*(4), 3217-3231. doi:10.1590/2179-8966/2017/31316

Lunbeck, E. (2014). *The Americanization of narcissism.* Cambridge: Harvard University Press.

Luthans, F., & Avolio, B. J. (2003). Authentic leadership development. *Positive organizational scholarship, 241*, 258.

Lyons, G. C., Deane, F. P., & Kelly, P. J. (2010). Forgiveness and purpose in life as spiritual mechanisms of recovery from substance use disorders. *Addiction Research & Theory, 18*(5), 528–543.

Lyons, H. Z., & O'brien, K. M. (2006). The role of person–environment fit in the job satisfaction and tenure intentions of African American employees. *Journal of Counseling Psychology, 53*(4), 387.

Lyons, P. (2008). The crafting of jobs and individual differences. *Journal of Business and Psychology, 23*(1–2), 25–36.

MacDonald-Dennis, C. (2015). *Making meaning: Embracing spirituality, faith, religion, and life purpose in student affairs*: Stylus Publishing, LLC.

Macey, W. H., & Schneider, B. (2008). The meaning of employee engagement. *Industrial and Organizational Psychology, 1*(1), 3–30.

Machell, K. A., Disabato, D. J., & Kashdan, T. B. (2016). Buffering the negative impact of poverty on youth: The power of purpose in life. *Social Indicators Research, 126*(2), 845–861.

Machonin, P. (1994). Towards sociological comparison of Czech and Slovak society, *26*(4), 333-+. Retrieved from <Go to ISI>://WOS:A1994QG72500002

Mackenzie, C., & Lewis, A. (1999). Morals and markets: The case of ethical investing. *Business Ethics Quarterly, 9*(3), 439–452.

Mackey, J., & Sisodia, R. (2013). *Conscious capitalism: Liberating the heroic spirit of business.* Cambridge, MA: Harvard Business School Press.

Mackey, J., & Sisodia, R. (2013). Conscious capitalism is not an oxymoron. *Harvard Business Review, 14.*

MacKinlay, E. (2002). Health, healing and wholeness in frail elderly people. *Journal of Religious Gerontology, 13*(2), 25–34.

Madison, G. (2006). Existential migration. *Existential analysis, 17*(2), 238–260.

Magat, I. N. (1999). Israeli and Japanese immigrants to Canada: Home, belonging, and the territorialization of identity. *Ethos, 27*(2), 119–144.

Major, L. E., & Machin, S. (2018). *Social mobility: And its enemies*. London: Penguin UK.

Malka, A., & Chatman, J. A. (2003). Intrinsic and extrinsic work orientations as moderators of the effect of annual income on subjective well-being: A longitudinal study. *Personality and Social Psychology Bulletin, 29*(6), 737–746. doi:10.1177/0146167203252867

Malott, C., Hill, D., & Banfield, G. (2013). Immiseration capitalism. *Journal for Critical Education Policy Studies, 11*(4).

Marcuse, H. (2005). *Heideggerian marxism*. Nebraska: University of Nebraska Press.

Marcuse, H. (2013). *One-dimensional man: Studies in the ideology of advanced industrial society*. New York: Routledge.

Marcuse, P. (2006). Security or safety in cities? The threat of terrorism after 9/11. *International Journal of Urban and Regional Research, 30*(4), 919–929. doi:10.1111/j.1468-2427.2006.00700.x

Margry, P. J. (2008). Secular pilgrimage: A contradiction in terms? In P.J. Margry (Ed.), *Shrines and pilgrimage in the modern world. New itineraries into the sacred* (pp. 13–46). Amsterdam University Press, Amsterdam.

Markow, F., & Klenke, K. (2005). The effects of personal meaning and calling on organizational commitment: An empirical investigation of spiritual leadership. *International Journal of Organizational Analysis, 13*(1), 8–27.

Marmor-Lavie, G., Stout, P. A., & Lee, W.-N. (2009). Spirituality in advertising: A new theoretical approach. *Journal of Media and Religion, 8*(1), 1–23.

Marsh, A., Smith, L., Piek, J., & Saunders, B. (2003). The purpose in life scale: Psychometric properties for social drinkers and drinkers in alcohol treatment. *Educational and Psychological Measurement, 63*(5), 859–871.

Martin, K. A. (2013). *Exploring a holistic approach for transformative change, learning, leadership & culture utilizing presencing as a vehicle: A case study*. (73).

Martin, R. A., MacKinnon, S., Johnson, J., & Rohsenow, D. J. (2011). Purpose in life predicts treatment outcome among adult cocaine abusers in treatment. *Journal of Substance Abuse Treatment, 40*(2), 183–188.

Martinko, M. J., & Gardner, W. L. (1982). Learned helplessness: An alternative explanation for performance deficits. *Academy of Management Review, 7*(2), 195–204.

Masferrer-Dodas, E., Rico-Garcia, L., Huanca, T., Reyes-Garcia, V., & Team, T. B. S. (2012). Consumption of market goods and wellbeing in small-scale societies: An empirical test among the Tsimane in the Bolivian Amazon. *Ecological Economics, 84*, 213–220. doi:10.1016/j.ecolecon.2011.08.009

Massey, D. S., & Akresh, I. R. (2006). Immigrant Intentions and mobility in a global economy: The attitudes and behavior of recently arrived US immigrants. *Social Science Quarterly, 87*(5), 954–971. doi:10.1111/j.1540-6237.2006.00410.x

Matteucci, X., & Filep, S. (2017). Eudaimonic tourist experiences: The case of flamenco. *Leisure Studies, 36*(1), 39–52.

Mattioli, F. (2017). *Losing values: Illiquidity, personhood, and the return of authoritarianism in Skopje, Macedonia*. (78). ProQuest Information & Learning.

Mattis, J. S. (2002). Religion and spirituality in the meaning-making and coping experiences of African American women: A qualitative analysis. *Psychology of Women Quarterly, 26*(4), 309–321.

May, D. R., Chan, A. Y., Hodges, T. D., & Avolio, B. J. (2003). Developing the moral component of authentic leadership. *Organizational dynamics, 32*(3), 247–260.

Mazlish, B. (1982). American narcissism. *Psychohistory Review, 1*(1): 56–72.

McAlexander, J. H., Dufault, B. L., Martin, D. M., & Schouten, J. W. (2014). The Marketization of religion: Field, capital, and consumer identity. *Journal of Consumer Research, 41*(3), 858–875. doi:10.1086/677894

McCabe, S., & Johnson, S. (2013). The happiness factor in tourism: Subjective well-being and social tourism. *Annals of Tourism Research, 41*, 42–65.

McCarthy, G. E. (1992). *Marx and Aristotle: nineteenth-century German social theory and classical antiquity*. London: Rowman & Littlefield.

McCrea, J., Walker, J. C., & Weber, K. (2013). *The Generosity Network: New Transformational Tools for Successful Fund-raising*: Deepak Chopra.

McDonald, M., & O'callaghan, J. (2008). Positive psychology: A Foucauldian critique. *The Humanistic Psychologist, 36*(2), 127–142.

McElroy-Heltzel, S. E., Van Tongeren, D. R., Gazaway, S., Ordaz, A., Davis, D. E., Hook, J. N., . . . Stargell, N. A. (2018). The role of spiritual fortitude and positive religious coping in meaning in life and spiritual well-being following Hurricane Matthew. *Journal of Psychology and Christianity, 37*(1), 17-27.

McGrath, S. J. (2016). The theology of consumerism. *Analecta Hermeneutica, 6, 23-35.*

McKnight, J., & Block, P. (2011). *The abundant community: Awakening the power of families and neighborhoods*: ReadHowYouWant. com.

McLendon, M. L. (2006). Tocqueville, Jansenism, and the psychology of freedom. *American Journal of Political Science, 50*(3), 664-675. doi:10.1111/j.1540-5907.2006.00208.x

McMurtry, J. (1973). Making sense of economic determinism. *Canadian Journal of Philosophy, 3*(2), 249-261.

Meglino, B. M., & Korsgaard, M. A. (2004). Considering rational self-interest as a disposition: Organizational implications of other orientation. *Journal of Applied Psychology, 89*(6), 946-959. doi:10.1037/0021-9010.89.6.946

Melamed, S., Meir, E. I., & Samson, A. (1995). The benefits of personality-leisure congruence: Evidence and implications. *Journal of Leisure Research, 27*(1), 25-40.

Menon, M., Pendakur, R., & Perali, F. (2015). All in the family: How do social capital and material wellbeing affect relational wellbeing? *Social Indicators Research, 124*(3), 889–910. doi:10.1007/s11205-014-0816-2

Merish, L. (2000). *Sentimental materialism: Gender, commodity culture, and nineteenth-century American literature*: Duke University Press.

Merrifield, A. (1993). The Canary Wharf debacle: From 'TINA'—there is no alternative—to 'THEMBA'—there must be an alternative. *Environment and Planning A, 25*(9), 1247–1265.

Mészáros, I. (2006). *Marx's theory of alienation*. Berlin: Aakar Books.

Metz, T. (2003). Utilitarianism and the meaning of life. *Utilitas, 15*(1), 50–70.

Meyers, M. C., & van Woerkom, M. (2017). Effects of a strengths intervention on general and work-related well-being: The mediating role of positive affect. *Journal of Happiness Studies: An Interdisciplinary Forum on Subjective Well-Being, 18*(3), 671–689. doi:10.1007/s10902-016-9745-x

Migone, A. (2007). Hedonistic consumerism: Patterns of consumption in contemporary capitalism. *Review of Radical Political Economics, 39*(2), 173–200.

Miles, M. S., & Crandall, E. K. B. (1983). The search for meaning and its potential for affecting growth in bereaved parents. In *Coping with Life Crises* (pp. 235–243). New York: Springer.

Miles, S. (1998). *Consumerism: as a way of life*. London: Sage.

Millán, R. (2016). Sociopolitical dimensions of subjective wellbeing: The case of two Mexican cities. In M. Rojas (Ed.), *Handbook of happiness research in Latin America* (pp. 297–323). New York, NY: Springer Science + Business Media.

Miller, P. M. (2011). Homeless Education and Social Capital: An Examination of School and Community Leaders. *Teachers College Record, 113*(5), 1067–1104.

Miller, P. M. (2012). Community-based education and social capital in an urban after-school program. *Education and Urban Society, 44*(1), 35–60. doi:10.1177/0013124510380910

Miller, W. (1990). Spirituality: the silent dimension in addiction research. The 1990 Leonard Ball oration. *Drug and Alcohol Review, 9*(3), 259–266.

Miller, W. R., & Bogenschutz, M. P. (2007). Spirituality and addiction. *Southern Medical Journal, 100*(4), 433–437.

Mills, A., & Codd, H. (2008). Prisoners' families and offender management: Mobilizing social capital. *Probation Journal, 55*(1), 9–24.

Mitrut, C., Balaceanu, C., Gruiescu, M., & Serban, D. (2015). The macro-economic framework of support analysis for sustainable businesses. *Amfiteatru Economic, 17*(40), 1068–1078.

Montgomerie, J., & Tepe-Belfrage, D. (2019). Spaces of debt resistance and the contemporary politics of financialised capitalism. *Geoforum, 98*, 309–317. doi:10.1016/j.geoforum.2018.05.012

Moorman, R. H., & Byrne, Z. S. (2013). How does organizational justice affect organizational citizenship behavior? *Handbook of Organizational Justice*, 355.

Moran, M. (2014). *Identity and capitalism*. London: Sage.

Morgan, A. R., Rivera, F., Moreno, C., & Haglund, B. J. A. (2012). Does social capital travel? Influences on the life satisfaction of young people living in England and Spain. *BMC Public Health, 12*, 12. doi:10.1186/1471-2458-12-138

Morgan, R., & Wang, F. (2018). Well-being in transition: Life satisfaction in urban China from 2002 to 2012. *Journal of Happiness Studies: An Interdisciplinary Forum on Subjective Well-Being*. doi:10.1007/s10902-018-0061-5

Morgeson, F. P., Dierdorff, E. C., & Hmurovic, J. L. (2010). Work design in situ: Understanding the role of occupational and organizational context. *Journal of Organizational Behavior, 31*(2-3), 351–360.

Morris, M. L., Messal, C. B., & Meriac, J. P. (2013). Core self-evaluation and goal orientation: Understanding work stress. *Human Resource Development Quarterly, 24*(1), 35–62. doi:10.1002/hrdq.21151

Morrison, E. E., Burke III, G. C., & Greene, L. (2007). Meaning in motivation: Does your organization need an inner life? *Journal of Health and Human Services Administration*, 98–115.

Muffels, R., & Headey, B. (2013). Capabilities and choices: Do they make sense for understanding objective and subjective well-being? An empirical test of Sen's capability framework on German and British panel data. *Social Indicators Research, 110*(3), 1159–1185. doi:10.1007/s11205-011-9978-3

Munck, R. (2003). Neoliberalism, necessitarianism and alternatives in Latin America: There is no alternative (TINA)? *Third World Quarterly, 24*(3), 495–511.

Munzel, A., Galan, J. P., & Meyer-Waarden, L. (2018). Getting by or getting ahead on social networking sites? The role of social capital in happiness and well-being. *International Journal of Electronic Commerce, 22*(2), 232–257. doi:10.1080/10864415.2018.1441723

Murgic, D., Rijavec, M., & Miljkovic, D. (2019). Initial validation of the shortened psychological capital questionnaire. *Ekonomski Pregled, 70*(1), 3–21. doi:10.32910/ep.70.1.1

Murphy, E., & Scott, M. (2014). 'After the crash': Life satisfaction, everyday financial practices and rural households in post Celtic Tiger Ireland. *Journal of Rural Studies, 34*, 37–49. doi:10.1016/j.jrurstud.2013.12.005

Murtaza, N. (2011). Pursuing self-interest or self-actualization? From capitalism to a steady-state, wisdom economy. *Ecological Economics, 70*(4), 577–584. doi:10.1016/j.ecolecon.2010.12.012

Myck, M., & Oczkowska, M. (2018). Shocked by therapy? Unemployment in the first years of the socio-economic transition in Poland and its long-term consequences. *Economics of Transition, 26*(4), 695–724. doi:10.1111/ecot.12161

Navarro, M., & Sanchez, A. (2018). Income and subective well-being. *Revista de Economia Mundial*(48), 153–178.

Naylor, T. H., Willimon, W. H., & Österberg, R. (1996). *The search for meaning in the workplace*: Abingdon Press Nashville, TN.

Negru-Subtirica, O., Pop, E. I., Luyckx, K., Dezutter, J., & Steger, M. F. (2016). The meaningful identity: A longitudinal look at the interplay between identity and meaning in life in adolescence. *Developmental Psychology, 52*(11), 1926.

Neilson, D. (2015). Class, precarity, and anxiety under neoliberal global capitalism: From denial to resistance. *Theory & Psychology, 25*(2), 184–201. doi:10.1177/0959354315580607

Nelson, J. A. (2018). *Economics for humans.* Chicago: University of Chicago Press.

Neulinger, J. (1982). Leisure lack and the quality of life: The broadening scope of the leisure professional. *Leisure Studies, 1*(1), 53–63.

Nicholas, B. R. (2012). *A qualitative investigation of the creation and use of social capital among street children in Bucharest, Romania.* (73). ProQuest Information & Learning.

Nicholson, T., Higgins, W., Turner, P., James, S., Stickle, F., & Pruitt, T. (1994). The relation between meaning in life and the occurrence of drug abuse: A retrospective study. *Psychology of Addictive Behaviors, 8*(1), 24.

Ning, L. (2017). *A comparative study on job satisfaction of employees in different classes: Based on the data of CSS2013.* Chengdu: Sichuan Univ Press.

Noonan, J. (2009). Free time as a necessary condition of free life. *Contemporary Political Theory, 8*(4), 377–393. doi:10.1057/cpt.2008.27

Norton, E. C., Nizalova, O., & Murtazashvili, I. (2018). Does past unemployment experience explain the transition happiness gap? *Journal of Comparative Economics, 46*(4), 1104–1121. doi:10.1016/j.jce.2018.04.004

Noviana, U., Miyazaki, M., & Ishimaru, M. (2016). Meaning in Life: A conceptual model for disaster nursing practice. *International Journal of Nursing Practice, 22*, 65–75.

Noys, B. (2014). *Malign velocities: Accelerationism and capitalism.* New York: John Hunt Publishing.

Nuñez, A.-M., & Sansone, V. A. (2016). Earning and learning: Exploring the meaning of work in the experiences of first-generation Latino college students. *Review of Higher Education: Journal of the Association for the Study of Higher Education, 40*(1), 91–115. doi:10.1353/rhe.2016.0039

Nur Iplik, F., Can Kilic, K., & Yalcin, A. (2011). The simultaneous effects of person–organization and person–job fit on Turkish hotel managers. *International Journal of Contemporary Hospitality Management, 23*(5), 644–661.

Nyqvist, F., Forsman, A. K., Giuntoli, G., & Cattan, M. (2013). Social capital as a resource for mental well-being in older people: A systematic review. *Aging & Mental Health, 17*(4), 394–410.

O'Brien, M. S. (2002). *Social capital and sense of community: The relationship of individual perceptions of community social dynamics and fear of crime.* (63). ProQuest Information & Learning.

O'Connell, M., Tondora, J., Croog, G., Evans, A., & Davidson, L. (2005). From rhetoric to routine: assessing perceptions of recovery-oriented practices in a state mental health and addiction system. *Psychiatric Rehabilitation Journal, 28*(4), 378.

O'Toole, J., & Lawler, E. (2008). *America at work: Choices and challenges.* New York: Springer.

Oakes, K. E. (2008). Purpose in life: A mediating variable between involvement in Alcoholics Anonymous and long-term recovery. *Alcoholism Treatment Quarterly, 26*(4), 450–463.

Oh, I. S., Guay, R. P., Kim, K., Harold, C. M., Lee, J. H., Heo, C. G., & Shin, K. H. (2014). Fit happens globally: A meta-analytic comparison of the relationships of person–environment fit dimensions with work attitudes and performance across East Asia, Europe, and North America. *Personnel Psychology, 67*(1), 99–152.

Oishi, S., & Diener, E. (2014). Residents of poor nations have a greater sense of meaning in life than residents of wealthy nations. *Psychological Science, 25*(2), 422–430.

Ojala, M. (2013). Coping with climate change among adolescents: Implications for subjective well-being and environmental engagement. *Sustainability, 5*(5), 2191–2209.

Okasaka, Y., Morita, N., Nakatani, Y., & Fujisawa, K. (2008). Correlation between addictive behaviors and mental health in university students. *Psychiatry and clinical neurosciences, 62*(1), 84–92.

Okazaki, S., & Abelmann, N. (2014). Religiosity and immigrant family narratives in Korean American young adults. In C. Kim-Prieto (Ed.), *Religion and spirituality across cultures.* (Vol. 9, pp. 355–369). New York, NY: Springer Science + Business Media.

Okulicz-Kozaryn, A. (2010). Religiosity and life satisfaction across nations. *Mental Health, Religion & Culture, 13*(2), 155–169. doi:10.1080/13674670903273801

Ollman, B., & Bertell, O. (1976). *Alienation: Marx's conception of man in a capitalist society*: Cambridge University Press.

Onyx, J., & Warburton, J. (2003). Volunteering and health among older people: A review. *Australasian Journal on Ageing, 22*(2), 65–69. doi:10.1111/j.1741-6612.2003.tb00468.x

Orlowski, J., & Wicker, P. (2015). The monetary value of social capital. *Journal of Behavioral and Experimental Economics, 57*, 26–36. doi:10.1016/j.socec.2015.04.007

Ostrom, E. (1990). *Governing the commons: The evolution of institutions for collective action*: Cambridge University Press.

Oteman, M., & van Lienden, H. (2014). Towards a trust and attention based management concept paying attention to attention first. In V. Grozdanic (Ed.), *Proceedings of the 10th European Conference on Management Leadership and Governance* (pp. 212–220). Nr Reading: Acad Conferences Ltd.

Ozcaglar-Toulouse, N. (2007). Living for "ethics": Responsible consumption in everyday life. In *Consumer culture theory* (pp. 421–436): Emerald Group Publishing Limited.

Pacifico, M., & Gomes, L. R. (2019). The ourselves spectacle. *Comunicacoes, 26*(1), 165–179. doi:10.15600/2238-121X/comunicacoes.v26n1p165-179

Pacquing, I. R. B. (2017). Neoliberalism and our precarious culture. *Kritike-an Online Journal of Philosophy, 11*(1), 129–148. doi:10.25138/11.1.a8

Palgi, Y., Ben-Ezra, M., Aviel, O., Dubiner, Y., Baruch, E., Soffer, Y., & Shrira, A. (2012). Mental health and disaster related attitudes among Japanese after the 2011 Fukushima nuclear disaster.

Palmarozza, P. (2006). *From principles to profit*. New York: Arcturus Publishing.

Palmarozza, P. (2019). Values based management: Guided by the Bhagavad Gītā. In *Managing by the Bhagavad Gītā* (pp. 231–247): Springer.

Pan, J.-Y. (2011). A resilience-based and meaning-oriented model of acculturation: A sample of mainland Chinese postgraduate students in Hong Kong. *International Journal of Intercultural Relations, 35*(5), 592–603.

Pan, J.-Y., Fu Keung Wong, D., Joubert, L., & Chan, C. L. W. (2007). Acculturative stressor and meaning of life as predictors of negative affect in acculturation: A cross-cultural comparative study between Chinese international students in Australia and Hong Kong. *Australian and New Zealand Journal of Psychiatry, 41*(9), 740–750.

Pan, J.-Y., Wong, D. F. K., Joubert, L., & Chan, C. L. W. (2008). The protective function of meaning of life on life satisfaction among Chinese students in Australia and Hong Kong: A cross-cultural comparative study. *Journal of American College Health, 57*(2), 221–232.

Panas, E. E. (2013). Homeorhesis and indication of association between different types of capital on life satisfaction: The case of Greeks under crisis. *Social Indicators Research, 110*(1), 171–186. doi:10.1007/s11205-011-9922-6

Pang, K. Y. C. (1994). Understanding depression among elderly Korean immigrants through their folk illnesses. *Medical Anthropology Quarterly, 8*(2), 209–216.

Pang, K. Y. C. (1996). Self-care strategy of elderly Korean immigrants in the Washington DC metropolitan area. *Journal of Cross-Cultural Gerontology, 11*(3), 229–254.

Park, C. L. (2005). Religion as a meaning-making framework in coping with life stress. *Journal of Social Issues, 61*(4), 707–729.

Park, C. L. (2010). Making sense of the meaning literature: An integrative review of meaning making and its effects on adjustment to stressful life events. *Psychological Bulletin, 136*(2), 257.

Park, C. L., & Ai, A. L. (2006). Meaning making and growth: New directions for research on survivors of trauma. *Journal of Loss and Trauma, 11*(5), 389–407.

Parker, P. F. (2014). *Evolving job competencies for the human resource professional in the 21st century*, (74). ProQuest Information & Learning.

Parsons, F. (1909). *Choosing a vocation*: Houghton Mifflin.

Patrizi, N., Capineri, C., Rugani, B., & Niccolucci, V. (2010). "Socio-economic design and nature": A possible representation through ecological footprint. In C. Brebbia & A. Carpi (Eds.), *Design and nature V: Comparing design in nature with science and engineering* (Vol. 138, pp. 527-+). Southampton: Wit Press.

Pattakos, A. (2010). *Prisoners of our thoughts: Viktor Frankl's principles for discovering meaning in life and work*: Berrett-Koehler Publishers.

Patterson, C. J., & Riskind, R. G. (2010). To be a parent: Issues in family formation among gay and lesbian adults. *Journal of GLBT Family Studies, 6*(3), 326–340.

Patton, K., Parker, M., & Pratt, E. (2013). Meaningful learning in professional development: Teaching without telling. *Journal of Teaching in Physical Education, 32*(4), 441–459. doi:10.1123/jtpe.32.4.441

Payutto, P., & Evans, B. (1994). *Buddhist economics—A middle way for the market place*.

Peck, J. (2002). Political economics of scale: Fast policy, interscalar relations, and neoliberal workfare. *Economic Geography, 78*(3), 331–360. doi:10.2307/4140813

Pei, Z. J. (2008). *Institutions, social capital and subjective well-being*. Chengdu: Univ Electronic Science & Technology China Press.

Pereboom, D. (2011). Free-will skepticism and meaning in life. In *The Oxford handbook of free will*.

Peters, G. (2012). The social as heaven and hell: Pierre Bourdieu's philosophical anthropology. *Journal for the Theory of Social Behaviour, 42*(1), 63-+. doi:10.1111/j.1468-5914.2011.00477.x

Peterson, B. E., & Plamondon, L. T. (2009). Third culture kids and the consequences of international sojourns on authoritarianism, acculturative balance, and positive affect. *Journal of Research in Personality, 43*(5), 755–763.

Pezirkianidis, C., Stalikas, A., Efstathiou, E., & Karakasidou, E. (2016). The relationship between meaning in life, emotions and psychological illness: The moderating role of the effects of the economic crisis.

Pharr, J. M. (2011). At the intersection of politics & consumption: A research agenda for investigating the effects of fair-trade marketing claims on ethical shopping behavior. *Journal of Leadership, Accountability & Ethics, 8*(5).

Piët, S. (2003). *De emotiemarkt*. Amsterdam: Pearson Education.

Pike, J. E. (2019). *From Aristotle to Marx: Aristotelianism in Marxist Social Ontology*. New York: Routledge.

Pine, B. J., & Gilmore, J. H. (1998). Welcome to the experience economy. *Harvard Business Review, 76*, 97–105.

Pine, B. J., & Gilmore, J. H. (2013). The experience economy: Past, present and future. In *Handbook on the experience economy* (pp. 21-44).

Pine, B. J., Pine, J., & Gilmore, J. H. (1999). *The experience economy: Work is theatre & every business a stage*. Boston: Harvard Business Press.

Pink, D. H. (2011). *Drive: The surprising truth about what motivates us*. London: Penguin.

Piontek, B. (2010). Contemporary conditions of socio-economic development (synthetics approach). *Problemy Ekorozwoju, 5*(2), 117–124. Retrieved from <Go to ISI>://WOS:000280795100012

Piston, S. C. (2014). *Sympathy for the poor, resentment of the rich, and their political consequences.*

Plaud, C., & Guillemot, S. (2015). Service interactions and subjective well-being in later life. *Journal of Services Marketing, 29*(4), 245–254. doi:10.1108/jsm-05-2014-0154

Plaut, V. C., Markus, H. R., Treadway, J. R., & Fu, A. S. (2012). The Cultural construction of self and well-being: A tale of two cities. *Personality and Social Psychology Bulletin, 38*(12), 1644–1658. doi:10.1177/0146167212458125

Podolny, J. M., Khurana, R., & Hill-Popper, M. (2004). Revisiting the meaning of leadership. *Research in Organizational Behavior, 26*, 1–36.

Polakow, V. (2007). In the shadows of the ownership society: Homeless children and their families. In S. Books (Ed.), *Invisible children in the society and its schools,* 3rd ed. (pp. 39–62). Mahwah, NJ: Lawrence Erlbaum Associates Publishers.

Polanyi, K. (1947). On belief in economic determinism. *The Sociological Review, 39*(1), 96–102.

Ponce, M. S. H., Rosas, R. P. E., & Lorca, M. B. F. (2014). Social capital, social participation and life satisfaction among Chilean older adults. *Revista de Saude Publica, 48*(5), 739–749. doi:10.1590/s0034-8910.2014048004759

Pontefract, D. (2016). *Flat army: Creating a connected and engaged organization*: Elevate Publishing.

Poon, K.-T., Teng, F., Chow, J. T., & Chen, Z. (2015). Desiring to connect to nature: The effect of ostracism on ecological behavior. *Journal of Environmental Psychology, 42*, 116–122.

Porritt, J. (2012). *Capitalism as if the world matters.* London: Routledge.

Portela, M., Neira, I., & Salinas-Jimenez, M. D. (2013). Social capital and subjective wellbeing in europe: A new approach on social capital. *Social Indicators Research, 114*(2), 493–511. doi:10.1007/s11205-012-0158-x

Prasch, R. E. (2013). *Aristotle, Adam Smith and Karl Marx: On some fundamental issues in 21st century political economy.* Taylor & Francis.

Prassl, J. (2018). *Humans as a service: The promise and perils of work in the gig economy*: Oxford University Press.

Pratt, M. G., & Ashforth, B. E. (2003). Fostering meaningfulness in working and at work. In K.S. Cameron, J.E. Dutton, & R.E. Quinn (Eds.), *Positive organizational scholarship: Foundations of a new discipline* (pp. 309, 327).

Pretty, J. (2013). The consumption of a finite planet: Well-being, convergence, divergence and the nascent green economy. *Environmental & Resource Economics, 55*(4), 475–499. doi:10.1007/s10640-013-9680-9

Price, L. L., Feick, L. F., & Guskey, A. (1995). Everyday market helping behavior. *Journal of Public Policy & Marketing, 14*(2), 255–266.

Provine, W. B. (1988). Progress in evolution and meaning in life. In M. Nitecki (Ed.), *Evolutionary Progress*, 49–74.

Purser, G. (2009). The dignity of job-seeking men: Boundary work among immigrant day laborers. *Journal of Contemporary Ethnography, 38*(1), 117–139.

Puvimanasinghe, T., Denson, L. A., Augoustinos, M., & Somasundaram, D. (2014). "Giving back to society what society gave us": Altruism, coping, and meaning making by two refugee communities in South Australia. *Australian Psychologist, 49*(5), 313–321.

Radcliff, B. (2001). Politics, markets, and life satisfaction: The political economy of human happiness. *American Political Science Review, 95*(4), 939–952. doi:10.1017/s0003055400400110

Raffaelli, M., Tran, S. P., Wiley, A. R., Galarza-Heras, M., & Lazarevic, V. (2012). Risk and resilience in rural communities: The experiences of immigrant Latina mothers. *Family Relations: An Interdisciplinary Journal of Applied Family Studies, 61*(4), 559–570. doi:10.1111/j.1741-3729.2012.00717.x

Rain, J. S., Lane, I. M., & Steiner, D. D. (1991). A current look at the job satisfaction/life satisfaction relationship: Review and future considerations. *Human relations, 44*(3), 287–307.

Ram, U. (2008). Why secularism fails? Secular nationalism and religious revivalism in Israel. *International Journal of Politics, Culture, and Society, 21*(1–4), 57–73.

Rand, A. (1964). *The virtue of selfishness.* London: Penguin.

Ranganathan, M. (2014). Paying for pipes, claiming citizenship: political agency and water reforms at the urban periphery. *International Journal of Urban and Regional Research, 38*(2), 590–608. doi:10.1111/1468-2427.12028

Ranta, E. (2018). *Vivir bien as an alternative to neoliberal globalization. Can indigenous terminologies decolonize the state?*: Routledge.

Reed, D. D., Reed, F. D. D., Chok, J., & Brozyna, G. A. (2011). The "tyranny of choice": Choice overload as a possible instance of effort discounting. *The Psychological Record, 61*(4), 547–560.

Reker, G. T. (1997). Personal meaning, optimism, and choice: Existential predictors of depression in community and institutional elderly. *The Gerontologist, 37*(6), 709–716.

Reker, G. T. (2005). Meaning in life of young, middle-aged, and older adults: Factorial validity, age, and gender invariance of the Personal Meaning Index (PMI). *Personality and Individual Differences, 38*(1), 71–85.

Reker, G. T., Peacock, E. J., & Wong, P. T. (1987). Meaning and purpose in life and well-being: A life-span perspective. *Journal of Gerontology, 42*(1), 44–49.

Ren, Z. (2009). On being a volunteer at the Sichuan earthquake disaster area (translated version). *Hong Kong Journal of Psychiatry, 19*(3), 123–126.

Renneboog, L., & Spaenjers, C. (2012). Religion, economic attitudes, and household finance. *Oxford Economic Papers, 64*(1), 103–127.

Rew, L., Slesnick, N., Johnson, K., Aguilar, R., & Cengiz, A. (2019). Positive attributes and life satisfaction in homeless youth. *Children and Youth Services Review, 100*, 1–8. doi:10.1016/j.childyouth.2019.02.021

Reyes-García, V. (2012). Happiness in the Amazon: Folk explanations of happiness in a hunter-horticulturalist society in the Bolivian Amazon. In H. Selin & G. Davey (Eds.), *Happiness across cultures: Views of happiness and quality of life in non-Western cultures.* (Vol. 6, pp. 209–225). New York, NY: Springer Science + Business Media.

Riaz, H., Riaz, M. N., & Batool, N. (2014). Positive psychological capital as predictor of internalizing psychological problems among flood victims. *Journal of the Indian Academy of Applied Psychology, 40*(1), 102–112.

Richards, L. (2016). For whom money matters less: Social connectedness as a resilience resource in the UK. *Social Indicators Research, 125*(2), 509–535. doi:10.1007/s11205-014-0858-5

Riggle, E. D., Rostosky, S. S., & Danner, F. (2009). LGB identity and eudaimonic well being in midlife. *Journal of Homosexuality, 56*(6), 786–798.

Riggle, E. D., Rostosky, S. S., & Horne, S. G. (2010). Psychological distress, well-being, and legal recognition in same-sex couple relationships. *Journal of Family Psychology, 24*(1), 82.

Riggle, E. D., Whitman, J. S., Olson, A., Rostosky, S. S., & Strong, S. (2008). The positive aspects of being a lesbian or gay man. *Professional Psychology: Research and Practice, 39*(2), 210.

Rindfleisch, A., Burroughs, J. E., & Wong, N. (2008). The safety of objects: Materialism, existential insecurity, and brand connection. *Journal of Consumer Research, 36*(1), 1–16.

Riza, S. D., & Heller, D. (2015). Follow your heart or your head? A longitudinal study of the facilitating role of calling and ability in the pursuit of a challenging career. *Journal of Applied Psychology, 100*(3), 695–712. doi:10.1037/a0038011

Robledo, M. A. (2015). Tourism of spiritual growth as a voyage of discovery. In *Tourism research frontiers: Beyond the boundaries of knowledge* (pp. 71–86): Emerald Group Publishing Limited.

Rockwell, D. (2019). A presidential address: The state of humanistic psychology. *The Humanistic Psychologist.* doi:10.1037/hum0000129

Rode, M. (2013). Do good institutions make citizens happy, or do happy citizens build better institutions? *Journal of Happiness Studies, 14*(5), 1479–1505. doi:10.1007/s10902-012-9391-x

Rodell, J. B. (2013). Finding meaning through volunteering: Why do employees volunteer and what does it mean for their jobs? *Academy of Management Journal, 56*(5), 1274–1294.

Rodgers, D. (2012). Haussmannization in the tropics: Abject urbanism and infrastructural violence in Nicaragua. *Ethnography, 13*(4), 413–438. doi:10.1177/1466138111435740

Ronkainen, N. J., Kavoura, A., & Ryba, T. V. (2016). A meta-study of athletic identity research in sport psychology: Current status and future directions. *International Review of Sport and Exercise Psychology, 9*(1), 45–64.

Ronkainen, N. J., & Nesti, M. S. (2017). An existential approach to sport psychology: Theory and applied practice. *International Journal of Sport and Exercise Psychology, 15*(1), 12–24.

Roos, C. R., Kirouac, M., Pearson, M. R., Fink, B. C., & Witkiewitz, K. (2015). Examining temptation to drink from an existential perspective: Associations among temptation, purpose in life, and drinking outcomes. *Psychology of Addictive Behaviors, 29*(3), 716.

Röpke, W. (2014). *A humane economy: The social framework of the free market.* London: Open Road Media.

Roscoe, P. (2014). *I spend, therefore I am: The true cost of economics.* London: Viking.

Rosenberg, R. S. (2013). *Our superheroes, ourselves.* Oxford: Oxford University Press.

Ross, G. (2013). Meaning making, life transitional experiences and personal well-being within the contexts of religious and spiritual travel. In *Tourist experience and fulfilment* (pp. 105–123). London: Routledge.

Ross, S. (2008). Ketamine and addiction. *Primary Psychiatry, 15*(9).

Rosso, B. D., Dekas, K. H., & Wrzesniewski, A. (2010). On the meaning of work: A theoretical integration and review. *Research in Organizational Behavior, 30*, 91–127.

Rousseau, J.-J. (1999). *Discourse on the origin of inequality.* Oxford: Oxford University Press.

Rubaltelli, E., Lotto, L., Ritov, I., & Rumiati, R. (2015). Moral investing: Psychological motivations and implications. *Judgment and Decision Making, 10*(1), 64.

Rubin, E. L. (2015). *Soul, self, and society: The new morality and the modern state.* Oxford: Oxford University Press.

Rucker, D. D., & Galinsky, A. D. (2008). Desire to acquire: Powerlessness and compensatory consumption. *Journal of Consumer Research, 35*(2), 257–267.

Russell, R. V., & Stage, F. K. (1996). Leisure as burden: Sudanese refugee women1. *Journal of Leisure Research, 28*(2), 108–121.

Rustin, M. (1992). No exit from capitalism. *New Left Review*(193), 96.

Ryff, C. D. (2017). Eudaimonic well-being, inequality, and health: Recent findings and future directions. *International Review of Economics, 64*(2), 159–178.

Ryff, C. D., Keyes, C. L., & Hughes, D. L. (2003). Status inequalities, perceived discrimination, and eudaimonic well-being: Do the challenges of minority life hone purpose and growth? *Journal of Health and Social Behavior*, 275–291.

Sachs, J. (2008). *Common wealth: Economics for a crowded planet.* London: Penguin.

Saito, C. (2014). Bereavement and meaning reconstruction among Japanese immigrant widows: Living with grief in a place of marginality and liminality in the United States. *Pastoral psychology, 63*(1), 39–55.

Saltman, K. J. (2013). Learning to be a psychopath: The pedagogy of the corporation. In Critical Pedagogy and Global Literature (pp. 47–62): Springer.

Salzinger, L. (1991). A maid by any other name: The transformation of 'dirty work'by Central American immigrants. In Ethnography unbound: Power and resistance in the modern metropolis (pp. 139–160). University of California.

Salzman, M. B. (2008). Globalization, religious fundamentalism and the need for meaning. International Journal of Intercultural Relations, 32(4), 318–327.

Samuel, R., Bergman, M. M., & Hupka-Brunner, S. (2013). The Interplay between educational achievement, occupational success, and well-being. Social Indicators Research, 111(1), 75–96. doi:10.1007/s11205-011-9984-5

Sanders, J. E., Hopkins, W. E., & Geroy, G. D. (2003). From transactional to transcendental: Toward an integrated theory of leadership. Journal of Leadership & Organizational Studies, 9(4), 21–31.

Sarracino, F., & Mikucka, M. (2019). Consume more, work longer, and be unhappy: possible social roots of economic crisis? Applied Research in Quality of Life, 14(1), 59–84. doi:10.1007/s11482-017-9581-0

Sartre, J.-P. (1974). Between existentialism and Marxism.

Sartre, J.-P. (2007). Existentialism is a humanism. New Jersey: Yale University Press.

Sarvimäki, A., & Stenbock-Hult, B. (2000). Quality of life in old age described as a sense of well-being, meaning and value. Journal of Advanced Nursing, 32(4), 1025–1033.

Savickas, M. L. (1997). Career adaptability: An integrative construct for life-span, life-space theory. The Career Development Quarterly, 45(3), 247–259.

Savickas, M. L. (2002). Career construction. In D. Brown (Ed.), Career choice and development, (pp. 149–205). San Francisco: Jossey-Bass.

Savickas, M. L. (2005). The theory and practice of career construction. In S.D. Brown & R.W. Lent (Eds.), Career development and counseling: Putting theory and research to work (pp. 42–70). Hoboken, NJ: John Wiley.

Savickas, M. L. (2013). Career construction theory and practice. In S.D. Brown & R.W. Lent (Eds.),Career development and counseling: Putting theory and research to work (2nd ed., pp. 147–183). John Wiley.

Savickas, M. L., Nota, L., Rossier, J., Dauwalder, J.-P., Duarte, M. E., Guichard, J., ... Van Vianen, A. E. (2009). Life designing: A paradigm for career construction in the 21st century. Journal of Vocational Behavior, 75(3), 239–250.

Sayre, S., & Horne, D. (1996). I shop, therefore I am: The role of possessions for self definition. ACR North American Advances.

Scarre, G. (2002). Utilitarianism. New York: Routledge.

Scerri, A., & Lam, C. (2015). From neoliberalism to neocommunitarianism: Opposing justifications in a dispute over privatized electricity infrastructure. Space and Polity, 19(2), 132–149. doi:10.1080/13562576.2015.1011371

Schaubroeck, J., Lam, S. S., & Cha, S. E. (2007). Embracing transformational leadership: Team values and the impact of leader behavior on team performance. Journal of Applied Psychology, 92(4), 1020.

Scheibehenne, B., Greifeneder, R., & Todd, P. M. (2010). Can there ever be too many options? A meta-analytic review of choice overload. Journal of Consumer Research, 37(3), 409–425.

Schlegel, R. J., Hicks, J. A., Arndt, J., & King, L. A. (2009). Thine own self: True self-concept accessibility and meaning in life. Journal of Personality and Social Psychology, 96(2), 473.

Schneider, K. J., & du Plock, S. (2012). Depth and the marketplace: Psychology's Faustian plight: A dialogue. In L. Barnett & G. Madison (Eds.), Existential therapy: Legacy, vibrancy and dialogue (pp. 193–208). New York, NY: Routledge/Taylor & Francis Group.

Schnell, T. (2009). The sources of meaning and Meaning in Life Questionnaire (SoMe): Relations to demographics and well-being. The Journal of Positive Psychology, 4(6), 483–499.

Schnell, T., & Hoof, M. (2012). Meaningful commitment: Finding meaning in volunteer work. Journal of Beliefs & Values, 33(1), 35–53.

Schnetzer, L. W., Schulenberg, S. E., & Buchanan, E. M. (2013). Differential associations among alcohol use, depression and perceived life meaning in male and female college students. Journal of Substance Use, 18(4), 311–319.

Schoene. (2015). Fair economics: Nature, money and people beyond neoclassical thinking. New York: Springer.

Schulenberg, S. E., Drescher, C. F., & Baczwaski, B. J. (2014). Perceived meaning and disaster mental health: A role for logotherapy in clinical-disaster psychology. In Meaning in positive and existential psychology (pp. 251–267). New York: Springer.

Schulenberg, S. E., Smith, C. V., Drescher, C. F., & Buchanan, E. M. (2016). Assessment of meaning in adolescents receiving clinical services in Mississippi following the Deepwater Horizon oil spill: An application of the Purpose in Life Test-Short Form (PIL-SF). Journal of Clinical Psychology, 72(12), 1279–1286.

Schulze, G. (1992). Die Erlebnisgesellschaft: Kultursoziologie der Gegenwart. Frankfurt am Main.

Schumacher, E. F. (2011). Small is beautiful: A study of economics as if people mattered. New York: Random House.

Schumpeter, J. A. (2010). Capitalism, socialism and democracy. New York: Routledge.

Schwanen, T., & Wang, D. G. (2014). Well-being, context, and everyday activities in space and time. Annals of the Association of American Geographers, 104(4), 833–851. doi:10.1080/00045608.2014.912549

Schwartz, B. (2004). The paradox of choice: Why more is less.

Schwartz, B. (2010). Be careful what you wish for: The dark side of freedom.

Schwartz, C. E., Keyl, P. M., Marcum, J. P., & Bode, R. (2009). Helping others shows differential benefits on health and well-being for male and female teens. Journal of Happiness Studies, 10(4), 431–448. doi:10.1007/s10902-008-9098-1

Schwartz, M. S. (2003). The" ethics" of ethical investing. Journal of Business Ethics, 43(3), 195–213.

Schwartz, S. H., & Bardi, A. (1997). Influences of adaptation to communist rule on value priorities in Eastern Europe. *Political Psychology, 18*(2), 385–410.

Schweitzer, R., Melville, F., Steel, Z., & Lacherez, P. (2006). Trauma, post-migration living difficulties, and social support as predictors of psychological adjustment in resettled Sudanese refugees. *Australian & New Zealand Journal of Psychiatry, 40*(2), 179–187.

Scott, B. G., & Weems, C. F. (2013). Natural disasters and existential concerns: A test of Tillich's theory of existential anxiety. *Journal of Humanistic psychology, 53*(1), 114–128.

Scott, K., Martin, D. M., & Schouten, J. W. (2014). Marketing and the new materialism. *Journal of Macromarketing, 34*(3), 282–290.

Scroggins, W. A. (2008). Antecedents and outcomes of experienced meaningful work: A person–job fit perspective. *The Journal of Business Inquiry, 7*(1), 68–78.

Sedlacek, T. (2011). *Economics of good and evil: The quest for economic meaning from Gilgamesh to Wall Street.* Oxford: Oxford University Press.

Seligman, M. E., Ernst, R. M., Gillham, J., Reivich, K., & Linkins, M. (2009). Positive education: Positive psychology and classroom interventions. *Oxford Review of Education, 35*(3), 293–311.

Selivanova, Z. K. (2017). Life goals and professional preferences of older adolescents. *Sotsiologicheskie Issledovaniya*(5), 51–56. Retrieved from <Go to ISI>://WOS:000403853200006

Sellman, D. (2010). The 10 most important things known about addiction. *Addiction, 105*(1), 6–13.

Semler, R. (2001). *Maverick!:The success story behind the world's most unusual workplace.* New York: Random House.

Sen, A. (2007). *Identity and violence: The illusion of destiny.* London: Penguin.

Sengupta, N. K., & Sibley, C. G. (2018). The political attitudes and subjective wellbeing of the one percent. *Journal of Happiness Studies: An Interdisciplinary Forum on Subjective Well-Being.* doi:10.1007/s10902-018-0038-4

Sennett, R. (1998). *The corrosion of character: The personal consequences of work in the new capitalism.* New York: WW Norton & Company.

Sennett, R. (2007). *The culture of the new capitalism.* New Jersey: Yale University Press.

Sennett, R. (2008). *The craftsman.* New Jersey: Yale University Press.

Sennett, R. (2012). *Together: The rituals, pleasures and politics of cooperation.* New Jersey: Yale University Press.

Sennett, R. (2017). *The fall of public man.* New York: WW Norton & Company.

Seppala, P., & Hellman, M. (2014). A as in atmosphere, Z as in zeitgeist: Trajectories in Helsinki dance club symbolism in the 1990s. *International Journal of Cultural Studies, 17*(4), 327–345. doi:10.1177/1367877913486533

Seuntjens, T. G., Zeelenberg, M., van de Ven, N., & Breugelmans, S. M. (2015). Dispositional greed. *Journal of Personality and Social Psychology, 108*(6), 91–933. doi:10.1037/pspp0000031

Sharp, Z. (2018). Existential angst and identity rethink: The complexities of competition. *Nonprofit and Voluntary Sector Quarterly, 47*(4), 767–788. doi:10.1177/0899764018760399

Shaw, D., Grehan, E., Shiu, E., Hassan, L., & Thomson, J. (2005). An exploration of values in ethical consumer decision making. *Journal of Consumer Behaviour: An International Research Review, 4*(3), 185–200.

Shaw, J. (2014). Destabilizing sexistentialism and hegemonic masculinity in Norman Mailer's An American Dream. *Canadian Review of American Studies, 44*(1), 44–64. doi:10.3138/cras.2013.030

Shek, D. T. (2005). Economic stress, emotional quality of life, and problem behavior in Chinese adolescents with and without economic disadvantage. In *Quality-of-life research in Chinese, Western and global contexts* (pp. 363–383). New York: Springer.

Sherman, J., & Fischer, J. M. (2002). Spirituality and addiction recovery for rehabilitation counseling. *Journal of Applied Rehabilitation Counseling, 33*(4), 27.

Sherman, N. E., Michel, R., Rybak, C., Randall, G. K., & Davidson, J. (2011). Meaning in life and volunteerism in older adults. *Adultspan Journal, 10*(2), 78–90.

Shin, J. (2018). Relative Deprivation, Satisfying rationality, and support for redistribution. *Social Indicators Research, 140*(1), 35–56.

Silver, H. C., Caudill, S. B., & Mixon, F. G. (2017). Human capital and life satisfaction in economic transition Econometric evidence from pre- and post-Arab Spring Egypt. *Economics of Transition, 25*(2), 165–184. doi:10.1111/ecot.12116

Singhal, H., & Rastogi, R. (2018). Psychological capital and career commitment: The mediating effect of subjective well-being. *Management Decision, 56*(2), 458–473. doi:10.1108/md-06-2017-0579

Sirgy, M. J., & Uysal, M. (2016). Developing a eudaimonia research agenda in travel and tourism. In *Handbook of eudaimonic well-being* (pp. 485–495): New York: Springer.

Sisodia, R., Wolfe, D., & Sheth, J. N. (2003). *Firms of endearment: How world-class companies profit from passion and purpose*: Pearson Prentice Hall.

Skevington, S. M. (2009). Conceptualising dimensions of quality of life in poverty. *Journal of Community & Applied Social Psychology, 19*(1), 33–50.

Skidelsky, E., & Skidelsky, R. (2012). *How much is enough?: Money and the good life.* London: Penguin UK.

Smircich, L., & Morgan, G. (1982). Leadership: The management of meaning. *The Journal of Applied Behavioral Science, 18*(3), 257–273.

Snel, J. M. C. (2011). *For the love of experience: Changing the experience economy discourse*. Amsterdam: Universiteit van Amsterdam.

Snir, R., & Harpaz, I. (2002). Work–leisure relations: Leisure orientation and the meaning of work. *Journal of Leisure Research, 34*(2), 178–203.

Sobol-Kwapinska, M. (2013). Hedonism, fatalism and 'carpe diem': Profiles of attitudes towards the present time. *Time & Society, 22*(3), 371–390.

Spence, R. (2009). *It's not what you sell, it's what you stand for: Why every extraordinary business is driven by purpose*: Penguin.

Spencer, J. H., & Le, T. N. (2006). Parent refugee status, immigration stressors, and Southeast Asian youth violence. *Journal of Immigrant and Minority Health, 8*(4), 359–368.

Spielmann, N., Babin, B. J., & Manthiou, A. (2018). Places as authentic consumption contexts. *Psychology & Marketing, 35*(9), 652–665. doi:10.1002/mar.21113

Spruk, R., & Kešeljević, A. (2016). Institutional origins of subjective well-being: Estimating the effects of economic freedom on national happiness. *Journal of Happiness Studies: An Interdisciplinary Forum on Subjective Well-Being, 17*(2), 659–712. doi:10.1007/s10902-015-9616-x

Stavrakakis, Y. (2000). On the critique of advertising discourse: A Lacanian view. *Third Text, 14*(51), 85–90.

Stavrositu, C. D. (2014). Does TV viewing cultivate meritocratic beliefs? Implications for life satisfaction. *Mass Communication and Society, 17*(1), 148–171. doi:10.1080/15205436.2013.816741

Stecker, R. E. (1981). The existential vacuum in Eastern Europe. *International Forum for Logotherapy, 4*(2), 79–82.

Steger, M. F., & Dik, B. J. (2009). If one is looking for meaning in life, does it help to find meaning in work? *Applied Psychology: Health and Well-Being, 1*(3), 303–320.

Steger, M. F., & Dik, B. J. (2010). *Work as meaning: Individual and organizational benefits of engaging in meaningful work*.

Steger, M. F., Littman-Ovadia, H., Miller, M., Menger, L., & Rothmann, S. (2013). Engaging in work even when it is meaningless: Positive affective disposition and meaningful work interact in relation to work engagement. *Journal of Career Assessment, 21*(2), 348–361.

Steger, M. F., Mann, J. R., Michels, P., & Cooper, T. C. (2009). Meaning in life, anxiety, depression, and general health among smoking cessation patients. *Journal of Psychosomatic Research, 67*(4), 353–358.

Steger, M. F., Pickering, N. K., Shin, J. Y., & Dik, B. J. (2010). Calling in work: Secular or sacred? *Journal of Career Assessment, 18*(1), 82–96.

Steger*, M. F., Frazier, P. A., & Zacchanini, J. L. (2008). Terrorism in two cultures: Stress and growth following September 11 and the Madrid train bombings. *Journal of Loss and Trauma, 13*(6), 511–527.

Steijn, B. (2008). Person-environment fit and public service motivation. *International Public Management Journal, 11*(1), 13–27.

Steptoe, A., Deaton, A., & Stone, A. A. (2015). Subjective wellbeing, health, and ageing. *The Lancet, 385*(9968), 640–648.

Sternberg, E. (1999). *The economy of icons: How business manufactures meaning*. New York: Greenwood Publishing Group.

Stetsenko, A., & Arievitch, I. M. (2010). Cultural-historical activity theory: Foundational worldview, major principles, and the relevance of sociocultural context. In S. R. Kirschner & J. Martin (Eds.), *The sociocultural turn in psychology: The contextual emergence of mind and self*. (pp. 231–252). New York, NY: Columbia University Press.

Stiglitz, J. E. (2012). *The price of inequality: How today's divided society endangers our future*. New York: WW Norton & Company.

Stojanovic, S. (2010). Collapse of communism, crisis of capitalism, and the state of humanity. *Philosophy & Social Criticism, 36*(8), 903–916. doi:10.1177/0191453710375590

Stolle, D., Hooghe, M., & Micheletti, M. (2005). Politics in the supermarket: Political consumerism as a form of political participation. *International Political Science Review, 26*(3), 245–269.

Stum, D. L. (2001). Maslow revisited: Building the employee commitment pyramid. *Strategy & Leadership, 29*(4), 4–9.

Suárez-Orozco, C., & Suárez-Orozco, M. M. (2009). *Children of immigration*. Boston: Harvard University Press.

Suhail, K., & Chaudhry, H. R. (2004). Predictors of subjective well-being in an Eastern Muslim culture. *Journal of Social and Clinical Psychology, 23*(3), 359–376. doi:10.1521/jscp.23.3.359.35451

Sullivan, S. E. (2011). *Self-direction in the boundaryless career era*.

Sundararajan, A. (2016). *The sharing economy: The end of employment and the rise of crowd-based capitalism*. New York: MIT Press.

Sundbo, J., & Darmer, P. (2008). *Creating experiences in the experience economy*. New York: Edward Elgar Publishing.

Sundbo, J., & Sorensen, F. (2013). *Handbook on the experience economy*. New York: Edward Elgar Publishing.

Super, D. E. (1957). *The psychology of careers; An introduction to vocational development*.

Super, D. E., Savickas, M. L., & Super, C. M. (1996). The life-span, life-space approach to careers. In D. Brown & L. Brooks (Eds.) *Career choice and development* (3rd ed., pp. 121–178). San Francisco: Jossey-Bass.

Sutker, P. B., Davis, J. M., Uddo, M., & Ditta, S. R. (1995). War zone stress, personal resources, and PTSD in Persian Gulf War returnees. *Journal of Abnormal Psychology, 104*(3), 444.

Swenson, R. (2014). *The overload syndrome: Learning to live within your limits*. London: Tyndale House.

Swinyard, W. R., Kau, A.-K., & Phua, H.-Y. (2001). Happiness, materialism, and religious experience in the US and Singapore. *Journal of Happiness Studies, 2*(1), 13–32.

Szymanski, D. M., & Mikorski, R. (2016). External and internalized heterosexism, meaning in life, and psychological distress. *Psychology of Sexual Orientation and Gender Diversity, 3*(3), 265.

Taber, B. J., & Briddick, W. C. (2011). Adlerian-based career counseling in an age of protean careers. *Journal of Individual Psychology, 67*(2).

Takahashi, B., Tandoc, E. C., Duan, R., & Van Witsen, A. (2017). Revisiting environmental citizenship: The role of information capital and media use. *Environment and Behavior, 49*(2), 111–135. doi:10.1177/0013916515620892

Takahashi, K., Nguyen, T. M. T., Poudel, K. C., Sakisaka, K., Jimba, M., & Yasuoka, J. (2011). Social capital and life satisfaction: A cross-sectional study on persons with musculoskeletal impairments in Hanoi, Vietnam. *BMC Public Health, 11*, 8. doi:10.1186/1471-2458-11-206

Takkinen, S., & Ruoppila, I. (2001). Meaning in life in three samples of elderly persons with high cognitive functioning. *The International Journal of Aging and Human Development, 53*(1), 51–73.

Taloyan, M., Johansson, L. M., Saleh-Stattin, N., & Al-Windi, A. (2011). Acculturation strategies in migration stress among Kurdish men in Sweden: A narrative approach. *American journal of men's health, 5*(3), 198-207.

Tandoc, E. C., & Takahashi, B. (2013). The Complex Road to Happiness: The Influence of Human Development, a Healthy Environment and a Free Press. *Social Indicators Research, 113*(1), 537–550. doi:10.1007/s11205-012-0109-6

Tang, Z. L. (2014). They are richer but are they happier? Subjective well-being of Chinese citizens across the reform era. *Social Indicators Research, 117*(1), 145–164. doi:10.1007/s11205-013-0339-2

Tcherneva, P. R. (2015). *When a rising tide sinks most boats: Trends in US income inequality.*

Teck-Hong, T. (2012). Housing satisfaction in medium- and high-cost housing: The case of Greater Kuala Lumpur, Malaysia. *Habitat International, 36*(1), 108–116. doi:10.1016/j.habitatint.2011.06.003

Tempany, M. (2009). What research tells us about the mental health and psychosocial wellbeing of Sudanese refugees: A literature review. *Transcultural psychiatry, 46*(2), 300–315.

Terkel, S. (2011). *Working: People talk about what they do all day and how they feel about what they do.* New York: The New Press.

Teschers, C. (2018). *Education and Schmid's art of living: Philosophical, psychological and educational perspectives on living a good life.* New York, NY: Routledge/Taylor & Francis Group.

Thaler, R. H., & Sunstein, C. R. (2009). *Nudge: Improving decisions about health, wealth, and happiness.* London: Penguin.

Thege, B. K., Bachner, Y. G., Kushnir, T., & Kopp, M. S. (2009). Relationship between meaning in life and smoking status: Results of a national representative survey. *Addictive Behaviors, 34*(1), 117–120.

Theurer, K., & Wister, A. (2010). Altruistic behaviour and social capital as predictors of well-being among older Canadians. *Ageing & Society, 30*, 157–181. doi:10.1017/s0144686x09008848

Thoits, P. A. (2012). Role-identity salience, purpose and meaning in life, and well-being among volunteers. *Social Psychology Quarterly, 75*(4), 360–384.

Thorpe, C., & Jacobson, B. (2013). Life politics, nature and the state: Giddens' sociological theory and the politics of climate change. *British Journal of Sociology, 64*(1), 99–122. doi:10.1111/1468-4446.12008

Thurang, A., Rydström, J., & Bengtsson Tops, A. (2011). Being in a safe haven and struggling against alcohol dependency. The meaning of caring for male patients in advanced addiction nursing. *Issues in mental health nursing, 32*(7), 401-407.

Thurnwald, R. (2018). *Economics in primitive communities*: Routledge.

Tian, T. (2010). Meaning economy: The nature of media economy. *Journal of International Communication, 7*, 23–35.

Tirole, J. (2017). *Economics for the common good.* Princeton: Princeton University Press.

Tjosvold, D., XueHuang, Y., Johnson, D. W., & Johnson, R. T. (2008). Social interdependence and orientation toward life and work. *Journal of Applied Social Psychology, 38*(2), 40–-435. doi:10.1111/j.1559-1816.2007.00311.x

Tkachenko, N. O., & Hromovyk, B. P. (2018). Scientific reasoning of the connection between the conceptual positions of the social responsibility theory and the social management elements of the pharmaceutical organization. *Research Journal of Pharmaceutical Biological and Chemical Sciences, 9*(5), 1552–1557.

Tosh, L. V., Ralph, R. O., & Campbell, J. (2000). The rise of consumerism. *Psychiatric Rehabilitation Skills, 4*(3), 383–409.

Tosone, C., Lee, M., Bialkin, L., Martinez, A., Campbell, M., Martinez, M. M., ... Riofrio, A. (2003). Shared trauma: Group reflections on the September 11th disaster. *Psychoanalytic Social Work, 10*(1), 57–7.

Toussaint, L. L., Kalayjian, A., Herman, K., Hein, A., Maseko, N., & Diakonova-Curtis, D. (2017). Traumatic stress symptoms, forgiveness, and meaning in life in four traumatized regions of the world. *International Perspectives in Psychology: Research, Practice, Consultation, 6*(1), 5.

Tran, A. L. (2013). *A life of worry: The cultural politics and phenomenology of anxiety in Ho Chi Minh City, Vietnam.* (73). ProQuest Information & Learning.

Trice, L. B. (1990). Meaningful life experience to the elderly. *Image: The Journal of Nursing Scholarship, 22*(4), 248–251.

Triplett, K. N., Tedeschi, R. G., Cann, A., Calhoun, L. G., & Reeve, C. L. (2012). Posttraumatic growth, meaning in life, and life satisfaction in response to trauma. *Psychological Trauma: Theory, Research, Practice, and Policy, 4*(4), 400.

Tronto, J. C. (2013). *Caring democracy: Markets, equality, and justice.* New York: New York University Press.

Troutman, M., Nies, M. A., & Bentley, M. (2010). Measuring successful aging in southern Black older adults. *Educational Gerontology, 37*(1), 38–50.

Tsai, M. C. (2009). Market openness, transition economies and subjective wellbeing. *Journal of Happiness Studies, 10*(5), 523–539. doi:10.1007/s10902-008-9107-4

Tsang, J.-A., Carpenter, T. P., Roberts, J. A., Frisch, M. B., & Carlisle, R. D. (2014). Why are materialists less happy? The role of gratitude and need satisfaction in the relationship between materialism and life satisfaction. *Personality and Individual Differences, 64*, 62–66.

Twenge, J. M., & Campbell, W. K. (2009). *The narcissism epidemic: Living in the age of entitlement.* New York: Simon and Schuster.

Twenge, J. M., & Foster, J. D. (2008). Mapping the scale of the narcissism epidemic: Increases in narcissism 2002–2007 within ethnic groups. *Journal of Research in Personality, 42*(6), 1619–1622.

Twitchell, J. B. (1999). *Lead us into temptation: The triumph of American materialism.* Columbia: Columbia University Press.

Tyler, M. (2011). Tainted love: From dirty work to abject labour in Soho's sex shops. *Human relations, 64*(11), 1477–1500.

Tyner, J. A. (2016). *Violence in capitalism: Devaluing life in an age of responsibility.* Nebraska: University of Nebraska Press.

Tziner, A., & Meir, E. (1997). Work adjustment: Extension of the theoretical framework. *International Review of Industrial and Organizational Psychology, 12*, 95–114.

Ulrich, D., & Ulrich, W. (2010). *The why of work.* New York: Tata McGraw-Hill Education.

Updegraff, J. A., Silver, R. C., & Holman, E. A. (2008). Searching for and finding meaning in collective trauma: Results from a national longitudinal study of the 9/11 terrorist attacks. *Journal of Personality and Social Psychology, 95*(3), 709.

Vaknin, S. (2009). *The narcissist and psychopath in the workplace.* New York: Narcissus Publishing.

van de Vliert, E., Janssen, O., & Giebels, E. (2002). Wat maakt een competitiever volk ongelukkiger? What makes a more competitive populace unhappier? *Gedrag en Organisatie, 15*(6), 317–330.

Van Dierendonck, D., Haynes, C., Borrill, C., & Stride, C. (2004). Leadership behavior and subordinate well-being. *Journal of Occupational Health Psychology, 9*(2), 165.

Van Gelderen, M. (2006). Opportunities in the market for meaning in life. *Journal of Enterprising Culture, 14.*

van Hoorn, A., & Sent, E. M. (2016). Consumer capital as the source of happiness: The missing economic theory underlying the income–happiness paradox. *Journal of Economic Issues, 50*(4), 984–1002. doi:10.1080/00213624.2016.1249746

Van Tongeren, D. R., Green, J. D., Davis, D. E., Hook, J. N., & Hulsey, T. L. (2016). Prosociality enhances meaning in life. *The Journal of Positive Psychology, 11*(3), 225–236.

Van Vianen, A. E., Nijstad, B. A., & Voskuijl, O. F. (2008). A person–environment fit approach to volunteerism: Volunteer personality fit and culture fit as predictors of affective outcomes. *Basic and Applied Social Psychology, 30*(2), 153–166.

Vanberg, V. J. (2014). Darwinian paradigm, cultural evolution and human purposes: On FA Hayek's evolutionary view of the market. *Journal of Evolutionary Economics, 24*(1), 35–57. doi:10.1007/s00191-013-0305-9

Vatter, M. (2009). Biopolitics: From surplus value to surplus life. *Theory & Event, 12*(2).

Vellem, V. S. (2015). Black theology of liberation: A theology of life in the context of Empire. *Verbum et Ecclesia, 36*(3), 1–6.

Vemuri, A. W., & Costanza, R. (2006). The role of human, social, built, and natural capital in explaining life satisfaction at the country level: Toward a national well-being index (NWI). *Ecological Economics, 58*(1), 119–133. doi:10.1016/j.ecolecon.2005.02.008

Vemuri, A. W., Grove, J. M., Wilson, M. A., & Burch, W. R. (2011). A Tale of two scales: Evaluating the relationship among life satisfaction, social capital, income, and the natural environment at individual and neighborhood levels in metropolitan Baltimore. *Environment and Behavior, 43*(1), 3–25. doi:10.1177/0013916509338551

Verduyn, P., Ybarra, O., Resibois, M., Jonides, J., & Kross, E. (2017). Do social network sites enhance or undermine subjective well-being? A critical review. *Social Issues and Policy Review, 11*(1), 274–302. doi:10.1111/sipr.12033

Verhaeghe, P. (2012). What about me?: The struggle for identity in a market.

Vermeir, I., & Verbeke, W. (2008). Sustainable food consumption among young adults in Belgium: Theory of planned behaviour and the role of confidence and values. *Ecological Economics, 64*(3), 542–553.

Vida, S. (2016). Precarious identities, governmentality, and violence. *Materiali per Una Storia Della Cultura Giuridica, 46*(2), 479–506. doi:10.1436/84839

Viviers, S., & Eccles, N. (2012). 35 years of socially responsible investing (SRI) research–General trends over time. *South African Journal of Business Management, 43*(4), 1–16.

Voelpel, S. C., Leibold, M., & Tekie, E. B. (2006). Managing purposeful organizational misfit: Exploring the nature of industry and organizational misfit to enable strategic change. *Journal of Change Management, 6*(3), 257–276. doi:10.1080/14697010600963076

Vogel, R. M., & Feldman, D. C. (2009). Integrating the levels of person–environment fit: The roles of vocational fit and group fit. *Journal of Vocational Behavior, 75*(1), 68–81.

Vos, A. (2017). *How to create a relevant public space*: Nai010 uitgevers/publishers.

Vosyliute, A., & Kaunas Univ Technology, P. (2008). Vilnius: Meanings of space and language. In *Nation and Language: Modern Aspects of Socio-Linguistic Development, Proceedings* (pp. 125–129). Kaunas: Kaunas Univ Technology Press.

Vuori, T., San, E., & Kira, M. (2012). Meaningfulness-making at work. *Qualitative Research in Organizations and Management: An International Journal, 7*(2), 231–248.

Wagner-Marsh, F., & Conley, J. (1999). The fourth wave: The spiritually-based firm. *Journal of Organizational Change Management, 12*(4), 292–302.

Wagnild, G., & Young, H. M. (1990). Resilience among older women. *Image: The Journal of Nursing Scholarship, 22*(4), 252–255.

Waisberg, J. L., & Porter, J. E. (1994). Purpose in life and outcome of treatment for alcohol dependence. *British Journal of Clinical Psychology, 33*(1), 49–63.

Walters, G. D. (2002). Fear, belief, and terrorism. In S. P. Shohov (Ed.), *Advances in psychology research* (Vol. 10), pp. 45–67). Hauppauge, NY: Nova Science Publishers

Walumbwa, F. O., Avolio, B. J., Gardner, W. L., Wernsing, T. S., & Peterson, S. J. (2008). Authentic leadership: development and validation of a theory-based measure. *Journal of Management, 34*(1), 89–126.

Walumbwa, F. O., Avolio, B. J., & Zhu, W. (2008). How transformational leadership weaves its influence on individual job performance: The role of identification and efficacy beliefs. *Personnel Psychology, 61*(4), 793–825.

Walumbwa, F. O., Mayer, D. M., Wang, P., Wang, H., Workman, K., & Christensen, A. L. (2011). Linking ethical leadership to employee performance: The roles of leader–member exchange, self-efficacy, and organizational identification. *Organizational Behavior and Human Decision Processes, 115*(2), 204–213.

Ward, S. J., & King, L. A. (2016). Poor but happy? Income, happiness, and experienced and expected meaning in life. *Social Psychological and Personality Science, 7*(5), 463–470.

Weckroth, M., Kemppainen, T., & Sorensen, J. F. L. (2015). Predicting the gross domestic product (GDP) of 289 NUTS regions in Europe with subjective indicators for human and social capital. *Regional Studies Regional Science, 2*(1), 312–331. doi:10.1080/21681376.2015.1037863

Weller, S. (2010). *Modernism and nihilism.* New York: Springer.

Wijk, H., & Grimby, A. (2008). Needs of elderly patients in palliative care. *American Journal of Hospice and Palliative Medicine, 25*(2), 106–111.

Wiklund, L. (2008). Existential aspects of living with addiction–Part I: Meeting challenges. *Journal of Clinical Nursing, 17*(18), 2426–2434.

Wilchek-Aviad, Y. (2015). Meaning in life and suicidal tendency among immigrant (Ethiopian) youth and native-born Israeli youth. *Journal of Immigrant and Minority Health, 17*(4), 1041–1048.

Wilensky, A. S. (1996). *Understanding the culture of nonprofit executives through stories: A qualitative investigation.* (56). ProQuest Information & Learning.

Williams, D. R. (2002). Leisure Identities, Globalization, and the Politics of Place. *Journal of Leisure Research, 34*(4), 351–367.

Williams, D. R., & McIntyre, N. (2001). *Where heart and home reside: Changing constructions of place and identity.* In Kim Luft & Sandy MacDonald (Eds.), Trends 2000: Shaping the future: The 5th Outdoor Recreation & Tourism Trends Symposium (pp. 392–403). East Lansing, MI:, Michigan State University:.

Williams, E. (2014). *Co-evolution of contextual structure and personal variables in decisions to stay or go: A qualitative study of women entrepreneurs' meaning making.* (74). ProQuest Information & Learning.

Wilson, J. (2000). Volunteering. *Annual Review of Sociology, 26,* 215–240. doi:10.1146/annurev.soc.26.1.215

Wilson, J. Q. (1993). The moral sense. *American Political Science Review, 87*(1), 1–11.

Wlodarczyk, A., Basabe, N., Páez, D., Reyes, C., Villagrán, L., Madariaga, C., ... Martínez, F. (2016). Communal coping and posttraumatic growth in a context of natural disasters in Spain, Chile, and Colombia. *Cross-Cultural Research, 50*(4), 325–355.

Wolcott, G. (2019). Restricting choices: Decision making, the market society, and the forgotten entrepreneur. *Journal of Business Ethics, 156*(2), 293–314. doi:10.1007/s10551-017-3560-0

Wolf, Y., Katz, S., & Nachson, I. (1995). Meaning of life as perceived by drug-abusing people. *International Journal of Offender Therapy and Comparative Criminology, 39*(2), 121–137.

Wong, Y. L. R., & Tsang, A. K. T. (2004). When Asian immigrant women speak: From mental health to strategies of being. *American Journal of Orthopsychiatry, 74*(4), 456–466.

Woo, M., & Kim, S. (2018). Does social capital always raise life satisfaction? A comparison of South Korea and Taiwan. *International Journal of Social Welfare, 27*(2), 121–131. doi:10.1111/ijsw.12293

Wood, D. J., Logsdon, J. M., Lewellyn, P. G., & Davenport, K. S. (2015). *Global business citizenship: A transformative framework for ethics and sustainable capitalism.* New York: Routledge.

Wright, L. L. (2011). *Principal identity and educational change.* (72). ProQuest Information & Learning.

Wright, R. (1995). *The moral animal: Evolutionary psychology and everyday life.* New York: Vintage.

Wrzesniewski, A., Berg, J. M., & Dutton, J. E. (2010). Managing yourself: Turn the job you have into the job you want. *Harvard Business Review, 88*(6), 114–117.

Wrzesniewski, A., & Dutton, J. E. (2001). Crafting a job: Revisioning employees as active crafters of their work. *Academy of Management Review, 26*(2), 179–201.

Wrzesniewski, A., Dutton, J. E., & Debebe, G. (2003). Interpersonal sensemaking and the meaning of work. *Research in Organizational Behavior, 25,* 93–135.

Wrzesniewski, A., McCauley, C., Rozin, P., & Schwartz, B. (1997). Jobs, careers, and callings: People's relations to their work. *Journal of Research in Personality, 31*(1), 21–33.

Wu, T. (2017). *The attention merchants: The epic scramble to get inside our heads.* New York: Vintage.

Wulff, E. (2009). Madness, sense, and meaning: How does the subject get outside of society and history? *Theory & Psychology, 19*(2), 235–243. doi:10.1177/0959354309103536

Wuthnow, R. (1995). *Rethinking materialism: Perspectives on the spiritual dimension of economic behavior.* Amsterdam: Eerdmans Publishing.

Xie, X., Xia, Y., & Zhou, Z. (2004). Strengths and challenges in Chinese immigrant families.

Xin, W., & Smyth, R. (2010). Economic openness and subjective well-being in China. *China & World Economy, 18*(2), 22–40. doi:10.1111/j.1749-124X.2010.01187.

Xue, L., Manuel-Navarrete, D., & Buzinde, C. N. (2014). Theorizing the concept of alienation in tourism studies. *Annals of Tourism Research, 44*, 186–199.

Yamaoka, K. (2008). Social capital and health and well-being in East Asia: A population-based study. *Social Science & Medicine, 66*(4), 885–899. doi:10.1016/j.socscimed.2007.10.024

Yani-de-Soriano, M., & Slater, S. (2009). Revisiting Drucker's theory: Has consumerism led to the overuse of marketing? *Journal of Management History, 15*(4), 452–466.

Yeatts, D. E., Cready, C. M., Pei, X. M., Shen, Y. Y., & Luo, H. (2014). Environment and subjective well-being of rural Chinese Elderly: A multilevel analysis. *Journals of Gerontology Series B-Psychological Sciences and Social Sciences, 69*(6), 979–989. doi:10.1093/geronb/gbu050

Yetim, N., & Yetim, Ü. (2014). Sense of community and individual well-being: A research on fulfillment of needs and social capital in the Turkish community. *Social Indicators Research, 115*(1), 93–115. doi:10.1007/s11205-012-0210-x

Yip, W., Subramanian, S. V., Mitchell, A. D., Lee, D. T. S., Wang, J., & Kawachi, I. (2007). Does social capital enhance health and well-being? Evidence from rural China. *Social Science & Medicine, 64*(1), 35–49. doi:10.1016/j.socscimed.2006.08.027

Yost, A. D., & Lucas, M. S. (2002). Adjustment issues affecting employment for immigrants from the former Soviet Union. *Journal of Employment Counseling, 39*(4), 153–170.

Young-Hall, G. B. (2001). *The addiction recovery experience: Transition to a satisfying sense of meaning-in-life.*

Young, M. (2017). *The rise of the meritocracy.* New York: Routledge.

Young, S. (2003). *Moral capitalism: Reconciling private interest with the public good*: Berrett-Koehler Publishers.

Yu, D. L., & Ren, Q. Y. (2014). On the features, status and role of adult education. In Y. Zhang (Ed.), *Proceedings of 2014 2nd International Conference in Humanities, Social Sciences and Global Business Management* (Vol. 26, pp. 139–143). Singapore: Singapore Management & Sports Science Inst Pte Ltd.

Yuan, Q. (2017). *Evaluating the effectiveness of a psychological capital development program on mental health, engagement and work performance.* (78). ProQuest Information & Learning.

Yuen, C. Y. (2013). Ethnicity, level of study, gender, religious affiliation and life satisfaction of adolescents from diverse cultures in Hong Kong. *Journal of Youth Studies, 16*(6), 776–791.

Yunus, M. (2010). *Building social business: The new kind of capitalism that serves humanity's most pressing needs.* London: PublicAffairs.

Yunus, S. (2014). *Increasing suicides amongst Asian teens—A sociological study.* In proceedings of SOCIOINT14–The International Conference on Social Sciences and Humanities, Istanbul, Turkey.

Zahra, A., & McIntosh, A. J. (2007). Volunteer tourism: Evidence of cathartic tourist experiences. *Tourism Recreation Research, 32*(1), 115–119.

Zatzick, C. D., Deery, S. J., & Iverson, R. D. (2015). Understanding the determinants of who gets laid off. *Human Resource Management, 54*(6), 877-891. doi:10.1002/hrm.21641

Zeng, Z. J., & Eisenman, J. (2018). The price of persecution: The long-term effects of the anti-rightist campaign on economic performance in post-Mao China. *World Development, 109*, 249–260. doi:10.1016/j.worlddev.2018.04.013

Zhang, R., Ewalds-Kvist, B. M., Li, D., & Jiang, J. (2019). Chinese students' satisfaction with life relative to psychological capital and mediated by purpose in life. *Current Psychology, 38*(1), 260–271. doi:10.1007/s12144-018-9849-z

Zhang, S., Liu, B. B., Zhu, D. J., & Cheng, M. W. (2018). Explaining individual subjective well-being of urban china based on the four-capital model. *Sustainability, 10*(10), 14. doi:10.3390/su10103480

Zhang, Y., Mei, S., Li, L., Chai, J., Li, J., & Du, H. (2015). The relationship between impulsivity and internet addiction in Chinese college students: A moderated mediation analysis of meaning in life and self-esteem. *PLoS One, 10*(7), e0131597.

Zhao, X., & Belk, R. W. (2008). Politicizing consumer culture: Advertising's appropriation of political ideology in China's social transition. *Journal of Consumer Research, 35*(2), 231–244.

Žižek, S. (1989). *The sublime object of ideology.* London: Verso.

Žižek, S. (2017). *The courage of hopelessness: Chronicles of a year of acting dangerously*: Penguin UK.

Zorondo-Rodríguez, F., Grau-Satorras, M., Kalla, J., Demps, K., Gómez-Baggethun, E., García, C., & Reyes-García, V. (2016). Contribution of natural and economic capital to subjective well-being: Empirical evidence from a small-scale society in Kodagu (Karnataka), India. *Social Indicators Research, 127*(2), 919–937. doi:10.1007/s11205-015-0975-9

Zou, T., Su, Y. K., & Wang, Y. W. (2018). Examining relationships between social capital, emotion experience and life satisfaction for sustainable community. *Sustainability, 10*(8), 16. doi:10.3390/su10082651

Zuboff, S. (2019). *The age of surveillance capitalism. The fight for a human future at the new frontier of power.* London: Profile Books.

Zygmuntowski, J. (2016). Profiling Western jihadists: Meta-analysis of intelligence reports and proposal of a standard jihadist radicalisation model. *The Polish Quarterly of International Affairs, 25*(3), 124–136.

Index

About the Cover Art

True art can open our eyes, hearts, and minds to our reality in ways that it would take academic authors hundreds of pages to do. A painting can, for example, not only make the viewer imagine being inside the depicted world but invites the viewer to look back from the depicted world to their own real-life world. Art can make us question ourselves, change our perspective on our own life, and make us aware of the changeability of all our perspectives. Just as a painting does not have one unchangeable meaning for everyone, so do our life, world, and self not have one unchangeable meaning. Thus, a true work of art frees our perspectives from their rigidity and reminds us of how we can live an authentic life with an openness for how things are—'the Being or Truth of beings' (Heidegger, 1950, *'The Origin of the Work of Art'*).

Of all approaches to art, cubism is possibly the most explicit in playing with the perspective of the viewers and making them aware of the contingency of their perspectives. Therefore, the cover of this book includes two cubist paintings by the artist Paola Minekov. The front cover shows the Lloyd's and Gherkin buildings in the City of London. These skyscrapers are more than imaginations; they are widely-known symbols of economics. Paola shows that economics does not only have one meaning or colour but can have many colours. The painting invites us to look at economics with an open mind, like this book showed that economics does not have one absolute meaning in different times and places. The painting breaks open traditional perspectives on economics and invites us to develop a meaning-oriented perspective.

Paola Minekov is a Bulgarian artist working and living in London and exhibiting her work in galleries around the world. She describes her art as a visual diary of her life: 'To paint is my way of analysing and understanding the world. My themes are always derived from everyday experiences and impressions. In my paintings I explore topics like movement, energy, contrast, and the mystery of emotions. I am interested in how they interconnect into body language as the true expression of the individual.' More art from Paola can be found on paola.art.

About the Author

Joel Vos, PhD, MSc, MA, CPsychol, is a psychologist, philosopher, researcher, and psychological counsellor in the United Kingdom, specialised in existential psychology and psychotherapies. He is researcher at the Metanoia Institute and leads the Professional Doctorate in Existential Psychotherapy and Counselling at the New School of Psychotherapy and Counselling. He is the organiser of the IMEC International Meaning Conferences and the London Critical University. He has over 70 research publications. Recent books include *Mental Health in Crisis* (SAGE) and *Meaning in Life: An Evidence-Based Handbook for Practitioners* (Palgrave McMillan).